£1-50

PENGUIN BOOKS

THE LATER CHURCHILLS

A. L. Rowse was born in Cornwall in 1903. The foremost Cornish writer of the day, a leading Elizabethan scholar, and both historian and man of letters, he went to Oxford as a Scholar in English literature at Christ Church, and won a Fellowship in History at All Souls. He has written a classic of its kind in *A Cornish Childhood*, with its sequel *A Cornishman at Oxford*; two portraits of a society with his *Tudor Cornwall* and *The England of Elizabeth*, which also has a sequel in *The Expansion of Elizabethan England*; and a pendant, *The Elizabethans and America*. Two biographical studies, *Sir Richard Grenville* and *Ralegh and the Throckmortons*, complement each other, while *The Early Churchills* and *The Later Churchills* set a model for a family history. His gift as a man of letters is displayed in the quartet consisting of his epoch-making biography, *William Shakespeare*, his edition of *Shakespeare's Sonnets*, *Christopher Marlowe*, and *Shakespeare's Southampton*, with his volumes of essays, *Time, Persons, Places* and *The English Spirit*. As well as his *Cornish Stories*, he has recently published *A Cornish Anthology* (1968) and *The Cornish in America* (1969). His latest book is *The Elizabethan Renaissance* (1971).

A. L. ROWSE

The Later Churchills

PENGUIN BOOKS

Penguin Books Ltd, Harmondsworth, Middlesex, England
Penguin Books Australia Ltd, Ringwood, Victoria, Australia

—

First published by Macmillan 1958
Published in Penguin Books 1971

—

—

Made and printed in Great Britain
by Richard Clay (The Chaucer Press) Ltd,
Bungay, Suffolk
Set in Linotype Times

To

RICHARD PARES

This tribute
to his heroism
no less than
to his scholarship

Contents

	Preface	xi
	Prologue	1
1.	Sarah's Grandsons	5
2.	Family Affairs and Finances	28
3.	Charles, Third Duke: at Home and Abroad	57
4.	A Young Family	89
5.	George, Fourth Duke, and Blenheim	126
6.	Whig Frolics	166
7.	Regency Generation	187
8.	The Complete Victorian	222
9.	Edwardian Reaction	256
10.	The Rise and Fall of Lord Randolph	295
11.	The Backward Son: A Varied Apprenticeship	338
12.	Liberal Minister	381
13.	The First World War	416
14.	Between the Wars	446
15.	The Heroic Years	484
	Epilogue	521
	Index	537

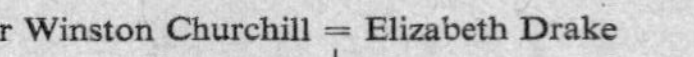

THE LATER CHURCHILLS

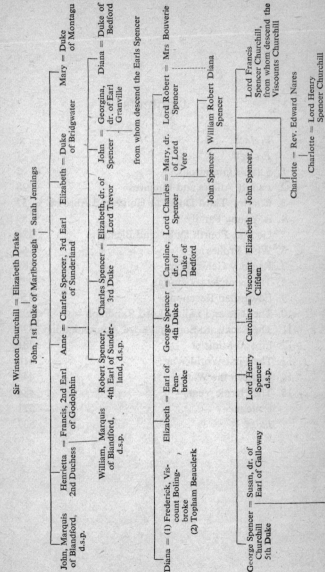

Sir Winston Churchill = Elizabeth Drake

John, 1st Duke of Marlborough = Sarah Jennings

John, Marquis of Blandford, d.s.p.
Henrietta 2nd Duchess = Francis, 2nd Earl of Godolphin
Anne = Charles Spencer, 3rd Earl of Sunderland
Elizabeth = Duke of Bridgwater
Mary = Duke of Montagu

William, Marquis of Blandford, d.s.p.
Robert Spencer, 4th Earl of Sunderland, d.s.p.
Charles Spencer 3rd Duke = Elizabeth, dr. of Lord Trevor
John Spencer = Georgina, dr. of Earl Granville
Diana = Duke of Bedford

from whom descend the Earls Spencer

Diana = (1) Frederick, Viscount Bolingbroke (2) Topham Beauclerk
Elizabeth = Earl of Pembroke
George Spencer 4th Duke = Caroline, dr. of Duke of Bedford
Lord Charles Spencer = Mary, dr. of Lord Vere
Lord Robert Spencer = Mrs Bouverie

John Spencer
William Robert Spencer
Diana

George Spencer Churchill 5th Duke = Susan, dr. of Earl of Galloway
Lord Henry Spencer d.s.p.
Caroline = Viscount Clifden
Elizabeth = John Spencer
Lord Francis Spencer Churchill, from whom descend the Viscounts Churchill

Charlotte = Rev. Edward Nares

Charlotte = Lord Henry Spencer Churchill

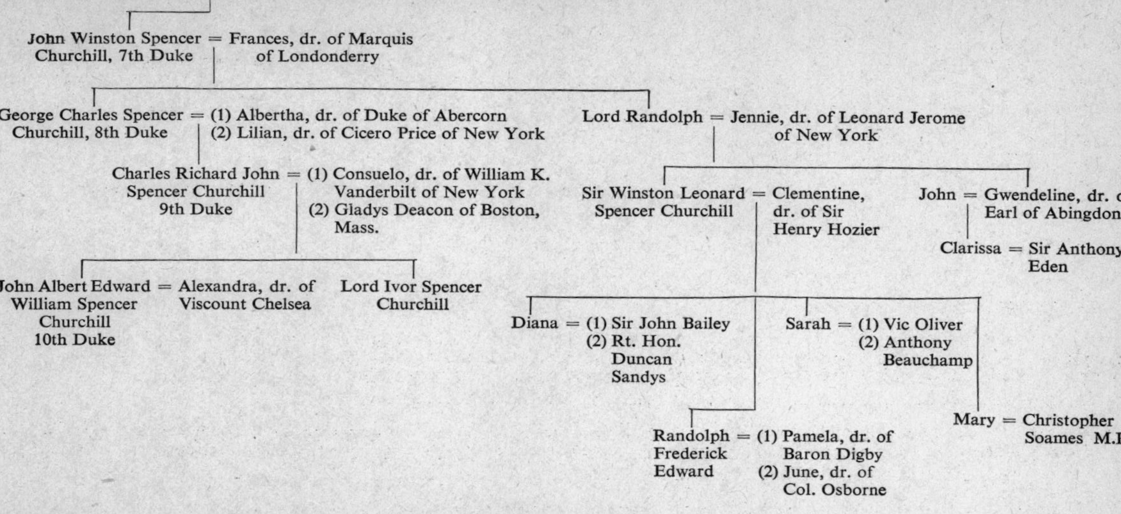
George Spencer Churchill 6th Duke = (1) Jane, dr. of Earl of Galloway
(2) Charlotte, dr. of Viscount Ashbrook
(3) Jane, dr. of Hon. Edward Stewart
John Winston Spencer Churchill, 7th Duke = Frances, dr. of Marquis of Londonderry
George Charles Spencer Churchill, 8th Duke = (1) Albertha, dr. of Duke of Abercorn
(2) Lilian, dr. of Cicero Price of New York
Lord Randolph = Jennie, dr. of Leonard Jerome of New York
Charles Richard John Spencer Churchill 9th Duke = (1) Consuelo, dr. of William K. Vanderbilt of New York
(2) Gladys Deacon of Boston, Mass.
Sir Winston Leonard Spencer Churchill = Clementine, dr. of Sir Henry Hozier
John = Gwendeline, dr. of Earl of Abingdon
Clarissa = Sir Anthony Eden
John Albert Edward William Spencer Churchill 10th Duke = Alexandra, dr. of Viscount Chelsea
Lord Ivor Spencer Churchill
Diana = (1) Sir John Bailey
(2) Rt. Hon. Duncan Sandys
Sarah = (1) Vic Oliver
(2) Anthony Beauchamp
Randolph Frederick Edward = (1) Pamela, dr. of Baron Digby
(2) June, dr. of Col. Osborne
Mary = Christopher Soames M.P.

Preface

MANY people have wondered, and not a few have asked me, what happened to the Churchills between the death of the great Duke of Marlborough and the recent return of the family to fame with Lord Randolph and his son, Sir Winston. The answer is that a great deal happened to them, though little enough of it is known; this book is an attempt to record it.

This is the second volume of my history of the family – the other wing of the diptych – of which the first, *The Early Churchills*, described their rise from West Country obscurity to the high and brilliantly lighted plateau of Blenheim. Here we begin with them established upon that eminence, though it was none the less not without an element of struggle to stick there. Nor is the story, for all their high place and social prominence, any the less without variety and diversity. In fact it has even more: a great deal of comedy and various humours, ripe and uninhibited characters with their amusing quirks and oddities, artists, politicians, bankrupts, bishops, Regency rakes; a duke (friend of George III) who takes to the pleasures of silence and astronomy; another, a full-blown Victorian prig, with his son (who was very far from it), who together scatter the wonderful art-collections of their ancestors – gems, pictures, china, the famous Sunderland library – that made Blenheim such a treasure-house. That is a story in itself.

And so we come to the latest phase in the family, in which they become American as well as English. The two streams, contrasting and sometimes conflicting, always complementary and in the end fortifying each other, exemplify the creativeness of cross-fertilisation. We are presented with a rich crop of exorbitant personalities: Leonard Jerome, one of the parents of the American turf, founder of race-course and jockey-club, the most attractive good fellow to appear on Wall Street and drive up Fifth Avenue four-in-hand in the nineteenth century;

his brilliant and flame-like daughter Jennie, who married Lord Randolph Churchill. There is his meteoric, brief, plunging course, and finally the Olympian career of their son.

I have had occasion to notice how closely and significantly the fortunes of this family reflect the tone and temper of English society contemporaneously, the rhythms of our history. Not least in its latest manifestation – the growing together of American and English fortunes under the stress and in the dangers of the twentieth century. Those two streams, English and American, come together in one of the grandest figures in all our history, who provides a bridge in both his person and the events and concerns of his career.

The last section of my book constitutes a biography of Sir Winston. But, much exposed to authors as he has been (himself among them), I hope I have something of my own to offer. My aim has been, not to write a full biography – the time has happily not come for that – but to set his career in historical perspective. In doing that it has worked out rather differently from what I expected, and proved even more revealing. Now Sir Winston sits on Olympus, above storm and criticism; but in fact his life has been as full of setbacks as ever of triumphs, punctuated with hard knocks and discouragements that would have disheartened a lesser man, of struggle and defeat no less than of achievement.

My chief obligation must be to him, both for his constant interest and encouragement, and on account of my large indebtedness to his own work, historical as well as autobiographical. I am deeply obliged to the Duke of Marlborough for his kind permission to work in the archives at Blenheim, without which this book could not have been written; to Madame Consuelo Vanderbilt Balsan, for helping me to shape, perhaps unaware, a passage of my book; to Lord Spencer, upon whose scholarship I have drawn concerning Marlborough House in Duchess Sarah's day; to Sir Winston's granddaughter, Miss Edwina Sandys, for telling me where to end my book.

I am most grateful to Richard Pares, to whom I have read the eighteenth-century section, and who, from his detailed knowledge of the period and his perspicacity of judgment, has saved me from several mistakes and helped me with various suggestions. Sir Lewis Namier, with whom, from the thirties, I have seen very much eye to eye about human affairs, has been kind and welcoming into the eighteenth century, and suggested two sources of material to me. Sir George Clark agreeably answered some queries from the archives at Oriel College. Miss N. McN. O'Farrell has helped me with research into original MSS. at the Public Record Office, the British Museum and Somerset House, as for previous books of mine. I am most of all indebted to Professor Jack Simmons for his unfailing literary judgment and critical surgery, from which this book has greatly benefited.

I am obliged to the Bodleian and Codrington Libraries on my doorstep; and it is a pleasure to recall how many hours I have spent at work in the large and friendly library of the University of Illinois. At home the Warden of All Souls gave me the free run of his library. I am grateful to Mr Cass Canfield of New York for advice in the presentation of the book and for an important help at one point to its content.

A. L. ROWSE

OXFORD,
31 *January* 1958

[illegible]

[illegible] Mr R. [illegible] O'Donnell has [illegible] with [illegible] MSS. in the Public Record Office, the British Museum and Somerset House [illegible] was greatly helped.

I am obliged to [illegible]

Prologue

No branch of history is more delightful than family history; nor, when all is said, is there any more real and truthful. Other kinds of history may give ground to abstractions, questionable assumptions, tendentious generalisations; afford opportunity for the specious, the disingenuous, the opinionated, those historians who would be clever at the expense of their subject. In pursuing the story of a family we must follow the record humbly and patiently. That need not exclude curiosity, intellectual interest and excitement, or profitable reflection. For there is all the strangeness of dealing with real beings – so much more various, coloured and shifting than grey theories, besides being more full of the juices of life. No wonder the sensible public prefers to read about people. Individuals, not arguments, are the real units of history; the families into which they are born, and which they carry on, their primary and concrete environment. The facts of life are more subtle, and more amusing, than people's theories about them.

The history of the Churchill family affords a remarkably representative introduction to the modern history of the English people. It is singular how well their story reflects the ups and downs, the set-backs and advances, the coils and involutions – in the end, quite simply, the central spine – of our story in the past three centuries. Emerging, like most good things, in the Elizabethan age, with the lawyer John Churchill, the family was caught up in the struggle of the Civil War, so decisive for the future of our society at home and overseas. Both John Churchill and his son, the original Sir Winston, took the King's side – as we saw in *The Early Churchills* – and suffered for their loyalty. Sir Winston, however, married into a Parliamentarian family, the Drakes of Ashe, and this may account for a certain ambivalence in the attitude and career of his son, the great Duke of Marlborough, first of English soldiers, the conscious and deliberate creator of his family's grandeur, of its position at the summit of English society.

Marlborough, a Tory by origin, was a good deal of a Trimmer. It should not be necessary to defend that concept. Its inventor, Lord Halifax – the great Lord Halifax – defined it for us in the seventeenth century: 'this innocent word "Trimmer" signifies no more than this, that if men are together in a boat, and one part of the company would weigh it down on one side, another would make it lean as much to the contrary'. It is clear that to be a Trimmer is an entirely good thing – in times of stress a necessary thing, to keep the boat from rocking. Marlborough's wife, the redoubtable Sarah, was not enough of a Trimmer: she became a vehement, partisan Whig; hence, in part, her celebrated quarrel with Queen Anne.

Though John and Sarah were successful beyond their dreams – a dukedom, an immense fortune, a palace to perpetuate his renown, a secure place in history – they did not succeed in perpetuating the Churchill name: their son died as a youth at Cambridge. By special remainder the dukedom devolved upon their daughter Henrietta, married to the son of Cornish Godolphin, John and Sarah's constant friend and confidant. The son of this marriage also died young and childless. So the Marlborough title and fortunes came to the lucky Spencers, the sons of John and Sarah's next daughter, Anne: young Charles Spencer became the third Duke and succeeded to his grandfather's inheritance; his brother John took over the Spencer estates, by special arrangement, and got the bulk of his grandmother's fortune.

With the Spencers a new strain came into the family. Whatever we may think of the talents of the original Churchills, no-one would accuse them of being connoisseurs or aesthetes. The Spencers were markedly both; to these avocations they added bibliophily, while some of them were artists in their own right. On the political side, however, the Trimmer tradition continued. Charles, third Duke, went to and fro like a weathercock – though Sarah's pressure upon her grandson was as much responsible as the political winds that blew. George, fourth Duke, sat pretty loosely to party: though really a Whig of the centre, with whom the motive of not offending George III was perhaps strongest, he was described by Lord Bute as a Tory – perhaps one small indication that the inner arcana of the politics of leading English families were not perfectly familiar to that doctrinaire Scot. This Duke and his brothers together occupied a spread from a position not far from the King's, through Shelburnite Whig and Pitt's following, to reforming Foxite principles. The family position did not settle down into a normal Toryism until after the Reform Bill of 1832.

Even so, after the unalleviated Toryism of our Sir Winston's grandfather, the Victorian seventh Duke, there comes the Tory Democracy of Lord Randolph Churchill: his son considered that had he lived this might have carried him over into Liberalism, as he himself was carried in 1905, not finding his way back till 1923. Perhaps we may conclude that where the country's interests (and their own) pointed, this fortunate family were mostly to be found.

For it was a thundering stroke of fortune that gave the family in its second phase a figure wider in his range, loftier in stature and of even greater significance in his country's history than Marlborough in the first phase. It was no less fortunate for this offshoot of the long line of Spencers and Churchills, fortified by an equally strong and idiosyncratic strain in the American Jeromes, to have expressed the ultimate will of the English peoples to resist and to survive in the heroic years 1940–1945. Perhaps that was the apogee of all our history – and marks the moment when, in the dangers of an atomic world, our separate history is merging into that of the English-speaking peoples all over the world. If so, there could be no more symbolic figure to stand beckoning on the threshold.

A couple of years after Waterloo, and perhaps under its inspiration, the family resumed the Churchill name. And, curiously enough, that coincided with a resumed dominance of Churchill over Spencer characteristics in the family. I do not think this a fanciful suggestion, for a family's conception of itself exerts a constant influence upon its members – nowhere more marked than in the family loyalty, the filial devotion, of its latest and grandest representative. At the same time it is worth noting how the Spencer characteristics come out in him no less than the Churchill traits: the artist in him is almost as strong as the politician and soldier.

The first volume of this history exposed the origins of the family, the struggle upwards, the ascent to glory; this volume deals with the story since. It has not been without a certain aesthetic satisfaction to observe a similar rhythm in the two phases. In the first, beginning quietly in the fields of Dorset and Devon, the family made its rise to the corridors and dependencies of Whitehall, and thence achieved its own wide sunlit plateau with Blenheim. In the second, beginning quietly with the education of Sarah's grandsons, the love-story during life of Charles and Elizabeth, the third Duke and his Duchess, passing through the long tranquil reign of the fourth Duke with his exquisite taste and sensibility, we ascend via the dizzy altitudes and declivities of Lord Randolph's exciting career to the rugged mountain-chain of his son's achievement in history. If the first period has the interest of the family's rise, while the second finds them already on the level of Blenheim, it has not been any the less a struggle to maintain themselves there.

If family history is more concrete and reliable, there is too the pathos and the poetry. It is nowhere more touching than in the places that knew these figures when they were alive: Ashe, ruddy now in autumn with the apple-orchards that surround the fragmentary Elizabethan house; Minterne church, dark and funereal with overhanging trees beside that Dorset road, the earlier Churchills gathered inside the narrow aisle; Blenheim in its splendour, to which they are all now anchored, those wide Oxfordshire spaces open to the moving skies, the fantastic roofscape reflected in the water of the lake, the lean shadow by the bridge, the great Duke on his column above the swaying trees; and now Chartwell, with its Elizabethan kernel, the radiant valley beneath the terraces, the sidelong view to the Downs whence came the planes in 1940. All stored away in those crevices of mind and heart to draw sustenance from in the horrors of the dark into which we go.

Chapter 1

Sarah's Grandsons

WHEN Marlborough died in June 1722 there was no likelihood of his vast inheritance coming to the Spencers. He was succeeded in the dukedom by his eldest daughter, Henrietta, who was married to the son of his old friend Godolphin; they had an heir, who now became Marquis of Blandford, with every prospect of carrying on the line. Sarah cared more for the Spencers, the children of her favourite daughter, Anne; on whose early death, as we have seen,[1] Sarah took charge of the orphaned girls – especially of the enchanting Di, who became her last love. In April of that year 1722 their father, the Earl of Sunderland, died suddenly and unexpectedly: an event that transformed the face of politics, for he was George I's leading minister and might have looked forward to many years of power. The way was left open for the long ascendancy of Sir Robert Walpole. Another consequence was that the care of the younger sons – the eldest succeeded to his father's estates and was soon old enough to look after himself – now fell also to Sarah. She assumed the charge with her usual energy and self-satisfaction, the familiar mixture of omnicompetence and exasperation.

The result is that there exist at Blenheim Sarah's detailed accounts of the brothers' expenses along with her correspondence about them, which gave one a fascinating picture of the upbringing of young sprigs of the English nobility in the second decade of the eighteenth century.[2]

The affairs of the family at Blenheim were a subject of gossip in the common rooms at Christ Church, as they have continued to be up to our own time. Dr Stratford was anxious to learn in what spirit the great Whig intellectual, the arrogant free-thinker whom Queen Anne could not abide, Lord Sunderland,

1. *v. The Early Churchills*, 374 foll.

2. Quotations and figures in this chapter are, unless otherwise stated, from unpublished MSS. at Blenheim, in drawers E 31 and E 54.

had faced death and 'whether he showed any sense of religion; I suppose not'.[3] Church affairs could never be on so bad a foot, to a Tory, as they were while he was in power. His correspondent, the son of Harley – Sunderland's old enemy – was able to assure him that he had some form of religion at his death. Dr Stratford was unable to see 'for what reason men of his opinion in which he was so open when he lived, as well as of his manners, should affect to act such a farce at that moment'. More important, for a bibliophile, was the disposition of Sunderland's famous library: 'I am afraid his death will throw a temptation in your way.... Here will be gleaning for my friend Mr Wanley.'

Shortly after we learn that 'young Lord Sunderland is going to Paris for this summer and returns about the time he is of age, towards the winter. He has refused being a Lord of the Bedchamber, which shows he is under his grandmother's influence.'[4] (Sarah had for some time been on unfriendly terms with her son-in-law and was now in opposition to the ministry.) A few days later this piece of gossip had grown: 'young Sunderland had a Garter offered him as well as a Bedchamber place'. This was improbable; not even canons of Christ Church are always infallible. 'His grandmother told him, if he would despise their baubles she would give him somewhat better than they would or could.' This was probable enough: it has the authentic ring. The young peer went off to Paris: the proper objective for a youth in his position and with his prospects.

Since the Sunderland Library came to be one of the most celebrated of the treasures with which Blenheim was packed, it will be as well to tell the story at this point of how it came to rest there.

Collecting books had been the delight of the somewhat unglad life of the intellectual statesman. Humphrey Wanley said that his keenness put up the prices of rare books in London. At the time of his death the parcels were still coming in – to be paid for by his executors Godolphin and Pulteney: the Earl had not expected to die. During the last three years of his life, with the profits of office, he was engaged in altering the old library

3. *H.M.C., Portland MSS.*, IV. 321–2. 4. ibid., 327, 329.

in his house in Piccadilly and then building a new one. A good many of the accounts remain: builders' and slater's bills, iron railing for the galleries; library tables with green baize covers, brass-plates for candle stands, hanging glasses and large mirrors over the chimney-pieces, a walnut table and a marble table in a gilt gesso frame.[5] An early eighteenth-century library: it must have been charming.

The year after Sunderland's death there was a proposal to sell the library to the King of Portugal. There are letters from Burnett, the English agent at Lisbon, complaining of the dilatoriness of the Court there and the difficulty of getting a positive figure out of the Secretary of State. The Court had incurred much expense by the recent Spanish marriages, but now that the fleet had arrived from Brazil with great riches Burnett hoped that the negotiation might be concluded. A Portuguese Jew who was employed to inspect the library reported that it was 'the most curious collection in Europe'. At length the Secretary of State offered 12,000 crusados, when the English price was £1200 sterling.

In April 1725 Godolphin wrote from Newmarket,

> since my Lord Sunderland approves so much of selling the manuscripts, my humble opinion is that Mr Burnett should be empowered to take £1000 for them, rather than miss the opportunity of parting with them. . . . Since he may truly affirm that £1500 was paid for one parcel of them only, I should hope that asking that sum for the whole might not be thought a demand too unreasonable for a king to comply with.

It fortunately turned out to be so and the library remained in England, to escape the Lisbon earthquake and grace the Long Gallery at Blenheim. Apparently it was Godolphin who, by advancing the young Earl the money on its security, enabled the library to be retained.

His younger brothers – Charles now fifteen, John eighteen months younger – were briefly at Eton.[6] Their dame was Mrs

5. Blenheim MSS., F I. 54 and 57.

6. Charles was born in November 1706, John on 13 May 1708. G. Baker, *History and Antiquities of the County of Northampton*, I. 110.

Naylor, to whom the Duchess paid £29 13s. for a quarter's board. In October they had two pair of buckskin breeches made for £1 16s. There was tea regularly for the young ladies, Di and her sister, at 8s. a pound; chocolate for the young masters. On 3 April Charles had a pair of shoes costing 7s., and eight more pairs in the next three months – in all four guineas. A Sagathy coat with breeches and a black camlet waistcoat, garters, buttons and buckles, cost £4 3s. Johnny's shoes from April 1723 to December 1724 cost £17 11s.; wigs, periwigs and bags, £19. The boys were left at Windsor Lodge for the winter, from 8 December to 2 March, when they went to St Albans with their grandmother. Their expenses while at Windsor were £253 13s. 11½d. (We must multiply by at least ten for a contemporary valuation.) One sees how expensive it was to be somebody in the eighteenth century – a recurring theme, we are reminded of it constantly.[7]

That summer the boys were having lessons in fencing and dancing. But it was time to send them abroad for their education. What Sarah thought of the purposes of foreign travel she expresses in her downright fashion. 'For my own part I never thought travelling was much use but to teach them perfectly the language and to keep them out of harm's way, while they are so young that they can't keep the best company in England; and to make them see that nothing is so agreeable as England, take it altogether.' From which we see what a patriot Sarah was – and also what a Philistine. A place was found for the brothers at Geneva, at the establishment of a M. Gallatin, a man of good family from which descended in the next generation the famous Secretary of the United States Treasury.

M. Gallatin became quite attached to the two Spencer brothers, especially to Charles, who remained with him for three years and had his share of the Spencer charm. On his departure M. Gallatin expressed his grief: 'toute la douleur que peut causer le départ d'un ami tendre et à qui je m'intéressais de tout mon cœur'. John was with him for a shorter period. From M. Gallatin's beautifully written accounts we perceive that he denied

7. These expenses were, of course, to come out of their inheritance, not just met by Sarah.

them, and himself, nothing. There are frequent payments of pocket-money, usually a score or so of *livres* at fourteen to the guinea. M. Gallatin did everything on a fine scale: there are clothes for their valet Abraham, payments for tea and sugar, damask *robes de chambre*; for riding school, masters in mathematics, *belles-lettres*; for *pension* and lodging, and of course extras.

John Spencer must have a flowered silk suit for the King's birthday, with stockings, hat and a peruke, costing 450 *livres*, while his share in the expenses of celebrating it came to 80 *livres*. Then there was a suit for his man, with a gold shoulder-knot, 276 *livres*; more for a scarlet riding-coat, with cape lined in velvet, a hat with silver edging, not to mention pocket-money, lodging and diet, and payment for the several masters. An entertainment at a tavern consumed fifty bottles of burgundy. There were the famous Duke of Marlborough's grandsons: no need to stint them (or oneself): they should make a good figure in the world.

We can hardly be surprised at Sarah's feelings as the accounts came in with their regularly increasing demands for extras. In September 1726 she is writing long letters to Gallatin complaining of the extravagance of Charles's stay – he was now moving from Geneva to the Court of Lorraine. She considers Gallatin's idea of a tour in Switzerland an unnecessary expense and 'worse than that, because it will lose him so much time in taking off from his study, which he wants much more than to see places that are very little worth'. The young man's time is being wasted in useless conversation: 'it is plain he does not write English well, which he will be ashamed of if you don't mend that before he comes into England, for it is better of the two for a man to be imperfect in any language than in his own'.

In October the Duchess was surprised to find that Gallatin had drawn bills upon her for £400 sterling. Whatever for? 'Charles's expenses at Geneva has [*sic.*] been extravagant and ridiculous' – indignation went to her grammar, and made it shakier than usual. But there is never any doubt about her meaning. Clothes? If he had to have a suit to appear at the Court of Lorraine, there was no need to have it made at Geneva:

better it were made in Lorraine, at least it would be in the fashion there. Linen? A great deal of linen has already appeared in former accounts, and he had a large provision of shoes on leaving Geneva, 'which seemed strange to me, for unless these things could not be had at Lorraine people don't choose to be encumbered with unnecessary things upon the road', et cetera. She concludes that Gallatin 'is far from being a disinterested man, as Charles thought him. Gallatin is making what bills he pleases and draws on me whether I will or no.' She suspects that behind these demands there must be *play* – a mania in that age, to which the Spencers, unlike the Churchills, had a hereditary addiction.

In May 1725 John had been sent abroad to join his brother, in the care of a young Guards officer, Humphrey Fish, who had been brought up as a page in Sarah's household and could therefore be relied on. At Paris two new suits of clothes were bought for 560 *livres* and there were the sights to see, the house, menagerie and woods at Chantilly, Versailles, the Trianon, Marly, Meudon and St Cloud; a berlin was hired to roll about in for a fortnight, with a French footman. On departing for Geneva there were post expenses, for dinner at Fontainebleau and seeing the palace; for supper and lodging and greasing the wheels at Montargis; for wine, biscuits and eggs; on the road for help to cross a river, for oxen to draw the carriage up the mountains. The high summer of 1725, the France of Cardinal Fleury and the *entente* with England, May and June along those scented flowering highways, youth and a millionairess of a grandmother to draw upon – what a delightful time they must have had!

The Duchess regarded Mr Fish's account as satisfactory and paid it at once: 'I shall never complain of any charge which is either useful or reasonable, but I mortally hate abuses or money foolishly thrown away'. Fish had left Johnny with Gallatin and then gone on with Charles to Lorraine. He was now able to report to the Duchess on the situation at Geneva: Gallatin had an affection for the two brothers but he was not industrious and had no notion of method or economy. In December 1726 he sent in an account for Johnny, which roused the Duchess again by increasing 'all those extravagancies of music, treats, allowances to the footman and feathers, notwithstanding that I writ positively that I would not allow of it'. Would people never be reasonable? Alas, it was not in nature. Charles at his age ought not to have been imposed upon by Gallatin. (It is fairly clear that Gallatin had kept on good terms with that young man by letting him do as he liked.) Now he asks for a velvet suit for John. The Duchess: 'I think to make things in such a place for the Court of Lorraine is just as if one was to make clothes at St Albans for a Birthday' (*i.e.* a royal birthday at Court). Gallatin's next account contains sums for playing on the flute, 'which as you know is a thing that I absolutely forbid and those things that he put so large a sum for making copies are to be bought here printed for 12 shillings'. Sarah has written Charles that 'I will not have him play for anything and I repeat the same as to Johnny'. Johnny's hand 'does not answer the care that I have taken to make him write handsomely and I could say the same for his brother'. As for his playing upon a pipe, 'I did not send him abroad to be a fiddler'.

She now took Johnny out of Gallatin's hands: he joined his brother in Lorraine in February 1727. Accounts with Gallatin were wound up, the Duchess paying all his demands as usual and protesting – as usual, in vain – against the expense of an equipage to ride post on the journey, when the horses they used for hunting should have done. After all Charles and John were younger sons with small fortunes: it was not expected that they should move about as if they were the Duke of Marlborough's heir: 'if they don't conform they shall make the best of the money that comes to them from their father's trust, and which is very far short of what they expect'. Gallatin closed his account with dignity, and no doubt with profit: 'Je suis mille fois plus sensible aux expressions dures et fâcheuses dont la lettre de Madame la Duchesse est remplie qu'à toute autre chose', that is to say, than to augment his own *petite fortune*.

The brothers were now together at the Court of Lorraine, where they were well received by the Duke, Leopold, who had made his duchy prosperous and agreeable and, moreover, had obligations to their grandfather. On his arrival Johnny was at once asked to sup privately with the Duke and Duchess who made much of him. Sarah acknowledged that this was a great honour, 'but I think he is too young to give up all useful improvements for that sort of entertainment'. The little Court at Lunéville and Nancy was very hospitable and gay, with frequent *fêtes* and entertainments. Sarah considered that 'they need not affect to be at the top of all that folly, nor wear fine clothes but upon proper occasions; which will make them last the longer. As for example: when I go a journey, stay at home or go to a dirty Indian shop, I don't put on my best mantua.' She does not like them going to Court so often, for 'they must expect only to live like country gentlemen upon small fortunes. And if they could have philosophy enough for that (which I believe is not their tempers), what a sad thing it is for men that had an opportunity of knowing everything that is valuable to be able to talk of nothing but hunting; and if they by chance have any estate, to know so little of accounts or business, as to be afraid of their stewards!' Sarah was anxious that her favourite grandsons – of whom she was clearly fond, at this time it is 'dear Charles' and 'dear Johnny' – should cut a worthy figure in the world. 'I have happened to be present at some of those conversations' – about books and classical authors – 'where some great men have been who could not say a word no more than myself, and I could not help reflecting upon Charles and John at that time and wishing that from all the pains I have taken they might not make the same sad figure at the end of their travels as I observed some did.' We observe here an underlying modesty in Sarah, a regret for her own lack of education, which rendered all the more acute her desire that her grandsons should do better.

To recommend her boys to the Duke and to recompense him for his kindness – he frequently invited them to his table and took them out hunting – Sarah sent them a present of a hundred bottles of Barbados water, 'which is worth all the cider in this country'. She hears that usquebaugh and good sack are very dear in Lorraine and is ready to send them some when she hears from them. The Barbados water was much appreciated and she follows it up with five dozen of cider for a trial. Her care of her boys extends to the minutest matters: do they take care of their teeth? 'Though a man were beautiful as Adonis he would be disagreeable with ill teeth. My Lord Sunderland has teeth that are as white as pearl and that, having good eyes, makes him look very well, though he cannot be said to have a handsome face.' There follows some interesting information on an esoteric subject – how people looked after their teeth in those days. The best way is 'to wash them always after eating and to take off something that naturally comes upon everybody's teeth after sleeping, with those quills that are round at one end, and never to clean them with anything that is harsh or that can hurt the gums. I think that honey mixed with bole ammoniac is a very good thing. And there is a white ashes that comes off from wood, if it be taken up carefully, that is very soft. But if the mouth is kept very clean, as I have already directed, they won't often want anything of that kind, and the seldomer they are rubbed the better and the longer the gloss will continue upon them. Burnt crust is harsh and the worst they can do, for it wears the gums.'

It is not long before Fish has to confess to an extra charge, like Gallatin before him. He writes, 1 May 1727, 'we have fallen into an expense which I must own was silly enough in itself, but 'twas but for once, and it could not be well avoided. It was upon the occasion of St George's day, the Patron of England, when all the English joined to give an entertainment to the people of the greatest distinction here. What gave occasion to it was the example of the Scotch and Irish that are here travelling, who had done something like it on St Patrick's and St Andrew's day. It comes to £17 for each of the Mr Spencers, which is what it costs every Englishman here. Of an unnecessary thing it was a very good one, for it was extremely well served and there was a good deal of company all very well satisfied with it.' The Duchess did not complain; she had given her view that these little entertainments in such vogue abroad were but 'an invention of the country for to make strangers spend their money'.

That month, May 1727, there was a rumour of war breaking out, and Captain Fish was rendered anxious at being away from his regiment. Sarah took the trouble to obtain Lord Scarbrough's assurance that there would be no war; and 'remember me very kindly to the two dear brothers'. Next month, 'tell Charles that I shall choose him of the House of Commons for the next Parliament, but that won't oblige him to come into England sooner than is reasonable, but only secure it for him when he has done his travels, and then John I will choose after he is of age, upon the first opportunity that I have'. That expresses the attitude of a patron, with borough interests, towards Parliamentary representation in the eighteenth century.

But Sarah was to find, not for the first or last time, her sanguine expectations not so simple to fulfil. For one thing, the election come upon them sooner than was expected.

The very next month, July 1727, the King died and that in those days necessitated an election. It set in motion a good many changes and even more hopes – especially for preferment, a prime preoccupation of the eighteenth century – Captain Fish's among others. He applied to the Duchess, who answered that she had 'no real interest at Court, I have not seen a minister but in the streets this many years and I know that in the late Queen's time, though I was a favourite, without the help of the Duke of Marlborough and Lord Godolphin I should not have been able to do anything of any consequence and the things that are worth naming will ever be done from the influence of men'. It is an interesting reflection, with its tinge of feminism. She was surprised and grieved to learn that the brothers wished to come into England to see the Coronation. Nothing was more ridiculous than to leave all the improvements they could have abroad to come into England 'only to see some old and odd people walk in red velvet upon green cloth, for handsome figures I know of none'. Gone were the days of her own beauty and John Churchill's, 'as handsome as an angel'; did she have a suspicion that she herself would provide one of the oddest spectacles at George II's Coronation? Would she have minded or cared?

She bestirred herself about more important matters. 'Tell Charles that I have been very busy to settle his being chose a member of Parliament for Woodstock, and with expense and a good deal of trouble I don't doubt of success; and I design to set up the Marquis of Blandford for St Albans. Not that he will ever sit in the House of Commons, for when he comes into England, which is not expected soon, he will be called up by writ into the House of Lords; so that is only keeping a place for Johnny to be chose where I have a natural right to recommend when he is of age.' All was not so simple, however. At St Albans she had expected to share the two seats between her grandson Blandford and Lord Grimston, both having local ties. But in the town there was a third interest so strong that 'your Lordship and my grandson cannot be chose without spending and bribing to the amount of a thousand pounds'.[8] From her experience she was sure that that meant a good deal more, 'and therefore I am determined to have no more to do with this election. I think it better to keep the money to help pay the taxes that a single member can't prevent.'

Meanwhile at Woodstock Sir Thomas Wheate discovered that Charles was not of age, 'which to prove he got a certificate from St James's church, and there being a law against choosing any member before they were of age, I was forced to set up my Lord Blandford an hour after I heard this blot was hit, to avoid a disagreeable petition in the House of Commons, which would have made this election void'. She was sorry for Charles's disappointment, 'but I hope he will bear it patiently since it was not my fault. And I think it very possible that many accidents may happen to give me an opportunity of bringing him into the house by the time he comes into England. And I assure him I will lose no occasion of doing it.'

These accidents happened, one of them of a nature to exclude Charles from the Commons for good: when his brother Sunderland died in 1729 he succeeded him in the Lords. Next year the disagreeable intruder into the seat at St Albans was dying; here was an opportunity for Johnny. The Duchess received a visit from Lord Grimston, head of the Bacon interest there, 'who seemed desirous to serve me; but I found before he went away that he only came with these professions to feel my pulse, and that his design is to set up his son, which I think would be very hard usage in St Albans to my family. I design to set up the

8. *H.M.C.*, *Verulam MSS.*, 121. Sarah to Viscount Grimston.

only grandson I have now that is a commoner, John Spencer, who has a very considerable fortune for a younger brother, and I will make it as good as most elder brothers. . . . Upon my certain knowledge Lord Grimston has never failed in contributing his vote in all those grievous things which this nation is now oppressed with.' That, in a word, meant the rule of the detested Walpole.

She did not get her way at St Albans. It was provoking that for all her money and being a Duchess and the condescension of having been born there, the ungrateful burgesses could not be brought to oblige her: they preferred to support Sir Robert. However, when Blandford died in 1731, Johnny could be brought in for one of the two family seats at Woodstock; and for Woodstock he sat so long as his grandmother lived – he did not long survive her.[9]

Abroad Charles 'received the news of the loss of his election with a great deal of firmness', Fish reported, 'as I believe he would any ill accident that he thought of consequence to him . . . the hopes you give him were enough to keep up his spirits were he less resolute'. The chief source of disappointment was that Charles would have now no excuse for returning home – and he was utterly bored with being abroad. In the early autumn they had been travelling about in Germany: 'we have entirely exhausted our fund of curiosity as to any further progress in that country'. In future years Charles as a soldier was to see more of it than of any other European land; he died as Commander-in-Chief of the British Army there. In October they were in Holland, at the Hague and at Utrecht where they dined with their cousin Lord Blandford: he knew nothing about his being chosen, by his grandmother, for Parliament and was on his way back to Paris.

Charles gave his voice for spending the winter in Paris, 'because he thought there would be a great many agreeable entertainments for the afternoons and evenings which would keep us in better humour and better spirits for the morning's application than if we should be at a place where we should be tired every day of our lives'. Mr John was indifferent; he would keep

9. cf. *Return of Members of Parliament*, II. 66, 77, 90.

his promise to pass the mornings in things that required some application, 'as to the afternoons he should find ways and means to divert himself tolerably wherever he was'. And so, equipped with Misson's *Travels* in three volumes with post maps lined with cloth, bought at the Frankfort fair – books make an infrequent appearance in these young gentlemen's expensive accounts – they travelled across country that had been fought over by their famous grandfather and that still echoed his name. At Brussels they were invited to dine with his old acquaintance Lord Ailesbury, who pronounced them 'two good young men, with Mr Fane and Mr Fish, old Mr Fish's grandson, a very pretty young man of the 2nd Regiment of Guards'.[10] Next day they left for Paris, where they were to spend the whole winter.

Meanwhile what progress were they making with their education? The Duchess demanded a report. Captain Fish replied that Gallatin had been neglectful and let them do what they liked. Yet their time was not utterly lost; they understood French very well and spoke and wrote it fluently. Their arithmetic was pretty well. Latin they understood better than when they left Geneva; they now had read and tasted the best part of Horace. They had a good notion of ancient history and geography, and a proper introduction to modern history. 'As to English I have got Madame de Sévigné's Letters, which are excellent, and Mr Spencers will translate three or four in a week, which I will likewise do and then we shall compare them and correct them.' As to their being weary of being abroad, 'I will tell you what is the truth of that matter. Mr Spencer has very little curiosity and looks upon all travelling as a very insipid entertainment, and thinks of Italy with a great dread as having no taste to the things he expects to see there.' In that we detect Charles turned after the Churchill side of his family, not after his bookish intellectual father – and Sarah sympathised with him. 'But Mr John is far from being in the same case; he thinks of seeing France with pleasure enough, but he is very eager in his desires to see Italy.' Mr Fane who has been with them thinks of going to pay court at Hanover. Would the Duchess care to engage Mr Fane's French tutor, M. Chais? – it would

10. *H.M.C., Ailesbury MSS.*, 232.

be 'like having a living dictionary always at one's elbow, which one may turn to immediately upon a hundred different subjects'.

The Duchess agreed to retain M. Chais: 'I never grudge any expense that my children are the better for, nor can be satisfied without rewarding a good man according to his merit.' Nor can she with a good conscience blame Charles's want of curiosity, 'because I have none myself for such things as you mention'. Then, 'I must ever wish Mr Montgomery well ... but I should be glad to know what you hear, in such a way that it may not be understood but by myself'. This relates to rumours of Blandford's attachment to the young lady at Utrecht whom he married. It is interesting to see that Sarah thinks of him by the affectionate name of her old friend Godolphin and that she is keeping her eye on him, though 'that is all in my power to do'; he was Marlborough's heir. The brothers' account amounts to £1500; this is for only three-quarters of a year and Lorraine is considered not expensive – in addition to all Gallatin's extras. It is far too much for younger sons to spend. As for Charles's return to England, she may consent to it in the summer, but John is much too young as yet.

To the Captain's demand for a directive as to the plan of studies they should pursue, the Duchess responds with a fine letter completely exposing her mind, with no hesitation or lack of clarity or decision, as her manner was.

You know my opinion long ago as to the use of travelling. I never had any taste for curiosities and I think they are of little value further than that they serve to kill time while you have nothing better to do and that it is not proper to be in England. Useful learning is what I have always earnestly recommended and next to that, to be sure, good company is the most desirable thing. But I should naturally have thought that the worse the company is at any place and the duller, the more likely it would be for young men to apply themselves to that sort of knowledge and learning that I am confident Charles and John are ignorant of. The mathematics I have always thought was the most desirable knowledge, and I remember once you gave me great hopes of Mr Chais's reading and explaining to them the classic authors. And I should have thought there are abundance of other books of letters which would be useful for young men to read, in order to make them write well. To speak the French language perfectly well is certainly very agreeable and upon many occasions it will be more useful even than Latin. But I was in hopes in so long time as the brothers have been abroad, being so young as they were, they would have been masters of that before this time. Dancing gives men a good air and fencing should be learnt, because it is possible that it may be of use. But if you have not learnt those things, what have you been doing this three-year? As to medals and antiquities, painting and sculpture, I don't look upon that to be the most useful knowledge to anybody, and much less to younger brothers who will have no money to lay out in such things.

Ironically enough, and according to the usual pattern by which such clear-sightedness and downrightness ask to be contradicted by the perversity of things, the contrariness of life – this was the very way that all the Spencers were to go. In fact they did get the money, and most of them became connoisseurs. Connoisseurship ran in their veins and they spent fortunes upon medals and antiquities, painting and sculpture – just what Sarah detested: that and gaming. If she could have known, she might have given all her money to the poor; but that she would have considered lunatic. What Swift did with his money was a case in point.

'As to architecture I think it will be of no use to Charles nor John, no more than music; which are all things proper for people that have time upon their hands and like passing it in idleness rather than in what will be profitable.' Here too she was proved wrong: on succeeding to Althorp Charles spent a great deal on refashioning it and he built himself a fine house at Langley, which he preferred to Blenheim. Perhaps we may consider that Sarah's very rationalism, carried to such extremes, bordered on lunacy; it certainly fortified her in her eccentricity.

But I find by your letters for some time that you are weary of being abroad. And I don't wonder at it, if there is little to be learnt there but such sort of improvements and seeing curiosities. As to the difference of the expense at Paris, I believe, if it is managed with reason it can't be very considerable, excepting in one thing, which I have forbid in all places, and that is *play*. I know in France they will all be wonderful civil in hopes of cheating you. And when they find people won't play, they grow very cool. And I think it is better to go without such civilities than to pay too dear for them.

All this was perfectly true. Their brother Lord Sunderland was corroborating it in his own experience at this moment in Paris. 'All the French women are cheats. The present Lord Sunderland that has money has been hurt by it and it has done so much mischief to the family, who never could command their temper, that it makes me uneasy when you but name play.'

To this tirade the Captain replied with spirit that 'Mr Spencers do not play, they are not finer than other people, they have the fewest servants that is possible and no debts are suffered to run on for tradesmen to charge more things than were delivered'. Yet their account is so large, for 'whoever will live cheap in a foreign country or indeed anywhere must have a constant attention and oeconomy in every article of expense that very few people are masters of'. (The Duchess was such a master.) As for Charles,

> he thinks of nothing but England and pines after it: the more he sees of foreign countries the more that desire increases. Paris does not answer his hopes, he is not easy nor happy. If he employs the morning in study, that is as much as one can well expect at one and twenty and when he goes out afterwards it is to return tired and disgusted. The world offers nothing agreeable to his imagination but England.

The footing of equality and mutual candour upon which the Duchess stood with her young Fish was much to the credit of them both. Sarah gave way and consented to Charles coming home.

> It is impossible for me to answer anything to generals that are very well expressed; but there must certainly be a great fault somewhere, since there are but few elder brothers that spend what they have done in travelling. I have nothing more to do now but to let them have what the produce of their fortune is, which they may dispose of as they think fit and which is more than my Lord Blandford had who is the heir to so great an estate. You tell me that the expense at Paris will scarce be less than £200 a month. That is more than the Duke of Marlborough and I spent when we were abroad with more than twenty horses and a houseful of servants.

Better if the brothers had laid out their money on a present to obtain an employment to add to their income, 'since 'tis plain they will spend more than they have'. Charles will feel the same uneasiness about play when he returns, 'for he will find everybody plays in this town: sharpers to get money and those that he will think fine gentlemen, to lose their estates. He has none to spare. And I am apt to think he will never be the better for play.'

Among the expenses for their Paris finery, powder and pomatum and silver swords, we find 360 *livres* for two mantillas they bought as presents for their grandmother and their sister Di. This was the only time they thought of anything of the sort for the old lady, who worked like a cart-horse on their behalf: the thought was much appreciated. There is a note of a physician for bleeding Mr Charles in his fever – he had the family tendency; and for loads and loads of wood. A cold time they had of it that winter in Paris. But Charles was coming home; what balance could be struck as to their education and equipment for all the money that had been spent on it?

> I have never yet had the satisfaction of finding that either of the brothers wrote their own language well; though their two sisters, that are of the simple sex, both write very correct. And here is a Frenchman that I believe is about three score, who has learned in a year's time to read all the English authors, and both to write and speak English: his name is Voltaire.

Evidently what Voltaire could do these very ordinary young lads were expected to be able to do likewise.

In February 1728 Charles at last came home. Sarah found that, having been abroad near five years, he still pronounced French like an Englishman. And he 'now has a little tone in his speaking English which seems to me affected, and if it happens that he does not speak French well it will be melancholy to have an ill accent in both languages'. His father had been a good linguist, fluent in both English and French, as well as a classical scholar; but then he was a remarkable and gifted man. The Captain replied that he could never cure Charles from pronouncing French like an Englishman: 'it always was his way . . . he has never had a familiar acquaintance that has not told him of it and at times rallied and laughed at him about it, which was the most probable way of curing it'. Sarah did not think Charles handsome, 'but he is well enough as the world goes and has a civil and modest behaviour'. But he has an ill habit of speaking through his teeth, one can't tell whether he says Yes or No; it is disagreeable not to speak distinctly, 'especially to a man that seems to have a great taste to be a senator. . . . There are several women in this country that don't articulate well and who think it pretty to make a noise like a bird.' We may be sure Sarah articulated only too clearly. Perhaps it was this that abashed Charles in the presence of his alarming grandmother. She complained that he never spoke but to answer her, and then she couldn't make out what he said and made him repeat it, 'which must make anybody weary of such a conversation'. In fact there could hardly be a more effective mode of self-defence on the part of a weak against an aggressive personality. Silence, lack of candour, disingenuousness, evasion – such is the familiar progression.

The time had come to concentrate on the last stage of Johnny's education. She longed to see him, for she had ever liked him since he was a child. What did he look like now? 'I thought he had once a good deal of his dear mother.' Back came the Captain's inevitable reply: 'he is changed since your Grace saw him from a boy to a man and his features are larger; he makes a very good figure, he is strong and well made, and is taller and larger every way than his brother'. Once before when Johnny had taken the trouble to write to her, she chaffingly sent her thanks 'for his directions how to dress myself, but more for having mended his hand'. Now she wrote charmingly to him,

> I never liked any fashion so well as this you have sent me of the mantillas, and your sister is so fond of it that I believe she will find some excuse to wear it even when the weather doesn't require it. Your direction is very particular in putting them on, and yet I doubt we have not yet attained to putting them on in the best air.

In May, having rejected the idea of places along the Loire because they were so full of English every summer, the Captain and John settled at Dijon in a little house with a garden, airy and convenient. They went to a public table near by, where the company was good, for dinner and supper. John got up at seven to fence; the rest of the morning was employed in translating and reading history: they were now half-way through Rapin's ten volumes on the History of England. (It was the current popular history that had appeared only a few years before in French and was shortly after translated.) John came home soon after dinner to divert himself with music till four, when a master came for mathematics. In the cool of the evening he made visits, went to public walks or assemblies or shooting or tennis or what amusements he liked. It was an idyllic existence for two young men attached to each other.

Johnny had been translating Madame de Sévigné's Letters, and Sarah expressed a desire to see some of them. He complied, sending her his translations of Voiture's too: 'they are highly commended'. Sarah had seen others that she liked better than this lady's. But she was pleased with her grandson and persuaded that he 'will be in everything what I desire, exact in keeping his word'. She was especially pleased at his keeping his word about play: ''tis a dangerous inclination to encourage and has been ruinous to his family'. She was willing now to give her permission for their going to Turin.

At the end of August John fell ill. He took rosemary and milk, was blooded next morning, and given a warm plaster of spices on his side next night. The Duke of Kingston came to see him with his governor who was a physician and took him home with him for a week. He had had a high fever, from which he was now better. In September we have a glimpse of them at Plombières, John quite recovered.

And so they pass out of our view; the delights and seductions of Italy lay before them.

When Charles returned to England he went to stay with his brother Sunderland at Althorp. The next we hear is of his brother's death in Paris next year, leaving a mass of gambling debts behind him to prejudice the estate. His dying letter to Charles, written 20 September 1729, is very affecting.

Dear Brother, I am now a-dying, and therefore desire when I am dead that you will do according to the directions in this letter. I owe Sir Michael Newton 220 guineas which I have borrowed of him at Paris. I owe Mr Meadows four score pounds. I also desire that the one thousand pounds Mr Lamb gave me credit for at Paris may be punctually paid him; I have drawn for it all. I beg of you to sell as much of my plate as will be sufficient to do it, and pay him immediately. I think you cannot have better servants than all my old ones; you can't do better than to keep them all. D'Olignon to be sure you will keep, but if ever you do part with him I beg you will give him a pension of twenty pounds a year as long as he lives. I have mentioned poor Oreillard in my will for a pension of thirty pounds a year. Pray be kind to that poor fellow. Mr Herbert has a mortgage of £6300 upon my estate, the interest of which I hope you will take care to pay punctually. Farewell, dear Brother.

Charles Stanhope wrote Charles a brief account of his brother's last days. He had

a severe fit of his fever on Monday night, sent for me at two in the morning, perfectly in his senses but expecting to die. He used the kindest expressions in relation to your lordship, signed this letter and bade me acquaint you that he desired to be buried by his father at Brington. He ordered D'Olignon to bring out all his letters and papers out of a box in the next room in a handkerchief and ordered me to burn them. I have been all day sending for tradesmen's bills to settle and settling with all persons employed about my late lord – and draw a bill for it upon your lordship.

A full statement of Sunderland's personal finances was enclosed. The physicians' charges were high, but they were the best. 'Your lordship may be surprised that the late lord had taken up his full credit and 210 louis besides, but we know from his own mouth that he had lost a considerable sum at play at Versailles.' Later we learn that he had drawn bills on Matthew Lamb the moneylender, for £1,128 18s. 1d. with interest; we have a note from Lamb suggesting that a gratuity had been promised him for his trouble.[11] The physicians' report confirmed that nothing could save the young lord; they had sent the corpse in the Calais coach with M. D'Olignon and a footman to attend it.

Charles replied that he believed his brother did not intend the large debt and the mortgage to Mr Herbert should be known. (It is unlikely, however, that Sarah had not already got wind

11. Blenheim MSS., F I. 57.

of it.) 'You knew my dear brother too well not to forgive me if I don't write as I ought after such a loss.'

Poor young man, afflicted by the double fever of his disease and of gaming, he passes a mere wraith across our view: nothing to show for all the famous blood in his veins, Marlborough and Sarah, James II's Sunderland, fascinating and reptilian, and the high intellectual interests of his brilliant father. Unmarried and unnamed he lies amongst the splendid monuments of his ancestors and his successors in Brington church in Northamptonshire.

Charles succeeded to an already embarrassed estate and the very next month was forced to apply to his grandmother as trustee under Marlborough's will. Punctilious as she was in money matters, conscientious as a trustee, she came to his help by advancing him now what was due to him at Christmas. Of this £1,000, £330 was deducted for interest due to the executors and he had lately received £210 from Sarah; there remained to him £460, which she enclosed. 'This is all that is due to you upon that head from the trust. I beg of you to enter what you receive of all kinds in some book. I am most tenderly yours.'

In the spring he had recourse to Sarah again, through his sister Di as intermediary who, after some delay, represents his necessities to his grandmother. She sends him her note, with a letter very much to the point: 'I hope it will answer all your purposes with it as well now. I wish you health and pleasure, dear Lord Sunderland, *in everything but play*, who am most affectionately yours.' So Charles was going the way of his brother at the gaming table. The reminder was resented by the recipient, as such things are. I cannot see why. After all, Marlborough and Sarah had made their money with much labour; why should she be expected to see the young man gamble it away and not protest?

Lord Blandford's death in August 1731 transformed Charles's prospects. He was now heir to the dukedom; the contingent arrangements of Marlborough's will by which, on succeeding to Marlborough's inheritance, he should hand over the Spencer estates to his younger brother, were now on the immediate horizon. He was already considerably in debt on his own account – to his uncle Godolphin, one of the trustees and Blandford's father, for one. We learn that during his four years' rule at Althorp he was engaged in making improvements to the house and the estates, that he revived the traditional hospitality of the place.[12] He was also gaming heavily. He was very neglectful of business and, like al the Spencers, extravagant, with no conception of making ends meet. The results were to be expected.

Unwilling to go into his own affairs for himself, taking no interest in business, he has recourse to Sarah again. She looks into his grandfather's settlement for him and makes the unpleasant discovery that, since his elder brother's death, Charles has received £1,000 a year that should have been John's. There was no penalty on his not handing over the Sunderland estate, but it was considered that when he was head of the family as Duke of Marlborough with £50–£60,000 per annum 'he would very readily part with the Sunderland estate to his next brother'. On her discovery Sarah took steps to stop selling Charles's South Sea annuity for him and to transfer £2,000 to John, *i.e.* to cover the past two years. She suggested tartly his discharging the mortgage he owed to Lord Godolphin, 'now that so great a sum has gone from his family with your £9,000 a year and Lady Blandford's £3,000, as you don't want money now'.

All this is quite clear. On Blandford's death his widow got her jointure of £3,000 a year; but Charles as their heir to Marlborough would now get £8,000 a year, plus £1,000 a year that Marlborough had left him – all this in addition to the Sunderland estates. He was a rich man, in prospect one of the richest in the country. He could gamble to his heart's content. He proceeded to do so. Sarah looked after his interests, working 'like a pack-horse', she complained, when he would take no interest himself. She came to town in November to put through these complicated transactions and make the transfer to Johnny – I spare the reader all the rebarbative arithmetic of her letters. Then she sold Charles's South Sea stock for him, at a considerably appreciated price.

In her letter she wrote, 'if your brother and you should die without issue male all this great estate will be tossed up and

12. cf. *D.N.B.*, *sub* Charles Spencer, Duke of Marlborough.

down backwards and forwards into other families'. She clearly, and not unreasonably, expected to have a say in the marriages of Marlborough's heir and her own. She had reckoned without the resources of those she considered weaklings and fools: silence and evasion. Benjamin Constant has a penetrating passage, written from bitter experience, on this subject.

> C'est une erreur de considérer comme un grand avantage d'avoir de l'ascendant sur les autres et de pouvoir les obliger à faire ce que l'on veut . . . Chacun cède, mais chacun s'écarte. On fait un vrai travail pour se mettre hors de l'influence de la personne qui vous domine, on ne lui dit jamais complètement la vérité . . . Il en est des personnes passionnées comme des princes. Sans le vouloir on les trompe, parce qu'on craint l'explosion si on leur parle franchement.[13]

Sarah was one of those persons, and again and again this pattern formed itself in her life: her friend Queen Anne, her cousin Abigail, her daughters – and now her grandson, Marlborough's destined successor – without her grasping why.

Charles fancied a career, and even a marriage, for himself. In the second objective he was aided and abetted by his spirited sister, Lady Bateman, who had inherited more than her share of her grandmother's characteristics: hence their mutual dislike. Charles seems to have succeeded in marrying without creating any attention – indeed, from the absence of public notice, almost surreptitiously. When Sarah learned who the bride was to be she was thunderstruck, as thunderstruck as when she had learned, after everybody else, that Abigail Hill had become Mrs Masham. She was even more furious, for Elizabeth Trevor was the granddaughter of one of the twelve Tories created peers in order to pass the Treaty of Utrecht – an offence against her beloved Duke never to be forgiven. What made Charles's choice still more difficult to tolerate was that he never regretted it: his marriage was a happy one, and he and Elizabeth remained lovers all their lives.

13. Benjamin Constant, *Journal intime, 1804–1816*, ed. Paul Rival, 38.

Chapter 2

Family Affairs and Finances

CHARLES'S marriage, 23 May 1732, to Elizabeth Trevor brought to a head all his grandmother's grievances against him, both latent and overt. There were other reasons for the disaccord between them, his extravagance, inattention to business, politics – perhaps his character, for which she had little (and insufficient) respect, as well as her own, which evidently got on his nerves. But to his marriage she never became reconciled, though she made a brief effort.

At first there was a good deal of thunder and fireworks, which reverberated around society like everything concerned with Sarah and the Marlborough family. Lord Egmont reports the rumour that she forbade Charles her house and offered to settle £40,000 on John immediately if he would engage not to see his brother.[1] John was credited with replying that he had always loved his brother and no sum on earth would make him desert him. Always a popular figure with people, this made him still more so. There must have been something in this, for in writing to their sister Di expressing her displeasure at John's presence at the wedding, Sarah said that even 'if I had not designed to make him my heir, surely my endeavour to have him educated well, my manner of living with him, the tenderness I showed him on all essential occasions was in reality a greater obligation even than an estate'.[2]

What vexed Sarah most of all in the affair was that she was convinced that the marriage had been arranged by her declared enemy among her grandchildren, Charles's other sister, Lady Bateman. The Batemans were favourites at Court and supporters of the administration; the Duchess was up to her neck, and up to every artifice, in opposition. At this moment Lord Bateman had been given the Order of the Bath: the ceremony

1. *H.M.C.*, *Egmont*, I. 279.
2. G. Scott Thomson, *Letters of a Grandmother*, 44.

to Sarah was 'the red riband show', at which Lady Bateman had taken her new sister 'by the hand several times in that great assembly like a fond lover'. From which Sarah inferred that 'she intended to manage her as long as she can. . . . For my part, I do believe that my Lord Sunderland, who is certainly a very weak man, will always be governed by his sister.' The old lady's forebodings were to be proved wrong. As to the new member of the family she could say nothing of her own knowledge, and that was most disagreeable: it affronted her sense of dynastic decency.

The sweet-natured Di got to work to improve her opinion of the offending couple and in particular to create a more favourable impression of Charles's wife. Back came the answer,

> I dare say your judgement of her is more likely to be a right one . . . but I wonder how she comes to have so easy and right a behaviour, who has always been used to low and ordinary company. I should think that must proceed from what I was told by one, that she has sense. I am not at all surprised at her being pleased at the great change of her condition nor of his being so fond of her at first, who has certainly so nasty a constitution.[3]

Coldness and ingratitude she charged to poor Charles's account, and to this she added, not unreasonably, a vein of obstinacy. 'He seems to be very proud and to think that if he makes a great expense, that is being a man of honour.' This throws a new light on Charles: it was precisely his pride and his tenacity that made him hold on and in the end make a very respectable figure in the world.

For more than a year Sarah's ill-humour with the couple continued; but she could not hold to her bad resolutions where the spoiled Johnny was concerned. Within a few months he was back in favour and she was designing to set him up as a candidate for Surrey – 'the expense should not hinder me from that undertaking' – or at Woodstock, 'where, if I can, I would settle so as to have that place always, as it ought to be, in the Marlborough family'. It was her sense of the Marlborough dynasty that impelled her: for thirty years she has been labour-

3. ibid. 50–51.

ing to serve the whole family and 'has done it with great success'. Now the unity of the family is imperilled by Lady Bateman's machinations and by her favour at Queen Caroline's Court, 'and that must be from the hopes the ministers have of dividing a family who, if they were wise, would be strong enough to make any ministry afraid of disobliging them. But they certainly think that by her means they shall get my Lord Sunderland. And I believe they will.'[4]

There was the rub. So long as Sarah was alive, as trustee of Marlborough's will, she wielded the effective financial power of the family. But when Charles became Duke of Marlborough he became a figure in politics in his own right. Between the desire to play a part of his own and possess his own soul on one hand, and on the other not to offend the Duchess irretrievably, the need at times to accommodate his actions to his exigencies and her demands, Charles was in a difficult position, sometimes a humiliating one. And this to some extent accounts for changes and about-turns in his political conduct – no more flagrant than other people's, but more galling to his pride from the source from which they arose. So that political discords came to increase the *gêne* between them, and the family, so far from acting in politics as a unit – as Sarah wished, and meant to direct it – was more often divided.

On 24 October 1733 Duchess Henrietta, on whom Marlborough's honours had devolved, died and Charles succeeded as Duke. At once dynastic and good sense impelled a reconciliation. The new Duke went to visit the Dowager at Windsor Lodge.

It is not easy for me to describe, without lessening it, the goodness of his behaviour in every respect. All that he said was so extremely good-natured and with good sense. . . . Before he went away he desired that his wife might come to me, just as I was going to speak to him of her: which, I told him, I was that moment going to do, and that I should be glad to see her when I came to London. For I never had anything to say against her. And that, as everybody gives her a good character, I hope she will behave to him in the manner I wish.

4. G. Scott Thomson, *Letters of a Grandmother*, 83, 86, 95.

Sarah considered this a very surprising turn; but she had been reading the Book of Job and concluded that hitherto God 'for a punishment of some sin of mine allowed me to be tormented, as he did Job, I need not say by whom' – Lady Bateman, of course.[5]

Charles followed up the good impression he had made by stopping a night with the old lady at Windsor within a week. Sarah was so much touched that she thought now that she had been too angry with him and

> for that I have asked him to forgive me with tears. He is of a generou nature and being very young has been a good deal imposed upon in money matters, and being in great circumstances and not loving money, he did not consider enough and thought it of no value; but if he is not yet sensible of that error I dare say he will in a little time and he will make a right use of it, and if he does he will have enough of it.[6]

Alas, at this moment that was precisely what Charles had not. His succession to the dukedom meant that the moment had come when he had to opt between renouncing the eventual reversion to all Marlborough's wealth and the immediate renunciation of the Sunderland estates to his brother. This might mean that during the interval, until Sarah herself died, he would be less well off than his younger brother. Such a situation would be certain to lead to his raising money on his expectations and thereby vastly increasing his indebtedness. And that was just what came about. It is to his credit that he did not shrink from doing his duty and opted for the uncomfortable position of reversionary, with the inevitable intensification of his jars with Sarah.

But now he was in a fix. Can it be that his visits to his grandmother were to prepare the way for resorting to her to help him out of it?

She was never without resource, and she at once thought of something that rubbed in the unwisdom of his marriage. What about his wife's dowry? Had he married without guarantees as to that? She, of course, had been kept in the dark; but she would find out. There was one person who should know: Nicholas Clagett, now Bishop of St David's, a client of the

5. ibid., 97. 6. ibid., 103–4.

Sunderland family who had risen in the Church by the patronage of Charles's father and had the confidence of Charles and the Trevors. In response to his request for help Sarah paid a call on the bishop, her description of which must rank among her finest efforts.[7]

I received your letter as soon as I came out of the City. And as I am always desirous to do everything that can possibly be of any use to you and could do no manner of hurt, I went immediately to the pious good Bishop of St David's. He was at home and, I think, could very willingly have spared my visit. He made a great many cringes and professions of what he owed to you and your family. I soon grew sick of his compliments and went to the point, telling him I heard he was one of your trustees and that as your affairs were now in a very bad way, I could not think of anybody that I knew so likely to inform me of some things which might be of use to you, under such great difficulties, as himself.

And therefore in the first place I desired he would tell me who were the trustees to the Duchess's mother's marriage settlement [*i.e.* the first Lady Trevor]. He presently assured me that he did not know. 'Why then,' said I, 'how could your lordship act the part of a faithful trustee to the present Duke of Marlborough, since without seeing that marriage settlement . . . you could not possibly know what fortune Mrs Trevor had a right to, and her mother was a considerable heiress and had no other child.'[8]

The pious good bishop averred that he knew nothing of it – he had heard people say it was £25,000 – but he had never spoken of it with the Duke of Marlborough – he was utterly ignorant.

I told him that there was not many that would believe that and that I thought he should have taken more care than to have brought such difficulties upon a family to whom he owed so much and that he ought to endeavour now to contribute all he could to bring my Lord Trevor to what he had been writ to upon, to do his daughter and the Duke of Marlborough justice. He knew very well your present circumstances and that in less than six weeks you must comply with your grandfather's will or forfeit the estate. And whatever misfortunes he [*i.e.* Lord Trevor]

7. Blenheim MSS., E 54.

8. Elizabeth was the daughter of the first Lord Trevor and his first wife; the other children of this marriage died young.

had brought upon the family, your having been deceived by people you trusted would not discharge him from being obliged to pay what was due to his daughter. If the Duke of Marlborough forfeited such an estate, if his lordship [*i.e.* the Bishop] would seriously reflect upon it, he must needs be sensible that he would be extremely censured in the world to have had a hand in a thing of this nature.

I said all this to fright him: for I know of no better way with anybody that has no principles, and I think it had an effect. For though he gave me an extraordinary good character of himself, he bowed and smiled and said he would be sure to write to my Lord Trevor this post; and he told me two or three times that if I knew him a little better I should think very well of him. But I am so thoroughly convinced what he is that I hope never to have a further acquaintance with him. The Bishop assured me with great solemnity that he knew no more of the settlements or marriage than I did and that I was the first that told him of it, when those melancholy letters passed between you and me, which you remember was not a great many days before all was completed. But indeed he said that after he did know it he wished mightily that you would have acquainted me with it. I do believe that last assurance will make you laugh.

A rather bitter laugh, no doubt, for the old Duchess does not conceal her sense of triumph at the consequences coming home to the weaker personality of not reposing trust in the superior wisdom of the stronger. It is the sort of triumph that the weaker never forgives, when the stronger goes on blithely and boisterously to forget. But the vividness of the scene, the vivacity and power of it are such that only a personality of Sarah's intensity and voltage can command.

The Bishop's description of the scene to Lord Trevor helps us to appreciate why the impression Sarah made on others was not uniformly favourable.

I told your lordship but a little of what passed on that occasion. The next time I see your lordship I will divert you with a relation of the rest. Besides the rudeness on one side (which was greater, I think, than I had ever before met with in my life) there was somewhat so exceedingly ridiculous on that side that, when told, it will hardly meet with belief. I discourse to her all along perfectly with temper and gave her very plain hints that I thought she did not herself do the same. I was tender of doing or saying anything that might exasperate her against my lord

Duke, my lady Duchess or yourself. I understand that at present she seems to like the young Duchess very well and carries herself with civility towards her. Better it should be so than otherwise. But as the French say, *N'importe*. It is no great matter, one way or another. For my part I am fully determined, on no account whatever, to see the grandmother more. If she comes again to my house I'll not see her, and if she sends for me I will excuse myself from going. . . . I am far from reckoning it a misfortune that I have quite broken with her. Your lordship's purpose of writing to her in the way you speak of is, I think, perfectly right.[9]

If that was all the result of Sarah's intervention in that quarter, it is not surprising that the new Duke's difficulties went on increasing. There was always the resource, for one of his vast expectations, of further borrowing.

At this point John saw fit to improve the occasion and recommend himself by making an approved marriage. His grandmother's choice fell upon a younger daughter of her political ally in the campaign against Walpole: Lord Carteret, Walpole's most dangerous enemy. It was a political alliance: it does not seem that John had even seen the lady. His grandmother wrote to Di blithely, 'I am glad that Torrismond [*i.e.* John] wishes they may like one another when they meet; for I think that looks as if he was under no sort of inclination or engagement. And though I must confess I am much more difficult to please than you are in a lady, yet I don't think Torrismond is extremely nice – provided that the person be not disagreeable, is healthy, has good sense and good humour.'[10]

Sarah was engaged in arranging the matter in this same month of December 1733 when she had the consequences of Charles's casualness about his marriage settlements to cope with. In her comments we discern another reason for her annoyance at his choice: she had thought of a better for him.

As young men won't take even the best advice without being delivered with good breeding and good sense, I know of nothing so desirable as the kindness and assistance of a father-in-law who, I think, must always make a considerable figure whatever way the world turns.

9. Blenheim MSS., F I. 34. 10. G. Scott Thomson, 110–11.

No one could deny that that was true of Lord Carteret. 'I think too that it is possible that this alliance may be an advantage even to your elder brother, who has been so miserably thrown away.' When Sarah met the elder Carteret daughter, now Lady Weymouth,

> I could not help thinking all the time what a delightful thing it would have been if she had been married to your brother Marlborough. She looks like a woman of quality and, by what I saw, I am persuaded she knows what is to be done and said upon every occasion. What a delightful thing it would have been if two brothers that have such a friendship for one another had married two sisters that love one another so well as they certainly do![11]

Writing to Di, she did not dwell on the political advantages that weighed even more heavily with her.

In February Jack's marriage was performed in great style, and with £30,000 down, at St George's Hanover Square between eight and nine in the evening. It was all very magnificent. Charles and his Duchess were present with Di and her Duke of Bedford – to whom Sarah had married her and provided *her* dowry of £30,000. Mrs Delany, then Mrs Pendarves, tells us: 'after they were married they played a pool at commerce, supped at ten, went to bed between twelve and one, and went to Windsor Lodge the next day at noon. . . . Her clothes were white satin embroidered with silver, very fine lace; and the jewels the Duchess of Marlborough gave.'[12] That is to say, Sarah. The *Daily Courant* reported that she had settled £5,000 a year on John and his heirs. Here was a marriage of which she could really approve, for she had made it herself. It must be added that it was an entire success; the couple were happy and fruitful, and established a new cadet line of Spencers at Althorp.

Later in the month John carried his new wife to Court to kiss hands, as the custom was, on their marriage. They went supported by all their relations, but they got a very cool reception. The King turned his back on them, and even Queen

11. ibid., 130.

12. *Autobiography and Correspondence of Mary Granville, Mrs Delany*, ed. Lady Llanover I. 427, 430.

Caroline, who usually made amends for his rudeness, neglected them for a long time and at length greeted John only with, 'I think, Mr Spencer, I have not seen you since you was a child.' He answered as coldly, 'No, Madam, I believe not,' and they all came away displeased. Lord Egmont comments that it is a pity the King does not conceal his displeasure, 'for the nobility of England are proud and presently take fire at any slight the Crown casts upon them'. The families on both sides of the marriage were well affected to the royal family, but they were no friends of Sir Robert Walpole; 'whoever are not friends to him are not to be countenanced at Court'.[13]

For the rest of the year a state of beatitude existed in the family. Sarah was having her grandsons' portraits painted for her new house at Wimbledon, though it was long before she could get Charles to sit for his. His letters to her showed his interest in Blenheim. The great place was lying deserted and neglected, for Sarah could not bear to live in it. Not long after young Horace Walpole, on an undergraduate tour from Cambridge, reported that he saw there

> nothing but a cross housekeeper and an impertinent porter, except a few pictures; a quarry of stone that looked at a distance like a great house and about this quarry quantities of inscriptions in honour of the Duke of Marlborough, and, I think, of her Grace too – she herself mentioned, as putting 'em up, in almost all of 'em.[14]

In June Sarah paid the Marlboroughs a visit at their Little Lodge in Windsor Park and approved of all, or nearly all, she saw. It was pretty and convenient, well-furnished and without any expense,

> excepting some pictures of horses and dogs and some old sort of Dutch pictures as I took them to be, with vast heavy carved frames almost as large as the cornice on the outside of a house, all gilt. I dare say they cost a great deal of money, and are worth a great deal more to those that like such things than the pictures that are in them, most of which I believe are very indifferent paintings.

13. *H.M.C.*, *Egmont*, II. 34.
14. Paget Toynbee, *Letters of Horace Walpole*, I. 15.

Her approval of Jack's wife was as lively as ever. 'She is bigger than she was, but not quick. I hope no accident will happen to her, for I do not hear yet that the Duchess of Marlborough is with child.'[15]

Charles had made various rearrangements with John prior to handing over the Sunderland estates. For one thing he bought John's share of Sunderland House in Piccadilly; for another he sold John his annuity of £1,000 a year from his father, to raise ready cash.[16] For the new Duke, so rich in prospect, was for the time less well off than his younger brother. This was a situation that had some part in spoiling their relations, though it was the position in which they stood in regard to Sarah, and the strain put upon them by it, that ultimately brought any friendship between the brothers to an end.

At this moment, somewhat improbably and as always ineffectively, Charles was trying to retrench. But, as Sarah saw,

> great as his fortune is, he will never be easy in money matters. For at a time that he saw his extravagance obliged him to retrench and did put away some very useless horses, he has made a much greater expense in building a ship. Where there must be a captain and seamen. And this I cannot help thinking a very odd thing, when he owed so much money and cannot live in a decent way without borrowing more. And except what he has of me, he must pay extravagant interest for it.

By this means he had now piled up 'vast loads of his own debts' and would not look into his expenses for himself. Everybody took advantage of him. Even his own servant making hay at the Little Lodge, Sarah found out with her eye for detail, charged him double: 'it is probable the Duke of Marlborough may think £20 nothing; but it is a great deal in £46'. She was 'labouring like a pack-horse every day to save him from the cheats', but he would not take the trouble to write ten lines in answer to matters that concerned only himself. It was all very well for Caesar to reply grandly, when asked to read a paper that concerned himself, that for that reason he would read it

15. G. Scott Thomson, 127–8.
16. Blenheim MSS., E 54.

last: he was a king; it would not do for the Duke of Marlborough to follow his example.[17]

By next year she complained that he was ceasing to answer her letters at all, though he was continuing his career of extravagance; at the end of the year there was a characteristic flare-up on her part that demonstrated her disapprobation better than any words and provided matter for gossip and amusement, as so often with her, all round society. The Duchess of Portland writes,

> the Duke of Marlborough has the Lodge in the Little Park and he has made very great improvements there and great plantations – a canal and a serpentine river and a mount that has cost a vast deal of money. The old Duchess came there a little while ago and brought a great many men from London to destroy everything that had been done, pulled up the trees and cut and hacked everything she came near.[18]

A rumour coming from Horace Walpole related that she had turned the Duke out of the Little Lodge, and 'then pretending that the new Duchess and her female cousins (eight Trevors) had stripped the house and garden, she had a puppet show made with waxen figures representing the Trevors tearing up the shrubs and the Duchess carrying off the chicken coop under her arm'. Everything concerning Sarah was apt to be exaggerated in the telling, hers was such an outsize personality; but that something of the sort happened was only too possible. For, from this time, her relations with the Duke worsened and he was forced to look elsewhere for a country home.

Vexed and embittered by his inroads into the fortune of which she was the guardian for the dead Marlborough and for the future of his family, she drew up a statement of what had come to Charles's possession already – before her death would give him undisputed control of the whole. And then what? His father, the third Earl of Marlborough, had left him £15,000, his grandfather, Marlborough, £5,000. On his brother's death the whole Sunderland estate came to him – £5,000 a year less a jointure of £900; that is to say, £4,100 a year, with Althorp and the house in Piccadilly, a great deal of plate and 'both better

17. G. Scott Thomson, 137–8. 18. Lady Llanover, I. 545.

furnished than most people of quality's houses are: no occasion to lay out a shilling for anything that was wanted'.[19] When Lord Blandford died he got £8,000 a year in neat money paid – and this he owed to Sarah's intervention in the making of Marlborough's will. By this he got a sum of £24,000, during the three years between Blandford's death and Henrietta, the second Duchess's. On that event, becoming Duke he was to have the overplus of the whole estate, after charges paid – £14,000 a year besides all arrears which were his. When his elder brother died £1,000 a year came to him in long annuities – and yet, loaded with debts and caring nothing for expense, he was eating into the Marlborough fortune at a rapid rate, prejudicing the whole future of the family.

That was what Sarah cared most about. In 1736 Mrs Pendarves reported to the Marlboroughs' old enemy, Swift: 'The Duke of Marlborough and his grandmother are upon bad terms; the Duke of Bedford who has also been ill-treated by her has offered the Duke of Marlborough to supply him with £10,000 a year, if he will go to law and torment the old Dowager.'[20] We are in a better position to judge on which side the ill-treatment lay. The dispute with the Duke of Bedford followed upon Di's death and related to her marriage settlements; this Duke was both acquisitive and tenacious: in any quarrel with Sarah it was six of one to half a dozen of the other.

We get occasional references to what Charles was spending his (borrowed) money upon in the correspondence of the time. In 1738 Lady Hertford went to see an island at Bray upon which he had spent some £8,000.

> He has a small house upon it, whose outside represents a farm, the inside what you please; for the parlour, which is the only room in it except a kitchen, is painted upon the ceiling in grotesque, with monkeys, fishing, shooting etc. and its sides are hung with paper. When a person sits in this room he cannot see the water, though the island is not above a stone's cast over: nor is he prevented from this by shade; for, except six or eight walnut trees and a few orange trees in tubs, there is not a leaf upon the island; it arises entirely from the river running very much below its banks. There is another building which I think is called a

19. Blenheim MSS., E 31. 20. Lady Llanover, II. 228.

temple. . . . It should seem that his Grace has taken a hint from the Man of Ross's public spirit; and in order not to copy him too slavishly, has bestowed a treat upon the eyes instead of the bellies of the passengers,

up and down the Thames.[21] It must have been charming, with its pretty decorations.

Turned out of the Little Lodge in Windsor Park, with Blenheim in Sarah's possession, though she did not choose to occupy it, and having handed over Althorp to his brother – where was the Duke to look for a home in the proximity of London? Across the Thames from Windsor, in the neighbourhood of Slough, lay Langley, the house and estate to which Lady Masham had retired with her Lord from the hectic excitements of those last days at the Court of Queen Anne. It was the rewards of their service at Court that had enabled them to buy the place and there Abigail spent the last twenty years of her life – not a sound emerging from that quiet place to disturb the silence and the discretion of her past, while the world still resounded with the indiscretions of her great enemy, and cousin, Sarah. In 1734 Abigail died there.

Now in 1738 the Duke's eye fell upon this, of all places, and he bought it from the widowed Lord Masham. He proceeded to build a large square house, in the plain Georgian taste, but with a suite of fine rooms for his growing collection of pictures.[22] Not content with this he set on foot improvements and began plantations which were continued by his son, to whom he transmitted his passion for landscape-design. In the end they not only rebuilt Langley and re-created the park with its long avenue, but created another large area of woodland to the north of it, Black Park, so called from the dark Scotch firs with which it was closely planted. Here Charles formed a large lake behind an immense, and expensive, embankment upon which he had at one time a hundred men working. This has now lapsed into natural woodland, a playground for the people.

21. *Correspondence of the Countess of Hertford and the Countess of Pomfret*, I. 7–8.

22. G. Lipscomb, *History and Antiquities of the County of Buckingham*, IV. 534.

The house itself – to which the Victorians added an entrance front with a baroque reminiscence of Blenheim – has become, in the general decline of the age, a temple of television with the squalid clutter of such things about it. In essence nothing has much changed: within, the house remains, marble floors and hall with noble staircase, classic urns; around the house, inside the ha-ha, the lawns overgrown, all mouldering into decay. Across the way is the fine red-brick range of stables – one sees Charles on his white horse coming over to say farewell to Elizabeth and take the road to Windsor on his way to the wars.

For there is no doubt that he loved this place: when away on campaign in Germany later this inexpressive man suddenly breaks into eloquence when he thinks of the glades and rides of Langley, the leaves falling in autumn and his beloved Elizabeth walking anxious among them, longing for him to come safe home.

For half a century Langley became the favourite residence of the family.

Children were now arriving, though with no great rapidity, their family forming around Charles and Elizabeth, making an enclosed circle within which intense affection and an exceptional sensibility prevailed. It would seem that this was due mainly to Elizabeth, who brought a strain of undue sensitivity into the family and set the prevailing atmosphere within it. Charles was very much a family man, who remained always in love with his wife, and – since he was never happy away from her and she was miserable away from him – very much torn between the claims of love and duty. It is to his credit that the latter prevailed as he grew older. Never a breath of scandal in regard to other women touched him, in this rather free-living age; nor did it in the case of his eldest son, who ruled at Blenheim right up to 1817 and carried this intensely respectable and rather uxorious tradition on to the threshold of the Victorian age.

Their first child, Diana – called after Charles's sister, Duchess of Bedford – was born 24 March 1734, in the honeymoon of their relations with the Dowager.[23] Not until three years later

23. *Collin's Peerage of England*, ed. by Sir Egerton Brydges (ed. 1812), I. 450–51.

was another child born – another girl, Elizabeth – 29 December 1737. Still no heir to the dukedom, which might indeed fall to John's children. So that when at length a son was born, 26 January 1739, Mrs Delany was able to record 'a great joy'. The year before, the Duke had made a sudden turn-round from the long and unrewarding course he had followed in opposition to the Court, for the sake of keeping in step with Sarah, made his peace with Walpole and accepted the colonelcy of a regiment from the King. Now the son and heir of the Marlboroughs was called after him, George. We learn from the Trevor side of the family, no friends of Sarah, that when the Duke sent news of the birth of an heir to her she sent for answer that 'to complete his joy she was very ill', though in reality she was very well and lived for some years after to annoy them.[24] A second son, Charles, was born 31 March 1740, and the youngest, Robert, some years after the others, 8 May 1747. This last lived right up to 1831. All these children made their mark in the world, in various individual ways, in addition to being notable figures in late eighteenth-century society by virtue of their position.

With this happy family life Charles was ill at ease whenever he was away from it; and this was rendered worse by Elizabeth's constitutional low spirits and the anxiety into which any absence threw her. We have evidence of this from a few undated notes to each other; when Charles was abroad his Duchess was plunged into deepest depression and most of his letters are concerned with trying to console her, coax her out of it. It must have been more than discouraging, positively lowering to the spirits – a very different state of mind from what Sarah's had been when her lord was away at the war: pride in him mingled with the wish that she were a man to go and fight as a soldier of liberty. However, the Marlborough correspondences have this in common: like John and Sarah's, Charles and Elizabeth's letters are all of them love-letters.

Here is Elizabeth:

My dearest Duke of Marlborough, you tell me you have a great deal of trouble, I wish I knew from *what* or rather from *who* it proceeded. . . . If you love me as you say, you will take care of your dear self when you

24. *H.M.C.*, *Trevor*, 243.

reflect how absolutely necessary you are to my happiness. I confess I am very miserable about you, though entirely ignorant of what you are about. . . . Yours with more true affection than I can express, my dearest Duke of Marlborough, or any but you conceive.[25]

This note has for postscript, '10 o'clock in bed', and sends good wishes to Henry Fox, the Duke's close friend and political associate. So presumably he was in London, at or near the Court. What he was likely to be about we know from an item of news passed on by Lady Hertford in January 1739, 'the Duke of Marlborough lost seven hundred pounds on Twelfth-night, which was all that was considerable'.[26] That would be at Court. It does not seem that the Duke ever won anything much; pride made him play, and lose, for high stakes; obstinacy made him continue. Sarah was justified in her prophecy to him as a boy that he would never be the better for play.

A characteristic note from Charles on a jaunt to Bromham, Elizabeth's old home, says: 'the journey has exceeded my expectations, yet I never will attempt another that will keep me so long from you, for I can now affirm by experience that when I am shooting or fishing, instead of enjoying the sport my thoughts are an hundred and fifty miles from the place'. He was always a man of few words – Sarah had complained of his taciturnity. He confesses to Elizabeth that

the real reason for my writing short is that I am not capable of writing or talking in a prolix way more than some are of being laconic, though perhaps I say as much in eight lines as some men do twenty eight; as for expressing how much I love you no number of lines could suffice . . .[27]

The long years of peace since the Treaty of Utrecht that had ended Marlborough's war – or, rather, of intermission from any general war – were drawing to an end. This happy and prosperous interlude associated with the long domestic rule of Walpole we owed to the Anglo-French *entente* maintained by the good sense and good relations of the English minister with the

25. Blenheim MSS., E 54.

26. *Correspondence of the Countess of Hertford and the Countess of Pomfret*, I. 49.

27. Blenheim MSS., E 57.

clever old ecclesiastic who ran French affairs from his seventies until he died in his nineties, Cardinal Fleury. This beneficent state of affairs was shattered by Frederick's sudden, swift seizure of Silesia in 1740 – a characteristic piece of German treachery – which called Europe to arms and set in motion the dreary war of the Austrian Succession.

For England it was another round in the secular struggle with France. We were drawn into it by our essential interest in maintaining a proper balance of power in Europe, *i.e.* one favourable to ourselves. George II had the additional interest of his concern for the safety of Hanover. This was a chief issue between the government and the opposition, mainly inspired by the young Patriots, Pitt and Lyttelton, egged on and patronized by Sarah. Their cant was to propagate the popular view that English interests were being sacrificed to Hanover. The injustice of this, along with the offensive tone in which it was urged, rankled with the King and made these young men, especially Pitt, extremely objectionable to him. Young Marlborough, who had also been objectionable under Sarah's pressure, had come round in 1738 and was now a supporter of Walpole and the King's government. He had been rewarded with the colonelcy of the 1st Royal Dragoons and then that of the 2nd Horse Guards. The soldierly instincts of his ancestry, the reputable ambition to deserve his name, grew stronger in him as he grew older and, ironically, as he moved farther away from Sarah.

The letters the Duke wrote on campaign to Elizabeth are preserved at Blenheim; their private interest is greater than their military.[28] This was Charles's first experience of active service abroad, and the Colonel was not yet a figure of any importance, save for his name. The General in command of the British forces was Lord Stair, an elderly officer who had served under the Duke's grandfather. But the situation was complicated by George II's spirited determination to go abroad and take command of both his British and his Hanoverian troops. That portended difficulties to come, disaccord between the two armies – the kind of situation in which the first Marlborough

28. They are in Blenheim MSS., E 55, from which I quote unless stated otherwise.

had displayed such diplomacy and been such a master. But now the Dutch had not forgotten their desertion at the Peace of Utrecht and there was some delay before they would allow British contingents to land in the Netherlands.

From Gravesend Charles writes to Elizabeth,

> I was in hopes to have been at Ostend by this time, but the damned transports have kept us here, some having forgot their water till this time. . . . David Morris is just come aboard and has brought me your dear letter with Di's at the bottom. I was on deck when I opened it, but was obliged to go into my cabin to finish it that the company might not see how I was moved.[29]

He may have seen her again before sailing, for there is an undated note: 'I have been in twenty different minds about coming back to you, but find at last that I cannot possibly live within twenty miles of you and not see you, though I must leave you again tomorrow noon.'

Arrangements were made with no very good grace to quarter the British troops in the Netherlands. The Duke crossed over in August; to begin with he was put up in 'a most wretched inn, with but one room for me and the servants to dine and sup in'. Arrived at Ghent on 21 August, 'I am now got into an exceeding good house, where I live very regular, dine at two without ever drinking, go to bed at ten without supper and rise before six, after which it is no wonder if I am very well in health.' He wrote to assure her – Elizabeth needed reassuring by every post: 'the French have not men enough out of Germany to venture upon any action and those at Prague are too far to attempt marching this way'. It seems that Lady Bateman had died – how Sarah had outlived enemies and friends alike! – 'I shall put no servants in mourning here, for I must not wear more than a black waistcoat myself, as we are all obliged to wear red or blue'.

The news of the King's joining his army increased Elizabeth's apprehension as to action.

> My dearest life, you seem apprehensive of the King's coming, which shows that you are unacquainted with military operations, for when the

29. ibid., E 57.

King is present the Guards don't go into the trenches but mount guard on the King s quarters, which is always out of the enemy's reach. . . . Forgive me, my dearest, for saying that there is one most unreasonable expression in your letter *that there is a possibility of your never enjoying a happy security*. I can't deny but that there is a *possibility* of the world's being destroyed; but for God's sake, my dear, don't afflict yourself for possibility when there is no probability joined. I really can't recollect what may not be called a *possibility* unless it is my ceasing to love you more than all the world.

He is 'beyond expression' hers. This is quite a dialectical and epistolary effort for Charles; but the lover in him makes him quite eloquent for an inexpressive man: 'love bade me write'.

In September he is presiding over a general court martial and 'as this is the first time I ever sat as judge upon life and death, my attention for fear of mistakes has quite tired me'. We observe that he was a conscientious officer, but that he always showed diffidence, mistrust of himself as a soldier: he had not been trained to it like his grandfather, nor had he the gift. 'I spend the same dull life as I did the last weeks sauntering about and thinking of you and when I shall receive your letters.' He is employed by regimental business in the morning and a French playhouse in the afternoon: they are said to be good actors, 'if what possess my thoughts was with me I might think so too. . . . My dearest dearest angel, ever inalterable yours.'

Now he hears from Morris that Blandford is in breeches: no doubt Elizabeth was keeping that for a surprise when he came home. For it was too late in the year to attempt anything now. 'If anything happens to you the principal reason for my living is gone or, to speak more properly, I shall have a strong reason against it.' In October the Duchess goes to Langley, which he thinks better for her health.

I can't join with you in wishing the leaves off the trees at Langley, but rather wish I may find 'em on when I come; not that I shall care or even know whether there are leaves or trees in the park if I find you well in the house.

Elizabeth has received a visit from the Dowager.

I am glad you kept the children out of the way when the old Duchess was there; if she wants to see 'em for any good purpose she will contrive to bring about a reconciliation, if it is only curiosity I hope she will always be equally disappointed. As for the question she asked about my building at Blenheim, that depends upon her: if she will be so good as to die soon that I may be able to clear my debts I believe I shall build; but if she is spiteful enough to live much longer, I fear I shall not build.

Such were his feelings for the old lady who had contributed so largely to his own greatness.

All thought of campaigning was over for that season. By November he is returning to England for the winter. He promises that he will not set out in a hurricane and he wishes their meeting to be at Langley, 'where I need not so much as speak to anybody else, for I own I shall hate anybody that does but ask me a question that don't relate to you'.

For the next campaigning season, which culminated at the battle of Dettingen, where the King was present and the Duke did good service, the Duchess was determined to accompany him to the Continent. Apparently she sent her sister in to the Duke's room to plead for her that if she did not go abroad with him she would die. The despairing Duchess evidently had no idea that conditions of service that year would keep them apart as effectively as if she had remained in England. Her step only added to Charles's concern on her behalf. From Dover in May he writes to learn what report Morris makes of the *Chandos* sloop for his Duchess's passage; 'if the King delays going over, if you'll send Mr Fox to Lord Winchelsea he will lend you a man-of-war for convoy'. At length the Duchess sailed in the same vessel as the King, who crossed over in a storm, giving Charles 'infinite anxiety upon every gust of wind when I thought you at sea . . . the thoughts of your being at sea in a storm makes me more unhappy than is possible to be expressed'.

Hitherto Charles had been rather enjoying himself, perhaps unconsciously at escape from the oppressive confinement of such sleepless solicitude. Out on the open heaths of Westphalia, in the breezy comradeship of men, he could breathe. In early May they were camping at Hoechst:

the soil is very dry and sandy, in the front of the camp there is a large wood and a very fine river in the rear, the situation is as beautiful as possible, but the heat of the sun beyond anything I ever felt; the warm weather agrees very well with my health, but I am not sure you will know me again at first sight, for I shall be a molotto at least.

What fun it must have been! – the early summer of 1742, health and the open air, marches that were like picnics, warfare that was more like a game of manoeuvre and not very deadly, at the end of it a safe return to the beautiful London of the early Georges, welcomed by Mr Handel's Dettingen *Te Deum.* The Duchess is not to be uneasy: 'the worst of seasons can't affect me who am strong and used to travel, so much as you in the best weather'.

The moment she had arrived in Holland she was agitating for Charles to come to her. It was out of the question: the army was moving up the Main. 'How can you imagine, my dearest, that I thought it would be so difficult for me to see you when I *consented* to your coming to Holland?' Elizabeth had brought the three children over with her; Betty was diligent to learn Dutch: he hoped it would not spoil her French, 'which I suppose Di now speaks without whispering'. At the Hague the Duchess was receiving more visits of ceremony than she liked – she was of a retiring disposition, a pure family woman; the Duke assured her that 'the approaching prospect of affairs will raise your spirits more than visits of ceremony will sink 'em'. The accession of the Dutch to the allied side made him think peace was probable. On the contrary, the war was drawing nearer, with the French and allied armies converging.

In June the combined British and Hanoverian forces were marching up the Main to Aschaffenburg. Charles had not been able to write for 'our forage was all gone and I was sent in the night with a detachment to this place' – he is too sleepy, from being twenty-four hours on horseback, to write any more. The summer was excessively hot,

but the heat makes no other alteration in me except my complexion, which will soon be of a fine olive colour. I mention this so often in my letters that you may not disown your once fair, but now tawny, husband when we meet, though I believe let my face alter ever so much my heart is entirely fixed, you must know me by that. The King has been here these two days and Lord Carteret with him, who gives me a bad account of your sloop that brought you to Holland. I hope you will never be in any more such distress without me.

Before Charles's next letter the battle of Dettingen had been fought.[30] It was more of a muddle than a battle, and led to grave recriminations on the part of the English commanders at the German influences around the King. Lord Stair, posted in a favourable position along the Main, had been most anxious to take advantage of it to attack the French army retreating from Bavaria across his path. From Hanover the King forbade any forward action – it was like the situation the great Duke had had to put up with so often at the hands of the Dutch. The result was that when at length the King arrived on the scene, the French were able to manoeuvre the Allied army into a mouse-trap of a place from which they should never have been able to escape. There was great disorder and confusion on both sides. The King cut rather a ridiculous figure, waving his sword and encouraging his troops in his absurd German accent; then his horse, to the unspeakable indignation of the peppery little man, ran away with him to the rear. George made his way back to the line, undaunted, on foot. Meanwhile, the French foot behaved in the most incompetent and cowardly fashion – symptom of the maladministration corrupting France and of *la grande nation*'s downward drift. Less than half the forces on either side were committed. The British infantry showed themselves steady in the *impasse* into which they had been led; their accurate fire had deadly effects and was more responsible than any generalship for extricating them. The French infantry were glad to get away – in fact fled in disorder over the Main. The unexpected turn of fortune was not followed up and there was no pursuit. It was all as far as possible from any action conducted by the first Marlborough – and so felt Lord Stair, who was an able officer and knew very well how a command should be conducted. Shortly after the battle he resigned his command and returned home. A decisive victory over the French in the present state would have meant peace; as it was, the war dragged on.

30. cf. J. W. Fortescue, *History of the British Army*, I. 91 foll.

In writing to Elizabeth the Duke, who had been in the front line in command of his brigade, played the action down. He had been marching day and night, he wrote; there had been a skirmish between a part of the English army and the French, who were driven back over the Main. He was in perfect good health, but 'with a beard three inches long, which I am just going to cut off in order to see what colour my face is now of, whatever it is, I hope it won't be long before you see it'. On 30 June,' we are now marching towards Frankfort and the French quite a different way, so you have not the least reason to apprehend any action from two armies that march different ways'. In July the Emperor's declaration of neutrality enabled Charles to assure her of the certainty of peace: 'I may venture to affirm that when we meet we will part no more.'

The news of Dettingen threw the Duchess into a fever of anxiety. Charles had to assure her that he had

> found a pretext at the end of the campaign to quit and then nothing in the world shall ever induce me to take any employment that divides me from you, for, believe me my dearest, I find by experience that nothing in the world can give me the least satisfaction in your absence.

The French have now marched home, and 'we did not endeavour to molest 'em in their going off, though I am very positive we might have destroyed at least half their army, with very little loss on our side. I never mention military matters to you but when they are conducive to peace.' Exactly – if he were to do so he might mention the seething indignation among the British commanding officers at the mismanagement of the campaign under Hanoverian influences. Of these, brother John's father-in-law, Lord Carteret, had made himself the spokesman and so had the King's entire confidence. Not that of his colleagues in the government at home, however.

Early in August the Duke was marching from headquarters at Hanau on the Main to the Rhine. From Wiesbaden, 14 August: 'I am so tired that I can hardly hold the pen. I have been forced to march in one day (God knows why) what the Hanoverians could hardly do in two.' Charles's fatigue at this point is very evident in his handwriting, no less than the prevailing anti-Hanoverian feeling in his expressions. On 20 August his brigade was ready to cross the Rhine; but in the next ten days he was ordered to make two days' marches away up the Rhine instead of down as expected. And so he could not name the day 'for my leaving this cursed country'. However, he repeated his resolution never to take service again away from her.

In September the ill feelings engendered by the campaign culminated in Stair's resignation. The Duke at last opened his mouth to the Duchess:

> the usage he met with was too much for anybody to bear and that proceeded from having differed in opinion from Lord Carteret about the operations of the campaign. ... If Lord Stair's scheme had been followed the French army must have been all destroyed and we should have made a great figure and a good peace, whereas now we must make a poor one and a bad peace.

Sharing Stair's indignation with his hereditary friendship, the Duke was bent on resigning too. It was impossible for him 'to have a moment's ease in your absence', and he was 'determined to suffer that inexpressible anxiety no more'. The only method of resignation he could think of was

> to make a *querelle d'Allemand* by asking a promotion for me alone. ... The King was so *Allemand* as not only to refuse me that, but even to please me beyond my expectations by making a promotion of a great number without taking me in. This is, God be praised, what I ought to resent even if I had no desire of quitting the army.

No wonder the King was angry with the Duke and expressed himself in very irascible terms.

Stair had a particular friendship for Charles for the great Duke's sake. He was returning home through the Hague: 'I beg you will show him the children. I am sure it will please him to see what I love and flatter my vanity by showing him with how much reason I love.' After his own return 'nothing but death shall ever part us more'. Charles kept his resolution for fifteen years, and then parted from Elizabeth to meet death on service once more abroad. At the end of September the Duke was journeying to meet his wife and family and take them back to England, where he would resume his place in Opposition

This could not but be agreeable to Sarah, and she was credited with a good *mot* on the subject: 'It is very natural: he 'listed as soldiers do when they are drunk and repented when he was sober'.[31] The move was in time yet, if not to reinstate himself in her favour, at least to prevent his young family from being cut out of all recognition in her will.

The past years had been full of bickering, in which the edge of Sarah's disapprobation at his behaviour over financial matters had been sharpened by his political conduct. Coldness and disapprobation may be read in a letter of January 1738, before he had gone over to the government.

> I am always desirous as soon as I can, to do anything for your Grace's ease, and therefore I have ventured to send the enclosed draft upon the Bank, though I cannot be sure what is due to you to Michaelmas last. But I know there is all the charges for the management of the estate for four years, besides other things that have not yet been computed or charged to your account. And I know likewise that the next half year will produce vastly less than it has ever done yet, from the vast sum that has lain so long dead, and a great deal more will be so very soon; notwithstanding that I have given much the greatest part of my time in labouring to do you service. But finding that it has not answered my reasonable expectations and wishes in any respect, I shall give myself more ease for the future.[32]

The accents of dislike and mistrust are unmistakable.

The vast investible sum that had been lying idle – owing to the disputes between Sarah and Walpole, and between Sarah and her grandson – was the capital sum at the disposition of Marlborough's trustees, in accordance with the trust, to buy estates for the endowment of the dukedom. Now, owing to his grandmother's justified distrust of him, the young Duke was undoubtedly suffering. On one side, estates were not being bought for him to dispose of; on the other, the capital was not being lent to the government, so that the trust was not profiting. In this *impasse* both sides, as usual, were losing. In the days of good relations with government Sarah had lent immense sums to enable it to reduce interest from 5 to 4 per cent on the public

31. Horace Walpole, *Letters*, *ed. cit*. I. 394.
32. Blenheim MSS., E 54.

debt – thereby reducing her own interest, a sacrifice she did not fail to point out. In return Sir Robert had given an assurance that the trust should be preferred to any other in placing money in the public funds. But he conveniently forgot that and, according to Sarah, preferred other people's money.[33]

In 1740–41, with war encroaching, the government was in need of money. The Duke wished a sum of £200,000, in addition to what had already been lent, to be advanced on the security of the salt-tax, which Sarah thought

> impossible to arise from anybody's advice but Sir Robert's, though he may not appear in it himself. Great statesmen have those ways of managing. No doubt Sir Robert finds it very difficult to get so great a sum as he wants. The salt tax is very unpopular. There is a great appearance of war everywhere . . . nothing is certain but that the government will want vast sums of money.

The government would be forced to increase interest. Sarah had already given her consent to the Duke's proposal to lend a great sum.

> I am not a nominal trustee, but by the Duke's will, and the decree too, my consent and approbation is to be had for disposing of the trust money. . . . I think myself obliged in honour and conscience to do all in my power to perform the trust put into me and therefore I can never consent to anything that is likely to be a prejudice to what the Duke so strongly designs for the security and benefit of his whole family.

A covering note outside says,

> I had no answer to this letter as I remember, for his Grace seldom gave himself the trouble to answer anything I said, unless he had occasion of borrowing money, or to desire that I would stay for money I had lent him, and let him receive the overplus before it was due to him, which he said would oblige him, and this was at the same time that he was very rude to me in everything else.

From the letter we perceive that they had been to law as to the interpretation of the trust, and the result had been to confirm Sarah's powers. So long as she lived she had the whip-hand.

She was not one to desist from using it.

33. These last letters, unless otherwise stated, are from E I. 35.

These financial *brouilles* ruined the old good relations between the brothers too. Charles owed John £3,000 for many years – doubtless the result of Sarah's discovery about the terms of their father's will – 'but would never pay principal nor interest, though I pressed him much to do it, saying what a shameful thing it was to have so great an estate and to refuse or delay paying such a sum to his younger brother'. So she obtained his bond to pay her the money, 'which he never would have done to his brother and I thought it disagreeable to have his brother go to law with him'. No doubt Charles considered that he had done far more than his duty in handing over the Sunderland estates, and incurring financial difficulties in consequence.

Sarah had no compunction in threatening him with the law. When the Duke was busy in the spring of 1741 attempting to save Walpole, her *riposte* was to write demanding the payment of the £3,000. 'It can be nothing but the great hurry of things of more consequence that has made you forget it. For nothing else I am sure could make a man of so great a character fail in sending what is due to me.' These are the accents of a real detestation. 'If your Grace thought of this matter at all, 'tis possible you might imagine that this money might be paid out of the overplus that is yours, arising from the Trust estate. But that cannot be. This bond for money owing to me has nothing to do with the trust.' She points out that there can be no overplus until she and Lord Godolphin are paid their jointures; that these have been stopped by the paying Mr Lamb, his money-lender, no less than £9,000 a year out of the trust estate;[34] that this is contrary to the will and that the Chancery has decreed that the Duke must pay their jointures immediately or lose possession of the estates. Does he want to put her to the trouble of going to the law for it? 'As I know your Grace very seldom thinks it necessary to write anything in answer to what I inform you of', she asks him to order a servant to write two lines whether he will pay or not; 'for 'twill be necessary for me to begin the suit as soon as I can, not doubting but your Grace will stand upon privilege'.

34. This large sum must have contributed handsomely to the Melbourne fortune. Matthew Lamb was father of the 1st Lord Melbourne.

In the last year of Sarah's life Charles hardly knew where to turn for money. Among his papers we find one of June 1744: 'a gentleman is willing to oblige your Grace with £3,000, either upon a *post obit* or by way of an annuity not to take place till after the demise of the Duchess Dowager'.[35] Of course this kind of thing got round to her ears: she was able to inform John, who replied, all good feeling gone: 'I dare say what you mention about my brother is true, it is so like the rest of his actions.'

Sarah was making her own preparations for her demise, doing her duty according to her lights for the Marlborough family, while leaving nothing that she could help in the power of her spendthrift grandson. She had heard about the post-obits.

> The last thing he has done, which I am sure is true, seems to me a little indecent: he has taken up £40,000 upon the Post Office pension [granted to his grandfather and his heirs] for his life, but that not being sufficient for his occasions, he has borrowed smaller sums, £500 or £1,000 of several people giving vast interest for them. But these people did not think it enough, so he told them that I was dying and that he would give them bond to pay them double the sum when I was dead. This contented the lenders, but I unluckily recovered and one of these creditors, who is a man of credit, told me himself that he had bought some of these securities, but he had sold them again; and I am told by others that these bonds are sold in the alleys like South Sea stock.

Considering all this, Sarah was preparing to be generous to the Duke's children, though the great bulk of her fortune was to go to John, and she left numerous large legacies to others. She was settling £3,000 a year on the heir to the Marlborough title, in clear money, free of all taxes; this was worth better than £4,000 a year in land. She would give portions to the other children,

> who will have, in spite of their father's madness and folly, their mother's portion which, I believe, will be £20,000 already settled in her deed of marriage on the children so that the Duke cannot take it from them. Lady Bateman, when she sold her brother to Lord Trevor, allowed him to keep the greatest part of that fortune till after his death. But as the children are very young, that and mine together will keep them at least

35. Blenheim MSS., E 54.

from being beggars. Marlborough House I have settled upon all the Duke of Marlborough's sons and to all that shall inherit the title of Marlborough, except himself, who would certainly sell it to Lamb or anybody if he had it in his power.

As for the heir –

I have ordered it so that he shall have the £3,000 a year after he has felt poverty in his father's house, a year before he is of age to do mischief. For I reckon the last year they will give him a great many sugar plums. Whether this project of mine will have the effect of preserving the Duke of Marlborough's estate as he has settled it to go to all his family, as he passionately desires throughout his will, nobody can be sure; but it is doing all that I can and what, I believe, everybody but Lamb and such as he will approve of. I am sure the Duke of Marlborough don't know what he owes, but I am pretty sure that his debts and what he has thrown away is not much less than half a million.

There is no reason to doubt Sarah's estimate: as we have given ample evidence to show, she was very exact where figures are concerned. It was a prodigious sum. Nothing that the Marlboroughs did was on an ordinary scale like anybody else, whether in saving originally or henceforth spending.

In October of that year 1744 Sarah died. The Duke was at last free to do as he liked: he was now the effective, as well as the titular, head of the family.

Chapter 3

Charles, Third Duke: at Home and Abroad

AGAINST this background of his private life – happy in marriage, unhappy about money in spite of all his grandfather's wealth coming to him – we may turn to Charles's public career.

It was natural that, with his family associations, he should belong at his entry into politics to the heart of the opposition to Walpole at the height of his power. There was Sarah – and for some years Charles may be regarded as her representative in the House of Lords; there was his brother-in-law the Duke of Bedford, with whom he acted in close concert; there was Lord Carteret, John's father-in-law, and Lord Chesterfield, Sarah's favourite, to give the group intellectual leadership. In the Commons there were the Boys, the young Patriots, of whom Lyttelton and Pitt were outstanding, whose popular line was to attack the Hanoverian commitments of George II's government.

Lord Hervey tells us that George II had always shown a dislike to Charles while he was Lord Sunderland, on account of his father, George I's minister, who could hardly help being involved in the quarrel between the King and his eldest son. Charles did not take much part in the proceedings of the Lords as Earl of Sunderland; when he did, it was to register an Opposition protest in accordance with Sarah's wishes and the policy of the group. They brought in a Bill to disable those who had pensions from government from sitting in the House of Commons.[1] The intention of the move was obvious and it was negatived by a large majority. Among those who signed the Protest on this, along with Marlborough's heir, were Harley's son and Samuel Masham. Politics produced strange bedmates and still more unexpected reversals.

On succeeding as Duke of Marlborough he was introduced, in January 1734, by the Dukes of Bedford and Manchester, appearing between them in his robes, with Black Rod, Garter king

1. *Journals of the House of Lords*, XXIII. 515.

of arms, the Lord Great Chamberlain and Deputy Earl Marshal, with all the paraphernalia proper to such an occasion.[2] In February the Opposition took the opportunity of the dismissal of the Duke of Bolton and Lord Cobham from their commands in the Army, for opposing Walpole's Excise scheme, to bring in a Bill to prevent officers from being deprived of their commissions other than by the Houses of Parliament or court-martial.[3] This was regarded by George II as personally insulting, as it certainly was an infringement of his rights in regard to the Army. The young Duke brought in the Bill, and, though it was negatived, there was a strong muster of Opposition peers to sign the Lords' Protest.

Hervey tells us that 'this step so strengthened his Majesty's enmity that "scoundrel, rascal or blackguard" whenever he spoke of him in private after that occurrence, never failed of being tacked to his name'.[4] The Duke of Bedford rose little better in the King's good graces.

> These two young dukes were of great consideration from their quality and their estates and were as much alike in pride, violence of temper and their public conduct as they were different in their ways of thinking and acting in private life. The Duke of Marlborough was profuse and never looked into his affairs; the Duke of Bedford covetous, and the best economist in the world. The Duke of Bedford was of such a turn as to have been able to live within his fortune if it had been fifty times less; and the Duke of Marlborough to have run his out had it been fifty times greater. . . . These two brothers were as unlike in their understandings. The understanding of the Duke of Marlborough was quite uncultivated, and that of the Duke of Bedford extremely cultivated without being the better for it. The one was incapable of application, the other had a great deal. The Duke of Marlborough wanted materials, the Duke of Bedford to know how to use them. And as the one in company, conscious of his ignorance, was generally diffident and silent the other was always assured, talkative and decisive; so that the Duke of Marlborough was sensible he wanted knowledge, whilst the Duke of Bedford had knowledge and was not sensible he wanted parts.

In these years when Sarah entertained high hopes of Walpole's overthrow, the Duke was fairly regular in his attendance

2. *Journals of the House of Lords*, XXIV. 320. 3. ibid., 344.
4. Hervey, *Memoirs*, ed. R. Sedgwick, I. 246–7.

at the House of Lords. We find him joining in Protests against Walpole's budgetary habit, to court popularity, of appropriating the produce of the Sinking Fund for current expenditure, 'the service of the present year'.[5] But it is interesting to observe that he never joins in the Protests against military measures, for limiting the number of troops the government thinks necessary to raise. This is a respectable line of conduct: it shows a certain consistency with his later line, in spite of his change of political affiliations, a consciousness of obligation attaching to the name of Marlborough, especially in regard to the Army, that grows upon him.

In the 1730s Opposition found a head, though a very unsatisfactory one, in George II's son, Frederick Prince of Wales. There was nothing to be said in his favour – except for his characteristically German love of music – and his mother and father were not given to saying it. The King said of his son, when he left St James's Palace after the *accouchement* of his wife, that he hoped he would never see the puppy again. The Queen said that her 'dear first-born is the greatest ass, and the greatest liar, and the greatest *canaille*, and the greatest beast in the whole world, and I most heartily wish he was out of it'. There was much to be said for their point of view, but English society was hardly accustomed to these Hanoverian antics in its royal family – such a contrast to the dignity, and fair family relations, of their predecessors. Hervey tells us that 'everybody talked of these quarrels, but the whole family was so little popular that few people justified any of the parties concerned in them or wished them reconciled'.[6]

Political dissension in such a close society did not interfere with the enjoyments of social life – it added a spice to them. That winter party-feeling and court-division extended itself to the realm of music. The Prince of Wales, with Charles's assistance, undertook a campaign against Handel, who was the King's favourite composer. They engaged an Italian company for the Opera in Lincoln's Inn Fields, where they opened their season with an *Ariadne*. Handel replied with a rival *Ariadne* at the

5. *Journals of the House of Lords*, XXIV. 421.
6. Hervey, *Memoirs*, 233.

Haymarket. The Italians then brought over the most famous of *castrati*, Farinelli, who made a fortune out of his favour in the Courts of Europe. Frederick's passion for music overcame his political feelings and he ultimately made it up with Handel.

These pleasurable feuds had their reflection in literature. Towards the end of the winter Fielding put on his tedious play, *The Universal Gallant*, which in opposition to Walpole he dedicated to Marlborough with a resounding platitude: 'Poverty has imposed chains on mankind equal with tyranny; and your Grace has shown as great an eagerness to deliver men from the former as your illustrious grandfather did to rescue them from the latter'. When Fielding published his *Miscellanies* the subscribers were headed by the Prince, followed by Bedford and Marlborough and what reads like a roll-call of the Opposition.[7]

At Frederick's marriage in 1736 Charles, resplendent in white and gold, almost eclipsed his friend the Prince – we may imagine the dazzling scene at St James's, the flowered silks and damasks, the jewelled headdress of the ladies, a thousand candles reflected in the mirrors, the thronged corridors and galleries. The Duke remained to put the Prince and Princess to bed in the formal French fashion – the King putting on the Prince's shirt, the Princess undressed by her ladies.[8]

Then there was the cost to be counted. George II, who was a frugal, saving man, had received £100,000 a year as Prince of Wales; he thought £50,000 a year enough for his son, who was extravagant and deeply in debt. Marlborough, to whom the Prince's difficulties could not but be familiar, approached Henry Fox on Frederick's behalf and a campaign was set on foot in Parliament to raise the allowance to £100,000. The ranks of the Opposition rallied behind this, all the politicians who, being now out of office, looked to the future and the reversionary interest of the heir to the throne. In the Commons the Opposition rallied a larger vote against the Court than at any time till Walpole's fall. The King and Queen were furious with their offspring.

7. W. L. Cross, *The History of Henry Fielding*, I. 172.
8. A. Edwards, *Frederick Louis, Prince of Wales, 1707–51*, 59.

Frederick afterwards published his resentment to the world by rushing his wife away in the pangs of childbirth from the Court, then at Hampton Court, to St James's so that the child should not be born under his father's roof with the Queen present. All this made an immense scandal: these events and the scenes that followed, as described by the corrosive pen of Lord Hervey, are justly famous. As soon as the Princess recovered, the Prince was ordered to quit St James's. Sarah at once offered to put Marlborough House at his disposal. Frederick, however, chose Norfolk House in St James's Square, where he established a rival court, the centre to which all the Opposition looked and resorted. Here, as a step in the campaign against his father and mother, the Prince entertained the Lord Mayor and Aldermen of London to dinner. Marlborough, with other Opposition peers, was in attendance distributing leaflets containing an account of the quarrel in the royal family, of the Prince's expulsion from St James's, with the exchange of letters between the Prince and his father, putting 'Poor Fred's' case in the most favourable light. Copies of the letters were assembled with delight by Sarah – and there they all are still at Blenheim.

These irritations vexed the last months of Queen Caroline's useful life. While she lay dying, the Prince sent frequent messages to St James's – so Marlborough himself told Hervey – to know how his mother was doing: 'Well, sure, we must have some good news soon. 'Tis impossible she can hold out long. I think I am a very good son: I wish her out of her pain.'[9] Courageous and philosophical to the last, she did not request the consolations of the Church. Archbishop Potter was able only to assure standers-by, 'Gentlemen, her Majesty is in a most heavenly frame of mind.' This, of course, was for the benefit of the people: it does not appear that the deistic Queen either desired or received the Sacrament.

Upon this consummation Frederick announced his intention of going to church; the Duke of Marlborough placed his seat at St James's, Piccadilly, at the Prince's disposal.

More important for Marlborough was his friendship with Henry Fox, which was a factor in the political grouping of the

9. Hervey, *Memoirs*, 889.

time and had consequences for the family into the next generation, for the best part of a century.

Their friendship was a case of mutual attraction that went back to early days – 'my most intimate and dear friend from childhood', Fox wrote of Charles when he died.[10] The Foxes had followed a course somewhat comparable to the Churchills. Starting as a West Country family in Wiltshire, they moved into Dorset; they were Royalists and subsequently Tories, tarnished with Jacobitism. They too were Household officials to the Stuarts, Sir Stephen Fox, like Sir Winston, an officer of the Board of Green Cloth; but as Paymaster he made a large fortune, 'honestly gotten and unenvied, which is next to a miracle', said Evelyn. The Game Books at Maddington show Marlborough as a frequent guest there in these years; and the Fox brothers were sufficiently interested in his well-being to lay wagers on the subject of Sarah's survival.

When Henry Fox fell in love with the Duke of Richmond's eldest daughter and won her parents' intense disapproval – for he was a younger son and they could not foresee that he would become one of the richest politicians of the time – Marlborough stood by him. Lady Caroline eloped from her parents' house and was married privately in Sir Charles Hanbury-Williams's residence in Privy Gardens; Marlborough as a friend of the Richmond family gave her away. The affair made a sensation and they were much abused for their part in it. Society, as usual in these affairs, took sides – mostly the side of the Richmonds, who were implacable and cut their daughter off, refusing to see her for years. In the end, they had to recognize that the marriage was blissfully happy and their unwanted son-in-law a foremost figure in politics: that mollified them. Whatever we may think of Henry Fox as a politician, in private life he displayed loyalty and charm. On the back of Richardson's portrait of Marlborough at Holland House he inscribed these words: 'Lord Holland loved and still loves his friend Charles Spencer better than any man living'. When Charles died Fox had to seek a change of scene to prevent 'continual thinking' of his dead friend: 'I came here in hopes that the journey and a little

10. Earl of Ilchester, *Henry Fox, Lord Holland*, II. 106.

Bath water might make me sleep better than, since I heard of his death, I have been able to do. I have not succeeded yet. Methinks the *anni recedentes* have particular disadvantage on these sad occasions.' There must have been something very attractive in Charles to inspire such devotion.

At a by-election at Windsor in March 1738 the Court candidate, Lord Vere Beauclerk, was opposed by Sarah and her grandson with all their might – Windsor Lodge and Langley Park being together on this. The voting turned out even: 133 votes for each candidate, Government and Opposition, so the decision was thrown into the House of Commons. There remains at Blenheim an account of the legal expenses incurred: coach-hire to Windsor to know the constitution of the borough and examine witnesses; further consultations at Westminster, warrants and the porterage thereof; for drawing the brief in very long folio and for dinners, of course – in all the lawyers managed to run up these expenses, apart from those of the election itself, to £202 5s. 10d.[11] In vain: Walpole's majority declared Lord Vere elected. Walpole's brother Horatio, writing to one of the Trevors, commented: 'the Duke of Marlborough in my poor notions of honour has acted a very precipitate and indecent part'.[12] This was the kind of situation he was placed in by Sarah's pressure, and it led nowhere.

He was now to emancipate himself, under the influence of Henry Fox. At the end of the same month we find Horatio Walpole writing to congratulate Robert Trevor

upon what I am persuaded will be as agreeable a surprise to you, as it has been to the whole town, of the Duke of Marlborough's having kissed his Majesty's hand yesterday and accepted a regiment. This was kept a secret from his nearest relations [*i.e.* Sarah] until, after having been yesterday morning with his particular friend Mr Henry Fox at my brother Walpole's, he appeared at the King's levee; where his Majesty received him in a most gracious manner. And after that his Grace wrote a letter to the Prince of Wales to take his leave of his Royal Highness, thinking that more decent than to wait upon him in person. . . . This agreeable news with respect to the King, as well as to my brother, was

11. Blenheim MSS., F I. 57.
12. *H.M.C.*, *Trevor MSS.*, 15, 16.

done in the handsomest manner and consequently must have given all our family infinite satisfaction, as indeed it does all honest men.

In the eighteenth century 'all honest men' means those who agree with one; other periods have their own cant.

Sarah, as we have seen, was unappeasable: she turned the screw on him financially; it must have been at this time that, in the course of the legal proceedings she instigated, she said that she had not handed over Marlborough's sword to him, though it was an heirloom, 'lest he should pick out the diamonds and pawn them'.

But her grandson had ceased to plough the sand; the rewards were not slow in coming. He had kissed hands for the colonelcy of the 38th Regiment of Foot in March; in August he was made a Lord of the Bedchamber. In January next year he was appointed Lord-Lieutenant of the counties of Oxford and Buckingham; in September he got the colonelcy of the 1st Royal Dragoons, and in May 1739 he was promoted to that of the 2nd Horse Guards. He was at last moving up the military ladder. Two years later he achieved the Garter. Such were the rewards, if not of virtue, of conformity and submission.

The long ascendancy of Sir Robert Walpole was drawing to a close under increasingly successful challenges to his policy and power, with the usual consequences of groups splintering and new ones forming. In April 1741 rumours were going round that Marlborough would drop Fox. A member of Parliament writes,

the consequences will be that your Grace can bring in nobody. Mr Fox must not forsake us, we are numerous and steady enough to serve you and him. . . . We are all impatient to see you in *broad daylight*, we have been clouded with too much darkness and underground work. Pray, my lord, let us see you and all will end well.[13]

The Duke had never been an intimate of Walpole's, but an undated letter from Walpole shows them in close understanding over some business that demanded the King's assent.[14] Walpole says that he has done all in his power but 'no orders from the higher powers could be had. . . . I most heartily wish you and

13. Blenheim MSS., E 54. 14. ibid.

Mr Fox through this detestable job. And you must play your own game the best you can.' But what was the job? and what the game?

When the colonial war with Spain merged into a general European war and Walpole's policy lay in ruins around him, a concerted attack was made on his prosecution of the war, which he was as ill-fitted to conduct as Neville Chamberlain was that of 1939. In February 1741 addresses to remove Walpole were brought forward with large support in both Houses of Parliament. For the moment they were rejected with unexpected majorities, owing to the abstention of the Tories. Thereupon Marlborough came to Walpole's defence against attainder or impeachment with a resolution in the Lords

> that any attempt to inflict any kind of punishment on any person without allowing him an opportunity to make his defence, or without proof of any crime or misdemeanor committed by him, is contrary to natural justice, the fundamental laws of this realm and the ancient established usage of Parliaments; and it is a high infringement on the liberties of the subject.

This was carried by 81 to 54.[15]

But nothing could save Walpole now with the war-fever heightening. In February 1742 he resigned. The Prince of Wales paid a visit in triumph to the King; crowds attended Frederick at Carlton House, where he refused to speak to Marlborough who had defended Walpole to the last.[16] There was talk that he would be rewarded with a command in Flanders; and in fact he did go on active service as brigadier to the Netherlands this year, as we have seen, and to Germany on the Dettingen campaign the year after.

He returned in disgust, as we saw, at the partiality which, the English officers considered, had been shown for the Hanoverians. On his return he went down to the country without paying his respects at Court, and on resuming Opposition he lost his post in the Bedchamber. Horace Walpole said that his motive was 'to reinstate himself in the old Duchess's will'. If

15. *H.M.C.*, *Egmont MSS.*, III. 191.
16. Horace Walpole, *Letters*, ed. P. Toynbee, I. 180.

this was so, he did not succeed. Other stories circulated about him, one of them to the effect that on coming to his quarters and finding them occupied by a Hanoverian general who claimed that the King had assigned them to him, the Duke had replied, 'Sir, I have but few words for you; if you insist on it, *Present and give fire*.'[17] This, though not convincingly in character, shows that the Duke was becoming known to the public in his own right. In December 1743 there was a motion in the Lords for an address to the King to dismiss his Hanoverian troops.[18] Though the Duke could not bring himself to speak to this, next month he seconded Lord Sandwich's motion 'that the continuing the Hanoverian troops is prejudicial to the King'.

Nevertheless, on the threat of a Jacobite invasion Lord Stair and Marlborough volunteered their services. Horace Walpole reports that 'immediately the Duke of Marlborough, who most handsomely and seasonably was come to town on purpose, moved for an address to assure the King of their standing by him with lives and fortunes'.[19] When the '45 Rebellion came England was denuded of troops, and there was no enthusiasm for the Hanoverian royal family at all. General Wade wrote, 'England is for the first comer; and if six thousand French land before these Dutch and English are here, London is theirs as soon as they can march to it'.[20] At this point the Revolution families and the City which had brought the Hanoverians in rallied to their aid: they had too much invested on that side not to do so. Marlborough and his brother-in-law Bedford, Montague and Cholmondeley all raised their own regiments for the King.

This effected a useful reconciliation with the Court, and it paid dividends. The Duke's career in the Army resumed its upward march: he was shortly after gazetted major-general, and two years later advanced to lieutenant-general.

Next year, 1746, brought a shock: the early death of his brother Jack Spencer 'at the age of six or seven and thirty',

17. Egmont, III. 274.
18. ibid., 278.
19. Horace Walpole, *Letters*, ed. Toynbee, II. 6.
20. Ilchester, *Henry Fox, Lord Holland*, I. 114.

according to Walpole, 'and in possession of near £30,000 a year, merely because he would not be abridged of those invaluable blessings of an English subject, brandy, small beer and tobacco'.[21] It is more likely to have been from the consumption all these children inherited from their mother. Jack had lived just long enough to get the bulk of Sarah's immense fortune, in addition to the Sunderland estates handed over to him by Charles. Now from the grave Jack administered a worse shock to his brother.

> The great business of the town is Jack Spencer's will, who has left Althorp and the Sunderland estate in reversion to Pitt, after more obligations and more pretended friendship for his brother the Duke than is conceivable. The Duke is in the utmost uneasiness about it, having left the drawing of the writings for the estate to his brother and his grandmother, and without having any idea that himself was cut out of the entail. An additional circumstance of iniquity is that he had given a bond for Mr Spencer for £4,000, which now he must pay, and the will and the bond are dated within three days of one another.[22]

To this had their relations come after the years of friction with and around Sarah, the bickerings and the increasing distrust; it is sad to think of, after the closeness and mutual affection of their youth and early manhood.

This country's duel with France, which was the dominant theme of our foreign affairs for most of the century, reached an inconclusive truce with the Peace of Aix-la-Chapelle in 1748. The rule of the Pelhams, in the years before and after, was described by Horace Walpole as 'a system of lethargic acquiescence in which the spirit of Britain, agitated for so many centuries, seemed willingly to repose'.[23] This was the Augustan age of Georgian England: everywhere country houses were being built or rebuilt in classic beauty, elegance of decoration and proportion, in admirable dignity and repose, or mere decency according to the good standards of the age. They embodied an ideal of civilization that was at the same time urbane and founded

21. Horace Walpole, *Letters*, ed. Toynbee, II. 204.
22. *Horace Walpole's Correspondence with George Montagu*, ed. W. S. Lewis, I. 34.
23. Horace Walpole, *Memoirs of the Reign of George II*, I. 323.

upon sane and healthy country foundations, pursuits, obligations. Never can there have been a better balanced, a more satisfying way of life. Everywhere the rural landscape was being brought into order and improved; the lines of woodland and plantation, park and wild, that have endured until our own unhappy day were then being laid down. These were the years when the Duke was making his park, with its lakes and plantations, at Langley and rebuilding the house there in the plain symmetry and distinction demanded by the taste of the time.

For the politicians there was the perennial sport of domestic politics, the ins and outs, the ups and downs, the snakes and ladders of office. Dukes – except for the absorbed Duke of Newcastle – sat more loosely to the game, though their stake in the country and their rank demanded some attention. Marlborough belonged to his brother-in-law Bedford's group, whose leading spokesman in the Commons was Henry Fox. Fox, who knew him well, described the Duke of Bedford as 'the most ungovernable governed man in the world' – for he was much under the influence of his second Duchess. Archdeacon Coxe adds that in middle age the Duke

> still retained his youthful fondness for cricket matches and other rural amusements, and was greatly attached to theatrical representations. These propensities, together with his social habits, rendered him impatient of restraint and negligent in the discharge of his official duties.[24]

At this time Secretary of State, he would come up from Woburn on Tuesday to return on Wednesday night. It was impossible to get any letters out of him. 'What would you have him write about?' said the King, 'there is nothing for him to do.' Or on other occasions: 'It is not to be borne; he never writes. . . . He has an easy office and receives his pay easily.'

Marlborough was in much the same case: equally dilatory and unwilling to support the routine burden of office. Perhaps being a Duke was a full-time job in itself. It was not that he was without ambition, or qualification for office. Even Horace Walpole, in his disparaging way, allowed that he had good judgement.

24. W. Coxe, *Memoirs of the Administration of Henry Pelham*, I. 108.

> The Duke of Marlborough had virtues and sense enough to deserve esteem, but always lost it by forfeiting respect. He was honest and generous; capable of giving the most judicious advice and of following the worst. His profusion was never well directed, and a variety of changes in his political conduct having never been weighed previously or preserved subsequently, joined to the greatest bashfulness and indistinction in his articulation, had confirmed the world in a very mean opinion of his understanding.[25]

We see once more how right Sarah had been to tell him to speak up, if he wanted to be a British senator – and how useless it is to wish people other than they are: only the rarest individuals can make themselves anew. We observe too Charles's natural diffidence that haunted him all his life.

Nevertheless, in spite of these disadvantages, pride and his sense of rank kept him to his last as a senator. In 1749 he was appointed Lord Steward of the Household: in a famous phrase of his descendant, Sir Winston, he had 'worked his passage'. In spite of diffidence and inarticulateness he spoke in the Lords when necessary. When a libellous tract of *Constitutional Queries* was circulated against Cumberland, the King's second son (in which the eldest son Frederick was suspected to have a hand), Marlborough moved in the Lords that it be burned by the common hangman. In Bedford's dispute with Newcastle over Nova Scotia, Bedford got Marlborough on to his side and so managed to hold on to office and receive his pay a little longer.

In 1753 there was an immense fuss about suspected Jacobite leanings among the preceptors of the young Prince George, heir to the throne. Two years before his father had died, regretted by no one: 'he had his father's head and his mother's heart'. The education of the boy who became George III was a matter of state importance. The old King appointed as his governor Lord Waldegrave, who was a personal favourite with him. Waldegrave was a great-grandson of James II by Arabella Churchill. The Hanoverians were as royalist in their prejudices as the exiled Stuarts. The charges against the young Prince's tutors created much excitement – just the sort of molehill to make a mountain of. Marlborough was called upon to put the

25. Horace Walpole, *Memoirs of the Reign of George II*, I. 483.

matter in its proper proportions and to report the sentence of the Cabinet Council, which gave no credence to the charges.

Since Sarah's death the Duke had been installed at Blenheim and we find him extending his interests in Oxfordshire. In 1751 Clarendon's descendant, Lord Hyde, was forced to sell beautiful Cornbury, which marches with Blenheim.[26] Marlborough's trustees bought the estate for £61,000, including the Rangership of Wychwood Forest. For the next century and a half this captivating property remained in the possession of the Duke's descendants, for part of the time under the name of Blandford Park. The name did not stick.

The contest for the representation of the county of Oxford at the approaching general election of 1754 made an immense stir. In the eighteenth century only a small minority of seats were ever contested, least of all the county representation; for where there were hundreds of freeholders to be paid, bribed or treated in some way or other for their vote, it was apt to be ruinously expensive. Tenants voted as they were instructed by their landlord or his agent; nevertheless 'it was at all times the first article of constitutional cant to describe the right of freely choosing representatives as "the most valuable privilege of every English freeholder" '.[27] Still the tenant had to be looked after for exercising his vote, that 'signal mark of citizenship', in the right direction and there remained those incalculable birds, independent voters, to be flushed and got into the right cage. No wonder the landowning class avoided contests as much as possible, and arrived at compromises representing the balance of family, landed and party interests in their area.

In Oxfordshire the bulk of the landed gentry were Tories – the Old Interest; so was the city of Oxford, so was the university, regarded by many as little better than a Jacobite seminary: here 'the old loves lingered sadly on'. But the magnates, the peers, were Whigs: the Marlboroughs, Harcourts, Macclesfields, Norths. The Marlboroughs controlled the representation of

26. V. J. Watney, *Cornbury and the Forest of Wychwood*, 191–4.

27. L. B. Namier, *The Structure of Politics at the Accession of George III* (1st edition), I. 88.

Woodstock, the Norths had their share in Banbury. To upset such arrangements was a challenge to political sportsmanship and received manners. Landlords respected each others' spheres of interest, and 'treating against a gentleman in his own town where he is residing is as great an incivility as treating in his parlour'.[28] Why, then, did the Duke decide in 1752 to upset the balance and invade the Tory representation of the county by putting forward, in agreement with the Macclesfields, Whig candidates?

The answer is fairly clear. The laconic Duke, who never explained himself any more than his grandfather had done, must have considered that his position in the county required this recognition. It would increase and ratify the recently acquired standing of his family there. It would enhance his importance in politics; the electoral influence of the Marlboroughs was inconsiderable compared with a Newcastle – this would help to enable him to look Newcastle in the face. We have noted that under Marlborough's diffidence there was a pertinacious determination to make himself felt, to deserve his name. And in fact, with Fox as intermediary, Newcastle was got to promise the government's help in challenging this Tory stronghold.

The approaching contest riveted attention all through 1753. Never was there such an outpouring of election literature, pamphlets, squibs, journalism, verses.

> Bravest lads, that have so lately
> Drawn your swords for Church and Laws,
> Sheath them not till you completely
> Crown by zeal the glorious cause:
>   Then to Marlboro', glorious Marlboro',
>   Give your votes, your hearts, your voice;
>   Our liberties he'll shield from danger,
>   Then in a bumper let's rejoice.[29]

Perhaps to them it was the last line that mattered most. To the Duke it was all very expensive: his campaign was regarded as another example of his reckless profusion. At race-meetings,

28. q. R. J. Robson, *The Oxfordshire Election of 1754*, 45.
29. q. Watney, *Cornbury and the Forest of Wychwood*, 196.

quarter-sessions and other times through 1753 lavish hospitality was dispensed on behalf of the Whig candidates. Lady Susan Keck, the aristocratic wife of the Duke's agent at Woodstock, wrote that it would cost a few guineas to have certain freeholders 'properly inspired when got together, since at present your Grace asks no mortal a question unpaid'. Elsewhere Marlborough's name went 'as current as the coin of the realm'; it was no doubt cashed in.[30] It was thought that the freeholders of the city of Oxford should be approached individually, 'to whom the compliment of being considered in the rank of gentlemen on this occasion may, I think, not improperly be made'.[31] The Old Interest was not to be out-done: the Dashwoods and Wenmans poured out money like water. A high old time was had by the freemen of (this corner of) England while the fun lasted and their betters contested for their favours. The Tory candidates were lauded as 'not impotent, but proper persons to propagate true Britons' – an aspersion upon the virility of one of the Whig candidates which called for the rejoinder, 'We hope so for their good ladies' sakes.'

As the election drew near the pace quickened. In January the Duke became High Steward of the Company of Blanket Weavers at Witney, with special intention. Incumbents were usually supposed to follow the political persuasions of their patrons. The Duke therefore was justifiably vexed when the vicar of Woodstock, though owing his preferment to him, publicly withdrew support from the Whig candidates when the government introduced a Bill to enable Jews to be naturalized. This measure was considered unchristian by a lot of the clergy: 'God did not permit the Jews to eat swine because this would have been a kind of fratricide'.[32] When the Duke sent the vicar not pork but venison, he returned 'no other answer than that if it was intended as a bribe, it would be lost upon him'. 'The loss of this one vote has surprised his Grace more than that of a hundred others would have done': no doubt the return of this one lost sheep by election day would have given great joy, if not in paradise, at any rate at Blenheim Palace.

Election day was not without the element of absurdity that

30. q. Robson, op. cit., 49. 31. ibid., 22. 32. ibid., 91.

often attends Oxford affairs. When the Whig cavalcade was pelted with dirt, Captain Turton discharged a pistol which accidentally killed a hostile chimney-sweep. The Duke was much agitated at this untoward event and posted off to Newcastle, 'the coroner, who is a most violent party-man, has given his inquest wilful murder. . . . The mob at Oxford already threaten to serve him as Porteous, if he is acquitted.'[33] It does not seem that anything much happened to Captain Turton:[34] silly of the sweep to get in the way of a gentleman's pistol.

When the count was over, for all the vast expense on both sides, the Tories were found to be in a majority. It took the Whig House of Commons three days a week for many weeks to put that right. Not for nothing had Newcastle been able to congratulate himself on the return of a manageable House: 'we have as good a body of friends in the House of Commons as ever men had'. He had seen to that. The House reversed the voting and declared the Whig candidates, Lord Parker and Sir Edward Turner, duly elected. The Tory election expenses were said to have been more than £20,000: in vain. The main burden on the Whig side fell on the Macclesfields; the government contributed only some £3,000. Marlborough had done his bit, and he had not much cash to spare. It remained for him to count the cost. He decided he must economize.

At Blenheim there is an account of the Duke's household expenses for the past two years, from Lady Day 1753 to Lady Day 1755, with suggestions where to prune.[35] The kitchen was to be cut £50, out of some £1,982, *i.e.* out of £991 per annum, 'by having more provisions of your Grace's own at Langley, which will also serve for the family at London'. The wine account was enormous – no less than £1,690 a year (multiply by ten or so!): it was to be cut £50 and 'by buying French wines only

33. ibid., 129. Captain Porteous, captain of the Edinburgh city guard, had been lynched by the mob in 1736.

34. Next year when returning the Commission of the Peace for Oxfordshire as Lord-Lieutenant the Duke named Captain Turton as J.P. though still under indictment for murder. The Lord Chancellor remonstrated with the Duke on his characteristic piece of carelessness. P. C. Yorke, *Life and Correspondence of Lord Chancellor Hardwicke*, II. 547.

35. Blenheim MSS., F I. 52.

when wanted'. Brewery £375 and Coals £439 were to be cut £25 each by proper care of the beer cellars and of fires; candles, which accounted for £178, by £20 with proper accounts and care. The Stables, which cost £1,223, were to be docked 'by having a post chaise and keeping eight horses at Chelsea'; with the Duke's neglectful ways we can see this growing into an extra charge. Household furniture at £300 should be reduced 'by having no more furniture for one or two years but what is necessary'. The chief saving proposed was £400, out of £1,730, by discharging several servants: it is unlikely that it was attained. Pensioners cost £185, bread £161 – to be cut £25 by proper accounts given; liveries and clothes for the household cost the large sum of £735. Taxes and parish dues ran away with £211, the dog kennel with £25. These figures with the comments of the steward are sufficiently eloquent of the state of affairs: what was needed was Sarah's broom.

Politically the Duke's demonstration achieved its end. An accommodation was reached in time for the next election, by which Whigs and Tories agreed to share the county representation: too expensive to fight. In the absence of a contest nomination was equivalent to election. In 1761 the Tory Sir James Dashwood returned to his former seat, with the Duke's second son, Lord Charles Spencer, as his companion.[36] Some member of the Blenheim family continued to represent the county until 1818 – over half a century's run rewarded the Duke's pertinacity. The representation of Woodstock remained a family perquisite, with Lord Randolph Churchill, up to the threshold of this century.

At the centre of affairs the Duke received an accession of strength in consequence. We learn that he was ambitious to succeed the Duke of Dorset in the expensive post of Lord-Lieutenant of Ireland; the rumour in Dublin was that he was appointed.[37] However, in January 1755 he got the high political post of Lord Privy Seal, which gave him an influential voice in affairs and brought him into the forefront of the complicated

36. *Members of Parliament* (Return 1878), II. 129, and *passim.*

37. T. W. Riker, *Henry Fox, Lord Holland*, I. 189; *H.M.C., Charlemont MSS.*, 198.

political manoeuvres on the eve and during the first years of the Seven Years War. It is impossible to describe these in detail – anyhow they are quite well known. On Henry Pelham's death in 1754 the old King exclaimed, 'I shall now have no more peace!' Nor had he. The clue to the situation was the weakness of Newcastle's administration in the Commons, where the two leading figures were Fox and Pitt; the problem how to accommodate them, or one or the other of them, without giving him control of the ministry. Marlborough's interest in the matter was very close, through his personal and political friendship with Fox. We shall see that he acted a part that was sincere in relation to his friend, self-sacrificing in regard to himself, and governed by his sense of duty to the country.

At the end of the year Newcastle was forced to bring in more of the Bedfords. To make this easier and at Fox's request Marlborough stepped down from his post as Lord Privy Seal to make way for Bedford's brother-in-law. Instead he accepted the office of Master General of the Ordnance. We may be sure that the change, though a demotion, was congenial to him: no more speechifying in the Lords, but a return to the Army. Moreover, it was an office his grandfather had held. At the same time Pitt and his few personal friends were dismissed from their subordinate positions in the ministry.

Hitherto Pitt and Fox had been as friendly as two pre-eminent rivals can be expected to be. One thing that drew them together was that Newcastle wanted neither of these men of superior abilities. But the country was already drifting into war and the sense of crisis was sharpening the conflicts of policy and power. There was only one man who could surmount the crisis, as in 1940, and carry the country through to victory: William Pitt. All the politicians were united to keep him out. He owed nothing to party and had few friends. Possessed by his own genius, cut off by illness and perhaps schizophrenia from normal commerce with average human beings, he soared alone. He had contrived to alienate many people in his twenty years in Parliament. The King detested him for his fulminations against Hanover, his self-consciously and highly dramatized patriotic line, and maintained a rigid veto against admitting him to any office that would bring him into contact with him. In all those years the King had only once spoken to him; at his levées George II was unable to recognize the greatest orator in the kingdom. Perhaps people may be forgiven for not discerning, underneath the orator, the 'daring pilot in extremity', the man who would dare all for his country and out of frustration and defeat raise her, in those years from his assumption of supreme power to the outbreak of the American Revolution, to the loftiest height she ever attained.

Horace Walpole points the contrast between these two, Marlborough's friend Fox and no one's 'friend' Pitt – for he did not regard anyone else as his equal; and perhaps he was right. Pitt was by far the greater speaker, Fox the better debater.

> Pitt could only attack; Fox, the boldest and ablest champion, was still more formed to worry. . . . Pitt's figure was commanding; Fox's dark and troubled – yet the latter was the agreeable man: Pitt could not unbend; Fox was cheerful, social, communicative.

Not far below the surface in Henry Fox was an inextinguishable jealousy of Pitt: one recognizes the familiar smell in his comment, after a superb speech of Pitt's, 'Pitt is a better speaker than I am; but, thank God, I have better judgement'. Some quality in Pitt daunted Fox: as the Prince of Vaudemont had said of John Churchill, there was 'something inexpressible' about him[39] – we need not forget that Pitt was a kinsman of the Churchills. Next year, when the country was bewildered by a succession of defeats, Pitt told the Duke of Devonshire calmly, 'My lord, I know that I can save my country, and that nobody else can'. There was something in the soul of William Pitt to make those who care for the English name, and know what he cared for it, to weep for him still.

Henry Fox was that rare thing in English politics, a confessed cynic. He knew what people are, and he did not mind. Now at this juncture Newcastle offered him a Secretaryship of State without the management of the Commons: in other words, that he should have the responsibility for the conduct of the war without the power. Fox unburdened himself to Marlborough:

39. cf. *The Early Churchills*, 207 (Penguin edn, 223).

'I then was to undertake this great office on the foot of being quite a cipher. . . . I thought it better to remain Secretary at War with, than to be Secretary of State without, control.'[40] Fox knew too well the want of veracity and candour in average politicians: 'I have within these three months, and indeed within these three weeks, seen such unaccountable behaviour as makes me very sure that people must be taken as they are'.[41] In fact this view justified Pitt in his lofty contempt for them, though at heart he would not accept it. Fox did and proceeded to profit from it. Pitt thought himself above that – as he was. Newcastle, with the not infrequent astuteness of the second-rate in dealing with the first-rate, was determined to leave Pitt 'under the uncertainty in which he now is' – and Henry Fox played his game. 'I do not desire to know, much less to determine, what Mr Pitt is to do or be.'[42] From that insincerity in his relations with Pitt, who was relying on him to make an entrance for him on equal terms into the Cabinet, flowed the ultimate frustration of Fox's political career, for when Pitt came to supreme power he excluded Fox from all share in it.

Marlborough, who had good judgement and did not lack courage, had at first advised his friend not to accept office without power and argued that Newcastle was at his mercy. Now Fox was left dependent on Newcastle, having to defend the government's failures in the Commons, without power. The war meanwhile was going from bad to worse. It had been brought on by Boscawen's attacking a French fleet off Louisbourg, capturing only two ships while all the rest of the ships got safe into harbour: the operation should either have been completed or not attempted at all. General Braddock's army was completely cut up by the French in the Ohio country and himself killed. Then came the surrender of Minorca. The country was both frustrated and furious; it was on this wave of indignation that Pitt was irresistibly borne forward, like his remote kinsman in 1940.

Fox had written to Marlborough:

what E. or P. will do, nobody can tell, nor should I care if it were not in concert with Leicester House. . . . They are capable of the shortest

40. Ilchester, op. cit., I. 207. 41. ibid., 215. 42. ibid., 240.

turns and Pitt already says that it is right to defend Hanover, but to what degree we should contribute to it is the question. Which is keeping himself for sale, but I own I do not see how they will buy him. . . . I don't see what Pitt can do with the Court, but had he meant opposition, he could not have thought it necessary to break so abruptly with me.[43]

Pitt had taken the measure of Henry Fox. What was Fox to do now? Marlborough, in perfect sincerity and like the honest man he was, wished to bring Fox and Pitt together in the present juncture: he was unaware of the sentence of exclusion passed in Pitt's uncompromising mind. Marlborough considered that no one could bring this about so well or with such authority as the Duke of Bedford, and he exerted himself to press this upon him.

In vain. Pitt would now never join with Fox. The disasters abroad forced him upon the politicians and the old King. At once the King's Speech in the new session revealed a new spirit, a master mind and a policy, which carried the nation through, even though a worse disaster and further frustrations were to come. Early in 1757 Pitt was again forced out – to find himself borne up to further heights of popularity by the nation outside the walls of Westminster. He came back with increased power to conduct the war as he pleased. In the negotiations to form a stable national government to carry the country through, Fox did all in all to prevent it. Horace Walpole comments: 'the rashness of throwing government into imminent confusion at such a juncture struck both the enemies and friends of Fox. His ambition was glaring; his interestedness not even specious.'[44] And that from a man who had no policy himself, and no belief! Pitt, who had no thought for anything but the war and his country's safety, permitted Fox to accept defeat with the lucrative job of Paymaster. With this Fox gave up the struggle. What it meant to him we may descry from an undated note at Blenheim, which must belong to this time, promising a visit there and to be at his friend's disposal, 'though it will be no pleasure to you to see me, so miserable, so contemptible in my own eyes as I am and ever must be'.[45]

43. Blenheim MSS., E 54. Fox's reference to E. means the Earl of Egmont.
44. Horace Walpole, *Memoirs of the Reign of George II*, II. 202.
45. Blenheim MSS., E 54.

Pitt went on to achieve undying fame, Fox to gain an immense fortune – and the not wholly deserved contempt of everyone.

The urgency of the war suspended the scuffling of factions for a time; in the summer of 1756 invasion was expected. The Foot Guards were encamped at Cobham and to raise morale a grand military parade was staged. Horace Walpole tells us that all the world was a-soldiering and that the great drum was to pass by to Cobham.

The Duke of Marlborough and his grandfather's triumphal car are to close the procession. What would his grandame, if she were alive, say to this pageant? If the war lasts, I think well enough of him to believe he will earn a sprig; but I have no notion of trying on a crown of laurel before I had acquired it. The French are said to be embarked at Dunkirk.[46]

When the emergency passed Marlborough was stationed at Byfleet in command of the artillery. In the winter a Parliamentary investigation went into the expenses of the Ordnance and found that his usual extravagance had faulted him. Among other undue expenses it appeared that the Duke had charged his own pay at 10s. a day, when 'the great Duke of Marlborough, the late Duke of Argyle, the Duke of Montagu, three men sufficiently attentive to their interest had touched but four shillings'.[47] Charles refunded all that he had received above that figure. He was at all times the target for much solicitation, especially from his wife's kin and from young officers. A request for a military appointment turns up in the correspondence of an Oxfordshire squire, Sanderson Miller of Radway.

I believe we all think him a little dilatory, but be that as it will we must keep it to ourselves and speak of the Duke of Marlborough as your nephew does in the fairest and handsomest terms. . . . His claim is so strong that it is impossible for the Duke of Marlborough to abandon him, unless he has some opportunity of picking a quarrel with him.[48]

46. *Horace Walpole's Correspondence with George Montagu*, ed. W. S. Lewis, I. 192.

47. Horace Walpole, *Memoirs of the Reign of George II*, II. 133.

48. L. Dickins and M. Stanton, *An Eighteenth Century Correspondence*, 350.

The young man obtained his promotion; this is how one got things in the eighteenth century: no 'damned merit' about it.

On the other hand, for some time after the Ordnance investigation, the Duke was regarded with disfavour by the King, who took a close personal interest in all that appertained to the Army. Marlborough wished for active service; the King would not give him a regiment. We find the Duke of Cumberland writing to Fox,

> you know the regard I have for the Duke of Marlborough and that I really have an opinion of him but always knew that the King would not be prevailed to give him a regiment. I will do and have done more than I care he should know about, but it won't do. Is he not as much in the Army as I am?[49]

Fox had written, 'His Majesty is still very severe in his opinion of the Duke of Marlborough: he will not consider him as in the Army.'

The advent of Pitt to power changed all this. Any officer who wanted to fight was regarded with favour by him; the Duke got his request and more.

Pitt was planning an attack on the French coast, to offset the ill posture of affairs in Germany and in the hope of diverting French forces; from this arose the Rochefort expedition. He found the Duke spirited and co-operative: 'the Duke of Marlborough showed great facility and promises to be ready very soon with the additions, and that the first train and stores shall sail with the transports'.[50] As usual at the beginning of this country's wars amateurishness and unpreparedness exacted their penalty: the expedition was a complete fiasco. The failure went to Pitt's heart, when with most politicians it would merely have gone to their temper: 'I feel more and more I shall never get Rochefort off my heart. Nor do I believe England (which is the misery) will cease to feel, perhaps for an age, the fatal consequences of this foul miscarriage.'[51] The country did not

49. *Letters to Henry Fox, Lord Holland*, ed. by the Earl of Ilchester, 112–15.

50. q. R. Sedgwick, 'Letters from William Pitt to Lord Bute', in *Essays Presented to Sir Lewis Namier*, ed. R. Pares and A. J. P. Taylor, 119.

51. ibid., 134.

hold him responsible; this was the spirit that changed the face of affairs in another year. Pitt appointed a court of inquiry into the miscarriage, of which Marlborough was the leading member. Everyone appreciated the fairness with which the inquiry was conducted, though not everyone understood, as Horace Walpole did, the artfulness of the move politically or its intention to stiffen the morale of the army command.

Pitt was full of expedients and schemes; he was ready to try anything. A new spirit was at work. What he liked was officers who, instead of making difficulties, found expedients to carry out his plans. For the Canada expedition he was planning he wanted Marlborough for the command. The King was making difficulties about Amherst: 'what a consideration that such commands go a-begging. We cannot be a country long.'[52] Here was the source of his inspiration: a burning zeal for England.

That winter there took place a very curious episode which gave rise to much comment.[53] The Duke received a warning letter signed by the name of Felton, that of the man who had assassinated the Duke of Buckingham.

> My present position in life is such that I should prefer annihilation to a continuance in it. . . . It has employed my invention for some time to find out a method of destroying another without exposing my own life. . . . I am desperate and must be provided for. I have more motives than one for singling you out upon this occasion; and I give you this fair warning, because the means I shall make use of are too fatal to be eluded by the power of physic.

The writer appointed a meeting on the Sunday morning near the first tree beyond the stile in Hyde Park in the foot-walk to Kensington. The Duke duly appeared at the hour appointed,

> on horse-back and alone, with pistols before him and the star of his order displayed that he might be the more easily known. He had likewise taken the precaution of engaging a friend to attend in the Park at such a distance, however, as scarce to be observable.

52. Pares and Taylor, op. cit., 141.
53. cf. T. Smollett, *Continuation of the History of England*, II. 415–23.

No one there. But riding away he chanced to turn back and saw a man near the tree standing at the bridge looking at the water, not far from Hyde Park corner. The Duke went back, bowed to the stranger and asked him if he had not something to communicate. The man said 'No, I don't know you', and on the Duke giving his name still persisted in knowing nothing.

A few days later the Duke received another warning, acknowledging his punctuality;

> the pageantry of being armed and the ensign of your order were useless and too conspicuous. You needed no attendant; the place was not calculated for mischief, nor was any intended. If you walk in the west aisle of Westminster abbey towards eleven o'clock on Sunday next, your sagacity will point out the person whom you will address by asking his company to take a turn or two with you.

This time the Duke had several persons in disguise on the watch, and shortly he saw the very same person with another man viewing the monuments. The Duke approached and asked if he had any commands for him, which the man denied; Marlborough forbore giving any signal that 'notwithstanding appearances he might run no risk of injuring an innocent person'. After this he received a third letter.

> My Lord, I am fully convinced you had a companion on Sunday: I interpret it as owing to the weakness of human nature; but such proceeding is far from being ingenuous and may produce bad effects. You will see me again soon, as it were by accident . . .

Nothing further happened until early next year, when he received another letter giving a clue to someone who 'is acquainted with some secrets that nearly concern your safety . . . it would be useless to your Grace, as well as dangerous to me, to appear more publicly in this affair'. This led to a further meeting between the Duke and the man he recognized from the Park and Westminster Abbey. The man was taken into custody – he turned out to be of respectable family and well-to-do. Various odd circumstances and coincidences came out in his trial at the Old Bailey, but no evidence could be found that the letters were in his handwriting, nor was there any presumption against him, except his happening to be in Hyde Park and the Abbey. So he was discharged, the mystery never solved. What added to its strangeness was that within the year the Duke was dead.

Pitt had another command for Marlborough in view, another attack on the French coast – this time St-Malo, the chief base for enemy privateers at the western end of the Channel. A considerable striking force was got together: a powerful fleet to cover the operations, a lesser force under Commodore Howe including transports for the troops to be landed: combined operations. Marlborough's name recruited a large number of aristocratic volunteers; he took his eldest son, Blandford, with him and the enchanting Di accompanied them to their embarkation at St Helen's. Horace Walpole writes with more than usual banter about it all:

> There! there is a Duke of Marlborough in the heart of France. Well! my dear child, I smile but I tremble; and though it is pleasanter to tremble when one invades than when one is invaded, I don't like to be at the eve even of an Agincourt. There are so many of my friends upon heroic ground that I discern all their danger through all their laurels.[54]

On his way down through the miry country this tempestuous summer he sent letter upon letter to the Duchess entreating her 'for my sake to keep up your spirits, you can have no cause for concern but that of my being absent'.[55] It was all like it had been sixteen years before, when he had first gone away soldiering in Germany. But now the children were growing up. Betty, the second, married to the irrepressible and rakish Lord Pembroke, was expecting her first child; if she is brought to bed before the fleet sails 'Di begs you will send her a letter when it happens'. They set sail on 1 June, but for several days were held up by contrary winds off the French coast and landed their troops only on 5 June in Cancale Bay, several miles from St-Malo. That spiked the enterprise from effecting a surprise, or at the

54. Horace Walpole, *Letters*, ed. Toynbee, IV. 143.
55. Blenheim MSS., E 56.

first onrush St-Malo might have been taken, strongly fortified as it was.

From Marlborough's letters to Pitt we may watch the expedition almost day by day: the landing carried out by the troops in excellent order and discipline, the march to St-Malo through enclosed country with very bad and narrow roads through which it was impossible to get the artillery, finding it impracticable to invest the city with their small forces so that enemy reinforcements and supplies poured in hourly.[56] Marlborough had sent small detachments into St-Servan under General Waldegrave, while General Boscawen threw up entrenchments to cover their withdrawal – one sees what a close circle conducted our affairs in the eighteenth century: here were two family connections of the Churchills under Marlborough's command. These measures enabled them to hold on long enough to fire the shipping in the harbour and burn the naval stores: practically all the privateers, of 30, 20 and 18 guns, were consumed – perhaps a hundred vessels.

One notices in his letters to Pitt the familiar diffidence, the emphasis the Duke places on the difficulties for fear more may be expected of him then he can perform. Unlike his grandfather, he was taking no chances: one feels that he is being over-careful of an untried reputation, afraid to expose the famous name to defeat. He was very anxious to secure the King's approbation for his conduct. Pitt writes the Duchess a kind letter to say that the attack on St-Malo itself had been found impracticable. He concurred with the Duke's withdrawal, on the supposition that superior forces under the Duc d'Aiguillon were converging on the city, at the same time remarking to Bute, 'May the next attempt answer better, and the British arms share one sprig of laurel with the rest of Europe.'[57]

Meanwhile the fleet and transports were wind-bound in Cancale Bay and could not get out. The Duke took the opportunity to reconnoitre Granville with Lord George Sackville and the engineers; but they found it too well fortified and guarded

56. These letters are among the Hotham MSS. in the East Riding Record Office at Beverley.

57. Pares and Taylor, 152.

by too strong forces to attempt. By 24 June the fleet had got clear of the Bay and was off Hogue. Marlborough wrote to Elizabeth, from the *Essex* rolling in contrary winds,

which makes this sort of service most extremely unpleasant, for schemes ever so well laid are prevented by some cursed wind. The ship rolls too much to write plain, but I don't believe I shall ever be seasick again; as for money I want none, for I don't know what to do with it: every time I open my box I see a purse of guineas that I am quite tired of and tempted to throw it overboard[58]

– a curious reflection that would not have recommended itself to his grandfather and perhaps reveals an odd psychological element in his attitude to money.

After reconnoitring the Normandy coast, Marlborough and Howe decided on an attack on Cherbourg. All the preparations for a landing on 29 June were made. At the last moment the wind blew so hard as to make it impossible: the transports would have been dashed to pieces. By this time they had only three days' hay left for the horses, the water for the troops was very bad and the men had grown sickly. There was nothing for it but to return to Spithead.

That great warrior, Horace Walpole, made fine sport with this disappointing conclusion. The Duc d'Aiguillon had sent a vessel under a flag of truce to restore the Duke of Marlborough's silver teaspoons which he had left behind in his hurry. Young Lord Downe 'makes the greatest joke of their enterprise and has said at Arthur's that five hundred men posted with a grain of common sense would have cut them all to pieces. ... How they must be diverted with this tea-equipage, stamped with the Blenheim eagles!'[59] We have more reason to appreciate the *politesses* of eighteenth-century warfare.

Actually the small results of the expedition may fairly be put down to the stormy weather that summer. Even so it may have had some effect in withholding French reinforcements for Germany – Prince Ferdinand of Brunswick was polite enough to say so. Nor was Pitt discouraged: the effect on him was to

58. Blenheim MSS., E 56.

59. Horace Walpole, *Letters*, ed. Toynbee, IV. 155.

make him reverse his veto on sending British troops to Germany. He determined to use the returned expeditionary force, refreshed and recruited in strength, to aid Prince Ferdinand. He at once made Marlborough Commander-in-Chief, with Lord George Sackville as second in command. Even Newcastle's apprehensive soul turned sanguine at the news of Ferdinand's victory over the French at Crefeld in June: 'Add to this that 9,000 British troops (the best, I hope, in Europe, both horse and foot) are going under a Duke of Marlborough to join Prince Ferdinand's army. If this will not do, nothing will.'[60]

By the end of July the Duke had already landed at Emden before the first regiments were embarked. He was back once more in the country he had known so well when he was young, in the days of the Dettingen campaign. Now he was Commander-in-Chief; but his letters to Elizabeth follow the familiar pattern, reassuring her, depreciating the chances of action, denying any danger.[61] His son was with him. In August they had made junction with General Fürstenberg with 3,000 men and would now halt until Prince Ferdinand joined them with the whole army. There was no danger of the Prince de Soubise attacking, though had he come up 'I should not have been over-alarmed though he was two to one; my troops are extremely desirous to meet the French.' But there was no probability. In the heavy rains the troops were marching up to their middles. Colonel Brown had just arrived with letters: 'I am very sensible I owe his coming solely to Mr Pitt, though the Duke of Newcastle in his letter to me takes the merit of it.'

Campaigning in Germany once more produced the old jealousies between English and Hanoverians that had made such a mark on the Duke's mind fifteen years before. He was incensed at a Hanoverian general being made full General of Foot over his head: this placed the Hanoverian next to Prince Ferdinand in rank and might have the deplorable consequences we saw in the Dettingen campaign. Charles at once wrote off a threatening letter to Newcastle – everybody knew that the way to get any-

60. P. C. Yorke, *Life and Correspondence of Lord Chancellor Hardwicke*, III. 216.

61. Blenheim MSS., E 56.

thing out of that poor dear was by bullying him. More to the point, he wrote to Pitt demanding a commission as full General dating from the time he was made Master General of the Ordnance – or he would retire from the Army and all employments for ever.[62] He had no intention of the English being cleavers of wood and drawers of water for the Hanoverians. Pitt at once got him his commission out of the King: no delay, no obstacles allowed to stand in the way now. And this was reflected in the good relations Marlborough established with Prince Ferdinand on joining up with him at Coesveldt. Charles was able to tell Elizabeth that the Prince treated him with much friendliness and consideration. All the same, it was better and safer for the Commander-in-Chief of the British forces to rank next to the Prince, and that Marlborough owed to Pitt's swift intervention. Charles, like everybody else, was won over to an intense, and unexpected, admiration for the great war-minister.

At the end of August news arrived of a shattering Prussian victory over the Russians at Zorndorf and their withdrawal into Poland. Charles writes that he is

quite stupified with reading, writing, looking over accounts, making contracts for bread, forage, wagons etc. etc., absolutely necessary for the existence of the English troops and what the Treasury ought to have done before we left England, but they [*i.e.* Newcastle] went to Claremont and forgot it . . . I have now two contractors, a paymaster and a secretary in the room with me and take this opportunity while they are turning Dutch money into English to assure you that Blandford and I are perfectly well. They have just cast up their bill. P.S. They shall stay till I give my love to Di. Be. Cha. Bo. and Lady Trevor.

A worse enemy than the French was stalking the lines of the British army. The wet summer had brought much sickness in its train; now dysentery spread through the ranks. In October the Duke was struck down. Jacob Bryant, his boys' former tutor whom he had taken with him as secretary, reported the event in his stilted language to Fox:

after much strength exerted and a train of favourable symptoms that served only to amuse and deceive, the affair came yesterday [20 October]

62. *Correspondence of William Pitt, Earl of Chatham*, I. 337, 348.

to a crisis and at last fatally determined. Lord Blandford (I cannot yet call him by any other title) is well, but in much trouble. In a few days, I imagine, he will set out for England.[63]

Bryant added that the 'poor Duke's lungs were so gone that had he survived this illness he could not have lived a year'. We see the background, the consumptive inheritance from his mother, against which his life's effort appears all the more gallant.

A month before he had sent home a messenger to Elizabeth with a ring of his own, 'rather too large for a lady's hand, yet you must keep it for my sake'.[64] It was the last token she received from him.

63. *Letters to Henry Fox, Lord Holland*, ed. by the Earl of Ilchester, 139.
64. Blenheim MSS., E 56.

Chapter 4

A Young Family

I

THE Duke's early death left a youthful family to Elizabeth's care; always nervous and apprehensive, she was oppressed by the responsibility. The two daughters were, however, already provided for. A good match had been found for the beautiful and virtuous Betty to Henry Earl of Pembroke; she was married at the age of nineteen in 1756: it turned out badly. Her elder sister, the talented and not so virtuous Di, found a rather unpromising match for herself in Frederick Viscount Bolingbroke; she was married at the age of twenty-three in 1757: it turned out worse. The three boys were not yet of age when their father died: George, who now succeeded as fourth Duke, was nineteen, Charles eighteen, Robert only eleven.

Responsibility for a family in such a position was a heavy one in the aristocratic scuffle for power and place in the eighteenth century – or even for survival when temptations were so many, opportunities to such young people so opulent and inviting. It was something to survive. We shall see how much Elizabeth and her eldest son leaned for counsel and guidance upon advisers from another class, especially tutors, more especiallly if they were clergymen in orders. Gone were the epic days when John and Sarah had piloted their own cool course through the treacheries and insincerities, the dangers and envenomed feuds of Restoration and Revolution, of the last years of Queen Anne and the Hanoverian Succession. Though politics were still all in all to the English ruling families, they hardly risked their heads or their necks.

At the same time we observe a marked change in the tone and temper of the family. Though this is chiefly a matter of heredity and personal characteristics, it also reflects a change in the temper of the time, in society. People were becoming more relaxed, or at any rate less hard, less rough and dangerous.

We note a decided improvement in the manners and way of life between the earlier and the later eighteenth century. We get an impression of boorishness and animal empty-headedness among so many men of good family in the earlier period, when a young man like Henrietta's son could die besotted with drink or the young Sunderland could think of nothing but the gaming table. If the mania for gambling continued and even increased in the later years of the century, it went along with marked intellectual interests in the circle of Charles James Fox and his friends the Spencers, a passion for books and reading, for collecting and connoisseurship.

We see all this reflected in the Marlborough family. And there goes along with it a relaxation of fibre; none of the tenseness, the hard hitting of Sarah who had found life such a struggle, or the unerring eye on the objective, the sleepless self-control of John, who had had everything to make. Life had been very hard for them. Though it was not altogether easy for their great-grandchildren, they could afford to take it more lightly, give themselves up to enjoyment, amuse themselves. *Their* position had been made for them. They could afford to be nicer. And in fact they were: there is noticeable in this generation an extreme degree of refinement and sensibility, a delicacy that became almost Chinese and certainly decadent in the case of the fourth Duke. It reminds one of nothing so much as the elaborate indirection, the formal consideration and oblique modes of expression habitual in the family of Louis XV, where *bon ton* was carried to such a point that in the end nothing could be said. And, in fact, the fourth Duke withdrew from the struggle of life into seclusion and silence.

On the other hand – and here is another contrast with Sarah's tough family life – the atmosphere of Charles and Elizabeth's family was one of easy mutual affection: a charm lay upon all its members, particularly evident in their relations with one another.

We discern this from early on with the schoolboy letters of George and Charles written from Eton, where they were at school from 1747 to 1754.[1] George writes to his sister Betty the

1. *The Pembroke Papers* (*1734–1780*), ed. Lord Herbert, 22–7.

sad unpunctuated news that 'My Poor Brother Monkey at Mr Days at Hounslow is dead therefore you and I must go in Mourning so pray tell Mama to send me down some new Mourning Cloaths. . . . My Tears hinder me from saying any more.' By the time of his next letter he has recovered his spirits with the news that his father is coming to Langley on Sunday, which means a visit. 'Charles & I are both of us very well & very happy, now I must tell you why I did not write sooner, which is because I had not time.' A few months later he is longing to know when his father is coming: 'I now expect him every day I long to see my Dear little Brother whom I dare say you love vastly I am sure I do'. In October, 'pray tell Papa I shall circumcaricumfricate him if he does not send for us soon, for I know he will say We shall come presently & presently till at last it will be too late. I am Dear Sister Betty your most Dutiful Son, Blandford. I beg your pardon for writing so short a letter, but my little finger itches so your Servant.' Two years later he is longing to see his father again at Eton, where he has not been a great while. The truth was that the Duke had been ill. He was to install the Prince of Wales as Knight of the Garter, acting on behalf of the King, at Windsor. The brothers were impatient for this chance of seeing their father: 'we hear the Installation will not be till next April (but to my mind it will not be at all)'.

It is evident how fond the boys were of their father; that other people appreciated the family atmosphere we see from the letters of Lord Trevor, Elizabeth's brother. When writing one spring to make interest for the presentation to a vicarage in the Duke's gift, he adds, 'the weather will now soon suit for Blenheim, where I propose great pleasure towards the end of May, in seeing both the natural and artificial beauties there'.[2] When May-time comes, it is a naval officer who wants a flag in the next promotion and 'has taken it into his head that a word from your Grace to some or one of the commanding courtiers may be of great service'. He wishes both Marlboroughs joy of 'the little folks' recovery from small-pox. Langley must be in perfect beauty.' How could it not be, with the attentions Charles

2. Blenheim MSS., E 54.

had lavished upon it, in this delightful fifth decade of the eighteenth century?

It is Charles's affection for Elizabeth that gives the note, sets the pattern for the family. In 1754 he is reading *Peter Wilkins*, a best-seller of the time, and the nonsense he writes to her while she is away at Bath is a sure sign of affection: 'I wish I was a Glumm with a Graundee that I might see my Gawry every other day. You see I studied my Peter Wilkin at my inn yesterday, I read both volumes.' Then, 'I did not wish you a Gawry that you might change, for no alteration in you (except your health) can possibly be for the better; but Gawrys can skim through the air at the rate of sixty miles in a minute, so you might easily dine at Blenheim from Bath every day'.[3]

In January 1755, gallant as ever, he writes from Marlborough House, 'I have just dined and drank your health in a pot of porter', and he has a pleasant surprise for her. 'I some time ago saw a very fine strong *seasoned quiet mare* at livery stables, the fittest for your riding that I ever saw, the man said she belonged to Lord Egmont and he believed he would part with her because he liked one with more spirit.' Charles got a gentleman to offer to buy the mare.

> This morning at nine a man brought her into the yard and asking for one of my servants delivered her to him. When my servant asked the man who she came from and what was to be done with her, he answered my orders are to leave her here, to answer no questions but to run away directly, which he did. This is an high punctilio of civility which I fear I shall never be able to return.

That summer the beautiful and entirely good Betty was being talked of for the rich young Lowther; 'but I very much doubt whether it will be a match', reports the sagacious youth, Harcourt, 'the Duke and Duchess being very cautious to whom they dispose of her. I am afraid Sir James is a little wild.'[4] He could hardly have been more so than Lord Pembroke, to whom Betty was married on 23 March 1756. Horace Walpole reports her appearance at a Russian masquerade where were all the

3. Blenheim MSS., E 57.
4. *The Harcourt Papers*, ed. E. W. Harcourt, III. 74.

beauties and all the diamonds and not a few of the uglies of London: 'like Rubens's wife (not the common one with the hat) she had all the bloom and bashfulness and wildness of youth, with all the countenance of all the former Marlboroughs'.[5]

Her spirited sister Di took matters into her own hands and an amusing situation, which ended up in a far from amusing way, is reported by gossipy Mrs Delany. Frederick Lord Bolingbroke, nephew of Sarah's old antagonist and later ally, was a no longer youthful rake who had passed through a good many women's hands.

They were together on a party at Vauxhall with the Duke and Duchess of Bedford; the company were teasing Lord Bolingbroke to marry, and he turned quick about to Lady Di and said 'Will you have me?' 'Yes, to be sure,' she replied. It passed off that night as a joke, but with serious consideration on his side of the lady's merit (which they say is a great deal) and the persuasion of his friends, he made a serious affair of it and was accepted. £1,500 a year jointure and £500 a year pin-money has cast a veil over the past. If *he* has sense they may be happy; for he must then see the absurd figure he has hitherto made and know how to value a woman of worth, though so long the dupe of beauty and folly.[6]

Alas, he did not.

It was time for the Duke to provide for the future, and with the outbreak of the war he took steps to do so by a private Bill in Parliament, which passed through all its stages between January and April 1756.[7] Its purpose was to provide a maintenance for Lord Blandford during his father's life, for the completion of the rebuilding of Langley and to confirm the provision made for the younger children. Sarah had left £3,000 a year to the heir to the title; Marlborough House to him after Jack Spencer's death – so that the family had had it to live in since 1746; and £5,000 each to Charles, Diana and Elizabeth. In 1752 a sum of £5,000 had been placed out at interest for their benefit and estates in Wiltshire and Oxfordshire devoted to the

5. *Letters of Horace Walpole*, ed. Toynbee, III. 285.

6. *Autobiography and Correspondence of Mrs Delany*, ed. Lady Llanover, III. 465.

7. Blenheim MSS., F I. 34; *Journals of the House of Lords*, XXVIII. 460, 503, 505, 509, 522, 547, 552.

purpose. Now the Bill sought to provide £3,000 a year from the Trust funds for five years – £2,000 for rebuilding Langley, £1,000 for Lord Blandford, then seventeen; afterwards the whole £3,000 a year to go to him.

These provisions had been in operations only two years when Charles died – to the advantage of the estate, as Horace Walpole was quick to comment. He reports that the third Duke's estate was £45,000 a year, £9,000 of which was jointured out. He paid but £18,000 a year in joint lives. The estate would save greatly by his death, as the young Duke 'wants a year of being of age and would certainly have accommodated his father in agreeing to sell and pay'.[8] The tight state of affairs which Charles's financial laxity had led to is reflected in Walpole's remark later, 'we shall be like the late Duke of Marlborough, have a vast landed estate and want a guinea'.[9] The situation is clear to read in Charles's brief will: everything was tied up.[10] Outside the settled estate he left only £2,000 to 'my dear wife, Elizabeth Duchess of Marlborough': a token of affection, for of course she had her generous jointure. After all his debts were paid the residue of his real and personal estate was to go to his younger sons, Charles and Robert.

Elizabeth now took up her task of looking after her sons, with the aid of their tutors. Tutors – a whole succession of them, Jacob Bryant, John Moore, William Coxe – came to occupy an important place in the house of Blenheim. Each of them was a remarkable man in his own right. Jacob Bryant was a Cambridge pedant, a Fellow of King's, whom Charles had recruited as Blandford's tutor and taken abroad with him on the St-Malo expedition and to Germany as his secretary. Bryant was an Etonian classical scholar who later developed an odd line of his own about mythology, for ever writing nonsensical books to reconcile the Homeric gods with Holy Writ and to prove that no such place as Troy ever existed. He became something of a favourite with George III, who would hold forth with him on summer evenings on the Terrace at Windsor, Miss Burney discreetly in the background.

8. *Letters*, ed. cit., IV. 219. 9. ibid., V. 99.
10. P.C.C., Hutton 341.

John Moore was the son of a Gloucestershire grazier; it is always said that Elizabeth took a fancy to him and would have married him; that he declined, pointing out the unsuitability of the honour, and that this was the foundation of his immense influence with her son and his duchess. I do not credit the story: such a flimsy foundation is hardly necessary to account for the influence of this excellent, wholly reliable man of virtue and good judgement, who became the indispensable confidant of the family. He made the right marriage for himself, marrying into the Eden family, a sister of Lord Auckland. His ecclesiastical career speaks for his unerring judgement, moving easily into a prebend at Durham and thence to a canonry at Christ Church; on to the deanery of Canterbury, whence he was whisked to become Bishop of Bangor. His correspondence with their Graces holds a tone of respect without sycophancy, until the day came when George III, rather than have an appointee of Charles Fox's foisted upon him, forked Moore into the see of Canterbury, whereupon it becomes the turn of the Duke and Duchess to address him respectfully as 'Your Grace'.

William Coxe was the best scholar of them all, an excellent historian, very industrious and judicious. But the Marlboroughs in their retirement from the world did not provide for his preferment; so he passed into the service of the Herberts, the house of Wilton. He ended up merely an archdeacon – yet he is remembered better than either of the others; posterity rates him higher.

Shortly after her husband's death the Duchess gave Bryant a handsome appointment, which was announced to him by her brother the Bishop of Durham. Immediately the pedagogue incurred her annoyance by soliciting a further favour, due, he said by way of apology, to wanting to be near 'that person of all others to whom I must ever look up with pride and admiration', evidently the young Duke.[11] He had made a further mistake in speaking for the latter's application to quit the army. (He had entered as ensign in the Coldstream Guards, and was now captain in the 20th Foot.) Bryant wished to be any assistance he could about the Duke's studies, 'the particular scope and direction you could wish him to take is a scheme not only very just but

11. Blenheim MSS., E 59.

very practicable; and I make no doubt it would prove a plan as entertaining as it is eligible'.

Later the Duchess had to administer another reproof: 'I have always found even during the happiest part of life many disagreeable circumstances arise from persons living in our house who had not real business in it.' She had therefore apprised her son of such inconveniences.

> You and he have a much better chance of being well together some time hence than if your desire had been complied with, and you will be of that opinion when you are weaned, pardon the word. Weaned we must be whatever it may cost us. He must launch into the wide world without us.... The foundations of learning which by your attention he has acquired may at any future time be taken up . . . but for the present I could rather wish him to apply himself to the Modern History of Europe and Laws of his own country in which he is born to be a principal actor, and I make no doubt a very shining and exemplary one.

As to that we shall see; but there is no doubt as to Elizabeth's good sense and her grasp of the situation. The young Duke was extremely handsome and very sweet-natured; he and his tutor were strongly attached to each other. Elizabeth did not succeed in marrying him off before her own disappearance from the scene. Bryant remained always unmarried, a great favourite with ladies of a certain age.

The Duchess had been more uneasy about Lord Charles. Bryant was able to assure her, from Eton, that

> one great test of a boy's sagacity, as well as goodness, may be drawn from the company he chiefly frequents and the friends he chooses.... Though he is, I believe, beloved by all yet he has been very sensible in distinguishing and has made friends of some of the best and most ingenuous I ever remember at this place.... A fairer mind and sweeter disposition is nowhere to be found.

That was true: sweetness of disposition was a marked characteristic with all these children.

Lord Charles had gone from Eton to Christ Church, where he matriculated in 1756 and took his M.A., evidently by a nobleman's privilege, in 1759. Now both of her elder sons were abroad; the Duchess asks the Bishop of Durham to speak to the King with respect to their longer stay, otherwise she will have to write to him herself. In the spring of 1760 we find her writing to Lord Charles about his 'strong attachment' to his friend Townshend: she finds that the latter wants frankness and openness, that he has a rough manner and is 'at best so illiterate and has had so mean an education that at your age he must be the greatest disadvantage to you in the eye of the world'. She was half dead at having to write such a letter, but she thought his future happiness at stake: 'nothing less could have made me write seven pages every line of which carried a dagger with two points, one for me and another for you'. We see indeed that Elizabeth Trevor brought too great a strain of sensibility and apprehensiveness into the family.

Her son replied robustly from the Hague that he wished her informant the Bishop of Durham would take the trouble to inquire into his friend Townshend's character from people who knew. He (Charles) had quitted the acquaintance of Barrington, 'who is a man that displeased me very much before I had been a month at Oxford'. Hence his friends' disapprobation of Townshend – it is not his fault if his father and mother are disagreeable. Ten days later he writes charmingly: 'I think I see you receive this letter, above half afraid to open it; there, now the seal is broke, you must begin to read it; and now you have finished it, are you contented?' The Prince of Weilbourg is to give a magnificent ball; he begs leave to stay for it and then set out for England. On his return the Duchess got her brother the Bishop to inform Bryant – such obliqueness of approach was characteristic of her – that she proposed to pay her son £500 till he was of age and after to settle that sum at least upon him 'out of his own power for his life that he may be entirely independent, in which state alone I suppose happiness to consist'. As for her youngest boy, Lord Robert, now thirteen, we find the Duchess in this summer of 1760 giving instructions that for the future Bob's money be paid to her; if there is any overplus she will invest it for him. We shall see how her anxious forethought for their well-being worked out.

Her eldest son gave Elizabeth no anxiety: the young Duke

was all virtue and promise – in addition to his magnificent looks. When he first arrived in London after his father's death, one professional politician whispered to another – a Jenkinson to a Grenville: 'the young Duke of Marlborough is lately come to town and by the advice of his mother has flung himself totally on Lord Harcourt to direct his conduct in the county of Oxford, and this was such circumstances as makes me think that Fox has no great influence over him'.[12] This was an accurate forecast, though the Duke was to find a much more effective political mentor than Lord Harcourt, in his uncle the Duke of Bedford. This was continuing his father's family-connection in politics; though we may say that young Marlborough was more consciously aristocratic than his father, more exalted and refined, far more withdrawn from the commerce of ordinary life. On 6 February he came of age, and two days later took his seat in the House of Lords.[13] In April he was made Lord-Lieutenant of Oxfordshire and we find him regularly present during the trial of Earl Ferrers for murder. Horace Walpole describes the scene: all the peerage there, many of the Royal Family in their box, and though the leading beauties among the peeresses were absent, 'there are so many young peers that the show was fine even in that respect. The Duke of Marlborough, with the best countenance in the world, looked clumsy in his robes. He had new ones, having given away his father's to the valet de chambre.'[14] An indication that the vein of extravagance in the stock was not to be abated. Other peers boasted of the antiquity of their robes, two of them pretending that theirs had been used at the trial of Mary Queen of Scots.

II

In October 1760 a more momentous accession took place: the old unrespected King died and his place was taken by his grandson, young George III, whose personality was to figure so large for the next half century.

12. q. N. S. Jucker, *The Jenkinson Papers, 1760–1766*, 18.
13. *Journal of the House of Lords*, XXIX. 581.
14. *Letters*, ed. cit., IV. 372.

At this mid-moment we may pause over a fine reflection upon the time by Horace Walpole.

A century had now passed since reason had begun to attain that ascendant in the affairs of the world, to conduct which it had been granted to man six thousand years ago. If religions and governments were still domineered by prejudices, if creeds that contradict logic, or tyrannies that enslave multitudes to the caprice of one were not yet exploded, novel absurdities at least were not broached; or if propagated produced neither persecutors nor martyrs. Methodists made fools, but they did not arrive to be saints; and the histories of past ages describing massacres and murders, public executions of violence and the more private though not the less horrid arts of poison and daggers, began to be regarded almost as romances. Caesar Borgia seemed little less fabulous than Orlando; and whimsical tenures of manors were not more in disuse than sanguinary methods of preserving or acquiring empires.[15]

The twentieth century has thrown a lurid glow upon that civilized complacency. We now know that men in the mass are less than rational and worse than irrational – that their folly can be criminal. Horace Walpole was an exceptionally civilized and exceptionally rational human being; the irony must have occurred to him that within a year or two of writing this passage we were involved in the most successful example in our history of acquiring empire by sanguinary methods. In the midst of Pitt's Seven Years War George III came to the throne.

In his *Memoirs* of that reign Walpole begins, 'the moment of his accession was fortunate beyond example',[16] and Lecky develops the theme.

The young King came to the throne when rather more than three years of almost uninterrupted victory had raised England to an ascendancy which she had scarcely attained since the great days of Henry V. The French flag had nearly disappeared from the sea. Except Louisiana, all the French possessions in North America, except St-Domingo, all the French islands in the West Indies had been taken and the last French settlements in Hindostan were just tottering to their fall. The wave of invasion which threatened to submerge Hanover had been triumphantly rolled back and the nation, intoxicated by victory and roused from its

15. Horace Walpole, *Memoirs of the Reign of George II*, II. 111.
16. idem., *Memoirs of the Reign of George III*, I. 5.

long lethargy by the genius of its great statesman, displayed an energy and a daring which made it a wonder to its neighbours and to itself. No sacrifice seemed too great to demand, yet in spite of every sacrifice commerce was flourishing and national prosperity advancing.[17]

Such was the situation just two centuries ago when George III became King and England was at her apogee in the world.

Everything conspired to give this the appearance of a new age, and not least the character of the new sovereign.

We now know that George III was a much maligned man. Generations of an undoubted literary superiority on the part of the Whigs, particularly in the writing of history, have done him some injustice in the English memory. We know now that he was completely innocent of any intention of straining, let alone extending, the royal prerogative – nothing shocked him more than such an accusation. He was intent solely upon his duty of maintaining the prerogatives that were constitutionally his. He was an exceedingly conventional man who adhered to the conventional constitutional position – indeed he might be described, without paradox, as a Whig himself (except that he detested party and desired to rule as monarch of all his people), adhering, as he constantly maintained, to the principles of the Revolution settlement that had brought his family to this country. Of course he was a pure German by blood, as all the Hanoverian line in England have been – the English have never minded that, though it gave him a defective sympathy with certain English traits where the disadvantage was not all on his side. For one thing, he had the typical German respect for experts, for efficiency, for regular attention to duty. It is fairly clear, though he did not say so, how much he detested the light-hearted amateurishness of English aristocrats, the calm assumption that the world was their oyster, that the loaves and fishes were theirs, whether they had earned them or no. He was a serious, deeply conscientious man, with more than his share of German *Ernst*. One sees how such a man would loathe the thought of Charles Fox.

And there was something German, too, in the very nature

17. W. E. H. Lecky, *History of England in the Eighteenth Century* (ed. 1921), III. 183.

and extent of George III's devotion to duty – the ruling principle in his mind: there was something rigid and inflexible about it; he was its sacrificial victim. Underneath the sense of duty, to which he sacrificed his own instincts and inclinations, there was a nature longing for affection, for he suffered from a deep distrust in himself. (Experience of what men are overcame this, but he paid a high price.) Brought up by the Princess Dowager in seclusion from savoury contacts with the world, with no knowledge of man and with the modesty of a girl which he always retained, he poured out all the ardent affection of his nature on his mentor Lord Bute, who took the place of a father-figure for him. With no confidence in himself, a retarded youth, he longed for certainty, the strength to fulfil his duty in the lonely exaltation of his position. Excitement, incessant work imposed upon a temperament naturally indolent, over-exertion of the will to make himself do what was demanded of him – all inflicted their strain: he had several slight attacks before the mental breakdown of 1788–9. On succeeding to the throne he was immensely taken with the attractive and vivacious Lady Sarah Lennox, sister-in-law of Henry Fox. He was not allowed to marry her – and indeed it would have been politically unwise. He was made to marry an ugly German princess, Charlotte of Mecklenburg, at the first sight of whom the young King started, visibly taken aback – though assured that 'the bloom of her ugliness will wear off with time'. Nature took its revenge and in his breakdown the poor King turned against the Queen, whom he had never really liked, and raved after Marlborough's sister, the charming Lady Pembroke, the Queen's favourite lady-in-waiting. How much happier both would have been if he had been able to marry *her* – for she had a miserable time with her irrepressible scapegrace Henry.

All this, however, was in the future.

At the moment everything marked the contrast between the old régime and the new. Like Queen Anne at her accession, asserting that her heart was 'entirely English' by way of contrast with William III's Dutch sentiments and affiliations, George III marked himself off from his grandfather with his first sentence, 'Born and educated in this country, I glory in the name of Briton.' (This aroused the enthusiasm of the populace; the instructed recognized the hand of a Scot.) The young King's first proclamation, against immorality, was another back-hander at the open immorality of his father, his grandfather and his great-grandfather. The régime of royal mistresses was at an end – until the turn of his sons came. George III's Court was not only respectable and decorous, it was also more dignified and formal, while at the same time more affable; none of the German churlishness of George I and George II: the new King was at least English in his manners. When the little Queen arrived she was made to be grand: she was never allowed to appear in public without a full parure of diamonds – as one sees her in Gainsborough still. The Philistinism of George II, who didn't like poetry and didn't like painting, was discountenanced by the expressed intention of encouraging literature and the arts. It was George III who purchased the magnificent royal collection of Canalettos and extended his personal patronage consistently to Gainsborough. He interested himself in scholars and scholarship, while the first pension of the reign went to the Tory, quasi-Jacobite Dr Johnson. The young sovereign was greeted with a genuine welcome such as the Hanoverian house had never yet received. Families that had failed to set foot inside the royal precincts flocked to pay their court. It was the Stuarts who were the foreigners now.

The King's accession meant a general election. For the family borough of Woodstock the family representatives, Viscount Bateman and Anthony Keck, the Duke's agent, were again returned.[18] But who would have the honour of occupying the county seats? There was a rumour that the Marlboroughs might lose their share in the county representation for which they had fought so expensively in 1754. Happily it was not so: the family retained the fruits of its victory. It was agreed that the second brother of the house, Lord Charles, should share the representation with the ancient fugleman of the Old Interest.

Lord Charles, just coming of age, was abroad; it fell to the youngest brother, Lord Robert, aged thirteen, to deputize for

18. *Return of Members of Parliament*, II. 129.

him.[19] Mr Keck prepared a wordy draft for him to read on the occasion, but the tutor John Moore knew better. He reports to the Duchess at Bath, 'I thought it was making a child of Lord Robert to suppose he could not make it in a proper manner. He is not at all apprehensive about it, but likes the consequence it gives him very much.' Moore enclosed his own draft of the words the boy was to speak:

> I am desired by my brother, gentlemen, to return you his most grateful acknowledgement for your support and protection. He hopes to be able very soon to attend his duty in Parliament, and begs leave to assure you his utmost endeavour shall not be wanting to deserve the confidence you have honoured him with.

Moore continues,

> he is to speak this as soon as Lord Charles and Sir J. Dashwood are declared duly elected in the Town Hall, just before he is chaired. I have no doubt of his acquitting himself as I wish . . . but my heart aches and will till it is over. P.S. It is not to be spoke to the mob but the gentlemen in the Town Hall.

Election day came, and the lad of thirteen acquitted himself like a great-grandson of the great Duke. By eight in the morning three hundred freeholders had assembled at Blenheim and more were dropping in till ten. 'Those who were and those who called themselves gentlemen were all introduced into the drawing-room to Lord Robert, who took them all by the hand and talked to them with as much address as if he had canvassed the county for the last three Parliaments.' Then the procession – that in the New Interest – set out, led by the sheriff's dozen pikemen, the flag with Lord Charles's name in gold letters, followed by Lord Robert on horseback with Mr Keck in attendance. There were four or five hundred freeholders with a mob of at least a thousand before they got to Oxford. Outside the city they met Sir James Dashwood's Tory procession of about the same number. Lord Robert and he made their compliments to one another and rode up the High Street at the head of the two bodies of freeholders joined together. The windows and housetops were

19. Blenheim MSS., E 59.

crowded, some ten thousand people were jammed together in the streets – the mob quite frightened the future archbishop, but fortunately they were all friendly. At the Town Hall the town clerk read out some Acts of Parliament, the members were named and declared duly elected by the sheriff. When Lord Charles was declared Lord Robert began to speak and went through without the least hesitation, very distinctly and as loud as his voice would carry. The boy of thirteen and the ancient Sir James then got into chairs and were carried round the cross at Carfax to their inn, where they dined.

The voice of the free men of England had spoken.

Before the proceedings were over Moore rushed off a note to the Duchess from Oxford:

> Lord Robert is quite well. All is happily over. Not one unpleasant thing has happened. He has been chaired. He will immediately after dinner go home in a chaise. Not one single word of opposition, nor one cry of the mob against Sir J. Dashwood has passed or against Lord Charles. He spoke like an angel. I hope this will make your Grace sleep the better for it at Bath tonight.

If the Duchess really had a *tendresse* for John Moore it was justified.

At Court the Marlborough family was in high favour with the young King; after all, he and the Duke were of an age and shared similar traits of character in their virtue and modesty, their shyness and diffidence. The Bishop of Durham was able to congratulate his sister on the offer of a lordship of the Bedchamber to her son: 'I wish the King had thought of Lord Charles; but that cannot now be hoped for, if it is offered to the elder brother. I did not show your letter to the Duke of Newcastle ... as *matters being unsettled* is too serious a truth, especially with his Grace at present.' That was all too true: the ancient crustacean was at last becoming unstuck, or frozen out, with the ascendancy of the favourite, Lord Bute; even the bishops, of whom he had made so many in his time, were beginning to forget their maker.

Not even a feeling of rivalry for the spirited Lady Sarah Lennox affected the King's feeling for Marlborough. He kept his confidences, however, for the ear only of his Dearest Friend, Lord Bute: 'the other day I heard it suggested as if the Duke of Marlborough made up to her. I shifted my grief till retired to my chamber, where I remained for several hours in the depth of despair. I believe this was said without foundation, at least I will flatter myself so.'[20]

The Duke's favour being such, his sister Di sought his help through the intermediary of their mother.

> The King has taken an almost unaccountable partiality for him and I am absolutely certain that there is no one request that he can now make to the King that will not be directly granted.... Our complaint is a common one, but not I am sure in the degree we feel it, I mean exceeding circumstances: which complaint, however disagreeable in itself, is ten times more so to me by perpetually seeing Lord Bolingbroke uneasy, who never would of his own accord have ventured to speak to my brother and therefore I determined to do it.... What I wanted him to ask for is a place, which, had he been here to ask, we should now have been in possession of... it is the Fox Hounds and Lord Denbigh is the man who has got them. It is a place of real value and would have so repaired Lord Bolingbroke's circumstances as to have made him easy for ever. The salary is no less than £2,000 a year. Good things, which alone are worth asking for, are as easily got, I observe, as little ones and therefore I wish my brother to ask for us, what has been already given, I know, a pension of about the same value upon Ireland.[21]

In the summer of 1761 Lady Sarah Lennox's hopes – and those of her ambitious brother-in-law Fox who was coaching her – received their quietus with the marriage of the King; and Di was able to do something herself to repair her husband's fortunes by being appointed a Lady of the Bedchamber to the Queen. She soon became the '*bon ton favorite de la Reine*', we learn, 'all the men in love with her.... She wears rouge and looks quite handsome.'[22] So long as her marriage lasted she was a favourite at Court, in the intimate circle of the royal couple, dancing gaily at their private balls and entertainments. In

20. *Letters from George III to Lord Bute, 1756–1766*, ed. R. Sedgwick, 38.

21. Blenheim MSS., E 59.

22. *Correspondence of Emily, Duchess of Leinster*, ed. B. Fitzgerald, I. 359.

September the Coronation was performed with great *éclat* – described for us as usual by Horace Walpole. The Marlboroughs were much to the fore: the Duke bore the sceptre and cross;

> Lady Pembroke, alone at the head of the countesses, was the picture of majestic modesty. . . . Lord Bolingbroke put on rouge upon his wife and the Duchess of Bedford in the Painted Chamber. . . . The coronets of the peers and their robes disguised them strangely; it required all the beauty of the Dukes of Richmond and Marlborough to make them noticed.[23]

A kindness on the part of the Duke was remembered by Arthur Young, who as a youth watched the traditional banquet from the gallery in Westminster Hall, 'and being in the front row above the Duke's table, I remember letting down a basket during dessert, which was filled by the present Duke of Marlborough'.[24]

Next month a familiar figure in these pages passcd noiselessly out of life, to which indeed she had always the air of not being much attached. Elizabeth died on 7 October 1761, asking that her funeral expenses might be 'no greater than common decency may call for'.[25] She left to her eldest son all her jewels, rings, watches, pictures, china, plate and other trinkets. To her two younger sons she left all the books which were her father, Lord Trevor's, and also her own, to be divided between them. All her money, bank bills, East India bonds similarly; all her horses, carriages and harness to be sold and the money likewise divided. She made the Duke her executor. He could not but be aware of the difference her death made; for the rental of the estates devoted to her jointure – on a scale that had infuriated Sarah years before – was upwards of £5,000 a year. Moreover, her son had generously made over Langley to her for life. She had, however, well done her duty by the family.

The marriage of the very handsome young Duke was the chief object of feminine diplomacy. After the King he was the leading prize – all the more desirable because of his express reluctance to marry young. He, too, had an eye for Lady Sarah,

23. *Letters*, ed. cit., V. 112.
24. *The Autobiography of Arthur Young*, ed. M. Betham-Edwards, 26.
25. P.C.C., Cheslyn 362.

but the strong-minded Duchess of Bedford had marked him down for her daughter, Lady Caroline Russell. We can watch the moves in the game, follow the progress of the campaign, in the letters of Lady Sarah's sisters. Early in 1760 Henry Fox's wife had written of her sister that Sal grew prettier every day.

The Duke of Marlborough sat by her and talked to her at the last ridotto, I hear. For him you have no notion how extraordinary it seems; 'twould be clever to be sure, but I'm determined not to think of it, all appearance of desiring it would do harm. He must be infinitely amiable: he has settled upon each of his brothers £2,000 a year for life, given his mother Langley for her life and to the man that was his tutor £600 a year. These are noble things and show a great and good mind.[26]

What would this amiable and beautiful young man not do for little Sal, if she could catch him?

But her sister already had doubts.

I'm quite sorry, dear siss, I express myself in such a manner about the Duke of Marlborough being smitten with Sal as to make you flatter yourself about it. I wish you had enough of my philosophy not to be disappointed at its stopping just where it was. He is scarcely ever in town, has not been since the ball one day, is not likely to see her three times these next six months, and a young man extremely determined not to marry young.[27]

A much more forceful person moved in on the scene, who was determined that he should: the horrid, designing Gertrude, Duchess of Bedford, whom nobody liked but who knew her own mind. In September 1761 Lady Sarah's sister reports, 'Alas! alas! the Duke of Marlborough is come, saw Sarah at Ranelagh, took no notice of her and walked all night with Lady Caroline Russell! Is not it quite mortifying? This is an unlucky year for our poor little Sal.'[28] It was: having failed to make the King she was now failing to catch the Duke. Shortly we hear, 'the Duchess of Bedford lives at Ranelagh now, where she seldom or never went before. It's taken great notice of, as it is since the Duke of Marlborough's arrival that their passion for it has

26. *Correspondence of Emily, Duchess of Leinster*, I. 281.
27. ibid., 277. 28. ibid., 110.

begun. My sister carried Sal one night, but to no purpose.'[29] For all her queer unattractive voice and her affected way of making up her mouth, Lady Caroline was winning the game.

Next spring, when the Duchess of Bedford thought Sal safe out of the way, she became

> so fond of her. The great lady has made herself more ridiculous than ever she has been, making a bustle about Lord Charles Spencer being so particular to Lady Caroline, which nobody but she ever found out, nor has that pretty boy the least thoughts of her. She went to Lady Bolingbroke about it and there is a fine *tracasserie* between them, which has I hear ended in the Duke of Marlborough being vastly angry with her Grace.[30]

However, what did that matter so long as she got her way? By August 1762 the matter was settled, the Marlborough campaign over. Sal's sister reports resignedly, 'Calcraft writes word from town that Lady Caroline Russell's perseverance will do at last, for that there is the greatest reason to think the Duke of Marlborough now intends to marry her. Madame l'Ambassadrice will then be completely happy.'[31] Horace Walpole clarifies the reference: 'the embassy to Paris is not the single glory of the Bedfords; after long hopes and trials on their side, and vast repugnance on his, the Duke of Marlborough has at last married their daughter'.[32]

Henry Fox in his Memoirs, years after, does not conceal his annoyance.

> On Monday August 23, the Duke of Marlborough married Lady Caroline Russell. The mean and unbecoming artifices the Duchess of Bedford made use of to bring this match on and which she had so little pride as to use in public too, exposing herself to the ridicule of the whole world, are not to be described.[33]

Nor did her artifices, unbecoming or no, stop with the marriage. When the young couple went down to stay at Woburn, it was

29. *Correspondence of Emily, Duchess of Leinster*, I. 112.

30. ibid., 319. 31. ibid., 337. 32. *Letters*, ed. cit., V. 241.

33. q. *Life and Letters of Lady Sarah Lennox*, ed. by the Countess of Ilchester and Lord Stavordale, 72.

noticed that the Duchess 'shortened her evenings from one (their usual time of going to bed) to eleven all the time they were at Woburn: is not that delightful?'[34] The result of this touching solicitude is reported next year:

the Duchess of Marlborough stays at Blenheim till March for fear of miscarrying. The Duke and she are quite taken up with one another, I hear, and don't mix with the world; the Bedford set talk of him as a very particular man, but extravagantly fond of her.[35]

Poor Lady Sarah married her Bunbury. Nearly forty years later she had not forgotten her disappointment: she wrote, as one woman will to another,

you may remember the great difference between the bouncing Lady Caroline Russell and the gentle Duchess of Marlborough. In the latter state she was very winning in her manners; those who live with her dislike her character, but to me she has always been pleasing from the moment she had *secured her Duke*.[36]

There was too much of her managing mother in Caroline to make her a likeable woman. But it must be admitted that she made her Duke an excellent wife. He was an exceedingly sensitive, over-refined man, with no confidence in himself, though with intelligence and gifts. From the moment he married her he was under her thumb: it was as well – he needed someone to manage for him. Soon, everyone noticed, they were inseparable; they continued inseparable for half a century.

In the same year, 1762, Lord Charles married the only daughter of Lord Vere of Hanworth, through whom there came Lady Betty Germaine's collection of antique gems to augment in time the famous Marlborough collection.[37]

There remained the financial settlements of the younger brothers. These, like all the financial affairs of the family, were of some complexity. But after decrees in Chancery, petitions and appeals, petitions to the House of Lords and references back to the Barons of the Exchequer, a simple outline emerges and a

34. *Correspondence of Emily, Duchess of Leinster*, II. 119.
35. ibid., I. 359.
36. *Life and Letters of Lady Sarah Lennox*, ed. cit., 465.
37. Mrs Steuart Erskine, *Lady Diana Beauclerk*, 50.

clear division.[38] The Duke treated his younger brothers with characteristic generosity. Lands in Lincolnshire were settled on Lord Robert; an estate in Oxfordshire on Lord Charles. This latter was at Wheatfield in the hill country outlying from the Chilterns, south-east of Oxford. There Lord Charles made his home, built a house that became a centre of agreeable social life for the member for the county. Nothing now remains there as one looks across those lush buttercupped fields in May-time down the slopes towards Oxford, nothing but the ageing elms and the stable courtyard with its well-proportioned cupola that reflects the distinction of the time.

Now the younger generation could go forward to play their hand, in the somewhat changed conditions of the game – with the King playing an active part, instead of exerting a mere negative. (In the event this added greatly to the difficulties, and in some respects worked out worse than under George II.) Pitt's resignation and the break-up of the strong national ministry that had transformed discouragement and defeat into triumph announced a new age.

For some time Pitt's colleagues had been groaning under his lofty, and indeed intolerable, ascendancy. He treated them all like the second- and third-raters he knew them to be, and strangely enough they resented it. But no one dared answer him back, such were his popularity in the country – re-echoed in America – and the astonishing results of his re-invigoration of the nation's spirit. Only the Duke of Bedford was unafraid and ready on occasion to stand up to him. No one could reason with Pitt. Horace Walpole, who had like the nation at large become converted to him, said perceptively that 'between the uncommunicativeness of his temper and the want of suite in his reasoning faculties, it was ever impossible to pin him down to any chain of definite propositions'.[39] The simple fact was that William Pitt lived by his intuitions; these were the intuitions of genius and his genius was all for action.

Was the war then to go on for ever – until France was so crushed that she could never raise her head again? The war

38. *Journals of the House of Lords*, XXX. 299, 300, 310, 326–7, 336.
39. Horace Walpole, *Memoirs of the Reign of George III*, I. 219–20.

had been won, but Pitt would give no indication of what peace-terms would satisfy him. All the cabinet, except his impossible brother-in-law Temple, wanted peace; so did the young King and, what was more important, his Dearest Friend, Bute. The situation was beginning to look like that which overtook Marlborough towards the end of his war, before the Peace of Utrecht. All reasonable considerations argued that the King and the majority were right. Unfortunately Pitt's sixth sense, and his first-class intelligence-service, told him that Spain was at that moment preparing to come in on the side of France. He was all for crippling Spain with a prior blow: an expedition to Cadiz that would capture the treasure-fleet on which Spain's capacity to wage a war depended. He could not carry his colleagues with him and, being a man of principle, as they were not, he at once resigned: October 1761. The treasure-fleet got safely across the Atlantic; the news of the Family Compact was made public and the ministry was forced to declare war on Spain after all.

All this only served to raise the Great Commoner to a still further height of popular acclaim and – maddening for his colleagues – they found they had to conduct, without him, a war which his strategic sense might well have shortened. However, the momentum that he had given to the national effort continued; his commanders, the expeditions he had planned, inflicted a series of disasters on Spain culminating with the capture of Havana, the heart of her West Indian empire. There remained the problem how to make peace. The ministers, and the favourite, could at least congratulate themselves on having the inconveniently great man out of the way – as indeed the favourite was congratulated by his toady, Bubb Dodington, author of the memorable lines:

Love thy country, wish it well,
Not with too intense a care,
'Tis enough that, when it fell,
Thou its ruin didst not share.

Dodington was able to write to Bute, 'I sincerely wish your Lordship joy of being delivered of a most impracticable colleague, his Majesty of a most imperious servant and the country of a most dangerous minister. I am told that the people are sullen about it.'[40] Bubb Dodington, however, was raised to the peerage; he was able to cover his ridiculous name under the respectable guise of Lord Melcombe.

Fox now had his hour of revenge upon the man who had won an immortal place in history. Incapable of leading the country in war, he made himself indispensable in putting through the peace. Walpole tells us that he hated Pitt and aimed at his destruction. 'Libels on libels were published against him, and he wrote none'; a coarse and loud-mouthed adventurer, Barré, was encouraged to assail him in the Commons, when no one else would. Pitt made no reply; the odium was laid quite rightly to Fox's account. It is to this time that the real detestation of Henry Fox dates.

In 1762 Bute came into the open, forced Newcastle to resign and himself assumed the leadership of the government. At this assumption of power by a Scot, a Stuart of quasi-Jacobite stock, the great Whig Revolution families, from whose control the King longed to emancipate himself, were offended and withdrew. The Duke of Devonshire, the Marquis of Rockingham and others resigned. In November 1762 the young Marlborough got office as Lord Chamberlain. At the formation of the new ministry Lord Charles was appointed Outranger of Windsor Forest, a post which, with the superintendence of the King's gardens, brought in a nice £1,200 a year. In the spring of next year there was something better for him — Comptroller of the Household and membership of the Privy Council. Bute, already apprehensive as to his capacity to control English politics and frightened of the consequences, wrote:

> I am to be arraigned in the Lords for the King's preferring the Duke of Marlborough a Tory, to the Duke of Devonshire a Whig, for making the peace and being an anti-German. . . . The whole is in reality aimed at the King himself, whose liberty is now to be decided on, liberty that his poorest subject enjoys, of choosing his own menial servants.[41]

40. L. B. Namier, *England in the Age of the American Revolution*, 38.
41. *H.M.C.*, *Lonsdale MSS.*, 131.

This view of the constitution was already out of date; we note from his reference to Marlborough as a Tory that Bute was also out of touch with the realities of English politics, and lastly that he was beginning to lose his nerve. And indeed it required a strong nerve to control them. Temple's comment to the demagogue Wilkes gives us a pointer: he made the charge that the Duke of Marlborough was made Lord Chamberlain 'to cover an infamous conclusion of a war more glorious than that which was so *feloniously* disgraced by the Treaty of Utrecht'.[42]

At the same moment, immediately after the appointment, the King was writing to Bute:

the Duke of Marlborough's letter would have caused me great surprise when I first mounted the throne, but I am now so used to find men wanting something more the day they are benefited that this only confirms me in my opinion of the greed that this age is cursed with.[43]

This reflection is one that has occurred to rulers in all ages; but the naïveté of its expression here arises from the fact that George III and his Dearest Friend had come to power with the idea of reforming not only politics but politicians. It was only two years since the young man had come to the throne: slow and stupid as he was, he was learning fast the facts of (political) life. It is not known what it was that the Duke was after; I conclude that it must have been the Garter, for that became the main object of his ambitions.

He does not seem to have cared for the office of Lord Chamberlain; perhaps it demanded too constant an attendance. From the first he wished to exchange it for that of Master of the Horse; but his domineering mother-in-law wanted that job for her brother, Lord Gower. In April when further changes were made Marlborough had to be content with the much grander office of Lord Privy Seal, 'though so very young', wrote the King, his senior by a year, sagely to Bute.

Millions of thanks to my friend for the best advice he ever gave me: the Duke of Marlborough made not the least hesitation, said if he could

42. *The Grenville Papers*, ed. W. J. Smith, II. 6.
43. *Letters from George III to Lord Bute, 1756–1766*, ed. cit., 168.

do anything that accommodated my affairs that he was too happy . . . The Duke of Bedford is full of the happiness of the Duke of Marlborough.[44]

This office he retained through the changes and the rising political temper of the next two years.

Bedford went off to make the peace in Paris, where he made rather more than the peace: he made money for himself on it – which cannot have been to the liking of the upright George III. However, that innocent young idealist had been forced, he said, 'to bring in bad men to govern bad men'. That must account for his bringing in the notoriously profligate Lord Sandwich, better known as Jemmy Twitcher, whose domestic life was so very unlike his own; upon whose appointment the *mot* ran round that 'the King read this verse in Psalm CI, "Whoso leadeth a godly life, he shall be my servant", upon which his Majesty immediately appointed Lord Sandwich Secretary of State'.

There was a large majority in Parliament for the peace, but Fox made sure of it by bribing where necessary. What was more objectionable was the rancorous persecution of its opponents from the grandest dukes down to the humblest tide-waiters among their followers – for in aristocratic England the spoils-system obtained as in democratic America. 'Strip the Duke of Newcastle of his three Lieutenancies', Fox wrote; 'then go on to the general rout.'[45] They did. At the end of it all, 'his object now was to withdraw from his uneasy pre-eminence and to carry into his retreat as much booty as he could contrive to pack. Loaded with sinecures and reversions for himself and his children, he was still unsatisfied unless he could obtain his peerage without losing his Paymastership', for that was worth at least £25,000 a year.

The ending of the war coincided with a spirit of popular restlessness, of domestic agitation, that came to centre on the ribald, not unattractive personality of Wilkes, ex-Nonconformist now professed unbeliever and rake, nothing in whose character

44. *Letters from George III to Lord Bute, 1756–1766*, ed. cit., 228.

45. Sir G. O. Trevelyan, *The Early History of Charles James Fox* (Nelson edn.), 45. 47–8

should have recommended him to Dr Johnson, yet whom the Doctor was unable to resist: in short, an artful demagogue, full of charm. In the *North Briton* he lashed the Court, the occult influence of Bute still operative, the government of George Grenville unsparingly, licentiously, libellously. Grenville was just the sort of politician who could not let well alone: a competent man of business, smug in the consciousness of his own rectitude, unimaginative, *borné*, blinkered, he made 'the ruin of one very insignificant individual a main object of the Executive'.[46] Not content with that, to produce £100,000 he imposed his Stamp Act on America, that led to the Revolutionary war and the disruption of the Empire.

Young Marlborough had no responsibility for these measures, but he was in rank the second member of the Bedford connection that was an important element in the government. The government issued a general warrant to take up the author and printer of the seditious libel constituted by No. 45 of the *North Briton*. In the first of the excited debates as to the legality of general warrants that disturbed Parliament and the nation, Walpole reports that 'a warrant to take up Lord Charles Spencer was sent to Blenheim from Bedford House and signed by his brother and returned for him; so he went thither – not a very kind office in the Duke of Marlborough to Lord Charles's character.'[47] But the division was a critical one: votes were brought down in flannels and blankets till the floor of the House looked like the pool of Bethesda. When the issue was raised again in January 1764 Lord Charles dared to vote in the minority with many other place-men against the Court, The tiresome Mrs Montagu reports, 'I hear the Duke of Marlborough is very angry with him; one is sorry so many divisions are made in families by party'.[48]

When the Poor-Law reformer Gilbert brought forward his first useful measure to organize relief by grouping parishes for the purpose and applying the funds more effectively – a measure which had passed the Commons – the Bedfords, Marlborough

46. Lecky, op. cit., III. 244.
47. *Letters*, ed. cit., VI. 11.
48. R. Blunt, *Mrs Montagu, 'Queen of the Blues'*, I. 46.

among them, were in the minority that supported the Bill.[49] It was defeated by the occult influence of Bute on behalf of the King, who was sick and tired of George Grenville and anxious to change the ministry. Nor did the King relish the hard and self-seeking personality of Bedford. As soon as he had an alternative ministry lined up, the government received its brusque dismissal. But the King showed his partiality for Marlborough by offering him the post he would most have liked, that of Master of the Horse, and giving any place he wished to his brother, Lord Charles, if he would take on with the new administration. This, Bedford reported, the Duke had in the handsomest manner declined.[50] When he resigned the Privy Seal, the King pressed him to keep it and consider of it again. This made for a little delay in resigning which was noted as 'rather extraordinary'; but the pull of 'connection' prevailed.

The chronic ministerial instability of this first decade of George III's reign was due as much to the politicians as it was to the King. Lord Mansfield, from the security of high judicial office, could say 'parties aim only at places and seem regardless of measures', and George Grenville, that man of virtue, could add, 'the cure must come from a serious conviction and right measures, instead of annual struggles for places and pensions'.[51] But the man who most of all stood for measures rather than personalities, Pitt himself, was not least responsible. For he was above all men intractable, touchy, difficult; and he was at one with the King in wishing to root out party. He wished for a government of national union, of men of all parties, under his own leadership; he did not see that to organize on the basis of common affections, common opinions and common interests was coming to be the only practical way of conducting the nation's business. Hence when the Rockinghams came into power in 1765 (with whom Pitt most agreed in matters of policy), to undo some of the damage Grenville had done – by their policy of liberal concessions to America – Pitt would neither join them, nor support them, nor even assume their lead as they besought

49. *Letters*, ed. cit., VI. 211.
50. *The Grenville Papers*, ed. W. J. Smith, III. 210, 217.
51. Sir G. O. Trevelyan, op. cit., 126.

him. Instead he made their position impossible, in the interest of the government of national concentration he envisaged round himself.

The result was that when the Rockinghams were dismissed next year to make way for him, they in return would give him no solid support and Chatham's administration that was to have been so strong was weak from the start. Already by October of the same year negotiations were in hand to strengthen the administration by the accession of the Bedfords. Their terms were high: in addition to office for their leaders, a Garter for Marlborough, a place for Lord Charles. The King thought their terms extravagant: his own brother had not yet got a Garter; he would show the Bedfords of what little consequence they were.[52]

The Duke of Bedford was left to report this upshot to the Duke of Marlborough in polite ducal language:

with regard to the promise to your Grace of the Garter, it was a most delicate subject and more proper to be looked at in prospect than in retrospect. His Majesty had a brother, now of age, who was not yet invested with it. . . . Lord Charles Spencer might immediately have one of the sticks at Court, I understand, the same he before had.[53]

On the last day of November, a Sunday noon at Blenheim, Marlborough replied:

I am rather surprised no place was mentioned for me, not but that I had much rather not have one at present. Your Grace will be so good as to tell Lord Chatham that the promise was a most absolute one to all intents and purposes of the next that became vacant, so that the brother was not then thought of. I don't in the least wonder at its being a delicate subject. That would be but a poor answer between man and man. [How much more so, Marlborough implies, between King and Duke!] However, if your Grace does receive the assurances from the King that are promised with regard to the Garter, and my friends are provided for, I shall be satisfied. I hope by assurances are meant a promise of the Garter after the brother at least; otherwise I shall be as far off as ever.

52. *Correspondence of King George III*, ed. Sir John Fortescue, I. 420.

53. *The Correspondence of the Fourth Duke of Bedford*, ed. Lord John Russell, III. 355–6.

From which we see how much importance dukes are apt to attach to these gewgaws.

For his brother, Marlborough answered, 'I imagine he will like the staff better than nothing. . . . I had a letter from him t'other day, in which he says he should not much like any place of that sort, as the expenses of a re-election would hardly make it answer.' And in fact Lord Charles declined the offer, on the ground that the expenses of re-election and the fees on the office would amount to a year's income, 'so that I should be out of pocket by it, which I could by no means afford if I were not to keep it that time'.[54] And what was to be done for Mr Keck, the Duke inquired. He had been awarded a secret service pension on the King's accession, simply because 'his Majesty was very glad of an opportunity to oblige your Grace'.[55] This he had lost with the Bedfords' loss of office in 1765. But Mr Keck would shortly need no earthly pension: he died in 1767.

Lord Bolingbroke took the opportunity to pipe up with a request for a lordship of the Bedchamber: 'I voluntarily gave it up to oblige a man [Marlborough] from whom I have in return received the most unmerited behaviour. Any connection therefore with him, my lord, is what my pride will for ever make me avoid.'[56] This was all on account of Lady Di's divorce from him. A Scotch peer, Lord Garlies, begged Marlborough to intercede to make an English peerage for himself a *sine qua non* of the party's acceptance of office: 'it is my *omnium*, the only thing in life I wish for and the only thing that I can be materially obliged in'. Marlborough duly testified for him – for the present to no avail. Lord Garlies had to live many years without his *omnium*, though later Marlborough's heir married Lord Garlies's daughter.

Lord Chatham had had enough of the negotiation; he retired in distress and ill-health to Bath, where he remained keeping some sort of contact with his ministry by correspondence until the spring. Then he suffered a complete nervous breakdown, which lasted for the next two years while he remained nominally

54. J. Brooke, *The Chatham Administration, 1766–1768*, 63.
55. L. B. Namier, *The Structure of Politics* (1st edition), I. 273.
56. J. Brooke, op. cit., 259, 261.

the head of a government that changed its very character without him, went in for a course of policy opposed to his dearest wishes: which he was powerless to prevent. By December 1767 the Bedfords had gained their point: the ministry came to them cap in hand to shore itself up. Marlborough got his Garter, Bolingbroke the Bedchamber; there were posts for Gower and Weymouth, for the horrid Sandwich and the detestable Rigby. 'The Bedfords made opposition pay.'[57] For Marlborough the Garter was the height of his ambition. Never again after the experiences of those years before and after the Peace of 1763 would he engage himself in the cut-throat hazards of the political struggle. Though besought often enough to take office, or rather to lend his name to some administration, the Duke persisted in a withdrawal that must have represented the deepest wish of his heart, an impulse, that ultimately became overpowering, to seclude himself from men's affairs.

That was in the future. But, meanwhile, an entertaining interlude showed that the Duke had no intention of abdicating his family interest in the politics of his own neighbourhood. For the election of 1768 the venal corporation of Oxford came into the market.[58] For generations the borough had looked to its country neighbours for support and nourishment – in Elizabethan days to the Knollys family, later to the Berties of Rycote. Returning thence on one occasion when they had been too well entertained, some of the aldermen came home drunk and fell off their horses. From Civil War days the corporation never managed to catch up with its debts, until by 1768 they amounted to the sum of £5,670. Thereupon the corporation offered to return their sitting M.P.s at the election if they would pay the debt. Those virtuous members refused and brought the matter before the House of Commons. The mayor and ten aldermen were committed for a day or two to Newgate, where they took the convenient opportunity to clinch the bargain with the Duke of Marlborough and the Berties. The Town Clerk carried off the corporation records that contained the evidence of the bargain

57. ibid., 332.

58. For this episode cf. R. Fasnacht, *A History of the City of Oxford*, 127 foll.

and everybody enjoyed the joke. In the House of Commons the Duke of Marlborough's friends exerted themselves on the aldermen's behalf; in the house of correction the gaoler at Newgate exerted himself to give them a good dinner before letting them out. The King made Lord Villiers tell him the whole story at the Opera and they were much diverted.[59] In gratitude the corporation inscribed the Duke's name on its list of benefactors.

The results were useful. For thirty years to come one of the town's M.P.s was nominated by the Duke, the other by the Berties. For well-nigh a century one Duke of Marlborough after another was High Steward of the city. For some twenty years, 1771–90, Lord Robert, that Foxite Reformer, sat for Oxford. The Marlborough influence on the representation lasted till 1812, when the reforming Lockhart 'at length reaped the fruits of his exertions by being elected member for the city and removing the long-standing stigma of its being merely a "Blenheim borough" and its freemen a "pack of Blenheim spaniels" '.[60] With the Reform Bill of 1832 the borough ceased to be a sphere of private influence and felt free to offer its favours less exclusively: bribes were spread more fairly, more democratically. The town of Oxford became notorious for the extent of its corruption; in 1832, in 1857 and again in 1880 the elected member was unseated for bribery. This jovial tradition continued right up to our own days, when in 1924 the Liberal member was unseated for the traditional reason.

Young Lord Robert, whom we last saw at the age of thirteen showing how well he knew how to handle the freeholders of Oxfordshire, was now abroad on the grand tour equipping himself for life and politics. In December 1766 John Moore, who was bear-leading him, writes from Vienna that they had been presented to the Empress-Queen, the famous Maria Theresa, who made Lord Robert a compliment on the services her father had received from his family.[61] 'She is still a very fine woman though greatly altered, as everyone says, since the death of the

59. *H.M.C., Carlisle MSS.*, 238.
60. ibid., 136.
61. Blenheim MSS., E 60.

Emperor.' Next day they were presented to her son, Joseph II: a great enemy to parade and finery, he had put an end to all gala days, some sixty in the year. Always dressed simply, he usually wore the uniform of one of his own regiments. Moore wished the Duke and Duchess could have been there

to laugh heartily at a certain Englishman in a light-coloured blue velvet embroidered with gold. I observed that people who talked with him called him sometimes M. le Comte, sometimes Milord and sometimes M. de More. When he happened to pass by a glass, he seemed to know less of himself than of anybody else in the company.

Charming old-fashioned Moore, whose head was never turned by any company he kept, was on his way to greater heights than these.

In January he sends descriptions of the Carnival in the snow-covered city, the streets crowded with horse-drawn sledges gay with carving and gilding. The whole Court was driving out, diamonds sparkling in the frost, liveries of every colour, harness and trappings shining in the winter sun – how it brings back the Hofburg of Fischer von Erlach, the narrow streets of Am Hof, the square in front of the Karlskirche with dome and columns newly built, the Prater and Schönbrunn. Lord Robert and he were dining out every night, never less than sixteen people. They were much taken with the extraordinary variety of costumes in the streets of this frontier-city of Europe. Beyond Vienna barbarism begins.

In the spring they made for Italy and in June were in Rome. Moore was moved by its beauty, by the thought of the thousands of columns of marble and porphyry from ancient Rome decorating the palaces, the exteriors of which looked dirty and desolate enough. The nobility held their assemblies from eleven at night till two in the morning, where the amusements were three:

they play at cards very low, make love or eat gingerbread nuts or a little of all three. Consequently an Englishman contents himself with the nuts, till at least he can talk the language. . . . Lord Robert and I had learnt Italian to read it before we came here and from necessity we have learnt to speak it pretty tolerably, so that for some time past we have left off the gingerbread.

They observed, as everyone did, the extreme poverty of the numerous servants and of the food, even of princes – everything was for show. At Naples there was the custom of receiving people when one was ill, the house full of noise, cards, etc., in the very sick-room; a dying man had had to ask the company to go into the next room, where they carried on till a servant came in to announce, 'il padrone è andato a Paradiso'. The ladies here wore no rouge, but when a cardinal died he lay in state with his face painted. Funerals were shocking, the body carried with the face uncovered, wig freshly powdered, all dressed up, sword by side.

In July they were travelling from Florence to Bologna, Parma, Verona, thence to Genoa and Turin, seeing the beauties and tormented by fleas, thousands of them – there was as much difference between English and Italian fleas as between a coach-horse and a race-horse. Mr Addison's book was deficient in not observing this circumstance. At Florence the thing was to meet on a bridge in the middle of the town from eleven at night onwards to take the *fresco*; 'the ladies go in undresses of different sorts and the men in general in straw hats and chintz night-gowns'.

By December they were in Paris and Moore was able to report that Lord Robert was growing more manly and amiable. Paris society consisted of those who play cards at least eight hours out of the twenty-four; 'the other, the *beaux esprits* or such as wish to be thought so pass all the same portion of their time in criticizing the plays and players, in talking of books which very few of them read and producing extempore *bons mots* which they have studied for a week beforehand'. It is a recognizable picture. London was much more populous and larger than Paris, 'but for the public walks, the clearness of the air, the goodness of the houses and the furniture, we can't dispute the point'.

Now Lord Robert's sister, Lady Pembroke, has arrived in Paris for a long stay and has taken a house, 'very dear, very dirty and very small. This is really a very serious misfortune. Especially as Lady Pembroke already knows five hundred people and is likely soon to know as many thousands.' Lord Robert has a numerous acquaintance, and practically lives with the French. There is no danger of his becoming a coxcomb or a *petit-maître*. 'I have the pleasure of assuring the Duke of Marlborough too that he does not play.' This was too good to last. One night

> he was presented to Mme du Deffand, an old blind lady, a *bel esprit* whose house is much in fashion. . . . She reached out her head in an odd manner. Miss Floyd, who was behind Lord Robert and very anxious for him to do all that was right, whispered him that she meant he should salute her. Not having an instant to reflect on the impossibility of her having any such thought, he did so. When Mme la Marquise immediately cried out, 'Je crois, qu'il me baise; il me paraît qu'il me baise; c'est pousser la politesse bien loin'.

The old lady seemed delighted at this from the young man, who was youthfully confused.

We hear the other side from Mme du Deffand's letters to Horace Walpole. She promises to tell him what success Lady Pembroke's beauty has: so far few have yet seen her.[62] By February her beauty is beginning to be noticed; she is 'aimable, douce et intéressante', but not exciting. There, perhaps, was the secret of her trouble with the tempestuous Henry: if she had been more spirited, had something of Sarah in her, she might have held him. But this generation of Marlboroughs were all of them too gentle. By the end of the year she was having a marked success: Lady Pembroke 'ne touche pas' – hardly puts foot to ground – your English women are so much given to pleasure – opera and comedy every day – a ball at the Prince of Monaco's, a fête at the Prince de Soubise's – next at the Palais-Royal, then to stay at Chantilly. These last decades of the Ancien Régime, this world painted by Boucher and Nattier – never was there a society more elegant and agreeable, more frivolous and fragile.

Now the old lady reports that Lady Pembroke grows on her: she has taste, discernment, grace, though she expresses herself with difficulty – like all this generation of her family, except her sister Di: they were apt to be silent. The Marquise

62. *Horace Walpole's Correspondence with Madame du Deffand*, ed. W. S. Lewis, I. 396; II. 26, 159.

is taking tea with her; she finds her 'agréable, delicate et juste'. At last she is completely conquered and comes out with a full-blown tribute. 'J'aime beaucoup la Milady; plus je la vois, plus je la trouve aimable; sa simplicité, son naturel, sa douceur, sa modestie ont quelque chose de piquant; sans être vive, elle est animée, elle a de la justesse dans les jugements qu'elle porte ... toutes ses manières sont extrêmement nobles.'[63] It was something to have passed the rigorous test of those sightless eyes.

Perhaps it was something of a consolation too, for there was no consolation in her marriage. Her very goodness and sweetness bored her husband: when he went off abroad with Kitty Hunter the actress in 1762, he left a note saying that he had done everything he could to make Elizabeth hate him – in vain. Then he wrote her a letter inviting her to join the party – which she nearly did out of sheer goodness of heart, but was prevented by the resentment of her family. The result of Henry's escapade was the little Augustus Reebkomp, whom Elizabeth accepted as a member of the family and brought up; she became very fond of him. And there were others. Henry she took back after this first escapade; in the end he became too much, even for her.

Nor did the spirited Di have any better luck with her Bolingbroke. He was a good deal of a rake and something of a brute: no intelligence to offset his displeasing character, nothing to hold her who was a very gifted and intelligent woman. She took him at his own valuation and consoled herself with the fascinating Topham Beauclerk. This gifted young man-about-town was a great friend of Dr Johnson and, being a Stuart by descent, could say anything to the Doctor – and did. A great-grandson of Charles II and Nell Gwyn, he inherited qualities from both: dark and rather saturnine, handsome and full of wit, he was very seductive and cared for nobody. He combined extreme charm with bad temper, bibliophily with a taste for women. London was soon full of the bad terms the Bolingbrokes were on, and the too good terms Di and Topham were on. But in those days it was exceedingly difficult to get a divorce.

In 1768 Di went through the distasteful proceedings with courage and success. A crucial point was the provision that

63. q. *The Pembroke Papers, 1734–1780*, ed. Lord Herbert, 37.

would be made for her. Her brother the Duke helped her and in the end Lord Bolingbroke, who was by no means well off, made her a small allowance. A private Act of Parliament, Royal Assent and all, was necessary to make the divorce absolute and enable the parties to marry again; so we can follow matters in the *Journals of the House of Lords.*[64] Dr John Moore gave his sedate evidence that he had married the parties in September 1757. The servants gave their less sedate evidence that Lord and Lady Bolingbroke never met or saw each other from 1765, that Mr Beauclerk frequently visited her, that he generally dined and supped with her and stayed till midnight, that they were usually alone together with the door locked – that once on entering the room the servant had found Lady Bolingbroke sitting confused on the couch, it looked as if she had been lying there; at another time there were shoe-marks at one end and a great deal of powder at the other. And so on. On 29 February 1768 the Bill was passed and immediately Di married her Topham. The date brought her no luck: in one way and another she had as much to put up with in her second marriage as in her first.

Life was catching up with these young people. With the passing of the seventeen-sixties they were no longer young.

64. *Journals of the House of Lords*, XXXII. 40, 110 foll.

Chapter 5

George, Fourth Duke, and Blenheim

WHERE the affections of the third Duke were fixed upon Langley, which was largely his creation, his son's were indubitably upon Blenheim. The pull of the place began to exert itself on the family which had taken so long to become acclimatized to the grandeur of the first Marlborough's conception. Now in the third generation from him Blenheim – disliked and neglected by Sarah, never occupied by Henrietta and only intermittently so by Charles – came into its own, became finally the centre and magnet of the family. And so onwards into the future.

Sir Lewis Namier has a perceptive passage on the importance of the 'place' for the continuity of the family.

> English history, and especially English Parliamentary history, is made by families rather than by individuals. . . . The English political family is a compound of 'blood', name and estate, this last being the most important of the three. . . . The name is a weighty symbol, but liable to variations; descent traced in the male line only is like a river without its tributaries. The estate, with all that it implies, is in the long run the most important factor in securing continuity through identification, the 'taking up' of the inheritance. The owner of an ancestral estate may have far less of the 'blood' than some distant relative bearing a different name . . . still, it is he who in his thoughts and feelings most closely identifies himself, and is identified by others, with his predecessors.[1]

George, fourth Duke, ruled at Blenheim far longer than any other member of his family – for just on sixty years; it is only natural, therefore, that he should have left an impress on it second only to John Churchill, first Duke, himself. Above all, we owe to the fourth Duke the dominant feature in the setting of the Palace as we see it today: the drowning of the river-valley of the Glyme to make that magnificent half-moon of lake upon which all the western windows look, that so enhances the fairy-tale

1. L. B. Namier, *England in the Age of the American Revolution*, 22.

quality of the scene and brings out the inherent romanticism of so classic a pile.

That wonderful house – a martial palace, a festive castle, conjured up out of the imagination of a dramatist – was almost as little appreciated in the Georgian age as it was in the Victorian. We know what Arthur Young thought of the exterior: 'a clutter of parts so distinct that a Gothic church has as much unity; and withal a heaviness in each part which is infinitely disgusting'.[2] Horace Walpole paid the place another visit just about this time, the high summer of 1760.

> We went to Blenheim and saw all Vanbrugh's quarries, all the Acts of Parliament and gazettes on the Duke in inscriptions, and all the old flock chairs, wainscot tables, and gowns and petticoats of Queen Anne that old Sarah could crowd amongst blocks of marble. It looks like the palace of an auctioneer who has been chosen King of Poland and furnished his apartments with obsolete trophies, rubbish that nobody bid for and a dozen pictures that he had stolen from the inventories of different families. The place is as ugly as the house, and the bridge, like the beggars at the old Duchess's gate, begs for a drop of water and is refused.[3]

This last criticism – the absurdity of such a magnificent bridge crossing so insignificant a stream – was just. Everybody recognized that it was unsatisfactory. An attempt had been made to reduce the marshy little Glyme to formal order, to canalize it and fill two ponds with its inadequate waters, one on either side of the immense bridge. It was this that was now to be transformed by a grand stroke of imagination.

The Duke's father had had no money left over from his works at Langley to spend on building at Blenheim, though he had thought of it. From the moment his son settled down to the possession of Blenheim he began to apply himself to embellishing it. He called in Sir William Chambers, the most fashionable architect at the time, with his French tastes and the patronage of George III, to lighten the declamatory effects of Vanbrugh. Chambers

2. Arthur Young, *A Six Weeks' Tour through the Southern Counties* (1768), 92.

3. *The Letters of Horace Wapole*, ed. cit., IV. 409.

designed a superb state-bed – bell-like baldachin and corner-plumes, pink silk and Sarah's lace – and went on to lighter and more elegant cornices to ceilings, chimney-pieces, pier-glasses. Outside he mitigated the severity of the east portal, with its cannon-balls supporting the piers, by laurel-wreaths on the superstructure. For the park he designed a Temple of Diana and a Tuscan gate, at Bladon an exquisite bridge across the Glyme; for the town of Woodstock a town hall of noble proportions, standing between the two streets that lead to park and Palace, a building that gives an air of foreign distinction to the Cotswold architecture of the little market-place.

Then the Duke called in a new man, Capability Brown, the leading exponent of the Back-to-Nature school of landscape-gardening, a conductor of the gathering romantic impulse of the time. Where the classic age had imposed the architectural forms of the house upon its environment, to extend the idea of the house to the garden, the new school sought to bring Nature right up to the doors. And this Brown, during the ten years he was employed at Blenheim from 1764 to 1774, proceeded to do with a vengeance.

It is extraordinary that that sensitive, compromising man, the Duke, should have allowed Brown to bring about such a revolution in his surroundings. But the Duke was a man of taste and fashion, a connoisseur, and he was young: it is doubtful if he would ever have undertaken such vast works later. Brown began by damming the river and creating the expanse of water that laps the Palace on its western side. As the valley filled and the lake came into existence, it gave sense to Vanbrugh's noble bridge at the same time as it reduced its size by drowning the ground-storey. Proportions were improved; a marvellous new scene created: from across the lake the Palace floats on the horizon, its gathered towers and turrets, the whole fantastic roofscape taking the skies.

Now Brown proceeded to bring the park up to the Palace. The bridge leads up to the grand and very formal entrance front – so grand it might almost be Escorial or Vatican. Brown grassed it over. On the south side of the Palace lay the *chef-d'œuvre* of Henry Wise, gardener to Queen Anne, who had designed and laid out the gardens at Blenheim.[4] This was an immense six-sided citadel of a garden – with Louis XIV's head taken from Tournai looking down on it – built within walls with bastions at each angle, walks and lime-alleys and fountains within; two great parterres running the whole length of the Palace, 'enriched with dwarf evergreens and coloured sands', raised walks from which one could look down the steep slopes to the valley, back to the house, forward to the tower of Bladon church on the axis running through park, garden, house, across the bridge to the Victory Column and beyond to the other horizon. All on a scale no other house in England could rival.

This superb formal garden was swept completely away. We must for ever regret it. Nothing took its place, nothing but grass: grass coming right up to the garden-front, grass extending in every direction, grass to infinity, nothing but grass and an immensity of sky. It, too, is rather magnificent in its way; but it is boring – as boring as a cricket-pitch, which it is, where once the fountains plashed and sun gleamed on evergreens or printed variegated patterns down those vanished alleys.

Perhaps Brown thought that the plain expanse of green set off his lake, as it certainly is a foil for it. One has to admit that on balance Blenheim gained greatly by his work: nothing could surpass the setting he gave the house; his natural romanticism curiously complements the rhetoric of Vanbrugh. Everybody feels this – that the strange house has now the providentially right setting. No less a judge than Wyatt expressed this sense: he

> never passed the road through the gate which leads from Woodstock to Blenheim without being exceedingly struck by the general effect, and had often stood to consider to what cause it could be owing, without being able to satisfy himself. It was not the building or the grounds, or the woods or the water singly . . . yet the whole together makes a forcible impression.[5]

The force comes from the striking harmony of it – as one enters that gate from the blind forecourt and the whole scene suddenly opens out before one's eyes.

Nor was this the end of Brown's works.

4. cf. David Green, *Gardener to Queen Anne*, cc. X, XI.
5. *The Farington Diary*. ed. J. Greig, I. 257.

The whole park, except for the north and east avenues and the kitchen garden, was replanted in Brown's famous belt-and-clump style. Beeches surrounded the park and guarded the Grand Bridge; chestnuts, limes and sycamores hung over the water; while in places of honour, for contrast and for their own peculiar grandeur, stood the cedars, in time to grow massive and lofty, spreading plane upon plane of dark foliage for the pale heron to rest on.[6]

In addition Brown wanted to see the park, the Palace itself romanticized. He managed to castellate High Lodge; he made detailed plans for a new granary, battlements and all. Where were the ramparts that should transform the Palace? He made a sketch to illustrate the effect of his plan, 'which would have involved not merely castellating the park walls but treating in like manner the walls of every visible Woodstock building . . .'

It was time to call a halt. For the years 1764 to 1774 the Duke paid Brown some £16,437 14s., and this can have been only a a part of the total sums spent on the improvements at Blenheim: money that was well spent: the country has this lasting memorial to show for it.

The family was steadily extending its holdings beyond the park-pale in Oxfordshire. The neighbouring estate of Cornbury in Wychwood Forest had been acquired in 1751, and we can watch the process of expansion through these years in the next-door parish of Wootton. This, like most Oxfordshire parishes, had had a number of small landowners. By 1770, when the common fields were enclosed – a desirable process which had the effect of greatly increasing productivity from the soil – the Marlboroughs were already leading landowners. In 1790 the Duke purchased the manor house of Dornford with two farms for £10,000, and by 1809 was also in possession of Hordley.[7] The historical interest of the process is this: Oxfordshire had always been a county of fairly numerous small estates; here we see a very large bird settling into the nest, pushing the others out. This is an oligarchical age: here is its economic underpinning.

This dominant position in the country involved many obligations. It was a point of honour for the county to turn up at the

6. David Green, *Blenheim Palace*, 187.
7. Charles Ponsonby, *Wootton*, 39, 94, 97.

Oxford Races. In September 1766 the Duke cannot be there and instructs his steward to give £20 or £30 to be run for by the freemen's horses.[8] Later he turned this into an annual subscription of £50, which he kept up for the rest of his life. Only once did he enter horses for the races: in 1776 when his horse Indian came in third (of five) for the subscription cup, and Critic won the sweepstakes. And that seems to have exhausted his interest.[9] In 1766 he subscribed £100 towards making the road over Botley causeway. Two years later, for making the Oxford–Banbury canal, he will subscribe a good round sum if it is not called for all at once: £5,000 and as much for Blandford; his brothers can subscribe what they choose themselves. In the accounts from 1767 to 1768 we find a note for moneys to Lord Robert to make his fortune equal to Lord Charles's when he comes of age; for annuities and pensions within the family, £4,378 6s. 10d.; for the town hall at Woodstock, £497 4s. $4\frac{1}{2}$d.; for Oxford Citizens, Election, etc. – which really means buying the corporation – the large sum of £4,974 4s. 7d.; for Lancelot Brown, £2,100; and an ominous item of interest-money, £1,237 11s.[10]

Within doors similarly expenses mount up. In 1764 a good deal of refurnishing was being done – hence upholsterers' accounts. It is of interest to go into the economy of such a household. Servants' wages for the half year Christmas 1770 to Midsummer 1771 amounted to £785 9s. $2\frac{3}{4}$d. There were seventy-five of them, of whom only seven have to sign by mark: even Diana Cooper, the still-room maid, can sign her name.[11] Charles Turner was the house steward for many years – paid £42. The clerk of the kitchen commanded £100 a year. There were a cook, a butler, a *valet de chambre*, a French hairdresser at £21; a chaplain, Mr Holloway, paid 10 guineas; Rebecca Hobson, housekeeper, £10. Outside, a waterman, a fisherman, a pheasant man, three gamekeepers, one gamekeeper for Wychwood Forest, one gardener. (No doubt Brown's abolition of the garden was

8. Blenheim MSS., F I. 36.

9. J. Weatherby, *The Racing Calendar, 1776,* 96. His brothers took not much more interest, Lord Robert entering a horse in 1775, and again in 1782; Lord Charles in 1778 and 1779.

10. Blenheim MSS., E 54.

11. ibid., F I. 37.

an economy.) Servants' wages remained at a fairly constant figure through these years, though with a slight upward tendency: from Christmas 1788 to Midsummer 1789, £858 10s. 10½d., from Midsummer to Christmas 1795, £886 17s. 3d.[12]

We get an insight into the life of the household from the general disbursements. In the 1780s private theatricals were much to the fore, but they cost little: from Midsummer to Christmas 1789, six guineas. William Tibbet, groom of the chamber, was paid seven guineas for music in August, and for music at Christmas, £8 16s. 6d.; there was also his pension. Musical instruments cost £22 16s., a music teacher £11 3s. 6d., while in December £20 12s. was paid to musicians for five nights' performance. By the Duke's order five guineas was paid to the Giant. There must have been a good deal of home-made fun at Blenheim in those days.

The children were arriving rapidly: first came two daughters, Caroline in 1763, Elizabeth in 1764. The eldest son, Blandford, was born in 1766, followed by Charlotte in 1769 and Henry in 1770; a third son, Francis, was born in 1779, and there were two more daughters: eight children in all. We know how their arrival was celebrated from the supper provided on the birth of the young lord (Henry), on 22 December 1770: roast beef, mutton and pork, loin and fillet of veal, pork and mutton pies; chicken, ducks, geese roasted; tongues boiled, hog's head and two dishes of souse; 2 plum puddings, one apple pie; in the housekeeper's room, for the upper servants, two roast chickens, one roast duck, one boiled tongue, one roast neck of mutton, one apple pie.[13]

For the Duke and Duchess to move anywhere with their children and a retinue of servants needed elaborate organization. Take a journey to Bath in November 1776. The Duke and Duchess were to go in the blue coach to Tetbury and in the chaise from thence; three servants in the hired chaise to Tetbury, with five menservants on post-horses. Four men and women were to go in 'our own chaise'; post-chaise horses to carry the chaise beforehand on Sunday to Tetbury: they must set out very early and wait some time at Burford and a good while at Cirencester. The coach-horses and two hacks were to go over to Burford on Sunday afternoon to carry the Duke and Duchess next day to Tetbury,

12. Blenheim MSS., F I. 57. 13. ibid., F I. 36.

where they would lie that night and wait to bring the children on to Bath in the landau – three girls and two women, with two menservants on post-horses. Read with the kitchen and laundry maids went ahead in a post-chaise, and the kitchen man with the waggon. H. Topping would be on Billy Bark, F. Taylor on Pennant, W. Tibbet on Pumpkin. It is somehow affecting to become familiar in these accounts with the names of these servants who have long gone to their account. We watch their names appear year after year, register their progress from boys to men, rising sometimes like Charles Turner or James Beckley to become house steward, or like Tibbet, groom of the chamber, until we come to their five-guinea funerals in the books and we read their names no more.

Whatever his expenses, the Duke continued to collect, for this was a collectors' age: 'an eclectic and inquisitive age', says Namier, 'primarily an age of collectors, with a passion for accumulating no matter what – books, manuscripts, shells, pictures, old coins or the currency of the realm'.[14] It was only in this last class that these later Marlboroughs were remiss. As early as 1762 Walpole, himself a most distinguished specimen of the collector's class, tells us that the Duke had bought most of the Zanetti collections of gems at Venice.[15] And this was only a beginning. The theme is brought into Reynolds's magnificent portrait of the Duke and his family painted in August 1777. In this canvas, painted in the grand manner with its architectural background, the Duke is holding a large cameo, while the heir is holding one of the crimson cases that held the Marlborough gems. The collector's mania was to run riot with this boy and ruin him.

Ten years later we find the Duke still bidding for gems. He went up as far as £120 for a damaged cameo of Augustus, but the Duke of Portland was determined to have it and his resources were now greater.[16] In earlier years Marlborough stinted himself of nothing: we find one goldsmith's account for a set of two dozen gold knives, forks and spoons engraved with his arms, for altering

14. L. B. Namier, op. cit., 37.
15. *The Letters of Horace Walpole*, ed. cit., V. 163.
16. *H.M.C., Rutland MSS.*, III. 311.

and adding festoons to a large tureen and gilding two ice pails – £332 5s. 7d.[17] It was with the fourth Duke as it had been with his father: this state of affairs could not go on. Between 1763 and 1782 the Duke had sunk just £100,000. It was necessary to retrench and, as with his father, we find a paper of suggested economies. As early as 1766 the Duke was writing, 'I don't know what we shall do for money to pay the quarter's bills'.[18] In the next year or two the number of servants was reduced from eighty-eight to some seventy-five. Nothing would do, however, except a major measure; and in 1788 he took the resolution to sell Langley. It must have fetched a very large sum and effected a considerable relief so far as this Duke was concerned. In the latter half of his life he was much less profuse and far more careful; his virtual retirement to Blenheim aided him to live within his income. But by this time his son had come of age and he proved the most extravagant and wasteful of this spendthrift stock.

Such is the background, such are the figures who appear in the accounts; we may now turn to the lives they lived, to give them life.

The Duke and Duchess went about a good deal, every year to Bath, and later on to fashionable Brighthelmstone where they had a house next the Pavilion; in London they lived at Marlborough House. But they moved about alone; they had always been wrapped up in each other since they were first married and they were sufficient to themselves. In time this cut them off from society so much that they became rather eccentric – the Duke notoriously so; but it had its effect on the Duchess too: as sometimes happens with very happy and exclusive marriages, husband and wife echoed each other, grew together.

These were the years in which Brooks's Club reached its apogee, with Charles Fox its most popular member, almost its tutelary deity. Marlborough's brother, Lord Charles, was an original member, and Lord Robert, Fox's intimate companion, for many years a leading spirit. Among its members were most of the dukes in the country, and Marlborough felt obliged to

17. Blenheim MSS., F I. 52.   18. ibid., F I. 36.

become a member in 1772, proposed by his youngest brother.[19] It does not seem that he attended or took any interest in it: he never proposed anybody else for membership, unlike his brothers, especially Lord Robert, who became one of the first Managers of the Club and introduced many new members.

The Duchess became a member of the Female Almack's, where the tiresome Mrs Montagu and the agreeable Mrs Boscawen reigned and where the Duchess of Bedford was blackballed.[20] We hear of the Duke's proficiency at quinze, for which he had a talent. Walpole says that at a ball in 1773 the Duke of Northumberland lost £2,000: 'the victorious name of Marlborough won most of it'.[21] Yet he was so shy that on one occasion when he made a master-stroke and staked all his cards on it, he lost what he had set on them rather than face the crowd that was collecting round him. To his pathological shyness – so handsome and so sensitive – he was now adding another neurotic symptom: silence.

In 1777 the Duchess went with her friends to hear 'Mr Garrick speak his last dying speech in the theatre. There was not a dry eye in the whole house. . . . If all the kings in Europe (except the King of England) were to abdicate, there would not be so much or so universal grief.' Afterwards they all had supper with Mr and Mrs Garrick. One of the ladies writes to Mrs Montagu, 'the Duchess is in hopes to bring the Duke into such company next winter in hopes to make him speak; that will fall to your lot, at least you will make him listen'.[22] It seems that the Duke evaded this fate.

In their curious withdrawn state from the world the Marlboroughs came to rely increasingly on Moore's letters for what was going on, as well as for counsel as to what they should do. It was the Duchess who kept the contact going; the Duke scarcely put pen to paper. Fortunately Moore was a good letter-writer and his letters to her form a gently amusing moving-picture of their lives and concerns.[23] In the summer of 1767 he writes from Durham, where he holds a fat prebend: 'my mornings are

19. *Memorials of Brooks's*, 19.
20. *Autobiography and Correspondence of Mrs Delany*, IV. 261.
21. *The Letters of Horace Walpole*, ed. cit., VIII. 238.
22. R. Blunt, *Mrs Montagu*, 365.
23. Blenheim MSS., E 60.

dedicated to signing death-warrants for turkeys and making bills of fare, and my afternoons to entertaining thousands of people whom I never saw before and half of whom I should esteem it a favour never to see again'. Elizabeth's brother the Bishop – hence no doubt Moore's prebend – 'has outlived the assizes, but not without the inexpressible fatigue of his apothecary, who has had double duty upon his hands all the time. I do really and seriously think he will eat himself to death in a short time. His appetite seems to increase every day.' This it took the good bishop four more years to accomplish.

In 1771 Moore became Dean of Canterbury and it was while he was there that we first hear of trouble with young Blandford. The boy was delicate and spoiled; it seems that Coxe, his tutor, was not successful in dealing with him. Moore, as usual, was called in to advise. He thought that Coxe had not shown enough firmness in dealing with the boy's fits; while his personal servant had taken advantage to demand new terms for himself. The Dean had no patience with this: if he did it again he should be turned out at an hour's warning. In all this correspondence we find the solid grazier's son trying to steel the Marlboroughs' resolution as they got odder and odder and more incapable of making up their minds.

It was after this experience, a whole year of it, that Coxe gave up his charge of the boy, though apparently retaining the Duke's favour. He wrote,

> I have too good an opinion of you and, I may say, too great a regard for you not to have read your letter without feeling great uneasiness; whatever may be the event of this, I shall never forget the care and attention you have shown to my poor little boy in all his illnesses and you will ever find me your sincere friend.[24]

The Duke made him his chaplain, promised to provide for him and 'even mentioned what he would give me, should it be vacant'. But Coxe found himself, in the event, mistaken: the Duke remembered no such promise. Coxe was not prepared for the absence of mind of great folks or, rather, not subtle enough to interpret their language. It sounds to me as if the Duke's polite

24. *The Pembroke Papers, 1734–1780*, ed. cit., 82.

words are a kind of *congé* and that when he asked Coxe to bear-lead his nephew, Lord Herbert, round Europe, it was really getting rid of him. Knowing the Duke's character, I detect a carefully concealed resentment at Coxe's giving up his charge. The charge became an almighty nuisance and Coxe was well rid of him. His tour provided the excellent letters we have from him and the material for an admirable book.[25] Coxe's career henceforth lay in Wiltshire and literature.

Meanwhile Moore had been made Bishop of Bangor and in the summer of 1776, while momentous events were taking place on the other side of the Atlantic and Congress was issuing its Declaration of Independence, was peacefully perambulating his diocese.

I have taken a journey which I believe no bishop of the diocese ever took before me, and though I am now quiet and in repose in my own house I can't help thinking I still hear rapid torrents roaring over immense fragments of broken rocks and falling in cataracts into the valleys. I have only to shut my eyes and I am surrounded with large mountains, stupendous rocks and dreadful precipices such as the romantic pencil of Salvator Rosa never exceeded.

In the summer of 1777, when Howe was occupying Philadelphia and Burgoyne on his way to Saratoga, the bishop was rambling in Anglesey, Sir Joshua painting at Blenheim.

It will amuse your Graces to have him there and it is a very good season for him to go on with the picture. I have no doubt but he will make a fine picture; but I hope the resemblances will be striking. I would have the countenances I have so long been used to see with pleasure handed down just as they are to posterity.

Sir Joshua made, all must agree, a splendid picture. The children, as so often with him, are particularly delightful: there is the smallest girl who was frightened of being painted, caught shrinking back, holding on to her sister's skirts; there is the little girl hiding behind the mask, the young heir looking fragile, the air of weakness already on him. The magnificent Duke displays his handsome calves while the Duchess is the centre of the whole.

25. *Travels into Poland, Russia, Sweden and Denmark*, by William Coxe, 1784.

But the family, which no doubt meant herself, considered she was done least justice. So next year Romney was employed to paint her portrait alone. The Bishop added that 'within this month or two people here have somehow heard of the rebellion in America and begun to talk of it'. Not until the surrender under the chestnut-tree at Saratoga did the country wake up to the seriousness of the situation in America and the task they had been let in for by the mismanagements of the past decade.

Saratoga brought France into the war and later Spain. Britain declared war upon Holland; and the hostile armed neutrality of the Northern Powers was formed against us. Soon Britain was fighting not only her revolted Colonies but half Europe, the more powerful half – fighting alone, without an ally, for her very existence. It was an extraordinary effort that she mounted, but it should never have come to such a pass. Sensible, conservative Coxe wrote from Italy,

> I know nothing in which our blessed Ministry are more blameable than in not having one ally. The moment that a war with America was necessary, they ought to have foreseen that one with France and Spain was unavoidable, and as well they ought to have formed some alliance with Russia, Denmark, Holland.[26]

That alliance had been Chatham's objective in 1766, but it was rejected by Frederick of Prussia. Pitt's genius had elevated this country to a dangerous ascendancy, for it raised up a world of jealous enemies biding their chance. Everything should have been done to purchase an ally: the combination of a defensive alliance in Europe with concessions to America would have made us safe and kept the Empire intact. This had been Chatham's policy. But he was a dying man, whom illness and the King had kept out in the years that mattered. The politicians gave themselves up to domestic dissensions – and the country, sunk in its eighteenth-century quiet, took no notice of what was piling up on the other side of the Atlantic: it was too far away, another world.

The unrespectable Lord Pembroke had been more sensible. He was now writing, 'Lord Chatham is not only the first Man, but alas the only man who can save this Nation'.[27] And then,

26. *The Pembroke Papers, 1734–1780*, 227. 27. ibid., 108, 116.

> Lord Chatham came down to the House today . . . a feeble shocking sight, a wreck . . . yet he made a spirited, short speech. A few minutes after he sat down and whilst the Duke of Richmond was speaking he – what they called fainted, fell back and was carried out. . . . I fear the attack was more than fainting.

Within a few weeks the great man – that 'trumpet of sedition' as the King had called him – was dead; George III was against his being given a state funeral. The country's affairs were less safe in the hands of those second-rate men, George III and Lord North, Sandwich and Lord George Germaine, than in those of the dangerous man of genius.

There had been a rumour in 1776 that Marlborough was moving into opposition; it seems that in June he was offered the Lord-Lieutenancy of Ireland and declined it.[28] 'Can your ladyship', wrote Coxe, '(unless it be some profound secret) give me any information thereupon – as who and who are together, and who has quitted with the Duke of M.?'[29] But by 1778 it was as much as he could do to review the local militia. Moore wrote to congratulate him on summoning up his resolution and to steel him to do it again. 'I have seen with pain how much your Graces have both withdrawn yourselves from the world of late, and I have feared it would grow upon you. . . . Your children are now growing up apace and they *must* mix with the world and how much better under your own eyes.' Moore was right as usual: their withdrawal was a factor in what happened to their eldest son.

He held up the example of Lord Charles who 'is so universally beloved in the militia' and whose example contributed 'much to the steadiness of your interest in the country'. Both Lord Charles and Lord Robert had jobs in the Administration, Charles as a member of the Board of Admiralty and Robert as a member of the Board of Trade and Plantations – both of them since the formation of Lord North's government in 1770. Now in 1779 Gibbon was coming to join Lord Robert as a sinecure member, along with the indispensable William Eden, now Moore's brother-in-law. We see what a family-party government was. Moore occasionally stayed with Lord Charles at Wheatfield. We find Lady Charles

28. *The Last Journals of Horace Walpole*, ed. A. F. Steuart, I. 560.
29. *The Pembroke Papers, 1734–1780*, 74.

writing to the Duchess, 'having a mob with me and Lord Charles never to be depended upon'. The mule the Duke gave her is 'so fond of the man who broke her that she sings to him whenever he goes to her. . . . I am writing with the dogs barking, the wind blowing and a loud organ roaring.'

Far stronger winds were blowing against the country. In 1779 Spain came into the war, with the object of taking Gibraltar and getting back Minorca and Florida. The first consequence was that a combined Franco-Spanish fleet of sixty ships-of-the-line entered the Channel where at first there was nothing to oppose them. They hovered off Plymouth threatening invasion. Moore's cool head makes an interesting assessment of their chances. He does not think highly of the state of the Spanish ships or of their willingness to fight under a French admiral. The English fleet is better manned and full of ardour – so that the combined fleets are not likely to gain such an ascendancy as to enable enough transports to cross and invade successfully. And so it turned out. Before the combined fleets appeared an immense fleet of merchantmen from the West Indies, one hundred and twenty-five sail, arrived home safe; and immediately after the enemy fleets had left, another equally big convoy came in from the East Indies. The combined fleets got back to Brest, ravaged with sickness, having accomplished nothing. The island-power was called on to make yet greater exertions; she was now fighting not only half the world but, now that conflict raged in India too, over half the world. The danger was extreme. Moore summed up episcopally: 'still, however, the crisis is very awful. If our calamities bring us back to a sense of Providence and Religion, they are a merciful dispensation.' If they brought the country back to political sense, it would be more to the point.

At the end of the year the Duke sent down to his agent at Woodstock the news of the striking success at Savannah, in the defence of which no less than a thousand American loyalists took part. After a month's siege the French under d'Estaing had been repulsed with the loss of 1,500 men, and he had returned wounded to France. 'I think there should be a bonfire in the Park and some beer given out, as was done for Keppel's acquittal.'[30]

30. Blenheim MSS., E 54.

This shows that in the recriminations between Admiral Keppel and his next in command, in which Opposition and people took Keppel's side, the sympathies of Blenheim were already with the Opposition.

The trouble was that the country was not united. United enough against its old enemies and to withstand invasion, it was not united against its own kith and kin across the Atlantic. Some of the best minds in England were with the Americans. From the moment France intervened, Charles Fox's friend, Fitzpatrick, declared, 'all people see the necessity of withdrawing the troops from America'.[31] It is true that neither were the Americans united: in some colonies there was a large number of loyalists or at least neutrally inclined. It was a revolutionary minority that was determined to break the connection. But in England, at the top, there was irresolution. Ten years before, even Henry Fox had at last wished to see Chatham in power, on the ground that he was the only man who did not know what it was to want resolution. Now the country was caught in a war that its minister Lord North had never believed in, driven on by the stubbornness of the King and the country gentlemen.

All these currents and cross-currents came to a head in the next few years of continual crisis until peace was made and Chatham's son came into power to give the country a long period of stable government. We cannot go into these complexities or the issues here: only show how they affected this particular family, head of which was an intelligent man but afflicted with a paralysis of the will. As the crisis deepened he did not know where to turn – except to Moore for counsel.

Party-spirit had invaded both navy and army. In January 1779 the Admiralty, of which the wicked Lord Sandwich was head, precipitately ordered the court-martial of Admiral Keppel. This was widely unpopular in the country and with the mob – and Keppel was a Whig. On this issue Lord Charles disagreed with the First Lord and determined to resign. He carried his brother with him, for Walpole tells us that the Duke and Lord Pembroke declared against Sandwich.[32] Marlborough, sensitive as ever, was

31. Lecky, *History of England in the Eighteenth Century*, ed. cit., V. 5.
32. *The Letters of Horace Walpole*, X. 366.

now feeling qualms about the Court's proceedings and, fearful for his brother, forbade him to attend Parliament during the trial.[33] On Keppel's acquittal the London mob took a hand. They broke most of the windows in Grosvenor Square, where the Bishop's house was: Moore had to light four flambeaux before his house and he 'has just heard we must again tonight. . . . We must illuminate for fear.' The mob was by no means a quiescent animal in the eighteenth century: one might describe government as oligarchy tempered by mob-protest.

But the Duke would go no further. Lord Pembroke, who was heart and head with the Opposition, writes to his son: '*entre nous*, the D. of M. takes a very silly, indecisive part for which he gets abused, justly enough I must say though I am sorry for it, in the newspapers: at which he is very sore'.[34] In May we hear: 'Lord Charles Spencer has resigned his place at the Admiralty, because he cannot in honour, he says, sit with the First Lord. Out Twitcher must, and the strong strange protection he has in one place only makes it the more absolutely necessary.'[35] But the government did not break up, nor did he go; the King's protection kept him there till the end. The King minuted Lord Charles's desire to resign, that he ought to be given an equivalent employment of £1,500 a year and that the Duke should be written to on this.[36] In September the King favoured removing Lord Lyttelton from the Treasury, 'whose private character makes him no credit to my service. Lord Charles Spencer may be placed much to his mind and the Duke of Marlborough consequently pleased, who is certainly very deserving of it from an uniform conduct towards me ever since I have known him.'[37] In December Lord Charles got the appointment of Treasurer of the King's Chamber. Honour was satisfied.

The Marlboroughs had not broken with the government and Lady Pembroke had to defend her brother against her easily exasperated husband and her son. Like the loyal soul she was, she did her best for both sides.

33. *The Last Journals of Horace Walpole*, ed. A. F. Steuart, II. 230.
34. *The Pembroke Papers, 1734–1780*, 163.
35. ibid., 182. Jemmy Twitcher was, of course, Sandwich.
36. *Correspondence of King George III*, ed. cit., IV. 352.
37. ibid., 451.

Pray do not consider my brother Marlborough as a party man, for he is certainly not that; he may be wrong and I think he is, but is in no shape attached or partial to anyone in the present ministry, quite the contrary; but he has a worse opinion of some of the Opposition who would come in if these were out, and he thinks it is *they* who by distressing ministry have occasioned our misfortunes, more than the bad conduct of the ministry. I think he judges wrong, but you may depend upon it that that is the principle he acts upon.[38]

This was still, on balance, the judgement of the country.

In February 1780 Lord Pembroke resigned his Court appointment and the King dismissed him from the Lord-Lieutenancy of Wiltshire. He instructed Lord North that 'a civil communication should be made to the Duke of Marlborough that regard to him alone made me not remove his brother-in-law; but he having chosen to resign, I could not think it right to leave the Lieutenancy in his hands'.[39] The pull of his family away from the government put the Duke into a great state of mind. At the same time Lord Robert's financial difficulties – the result of his mania for gambling – resulted, like Fox's, in bankruptcy. In régard to both worries the Duke had resort to Moore, who addressed his longest and most interesting letter to the subject.

Moore never allowed himself to think of unpleasant circumstances until the matter was settled.

I am afraid that emphatical word *Fuss*, which your Grace uses, is not always confined to one side of the fire. Indeed if that word was struck out of the language or rather the thing itself turned out of the doors at Blenheim, I do think it would be the pleasantest place and the possessors of Blenheim would be the happiest persons in the world. But, alas, there is not resolution enough to resist his intrusions. In some shape or other he conveys himself into the house daily and hourly. If no visitor introduces him before dinner; if Mr Cole does not convey him into the house in the course of the day, still it is a hundred to one but he comes by the post and, seeing himself made so much of, it is no wonder that he is not in a hurry to quit the house.

38. *The Pembroke Papers, 1734–1780*, 366.
39. *Correspondence of King George III*, V. 17.

As to the Duke's anxiety about what line he should take towards the government:

when the judgement of his brothers and sisters is unprejudiced and dispassionate and their arguments are conclusive to his own unbiased judgement, that judgement being formed by the best information he can get, let him come into their sentiments and act accordingly. But I hope he will never give up his own understanding, nor abandon the respectable and manly character he maintains, to mere importunity and teasing. He will hold a very inferior rank in the minds of all men, if he should cease to support government because Lord Robert is the friend of Mr Charles Fox, or because Lord Pembroke is an enemy to the Administration – or because Lord Charles, with the best of hearts but a ductile mind, is now and then impressed strongly with the sentiments of warm party men with whom he lives in habits of friendship.

The Duke of Marlborough is the head of the family by birth and in parts has as good judgement as any of them. The Bishop sees nothing like perfection in the present Administration,

but have we another administration to look to of sounder hearts, or sounder heads? I don't see where it is to be found. . . .

As to the other points mentioned in your Grace's letter, the necessity of employment, society etc., I have stunned your ears and rung the changes upon them so often that I have been quite ashamed of myself. . . . The truth is the Duke of Marlborough need never want employment, nor either of your Graces society. But both will be wanted till the Duke resolves not to be afraid of a little employment and both your Graces resolve not to be afraid of society. At present the Duke uses himself to look too much at difficulties in everything that comes in the shape of employment, and I much fear that both your Graces would look upon it as a distress if four or five of the best friends you have in the world should be announced to you unexpectedly any day in the week. While this is the case you will never enjoy society as other people do. The same people are not the same thing to you as to others. They wish to be so, but they can't. They are *gênés*, because they see your Graces so, for there is no distemper more catching.

There is the whole position set out: the Bishop was a true confessor, and a very rational and sensible one. Here was the upshot of a too happy, too exclusive marriage upon over-refined, over-sensitive temperaments. The position was, in fact, beyond repair.

Lecky says that

> the aspect of affairs at the close of 1780 might indeed well have appalled an English statesman. Perfectly isolated in the world, England was confronted by the united arms of France, Spain, Holland and America; while the Northern league threatened her, if not with another war, at least with the annihilation of her most powerful weapon of offence. At the same time, in Hindostan, Hyder Ali was desolating the Carnatic and menacing Madras; and in Ireland the connection was strained to its utmost limit and all real power had passed into the hands of a volunteer force which was perfectly independent of the government and firmly resolved to remodel the constitution.[40]

Strangely enough, in this situation, at war with half the world, the country was not appalled. The tremendous struggle swung to and fro with varying fortunes. Gibraltar, surrounded on all sides and subjected to a terrific bombardment, refused to yield and held out unconquered to the end of the war. With the capture of St Eustatius, Rodney took one hundred and fifty merchantmen of all nations, enormous stores on the island and a Dutch merchant fleet to boot. In America Washington was anything but confident: he knew that it depended entirely on whether France made an effort large enough to turn the scales. At last she made a supreme effort: dispatched a fleet of twenty-five ships of the line under de Grasse, a convoy of between 200 and 300 ships, and 6,000 regular soldiers; enough to turn the scales and force Cornwallis to surrender at Yorktown, October 1781.

At home the country was turning against the government; the majority that had held firm so long was breaking up. George Selwyn reports to us the agitation in Parliament – and that Lord Robert, brought in by his brother the Duke, was voting against the government. The Duke says

> he cannot now give one third to his own younger children of what he has given to his two brothers, who have left him to be seduced by Charles Fox. Here is a Fox running off from Marlborough House a second time with their geese, as the old Duchess used to say.[41]

Early that year Lord Robert resigned from the Board of Trade – all for the misleading *beaux yeux* of Charles Fox.[42]

40. Lecky, *History*, V. 73–4. 41. *H.M.C.*, *Carlisle MSS.*, 754.
42. ibid., 454.

At the news of Yorktown Lord North, pacing up and down his dining-room, exclaimed, 'Oh God, it is all over!' It was with him, and the Whigs came in – led by Rockingham and Shelburne who had opposed the war all along – to end it, make the peace and introduce the reforms which were to diminish the influence of the King, and the number of placemen, in the Commons. One of the first places to go was that of Lord Charles at the Treasury. Shelburne took his interest under his wing, Rockingham Lord Robert's as a follower of Fox: the ministry was divided between these two sections. Shelburne wrote to Marlborough his regret that it was impossible to save Lord Charles and suggested, rather Jesuitically, to the King that he should express his regret to Lord Rockingham at Lord Charles's being left out of the government and his Majesty's great consideration for the Duke. Shelburne had already sounded the Duke whether he would accept the office of Groom of the Stole: he desired time to consider this.[43]

A few days later Shelburne announced his intention to tell the Duke

> as I have great facility with him, the pains I have taken to serve his brother and my wish that the Steward's staff should be offered to him in the handsomest manner, on account of his own importance as well as of your Majesty to whom I know he was always acceptable but must be particularly so in the present moment.

The King approved: 'Lord Shelburne's proposed language to the Duke of Marlborough is highly proper and will at least keep him right'.[44] Though Marlborough declined the office Shelburne gained his support by making it.[45]

The office Shelburne had in mind for Lord Charles was that of a Vice-Treasurer of Ireland; Rockingham had it in mind for Lord Robert. It became a tussle between these two principals. The proper thing to do was to submit the matter to the Duke and that meant calling in Moore. Lord Shelburne to the King:

> the Bishop of Bangor, whom I have seen three times and is this moment left me, has not been able to bring the Spencer family as yet to any good

43. *Correspondence of King George III*, V. 486, 494.
44. *The Last Journals of Horace Walpole*, ed. A. F. Steuart, II. 440.
45. *Correspondence of King George III*, VI. 19, 23.

understanding. In this situation, if I fail in all my endeavours and Lord Rockingham presses your Majesty further on the subject of Lord Robert Spencer, I would submit to your Majesty whether you would think it improper to mention to Lord Rockingham my claim in favour of Lord Charles Spencer, intimating as much as you think proper of your Majesty's own inclination, your dislike of competition among [*i.e.* within] the great families of your kingdom, and particularly the Spencer family on account of your Majesty's great regard and consideration of the Duke of Marlborough, and your desire that Lord Rockingham or Lord Shelburne should wait on the Duke of Marlborough to know his own mind in regard to his own family.[46]

William Eden considered this offer 'a very awkward and indelicate one. They should have found some other office for Lord Charles. The Duke leaves it to Lord Charles to decide as he likes.'[47]

Lord Rockingham, though a dying man, would not yield the point. The King: 'I feared Lord Rockingham would be obstinate as to Lord Robert Spencer, but Lord Shelburne has now put it into a train that will oblige the Duke of Marlborough, and that is what I wish may be effected by his knowing who are his friends and who are not'. In the last days before Lord Rockingham died Lord Robert got the appointment. A few days after Charles Fox left the government and Lord Robert with him. Shelburne, victorious, to the King, 9 July: 'Lord Robert Spencer having desired his resignation to be laid before your Majesty, I have taken the liberty to offer his employment to the Duke of Marlborough for Lord Charles Spencer'. The King: 'Lord Charles Spencer very properly succeeds his brother'.[48] It was the correct solution and in keeping with family etiquette for the much junior brother to yield to the senior. It does not seem to have led to any ill-feeling.

We see the amount of time and energy expended in this aristocratic age on places and pensions, providing for younger sons, the consideration for great families, keeping them sweet, keeping them together.

46. *Correspondence of King George III*, VI. 503, 504.
47. *Journal and Correspondence of Lord Auckland*, ed. by Bishop of Bath and Wells, I. 6.
48. *Correspondence of King George III*, VI. 24, 25, 77, 79.

Events did not stand still for these manoeuvres and petty disputes. It was conceded that the war was over in America, independence virtually recognized. In the last stages of the war, however, the island-power showed both toughness and resource. Rodney's great victory over a big French fleet at Les Saintes in the West Indies, with the destruction he wrought upon it, and the triumphant resistance to the last combined assault on Gibraltar, enabled peace to be discussed in a better atmosphere. Shelburne favoured the most generous concessions to the Americans – far more so than the French wished. The Peace of 1763 had recognized the country across the Great Lakes and to the Mississippi as forming part of Canada. Now Shelburne with his long-sighted vision of Anglo-American partnership was all in favour of handing over these vast interior territories to the new nation. In the last stages of the peace-preliminaries there came into being an understanding between English and Americans against the French – to the indignation of the latter who had bankrupted themselves in support of the American Revolution and were now on their way to a revolution of their own. Shelburne was bent on an English-speaking future for the North American continent; the new nation came into existence with many immediate difficulties but tremendous ultimate prospects.

That summer Bishop Moore had more business than usual, moving about his draughty diocese 'in spite of perpetual rains and such winds as one may pass a century at Blenheim without having any idea of'. He had received a letter from London which puzzled him exceedingly – from the First Minister. For once he asks their Graces' advice, whether to answer and, if so, how.

> 'Lord Shelburne presents his best compliments and many thanks to the Bishop of Bangor.' 'Thanks for what?' says the Bishop. 'Did your Lordship send him any Welsh mutton?' says the Chaplain. 'No such thing.' 'Did you write to him?' says Lady Eden. 'No, indeed, Madam.' 'Why,' says Mrs Moore, 'that's what he thanks you for, to be sure. He is tired to death of receiving letters and so thanks you for not sending any.'

The fact was that the Bishop was on the threshold of higher things.

In November, with the preliminaries of peace under discussion, he wrote to spur the Duke on to do his duty. 'The moment is indeed very critical: too important in my opinion for a man who has such a stature as yours in the country to allow himself to be absent from the great scene of business. I hope therefore your Grace is coming.' Marlborough's name was being once more brought forward for office. Lord Carlisle had resigned as Lord Steward and Shelburne thought of the Duke, but was apprehensive that he might hesitate, 'especially as there is no offering it to him except by letter'. The King:

after what passed last year on the subject of the Steward's staff, the Duke of Marlborough would have reason to be displeased with Lord Shelburne if it was not offered to him. I cannot see the smallest inconvenience to that being done by letter and think therefore Lord Shelburne ought immediately to write to him.[49]

Nothing came of this and, in any case, Shelburne was shortly after turned out of power – not by the King but by the majority of the House of Commons. It is difficult to understand the detestation with which this remarkable man – of political imagination and even vision, a genuine reformer, a man of ideas whose ideas were in line with the future – was regarded by everybody. *Everybody* hated Shelburne: one sympathizes with him. The fact was that, though a politician, he was not a professional: he was not one of them. Something of a doctrinaire who cared for ideas rather than men, he did not trust people and they did not trust him. A devious and secretive man, they called him 'the Jesuit of Berkeley Square'. 'It was strange,' said young Pitt's friend, Dundas, 'the impression entertained of Lord Shelburne's character, but it was so.'[50] The King bitterly resented his resignation: *he* had more nerve and would have faced it out. George III was even more furious at what took his place: the famous, and unprincipled, Coalition of Charles Fox with, of all people, Lord North.

Fox had spent the greater part of the American War – such time as he could spare from the gaming-table – in attacking Lord North and his policies with the utmost moral indignation.

49. *Correspondence of King George III*, VI. 232, 233.
50. q. Lecky, *History*, V. 219.

Fox, now the leader of Rockingham's Whig party, was a leading advocate of reform, the violent assailant of the royal power in politics; Lord North, its incarnation during twelve years of rule, representing all that the Foxites meant by corruption. The Coalition effected an astonishing, and rather shocking, transformation of the political scene; Fox himself said, with something of his father's cynical candour, 'Nothing but success can justify it.' And it looked certain to succeed, for it had an irresistible majority in the House.

For months George III tried to resist this servitude, tried to find someone who would undertake the government and deliver him from the yoke of Charles Fox. But the King could find no one willing and had to submit. At the end of the year Fox's India Bill gave him his chance. Fox, knowing that he could never win over the King, brought in a Bill which would have the effect of annexing the vast patronage of the reconstructed East India Company to the government and thereby make it independent of royal power, himself the arbiter. This roused the intense hostility of most of the East India interest in the City, increased the distrust of the unscrupulous Coalition in the country and gave the King his opening. Fox's Bill passed the Commons with large majorities, in spite of the antagonism it aroused outside. In the Lords the King let it be known that whoever voted for it he would regard as an enemy; and the measure was defeated. Having ascertained that Pitt was now prepared to form a government, considering in his strangely mature judgement that the moment was at last ripe, the King contemptuously dismissed the ministers, still in possession of their large majority in the Commons.

George III did all he could to strengthen the hands of the young minister fighting against such odds, and there is an interesting exchange of letters at Blenheim that illustrates the efforts he made. The King wrote from Windsor, 29 December 1783:

the Duke of Marlborough may be surprised at receiving this from me; but when he reflects on the personal regard I have uniformly expressed for him, which arises from the purity of his conduct and the attachment he has ever expressed for me, that will subside. The times are of the most serious nature, the political struggle is not as formerly between two factions for power, but it is no less than whether a desperate faction shall not reduce the Sovereign to a mere tool in its hands; though I have too much principle ever to infringe the rights of others yet that must ever equally prevent my submitting to the executive power being in any other hands than where the Constitution has placed it. I therefore must call on the assistance of every honest man and I trust the Duke of Marlborough will zealously engage his friends to support Government in the present most critical occasion. I know too well the Duchess of Marlborough is ever friendly to me and hope she will also warmly espouse my cause, which is indeed that of the Constitution as fixed at the Revolution and to the support of which my family was invited to mount the throne.[51]

The draft of the Duke's reply from Blenheim the same day confesses that he did not see the East India Bill in a dangerous light: he thought that it was calculated rather to increase than diminish the power of the Crown or he should not have given his proxy in support of it. He hopes to pay his duty to the King in London in a week or ten days and wishes he may be able in the meantime to find out the best method of doing what he can for the King's service, but confesses that at the present moment he does not well know how to set about it.

It does not need any special knowledge of the Duke's peculiar style to perceive that this was a polite negative to the King's request: the Marlboroughs were with the Fox–North Coalition.

Fox could at first hardly take the youngster's government seriously and was convinced that the Coalition must necessarily return in a short time to power. Amongst the many failings of this all too human person was that he was always too sanguine. Another, that was fatal for a political leader – and all the stranger in a man of such gifts and power of personality – was shocking bad judgement. He declared against a Dissolution and proceeded to hold up government. This played straight into the hands of his young rival, who in the epic struggle that ensued never made a single mistake of tact or judgement, never allowed himself to be daunted in debate night after night, though he was the only member of his Cabinet there to face the combined eloquence and onslaughts of all the leading parliamentary figures in coalition against him. Meanwhile opinion was turning in his favour in the

51. Blenheim MSS., E 62.

country: he would wait, give Fox all the time he needed to destroy himself.

The line the Opposition took was that Pitt's government had come into being in contravention of constitutional principles. In fact the constitutional position at this time was that the King could call in what ministers he chose – it was for them to survive – and Pitt consistently asserted what could not be denied to be the royal prerogative. The Opposition brought forward a series of resolutions, meanwhile holding up government, which was virtually at a standstill. On 16 January 1784 Lord Charles Spencer was put up to move the resolution that the continuance of the ministers in office was contrary to constitutional principles.[52] He apologized for want of the habit of speaking in that House (after a membership of twenty-three years!) and for a natural timidity in that respect. He proposed a vote of no confidence in the present administration. By what arts they still maintained their situation he knew not; certain it was that when his Majesty was convinced that the House of Commons could not confide in the present ministers he would that instant withdraw his confidence from them. His resolution followed naturally on those to which the House had already agreed, namely that 'the appointment of his Majesty's present ministers was accompanied by circumstances new and extraordinary and such as do not conciliate or engage the confidence of this House'.

The resolution was carried against the government by 205 to 184; but his Majesty was not convinced.

This led to another exchange between King and Duke. The very morning after the debate the Duke wrote from Marlborough House that

> he has felt himself much distressed lest your Majesty should have thought him unmindful of the commands laid upon him in your Majesty's letter of 29 December last. . . . He has found it impracticable in the present posture of things to obey your Majesty's commands to their full extent. He begs leave nevertheless to assure your Majesty that his friends and some of their friends are cordially disposed not only to check violent measures but to use their best endeavours to promote a moderate spirit in these turbulent times . . . and although the Duke of

52. *Parliamentary History of England* (ed. Cobbett), XXIV. 359–60.

Marlborough cannot help thinking that in the present state of things it would contribute to the ease of your Majesty's mind and to the strength of government that the fermentation now subsisting should be brought to some crisis, yet he must assure your Majesty in justice to himself that the motion made by one of his brothers yesterday in the House of Commons was agreed to in a hurry by Lord Charles Spencer himself when it was proposed to him and earnestly requested by some of your Majesty's late servants and this in a great measure proceeded from Lord Charles Spencer's ignorance of your Majesty's late gracious communication of your wishes to the Duke of Marlborough, which the Duke of Marlborough had not yet thought himself at liberty to disclose to his brother. The Duke of Marlborough implores your Majesty's forgiveness if anything should have dropped from his pen which may not be perfectly pleasing to your Majesty, flattering himself if that should be the case that your Majesty will impute the fault to his head and not to his heart.

This language of almost Oriental courtesy does not conceal that there had been an explanation between the brothers, that Charles had been caught on the hop by Charles Fox, probably at Brooks's, and told off to move the resolution, without time to consider the Duke's position.

The King replied the same day from the Queen's House, now Buckingham Palace, with equal politeness but more robustly:

The Duke of Marlborough's stating his ignorance of Lord Charles Spencer's intention of moving the resolution of last night I look upon as a fresh mark of his attachment; but I should have done great injustice either to his head or heart if I could have harboured such an opinion. So strong a measure can hurt none but the promoters of it, as it must open the eyes of all moderate men as to their intentions.

Pitt held on with unshaken tenacity throughout these months. Lecky is right in saying that there is nothing in English parliamentary history more wonderful than the fight he put up. He showed that he possessed all his father's indomitable political courage and much more sense. All the time, like his father, he had his eye on opinion outside the House. The night came when he had worn down the Opposition's immense majority to one, and when he had got the necessary business through the Commons he did not hesitate any longer to seek a Dissolution. Nothing was neglected in the appeal to the country, no chances lost. John Robinson summed up the prospects.[53] The Duke of Marlborough had five seats at his disposal. At Woodstock 'probably the Duke of Marlborough will again return the same members'. He returned one of the two members for the county of Oxford, one for the city and one for Heytesbury. No money would pass in this case.[54] Lord Charles, like the Duke, was something of a waverer: Robinson, writing before the change of government, said that he 'is now *con* as in office, but on a change would be *for*'. But he was wrong in this forecast; nor did the Duke make any move till later. In January 1784 the Duke of Dorset had written to Lord Sackville: 'the Duke of Newcastle and the Duke of Marlborough are both come over and Robinson says *it will do*'.[55] It did. The Opposition went to the constituencies fore-doomed to ruin and were utterly shattered. A hundred and sixty of their members were driven out of Parliament. The nation had found in Chatham's son a leader, and a long period of stable government ensued under his direction.

In the interval between Shelburne's resignation and the Fox–North Coalition coming in, the King had made Moore Archbishop of Canterbury. With his conscientious desire to get the best man instead of a party-appointee the King had offered it to the two most distinguished prelates in the Church, Bishops Lowth and Hurd, both of whom refused and concurred in recommending Moore as the man. The King communicated his nomination first to Marlborough as a mark of favour.

The Duke of Marlborough will, I am certain, receive the intelligence of my having just wrote to Lord Sydney that the *congé d'élire* and recommendatory letter to the Chapter of Canterbury in favour of the

53. *The Parliamentary Papers of John Robinson, 1774–1784*, ed. W. T. Laprade (Camden Soc.), 52, 69, 88, 109.

54. By contrast with Cornish borough-owners, who would receive an average of £3,000 a seat; *e.g.* Lord Edgcumbe for 6 seats £18,000, Sir Francis Basset for 5 seats £12,000, Lord Falmouth for 3 seats £9,000, Mr Eliot, it is supposed, £10,000 (he got a peerage into the bargain), Mr Buller £6,000, Mr Praed £35,000.

55. *H.M.C.*, *Stopford Sackville MSS.*, I. 84.

Bishop of Bangor be prepared. I hope the Duke will acquaint the Bishop that he must kiss hands tomorrow.[56]

With this appointment the former tutor now takes precedence of the Duke. In the next few years Moore's correspondence with the Duchess flags: no doubt he had plenty to do on becoming Archbishop of Canturbury. Then, too, there were the domestic duties of a family man. Moore had married again, into the up-and-coming Eden family. The day comes when he has to inform the Duchess that Mrs Moore is brought to bed – hardly a suitable item of news, one feels somehow, from Lambeth.

Politics over, polite exchanges continue, on the gilt-edged writing paper used by these eighteenth-century grandees, between the Marlboroughs and the royal family. The Duchess was still breeding and old Princess Amelia, George III's aunt, stood sponsor for their last child. Courtesies now pass between members of the next generation. The Princess Royal – a Charlotte Augusta Matilda – writes to the Duchess,

as you expressed to Mama last night a desire of seeing some of my poor performances, I beg that you will accept of the etchings that accompany this note, which I feel the more ashamed of sending you since Mama has been so good as to indulge me with the sight of some beautiful drawings which Lady Caroline and Lady Elizabeth made her a present of some time ago.

Then there was a dreadful rumour that a royal visit to Blenheim was intended. It did not take place that autumn but materialized in the summer of 1786, when the King and Queen paid a visit to Oxford. The Duke was thrown into a state of agitation and had to be led firmly up to the hurdle by Archbishop Moore. He had heard at the Drawing Room that they were going to Lord Harcourt on Saturday and were not to return until Tuesday. Oxford would take a day and 'if proper invitation is given, Blenheim another at least'. Moore urges that

nobody has so fine a family in so fine a place to show and my lord Duke will be amply paid for all his misgivings on the occasion by the reflection that what is done is right and that the omission would scarcely be doing

56. Blenheim MSS., E 62.

justice to his family or himself, and certainly condemned by the world, as well as crossing the reasonable expectations of the Royal Family. Long deliberation won't do – your first thoughts will deserve to be followed by immediate act; and I am sure you will all think it right when over.[57]

Thus firmly propelled, the invitation was given. An attempt had recently been made on the King's life, so that the royal visit to loyal Oxford took place in an atmosphere of emotionalism that was more characteristic of the Regency. The Duke, as High Steward of the university, received the royal family in the Sheldonian – Miss Burney discreetly in attendance, noting it all down.[58] A loyal Address was read, the Princesses wept, there were tears in even Queen Charlotte's eyes, hardly a dry eye in the Sheldonian. There was much kissing the King's hand, old dons who couldn't get up from their knees, others who tried to walk backward and fell down, the mix-up and general confusion one knows so well on these occasions.

Next for Blenheim. The Duchess reports to Moore:

Considering the shortness of the notice, it all went off very well. They stayed here from eleven till six. We had breakfast for them in the Library and, after they returned from seeing the park, some cold meats and fruit. Lord and Lady Harcourt told us we were to sit as lord and lady of the Bedchamber all the time they stayed here; and poor Lord Harcourt seemed quite happy to be able to rest himself, the Duke of Marlborough found him sitting down behind every door where he could be concealed from royal eyes. We were just an hour going over the principal floor as they stopped and examined *everything in every room*; and we never sat down during that hour or indeed very little but while we were in the carriages, which fatigued me more than anything else. Lord Harcourt told the Duke of Marlborough that he had been full-dressed in a bag and sword every morning since Saturday; but the Duke of Marlborough could not follow his example in that, as he had no dress-coat or sword in the country. He desires me to tell you that he had no misgivings. All the apprehensions were on my side. Nobody could do the thing better or more thoroughly than he did.[59]

57. Blenheim MSS., E 60.
58. *Diary and Letters of Madame d'Arblay*, ed. Austin Dobson, II. 466.
59. J. H. Jesse, *Memoirs of the Life and Reign of George III*, III. 7.

The King was very much taken with everything and his comment, 'We have nothing equal to this', very gracious. King and Duke shared a keen interest in astronomy, which was becoming an obsession with Marlborough: he was fitting up one of Vanbrugh's towers as an observatory. At the end of August George III wrote,

> the Duke of Marlborough is so skilful and practised an astronomer that I am happy in having got Dr Herschel to complete the 10 ft telescope so soon after his return from Germany. I can answer for the excellency of this instrument, having twice compared it with the one in my possession and indeed sent the one that proved the most perfect.

Family man spoke to family man: 'I am certain the Duke, who is a tender father, will share in my joy at my third daughter being totally now without complaint'.[60]

Next year there was talk of another royal visit to Blenheim and the Duke wrote expressing his apprehensions to the Archbishop. The Duchess was unwell. It would be too much. It did not take place.

In 1788 the correspondence picks up briskly with the King's madness. Moore keeps the Marlboroughs regularly posted down at Blenheim. But we have a nearer source of information in the diary of one of the King's equerries in attendance on him.[61] Years of overstrain and overwork, of incessant anxiety and exertion of the will, the terrible burden of the American War and carrying Lord North with it, the political agitations that followed and now the private, or all too public, worries of the way his son the Prince of Wales was going – all told on him, until a slight breakdown of his usual good physical health caused a complete mental collapse. What made him so pathetic a figure was that from time to time he came to his senses and realized what had overtaken him. With the contradictoriness common in such states he abused Pitt and called Fox his friend. The most chaste of men, he began to lust after Lady Pembroke – which was more than Lord Pembroke did: with him, almost anyone rather than his wife . . . after later escapades than Kitty Hunter, she had at

60. Blenheim MSS., E 62.

61. *The Dairies of Robert Fulke Greville*, ed. F. M. Bladon, cf. 139, 162, 165, 167, 170, 188, etc.

length parted from him and was living contentedly on her own in Richmond Park.

In December Colonel Greville writes of the King: 'in his more disturbed hours he has for some time past spoke much of Lady Pembroke. This evening he recollected what he had at times said of her . . . he very feelingly said to one of his pages, he hoped nobody knew what wrong ideas he had had and what wrong things he had said respecting her.' But he went on talking about her and against the Queen. Sometimes he called her Esther and sometimes Queen Elizabeth. In mid-January he had to be put into a strait-jacket. He was talking of Lady Pembroke under the name of Minerva. 'While playing at piquet he distinguishes her by the Queen of Hearts, kissing it whenever he saw it. This evening he had the King of Hearts himself and said, "Oh, if the Queen of Hearts would fall to the King".' He said he meant to visit Richmond Park and thought that the Queen had consented that Lady Pembroke should see him. Then, recovering a little, he asked for release from his jacket, promising 'he would try all he could to be quiet, which was all a man could do'.

He talked a good deal in German, and in lucid intervals would read Shakespeare and Gray's *Elegy*, pathetically pulling down the long sleeves of his strait-jacket 'to tell his situation to all the world'. He knew that Langley was at this time for sale and often talked of purchasing it for his Eliza. He called the chair of coercion he was sometimes confined in the 'Coronation chair', and prayed that he had left undone those things which he ought to have done and done those things he ought not to have done, asking that God would be pleased to restore him to his senses or permit that he might die directly. When he was somewhat better he would himself put on the jacket and help with the long sleeves sadly.

These months were a time of intense political crisis. For the second time in his career Pitt showed that he had the highest political courage – and again that his judgement was not at fault. Fox made the cardinal mistake of claiming an inherent right on the part of his crony the Prince to succeed as Regent with all the prerogatives of the King. It was understood that in these circumstances the Regent would call on Fox at once to form a government.

But the circumstances never became ripe. By the end of February the King was recovering. Early in March the Duke spent half an hour with him one morning; the King recognized this kindness with the gift of an astronomical watch. Marlborough told his protégé Eden, who had just been rewarded by Pitt with a peerage, 'I behaved like a fool twice whilst I was with him, but the account of his feelings etc. moved me so much that I could not help it, and he took it very kindly and was a good deal affected himself.'[62] One day the King was out walking along the terrace at Kew when the boatmen on the river caught sight of him and shouted 'God bless your Majesty', and 'Glad to see you abroad again'. The King was much touched by their kindness and good feeling; he took off his hat to them and bowed. Soon the round of audiences and incessant business began once more. He returned to his favourite brisk 'What! What! What!' – Horace Walpole called it 'coming to his nonsense'. But when he went to St Paul's to give thanks for his recovery, it was evident that his people had at length taken him to their hearts. It was George III's madness that made him popular with the English.

At Blenheim the children were growing up, on the threshold of their entry into the world; in the background – or rather in the foreground now at Lambeth – there was Moore, willing as ever with counsel and more practical help over this generation as he had been with their parents and all along. He was an elderly man now, but in a position to advance the interests of his old friends' children.

Nothing much could be done with Blandford, though he was not without talent. Indeed a marked vein of talent appeared in both these generations, as it had not done in the previous one, that of Sarah's grandchildren – to her intense annoyance. This young Blandford was at Eton during the years of the American War, 1776 to 1783. When he left the Duke sent him to Paris for three or four months with a tutor, Mr Hind. 'What a man to

62. *Journal and Correspondence of Lord Auckland*, ed. cit., II. 300–301. The Duke assured the new Lord Auckland that he would have been very welcome to take Woodstock for his title, but that the Duke of Portland had got that.

send,' wrote Lord Herbert to Coxe, 'a very good scholar, a very good University tutor, but totally ignorant of any modern language except his own mother tongue and as ignorant to the world. What strange people they are!'[63] It did not answer and Moore was called in to advise. He thought they should come home: 'two or three months more abroad can produce no material improvement. They will be thrown away at best. When he comes home your Graces will consider whether he shall go to Oxford or abroad.'[64] The Duke replied with a fine haunch of venison, which came very conveniently for a New Year's dinner at Lambeth. The young man was sent to Christ Church, where no doubt he enjoyed himself.

The hopes of the family rested on the second son, Henry, who was a clever boy of much promise. At Eton he was, with Canning and Hookham Frere, one of the founders of *The Microcosm*, earliest and most famous of school periodicals. At Christ Church he was again with Canning, and one of a group of young men of brilliant promise who came under the celebrated Dean Cyril Jackson. To all the family charm – and family reserve and shyness – he added a keen wit and precocious ability. He was marked out for diplomacy, and one cannot but think that it was old Moore who marked him out. For he was brought into the foreign service under the wing of Moore's brother-in-law, the very able administrator William Eden, now Lord Auckland. Eden was an Eton and Christ Church man who had come into Parliament under the patronage of the Duke, who returned him to Parliament as one of his members for Woodstock from 1774 to 1784 and for Heytesbury in the election that confirmed Pitt in his tenure of power. Eden, in conformity with the Marlboroughs, had belonged to the Fox grouping, their sympathies inclining them to the Opposition. Eden went over to Pitt and a good thing he made of it; for Pitt was anxious to recruit young men of ability and used Eden's capacities to the full to negotiate the commercial treaty with France and subsequently in diplomacy. No doubt it was through this connection that Moore made his Eden marriage. We see how these things tie up so nicely for those who are in the swim and know how to.

63. *The Pembroke Papers, 1780–1794*, 217. 64. Blenheim MSS., E 60.

In January 1789 Lord Henry gratified the Archbishop and Mrs Moore with his company: 'his goodness and good nature, and mild and unassuming manners will make him most acceptable and contribute much to his happiness in any situation he can be placed in'. Right again: they did. The Archbishop would be delighted to have him any time he was in town on business: 'we are almost as near the Secretary of State's office as Marlborough House is'. Lord Henry was on his way abroad to equip himself by a foreign tour. On his return the Archbishop offered him an apartment at Lambeth if he came to town alone. But he hoped that the Marlboroughs would come.

In answer to the Duke's question 'How shall we keep up the acquaintance with Mr Pitt?' – nothing is more easy. You have only to give him a dinner or two and make the *entrée* of Marlborough House easy and familiar to him when you come to stay in town. He said a great deal to me about his visit at Blenheim, much of the splendour of the place and more of the family.

This is all we know of a visit by Pitt to Blenheim; for all the Archbishop's bolstering up morale it is unlikely that the Duke got round to being familiar with Mr Pitt.

But Lord Henry was safely launched: he was to go abroad as secretary to Lord Auckland, ambassador to the Netherlands, where the young man, left in charge of the embassy at a critical time, had a resounding success. Now in December 1789 he was to kiss hands on his appointment. The Duke of Leeds was awaiting instructions as to presenting him, 'which his Grace's relationship and office seem to me to point out as particularly proper'.[65] If Lord Blandford is to be presented at the same time the Archbishop will be very happy to present him. (No amount of kissing hands would do him any good.)

Now the Duchess has a favour to ask of his Grace, on behalf of the Dowager Lady Clifden, mother-in-law of her dearest Caroline, who wants a presentation to a living. The Archbishop promises to favour this request as soon as it is in his power.

65. The Duke of Leeds was the son of Henrietta Churchill's daughter, Lady Mary Godolphin, and was therefore a cousin; *v. The Early Churchills*, 406.

This very choosey young woman, Lady Caroline, had already rejected first the heir to the Duke of Sutherland and then the heir to the Earl of Pembroke before finally deciding on Lord Clifden. In the first case she was so late in discovering that she did not love the young man enough to marry him that her wedding clothes were already bought, the settlements completed and her lover was at Blenheim to execute them.[66] The Duke was much vexed. When her cousin Lord Herbert fell in love with her, the Duchess had to tell him 'that she is much obliged to you for the favourable opinion you have of her, but that she cannot either now or hereafter comply with your proposal, though she agrees with the Duke of Marlborough and myself in having a thorough good opinion of your character'.[67] Lord Herbert could not give up the thought of her so easily: Uncle Charles was called in to see what he could do. He reports to the poor young man,

> I am grieved that I have nothing good to tell you; I have talked a great deal upon the subject, first with my brother and the Duchess together, then with her separately for a very long time, and what is more to the purpose I have talked for a good half hour with Caroline alone: the result of which was that she hoped you would drop all thoughts of the business, for that though she has an exceeding good opinion of you and is far from any dislike to you, yet she has not that *kind* of *liking* for *you*, without which she is determined not to marry any man. . . . As this is the case, forget her as soon as you can; it is quite surprising to me how she could refuse you, but there is no accounting for the fancies that are in the world.[68]

Lady Caroline found the man for whom she could have that kind of liking in Lord Clifden, whom she married in 1792. It took Lord Herbert six years before he could find somebody else to his liking – and then it was another cousin, daughter of Lady Di Beauclerk. The next sister, Elizabeth, found happiness in marrying her cousin John, Uncle Charles's eldest son, at Wheatfield. The third daughter, Charlotte, went further even than her aunt, Lady Di, in the matrimonial handicap. She was very good at the amateur theatricals, which passed the time agreeably that went so

66. *Journal and Correspondence of Lord Auckland*, I. 24.
67. *The Pembroke Papers, 1780–1794*, 314.
68. *The Pembroke Papers, 1780–1794*, 316.

slow at Blenheim.[69] One April day in 1797 she put on a surprising performance of her own: she went off with an Oxford don.

Time indeed went slow over those slopes, to Vanbrugh's bridge and up to the Victory Column, over lake and parkland and pasture, in the last decades of those long lives while Mr Pitt ruled and the country was once more at war, the never-ending struggle with Revolutionary France and Napoleon. Not much changed in that household in the grip of a lethargy so deep it might be inhabited by a Sleeping Prince and Princess under their gathered towers beside the lake. Taxes went up: Mr Pitt's new taxes upon menservants, on horses and carriages, houses and windows – there were hundreds of windows in Blenheim.[70] Costs went up; servants' liveries, from Scarpelain and McCarty, consumed £166 a year[71].

One summer evening in 1790 the Marlboroughs arrived on ancient Horace Walpole at Strawberry Hill: 'the sun being setting and the moon not risen, you may judge how much they could see through all the painted glass by twilight'.[72] Once before they had been unlucky in going to breakfast there with Horace, for it 'rained the whole time with an Egyptian darkness'.[73]

The Duke and Duchess still went to Bath in the autumn, to Brighthelmstone for the season. Their summer there in 1795 cost them £839 18s. 7½d.: many gratuities to the Rector, Sunday school, the woman that keeps the church tower; to a French prisoner, a puppet-show man, musicians on the Steyne; for servants to the plays, hot and cold baths, sea-water, fruits, a pianoforte – the world of the Regency approaching.[74] The day came, the summer of 1802, when they decided they would go no more to Brighton, and the Prince wrote 'should this really be so, after having for so many years had such very agreeable neighbours I could not bear the thoughts of having anybody else so very near me' – would they favour him with their preference as a

69. Sprightly William Coxe said that life there was '*ennui* itself'. ibid., 152.
70. Taxes on the establishment at Blenheim amounted to £340 1s. 5¼d., in 1794.
71. ibid., F I. 52.
72. *Letters of Horace Walpole*, XIII. 164.
73. ibid., XIV. 261.
74. Blenheim MSS., F I. 57.

purchaser?[75] Marlborough House too was a burden, with the taxes upon it. Before the end it was let to the Princess Charlotte and Prince Leopold – the Duke no longer subscribed his guinea for watering the Mall in summer. On his death it would revert to the Crown.

News of the war sometimes penetrated the gathering silence. The Archbishop communicated the news of the victory of the Nile and of its effect on the lower sort. 'They are always captivated with bravery and success', he wrote.[76] Thousands who were disaffected were made friends to government by this victory. Last year when Mr Pitt dined in the City he had to change his carriage for security; this year the horses were taken out and his carriage drawn in triumph by the very mob who would have pulled him to pieces – *varium et mutabile vulgus*. Such was Georgian England. But when the victor of the Nile himself turned up with Emma and Sir William Hamilton on a July day in 1802, during the peace – as sooner or later everybody did turn up to see Blenheim – it was more than the Duke could do to summon up the spirit to receive him. 'After a lengthy pause, refreshments in the park for Lord Nelson and friends were announced', wrote a Woodstock cleric – to be refused with indignation. The questionable trio were mightily offended, but Lady Hamilton's 'superior mind' rose to the occasion. She said that if Marlborough's services had been rewarded with Blenheim it was because a woman had then reigned and 'women have great souls': if she were queen, Nelson should have had a principality such that Blenheim Park would be only a kitchen garden to it.[77] The hero with the woman's sensibility was mollified and touched to tears.

Old friends were dropping away: in 1804 Jacob Bryant, full of years and smug contentment, of his conversations with the royal family, of being introduced to Mr Pitt on the Terrace at Windsor, his great neighbours in spirits with all the reviews and galas. Next year, the year of Trafalgar, died that other tutor and friend of the family, old Moore, Archbishop of Canterbury. Carefully folded away by the Duchess in the archives at Blenheim among the news-

75. Blenheim MSS., E 62.
76. ibid., E 61.
77. E. Marshall, *The Early History of Woodstock, Supplement*, 45–6.

paper cuttings recording these faithful lives are others, of which she was evidently not less proud, tributes to her and the Duke's charity and goodness to the poor of Woodstock over many years, the continual happiness he and she reaped from the 'pleasing domestic scene', his 'probity and disinterested justice in public life, benevolence and conjugal affection in domestic retirement'. She herself built the almshouses for poor widows one sees along the road into Woodstock – plain, decent Georgian buildings in honey-coloured Blenheim stone beside the East gate. Then, rendered unhappy by the character, the scrapes, the extravagance of her eldest son, full of foreboding for the future, in 1811 she died.

The Duke retired further than ever into himself, into his passion for astronomy, communing with the stars. There are pages and pages of astronomical calculations, corrected by Dr Hornsby, Savilian Professor at Oxford, with a paper of the Duke on the Harvest Moon.[78] Nothing disturbed the silence – until one day on the announcement that clamouring at the gate to get in was the famous, the aggressive, the intolerable Madame de Staël, the Duke broke out to his astonished attendants with 'Take me away! Oh, take me away!'

It was his last recorded utterance. When he died in 1817 a great change came over Blenheim.

78. Blenheim MSS., F I. 44 and 45 contain these. It may be said that the Duke's election as Fellow of the Royal Society in 1786 was rather more appropriate than that of his ancestor Sir Winston Churchill. He presented the university with a large telescope, as well as a number of paintings.

Chapter 6

Whig Frolics

FROM the seventeen-eighties onwards one discerns a new tone, a new spirit abroad in society, and with the coming of age of the Prince of Wales this found its leader at once glamorous and questionable. As Edwardian society took shape long before the end of Victoria's reign, so we see Regency society coming into being, with all its fruity characteristics, and taking possession of the scene years before the Prince became Regent. The keynote of his world was a somewhat promiscuous joyousness; its characteristics a taste running to fantasy, sentiment and sensibility that easily overflowed into insincerity, an attention to fashion and the *chic* that was yet spontaneous and unselfconscious, a lack of self-control, an extravagance that went with chronic indebtedness. In the highest ranks of this society one wasn't quite sure who slept with whom or who was whose child – as Lord Melbourne said, 'Who the devil knows who one's father is, anyway?' (his own father was probably not Lord Melbourne but Lord Egremont); illegitimacy ran riot; a fine old time was had by (almost) all. It was like the Restoration come again; the *beau monde* shaded off into the *demi-monde*.

All this was in marked contrast to the domestic life of the dear King and to no small extent in direct reaction to his dull, economical, restrictive virtues. There was much shaking of heads in the royal circle and among respectable persons like Archbishop Moore and his elderly friends at the capers and the behaviour of the younger generation. But there was nothing they could do about it, except tighten the reins financially and shorten the allowances – and then the young men piled up mountains of indebtedness on their expectations. Before George III's heir became Regent he had accumulated debts amounting to £630,000 – and some £160,000 had once before been met.[1] Before Marlborough's heir succeeded as fifth Duke, his father had tried

1. Roger Fulford, *George IV*, 49, 78.

keeping him short: the young Marquis simply borrowed at outrageous interest on his expectations – and there was no Parliament to meet his indebtedness.

Respectability, and his troubles, had endeared George III to the heart of the English middle class. Nothing about the Prince Regent endeared him to that great organ, for there was nothing about him that was quite respectable: neither his morals nor his politics, his marriage nor his finances, his companionships nor his taste. Perhaps it was his taste that offended most: it was so shockingly regardless of what they chiefly valued, decorum, running as it did to the Oriental fantasy, the minarets, domes and turrets, the lacquer and gilt of the Brighton Pavilion. A Regency poet wrote:

> In Xanadu did Kubla Khan
> A stately pleasure-dome decree;

another Regency artist called into being an evocation of those lines, in bricks and mortar, by the seashore at Brighton. (The irreverent Sidney Smith said it was as if the dome of St Paul's had gone down by the sea and pupped.)

Within was the exquisite gilt dolphin furniture, all curves and plush and fish-tails; the pretty wall-papers patterned like muslin, festooned and wreathed; the Chinese screens and lanterns, the corridors lighted behind coloured glass; the tented ceilings from which hung astonishing chandeliers like Oriental fruits dropping succulently above the guests feasting off the gold plate Parliament had ultimately to pay for. At Carlton House was the ebony furniture for which the Regent had a fancy, the magnificent collection of snuff-boxes and *étuis* that now adorns Buckingham Palace. There was his patronage of artists, of the brilliant, too scintillating Lawrence; his purchase of the Dutch pictures that are now a glory of the royal collections; his admiration for Walter Scott and Miss Austen – a set of whose novels appeared chastely among the more exotic ornaments (and personages) in each of his residences.

It was the personality above all, the character, that counted. Along with the feeling, the aesthetic sensibility, there was a levity, an absence of *suite* that gave the tone to so much of his doings and made him a figure of fun. There was the utter disregard of money in reaction from the economy of his father, the lack of any self-control, the romantic fantasy ministered to by such spirits as Sheridan and Lawrence, Nash and Wyatt, that announced a new age. His life was a romantic extravaganza; his personality well summed up by Wellington, 'the most extraordinary compound of talent, wit, buffoonery, obstinacy and good feeling – in short a medley of the most opposite qualities with a great preponderance of good – that I ever saw in my life'.[2] The preponderant good, however, was apt to be nullified in other people's opinions by the fact that the First Gentleman of Europe was also a good deal of a cad. Of course he was a German, and all his characteristics were German: place him beside those subjects who made the glory of his age and rule – Wellington and Nelson, Pitt and Fox, Wordsworth and Scott – and one sees the difference. Like many Germans who are good-looking in youth, he grew gross when old.

However, he had the vitality and the gifts to set the tone to the society of his day and for his extravagance we have at least something to show – the fantasy of the Pavilion at Brighton, the skyline of Windsor with all its gathered towers and battlements, the fragments left of his splendid conception of the West End of London from Carlton Terrace, up the Quadrant through Regent's Street to the grandeur of Regent's Park, however much fractured and fissured by the combined Philistinism and squalor of later times.

Such was the background to our story.

Of Marlborough's brothers and sisters, Diana and Robert were prominent figures in the social life of their time, and they were much the closest together of the family. Diana's contribution was the more valuable and idiosyncratic, for she became an accomplished artist. In her art all the charm that was in this family achieved a most appealing form; while its characteristic notes – gaiety, enjoyment of life, naturalness and fantasy, all in a

2. q. *The Journal of Mrs Arbuthnot*, ed. F. Bamford and the Duke of Wellington, xv.

feminine key – made it a no less authentic expression of the society they created and lived in.

After her deliverance by divorce from what she called Court-slavery, Lady Diana, through her new husband, Topham Beauclerk, became free of the society of the most gifted men of the time – Johnson and Gibbon, Reynolds, Garrick, Horace Walpole, Charles Fox. It was a profitable exchange for the conversation of Queen Charlotte, the life of boredom and thraldom that wore down the sprightly Fanny Burney. Not that Diana had not a good deal to put up with from Topham. As sometimes happens with men of extreme charm, he had a corresponding vein of cruelty in him, and this came to be exacerbated by many illnesses through which Diana dutifully nursed him. Like his great-grandfather, Charles II, he was dissolute. 'The moral, pious Johnson and the gay, dissipated Beauclerk were companions,' said Boswell. 'What a coalition! I shall have my old friend to bail out of the Round House,' said Garrick. Beauclerk was one of those handsome men who do not like washing; when the Beauclerks went to stay at Blenheim the very correct Duchess complained that 'his habits were beyond what one could have thought possible in anyone but a beggar or a gipsy'.[3]

Topham could plead the excuse of being a bibliophile. He collected an immense library; when he added on a room to his house in Great Russell Street to hold it, Horace Walpole said that it reached half-way to Highgate. There was no doubt about the charm; one sees it in his pleasant threat to the Earl of Charlemont, if he won't come over from Dublin, to bring over all the Club upon him in Ireland: 'Johnson shall spoil your books, Goldsmith pull your flowers and Boswell talk to you'.[4] (What would one not give for half an hour of such company?) Neither of the Beauclerks had any idea of money, and Diana was always busy, always in a hurry. From Bath she ends a letter, 'part of this letter was dictated by Mr Wade; part by my footman; part by my maid; which makes an agreeable mixture of style: I hope you like it'.[5]

Well-off as Topham was – his father had been a shameless

3. Mrs Steuart Erskine, *Lady Diana Beauclerk*, 116.
4. ibid., 125.
5. ibid.,164

captator, a legacy-hunter – the day came when he needed money so badly that he mortgaged his library to the Duke for £5,000. On his death in 1780 the sale lasted forty-nine days and each day the money was paid over to the Duke: it totalled £5,011.[6] Diana was forced to resort to her brother for cash; but in contrast to his earlier open-handedness, she complained that he did not omit to take interest on it and dunned her when she had not five guineas in her purse.

Quit of men at last she was free to deploy her own talents, to develop her remarkable gift as a painter. She had a house at Twickenham, near Horace Walpole, Little Marble Hill – lawns sloping down to the river, garden designed by Pope; and there she proceeded to decorate the rooms in her own delightful festive style. Old Horace grew lyrical about her work, and her. One room was festooned with lilac painted on a pale green background; geranium, ivy, periwinkle in the panels at the base. Horace wrote a poem about it. He describes for us another room painted with honeysuckle wreathed round children – Diana adored children, her art, like her life, came to be designed round them: 'there is a baby Bacchus, so drunk! and so pretty! borne in triumph by Bacchanalian children'.

Nearly all her decorative work has perished with the houses she decorated; but her pastel portraits remain, her water-colours and designs for ceilings, illustrations for books, Wedgwood china plates and jars. For she was a prolific artist, quick at expressing herself with spontaneity and freshness, a natural distinction. From her treatment of landscape, especially her trees, we see that she had studied Gainsborough, and from her children, Romney. She delighted in the rose-pink and pale blues of the Regency. Her work conveys the airy lightness, the sense of fun and mischief of her world; its naturalness and superficiality are disarming, while its very femininity saves it from the sentimentality of a Cipriani, the artificiality of a Loutherbourg. Above all, like the time, it was spontaneous and released; there is an innocence about its pastoral fantasy, the woodland Arcady peopled by cherubs and children, Cupids and Pans making love or quarrelling, with the goat-footed creatures lurking in the background

6. *H.M.C., Charlemont MSS.*, 382.

to make mischief. (Perhaps these were creditors, for there was never any money.) It is all a transcript into the world of fantasy of her own gay, chequered, sunny life.

She was an amateur and most of her work was known only to the select circle of her friends – though she was besieged by invitations from people who wanted to see her rooms and decorations: she had to issue tickets. It was known to the public chiefly by the engravings Bartolozzi made of her illustrations for Horace Walpole's Gothick tragedy *The Mysterious Mother*, for Dryden's *Fables* and her nephew William Robert Spencer's translation of Bürger's *Leonore*. This young man, son of Lord Charles, had his share of the family talents too: he was well known for his *vers de société* and the distinction of being favourably reviewed by Byron. (After all, was he not a fellow-aristocrat, in a literary world increasingly dominated by the middle class?) Horace Walpole was beside himself with admiration for Lady Diana's drawings – no doubt there was a similar element of fellow-feeling in his enthusiasm. 'Such figures! such dignity! such simplicity! Then there is a cedar hanging over the castle, that is more romantic than when it grew on Lebanon.' We see that her art has its place in the immense romantic transition – flood or cataract or geological fault – that marks off the time from the classic eighteenth century.

She did some portraits of the circle she lived in: an enchanting caricature of Gibbon, laurel-wreath and that face Madame du Deffand thought it a *mauvaise plaisanterie* to lay hand on.[7] (Gibbon thought Lady Diana 'handsome and agreeable and ingenious far beyond the ordinary rate'.) She painted a portrait of the exquisite – and ruinous – Georgiana, Duchess of Devonshire, goddess of that society, 'all flowing elegance, melting glances and shifting silken colour';[8] the friend of Fox and addict of the gaming-table, who cost her husband (he lived *à trois* with her and her friend Lady Elizabeth Foster) hundreds of thousands in gambling debts. Like Charles Fox, she had constitutional ill-luck. Marlborough paid for this portrait to be engraved.

Lady Diana's relations with Blenheim grew frostier and

7. This drawing is in the British Museum.

8. Lord David Cecil, *The Young Melbourne*, 59.

frostier as she grew poorer – largely owing to the selfishness and pride of the Duchess, whom Queen Charlotte considered the proudest woman in the kingdom. Diana's real friend within the family was her brother Lord Robert. Her letters ring the changes on the constant theme: lack of money. In 1797, 'we are so poor here. I have not means to pay for a letter even.'[9] In 1799 she cannot pay her taxes, 'all my real friends are so poor I will not mention it to them'. That same year, 'my brother Robert has sold his charming house in town and pictures and all from poverty' – all from gambling, in fact. Next year, though she considered Robert 'the real guardian of all the family . . . we are all in a bad way as to money'. Two years later, 'if I can sell some more old candlesticks (as I did last year) I will go to town for two months, as it is too cold for me here all winter'. Then Robert brings her back two beautiful candlesticks from his visit to Paris with Fox. Next year, 'I am poverty itself, and so is everybody I believe except a few great people, and they keep all snug to themselves'.

In 1806 Lord Robert's luck turned with Pitt's death and Fox and his friends at last coming in, after twenty years in opposition.

> Mr Pitt being gone, Charles Fox and all my friends are just coming in, I believe. When I say 'all my friends', I only mean Charles Fox and my brother Robert, for I know few of the others by sight – but they are reckoned to possess all the abilities of this kingdom.[10]

In fact her sight was going: no more drawing now: nothing to employ her time except visits to Robert, now installed at Woolbeding with the remains of his possessions around him. There, in that charming, comfortable house, surrounded by affection and pretty objects to remind her of the past, she was always happy.

Her friends were passing away, Charles Fox that same year: she had left him her portrait of his closest friend, Lord Robert; now she must alter her will. To Robert she left a portrait of her son, Lord Bolingbroke, her marble busts and all her pet green-

9. These quotations are from Mrs Steuart Erskine, op. cit., 264, 269, 271, 276, 287, 295.

10. ibid., 304.

house plants; to her son Lord Robert's miniature. Her daughter Mary was provided for: for years she lived with her aunt, Lady Pembroke, who went peacefully on, in spite of her earlier troubles, to a great old age. One day her aunt 'carried her to Marlborough House on a visit! only think of that?'[11] A long vista of separation within the family unfolds – her gladness is touching: shortly after she was dead.

A closer contact with Blenheim was for some years maintained by the second brother, Lord Charles, from Wheatfield. In the theatricals of the seventeen-eighties he was a frequent performer. In 1790 a marriage between these two branches of the family should have brought them together: the Duke's daughter Elizabeth married the elder son at Wheatfield. Lady Stafford reports that the 'Duchess of Bedford says that it is the *most charmingest* match that can be, that Mr Spencer is a good actor, a good musician and a good composer, and that they will be very happy'.[12] Then, with feminine malice, 'don't you like the reasons her Grace gives to constitute their happiness?' The marriage seems to have led to a quarrel between Blenheim and Wheatfield, perhaps over settlements. Old Moore had, as usual, to be called in and he wrote to the Duke and Duchess enjoining silence and no talk whatever on the matter in public, especially under the present anger.[13]

At the same time there seems to have been a separation between Lord Charles and his wife, though they kept silent about it. The family *penchant* for silence came in useful, for nobody could extract any information. Not even the Archbishop, who could bring about no reconciliation, either in the Wheatfield or Kimbolton households – the Duchess of Manchester was Lady Blandford's aunt. Everybody in the Regency world had either wife-trouble or husband-trouble – except the ducal couple at Blenheim, and they paid a price for their mutual contentment. The coldness between Blenheim and Wheatfield continued;

11. ibid., 305.

12. *Private Correspondence of Lord Granville Leveson-Gower*, ed. Countess Granville, I. 20.

13. Blenheim MSS., E 60.

when Moore went to stay at the latter in 1796 he could still get no information on the subject.

To personal reasons for the breach we may have to add a political one. Lord Charles represented Oxfordshire in Parliament from that day in 1761 when his brother Robert as a boy deputized for him at the declaration right up to 1790 – nearly thirty years. In that year he had to make way for the feckless youth, his nephew Blandford, and remained out for the Parliament of 1790 to 1796.[14] He cannot have liked this, nor can it have been appreciated by the county, for he was a popular member. In 1796 he was returned once more and Blandford was left out in the cold. Not until 1802 was a seat found for the heir – or more probably bought for him, since it happened to be Tregony.[15]

True to the tradition of his family Lord Charles was a good deal of a Trimmer. In Addington's administration from 1801 to 1804 he was a Postmaster-General, along with Lord Auckland. When Pitt resumed power Lord Auckland was dropped – Pitt had not forgotten Auckland's intervening with the King behind his back against Catholic Emancipation. Lord Charles was continued. On Pitt's death Auckland pressed that Lord Charles might remain Postmaster-General: 'I shall hardly venture to write to Blenheim till I know how the matter rests.'[16] A place was found for him as Master of the Mint, but he held it only till October. After that he went into retirement; a pleasant pension of £1,000 a year made him comfortable.

Lord Robert was all his life an undeviating Foxite Whig, a pure party-man, as befitted the boon-companion of Charles Fox. They were at Oxford together. Lord Malmesbury describes the very pleasant life they enjoyed there, the bone-idleness, while waiting to take the chances held open to these fortunate youths in Parliament, the law or the Church.

> Our life was an imitation of High Life in London; luckily drinking was not the fashion, but what we did drink was claret, and we had our regular round of evening parties to the great annoyance of our finances.

14. *Return of Members of Parliament*, II. 192, 206.
15. ibid., 216.
16. *H.M.C., Fortescue MSS.*, VII. 350.

It has often been a matter of surprise to me how so many of us made our way in the world, and so creditably. Charles Fox, Lord Romney, North, Bishop of Winchester, Lord Robert Spencer, William Eden (now Lord Auckland), were amongst the number.[17]

It is no surprise to us: Foxes, Spencers, Norths – the world was theirs for the taking. Trevelyan describes theirs as

that most enviable of all the aristocracies of history, the men who look out from the canvasses of Gainsborough and Romney with a divine self-satisfaction, bred of unchallenged possession of all that was really best in a great civilization. . . . They felt themselves above the censure of any class but their own, and they had not yet been frightened by the French Revolution or reclaimed by the Evangelical Revival.[18]

The mania of that society was its insatiable passion for gambling. All the literature of the time bore witness to it – and not a few roofless country-houses and ravaged woods. 'The dryads at Hagley are at present pretty secure', writes Lord Lyttelton, but he trembles to think that the rattling of a dice-box at White's may one day or other shake down all his fine oaks, if his son should happen to become a member of that famous academy.[19] 'The gaming', writes Horace Walpole, 'is worthy the decline of our Empire. The young men lose five, ten, fifteen thousand pounds in an evening.'[20] At the age of sixteen Charles Fox and his brother cost their father £32,000 for three days and night's play. Some ten years later Fox's debts amounted to £140,000, which his father met with hardly a complaint – such had been the profits of the Paymaster-General's office. They were mad.

If White's were not sufficient to lose a fortune, there was Brooks's across the way; if London flagged, there was Paris. Fox and Lord Robert were in Paris together in 1771. They were often at Madame du Deffand's: those blind eyes saw through the young Fox, 'dur, hardi, l'esprit prompt', she said. As for Robert, he neither spoke nor ate but played tric-trac the whole time with

17. *Diaries and Correspondence of the 1st Earl of Malmesbury*, ed. by the 3rd Earl, I. ix.

18. G. M. Trevelyan, *Lord Grey of the Reform Bill*, 16.

19. Algernon Bourke, *The History of White's*, 94.

20. *Memorials of Brooks's*, xi.

the Marquise de Boufflers, who tried to fleece him. 'Ce petit Milord est bien borné: l'oiseau de proie s'en était emparée et aurait bien volulu le plumer.'[21] (What had Sarah warned his father years before about these French women cheating silly young Englishmen?)

But Brooks's offered one incomparable opportunities of ruining oneself in the best company, the irresistible company of Charles Fox, and this Lord Robert proceeded to do. Before long he was in financial difficulties and had to resort to his brother to help him. This meant calling in Moore, who drafted the letters that passed, for the Duke could not bear the thought of it.[22] Moore had extracted a promise from Lord Robert that 'certainly went to leaving off play, to living upon his income, to contracting no more debts'. What was the value of a promise from these young addicts? – the Duke 'must consider him as having broken his word'. By 1777 Lord Robert was reduced to selling his estate:

> I grieve to see him carried away by the prevailing torrent, and without making a struggle against it. My attachment to him from his childhood will never let me see him unhappy without being a partner in his distress. But I have one satisfaction in my own mind, I have not to accuse myself of ever having given him a single piece of advice or a single opinion that I can think of with disapprobation in my last moments.

Lord Robert mortgaged his Lincolnshire estate to his brother to meet his debts.[23]

But the story continues: the debts piled up. In 1779 we learn from Moore that Lord Robert had gone to the gaming table with £300 received from his place at the Board of Trade and won between £3,000 and £4,000. It had been a desperate venture, for he needed all the money to pay debts. He told Moore that he did not intend to go in for high play again but had 'got himself chosen at Stapleton's, where the play in general is guinea whist. He thinks there is no doing without a resource of that kind, but

21. *Horace Walpole's Correspondence with Madame du Deffand*, ed. W. S. Lewis, III. 150.

22. Blenheim MSS., E 60.

23. *Journals of the House of Lords*, XXXV, 69, 86, 173.

protests he will confine himself to that.' The good Bishop had scolded, begged and prayed – all to no avail.

In the early seventeen-eighties the financial affairs of Fox and Lord Robert, always unsteady, reached a crisis along with their politics. They were constantly together: in the notices of the time their names are inseparable: at parties given by the Prince at Carlton House, going down to Norfolk with him, dining at Fox's with General Burgoyne returned from Saratoga. George Selwyn gives us frequent news of the circle, breaking frequently – as their habit was – into French. Early in 1781, their opposition to Lord North and the American War coming to a head, Lord Robert resigned from the Board of Trade and Plantations and went bankrupt. Selwyn tells us that after this patriotic effort Lord Robert was in a delirium for a couple of days and still had a fever: 'although I am obliged to condemn him, my conjecture is that vexation in reflecting upon the whole of his conduct has contributed to this illness'.[24] On his recovery, 'he seems very much vexed at the part he has transacted and has been very much condemned for it. Charles denies having taken any steps to persuade him to it. If he had persuaded him against it, he would now have made me believe with reason what he has made Lord Robert believe without it.' Even their friends evidently thought that Fox was a bad influence.

In May the bailiffs took possession of Fox's effects in St James's Street: his furniture was thrown out into the street – everybody noticed what a filthy lot of odds and ends it was; for two days the Jews were filling carts with his goods, his clothes and books – presentation copies from Gibbon and so on. While this execution was going on in one part of the street, in another Fox and his friends were holding a faro bank of £3,000, by which they soon got near £2,000. 'Lord Robert since his bankruptcy and in consideration of his party principles is admitted to some small share.'[25] (Is it any wonder that George III objected to these young men having any share, however small, in running the Treasury?)

However, the faro bank prospered. In June it made £2,300; Hare and Lord Robert had their six guineas an hour, likely to

24. *H.M.C.*, *Carlisle MSS.*, 461, 463. 25. ibid., 488.

produce more than the pension of a Lord of Trade. 'He has let his own house to Sir George Rodney's son and is now in Foley House: *voici les ouvrages de la fortune.*'[26] Shortly Charles Fox was able to go out of town with Lord Robert: 'he talks upon the funds, sets up drink and spews to an immoderate degree'. By November Selwyn thought that between Foley House and the run of Mr Bouverie's kitchen, with his credit at Brooks's, his share in the opulent faro bank and flourishing trade, Lord Robert might find a subsistence. He did. On Christmas night one of their friends lost £7,000 to the bank, in which Hare and Lord Robert had a twelfth. They proposed that their share should be raised to an eighth. 'The whole manoeuvre, added to their patriotism, their politics etc. are incredible.'

Lord North's government was coming to an end. In February Lord Robert and Lord Ossory thought that they would carry the question against the government by a majority of ten, but that ministers would give up without.[27] In March Charles was giving audience to everybody at Brooks's; at Court only the Queen stood between Lord Robert and the King at the Drawing Room. When offices were distributed Lord Robert and Hare were for a time unplaced: 'how they are to be satisfied for their virtue, their patriotism and their fidelity I do not know'. We know that Lord Robert held his Vice-Treasurership of Ireland only for a moment, until Charles Fox left Shelburne's ministry in high dudgeon. His triumph, by the coalition with North, lasted only a few months: the moment George III could get rid of him he did. They were out for more than twenty years.

Trevelyan says that 'it is indeed hard to discern any principle, least of all of a Liberal character, in the actions of the Opposition during the years when they were denouncing Pitt's Free Trade and pacific policy towards France and plotting to climb back to power on the shoulders of the Prince Regent'.[28] Lady Holland tells us, years afterwards, that 'the fashion was to be in Opposition; the Prince of Wales belonged to it; all the beauty and wit of London were on that side'.[29] However, common sense and

26. *H.M.C., Carlisle MSS.*, 495, 499, 501, 512, 540–41, 552, 554.
27. ibid., 580, 602, 622.
28. G. M. Trevelyan, op. cit., 11.
29. q. ibid., 13.

responsible statemanship were on the other, led by a man who was as much above these aristocratic irresponsibles in integrity and loftiness of purpose as he was far more than a match for them in sheer tactics. It was not they, for all their brilliance and wit, who caught him out; he invariably caught them out. He ruled the country for practically the rest of his life; he gave his life to it.

The long years passed in the twilight of Opposition. These people who considered themselves so much cleverer than ordinary mortals proved again and again how much sillier they were. As France, with the unfolding of the logic of Revolution, became more aggressive and more dangerous to Europe, Fox, who had opposed Pitt's admirable commercial treaty on the ground that France was 'the eternal enemy', now became the champion of Revolutionary France. When France passed over from the defensive to become a danger with the victory of Valmy in 1792, 'no public event, not excepting Saratoga and Yorktown, ever happened that gave me so much delight', he brayed.[30] Next year, for his services to the country, his party raised another enormous sum to pay off his debts once for all and allow him an annuity to live in comfort for the rest of his life with Mrs Armisted.

This lady (it does not appear that there ever was a Mr Armisted), though the daughter of a Methodist shoemaker, spent her early life in frolicsome company. Lord Bolingbroke first raised her from the lower ranks of her profession and introduced her into better society. She became Lord Derby's mistress, had a turn with the Prince of Wales and finally hooked Charles Fox. In those capacious arms she rested, and in 1795 Fox married her, though they did not declare the marriage till seven years later, when he took her on his celebrated visit to Paris, with Lord Robert, after the Peace of Amiens, to see the pacific First Consul. The fact was that Mrs Fox was a good sort, a kind heart, devoted to looking after her famous husband: their marriage was idyllically happy. As Lord Egremont, who knew, truly said: 'Mrs Fox is a very kind-hearted woman and now very religious. And she seems to have taken the good qualities of our God

30. E. Lascelles, *Charles James Fox*, 242.

Almighty without his atrocious ones, by showing mercy unto the third and fourth generation of, not quite, thousands of those who have loved her and kept her commandment.'[31]

Politically a disastrous lot, privately they had a very good time. The grandest houses were open to them (without Mrs Armisted): Devonshire House and Holland House in London, Woburn and Holkham in the country. And how they enjoyed themselves! Every year they had a large party of friends at one or other of their houses; there they spent the time riding, shooting, walking and talking, reading, playing games or making love. But above all in talking, listening to Charles Fox's talk, for there was no doubt about the fascination or the energy of his mind. One sees it in his letters, where he is capable of breaking off and finishing in Spanish, for he has been reading Cervantes, or in Italian, having just finished Ariosto; passages of Latin or Greek come no less spontaneously to his mind or easily to his pen. No very exact scholar, he was a naturally intellectual man and theirs a cultivated society; while, when Fox was among friends – he was not good-natured with opponents – 'a lazy sunshine of good humour shone round them, softening the edge of their sharpest sayings'.[32] His good temper was such that, long after he was dead, his memory was carried on far into the Victorian Age: old gentlemen who had known him could not hear his name without tears bedewing their ancient cheeks. He is still the god who is worshipped at Brooks's.

The wry Wraxall tells us,

> no sooner had the shooting season commenced than he constantly repaired to Norfolk. Lord Robert Spencer generally accompanied him; and after visiting various friends they sometimes hired a small house in the town of Thetford, rose at an early hour and passed the whole day with a fowling-piece in their hands, among coveys of partridges and pheasants, for successive weeks during the autumn.[33]

Thus they restored the health they had prejudiced by late nights at Brooks's and in the House of Commons. So they enjoyed

31. The Earl of Ilchester, *The Home of the Hollands, 1605–1820*, 182–3.
32. Lord David Cecil, *The Young Melbourne*, 38.
33. N. W. Wraxall, *Historical Memoirs of My Own Time*, ed. 1904 345.

London at its most elegant, the English countryside at its loveliest. War might rage on the Continent or in America, but they were safe, behind the wooden walls of the Navy. Their double security gave them ease and naturalness, 'that delightful unassertive confidence', Lord David Cecil tells us, 'possible only to people who have never had cause to doubt their social position'.[34] It was this too that accounts for the paradox that they were the more democratic politically as they were more aristocratic socially: they could afford to be the one because they were the other.

And so it came about that Fox never failed to be elected by the popular electorate of Westminster, the beautiful Duchess canvassing for him assiduously, voluptuously (an Irishman said he could light his pipe at her eyes), the Prince, taking a hand in the election, sporting a fox's brush and escorted by a bevy of prize-fighters. When the famous election of 1796 was over, Fox was drawn in triumph in Lord Robert's carriage from Devonshire House to a popular dinner at the Shakespeare Tavern.[35] The Prince gave a public breakfast in the garden of Carlton House with singing and dancing, while his father drove mutely by in state to open Parliament.

The war went on and on, with its increasing burdens on the country. When a truce was established at Amiens in 1801, the whole of Whig society flocked to Paris to make up to the famous First Consul. Charles Fox took Mrs Fox abroad with him, recognizing her publicly for the purpose; people who did not in the least mind his having a mistress were shocked at his having married her, above all at having married so long without their knowing. Lord Robert and his friends were there, and both Fox and he had audiences at the Tuileries.[36] Napoleon regretted the necessity for a great military establishment; his inclinations were all for peace (he too, like Hitler, was an artist) and he was 'to the last degree' opposed to war with Britain. When, however, he attacked Pitt with the disgraceful lie that he was party to plots for his assassination, Fox came to Pitt's defence, asserting the

34. Cecil, op. cit., 15.
35. *Diary and Correspondence of Lord Colchester*, I. 60.
36. E. Lascelles, op. cit., 295–7.

impossibility of such an idea. Napoleon turned away in silence. He talked to Lord Robert about his admiration for his ancestor Marlborough – which was genuine; a figure of the Duke was being set up on the Tuileries at the time.

They came home persuaded that all the First Consul wanted was peace; nor were they perturbed by his annexation of Piedmont and Elba in the interval, nor by the 'mediatization' (*Gleichschaltung* was the word in our time) of Switzerland. Fox was, however, disquieted by Napoleon's unrepublican claim to Sicily for his brother Joseph. When the spectre of Napoleonic aggression all over Europe was at length laid, after years of war, and the man was laid by the heels in St Helena, Lord Robert sent him the Life of Marlborough they had talked about at the Tuileries in 1802.[37] Lady Holland bustled about among her Whig friends organizing sympathy and sending out presents. The cult of the First Consul with these intellectual liberals was almost as silly, though nothing like so disastrous, as the appeasement of Hitler in our time.

In 1803 Creevey supped with Fox and the Whig leaders at Mrs Bouverie's – she lived in tranquil amity with Lord Robert, Mr Bouverie raising no objection: he formed the third in a friendly, inseparable family-trio. Creevey was astonished at

> the vigour of body, the energy of mind, the innocent playfulness and happiness of Fox. The contrast between him and his old associates is the most marvellous thing I ever saw – they all having the air of shattered debauchees, of passing gaming, drinking, sleepless nights, whereas the old leader of the gang might really pass for the pattern and the effect of domestic good order.[38]

Pitt returned to power in 1804, with the renewal of the war, to carry its burden virtually alone; for the King would not have Fox, and the others would not come in without him. Pitt knew that it would cost him his life; after the news of Austerlitz, that look never left his face. Within a few weeks he was dead, those last words – 'Europe is not to be saved by any single man' – still ringing in the ears of his countrymen, to inspire a decade of effort to free Europe. He was forty-six, utterly worn out, having

37. Ilchester, op. cit., 326.
38. *The Creevey Papers*, ed. Sir H. Maxwell, 13.

been Prime Minister for twenty years. It needed a coalition of All the Talents to take his place, and at last George III had to have Fox to lead it.

Fox at once inherited the difficulties that had overwhelmed Pitt. In one respect, worse; for everybody rushed upon him for office, places, pensions, harmless little jobs for their relations. 'Can I give up Jack Townshend, or Fitzpatrick, or Lord Robert for any of these young Lords? Indeed, indeed, my friends are hard upon me.'[39] Lord Robert became Surveyor-General of Woods and Forests – a small reward for twenty years in Opposition.[40] He and Mrs Bouverie joined forces to press for promotion in the Church for a son of Bouverie's.[41] A worse disillusionment awaited Fox when he opened peace negotiations and found that Napoleon did not mean business. 'It is . . . the manner in which the French fly from their word that disheartens me. It is not Sicily but the shuffling insincere way in which they act that shows me they are playing a false game.'[42] To make concessions would only be to betray our allies. So Pitt had been right after all; in the last months of Fox's life, too late, he found himself following in Pitt's footsteps. Before the year was out he too was dead; we remember how the news affected Wordsworth when he heard it on a remote road in Cumberland.

Fox's will mentioned by name all those he loved as his oldest companions, all those who, devoted as they had always been, waited anxiously for news as he lay dying. It was Lord Robert who, finding words at last, spoke the truest eulogy of his friend: 'beloved, esteemed, renowned, lamented', he began. With Fox gone the centre went out of their lives; nor was it long before the Talents showed their silliness of judgement once more, lost office almost by inadvertence and went once more into Opposition for which their talents were better fitted. They spent another twenty years in the wilderness, while other, more sensible men got on with the laborious job.

After 1807 Lord Robert was out of Parliament for ten years

39. E. Lascelles, op. cit., 322.
40. *Diary and Correspondence of Lord Colchester*, II. 38.
41. *H.M.C., Fortescue MSS.*, VIII. 28.
42. E. Lascelles, op. cit., 323.

and only returned for the years 1817–20, as an elderly man. Perhaps we should look into his Parliamentary career, which was rather *mouvementé*: he had not the distinction, unlike his older brother, of holding a county seat for most of a lifetime, and the disasters to the Foxite Whigs, during Pitt's long reign, made him skip about for a seat.[43] He first sat for Woodstock from 1768 to 1771, and then represented Oxford city for close on twenty years, 1771 to 1790. In that year he had to find another seat and got one at Wareham, for which he sat from 1790 to 1796. At the height of Pitt's power, the doldrums for the Foxites, when they seceded from Parliament (rather against Charles Fox's conscience), Lord Robert was out: from 1796 to 1802. In this last year, after some uncertainty as between Wareham and Tavistock, he was returned by his Whig relations, the Russells, for Tavistock, which he represented till 1807. After ten years out he was elected again for Tavistock in 1817, but made way for one of the young Russells there in 1818, to return to Woodstock till 1820. At that election both Woodstock seats went out of the family: to Gladstone's father, a Tory, and a Mr Langston. The sympathies of the new Duke were rather Tory; but, more important, he needed the money badly.

The social life of the Whigs continued, vivacious, convivial, controversial: dinners at Holland House, visits to the Pavilion at Brighton, nights at Brooks's. Coming back from Brighton Creevey would look in at Brooks's to find all the regular gang there – Whitbread, Fitzpatrick, Morpeth, Sefton and Lord Robert. Lord Robert had the appellation of 'Comical' among his friends: there must have been something amusing about him, in expression and turn of speech. During Fox's life Lord Robert had often acted as a channel of political communication between him and his friends. For long after an active political role was over, he did not cease to be a sprightly, humorous figure in society. In 1828 Creevey had to do the honours to him, and

really my *tête-à-tête* with old 'Comical' was both curious and entertaining. He, aged eighty one, was just returned from a visit to his sister, Dowager Pembroke, in Richmond Park, aged ninety four and quite

43. cf. *Return of Members of Parliament*, II. 141, 190, 202, 203, 217, 237, 259, 276.

well. In our unreserved moments his criticisms upon men were quite delightful. He considers the wit Sydney Smith as a 'boisterous mountebank'.[44]

Lord Robert was a little man; however, he was man enough to give Mrs Bouverie pleasure. In 1810 her husband died and Lord Robert was free to marry her. Before this rather superfluous event, after so many years, they made an excursion together to stay with Grey, the new leader of the party, at Howick. 'Their marriage (which it is to be presumed will soon take place) is a comical enough event', considered Lord Dudley.[45] One of Mrs Bouverie's children, Diana, was Lord Robert's: 'the tell-tale Bouverie,' wrote Lady Louisa Stuart, 'for there never was such a perfect indisputable Spencer, Lord Robert's walking picture, and the very prettiest creature that ever was seen'.[46] To her he left Woolbeding, with his treasured possessions: so many mementoes of them all, of his sister, Diana Beauclerk, and the friends of Charles Fox, in that undisturbed temple of Foxite doctrine and Whig society.

When Lord Robert sold his town-house and the greater part of his collection of pictures in 1799 he moved the remainder and his fine library to Woolbeding, the country-house near Midhurst which his gains from the faro bank had enabled him to buy. It was a pretty place, which he proceeded to improve by attentive care and judicious planting. Charles Fox's nephew visited it in 1823 and found it a pleasant contrast to the vast discomfort and untidiness of Petworth:

> small, comfortable and quite luxurious from the perpetual attentions of its owners to the comfort and convenience of their guests and of themselves – the eating and the whole *façon de vivre* exquisite. The fault of the house is the excessive violence of their politics . . . to me such party-violence and such bigoted opinions are quite incomprehensible.[47]

Everyone recognized that Lord and Lady Robert belonged to the extreme wing of the Foxite party.[48] A lifetime in opposition

44. *Creevey*, ed. by John Gore, 282.
45. *Letters to 'Ivy' from the 1st Earl of Dudley*, ed. S. H. Romilly, 144.
46. q. Mrs Steuart Erskine, op. cit., 208.
47. *The Journal of H. E. Fox*, ed. by the Earl of Ilchester, 185.
48. cf. *Memoirs, Journal and Correspondence of Thomas Moore*, ed. Lord John Russell, IV. 223.

is hardly a recipe for political good humour – only the temper of a Charles Fox could support that; Lord Robert died, a very old man, just before his party and his opinions triumphed with the Reform Bill.

A few years before, Mr Creevey paid Woolbeding a visit and his account corroborates the impression of charm, breeding, taste.

> This place is really exquisite – its history not amiss. This venerable grave old man and offspring of Blenheim purchased it thirty-five years ago with the money he won as keeper of the faro bank at Brooks's, and he has made it what it is by his good taste in planting etc. . . . There is only one fictitious ornament to the place and the 'Comical' seems to have shown as much address in converting it to his property as he did in winning the estate. It is a fountain, by far the most perfect in taste, eloquence and in everything else I ever saw. I am always going to it. It came from Cowdray, three miles off, Lord Montagu's. When Cowdray was burned down thirty years ago, this fountain, being in the middle of a court, was greatly defaced and neglected. Lord Montague was drowned in the Rhine with Burdett's brother at the precise time his house was burnt and so never knew it; and as there was no-one else on the spot to look after the ruins, Bob thought it a friendly office to give the fountain a retreat in his grounds. It cost him £100 to remove it and put it up here.[49]

And there it still is.

49. *The Creevey Papers*, ed. Maxwell, 504.

Chapter 7

Regency Generation

LORD ROBERT's long career spanned the lives of several of the generation younger than his own. Of these two interest us.

Lord Henry, the second son at Blenheim, was the hope of the family. We left him under the kindly wing of Archbishop Moore, on the threshold of his career, going to be presented at Court. In 1790 he was returned for the family seat at Woodstock.[1] Next year he got his first diplomatic post as secretary of legation at The Hague, where Lord Auckland was ambassador. When Lord Auckland came home on leave, full responsibility fell upon a young man totally without experience. However, there was a lull in foreign affairs; Mr Pitt's government had managed so well that there was not even any concern for what was happening abroad. 'And this indifference as to foreign affairs', Auckland wrote Lord Henry,

> is general throughout the kingdom; you may find it even in our newspapers; perhaps it may be justly attributed to the great prosperity of the country, which confines all attention to interior and insular details. I have lately much wished to pass a day at The Hague for the sake of a little rational conversation.[2]

During these months the novice acquitted himself with much credit in the slow, intricate negotiations taking place with Holland and Austria in regard to the Austrian Netherlands. The object was to spin these out and maintain the *status quo*. Having achieved this there was not much else to do; 'but you must not flatter yourself that in this eventful age', wrote Lord Auckland, 'you will be long without occasion to exercise both your judgement and your activity'.[3] Curiously enough, this was some time in coming: we had no wish to embroil ourselves in the sequence of

1. *Return of Members of Parliament*, II. 192.
2. *Journal and Correspondence of Lord Auckland*, ed. cit., II. 398.
3. ibid., 390.

events unleashed by the French Revolution and were pressing Holland not to take part with Prussia and Austria against Revolutionary France. Already Lord Henry was winning golden opinions; the Foreign Secretary himself, the cool, unexcitable Lord Grenville, wrote: 'it is not possible to have acted with more judgement and good sense than he has done'.[4] The King spoke of him with marked kindness; when the Duke feared that parental partiality led him to think too well of his son, George III assured him it was 'impossible to think better of him than I do'.

After such a promising start, what next for the young man? In the summer of 1792 he was sent *en mission* to Vienna to compliment the Emperor on his accession – a distinction that gave much pleasure to the Marlboroughs and their friends. On his way there he fell in with that lady who became celebrated as Lady Holland: he may be said to have had a narrow escape.

Lady Webster, as she then was, was talented, vivacious, perhaps beautiful, unhappy – and rich. Partly Jamaican and partly American, she had been married at the age of fifteen to a man twenty-three years older, and in her defence it must be said that he was moody, unkind, inclined to be stupid and no company for her. She was not the woman to put up with it. In these years she was journeying about the Continent sometimes with her husband, more often without him. Whatever may be said against the famous Lady Holland – and many people detested her, her minatory manner, her domineering voice, her egotism and caprice – nothing gives a worse impression than what she wrote about herself. At Dresden in July 1792 was a numerous company of English:

> Lord Henry was there on his way back to Vienna, whither he was to carry the compliment upon the accession of the Emperor. He was then Secretary at The Hague under Lord Auckland. His abilities were spoken highly of. . . . His shyness embarrassed him and rendered his manner awkward. He was very witty and possessed a super-abundant stock of irony. In short, he became ardently in love with me, and he was the first man who had ever produced the slightest emotion in my heart.[5]

4. *H.M.C., Fortescue MSS.*, II. 251.
5. *Journal of Elizabeth, Lady Holland*, ed. the Earl of Ilchester, I. 13.

She took pride in not going to Court, but at a royal villa in the neighbourhood Prince Anthony mistook her for Lord Henry's wife, and

complimented him upon my beauty, *agréments* etc. and concluded by saying, 'I see by your admiration and love for her you are worthy to possess her'. This, said before ten people, was too painful to bear. Had I been very accessible to vanity on the score of person, I could not have resisted the flattery I everywhere met with.

However, Lord Henry had to go on his way. From Berlin he reports interestingly to Auckland,

the King is coming here today very privately from Potsdam for no other purpose but to toy a young girl who has been provided for him by Madame de Ritz, a lady much celebrated in that line. I believe I shall be presented to his Majesty tomorrow or next day. The Prince Royal, of whom I have seen a good deal, seems more in opposition than ever the Prince of Wales was. . . . I lately supped with the old Queen Dowager at her house in the country and the Prince Royal took us all out to the neighbouring village with a parcel of maids of honour. All at once I saw him dancing about in a most extravagant style, with all sorts of gestures, which the company present seemed perfectly to understand and enjoy.[6]

He was mimicking his uncle, the Stadholder of Holland, who was little more than a natural: 'I could not help admiring the exactness of the resemblance'.

In the autumn he came home on leave – at the time when revolutionary fervour was reaching a new height with the September massacres in the prisons of Paris and the call for a war of aggression to carry the Revolution across the frontiers. The English upper classes were at least thoroughly alarmed – as well they might be, not only for themselves but for the country. At Blenheim Lord Henry, evidently a Pittite without qualification, was disturbed by reports that Tom Paine's book had been translated into Erse and was in the hands of the common people in the Highlands; the book was being read by all the factory hands in Manchester and had appeared recently in Welsh.[7] (We see that Lord Henry was still very young, and had an aristocrat's over-estimation of the people's literacy.) In December he made

6. *Fortescue MSS.*, II. 290. 7. *Auckland*, ed. cit., II. 469.

his maiden speech in the House, much to the point, and, since he was able to contradict Fox on a point of fact, it was considered effective.[8] On kissing hands at going abroad again he had a very kind reception from the King, who was 'distressingly gracious' and said he had read all Lord Henry's reports – as no doubt he had, for he was very conscientious.

Lord Henry did not want to go back to the boring Hague, where there was not enough to do; he was ambitious and he wanted an independent post. However, back he had to go. Lord Auckland stayed there until the French advance on Holland was halted and then returned: Lord Henry would have a fine position taking his place there. The young diplomat inquired whether he could have the rank of Envoy and an increase of pay?[9] In July he got his first independent posting, as Minister to Sweden: he was not at all pleased at being sent to a country where there was no business to transact.[10] According to Lady Holland he was out of spirits, complaining of solitude – naturally, away from her. In August, 'Lord Henry talks of coming to meet me; he can be absent from The Hague only by stealth. Wrong as it will be, my inclination would get the better of my reason if I had the measure to decide upon, but as I have *not*, it must take its chance; only I do not think he can arrive before I go. My children are perfectly well.'[11]

The lady returned to England in no very good temper. In her circle she was bored by Gibbon's 'tedious witticisms'; for his part he could not bear her. She went down to Brighthelmstone, where 'the Prince chose to *combler* me with every attention and civility. . . . I heard from Lord Henry, very miserable at not being able to catch me anywhere on my return, but ordered to repair immediately to Stockholm.'[12] Across northern Europe he made his solitary way, pausing in Copenhagen which charmed him. At home the Dutch Grand Pensionary was in England, but Lord Henry had not given him letters to his family, 'because

8. *Auckland*, ed. cit., II. 474.
9. ibid., 502, 503.
10. ibid., III. 83.
11. *Journal of Elizabeth, Lady Holland*, I. 86.
12. ibid., 97.

I did not choose to put it into their power to be rude to him. You will perhaps have an opportunity of explaining to him that we are an odd set of people.'[13] (When an Austrian Archduke visited Blenheim a few years before, he was not asked even to have a glass of wine, nor, though rain kept him in the house some four hours and in the very room where the table was laid, given anything to eat.)[14] Auckland replied that he had apprised the Duke and Duchess of the Grand Pensionary's visit, but 'I apprehend they will not have the courage to molest him'. However, for once they did their duty and received him: could it have been the stirring of some ancestral memory of the first Marlborough's relation to the celebrated Heinsius, or, more likely, the desire to advance their brilliant son's career?

He was meanwhile being bored to distraction in Stockholm. Foreign diplomats were hardly received at Court, and etiquette prevented them from being welcomed in the homes of the Swedes. Lord Henry had not met with such a way of life since he left college.

> There is, however, a court and Swedish opera once a fortnight, and it is then only that we get a sight of the fair sex, which in this country consists of about thirty or forty elderly women, who are said to be very lively and very amorous. There is only one female in the *Corps*, who never goes out; and if a foreign minister should get admitted into a Swedish house, he is expected to go away at eight o'clock.[15]

Winter was approaching and there were six hours of daylight It was as if a man had suddenly fallen into a coal-pit.

Lord Auckland consoled him with the miseries *he* had endured on his way across the Atlantic in December 1778: every December had been a source of happiness to him ever since. For some time Lord Henry had no news to communicate worth knowing from his Eddystone Lighthouse, then suddenly life was enlivened by all the excitement of a plot: an attempted *coup* by the adherents of the late murdered king, on behalf of a foreign power, a lady at Court, mistress of the exiled leader, love-letters – all the agreeable ingredients of a melodrama. 'Nobody knows how

13. *Auckland*, III. 102, 105. 14. *Fortescue MSS.*, I. 267.
15. *Auckland*, III. 121.

far the plot extended, but we are now dancing and playing at cards with people one day, and hearing of their being in prison the next.'[16] However, the prisoners were not without spirit: one of them, the night before his execution, asked whether he had any favour to request – it was hoped he would ask for mercy – replied, 'I have nothing to ask but that I may never see your face again', and immediately blew out the candle.

While Lord Auckland was writing from Kent on 'a beautiful autumn morning, the sky blue, the woods yellow, the lawn green', or having tea on the lawn 'with the addition of tame lambs, turkeys, peacocks, bantams, ducks, doves, dogs, etc. etc.', or boasting of the three thousand peaches he had grown that summer, poor Lord Henry was able only to say

> we have had just *three*, and very bad ones. There have, however, been plenty of currants, raspberries, gooseberries, cherries and so forth. In winter we have no vegetables but what are preserved in salt, which is a great grievance. The Swedes live almost entirely on salt meat and brandy. In consequence of this they are very subject to the scurvy, and the peasants have all the itch to a man. It is literally true that when the workmen in the forges perspire very profusely, their shirts are covered with the salt that oozes out from their bodies. So much for the manners and customs of Sweden.[17]

He was very ready to depart.

For some time he had been destined for a much more important post – at Berlin where matters were becoming critical: the pro-French party led by Prince Henry was pulling Prussia out of the war. Before leaving Stockholm Lord Henry had an unpleasant surprise. It was usual for monarchs to give miniatures of themselves set in brilliants to departing envoys: the young King Gustav presented Lord Henry with an indecent picture. This must, of course, be regarded in the light of a calculated insult: it was firmly returned to Court and the incident reported in the proper language of diplomatic cant.[18]

Lord Henry was suddenly ordered to hurry to Berlin in the depth of winter. There the peace-negotiations were far advanced,

16. *Auckland*, III. 165–6, 249.
17. ibid., 221, 249–50, 255.
18. ibid., 277, 281.

and on his arrival he reported that he expected the peace-treaty with the French Convention to be followed by an alliance between the two countries, as against the triple league of Russia, Austria and Britain. 'Under these circumstances', he wrote to the Foreign Secretary, 'I apprehend that the presence of an English minister at this Court would be as little advantageous to the public service as agreeable or creditable to himself and that I may look forward with a great degree of confidence to the leave of absence which I have so long solicited for my private affairs.'[19] (What were these affairs? – thoughts of marriage, pursuing his far from reluctant lady?) Lord Grenville replied with a snub, which at the same time reflected the high value he set upon Lord Henry's services:

it will, I am persuaded, be sufficient for me to mention to you the importance of an English minister of your lordship's rank being resident at Berlin at the present moment in order to induce your lordship to abandon a request which I should not think myself justified in recommending to his Majesty at so critical a period.

So Lord Henry stayed. The game was by no means lost. Though Prince Henry of Prussia was pro-French, the King was friendly to Britain, and Lord Henry had an influence with him through his mistress, who was amicably disposed. Lord Henry's letters continue vigorous and informative; then suddenly, in the heat of July, he was struck down by fever and died.

With this young man there died the hope of the family, not only for this generation but for the next. Everybody was struck by his loss. Mr Pitt himself wrote the news to the Foreign Secretary; Lord Spencer wrote to inform the Archbishop, who had entertained such hopes; Lord Auckland had to break the news to the Duke. Lord Grenville lamented the loss to the public service on every account, 'having always entertained the highest opinion of his talents, his discretion and his principles'.[20] From abroad even Prince Henry of Prussia, 'whose disposition in general is adverse to English characters, has shown peculiar attentions to our late excellent young friend, whom he constantly mentioned as one of the best young men that he had ever seen

19. *Fortescue MSS.*, II. 561–2. 20. *Auckland*, III. 310.

from any country'.[21] The Prince had requested some trifle as a memento of him and had been sent a gold tooth-pick case found among his effects; in return the Prince sent a porcelain *déjeuné* of the most handsome kind. Carefully folded away among the archives at Blenheim is the draft of the Duchess's reply – for it fell to her to do everything:

> Les bontés dont vous avez déjà honoré mon fils pendant son séjour à Berlin, l'intérêt bien particulier que vous aviez daigné lui témoigner et dont j'avais souvent été instruite par lui-même vous avez déjà donné bien des droits à ma reconnaissance aussi qu'à celle de sa famille qui ne les oubliera jamais.

It was Lady Holland, as usual, who had the last word. In the summer of Lord Henry's death she hooked Lord Holland. Four years later, down at Saltram, 'I had the misfortune – and a most severe, heartfelt one it was – to lose my faithful companion, my attached Pierrot'. This was the pretty yellow and white Blenheim spaniel one sees in her lap in a portrait of her. 'He died! . . . He was the gift of Lord Henry. He faithfully maintained the love for me his master felt whilst living. Peace to them both!'[22]

Another blow that befell the Marlboroughs in these years was entirely their own fault. Closest to Henry among his sisters was Charlotte, just a year older; and among his Oxford friends was a very good-looking Merton man, son of Judge Nares – fine large nose, blue eyes and a mass of fair wavy hair. The Blenheim theatricals threw these two much together and Nares became an intimate of the house.[23] Years after he wrote, 'those who have been at Blenheim since can have no idea how princely the whole establishment was at that time and yet how little the family mixed with the world at large'. They lived in an enclosed world of their own.

21. Blenheim MSS., E 61.
22. *Journal*, II. 19.
23. For the facts of Nares's life and the quotations above *v. Edward Nares. A Versatile Professor: Reminiscences*, ed. G. C. White.

The theatre was fitted up to hold from two to three hundred people, scarlet cloth boxes for the family on either side of the stage. Each performance was given on four successive nights; invitations went out to the neighbourhood, the town of Oxford, the university, the county, friends – each audience ascending in the social scale. On the fourth night of the November performances 1789 the authors of the two plays presented sat in the front row before the stage: Horace Walpole's friend, Field-Marshal Conway, who had written the comedy *False Appearances*, and General Burgoyne who, more accomplished on the stage than at warfare, was the author of *Maid of the Oaks*. All the younger generation acted; Lord Charles came over from Wheatfield to take a part, and young Mr Nares from Merton won much applause at his first appearances.

In the years following he appeared frequently at Blenheim and won more than applause: he captured Lady Charlotte's heart. No other more eligible suitors appeared and these girls were allowed little contact with the world. Lady Charlotte was a bridesmaid at the unhappy marriage of the Prince of Wales to the dotty Caroline; but Lady Charlotte was not to leave Blenheim until the Princess had actually landed. (It was proposed that the Duke should carry the sword of state at the wedding: he declined on the ground that he was not strong enough.) Nares was given no reason to suppose that his attentions to Lady Charlotte were unwelcome; they had known each other for seven years and she was over twenty-seven when he asked the Duke for her hand and got a direct refusal. It seems that the Duchess was responsible; Horace Walpole said that her 'wavering weathercockhood always rests at forbidding the banns'.[24]

The couple took matters into their own hands; in April 1797 they went over to Henley and got married. Next day the steward from Blenheim informed Lady Charlotte that the Duke would allow her £400 a year, but they were forbidden the house, and she never saw her home again. Nares got a living in Kent – he had been ordained five years before – to which he took his wife. She bore him a daughter and they were tenderly devoted to each

24. *Letters of Horace Walpole*, ed. cit., XIV. 280.

other; but after five years she died, leaving him deeply afflicted. He wrote a poem in her memory:

How without rule are the decrees of God!
How He chastises! How He spares the rod!
Scarce does it ever seem that Right prevails;
How oft guilt flourishes and virtue fails!
What must I think of this severe decree
Which, through the will of God, now humbles me?
Am I to think Him kind who could destroy
The fondest hope I had of lasting joy?
Am I to think Him merciful who knew
The pangs I felt and yet His aid withdrew?

It does not appear that the poem provides satisfactory answers to these questions.

But Nares was a clergyman. He gave the Bampton Lectures in the year of Trafalgar, *A View of the Evidences of Christianity at the Close of the Pretended Age of Reason*. He had greater success, and was more convincing, with his best-selling miscellanies, by which he became widely known to the public: *Thinks-I-to-Myself, a serio-ludicro, tragico-comico tale*, followed by *I says, says I.* (His was a Regency brand of humour.)

Lady Diana Beauclerk's kind heart was touched by her niece's fate.

> Poor thing, the story is too horrid to write. Her husband behaved with the utmost affection during her illness (others not so!); there are sad hearts about the world. . . . Her parents' hard heartedness helped to break her heart, I fear – they really are become callous to all (but themselves), when I say 'they' I mean more particularly the female.[25]

And this seems to have been the case, for after the Duchess's death the Duke invited Nares to bring his and Lady Charlotte's daughter to Blenheim. It was in December 1813 that he came back – sixteen years after; the old ones among the servants remembered him with affection and Nares was touched. The old Duke was confined to his bedroom, but Lord Francis showed him up after dinner, and both the Duke and Nares were deeply affected.

Next day he was gratified by the news of Nares's appointment

25. Mrs Steuart Erskine, op. cit., 285, 292.

as Regius Professor of Modern History at Oxford, and henceforth relations were renewed. As Professor coming up to deliver his lectures, Nares became intimate with Lord Charles's family, while Lord and Lady Churchill came in to Oxford from Cornbury specially to meet him and his daughter. In May 1814 the Regius Professor was presented to the Regent – he went to the levee from Marlborough House. Later on they stayed with Blandford at Whiteknights. Nares, who never had an ill word for anyone and had borne with the treatment he had been accorded without a murmur, put in a good word for the spendthrift Blandford and pointed to 'the many disadvantages under which he laboured. . . . I shall always consider him an injured man.'

Another close tie re-knitted the family. Lady Charlotte's daughter married Blandford's son, Lord Henry Spencer Churchill – the old name had been resumed. He died young and his widow looked after his mother, now Duchess, to the last; she is remembered in her will.[26] This girl had been handsomely provided for as his grand-daughter by the old Duke: first £6,000 in trust and then another £3,000.[27] A more touching thought appears in a last codicil: he asked that his daughter's body might be brought back to Blenheim to rest beside him.

Nares himself is known to literature through a celebrated review by Macaulay. The Professor went on peaceably producing an occasional textbook or sermon; but when in 1831 he produced his *magnum opus*, the *Life of Lord Burghley*, Macaulay fell on him.

> The work of Dr Nares has filled us with astonishment similar to that which Captain Lemuel Gulliver felt when first he landed in Brobdingnag and saw corn as high as the oaks in the New Forest, thimbles as large as buckets and wrens of the bulk of turkeys. The whole book, and every component part of it, is on a gigantic scale. The title is as long as an ordinary preface: the prefatory matter would furnish out an ordinary book; and the book contains as much reading as an ordinary library. We cannot sum up the merits of the stupendous mass of paper which lies before us better than by saying that it consists of about two thousand closely printed quarto pages, that it occupies fifteen hundred inches

26. She left her £200. P.C.C. 1842, 353.
27. P.C.C., Effingham, 318.

cubic measure, and that it weighs sixty pounds avoirdupois. Such a book might, before the deluge, have been considered as light reading by Hilpa and Shalum. But unhappily the life of man is now threescore years and ten; and we cannot but think it somewhat unfair in Dr Nares to demand from us so large a portion of so short an existence.[28]

And so on for several more pages, in tearing spirits.

The Blenheim family seem always to have come in for hard treatment from Macaulay. As a matter of fact Nares's is not a bad book, and it consists of much the same number of pages, occupies a similar cubic measure and weighs about the same number of pounds avoirdupois as Macaulay's *History of England.* History does not record what Nares felt about the trouncing he got. He shortly after died.

The heir to Blenheim, the Marquis of Blandford, first burst upon public attention on account of the celebrated, the fantastic Gunning scandal of 1790–91. Appropriately enough, for he was a fantastic character, though it must be added that in this case he was not to blame. His marriage was naturally the concern of all the designing mothers in town, but no one could have supposed that it would take on all the elements of a Regency novel in real life.

Blandford was a figure made after the model of the Regent, both gifted and absurd. Their personalities had several points in common: neither of them was a bad man, in both sentimentality and kindness of heart prevailed; each of them lived in a dream world, each had his 'pleasure-dome' floating flashily and crazily on a foundation of debt. In the case of the Regent Parliament paid up; in Blandford's case not all the remains of the Marlborough fortune were enough to meet his liabilities. The edifice of dream in which he had lived so long at length crashed about him.

In 1781 his mother was laying a scheme to marry him to a great fortune – Sarah Child, who was as beautiful as she was good and, more important, was the only offspring of the immensely rich banker of Osterley Park.[29] The Pembrokes were scheming after

28. Lord Macaulay, *Critical and Historical Essays*, ed. 1891, II. 1–2.
29. *H.M.C., Carlisle MSS.*, 541.

her too, but she went to the Earl of Westmorland. Some years later, the young man being still unprovided with a wife, Mrs Gunning the novelist took a hand – and the novel she proceeded to write with these materials, for she had a daughter to marry, rivalled the Pavilion in proportions, in exotic decoration and labyrinthine detail.

Mrs Gunning was the sister-in-law of the lovely Gunning sisters, one of whom was twice duked. (This one had first married the Duke of Hamilton surreptitiously with a ring of the bed-curtain, according to Walpole, and secondly the Duke of Argyll.) Mrs Gunning fancied a duke for her daughter and her choice fell upon the Marlborough heir. The daughter preferred the Argyll heir, but the mother brushed this preference aside. Her husband, the Irish General Gunning, had done not badly at Bunker's Hill; he played a humiliating part in the matrimonial drama that ensued, being completely taken in by the tricks of his women-folk and rendered a ridiculous figure.

In August 1790 the news broke upon the town that another Gunning was to become a duchess, and that Miss Gunning was to have the same generous jointure as her future mother-in-law, the Duchess of Marlborough. The match-making old Duchess of Bedford was behind the scheme: 'it took its rise solely in poor old Bedford's dotage, that still harps on conjunctions copulative, but now disavows it, as they say, on a remonstrance from her daughter'.[30] But the rumour grew mysteriously, with a number of letters being bandied about, with affirmations on one side, denials on the other. Then the newspapers came out with a statement of the General's descent from Charlemagne, to prove that his daughter was equal to any such match.[31]

Meanwhile more and more love-letters reached Miss Gunning from the Marquis, until the General considered it his duty to ask him in form what his intentions were with regard to his daughter. The Marquis denied that he had ever entertained any. At that the General confronted him with all the letters. The

30. *Letters of Horace Walpole*, ed. cit., XIV. 279, 281, 361.

31. This turned out to have been inserted by his wife. When told of it later the General said, 'It is true I am well-born; but I know no such family in Ireland as the Charlemagnes.' – ibid., 397.

Marquis immediately owned the few letters disclaiming any inclination for Miss Gunning and disavowed the rest. Her father proceeded to lay the matter before the Marlboroughs, sending his own groom, who returned with a letter saying how delighted they were 'at their son's having made choice of so beautiful and amiable a virgin for his bride . . . and how chagrined they were that, from the lightness and inconstancy of his temper, the proposed alliance was quite at an end'.[32] People hardly knew what to think, for the Marlboroughs were regarded as so odd in their conduct to their children that this might well be true. The General was ready to take proceedings when the groom confessed that he had been bribed by Mrs Gunning. Revealed as a dupe all along, Gunning turned his wife and daughter out of house; the latter, the fair Gunnilda, was taken in by the Duchess of Bedford, who continued to support her cause.

The saga was by no means at an end. Gunnilda stuck to her story that the Duchess of Marlborough had given her every encouragement; so

> the Signora Madre took a post-chaise-and-four and drove to Blenheim; but not finding the Duke and Duchess there, she inquired where the Marquis was and pursued him to Sir H. Dashwood's: finding him there, she began about her poor daughter; but he interrupted her, said there was an end put to all that, and desired to lead her to her chaise, which he insisted on doing and did.[33]

It was said that Mrs Gunning tried to get the Marquis into her chaise, but that he would not venture being carried to Gretna Green and married by force. Miss Gunning remained with his Bedford grandmother.

She now confessed to her preference for Lord Lorne, of the two ducal aspirants to her hand, and this brought in the Argylls with affidavits and counter-affidavits as to her, her mother's and the groom's veracity. A new narrative was sent down to Blenheim maintaining Gunnilda's story that she had passed three days with them that summer, when it was in fact but three hours. The Duchess of Bedford interceded on behalf of her darling with

32. *Letters of Horace Walpole*, ed. cit., XIV. 371–3.
33. ibid., 376, 378–9.

the Argylls. The scandal reached enormous proportions with prints beginning to appear: one, 'The New Art of Gunning', depicted 'Miss astride a cannon firing a volley of forged letters at the castle of Blenheim, and old Gertrude, emaciated and withered and very like, lifting up her hoop to shelter injured innocence, as she calls her'. Mrs Gunning followed with a whole book of 246 pages replying in kind to the aspersions on her with aspersions on everybody else in the farce, with 'endless tiresome encomiums on the virtues of her *glorious darling* and the unspottable innocence of that harmless lambkin'.[34] They then went off to France. (At this point Madame du Barry came over after her stolen jewels, and returned to be taken, screaming, to the guillotine.)

Further pamphlets appeared in the Gunnings' absence and many squibs were passed about, one of them sung to the tune of 'The House that Jack Built': 'this is the note that nobody wrote, this is the groom that carried the note that nobody wrote', etc. etc. It became apparent that most of the Blandford letters had been fabricated by Mrs Gunning, though when she and her daughter returned from Paris they were still upheld by the Bedford grandmother. The Marquis had had such a narrow escape that he perhaps felt that there was safety only in marriage; so a match was suddenly patched up for him that summer

> with a little more art than was employed by the fair Gunnilda. It is with Lady Susan Stewart, Lord Galloway's daughter, contrived by and at the house of her relation and Lord Blandford's friend, Sir Henry Dashwood; and it is to be so instantly that her Grace, his mother, will scarce have time to forbid the banns.[35]

Retribution came for Gunnilda when 't'other day poor old Bedford made Miss Gunning read her daughter Marlborough's letter on Lord Blandford's marriage to a lady that came to visit her'.

His mother resented the marriage, and good old Moore had to patch things up: he wrote he was glad Lord Blandford had married into a family of rank and good connections. He advised the Duke and Duchess 'as soon as possible to receive both son

34. ibid., 389–90, 394. 35. ibid., XV. 56–7, 80.

and daughter and give them every mark of your love and forgiveness'.[36] The truth was that the Marlboroughs were disappointed in their eldest son, and at the back of their disapprobation was his frivolity and thriftlessness. They therefore kept him on a short allowance, one that was insufficient for a person in his position. While the Duke and Duchess resided in state at Marlborough House, he lived in lodgings at Triphook's in St James's Street. The consequences were what might be expected: Blandford had recourse, in regular Regency fashion, to moneylenders who advanced him large sums at exorbitant rates of interest on his expectations. The very length of his father's life made the situation worse: when Blandford succeeded to the dukedom the whole edifice was undermined.

To music, botany, gardening, the Marquis added another expensive interest – a mistress. Lady Mary Ann Sturt was the wife of a rich Dorset M.P.; her brother, Cropley Ashley, was married to one of Blandford's sisters, so it was all within the family. When Mr Sturt brought his case before the courts the celebrated Whig advocate Erskine surpassed himself in moral objurgation.[37] This was the gravest injury which it was possible for one man to recieve from another – the seduction of his wife. Over and over again the Courts of Justice had felt themselves called upon, by the most solemn duty they owed to the public, to repress, by the greatest possible severity, the commission of this crime. Unfortunately, however, it had had very little effect; he was sorry to say that the morals of the public, in that respect, seemed to be very little improved. This was all by way of asking for large damages.

The connection was not denied and letters were read which revealed the Marquis in a very sentimental light – much in the style of the Prince Regent, as it might be to Mrs Fitzherbert. Blandford regarded his Mary Ann as his spiritual wife, and wrote after the birth of a child,

> that that Providence which has watched over you in your recent dangers may ever continue to shower down its choicest blessings on the worthiest object of its care is and ever shall be my constant prayer. To one point

36. Blenheim MSS., E 61. 37. *The Times*, 28, 29 May 1801.

we must both look – the education of the dear pledge of our eternal love. My wife, my dear wife, the adored mother of my beloved child, my affection to you is ten millions of times stronger than ever. Suffer this innocent babe to cement our union, so that it may know no end. Love the little Georgiana for the sake of your George, of your Blandford, of your faithful husband.

The injured husband deposed that the guilty couple dressed very fine; 'Lord Blandford's fingers were loaded with trinkets, while his wife was bedecked with ear-rings, necklaces, lion clasps and handsome gowns the Marquis had given her; he made her presents which would have been more properly bestowed on the Marchioness.' On the discovery of their correspondence the Marquis wrote that he was 'on his way to Switzerland, that he might indulge his melancholy amidst the horrors of the Alps. One consolation he would have in his solitude: he carried along with him a miniature of his Mary Ann, which he had received from her in the days of their love.'

It transpired in the course of the case that the injured husband was not so innocent: he was more or less accessory to the footing upon which the Marquis stood with Mary Ann, while himself 'had been living for several years past in adulterous concubinage with Madame Krumpholtz, who played upon the harp and by whom he had five children'. In place of the £20,000 damages hoped for, the jury awarded him £100.

This extravagance was nothing compared with the money he spent on curious plants and rare books, on music and musicians – he was a fair amateur composer, though we do not know if he composed for Madame Krumpholtz's harp. At Whiteknights near Reading he had a place with a superb garden kept up like a royal residence with more than twenty gardeners. The King of Prussia sent his head gardener there to pick up tips.[38] There was a vineyard producing and a shrubbery of forty acres in which rare American plants only just beginning to be known in England were cultivated. The Marquis thought nothing of paying £500 for a rarity. In the greenhouses aquatic plants from the Ganges were kept afloat in tepid water. Some exotics unique

38. G. C. White, *Edward Nares*, 247.

in England he reared with his own hands, for he had exceptional botanical knowledge.

His attitude to books and music was similarly in the family vein of expensive connoisseurship. He collected a fine library at Whiteknights, which contained the fifteenth-century Duke of Bedford's Missal and the Valdarfer Boccaccio, for which he paid £2,260. The purchase of this *Decameron*, it seems, was the occasion of the founding of the Roxburghe Club of which he was an original member. When Nares went to stay with him a military band of seventeen musicians played all through dinner. The Marquis himself composed: in 1798 he published a collection of twelve glees, for three and four voices.[39] Like many people of an extravagant turn of mind and no aptitude for business, he longed to manage something – perhaps with a feverish hope of recouping his losses. Wyatt's Pantheon in Oxford Street had twice burned down;[40] Blandford took it over in an unsafe condition to run it as an opera house. The Lord Chamberlain ordered it to be surveyed before reopening to the public; characteristically Wyatt could not be traced. When found he reported that it was unsafe: nothing but a new roof and walls would do. The Lord Chamberlain insisted on the public being warned if the Pantheon opened, and then refused a licence. Blandford's letters about this remain at Blenheim, feverish and illegible; it is unlikely that he did anything but lose more money over it.[41]

The consequences were what one would expect. A solitary note of interest due during eighteen months, June 1808 to January 1810, speaks volumes.[42] There was interest to be paid on his bond for £6,000, on a first mortgage for £11,360 12s., on a second for £5,472 8s. 8d. – simply in interest £2,488 9s. 6d. engulfed. There were the accountant's costs for preparing different securities. But this did not discourage his ostentatious extravagances: coachmaker's work for 1808, £482 4s., for 1809, £805 8s. He was a great fool, in spite of his varied talents. When Captain Gronow travelled down with him to White-

39. *Bodleian Library Record*, V, no. 6, 335.
40. Anthony Dale, *James Wyatt*, 6–14.
41. Blenheim MSS., F 1. 37.
42. ibid., F I. 57.

knights in his coach, he opened a cupboard, constructed in the side of the roomy vehicle, that contained a capital luncheon with different wines and liqueurs. Another cupboard contained a secretaire with writing materials and a large pocket-book with a wad of fifty Bank of England notes for £1,000 each, borrowed the day before from Levy, to whom he had given a post-obit on his father's death for £150,000. Even if we allow for exaggeration, it hardly misrepresents the situation:

> You see, Gronow, how the immense fortune of my family will be frittered away. But I can't help it; I must live. My father inherited £500,000 in ready money and £70,000 a year in land; in all probability when it comes to my turn to live at Blenheim, I shall have nothing left but the £5,000 a year on the Post Office.[43]

And that was about what came to pass.

There was nothing that the Duke could do effectively to protect the family from this idiocy. As early as 1793 the Duke was hardly on speaking terms with his son: Lord Henry wrote that his father would not return to Blenheim when Blandford was to be steward of the Oxford races.[44] After Henry's death Lord Francis became the favourite son on whom his parents relied. Blandford was not put up for Parliament again either for the county or for Woodstock. His brother, Lord Francis, represented the county from 1801 up to 1815, when he was made a peer; and he took what should have been his brother's place in the life of the county, commanding the Oxfordshire Cavalry volunteers, then the Oxfordshire Militia, lastly the Yeomanry all through the long war and beyond.[45]

Lord Francis drew near to Pitt and was given the job of moving the Address in January 1806, when he congratulated the government on its brilliant successes at sea culminating in Trafalgar and regretted the defeats of our allies on the Continent. We had nothing to fear from Napoleon's menaces, 'defended by the known loyalty and valour of his Majesty's subjects and the unexhausted resources of this empire'.[46] But in accordance

43. J. Grego, *Reminiscences . . . of Captain Gronow*, 314 foll.
44. Auckland, III. 112.
45. Watney, *Cornbury and Wychwood Forest*, 200 foll.
46. *Cobbett's Parliamentary Debates*, VI. 13.

with the trimming tradition of his family he veered away from the Tories towards the end of 1809. Auckland sent the information to Grenville, hoping that the Grenvilles would have the whole support of the Marlborough family and its connections, though in some degree divided against itself.[47] It was indeed: Blandford was a Pittite Tory at one end – made a Commissioner of the Treasury (!) by Mr Pitt in 1804; Lord Robert an extreme Foxite Whig at the other end. In between were the Duke, whose main idea was not to upset George III, and Lord Francis, whose leading idea was not to upset his father.

His father rewarded him and marked his disapprobation of his eldest son so far as he could. He was anxious to have Lord Francis made a peer and to have the name and title of Churchill revived in him. To this end he settled the Cornbury estate upon him and the manors and lands purchased from the Earl of Clarendon, away from the Dukedom. In his will he left him for life the beautiful house in Oxford Lord Francis occupied – now the Judge's Lodgings in St Giles's; all the books, prints and drawings in his dressing-room, together with bronzes and china, to his wife.[48] In 1812 the Duke wrote to the Regent soliciting a barony for his son; the Regent was willing, the Tory Prime Minister Perceval against.[49] However, they got it in 1815, and Lord Francis became Baron Churchill of Wychwood, the first of a cadet line.

Two years later Blandford succeeded as fifth Duke and took back the old surname of Churchill. This may have been partly out of rivalry with his brother, but perhaps even more inspired by these years of victory culminating in Waterloo and the thought of the earlier military glories of John Churchill. On a summer evening in 1817 the new Duke invited over seventy people to dinner to celebrate his accession.[50] The arrangements were in accordance with the elaboration of his taste: the stable people stationed on the steps when the company arrived, lamps round the courts, steps and portico lighted at nine, the other servants in

47. *H.M.C., Fortescue MSS.*, IX. 435.
48. P.C.C., Effingham, 318.
49. *The Letters of King George IV*, ed. A. Aspinall, I. 25.
50. cf. D. Green, *Blenheim Palace*, 192–4.

the hall to conduct the company through the Bow Window room to the Grand Cabinet. The band played in the hall and then in the dining-room while the guests passed to the saloon; later, in the Library while refreshments were served in the colonnade.

The new Duke's fantastic tastes soon displayed themselves in the gardens. He added wings to the Temple of Health to form an aviary for his exotic birds, and soon gardens were forming down the slopes below it: an Arcade Flower Garden, the Botany Bay Garden, the Chinese and Terrace Gardens, the Dahlia and Rose Gardens. Admittance to the Rock Garden was through a revolving mass of rock that gave way to the touch, opening upon a picturesque scene. The Bernini fountain was at last set up; there was also a Druid's Temple, with romantic altar supported on unhewn monoliths overgrown with moss, a Garden of Springs, a Valley of Streams, grottoes, rustic bridges, islands. Within doors, under the Long Library, the Duke fitted up a room in Waterloo-blue drapery hung from an immense rosette in the ceiling. This room looked out on the Arcade Flower Garden and a new octagon pavilion of coloured woods. Further apartments were formed: an Italian refectory of *verd d'antique* and Sienna marble, a Japanese drawing-room with a fresco of an Indian tiger-hunt.

It is the same spirit of Regency exoticism that was at work in Beckford's mind, at Sezincote and the Brighton Pavilion.

Who knows what the fifth Duke would not have made of Blenheim as his plaything if creditors had not shortly called a halt? The vultures came home to roost – bailiffs in the Palace; the melancholy mournful knell of Debt clanged in his ears for the rest of his life. It was only on succeeding as Duke that he could pay the Rev. Vaughan Thomas for the charges he had incurred for his sons at Eton and the interest that had mounted up since: these included Montem expenses, a portrait of Sarah bought at an auction and a marble chimney-piece for Whiteknights – in all £637 10s. 6d., discharged in 1817.[51] His own personal collections there had to go under the hammer; the Boccaccio he had paid £2,260 for was sold to his cousin, Earl

51. Blenheim MSS., F 1. 37.

Spencer, for 875 guineas; the whole library fetched £14,482, far less than he had spent on it.[52]

Before Whiteknights was sold the Duke of Wellington rode over with a large party from Strathfieldsaye to see the gardens. It was January, but

from the profusion of evergreens the place looked quite like summer and it is impossible to express the beauty of the American plants. . . . It has been seized by a Sir Charles Cockerell, to whom the Duke owes a large sum of money. It is said that the gardens have cost the Duke £40,000 or £50,000 and that he owes Lee and Kennedy of Hammersmith £10,000 for plants.[53]

Meanwhile, at Blenheim when one of the younger generation of Foxes was asked to dinner,

I was very much amused with the Duke and surprised at the splendour of the establishment. The party were chiefly (with the exception of some hungry curates) Oxonians. The house ill-lighted and all the servants, I believe, *bailiffs*. I was astonished at the invitation, for I never had seen him in my life. [To be a Fox was no doubt enough.] He is pleasant, but looks like a great West India property overseer.[54]

When Wellington took Mrs Arbuthnot to see Blenheim in 1824 she

could not but regret the difference of times which rendered it impossible for a second Blenheim to be erected to the hero of Waterloo. Such a house could not be erected under millions. . . . The family of our great General is, however, gone sadly to decay and are but a disgrace to the illustrious name of Churchill, which they have chosen this moment to resume. The present Duke is overloaded with debt, is very little better than a common swindler and lets everything about Blenheim. People may shoot and fish at so much per hour! and it has required all the authority of a Court of Chancery to prevent his cutting down all the trees in the park. He did melt and sell the gold plate given the great Duke by the Elector of Bavaria, substituting ormolu ones to deceive the trustees. His second son took the benefit of the insolvent act lately.[55]

52. *The Farington Diary*, ed. J. Greig, I. 266.
53. *Journal of Mrs Arbuthnot*, I. 63.
54. *The Journal of H. E. Fox*, ed. the Earl of Ilchester, 88.
55. *Journal of Mrs Arbuthnot*, I. 304.

Nor was the elder son, it must be added, in a way to retrieve the position.

At some point there had been an execution in the Palace. The Rev. Vaughan Thomas thought that Marlborough's famous note to Sarah from the battlefield of Blenheim had been abstracted 'by some of the gang of bailiffs let into Blenheim upon Neate's execution – Neate and Bartlett forced open the latticed press which used to be under the Van Dyck picture of Charles I in the drawing room and seized the papers'.[56] As the years went on the Duke was forced to close down more and more on the establishment; for years he was more confined within the walls of Blenheim by debt than even his father had been by eccentricity. Of course he could jog along on the game and venison from the park, beef, poultry and eggs from the estate, fish out of the lake, and he had a good cellar of wine. But he could obtain credit neither in London nor Oxford, nor did he dare to show his face there. His melancholy forecast that he would come to depend on the famous Post Office pension of the first Duke was fulfilled. It was fortunate for the family and the future that the Blenheim estate and the heirlooms were strictly entailed, or they would surely have gone the way of the rest.

In this reduced state the Duke had the honour – and, like his father before him, the anxiety – of a royal visit: in October 1835 Queen Adelaide and her sister descended on him.[57] The Duke in a great state had to ask Lord and Lady Churchill to come over and help him do the honours: it does not appear that his Duchess was living with him. The Churchills arrived in time, shortly before the Duke of Wellington. Lord Churchill's band was stationed in the Grand Court, at the centre gate of which the royal party entered, which had a good effect. The Duke handed out the Queen and Lord Churchill her sister. After seeing over the Palace there was a handsome luncheon, and an address from the borough of Woodstock. 'Everything went off *surprisingly* well', reported Lady Churchill to the absent Duchess.

The heir, known as Lord Sutherland while his father was still Marquis of Blandford, was not the man to retrieve the situation.

56. Blenheim MSS., F 1. 54. 57. ibid., E 54.

His schoolfellow at Eton, Lord Monson, described him as 'one of the handsomest lads I ever saw'; but at that ancient house of learning he signalized himself, so far as is known, only as the ringleader in the riots against the ferocious Keate, the headmaster. Dr Keate, however, bore no malice, nor did the boys. When all the English flocked to Paris after Waterloo they were astonished to see the Doctor eating an ice at Torloni's on the Boulevard like any other human being.[58] His pupils – many of whom had suffered as much from him as Dr Busby's – determined to give him a dinner at Beauvillier's, the best dining place in Paris. There were Sunderland and his friend Lord James Stuart; the dinner was an immense success, the Doctor ate as he had never eaten before and paid his addresses in large bumpers to every description of wine. *Floreat Etona!*

In those blissful Waterloo years the young Duke of Devonshire was being hunted down by scheming mothers for their daughters, with all the vulgarity, according to Gronow, of the British matron in full cry after a duke. Lady Conyngham, the Regent's Egeria, was after him for her daughter, Lady Elizabeth. (The Duke of Devonshire remained obstinately, inexplicably, the Bachelor Duke.) Lord Sunderland, more susceptible, fell desperately in love with Lady Elizabeth and proposed to her. Her mother refused him, hoping against hope that the besieged Duke would yield.[59]

Whether off the rebound or no, Lord Sunderland – who, everybody agreed, was a fine young man – engaged immediately in an adventure for which he more than merited Dr Keate's cane. At twenty-three he wanted a girl and he found one aged between sixteen and seventeen, the daughter of parents in a respectable position.[60] Whether there was collusion between the mother and the Marquis or no, the way to the girl's charms was a marriage ceremony. The young lord had a brother who was a clergyman, he said, and would perform it. The ceremony took place privately in the mother's

58. J. Grego, *Reminiscences . . . of Captain Gronow*, 208.

59. ibid., 302.

60. cf. *The Times*, 10, 23 November 1838; Adolphus and Ellis, *Reports of Cases in Queen's Bench*, VIII. 907–10.

presence and in her room – she must have known that it was not legal, though she may not have known that the 'clergyman'-brother was actually an army officer. The ceremony was entered up in the Prayer Book and the young woman received a 'settlement' of £400 a year. On that she went to live with the Marquis – his father had just become Duke – as his wife in private.

When he went down to Scotland for the grouse-shooting next summer he travelled in his own carriage with his valet, 'Mrs Lawson' went by the Edinburgh mail with her child and one servant. It was this that got him into trouble subsequently; for twenty years later a horrid paper, the *Satirist*, claimed that this was a Scots marriage by recognition and admission and invalidated his subsequent marriage to his Galloway cousin. This was a matter of the first importance to his son, heir to Blenheim in turn, and a case was brought before the courts to settle the issue. There had been no legal marriage with the girl, of course, and subsequently she herself married. The Marquis's mother, the Duchess, paid her her £400 a year for a number of years, in return for which she gave up many of his letters signing himself as her husband. Like father, like son: both lived in a world of Regency extravaganza and fantasy.

Father could hardly complain when the consequences of his own way of life were visible all round. His nephew, the sainted Lord Shaftesbury, gives one an impression of the interior. This earnest young neophyte did not get his religion from his parents. 'His mother', writes his Victorian biographer, 'was a fascinating woman attached, after a certain manner, to her children; but too much occupied with the claims of fashion and of pleasure to be very mindful of their religious training. . . . He received no help from his parents in his religious life.'[61] He got it from a servant, who had been a maid at Blenheim. This young Ashley was a sport in his stock; certainly nothing would have been a greater shock to his cynical ancestor, the first Shaftesbury, than the appearance of this Evangelical reformer. With him the Victorian age is on the way.

However, he was a son of the family and in 1826 was returned

61. E. Hodder, *The Life and Work of the 7th Earl of Shaftesbury*, I. 36.

along with the naughty Blandford – an otherwise improbable coupling – as member for Woodstock. In February 1828 he had to go down and be re-elected on his appointment as Commissioner of the India Board of Control.

> Feb. 6. Woodstock. All has been going well, too well; my whole condition is so bettered that I fear reverse of fortune. Last night I dined with the Duke of Marlborough. Never did I feel so touched as by the sight of his daughter Susan – his natural daughter. She is Charlotte, our dear Charlotte over again, in voice, in manner, in complexion, in feature, in countenance. I could hardly refrain from calling her Sister. O Great God, have compassion upon her forlorn state! What will become of this poor girl? What danger is she beset with! May *I* have the means of doing her some real lasting service! Father of mercies, grant thy protection and keep her from the awful perils that are on every side.[62]

The best service this young prig could have done her would be to marry the girl. He had the good looks of the family. He married the respectable daughter of an Earl. But indeed in such a passage we have our finger on the pulse of the transition to full, high, unbreathable Victorianism.

Blandford added political divergence to other disagreements with his father.[63] The family representatives in both Houses had been so silent for so long that it is curious to find this member of it speaking frequently and fully during a very short period, the sessions of 1829 and 1830, before silence descends again.[64] What makes it all the odder is that he gives the impression of an accomplished speaker, rather stylish, with quotations from Bacon and Locke, Chatham and Burke. One would say that he was on the way to becoming a figure in politics, except that his position was such an eccentric one; and then something cut it short. Altogether it makes an odd episode.

62. E. Hodder, *The Life and Work of the 7th Earl of Shaftesbury*, I. 81.

63. In 1818 the Marquis brought a case to restrict the Duke from treating the Blenheim estate as if he were absolute owner in fee-simple, *e.g.* to stop him cutting timber. He lost the case. *Annual Register*, 1818, 336–8.

64. He sat first for Chippenham, 1818–20. *Return of Members of Parliament*, II. 278.

He made his maiden speech, conventionally enough, with a defence of spring-guns: if they were prohibited

armed bands must be marshalled against the midnight invaders of property, and the conflicts of the two parties would produce much more human suffering than ever had resulted, or ever could result, from the setting of spring-guns. He had himself for several years made use of these instruments for the protection of his property; he considered the objections urged against them to arise from a kind of morbid sensibility.[65]

In a flash one sees the rural background to aristocratic ascendancy: game-laws and poachers, spring-guns and man-traps, pauperism, misery, rick-burning in these years of distress. It is to his credit that he came to see that spring-guns were no remedy for agrarian grievances.

But his real hobby-horse was a detestation of Roman Catholic Emancipation; this rather free young man stuck to the Protestant tradition of his family and class. March 1829: 'he had always observed that national calamity followed the introduction of Catholics to political power in a Protestant community. . . . A House of Commons which was not faithful to the exclusive principle of a Protestant King and Protestant parliament was calculated to give due cause of alarm to the people.'[66] But he was being deserted by his leaders, for Wellington and Peel capitulated to the demand for votes for Catholics as an alternative to civil war in Ireland. This had the paradoxical effect of precipitating Blandford into the arms of the Parliamentary Reformers, on the ground that a more representative legislature would not have passed Catholic Emancipation. 'Let the question be sent to the hustings in every county in England – let the genuine opinions of the people be had on this question – let their representatives be sent back to them and the House would soon see that this measure was odious to the nation.'[67] No doubt – but it was not England that was in question. The concession to Ireland made him conclude that 'the period had come when it was expedient and highly necessary that they should without

65. Hansard, *Parliamentary Debates*, New Series, XVII. 25.
66. ibid., XX. 853–4.
67. ibid., 1502.

delay enter upon the question of parliamentary reform', and he now tendered his support to the reformers.

In May he announced his going over into opposition to a government that had given Catholics the vote.[68] In June he brought forward his own resolutions in favour of the extinction of rotten boroughs and the extension of the franchise. (That his lead was noticed in the country we know from the fact that the first meeting of the Birmingham Political Union petitioned in favour of his Bill.)[69] His speech on this occasion was fluent and well made.

> The whole internal constitution of this House has been revolutionized. An imperious necessity has been super-added to the already existing propriety of putting down the borough-monger and his trade. . . . I am speaking of a large and powerful party of six or seven millions of men, a party acknowledging a common head and centre of union, a spiritual sovereign and that sovereign residing in a foreign country. . . . Seats in this House will be bought up by the agents of this wealthy, powerful and enterprising body, and thus to their county strength in Ireland will be added their burgage tenure strength in this country.[70]

It seems to us a somewhat esoteric reason for extinguishing rotten boroughs, but as long as they remained there was this possibility. He opened out into a general attack on the system. 'Can there be anything in more open defiance of common sense and political expediency than that 354 voters should send 56 members to parliament – a ninth part of the whole House of Commons?' He goes on to attribute to the 'fatal majorities' constituted by members for rotten boroughs in the House 'the success of the odious principle of free trade'. We see that his was simply the point of view of the landed interest fearful of its ascendancy being overthrown by the Catholic vote and by the rotten boroughs being bought up by the superior financial resources of the growing industrial interest. That indeed might well have happened – from that point of view the Reform Bill may be held, paradoxically, to have prolonged the hold of the landed interest. Blandford concluded that the 'nation felt' that it was

68. Hansard, XXI. 1074–6.
69. W. M. Torrens, *Memoirs of Lord Melbourne*, I. 332.
70. Hansard, XXI. 1672–9.

'not safe to trust to burgage tenures and proprietary influence what should be confided to a chaster representation'. And more of the usual Parliamentary cant of this sort.

Byron's friend, Hobhouse, 'voted and spoke in favour of Lord Blandford's resolutions in favour of parliamentary Reform; but I was obliged to say I did not approve his reason, nor his plan of doing away with the seats, which were to be bought with money'.[71] Naturally friends of government were outspoken in their disapprobation. Wellington's friend, Mrs Arbuthnot, wrote:

our opponents are just such as we might have chosen for ourselves – Lord Blandford, who is said to have lost £26,000 at Doncaster Races and not to have paid the debt. These are the careful guardians of the public purse and the persons who are to din economy into our ears. Last night after listening for hours to Mr Hume's nonsense, when the business of the country began Lord Blandford stopped it by moving repeated adjournments.[72]

The debate on the Address at the beginning of the next session found Blandford supporting the Irish Catholic leader, O'Connell – Parliamentary causes produce strange allies; they were in a tiny minority of 11 against 96.[73] His course led him into a still stranger alliance with the Radical member, Joseph Hume: a minute group of 9 voted against Supply until the distress of the people was taken into consideration.[74] In that same active month of February Blandford brought forward his own proposals for Parliamentary Reform in a lengthy and well-phrased speech. By now he was eloquent against corruption, arguing for wholly transferring 'elective franchises from old foss-ways and crumbling castles, from the solitude of the plain and the ploughed field to the busy haunts of men – to the industrious and the intelligent and the independent among the sons of agriculture and commerce'. He paid a tribute to the dauntless (if unrespectable) Reformer, Horne Tooke, quoted Lord Chatham and Pitt in

71. Lord Broughton, *Recollections of a Long Life*, ed. by Lady Dorchester, II. 322.

72. *Journal of Mrs Arbuthnot*, ed. cit., II. 334.

73. Hansard, XXII. 170–78.

74. ibid., 325–6, 391.

favour of reform, taking up the position that he wished 'to restore the Constitution to its proper form and energies and to do it upon ancient principles'.[75] But he had now advanced so far as to propose the abolition of rotten boroughs without compensation to the proprietors and the enfranchisement of populous places instead, the extension of the vote to all taxed householders and the payment of members.

For these Radical motions – Blandford's chief Parliamentary effort – for which he and Joseph Hume acted as Tellers, a minority of 57 voted.[76] Among them were his cousin, Lord John Russell, a framer of the Reform Bill with which the cause ultimately triumphed: Lords Althorp, Ebrington and Howick, the heirs of Earls Spencer, Fortescue and Grey; with such notable figures as the Whitbreads, Brougham, Sir Francis Burdett, Lord Nugent and Daniel O'Connell.

This session witnessed Blandford's parliamentary high-water mark. In March he drew attention to the people's distress and called, eloquently but vaguely, for 'the repeal of all taxes on labour and industry'.[77] This winter was one of widespread distress, of misery and starvation for the poor, and Blandford returned to the charge once more this month: ministers 'ought to remove at once from £10 millions to £12 millions of taxation and to accompany that removal by a considerable reduction of expenditure. They ought to abolish all sinecures, pensions and useless places.'[78] This thought can hardly have given unalloyed pleasure at Blenheim, where his father was jogging along on the Post Office pension of £5,000 a year.

Lord Blandford's last speechifying in the Commons was on what one would have thought a congenial subject: Lord Ellenborough's divorce. This portentous matter consumed days of parliamentary time and pages of Hansard. Lady Ellenborough, a young lady of great beauty and artistic talents, found herself neglected for her husband's passion for politics. Prince Schwarzenberg came to console her – and later she had a fantastic, dubious career across Europe, ending in the arms of an Arab sheik near Damascus. Meanwhile she had to be divorced. A

75. Hansard, XXII. 678–98.
76. ibid., 726.
77. ibid., 805–6.
78. ibid., XXIII. 805.

lady in distress was too much for Blandford's gallantry – or was it party-spite against a minister of the party he had abjured? Anyway he opposed the divorce-bill. He thought that

> the long-continued neglect of Lord Ellenborough deprived him of all right to the relief he claimed at their hands. He believed in his conscience that Lady Ellenborough had been neglected, abandoned and sacrificed. And when the youth and inexperience of her ladyship were taken into consideration, and when it was remembered that she was subjected to the mischievous influence of gay and profligate associates, in disregard of warning given, and suffered with a blind confidence on the part of his lordship to roam about unprotected, he thought there could be little doubt that she had been sacrificed and he had as little doubt that Lord Ellenborough was not entitled to the relief he sought.[79]

These were high moral considerations; on such matters the Marquis should know. But, with Hume and himself as Tellers, he was in the minority again: 16 against 86. Whatever the reason, the Marquis took no further part in Commons' debates or discussions.

Affairs were reaching a grave crisis with regard to Parliamentary Reform; agitation spread all over the country and people began to think a revolution not out of the question here if the House of Lords held up the national demand for the Reform Bill any longer. The sweeping character of this measure astonished Whigs and Tories alike.[80] It took the wind out of the sails of Lord Blandford; the whole thing may have gone further than he liked, to judge from a hint of the Tory Croker in January 1831.

> Had some serious talk with Lord Blandford in the vote-office and took leave of him with a 'Good-bye, Citizen Churchill'. How men of rank and fortune, and above all those who have nothing but rank and fortune, can lend themselves to a faction that seeks to annihilate them, passes my comprehension. To do Citizen Churchill justice, however, he seemed to me to be alarmed and inclined to train off.[81]

79. ibid., 1389.

80. cf. E. L. Woodward, *The Age of Reform, 1815–1870*, 78.

81. *Correspondence and Diaries of J. W. Croker*, ed. L. J. Jennings, II. 100.

Alarmed or no, his name was among those to be made peers to carry the Reform Bill in 1832, if necessary.[82] In the end it was not: enough Tories gave way to let the Bill pass.

The differences between Lord Blandford and his father were reflected in the representation of Woodstock, the family borough. In 1830 Blandford was returned with his brother, Lord Charles Spencer Churchill, for the two seats.[83] In 1831 Blandford was left out and Viscount Stormont took his place: no doubt the Duke disapproved of his extreme Reform views. The Reform Bill reduced Woodstock to one seat, and in 1833 Blandford had it. In 1835 he made way again for Lord Charles. In the election on Queen Victoria's accession in 1837 Lord Charles was defeated at his own gates by an Oxfordshire gentleman, Henry Peyton.[84] The majority was only ten; Lord Charles petitioned against Peyton's return on the ground of bribery and corruption. Lord Charles did not enter into recognisances in respect of the petition – he was probably unable to – and so it was discharged.[85] However, Peyton had the goodness, or was prevailed on, to withdraw, and in May 1838 there was a by-election in which Blandford fought his brother, Lord John. Now Lord John petitioned the House that his brother's election had been procured by bribery, undue influence, the admission of persons not qualified to vote. The House rejected this plea, declared Blandford's election valid and pronounced the disqualification of three Woodstock voters.

In 1839 there was some question of Sir James Graham, the Duchess's nephew, succeeding to the seat. Graham was an able administrator, but as difficult as he was distinguished, and he had forked himself out of a more honourable county seat for Cumberland. A letter of his is revealing:

if Blandford and the Duke cordially agree to support the same candidate at Woodstock, the seat is a close one; but, alas, I know my relations too well, and I am afraid that no trust can safely be reposed in them. They

82. *The Greville Memoirs, 1814–60*, ed. Lytton Strachey and Roger Fulford, II. 283.

83. *Return of Members of Parliament*, II. 319, 332, 344, 355.

84. N. Gash, *Politics in the Age of Peel*, 226.

85. *Journals of the House of Commons*, 1837–8, 131–2, 166, 215, 477, 513 foll., 581 foll., 600.

would both try to screw money out of the transaction; and one or other at the critical moment would fall away. I admit, however, that as trustee by their joint consent and as one of their nearest relations I am the candidate in whose return they are most likely to agree. My belief is that Blandford does not wish to hold the seat in another Parliament, his sole object being to keep it open for his son, who is about seventeen years of age.[86]

This turned out to be so: when Blandford succeeded as Duke in 1840 Frederick Thesiger got the seat.[87] On Thesiger's appointment as Solicitor-General in 1844 he resigned for re-election; but the new Lord Blandford took his seat and when he resigned it after a year, it was to Viscount Loftus who made way for a younger son of Blenheim, Lord Alfred Spencer Churchill. This Blandford's resignation was due to a disagreement with *his* father in turn – over Free Trade. The father on becoming Duke became noticeably more conservative than he had been; and, in spite of his earlier Reform ideas, had never approved of Free Trade. It is refreshing to see the differences that could take place in regard to policy within the bosom of a privileged landed aristocracy – even if we observe that the views of the holder of the title and estate conformed more closely to what he considered his economic interest than those of the heir: politics were not simply a question of class-interest. This Blandford sat henceforth for Woodstock until his succession as Duke in 1857, when his brother, Lord Alfred, followed him.

The spendthrift, spend-all fifth Duke, the Regency buck who had undermined the family's finances, died in 1840. He left a curious brief will, leaving 'all and singular my goods, chattels and effects unto Matilda Glover now living in my family at Blenheim. And I do hereby nominate, constitute and appoint the said Matilda Glover to be the sole executrix of this my will.'[88] The will was made in 1838; it was attested as valid in 1841 and proved by Matilda Glover. Who was Matilda Glover? I do not know.[89]

86. British Museum, Add. MSS. 40616, f. 128.

87. *Return of Members of Parliament*, II. 369, 386, 403, 420, 436, 451.

88. P.C.C., Wills 1841, f. 42.

89. The answer is now provided by V. H. H. Green, *Oxford Common Room*, 71.

The Duchess died next year, leaving a large number of small legacies – but nothing to Matilda Glover.[90] It does not seem that the Duchess had been living at Blenheim, but occupying a grace-and-favour lodging at Hampton Court. She had a little money to leave, a little furniture and a number of family miniatures by Craig copied from Cosway. Nothing attests the decline of the family fortunes more than this pathetic bequest. On the Duke's death the *Annual Register* recorded that the collections he had made were dispersed in his lifetime, and 'during the latter years of his life he lived in utter retirement at one corner of his magnificent palace: a melancholy instance of the results of extravagance'.[91]

Of the rule of the sixth Duke at Blenheim there is nothing to say, for he left instructions at his death for all his personal papers to be destroyed – the fragmentary evidences of the life of the man who had been the handsomest boy at Eton. He made three marriages: the first to his cousin of the Galloway family – his mother's family.[92] She had been born at Blenheim in 1798, and died there in 1844. He next married a daughter of Lord Ashbrook, who died in 1850. For his third wife he went back to his mother's family and married a Galloway cousin; but, strangely enough, in his will he says nothing about her and leaves her nothing. She lived up to the threshold of our day, dying in 1897, one of the five Duchesses of Marlborough above ground at one and the same time.

The various vicissitudes, financial, matrimonial, personal, of these two dukes did not prevent the university of Oxford from honouring their great neighbours. The fifth Duke had received the degree of D.C.L. as long ago as 1792; the sixth after his accession at the Encaenia of 1841. He was also Lord-Lieutenant of the county from 1842 till his death; not all the mighty shades of Blenheim could prevail on the Crown to make his bankrupt father its representative.

It is only from the will of the sixth Duke that we glean some pathetic particulars about him.[93] He was dying in 1857, not old,

90. P.C.C., 1842, 353. 91. *Annual Register*, 1841, App., 155.
92. *The Complete Peerage*, by G. E. C., VIII .501–2.
93. Somerset House photostat.

only sixty-three, leaving a family of young children to provide for, about whom he was anxious. For the past seven or eight years he was an invalid, confined to a wheeled chair. He had been a sportsman, keen on shooting, fishing, yachting. He left his chronometer, ship-watch, sextant and telescope to his son, Lord Alfred; all his sea-telescopes, some Vulliamy clocks and a painting by Condy of the *Wyvern* yacht to Lord Alan; his guns, fishing-rods and tackle to be divided between them. His daughter, Lady Clementina, was to have, when twenty-one, the diamonds her mother had converted after her marriage into 'a splendid tiara'; a guardian was appointed for her, while his eldest son and heir was to be sole guardian of young Lord Almeric during his minority, with the express wish that he should go to Eton and then to Oxford. So we deduce that there was entire confidence between the sixth Duke and his eminently respectable, public-spirited successor.

The will is of immense length and complexity, for there were various trusts to provide for these younger children; the entailed estates to go to Blandford, with the addition of most of the household goods, furniture, garden tools and wines in the Blenheim cellars. A more touching reference is provided by the Duke's solicitude for his housekeeper, Sarah Licence: she had £50 down, £3 a week for life, the Duke's little brass bedstead, his black marble clock and rosewood writing-table, 'also the large arm-chair with high wheels in which I have daily sat for the last five years'. This was in 1854. Later that year, solicitous for her, he purchased a house for her to dwell in for life. His funeral expenses were not to exceed £100 – a far cry from the magnificence of the funeral of John Churchill, first Duke.

Chapter 8

The Complete Victorian

WITH John Winston, seventh Duke, respectability set in with its usual severity. No more Whig frolics, no more Regency extravaganzas. From his early youth this Blandford, unlike his predecessors of that name, was sober-sided and serious-minded, devout and chaste, devoted to the interests of the Church, for most of his life his horizon bounded by ecclesiastical legislation. A one-track mind, he was yet a man of ability, pertinacious and industrious in the cause he served; needless to say, he was a Tory of a narrow dispensation. The astonishing house of Marlborough holds yet another surprise for us: for the first (and last) time it produces a complete, full-blown, Victorian prig.

It is a sobering thought that this was the grandfather of our Sir Winston, and it is difficult to account for him: John Winston was decidedly a sport in the line. But there is this historical interest in such an apparition: it shows how the family reflects the varying temper of the society – a continuing theme of this book.

Is he to be accounted for by his education, as the original Sir Winston was? We saw that the first Winston remained always what St John's College at Oxford made him – High Church but obstinately Protestant, a royalist and divine-right-of-kings-man, a loather of Puritans and Republicans. His descendant, John Winston, may have similarly been affected by his Oxford college; for, contrary to family tradition, he did not go to Christ Church – which was apt to be broad-minded in all senses of the word – but to Oriel, the seminary of the Tractarian movement, and at its critical apogee in the midst of the *Tracts for the Times*. He matriculated from Oriel in the Michaelmas term of 1840 and remained there under the tuition of a devout clergyman who died young.[1] John Winston seems always to have been affected by the Tractarian influence, though later

1. I am indebted for this information to the former provost of Oriel, Sir George Clark.

something confirmed his Protestantism to the point of being very anti-Roman, as so many Victorians were. This circumstance may equally have been his marriage to a strong-minded Ulster-woman, the influence of his cousin, Lord Shaftesbury, or the reaction against the creation of a Roman hierarchy in England.

In 1845 he supported Peel in increasing the grant to Maynooth College. Seven years later: 'if at that time I did not entertain the strong opinions I now do, it was owing to the absence of a full inquiry into the true nature of the Roman Catholic religion'.[2] He now thought Canning mistaken in advocating Catholic Emancipation and he wished to end the Maynooth grant as 'repugnant to the feelings of the people of this country, opposed to their conscientious religious convictions and repudiated even by the very persons whom we desire to benefit'. When the sprightly Lady Knightley met him twelve years later at Lady Waldegrave's – how these names re-echo from century to century in an old society – she found that the Duke 'talked too much Toryism even for Charley, about the divine right of kings and the duty of submitting to the powers that be, and abused Garibaldi like fun'.[3] When we consider that 'Charley' thought that the national agitation in Germany was got up by the Jesuits we see what a reactionary and stupid frame of mind we have fallen in with.

There was no challenge to virtue in dining at Blenheim with this Duke – nothing but confirmation of one's prejudices. Mrs Jeane, the wife of an Oxford don on his way to becoming a Victorian bishop, dined there on a cold night in November 1858: 'furs and hot-water bottles kept us warm and prevented any evil results'.[4] There were Lord and Lady Shaftesbury, the Dean and Mrs Liddell from Christ Church. Conversation was not very lively:

the Duchess sat evidently racking her brains for some subject for conversation, but was unsuccessful in finding any sufficiently interesting to excite more than a sentence or two from either of her two supporters.

2. Hansard, *Parliamentary Debates*, 3rd Series, CXXI. 523.
3. *The Journals of Lady Knightley of Fawsley*, ed. Julia Cartwright, 74.
4. *Pages from the Diary of an Oxford Lady, 1843–1862*, ed. M. J. Gifford, 73–4.

She seems a kind-hearted motherly sort of person – neither clever nor at all handsome. The Duke also is a 'plain' man in all its meanings, but it is in itself an immense merit to be a religious Duke of Marlborough, and this his Grace has.

Perhaps when clever Mr Max Müller of All Souls went there to stay next year, he carried his engaging conversation with him, for the Marlboroughs asked him to stay longer.

Dinner was splendid; we dined in the Rubens room, and opposite me hung Rubens and his wife, Andromeda, and Philip of Spain. We were twenty four at dinner. After dinner we wandered about the rooms. There was a splendid Erard in one room, and we had some music; the next day I saw pictures in the private rooms, which one cannot see otherwise, the gems, the sketches, then more music.[5]

But the over-riding tone is the same: 'you are right when you say that I cannot be grateful enough to God for all the goodness He has shown me, my whole life long. My present position is really, of its kind, quite perfect, and if I only keep well I am thoroughly satisfied.'

It is the tone, earnest and moralizing – of some complacency for all its conscious seeking – of the Victorian age.

John Winston became well known, some years before he succeeded as seventh Duke, for his prolonged campaigns for Church reform. When he died, having widened his experience and interests as Lord President of the Council and as Lord-Lieutenant of Ireland, *The Times* said of him, 'perhaps his name will be held longest in remembrance as the author of the Act which he helped to pass as Lord Blandford and which bears that name, for the purpose of strengthening the Established Church in our large towns by the subdivision of extensive parishes and the erection of smaller vicarages or incumbencies'.[6] It is unlikely that anyone remembers the Act of that name now, but to get it passed involved Blandford in a strenuous one-man campaign over some years.

5. *Life and Letters of F. M. Müller*, ed. by his wife, I. 217–18.
6. *The Times*, 6 July 1883, 10.

We find an early characteristic performance of his over an Education Bill introduced by the Radical member for Oldham in 1850.[7] All the religious reactionaries were up in arms against it, on the ground that it violated religious scruples: no one voting for the Bill could claim to be a friend of religious liberty, et cetera. The Duke of Norfolk's heir was shocked; the sainted Lord Ashley (later Shaftesbury) was shocked; his cousin, Blandford, wound up solemnly, 'every lover of his country's truest welfare would unhesitatingly reject the Bill. . . . You will have taught them [the people] to desire great things without giving them instruction which from God's Word teaches them to be loyal and contented subjects.'

The House had no difficulty in rejecting this early Education Bill by a large majority: everybody rolled up against a Radical measure. It was another two decades before the obstruction of the religious sects, and their mutual dislike, permitted a national system of education.

Next year Blandford raised the question of Church Extension, 'an object which ought to be upon the hearts of all good men . . . but the interest which is shown in ecclesiastical affairs is not great'.[8] He proceeded to devote his energies entirely to them, becoming a kind of Lord Hugh Cecil of his time. He embarked on a campaign for the subdivision of parishes, for founding new parishes in overburdened industrial districts with no clergy or church provision; he demanded an inquiry into the surplus revenues of the bishops and of the deans and chapters, which might be devoted to this purpose. He proposed an Address to the Queen 'to lay the wants of the people at the feet of Her who in this country is the fountain of worldly honour, ecclesiastical as well as civil'. The Radical member Hume was able to get some of his own back by drawing public attention to a document on the revenues of the bishops 'so tardily furnished by themselves'.[9] From this it appeared that the Archbishop of Canterbury had averaged over the past seven years £22,907 a year, the Bishop of Durham £26,786, the Bishop of London £16,513, the Archbishop of York and the Bishop of Winchester

7. Hansard, CX. 479; CXI. 791.
8. ibid., CXVIII. 30. 9. ibid., 58.

over £12,000 each. In all, a sum of £192,024 a year went on twenty-six bishops. It is the world of Trollope, of Barchester and scuffling for preferments, of Mrs Proudies and underpaid starveling curates.

This state of affairs forced Blandford, with his passionate concern for the welfare of the Church, to become a reformer in his way. He urged that the management of Church lands should be placed in the hands of laymen: was it fitting that persons of spiritual character should spend so much of their time managing property?[10] He wanted a central body to take over the estates of the Church. The member for the university of Oxford – a largely clerical constituency – thought this would be fatal to the Church's interests. The proposal was lost in the Lords, where the bishops sat in strength. But Blandford persevered: years of parliamentary time and acres of Hansard went on this campaign for sensible reforms.

In 1854 Blandford brought forward his Bill again. The Crimean war had now begun. He thought that 'if it was desired to obtain the Divine blessing for the country – its prosperity at home and its immunity and protection from invasion from without – no surer method could be adopted . . . than by that House having due regard to the spiritual interests of the people'.[11] Some people thought that in the midst of a war other things were more important than Lord Blandford's Episcopal and Capitular Estates Bill. Not so John Winston: with characteristic obstinacy he brought it forward again – this was peculiarly the time to bring down the favour of God on the people of this country.[12] He ferreted out a few more damaging facts; he found that the Dean and Chapter of Canterbury, out of a revenue of £25,000 a year, devoted £71 to augment their poor vicarages and £1,306 for schools and charitable purposes. Durham Cathedral Chapter, with an income of £60,000 a year, provided £4,000 for these purposes; Westminster, with £30,000 a year, ear-marked £474 for their vicars and £426 for charities. Truly these deans and canons were at ease in Zion: the earth was theirs and the fulness thereof.

10. Hansard, CXXIX. 1220, 1236.
11. ibid., CXXXII. 3.
12. ibid., CXXXVI. 2032 foll.

They were not letting go so easily. Blandford was once more checkmated by the Church he wished so ardently to serve.

In 1855 a motion was brought before the Commons that 'it would promote the moral and intellectual improvement of the working classes of this metropolis if the collections of natural history and of art in the British Museum and the National Gallery were open to the public inspection after morning service on Sundays'.[13] Blandford thought that it would lead to 'the desecration and destruction of an institution the pride, the treasure and the glory of every Christian country'. He trusted that the House would never sanction such a measure, but ensure 'sanctifying the Sunday as a day of rest, believing that such a policy would bring its abundant reward according to the promise, "Them that honour Me, I will honour"'. The House easily rejected this sensible motion, by a very large majority.

With his views Blandford was strongly opposed to any form of Sunday trading and pressed forward legislation 'to obtain the solemn and decent observance of the Lord's day'.[14] He regretted the inability to curtail the sale of liquor, 'when it was known that from six to ten on Sundays, the public houses were filled with persons carousing and reducing themselves to the level of beasts'. With fatiguing consistency, for Blandford was a singularly consistent man, all of one piece, he was opposed to the government allowing military bands to play in the parks an Sunday. This was 'affording amusement to the public of a Sunday.... Some colonels would rather cut their right hand off than offend their religious scruples.'[15] It does not appear that the British Army was seriously inconvenienced by self-mutilation on the part of colonels when the bands did ultimately play in the parks.

At the end of the Crimean war the government in proposing peace celebrations forgot to order a Day of Thanksgiving – so like Palmerston, who was no Victorian prig, but a Regency buck who had survived into the clime of Queen Victoria. Blandford protested that 'our thanks were due to the Disposer of events', not only for peace 'but for the signal mercies which had

13. ibid., CXXXVII. 922. 14. ibid., CXXXVIII. 57. 15. ibid., CXCI. 1913.

accompanied the British Army through the whole course of the expedition to the Crimea'.[16] At our distance it is difficult to descry what these were; perhaps it may be taken to refer to our lucky escapes from the consequences of the incompetence of the Crimean generals.

War or no war, through Balaclava, Inkermann, Sebastopol, Blandford had gone on with his own campaign. In February 1856 he brought in his Episcopal and Capitular Estates Bill a fourth time, his Formation of Parishes Bill a second time.[17] In introducing the latter he instanced the confusion in over-populated parishes like Manchester, where the number of baptisms at one service sometimes exceeded a hundred; the consequence was that the parties and sponsors collected in the neighbouring pubs and everybody, except presumably the infants, appeared at the font in a state of intoxication. Marriages similarly.

In the summer of this year Blandford at length got his Bill for the subdivision of parishes through – the reward of long pertinacity. But it was only one part of his programme: he was unable to get his clutches into the fat surpluses of bishops, deans and canons. He had been radical enough to propose putting these prelates and clerical persons on fixed incomes. No such luck: these birds eluded him. Meanwhile he went after such of the bishops as were too debilitated to perform their functions. He raised the question of suffragans. He had great respect for prelates, but it was necessary to bring forward the matter 'in consequence of infirmities over which those reverend personages had no control'.[18] In consequence of their state of health 'several of the prelates of the Church were unhappily disabled from attending their dioceses'. Wiser now, Blandford proposed no disturbing measure, merely asked that the Act of Henry VIII (!) for Suffragans might be put into force.

This frightened a brace of moribund bishops into retirement. Whereupon an impolite Liberal M.P. pointed out that the Bishops of London and Durham over a period of twenty years had together absorbed a matter of £973,000.[19] The good old days were beginning to be over when these Victorian reformers

16. Hansard, CXCI. 1541.
17. ibid., CXL. 181, 681.
18. ibid., CXLII. 590.
19. ibid., CXLIII. 1357.

got to work. Blandford was one of them. He himself had pointed out that over the past thirty years £191,000 had been paid to the Dean and Chapter of Durham alone, simply for fines on the renewals of leases: no portion of this had been funded for the benefit of the Church, it just went into the pockets of the Dean and canons. 'When we remember that this is the return from one proprietary only, we shall be able to form some estimate of what enormous sums are being annually lost to the Church.'[20] In March 1857 Blandford introduced an Ecclesiastical Corporations Bill into the Commons.[21] It was withdrawn, and shortly he left the Commons for the Lords. However, there is no doubt that in the end his campaign bore fruit: in strengthening and recasting the Ecclesiastical Commission, and so on. In our time his proposals have come about: the properties of the Church are administered by the Commissioners; bishops, deans and canons live on fixed stipends. Mrs Proudie's day (financially speaking) is over.

From his place in the Lords the Duke continued to advocate the causes he had so much at heart. In April 1858 it was a motion for a Select Committee to inquire into the Spiritual Destitution of England and Wales: 'enormous evils grew out of the degraded moral state of the people'.[22] In May he was supporting an Ecclesiastical Commission Bill.[23] In June he opposed the removal of the political Services from the Prayer Book – the commemoration of Charles I and of Gunpowder Plot; for this might be a stepping-stone to further alterations in the Liturgy.[24] In February 1859 he wanted a public thanksgiving on the suppression of the Indian Mutiny.[25] A propos of Indian Education he was opposed to the government's neutral attitude as between religions: the moral advancement of the people of India was 'by extension among them of a knowledge of the great truths of the Christian religion.'[26] Time has deposited a sediment of dust upon those antique aspirations.

In 1860 Lord Shaftesbury was agitated by the question of divine

20. ibid., CXX. 1334.
21. ibid., CXLIV. 2182.
22. ibid., CLI. 1568.
23. ibid., CL. 6.
24. ibid., CLI. 492.
25. ibid., CLII. 852.
26. ibid., CLIII. 1789.

service in theatres: could that possibly be right? His cousin was more broad-minded: though he was not in favour of those venues, services were held there when no other suitable places could be found.[27] In the same month, on the Endowed Schools Bill, the Duke introduced an amendment to see that the Dissenters did not introduce their disagreeable teaching into Church schools.[28] In May he gave his support to a Bill for stopping selling and hawking goods on Sunday.[29] In July he returned to the question of the Bible in government schools in India, introducing a motion that it should not be excluded.

As usual he had got up the subject with care and in detail; he had organized a campaign; his speech, fortified with the facts of past legislation, with letters and opinions on the subject, was published as some others of his had been.[30] That night he had presented four hundred petitions to the House, but he believed there were fifteen hundred altogether. People were attached to toleration, but another principle to which they were equally attached was a devotion to the Word of God. He protested against education in the government schools in India being secular. Indian religions were founded not only on false doctrine but false science. The student for every purpose of religion was left no better but to become worse, 'a shallow, hollow Deist'. Over the reception accorded his campaign the Duke expressed himself testily, as he had before where his religious convictions were concerned: there was this streak in him. The Duke's diocesan, Bishop Wilberforce, whom even the Victorians thought of as Soapy Sam, opined that 'the religious mind of the people of this country was to a remarkable degree unanimous' on this.[31] No doubt. The Lords had more sense, where India was concerned: they negatived the motion.

Enough of this sort of thing: let us get on to the Duke's active career, not so much what he preached as what he practised.

In spite of his religious preoccupations the seventh Duke led a more effective social life, much more in the public eye, than

27. Hansard, CLVI. 1689. 28. ibid., 1564. 29. ibid., CLVIII. 553.
30. *Speech on Education (India), 2 July 1860.*
31. R. G. Wilberforce, *The Life of Bishop Wilberforce*, II. 451.

any of his three predecessors. In 1843 he had married a daughter of the Marquis of Londonderry, 'a woman of remarkable character and capacity, judicious and tactful', as the *Complete Peerage* tell us.[32] She was a figure in her own right, warm-hearted and forceful, ambitious for her brilliant younger son, Lord Randolph. Together the Duke and Duchess proceeded to revivify the life of Blenheim, melancholy and moribund for so long; and there they gave entertainments such as the Palace had never seen. The new Duke succeeded to the Lord-Lieutenancy of Oxfordshire and certainly did his duty by the county, city and university.

Mrs Jeune describes for us a ball given for the Prince of Wales when staying at Blenheim in 1859. It was November and cold again; but

> it looked *very* grand, well lighted and with a dozen footmen in the showy Marlborough livery drawn up at the entrance – when the servant conducting us, being evidently on the watch, turned and announced 'the Prince is coming'. H.R.H. was coming from his rooms with his suite and in his gracious pleasing manner advanced at once to us to shake hands, and then we followed him into the Grand Cabinet where a large party was already assembled.[33]

There, too, were the inevitable Liddells from Christ Church, along with the Austrian Ambassador and Ambassadress, Macclesfields, Portarlingtons, Vanes and who not in the county of Oxford.

Dinner was in the Grand Saloon, brilliantly lit by candles and gas below, dark suggestive shadows in the high vault above. Little Mrs Jeune was dazzled by the display of jewels around the table, the Ambassadress's shoulder-knots of rubies and diamonds, the Duchess's necklace, Lady Macclesfield's tiara. At ten the evening company began to arrive and they all proceeded to the ballroom. There was dancing in two of the Tapestry rooms too, and all would have been perfect 'if the Duchess had requested those who knew more of her company than she knew herself to make more introductions; but she has not very agreeable manners herself and is very deaf, which gives her an appearance of awkwardness unfortunate in her position'. However,

32. *The Complete Peerage*, by G. E. C. Revised ed. VIII. 503.
33. Gifford, op. cit., 92–4.

his Royal Highness enjoyed himself thoroughly with the ladies, dancing 'every dance of every kind and was still dancing the Cotillion when we left a little before four o'clock'.

The Prince was there again for an even grander party another year.[34] He had come to shoot with three or four friends, including Colonel Keppel. After the shoot there was a banquet *à la russe* in the Grand Saloon, with a vast bill of French fare. There was an evening party for three hundred; 'the display of diamonds and jewelry was dazzling in the extreme'. All the apartments along the whole south front of the Palace were illuminated and thrown open to the autumn night and the gaze of hundreds of spectators gathered on the site of Henry Wise's vanished parterres. The first and second state drawing-rooms had been furnished anew for the occasion, the Prince's apartments fitted up in enamelled white and gold furniture. Altogether, the newspaper concluded, it was the most brilliant spectacle in the county for a century.

The Bishop of Oxford, in the intervals of trying to squash Bishop Colenso and make T. H. Huxley look ridiculous, found time to stay at Blenheim. In November 1865, for example, there was a large party for Blandford's coming of age, with the Duc d'Aumale, Lord Hardwicke, etc. etc. 'The Duke is doing it very handsomely and I want to back him up in everything. He is quite a capital fellow really.'[35] Two years later the Bishop was invited to meet Disraeli. 'Nothing can be kinder than the Duke and Duchess have been. I enjoyed meeting Disraeli. He is a marvellous man. Not a bit of a Briton, but all over an Eastern Jew; but very interesting to talk to. He *always* speaks as if he did believe in the Church.' Dizzy always knew which side his bread was buttered: was he not the Conservative leader, and had he not described the Church of England as the Conservative party at prayer?

However, the grandest society would not be what it is without its mortifications to complain about and cause the blood to flow. At the wedding of the Prince of Wales to Princess Alexandra in St George's chapel at Windsor in 1862, space was so

34. From an undated newspaper cutting, Bodleian, G.A. Oxon 73 (5, 6).
35. R. G. Wilberforce, op. cit., III. 173, 233.

limited that though Mr and Mrs Disraeli were bidden as the Queen's guests, the Marlboroughs were not. 'There is no language which can describe the rage, envy and indignation of the great world. The Duchess of Marlborough went into hysterics of mortification at the sight of my wife, who was on terms of considerable intimacy with her, and said it was really shameful after the reception which the Duke had given the Prince of Wales at Blenheim.'[36]

By now Dizzy had 'climbed to the top of the greasy pole' – a remark that earnest Victorians could hardly approve. (Can one imagine Mr Gladstone making it?) Marlborough was a friend of Dizzy's and was first given office as Lord Steward of the Household – a post the fourth Duke had held – in 1866. Next year there was a reconstruction of the cabinet upon the resignation of Cranborne (later Lord Salisbury) in disgust at Disraeli's democratic Reform Bill. Disraeli replaced him by no less than three dukes, of whom Marlborough became Lord President of the Council. It was an arrangement that provoked many a smile: so characteristic of Dizzy – an artful combination of reactionary dukes with democratic measures. The author of *Coningsby* and *Sybil* was writing a novel in real life.

Disraeli, however, was not without effect in influencing the minds of his dukes: he reported with some complacency to the Queen Marlborough's speech in favour of his Reform Bill. The Duke 'spoke with much ability on the point and adjured his colleagues to take the step of necessary boldness'.[37] In a few years Marlborough had come a long way from divine-right-of-kings nonsense. But at the end of the year he was alarmed by Fenian news from New York: a couple of small vessels had left harbour carrying armed Fenians who planned to murder the Queen. The Queen for her part was not alarmed, merely irritated, and refused to leave Osborne. 'It is most unpleasant to feel one's liberty now so much interfered with, and every step and turn having to be calculated.'[38] The dreary Irish question was beginning to raise its head in its usual murderous form.

36. G. E. Buckle, *Life of Benjamin Disraeli*, IV. 386.
37. *Letters of Queen Victoria, 1862–78*, ed. G. E. Buckle, I. 413.
38. ibid., 483.

In this last year of Derby's administration, with the Prime Minister away at Knowsley nursing his gout, Disraeli willingly shouldered the burden of government. In January Disraeli reports, 'the Duke of Marlborough has been with me all this afternoon and has unfolded the project of the Council Office. I think it excellent: large, I would almost say complete, and yet moderate and prudent. But it is a scheme which would require frequent cabinets and minute discussion.'[39] As Lord President the Duke had to concern himself specially with education, since there was no Minister of Education and the question of introducing a national system was coming to the fore. Marlborough took up the matter with his usual energy and keenness. Disraeli reported to the Queen that the Duke wished 'the Lord President to be the ex-officio Education Minister on a great scale, which is not an arrangement which would be popular in the House of Commons, as it would seem to close the House of Commons to the Minister for Education'.[40] To Derby he wrote more cynically:

> All going on very right with the Duke of Marlborough. . . . But, so far as I can judge, the Education flame is more bright than lasting, and in a month's time I am not sure the Lord President may not bring in a strictly preparatory measure in the House of Lords and keep the great question for the next Parliament. But it must be in the Lords now; at any rate, we want education discussed by Dukes and Bishops. It will have a beneficial effect on all.

Within the month, February 1868, Disraeli became Prime Minister; he wanted Marlborough to lead the House of Lords. After the Lord Chancellor, 'I think the Duke of Marlborough the most competent man in our ranks to address a senate. He has culture, intellectual grasp and moral energy – great qualities, though in him they may have been developed, perhaps, in too contracted a sphere.'[41] Naturally Dizzy preferred a duke, and the Duchess's mother, Lady Londonderry, was one of his most intimate friends. But Marlborough told the Prime Minister that Lord Malmesbury, who had filled the place in Lord Derby's frequent absences, had the prior claim and he insisted on standing down.

39. Buckle, *Disraeli*, IV. 577. 40. ibid., 581. 41. ibid., 585.

In April Gladstone carried a resolution against the government in favour of disestablishing the Irish Church, and Disraeli decided on a dissolution of Parliament, hoping for gratitude from the electors he had enfranchised on so generous a scale. Marlborough disagreed with the policy: he preferred a simple resignation, leaving the onus upon Mr Gladstone to form a government. The Duke was ready to resign from the cabinet, but Malmesbury dissuaded him. He remained to introduce the Education Bill upon which he had been at work.

> It had the great merit of recognizing the importance and dignity of education by constituting a comprehensive education department under a Cabinet Minister, a reform which Disraeli had advocated in 1855 but which Parliament did not accept till 1899. . . . It was a measure, in Disraeli's word, 'preliminary, but of magnitude'; but there was no time to consider it, and the whole question was left over to the next Parliament.[42]

On appealing to the country Disraeli's new electorate expressed their gratitude by throwing out his government and returning his opponents with a triumphant majority. Disraeli and Marlborough alike spent the next six years of Mr Gladstone's government in opposition.

The Duke's short experience as Lord President had expanded his mind and enlarged his interests considerably. In April he had come to the rescue of his friend the Bishop of Oxford, attacked by an Irish Protestant peer for dedicating a bell at Bampton.[43] This was held to be ritualistic – surprising the amount of time consumed then on the subject by supposedly sane persons. In May he had to handle the more useful matter of the Contagious Diseases (Animals) Bill. As Lord President he dealt with a variety of government business, Irish Church Commission, Irish Land Commission, London Museums, but especially Education – Technical Education, the Parochial Schools of Scotland, in addition to the government's Bill.

He still found time to urge an increase in the episcopate, and this also achieved results in a few years with the founding

42. ibid., V. 46–7. 43. Hansard, CLXXXVI. 1330.

of new sees like Truro and Manchester. In Opposition he brought in a Benefices Bill, to prevent the sale of the next presentations to livings and in certain cases making the sale of advowsons illegal, for example when a financial bargain was made and the sin of simony thereby committed.[44] A Liberal House of Commons passed this with alacrity, but the Lords objected – interference with the more sacred rights of property. Marlborough withdrew his Bill for further inquiry. Forster's Elementary Education Bill of 1870 he welcomed and, surprisingly, accepted its conscience clause which embodied a compromise between the Church and the Nonconformists on religious teaching: roughly, the Bible but no Church Catechism.[45] The Duke was indeed becoming more broad-minded; it was not to be expected, however, but that he should urge extending the voluntary schools instead of pressing on the building of national schools, and argue for more religious instruction. In 1872 we find him speaking on a variety of subjects – the peculiar question of the Marriages of Friends or, in case anyone misunderstands, of Quakers; on Church Seats, the Resignations of Deans and Canons, and the more appealing topic of the Brigade of Guards.

On the return of the Conservatives to power in 1874 Disraeli was faced with the familiar difficulty of finding a suitable Lord-Lieutenant for Ireland. This most exalted position under the Crown, viceregal in state and consequence, was a place of great responsibility where a career might be marred – though it might not be made, for the position was now without power. On the other hand, it cost a fortune to maintain its pomp and circumstance: regular Courts at Dublin Castle, balls and official receptions, at Viceregal Lodge in Phoenix Park week-end parties, the unceasing hospitality of Irish life expected and given; a glittering staff, a retinue of servants, postilions and outriders; races and hunting, feasts and charities. It may be seen that the number of political persons from whom to draw upon to support all this was comparatively few and select. Disraeli turned first to Marlborough and proposed his name to the Queen, who minuted 20 February 1874: 'I saw Mr Disraeli

44. Hansard, CCII. 1338. 45. ibid., CCIII. 834.

at quarter to three today. He proposed the Duke of Marlborough for the post of Lord Lieutenant and thought the Duchess and her daughters would do well there. I approve this.'[46]

But the Duke of Marlborough was no longer a rich man and there were troubles enough at Blenheim to detain him. For the time he had to refuse.

When we scrutinize this apogee of the Victorian age we are struck by the fantastic wealth of a number of the peers at the head of English society.[47] The Earl of Derby had a revenue of over £150,000 a year from Lancashire alone; the Duke of Northumberland had over £160,000 within his county: both these magnates had estates elsewhere too. From Dumfries, Lanark, Roxburgh and Edinburgh the Duke of Buccleuch drew some £160,000 a year. The Duke of Bedford enjoyed an income of £120,000 from his agricultural estates, while his London properties yielded at least as much again. So too with the Duke of Westminster. While the Duke of Norfolk's revenues from Yorkshire were some £231,000 a year – though this was gross and would far exceed the net income; Sussex yielded him nearly £30,000 a year to jog along on.

In comparison with these magnates the Marlboroughs were no longer wealthy. Their Oxfordshire estates brought in £35,541 a year, Buckinghamshire £5,135 – a total of not much above £40,000 a year, and with the immense expense of a Palace to keep up.[48] They had reason to regret the fourth Duke's alienation of Cornbury to a younger son – an estate of 5,000 acres worth another £6,000 a year.[49] There the cadet branch of the Churchills, with a separate peerage, was in possession. The family had still more reason to regret the fabulous extravagance of Charles, third Duke, the £100,000 sunk on the gardens at Blenheim by the fourth Duke, the incalculable and ruinous waste, ending in virtual bankruptcy, of the fifth Duke. Even the seventh Duke had himself not been niggardly in his expenditure. And not a single one of the whole lot of them had as much as married an heiress.

46. *Letters of Queen Victoria, 1862–78*, II. 321.
47. These figures are taken from the *Return of Owners of Land*, 1873.
48. ibid., II. 14.
49. ibid., 4.

The result was that circumstances at Blenheim in relation to the demands upon it were decidedly pinched – and this at a time when the agricultural depression of the mid-1870s was bringing ruin to many landowners. In addition there was the family now grown up to provide for – six daughters as well as two extravagant sons, both addicted to society with all its expensive allurements. Blandford was a sad disappointment to the Duke, for all Soapy Sam's moral support; no one now had any expectations of him, though he was not without odd talents – like his great-grandfather, the botanizing Blandford of Whiteknights: a return to the Regency. Lord Randolph, early addicted to politics and the hope of the family, in 1874 married Jennie Jerome, daughter of the celebrated Leonard Jerome of New York, who, having made two fortunes on the Stock Market and lost them, now had not much to bestow. Nor had the Duke. What was he to do? Where was he to turn for money?

It is ironical that where the Regency rips and rakes, the Georgian extravagants, had left the treasures and heirlooms of Blenheim intact, the virtuous Victorian should have begun its systematic spoliation. But then, dead keen as he was on religion and the Church, there is no evidence that he had any taste. Lady Randolph observed on coming into this Victorian family, surrounded by magnificent pictures, Rubenses and Van Dycks, that none of its members ever looked at them. The Duke may have been proud of the splendid Sunderland Library that occupied the Long Gallery, for in 1872 he got the Rev. H. O. Coxe to catalogue it and had the result printed in fine big quarto; but it was he who nine years later sold it.

There naturally had been sales of surplus stuff from Blenheim at intervals before – usually upon the demise of a duke and the beginning of a new régime. On the death of the fifth Duke there was a four-day sale at Oxford of surplus books, mostly light literature but some earlier editions, a collection of prints and drawings, another of musical instruments.[50] One sees the interests of this curious man in the botanical prints, American Ornithology, Cruikshank engravings; the quantities of music, including his own compositions, *Arie composte dal Marchese di Blandford*, in

50. Bodleian, Mus. Bibl. III. 465.

two volumes. In London Thorpe sold a quantity of rarer books he had himself collected, including an early Dekker item and the Roxburghe Club volumes he had initiated.[51] In 1853 more music and engravings were sold, with several parcels of English and French literature, and a few miscellaneous items which had belonged to the great Duke, including – of all things – his badge of the Garter in onyx.[52] (Was this perhaps the one that came into the possession of the Wellington family, and that one sees now at Apsley House?)

In 1856 a still larger collection of the fifth Duke's music and musical instruments was sold: pianofortes, harps, violins, cellos; plate, bijouterie, clocks, china, Sèvres and Wedgwood. There was a small library, then the Duke's own glees, Moore's Irish melodies, Czerny, Haydn and Beethoven, Crotch, Green and Purcell, Croft and Handel, with full scores of Mozart and Donizetti: a complete Georgian and Regency collection. In 1870 a selection of duplicate and surplus books was sold.[53] Now in 1875, hard put to it, the Duke decided on the sale of one of the greatest treasures of Blenheim, the famous Marlborough Gems.

As we have seen, the formation of this collection was the real life-work of the connoisseur fourth Duke: it was on this that he spent his time, his money, his passion.[54] To collect it, to get rare gems – antique, Renaissance or modern – into his possession he had been in correspondence with agents all over Europe. In this channel and in the collection of pictures we see something of the acquisitiveness of his great-grandfather, John Churchill, reappear. It was over his gems that he pored hour after hour with Jacob Bryant, getting their scholarly descriptions right for the superb volumes he had printed, in Latin and French, with the Bartolozzi engravings, to present to the crowned heads of Europe.[55] There they were, these exquisite works of art, 739 in all in their red morocco cases: about a half of them he had collected himself; the remainder contained such collections as

51. ibid., 2593 f. 9 (5).

52. ibid., Mus. Bibl. III. 524 (12).

53. ibid., 2591 d. 3.

54. cf. M. H. N. Story-Maskelyne, *The Marlborough Gems*.

55. *Gemmarum Antiquarum Delectus* (*Choix de pierres antiques gravées du cabinet du duc de Marlborough*), 2 vols., 1780.

the Earl of Arundel's cabinet, the second Earl of Bessborough's, the Earl of Chesterfield's. Some of the gems were signed by famous gem-cutters, like the celebrated example of the dog-star Sirius, a ring-set gem cut into a splendid garnet. Of the Pallas with helmet, breast-plate and Medusa's head *The Times* said, 'nothing can be more singularly fascinating than this gem into which one looks as into deep water, to discover a beautiful vision of the stern goddess'. And of the collection as a whole, 'most of the finest cameos and intaglios are cut in Oriental stones of rare quality such as are scarcely ever met with in modern commerce'.[56] There were chalcedony and onyx, sardonyx and sard, amethyst, garnet, sapphire and agate, occasionally lapis lazuli.

The sale at the end of June at Christie, Manson and Woods created much excitement, all the leading amateurs and experts from both this country and the Continent being present. A reserve price of £35,000 was put on the gems. After a brief pause, Mr Agnew bade 35,000 guineas – to the loudest applause ever heard in the saleroom. The collection, it was understood, passed *en bloc* to a Mr Bromilow; what happened to him or it subsequently I do not know. On the whole the Duke must be held to have been lucky to realize such a price with so little trouble. Only Blenheim was the poorer.

Upon the family, Blandford's misconduct brought increasing trouble. He had alienated the Prince of Wales by his affair with Lady Aylesford, and Lord Randolph, taking his brother's side with an effective aggression that was characteristic of him, wrecked his friendship with the Prince for several years to come. Lord Randolph found himself, newly married, ostracized by the society of which he and his wife were already scintillating ornaments. It was a bitter experience. Clever old Disraeli, now Lord Beaconsfield, took his opportunity to renew the offer to the Duke to go to Ireland as Viceroy, adding the argument that if he took Lord Randolph over with him resentment in London would blow over the sooner in his absence. The Duke reluctantly consented, Sir Winston tells us: 'Blenheim was handed over to housekeepers and agents and its household was bodily trans-

56. *The Times*, 25 June 1875.

ported to the Viceregal Lodge'.[57] The Duke had hoped that Lord Randolph might go over as his official secretary; not at all: he had to pay for him out of his own pocket.

From a photograph published at this time by the London Stereoscopic Company, we derive a convincing likeness of the Duke on the eve of his Viceroyalty.[58] It is a very Churchillian face, square and set; there is the pugnacious lower lip thrust out, the short snub nose with long upper lip, and the extraordinary expression of those strange eyes, full of latent vigour. The countenance has a dogged, muffled expression – the melancholy of the virtuous Victorian, chaste and stern, somewhat remote and very aristocratic.

Such was the man who disembarked from the *Connaught* at Kingstown on 12 December 1876, to preside over the last years of comparative quiet before the Irish question was given a new and bitter twist by the personality of Parnell, and the rising storm over Home Rule divided and bedevilled British politics for half a century. It was bitterly cold and the people on the landing pier waited with exemplary patience.[59] The Viceroy was accompanied by Lord Randolph and was received by the Household, of which Lord Caulfield was Controller, and the viceregal staff. There was a special train and a state entry into Dublin; in the procession that followed was Lady Randolph with her child, the two-year-old Winston. At the Castle the Lord Justices and the Irish Privy Council received the Viceroy, who took the oaths – a salute of fifteen guns going off; he proceeded to the Presence-Chamber and took his seat on the throne – a salute of twenty-one guns. Such were the centuries-old formularies: brought to an end in our time.

In spite of the assassination of Lord Leitrim in Donegal, Marlborough's first year was fairly quiet. Over in England, in July 1877 he was able to give a good report in the Lords of the diminishing number of outrages: in 1870 there had been 4,321; in 1872, 3,238; in 1874, 2,096: now in 1876, 2,048.[60]

57. Winston S. Churchill, *Lord Randolph Churchill*, I. 75.
58. *Illustrated London News*, 28 October 1876.
59. *Annual Register*, 1876, 114.
60. Hansard, CCCXXV. 1307.

Agrarian crimes had gone down from 767 in 1870 to 212 in 1876. Occasionally, when over in England, we find him taking the opportunity to speak on Irish matters – railways, inland navigation, piers and harbours.

But 1878 was excessively rainy; the potato crop failed and there was a fuel shortage. We see that Ireland's agrarian economy existed on a shoe-string and no one could do much about that. The Duchess came to the fore with a vigorous campaign for a Relief Fund; she got a warm response from the English press and a lot of money was subscribed – though never enough. Not to be outdone, the Catholic Lord Mayor of Dublin initiated a rival fund. The Dublin Municipal Council passed a resolution in favour of public works: no response from Disraeli's government. (Disraeli was preoccupied with the Russo-Turkish war and the Congress of Berlin.) Parnell, an Irish Protestant landowner himself, took the opportunity to launch an Anti-Rent agitation and to press for a more aggressive Home Rule policy. Hitherto the Irish members in the House of Commons had followed the gentlemanly lead of Isaac Butt – with whom Lord and Lady Randolph were on friendly terms. Parnell's slogans – 'No rent to the landlords, the land of Ireland restored to the people of Ireland' – were effective in capturing the leadership of the Home Rule movement from Butt.

Lord Randolph threw himself with his usual gusto into Irish life, which had, as always, a hospitable warmth and charm to make up for its political disagreeableness. He and Lady Randolph lived in the Little Lodge, a short distance from the Viceregal Lodge in Phoenix Park, and here they too kept open house, entertaining company far too Nationalist for the Tory grandees that surrounded the Viceroy. Soon Randolph knew everybody and had travelled all over the country. He hunted every winter with the Meath and Kildare hounds; he fished the lakes and streams, or sailed in Dublin Bay; he went after snipe in Donegal or Connemara. 'But wherever he went, and for whatever purpose, he interested himself in the people and studied the questions of the country.'[61] Soon he was speaking at the Trinity College Historical Society, a parallel to the Oxford Union he

61. Winston S. Churchill, op. cit., I. 78.

had known. He became a regular member of Fitzgibbon's Christmas parties that met at Howth.

It was not long before Lord Randolph was speaking about Irish affairs in a tone not agreeable to Tory ears. At Woodstock in 1877 he proclaimed, 'I have no hesitation in saying that it is inattention to Irish legislation that has produced obstruction. There are great and crying Irish questions which the government have not attended to, do not seem to be inclined to attend to and perhaps do not intend to attend to . . . and so long as these matters are neglected, so long will the government have to deal with obstruction from Ireland.'[62] It may be noted here that Lord Randolph's subsequent obstructive tactics against Mr Gladstone's government owed something to Parnell's example.

This outburst created trouble for his father, the Viceroy, who had to answer the remonstrances to the Chief Secretary.

> The only excuse I can find for Randolph is that he must either be mad or have been singularly affected with local champagne or claret. I can only say that the sentiments he has indulged in are purely his own; and, more than this, I was as much amazed as you in reading them, and had no conception that he entertained such opinions.[63]

The Duke had to point out that Randolph's position was quite unofficial and that it was unwarrantable to represent Randolph's views as his father's. But Lord Randolph, as usual, was unrepentant. In 1878 he pushed forward a motion in the House of Commons for a Select Committee to inquire into the condition of the (Protestant) endowed schools of Ireland and to report on how far they were promoting intermediate education there without distinction of class or religion. This pleased the Irish Nationalists as much as it disgusted the Irish Tories. In the course of the work of the commission appointed, he 'travelled all over Ireland – north, west and south – collecting information and examining schools'.[64] In fact it may be said that Ireland provided Lord Randolph's real political apprenticeship.

Lady Randolph enjoyed her time in Ireland no less. The Marlboroughs took various houses in different parts of the country so that they saw a great deal of it.

62. ibid., 90. 63. ibid., 92. 64. ibid., 96–8.

At Knockdrin Castle in Westmeath, where we stayed for a few months, we enjoyed the hunting, for the foxes were as wild as the people were untamed.... One winter my father-in-law had Lord Sligo's place at Westport, County Mayo, where the snipe-shooting afforded excellent sport.[65]

They went to Galway and Connemara, and often stayed at Muckross Abbey on the Lake of Killarney, from which they visited Kenmare, one of the show-places of Ireland then. Altogether they hunted with almost every pack of hounds in the country: what better way of seeing it?

Lady Randolph herself did not go unobserved. Lord D'Abernon, a notable amateur of women's beauty, describes her as she was in those years. 'I have the clearest recollection of seeing her for the first time. It was at the Viceregal Lodge at Dublin. The Viceroy was on a dais at the farther end of the room surrounded by a brilliant staff, but eyes were not turned on him or his consort, but on a dark lithe figure, standing somewhat apart and appearing to be of another texture to those around her, radiant, translucent, intense. A diamond star in her hair, her favourite ornament – its lustre dimmed by the flashing glory of her eyes ... With all these attributes of brilliancy, such kindliness and high spirits that she was universally popular.... Her courage not less great than that of her husband – fit mother for descendants of the great Duke.'[66]

The youthful eyes of one of these descendants were beginning to take in the scene. By one of those pleasant proprieties of history the first memories of our Sir Winston go back to the town where the first Sir Winston ploughed away at the land-settlement of Ireland in the draughty King's Courts of Restoration Dublin. (That land-settlement was now in the throes of dissolution, about to be undone.)

I can recall scenes and events in Ireland quite well, and sometimes dimly, even people.... I remember my grandfather, the Viceroy, un-

65. Mrs Cornwallis-West, *The Reminiscences of Lady Randolph Churchill*, 78 foll.

66. q. Winston S. Churchill, *My Early Life*, 18–19.

veiling the Lord Gough statue in 1878. A great black crowd, scarlet soldiers on horseback, strings pulling away a brown shiny sheet, the old Duke, the formidable grandpapa, talking loudly to the crowd. I recall even a phrase he used: 'and with a withering volley he shattered the enemy's line'. I quite understood that he was speaking about war and fighting, and that a 'volley' meant what the black-coated soldiers (Riflemen) used to do with loud bangs so often in the Phoenix Park where I was taken for my morning walks. This, I think, is my first coherent memory.[67]

There were other memories. There was the long dark procession of men whom his nurse took to be Fenians approaching and the house amid the shrubberies where the Under-Secretary lived, Mr Burke, who gave the boy a drum. It was at the Little Lodge that he was first 'menaced with Education. The approach of a sinister figure described as "the Governess" was announced.'[68] When 'the fateful hour struck and the Governess was due to arrive, I did what so many oppressed peoples have done in similar circumstances: I took to the woods'. The 'woods' were the shrubberies amid which the Chief Secretary, Lord Frederick Cavendish, and Mr Burke were murdered two or three years later.

For the political situation deteriorated rapidly in the last months of Marlborough's Viceroyalty. In October 1879 the National Land League was formed; seven of its first chosen officers were either Fenians or ex-Fenians.[69] The government, alarmed by further murderous attacks on landlords and their agents, suddenly arrested four of the agitators, including the popular Michael Davitt. After some days, realizing that no jury would convict them, the government released them – and was ridiculed by both sides all over the country. There is never any satisfactory dealing with such situations: they are intractable.

Nothing remedied the distress owing to the persistent bad harvests in Ireland since 1878, and the relief measures introduced by the government on Marlborough's advice were as persistently obstructed by the Parnellites in Parliament. At length Beacons-

67. ibid., 15. 68. ibid., 17.
69. R. B. O'Brien, *C. S. Parnell*, I. 195.

field, deciding on an appeal to the country, sought to make Ireland the issue. In a historic letter to the Duke he stated that

> a danger, in its ultimate results scarcely less disastrous than pestilence and famine, and which now engages your Excellency's anxious attention, distracts that country. A portion of its population is attempting to sever the constitutional tie which unites it to Great Britain in that bond which has favoured the power and prosperity of both.[70]

This uncompromising statement united both sections of the Home Rule movement, moderates and Parnellites, against the government and helped to give Mr Gladstone a sweeping majority.

Before the Viceroy laid down his charge the Duchess was able to report to the public on the work accomplished by her Relief Fund. Her grandson sums up: 'she was a woman of exceptional capacity, energy and decision, and she laboured earnestly and ceaselessly to collect and administer a great fund'.[71] Its purposes were to supply food, fuel and clothing, especially for the aged and weak; to give grants to schools for free meals for children; to provide seed potatoes for tilling. In spite of the rival fund set going by the Lord Mayor of Dublin, the Duchess ultimately raised £135,000; of which £80,000 went in relief through local committees, £37,000 on seed, £10,000 on clothing. The working expenses were under £1,700, for all the viceregal family were brought into the work.

The Duchess was proud of the work she had accomplished, and treasured the personal letter she received from the Queen in recognition of it. Just before her death she gave the letter to her grandson for the archives at Blenheim, with the touching words, 'I may seem a useless old woman now, but this letter will show you I was once of some importance and did good in my day'.[72] In that are expressed two sides of the Victorian spirit.

The Duke came back from his ungrateful charge to find everything at Blenheim wanting attention. His grandson tells us

70. G. E. Buckle, op. cit., VI. 514–16.
71. Winston S. Churchill, *Lord Randolph Churchill*, I. 110–11.
72. *Reminiscences of Lady Randolph Churchill*, 74.

that the 'estates had suffered from the absence of their owner and those dependent upon them felt acutely the diversion to Ireland and Irish purposes of that personal sympathy and care' which was customarily devoted to the neighbourhood of Blenheim.[73] The life there that Lady Randolph observed with a fresh eye – the family took it all for granted – was resumed. But Randolph had a deep ancestral pride in the place: it was a pity that he was not the heir – except that if he had been a duke the career of his famous son would, nowadays, have been impossible. As the young married couple had been drawn by the loyal inhabitants of Woodstock through Sarah's archway and the scene suddenly, as he had planned, opened out before them, Randolph said to his American bride, 'This is the finest view in England.'

She found the life conducted by the elderly Duke and Duchess of an old-fashioned formality. 'At luncheon rows of *entrée* dishes adorned the table, joints beneath massive silver covers being placed before the Duke and Duchess, who each carved for the whole company, and as this included governesses, tutors and children it was no sinecure.'[74] Sir Winston remembers that after the meal it was the regular thing for the Duchess to fill small panniers with the food that remained over for the children to distribute among the sick and poor of Woodstock and Bladon following the list she gave them. He had the impression that there was nothing to waste or indeed much to spare at that time.

Under the rule of the Duchess when the family were alone the big household went like clockwork: part of the morning devoted to the newspapers, for the conversation at dinner was invariably political; in the afternoon drives to visit neighbours or in the grounds; dinner a rather solemn full-dress affair, and afterwards all would repair to the Van Dyck room. However sleepy,

> no one dared suggest bed until the sacred hour of eleven had struck. Then we would all troop out into a small ante-room and, lighting our candles, each in turn would kiss the Duke and Duchess and depart to

73. Winston S. Churchill, op. cit., I. 115.
74. *Reminiscences of Lady Randolph Churchill*, 58 foll.

our own rooms. . . . The Duke was extremely kind and had the most courteous and *grand seigneur* appearance and manner. His wife was a very remarkable and intelligent woman with a warm heart, particularly for members of her family, which made up for any overmasterfulness of which she might have been accused. She ruled Blenheim and nearly all those in it with a firm hand. At the rustle of her silk dress the household trembled.

Blenheim still possessed most of its treasures. There had been a serious loss when, in February 1861, part of the north-east quadrangle was burnt out and the Titian gallery with all its pictures destroyed. When the intelligence spread to Oxford that the Palace was in flames, 'with equal rapidity several fire-engines and thousands of persons on horseback and on foot were on the way to the spot'.[75] This fine room had contained the series of nine large paintings, attributed to Titian, on gilt leather and given to the great Duke by Victor Amadeus II of Savoy. It also contained a Rubens 'Rape of Proserpine' and a number of family portraits.[76]

What a treasure-house Blenheim must have been! Lady Randolph writes,

when I first went there the far-famed Sunderland Library was still in existence. The beautiful old leather bindings decorated as nothing else can the immense long gallery with its white carved bookcases and vaulted ceiling. Cabinets of Limoges enamels gave the old-world look and Renaissance colouring to the Duchess's sitting-room. There, too, were the Marlborough Gems, besides rooms full of priceless Oriental, Sèvres and Saxe china. And what of the four hundred and fifty pictures all recklessly sold regardless of the remonstrances and prayers of the family and without a thought of future generations! Little did Lord Cairns think when he made his Act affecting the sale of heirlooms that it could be stretched to such a point.[77]

75. *The Times*, 6 February 1861.

76. G. Scharf, *Catalogue of Pictures at Blenheim*, 1860. Consuelo, former Duchess of Marlborough, tells us that 'the gallery was kept locked, since the ladies were not allowed to view the pictures, and great was their delight when it was destroyed by a fire'. – Consuelo Vanderbilt Balsan, *The Glitter and the Gold*, 34.

77. *Reminiscences of Lady Randolph Churchill*, 62.

The Lord Chancellor was a colleague and the Duke was enabled to put through the Blenheim Settled Estates Act in 1880, by which the argument that the Sunderland Library was deteriorating 'through age and other circumstances' was allowed to over-rule the entail.[78] The Duke felt forced to sell the Library, but he cannot have realized what a flood-gate he was opening for his miscreant of an heir to take advantage of. *The Times* urged that this famous Library should be bought for the nation and suggested a figure of £40,000. But those were the days of *laisser-faire* and privileged Philistinism in the highest quarters – the Prince of Wales could have bought it with a fraction of what he spent on his vulgar social life, or the Queen easily from what she saved for her family.

The Duke needed to sell, and this splendid collection of books, monument to the scholarly tastes of the third Earl of Sunderland, passed under the hammer. It contained a fine body of early editions of the classics, a large section of Bibles and Testaments in various languages from early presses; more congenial, there was a large collection of Renaissance authors, including a Valdarfer Boccaccio; a greater number of early books printed on vellum than any private library in Europe possessed, large collections of English county histories, medieval chronicles and of Americana. There was an extraordinarily full section of English pamphlets and tracts ranging from Elizabeth I to Anne, a large number of books on canon and civil law and a unique collection of French controversial tracts of the sixteenth and seventeenth centuries. The Library was sold in two portions, each taking ten days in December 1881 and July 1882. It realized altogether £56,581 6s.[79]

This sum, by the Act, had to go back into the family estate, but the Duke was allowed £2,000 to convert the Library into a picture gallery. The splendid early Georgian woodwork of the bookcases was torn out to instal inferior family portraits ransacked out of obscure corridors. Shortly before he died the

78. D. Green, *Blenheim Palace*, 201.

79. Auction Catalogue of Puttick & Simpson, Bodleian, Mus. Bibl. III. 738, 739, gives this concrete figure; Mr Green gives an estimate of 'about £30,000'.

Duke sent from Blenheim to the saleroom the very fine collection of over eighty Limoges enamels, mostly of the Renaissance. The sale drew a large attendance of amateurs and dealers, but the prices did not reach the figures of the recent Hamilton Palace sale.[80] Several of the items did not come up to their reserve, and Marie-Antoinette's table of Sèvres with painted panels and ormolu was withdrawn. A sum of merely £8,226 was netted: one can imagine the prices these things would fetch today.

Truly, the combination of Victorian piety and politics was not propitious to the arts.

With his Irish experience fresh in mind, the Duke's interventions in the Lords were, in these last years, wholly devoted to that topic. Indeed it dominated British politics throughout Gladstone's second administration and beyond. The Irish Land League, Parnell's obstruction in Parliament, his agitation outside, in Ireland and America, the increasing demand for Home Rule, the deterioration of law and order in Ireland reinforcing the Tory determination against it, the mounting bitterness of the conflict – the dreary question was entering a new and more sinister phase. Marlborough's withdrawal coincided with the effective spread of the weapon of 'boycotting' and the miraculous appearance of the Virgin Mary at Knock, to which thousands of pilgrims arrived from all over the country, though it did not prevent the murders from continuing. In 1880 Lord Mountnorris was murdered, and a deputation of more than a hundred landowners and agents laid their position before the new Liberal Viceroy, with their recommendations of means for restoring law and order.

Mr Gladstone's government was anxious to meet the Irish case and began by suspending coercion. Marlborough expressed the doubt whether they were warranted in so doing, with the situation becoming not less but more threatening.[81] Inevitably there was a further increase in crimes and outrages. The Duke, who knew, pointed to the activities of the secret societies as 'the kernel of the whole state of things'. He had had to witness a record of outrages – murders for which not a tittle of evidence was found, destruction of property without any information

80. *The Times*, 15 June 1883.

81. Hansard, CCCLII. 78.

coming to light, the collision of arms-carrying processions; it was not possible to control such a situation if the government removed the mild measures of repression that were necessary in the interests of public order. And so indeed the government found – much against Mr Gladstone's liberty-loving convictions. As J. L. Hammond points out, Ireland's best friends were increasingly alienated by Irish lawlessness.[82]

It was against this background that Gladstone introduced his Bill for Irish land reform. In August 1881 the Duke made an effective speech against the measure.[83] He said that it was the result of the agitation of the Land League, and there he was right: the British government was conceding to violence and crime what it had not granted to justice and reason. Marlborough claimed that there was ample refutation of the principles of the Bill, from the mouths of its present supporters, in Hansard, 'which records the opinions of public men and which is full of retractations and recantations and disavowals of previous opinions'. True enough: he himself had displayed a remarkable consistency in his public life, where greater men, like Disraeli and Gladstone, had found it more difficult. Nor would the Bill assuage the land-hunger of the Irish; on the contrary –

> Crescit indulgens sibi dirus hydrops,
> Nec sitim pellit, nisi causa morbi
> Fugerit venis, et aquosus albo
> Corpore languor.

'The destruction of the National Church in Ireland was one, and this will be another, among the many monuments to the transcendent ability, but at the same time ill-regulated optimism,' of Mr Gladstone.

The result of this generous optimism was soon to see: 'the number of agrarian outrages, instead of declining, had risen by 60 per cent, while the number of homicides and cases of firing at the person had trebled'.[84] The Liberal Viceroy and his Chief Secretary resigned, and their places were taken by Gladstone's

82. J. L. Hammond, *Gladstone and the Irish Nation*, 208.
83. Hansard, CCCLXIV. 478 foll.
84. R. C. K. Ensor, *England, 1870–1914*, 74.

friend (and Marlborough's remote cousin) Earl Spencer, with Lord Frederick Cavendish as his Chief Secretary. After the pageantry of the state-entry, Lord Frederick and Mr Burke, the permanent Under-Secretary, were surprised within sight and hearing of the Viceregal Lodge by the emissaries of a Dublin murder-club, who hacked them to death with long surgical knives. Even the iron Parnell was appalled. The Duke paid his tribute in the Lords to Mr Burke, acknowledging that it was he who had foreseen the famine and scarcity of the winter of 1879–80 and that it was due to him that steps were taken which were 'the means of preventing a vast amount of want and distress in that country'.[85]

The Duke's last appearance in the Lords, in June 1883, was to make a long speech on a more congenial subject, the Marriage with a Deceased Wife's Sister Bill.[86] One would have thought that the long record of his heir's misconduct, which was now public property through a divorce case before the courts, might have made the old Duke take this subject less seriously. Not so: he ended, as he began, with the defence of the Church. It is somewhat difficult, after the experiences of our age, to feel with their full intensity the force of the sacred objections to marriage with a deceased wife's sister.

The Duke did not rest his case upon an Old Testament prohibition, for there was none; but with Christianity 'a higher law and a higher morality had been introduced'. A Liberal Earl had said that the universal opinion in America was in favour of these marriages. The Duke read a letter from a clergyman in Ohio to the effect that repugnance to them was growing. Moreover, a resolution against the marriage of relations was about to be presented to the General Convention of the Episcopal Church in America. 'A large portion of the American people looked with great interest to the vote their lordships might give on that occasion.' (Was this likely? The Victorian Duke never at any time betrayed, among his immense possessions, a sense of humour.) He ended by letting a decipherable cat out of the bag: the real objection to the Bill was that

85. Hansard, CCCLXIX. 317.
86. ibid., CCCLXXX. 1653.

it was pushed by the Dissenters, and they were the enemies of the Established Church; the end of the Establishment was 'the great object for which every Dissenter in the kingdom had long been striving and which every Radical in the kingdom desired should become an accomplished fact'.

This was the Duke's last battle on behalf of the Church. He had not been able to accomplish much, to arrest the movement of the time; but he managed to hold up a small fraction of the tide at this point. The vote on the Bill in the Lords was a near thing: 140 voted for it, including, very sensibly and understandably, the Prince of Wales; 145 voted against, including 18 bishops, and the Duke as Teller.

The result was that this matter remained over to waste more parliamentary time and people's tempers in the next generation. And appropriately enough the subject was made the special concern of that confirmed bachelor, Lord Hugh Cecil, the Duke's successor as the self-dedicated defender of the Church. The Duke's grandson tells us that he had scarcely got into Parliament when Lord Hugh

> drew me into his vehement resistance to the Bill for allowing a man to marry his deceased wife's sister. I was myself at first sight inclined to think this might be a very excusable and often reasonable arrangement. . . . But when I pointed out these considerations to Lord Hugh Cecil, he was scandalized at my ignorance of Ecclesiastical Law.[87]

Lord Hugh bore him down with a complexity of arguments 'enforced with splendid eloquence and flame of faith which induced me to assist Lord Hugh in the prolonged and successful obstruction of the Deceased Wife's Sister Bill of 1901 in the Grand Committee'. After weeks of obstruction – during which Lord Hugh *loitered in the lobby*! and the venerable Hicks-Beach 'literally crawled inch by inch across the matting which led to the portals where the votes were counted' – the Bill was killed: an enjoyable time had been had by all, except the Deceased Wives' Sisters.

Years after, Sir Winston admits that 'in the growing tolerance of the age I was ultimately induced to acquiesce in the legalizing

87. Winston S. Churchill, *Thoughts and Adventures* (1947 ed.), 35–8.

of a man's marriage with his deceased wife's sister'. It is obvious that he can no longer remember what it was that he found so compelling in Lord Hugh's arguments against this sensible measure. Perhaps it was the sheer joy of obstruction.

A few days after his last speech in the Lords the Duke died, of a sudden heart-attack on 5 July 1883.[88] His body was taken to Blenheim where he lay in state; some three thousand people passed before the coffin, a genuine tribute to a man worthy of respect. There was fine weather for the funeral – the mayor and corporation of Woodstock in their robes, tenantry lining the steps, a gathering of his political colleagues, Blandford and Lord Randolph present. The coffin was lowered into the vault at the foot of Rysbrack's monument to the great Duke, while they all sang 'I heard the voice of Jesus say'. There was a *contretemps* over the solitary cross of white lilies, roses and maidenhair said to have been placed there for the Marchioness of Blandford, now definitely parted from her erring husband; two days later this was contradicted – it had been placed there, of course, at the express wish of the widowed Duchess. Lord Randolph incontinently left Blenheim for the Continent.

There is little to reveal this reserved, discreet, dutiful man in his will.[89] The long and wordy document is chiefly content to recite and confirm previous settlements: little that is personal in it. His Duchess was provided for by the terms of her marriage settlement; but the Duke left her £2,000 for her immediate use and convenience, all the contents of his town-house in Berkeley Square, from Blenheim what furniture she should select, with all the jewelry and trinkets she wore, 'except the three large diamonds set now in her necklace and which have been substituted for diamonds formerly set in the sword of John Duke of Marlborough and subjected to the trusts and provisions affecting the said sword as an heirloom'. (This was the famous sword that Sarah had refused to make over to her grandson Charles, on the ground that he would pawn the diamonds.) Several clauses are concerned with the settlements he had made on his daughters at

88. *The Times*, 6 and 11 July 1883.

89. Somerset House. Proved 15 September 1883, at above £146,000, according to *The Complete Peerage*, VIII. 502.

the time of their marriages, Lady Wimborne, Lady Rosamond Fellowes, Lady Fanny Marjoribanks, the Duchess of Roxburghe – each of whom had received £8,666 13s. 4d.; and there were two unmarried daughters. His aim seems to be to raise their portions to £10,000 apiece. The residue of his personal stocks and shares were to form a trust, with the income for his widow for her life, afterwards to go to Lord Randolph.

Nothing in his life contradicts, everything corroborates, the verdict on him of the *Dictionary of National Biography*: 'a sensible, honourable and industrious public man'.

Chapter 9

Edwardian Reaction

LONG before Queen Victoria died Edwardian society proclaimed itself and took possession of the scene. It was with her reign as it had been with her grandfather's – with George III and the Regent – the withdrawal of the monarch from general society left the heir to the throne to take the lead and set the pace. And in both cases a very fast pace was set – a marked reaction from the sedateness and sobriety of the parents. In both cases it was very understandable. Queen Victoria's exaggerated grief for the Prince Consort, the cult she vowed to his memory and morosely inflicted on her family and entourage, with the impression she gave of resentment against Providence for delivering him from her – one sees it in the expression of her face, the turned-down corners of the mouth – all testified to the emotional extremism of her pure German blood. Nothing could be more un-English. Though the heir to the throne again spoke English with a German accent he was at least gay, did enjoy life, was a sport – though perhaps not always a sportsman – and was in full touch with the commoner currents of the nation's life.

The Prince of Wales was a kind of Prinny come again, with all his social gifts, his immense gusto and conviviality; wherever he went a troupe of companions surrounded him, of both sexes: he was never alone and never in the same place for long. If he had not the Regent's artistic flair, his fantasy or his taste, he was even more an amateur of the beauty of women. Apart from that he had as good as no taste at all. With him dress and the punctilios of social behaviour took the place that high politics, and the affairs of her family, took in his mother's mind. He could not bear women, for whom he had such a nose, to be ill-dressed. To the remarkable Lady Salisbury, who had a mind above such things, he one day said reprovingly: 'Lady Salisbury, I think I have seen that dress before'. 'Yes, and you'll see it again', replied that lady, undaunted but most improperly.

By the 1870s society had found its acknowledged leader: people looked to Marlborough House and Sandringham, where the Prince and Princess of Wales ruled and entertained continually, as in the earlier years of the century they had looked to Carlton House and the Pavilion at Brighton. Marlborough House had undergone some interesting changes since the Marlboroughs' lease had come to an end: first came Princess Charlotte and her husband, Prince Leopold, then William IV's widow, Queen Adelaide. Latterly it had been a National School of Design: the pictures were removed to the National Gallery, the drawing classes to South Kensington and the house a good deal altered to make room for Albert Edward and Alexandra. A large state dining-room was added for their entertainments, three of Sarah's original small rooms on the ground floor were thrown into one long Red Drawing-Room; a third storey was added to spoil the proportions, the windows given plate-glass to impair the look of the house. Yet not even these characteristic Edwardian improvements – they might have been worse – succeeded in destroying the distinction of the house Wren, and Sarah, conceived.

The Marlborough House set led the younger generation and was in every way more liberal-minded, more Continental in its outlook, its manners and modes, than the stuffy closed atmosphere of the Court, ruled by the standards of the Queen and her ladies, intensely conservative, dedicated to duty without pleasure, the monotony of endless work and routine – Windsor, Balmoral, Osborne, with rare appearances in London. Marlborough House was essentially cosmopolitan, its *habitués* as much at home at Auteuil, Longchamps, Chantilly as at Newmarket, Ascot, Goodwood; the Prince and Princess of Wales were accustomed to spend several months of the year abroad, their regular routine including Biarritz, Homburg, Marienbad, with frequent appearances in Paris or at Monte Carlo. (When the great Lord Salisbury made one appearance there he was, to the delight of his family, rejected from the Casino on the ground that he was unsuitably dressed.) To the familiar figures of the Austrian and Portuguese ministers, Count Mensdorff and the Marquis de Soveral, Marlborough House added a distinctive American element: there were Minnie Stevens of New York, later Lady Paget, Mrs Cavendish Bentinck, and Consuelo, Duchess of Manchester. Upon these followed Jennie Jerome, who married Lord Randolph Churchill, and later Consuelo Vanderbilt, who became Duchess of Marlborough.

The America of those days must have been essentially a man's world: the movement of menfolk was westward to its wide-open spaces and wider opportunities, while it was the women who came east, crossing the Atlantic to lay London and Paris at their feet. They were not without the prizes of conquest: Lady Randolph Churchill herself noted that nowhere in the world had women so much influence in politics as they had in London.

And what a time they all had! These were the last days of a privileged society to whom all the earth was open: from Vladivostok or Kyoto all the way across the Old World and the New to Wyoming, where there were buffalo still to be shot. The massacre of big game all over the world at the hands of these gentlemen – tiger-hunts in India, lions, rhinoceros, elephants in Africa – makes characteristic (and sickening) reading. 'He was a magnificent specimen, 9 feet 7 inches in length, and a splendid skin, which will, I think, look very well in Grosvenor Square', writes Lord Randolph home to his wife.[1] 'Tigers in the Zoo give one very little idea of what the wild animal is like.' (One wonders what has happened to all the tiger-skins that garnished Edwardian houses.) Or it is,

> yesterday we hunted one leopard, which ultimately escaped after being much fired at and, I think, grievously wounded. I shot a very nice swamp deer, and Thomas a nilghai or blue bull. We also shot pea-fowl, bustards and partridges, and every variety of bird. We have fifteen elephants, and these creatures are an unfailing source of interest and amusement.

At home it was much the same sort of thing: massed battues of birds over thickly-preserved coverts in East Anglia or Yorkshire; or the expensive routine of deer-stalking in Scotland. Every county had its hunts, though hunting was at its most opulent in the Midlands, especially Leicestershire. (This was an

1. *The Reminiscences of Lady Randolph Churchill*, 114–17.

opulent society, apt to judge – and include – by capacity to spend.) There was the still more extravagant interest in horse-racing. All these avocations went with constant entertaining, large country-house parties, complete with baccarat, bridge or billiards, with the singers, variety artists, orchestras of the day to help to entertain them. At the top it was a European society with its Courts all the way from St Petersburg to Seville, in which its glittering denizens were – if not equally, at any rate everywhere – at home.

What added a peculiarity to the English version and gave it its flavour was that here there was a national sport, in which the privileged and the unprivileged were equally judges of form: politics. Nothing could exceed the passionate interest taken in politics in that age, whether by society in the narrow and exclusive sense or by society at large – when the appearance of a national figure like Mr Gladstone or Lord Randolph Churchill could hold up the traffic and suspend the life of a large city for hours. Lord Randolph's son, who was born in that age, tells us how things were:

> I was a child of the Victorian era, when the structure of our country seemed firmly set, when its position in trade and on the seas was unrivalled, and when the realization of the greatness of our Empire and of our duty to preserve it was ever growing stronger. In those days the dominant forces in Great Britain were very sure of themselves and of their doctrines. They were sure they were supreme at sea and consequently safe at home. They rested therefore sedately under the convictions of power and security.[2]

Such was the high Victorian position. We may not be wrong in diagnosing an increase of tempo, a certain loosening of morale, a feverishness and a brittleness, that differentiated the Edwardian tone from the high Victorian. Some of its glitter we may impute to the phosphorescence of decay.

The two sons of the seventh Duke were yet another George, Marquis of Blandford, and Lord Randolph – a new name to appear in the family: whence it came I do not know. Throughout

2. Winston S. Churchill, *My Early Life* (*A Roving Commission*), 9–10.

their short, and rather hectic, lives they remained firmly attached to each other – except for one brief interval, when they had a serious quarrel, and not without good reason. The elder was born 13 May 1844, the younger 13 February 1849. Both were sent to Eton, though with such a gap in age between them they did not overlap.

Young Randolph's home-letters from Eton remind one of his ancestor's, the fourth Duke, when a boy: there are the similar concerns of their small world, the family's doings, the dogs and ponies, sport, the birds, the successes of the Heythrop hounds, occasionally some political event that impinges, an election at Woodstock or a visit from Mr Disraeli. One March day in 1863 came the wedding of the Prince of Wales to Princess Alexandra, which caused his mother such mortification and gave Mrs Disraeli such a triumph. As an Eton boy Randolph had a first-class view inside Windsor Castle and describes it all graphically in a letter to his father.

> We were all mustered in the school-yard about eleven o'clock, and then marched up Windsor into the Castle by Henry VIII's gate. There we had to stand for a tremendous time without anything coming. At last the first procession came; it was the King of Denmark and all those people. We had a beautiful view of all the people. Then we had to wait about a quarter of an hour, and then came the Princess Royal. She was sitting on our side, and she bowed away as hard as she could go. (I think her neck must have been stiff.) And then came the Prince; he looked extremely gracious. And last of all came the Princess. And then there was such a row, in spite of the Queen's express commands that there was to be no cheering. I never heard such an awful noise in all my life. I think, if the Queen heard it, she must have had a headache for a long time afterwards.[3]

When the Prince and Princess came out after the ceremony, the Eton boys – pent up with so long waiting – rushed after their carriage down the hill, Randolph in the van.

> I was right in the front of the charge; it was a second Balaclava. Nothing stood before us; the policemen charged in a body, but they were knocked down. There was a chain put across the road, but we broke that; several old *genteel* ladies tried to stop me, but I snapped my fingers in their face and cried 'Hurrah!' and 'What larks!' I frightened

3. Winston S. Churchill, *Lord Randolph Churchill*, I. 9–11.

some of them horribly. There was a wooden palisade put up at the station (it was the Great Western), but we broke it down; and there, to my unspeakable grief, I was bereaved of a portion of my clothing, viz. my hat. Somebody knocked it off. I could not stop to pick it up. I shrieked out a convulsive, 'Oh, my hat!' and was then borne on. I got right down to the door of the carriage where the Prince of Wales was, wildly shouting 'Hurrah!' He bowed to me, I am perfectly certain; but I shrieked louder. . . . At last the train moved off while the band played 'God save the Queen'. There I was left, in the station, hatless.

It was his first introduction to the Prince, with whom his life was to be variously associated: first friendship, then a breach that reverberated all through society, last reconciliation and frequent meetings. This vivid school-boy letter may also be taken to pre-figure a good deal else in Lord Randolph's career and fortunes.

Subsequent letters show the terms of mutual concern and confidence upon which the Duke was with his gifted son. Randolph: 'I cannot tell you how delighted I was when you wrote and told me that you had accepted the office of Lord President of the Council. I think it is just the office that you would like best.'[4] One notices the characteristic 'I think'. Pride in his younger son did not induce the Duke to spare him censure for some equally characteristic act of rebelliousness: 'to tell you the truth, I fear that you yourself are very impatient and resentful of any control; and while you stand upon some fancied right or injury, you fail to perceive what is your *duty*, and allow both your language and manner a most improper scope'.[5] That scored a bull's eye: it remained true of Randolph all his life, his greatest failing. As his mother who adored him wrote, with touching humility,

Alas! had I been a clever woman, I must have had more ability to curb and control his impulses, and I should have taught him patience and moderation. Yet at times he had extraordinary good judgement, and it was only on rare occasions that he took the bit between his teeth, and then there was no stopping him.[6]

It must be said that there was a Churchillian vein of unamenability in him, that all his life he was incorrigible.

4. Winston S. Churchill, *Lord Randolph Churchill*, I. 23.
5. ibid., I. 12–13. 6. ibid., I. 14–15.

After Eton he went up to Oxford, at the same time as the school-friend who became Lord Rosebery. There their friendship was confirmed for life: after the Conservative leader's early death the Liberal Prime Minister wrote the most perceptive and the most generous account of his personality. In yet another generation the house of Blenheim refrained from sending its son to Christ Church: Lord Randolph went to Merton, where he came under the encouraging tutorship of the politic Creighton. Here he narrowly missed a First in the Schools – no mean achievement for a young aristocrat who was giving the greater part of his energies to the Blenheim Harriers he had started and whose affairs he was conducting most methodically.

Meanwhile, his brother was serving as an officer in the Blues, enjoying all the delights of life proper to a young man of his station. After a considerable experience of these he fell in love with a beautiful daughter of the Duke of Abercorn: Lady Albertha Hamilton was as good as she was beautiful, as pious as she was innocent, and really rather stupid. He was neither pious, nor innocent, nor stupid. In fact he seems to have been a clever man whose cleverness ran all to seed; a hedonist whose pursuit of pleasure (in the form of women) brought him no satisfaction; a very *désabusé* man of whom no one approved, a man to whom life gave a decided chip on the shoulder. Everyone keeps quiet about him, he was so very much disapproved of in his day: his elusive, unhappy, buried personality intrigues one the more. There was some inner source of restlessness incapable of satisfaction in him, as there was in his brother. There was an element of reaction against the religiosity of their parents – though both sons, natural rebels as they were, deeply respected their father, while Randolph adored, and was spoiled by, his mother. Perhaps it was too high breeding: too many marriages within an exclusive aristocratic circle, and what was wanted was a good middle-class marriage like that which revivified the stock with the Cecils – or an American marriage bringing in a renewal of spirits, confidence in life, boundless zest and unfaltering courage. That was on the way for one of the brothers – with what incalculable, what historic, results!

The Marquis of Blandford married his ducal bride in Westminster Abbey, 8 November 1869, and was at once bored with his treasure. Her chief accomplishment seems to have been practical jokes. At a Blenheim dinner-party she once placed small bits of soap indistinguishably among pieces of cheese. A rich guest, too polite to spit this out, was rendered extremely sick and – 'Fancy, he never forgave me'. Her husband would open a door, to receive the contents of an ink-pot on his head. When he took up chemistry, in which he became passionately interested – like the fourth Duke in gems and astronomy, the fifth in botany and music – Albertha mixed up his chemical experiments for him. As if these were not sufficient grounds for divorce, he added others, more savoury, on his part.

A few years later Lord Randolph found for himself a most unexpected bride. In the high summer of 1873, now aged twenty-four, he was at Cowes when a ball was given in honour of the Tsarevich and the Tsarevna who had arrived in the *Ariadne*. Here he met Miss Jennie Jerome, whose mother had taken a cottage there for the summer. Next night he went to dinner with them. The third evening he went for a walk with Miss Jerome, proposed to her and was accepted.

This sudden train of events was not easy to explain to Blenheim. To the Duke he wrote,

> I must not any longer keep you in ignorance of a very important step I have taken – one which will undoubtedly influence very strongly all my future life. . . . I know, of course, that you will be very much surprised and find it difficult to understand how an attachment so strong could have arisen in so short a space of time; and really I feel it quite impossible for me to give any explanation of it that could appear reasonable to anyone practical and dispassionate.[7]

In short, this was, what one often hears about but seldom meets, a romantic instance of love-at-first-sight. And her family? 'Mr Jerome is a gentleman who is obliged to live in New York to look after his business. I do not know what it is.'

This could hardly be expected to be thought good enough by the Duke, who wrote back, 'it is not likely that at present you

7. Winston S. Churchill, *Lord Randolph Churchill*, I. 41–3.

can look at anything except from your own point of view; but persons from the outside cannot but be struck with the unwisdom of your proceedings, and the uncontrolled state of your feelings, which completely paralyses your judgement'. Blandford was now able to support this view with a set of witty, but presumably unprintable, verses on what happens to those who marry in haste.

Who was Jennie Jerome anyway?

She was the daughter of one of the finest men, certainly one of the sunniest and most golden natures, to arise out of the hurly-burly of New York in the middle of the nineteenth century. Leonard Jerome, born at Syracuse in New York State, was descended from an old Huguenot family of La Rochelle who had left for America as early as the time when the Tories were coming back into power under Queen Anne and Marlborough was on his way out. As a boy Leonard Jerome had moved westward to Palmyra, whence he went to Princeton quite poor, though this did not prevent him from enjoying himself, as he did everywhere all through life with a zest that people, but especially women, found irresistible. Tall, good-looking, abounding in vitality, he married dark Clara Hall, who was one-quarter Iroquois from those woods. So that her eldest grandson, Sir Winston, in the middle of some war-time dispute with the Americans, was able to claim in his own right, 'Tell them I was there before they were!' (This, in addition, to an unbroken male descent five generations back on his mother's side to a lieutenant in Washington's army: too unfair for argument.)

Leonard Jerome brought his bride to New York in 1850, where he proceeded to make (and lose) his first fortune, make a second and bigger one on Wall Street, and fall for the singing of Jenny Lind – hence his second daughter's name. Appointed consul at Trieste for a time, he gave himself up to the delights of sailing in the Adriatic as he had done to making money and music, making up to women. Mrs Jerome lost her heart to Europe, and when she paid a visit to Paris later – the adorable, gimcrack Paris of the Second Empire, of Eugénie and Princesse Mathilde, of Morny and Offenbach and Meyerbeer, of the brilliant blue uniforms of the Imperial Guard, parties at Compiègne and the new boulevards of the Baron Haussmann – 'I have found the Court I want', she said.

Back at home it was the New York of *The House of Mirth*. In partnership with Commodore Vanderbilt – Consuelo's grandfather – Leonard Jerome could only prosper, but he knew how to spend his money more agreeably. It is said that some $10 millions ran through his fingers; it is certain that he gave a quarter of a million dollars to the sufferers from the New York riots of 1863. He owned one-quarter of the *New York Times* at one time, and on the conclusion of the war he backed the Southern Relief Fund: 'we must ease the bitterness', he declared. No more generous spirit ever existed, and no more joyous. He built himself a house on Madison Square with a private theatre and a stables at the back. From the one he brought forth the singers he launched upon their careers – Minnie Hauk, America's first prima donna, and Fanny Ronalds, her second; from the other he produced the horses with which he created and refined flat-track racing in America and became, with August Belmont, a Father of the American Turf.

He was the first in the States to drive four-in-hand. One sees him driving up the more spacious, rattling Fifth Avenue of those days, soon reaching country where now Central Park begins –

> gay and laughing ladies in gorgeous costumes filled the carriage. Lackeys, carefully gotten up, occupied the coupé behind; Jerome sat on the box and handled the reins. With a huge bouquet of flowers attached to his button-hole, with white gloves, cracking his whip, and with the shouts of the party, the four horses would rush up Fifth Avenue, on toward the Park, while the populace said, one to the other, 'That is Jerome'.[8]

They were on the way to the race-track he had created: Jerome Park. Not content with triumphs on land, he backed the *Henrietta* on the first ocean sailing race, sailed the Atlantic in her through the storms of mid-winter, narrowly missed being presented to Queen Victoria on landing at the Isle of Wight – and won $100,000 on the result.

8. q. Anita Leslie, *The Fabulous Leonard Jerome*, 85.

Everyone had to admit that Jerome made his money honestly: 'that damn fellow has cashed in on honesty'. But in the years after the Civil War his luck turned: he suffered enormous losses on Pacific Mail, and in a default on Indiana bonds; he was involved in a friend's failure with Georgia stock. With the remains of his fortunes he was engaged in giving the best he could to wife and daughters now set up in Paris in the last days of the Empire.

His daughter has written well on what life was like in those years. 'The last flicker of the candle, the last flame of the dying fire, is ever the brightest; and so it was with Paris in 1869. Never had the Empire seemed more assured, the Court more brilliant, the fêtes more gorgeous. The Bois de Boulogne and the Champs-Elysées, where we were living at that time, were crowded with splendid equipages. I remember often seeing the Empress Eugénie, then the handsomest woman in Europe, driving in her daumont, the green and gold liveries of the postilions and outriders making a brave show.'[9] But it was not a question of observing this pageantry, these cavalcades, from the outside: *la belle Américaine* and her daughters were invited not only to the formal receptions at the Tuileries, but to the Empress's favoured *petits Lundis*, the Emperor's hunting parties at Compiègne.

It was after one of the *petits Lundis* that a sinister note was sounded by a German diplomat. Count Hatzfeldt remarked, 'I never saw their Majesties in better spirits than they were last night, and God knows where they will be next year at this time.'[10] He knew. In the interval Bismarck had his war; the Second Empire crashed in ruins and that is how Mrs Jerome and her daughters came to be spending the summer at Cowes. She had meant to marry her daughters to French noblemen. Fate (in the shape of Bismarck) ordained otherwise: all three of them married Englishmen, so that all Leonard Jerome's grandchildren – himself the most American of men – grew up English.

Mr Jerome, who was as proud as any duke, was displeased by the Duke's attitude; he considered his daughter good enough for any duke's son – as indeed she was. And yet the Duke's attitude was not at all unreasonable: how could he be sure, especially

9. *Reminiscences of Lady Randolph Churchill*, 4–5. 10. ibid., 7.

with Blandford's experience before his eyes, that Randolph's three-day infatuation would last, was a strong enough foundation for marriage? He knew, none better, his son's impulsiveness, his wilfulness and impatience. He did not reject Lord Randolph's request; he imposed a year's delay: 'if this time next year you come and tell me that you are both of the same mind we will receive Miss Jerome as a daughter and, I need not say, in the affection you could desire for your wife'.[11]

The fact was that the Duke was expecting an election this year and was determined that nothing should stand in the way of his brilliant son being returned for Woodstock. 'It is for this that they have kept me idle ever since I left Oxford, waiting for a dissolution', he wrote to Jennie.

I have two courses open to me: either to refuse to stand altogether unless they consent to my being married immediately afterwards; or else – and this is still more Machiavellian and deep – to stand, but at the last moment to threaten to withdraw and leave the Radical to walk over. All tricks are fair in love and war.

One recognizes the authentic Churchillian note.

The election came early in 1874 and Lord Randolph – perhaps his situation aroused sympathy – got a record majority. He reported to Jennie:

the poll was not declared till eleven, and the hours of suspense were most trying; but when it was known, there was such a burst of cheers that must have made the old Dukes in the vault jump. . . . There is nothing more to be done except to pay the bill, and that I have left to my father.[12]

After this there was no more resistance on either side. The Duke capitulated; Mr Jerome capitulated, and added £6,000 a year to the young couple – never enough as it was, at the pace they went and the rate they spent. What was more, Mr Jerome became the staunchest believer in Lord Randolph in all his ups and downs: he recognized a man after his own heart, a man ready to take his life in his hands, a gambler and a sport; though he complained that none of his grandchildren was American, Randolph's son, named Leonard after him, was

11. Winston S. Churchill, op. cit., I. 46–7.   12. ibid., I. 55.

always his favourite grandchild. And indeed the boy turned greatly after him.

The impatient young couple were married in Paris in April; we have noted their welcome to 'the leafy glories of Blenheim in the spring'. At the end of November Lady Randolph, prancing about with too much vivacity for her condition and out in the park that very day with the guns – the child no doubt eager to arrive on the public scene and start his career without further delay – had to be hustled back into the house and there, in a drab downstairs back room, gave birth. This room had been the original chaplain's, Dean Jones – the gluttonous-looking old cleric one sees painted by Laguerre in the saloon – who was said to haunt it still. Such was the force of the new arrival, or the influence of the event, that it exorcized that baleful presence; at any rate he has not been seen there since. (We remember from Shaw that a miracle is 'an event which creates faith'.) The boy was given the names of his two grandfathers: Winston Leonard Spencer Churchill.

With this agreeable event out of the way Lady Randolph was able to throw herself and her younger sister, Clara, into the delights of London society, and a dazzling season they had of it in 1875. For Jennie there was entertaining the Prime Minister, fascinating old Mr Disraeli, to dinner at their little house or being taken to the opening of Parliament by Lord Rosebery. The purely social side of life is depicted in Clara's artless letters to Mrs Jerome; and from them we see that there was a certain *froideur* between the elderly Marlboroughs, of Queen Victoria's generation and outlook, and the Randolph Churchills, who were at once taken up by the Prince of Wales's fast set – Jennie was made much of by them – and made free of Marlborough House.

In June they were all at Ascot. 'Jennie wants me so much to be nice to Sir William Gordon-Cumming and wants him to make up to me. He began *très sérieusement à faire la cour* to Jennie, but last night he would not leave me in the hall. But I could not think of him at all as he is very poor and not *sympathique*.'[13] (Though not *sympathique*, he was in fact rich: famous for his tiger-hunting exploits in India.) 'Tonight there is this dreadful

13. Anita Leslie, op. cit., 197–202.

dinner at the Square [Berkeley Square, the Marlboroughs' town-house] which will be such a bore. I can't tell you how jealous Randolph says the Duchess is of Jennie and I [*sic*.]. She is always very kind and amiable but *une certaine aigreur* in the way she talks.' No doubt there were the usual feminine jealousies.

Next day:

I never saw such wonderful *toilettes* and the Royal Enclosure was very swell and select. Lord Hartington took me to lunch in a private room with the royalties, the Prince himself giving his arm to Jennie and altogether the day was *très réussi*.

Clara 'took lunch' with the editor of *The Times*:

he has a charming house on the other side of the course and we only had chic people. Mr and Miss Stevens were there[14] and Mrs Stevens told Mrs Farquhar, it seems, that she 'hoped little Lady Randolph had better manners than she had last year'. Such a common vulgar creature she is. Jennie took her Sir William Cumming all to herself, he being the swell of the party, and does not let anyone else talk to him.

Back in London there was a ball, at which 'the Prince gave me his bouquet in the flower figure and I saw Rosamond [Randolph's unmarried sister] and Miss Stevens *green* with jealousy. He (the Pce) was very civil to Jennie and I talked to the Princess, so taking it all in all it was most satisfactory.' At the Westminsters' ball, 'the Duchess and Rosamond looked so jealous when Jennie and I appeared in our new dresses'. It was for this that poor Mr Jerome was working so hard now in New York.

At the end of the season the Prince proposed himself for an Indian tour – tiger-hunting included. The Queen took alarm at the proposal: there was her jealousy of her position as Queen, there was her specifically Hanoverian jealousy of the heir who was to succeed her. (At this time she could not look at him without shuddering, she said, and communicated with him through her Cabinet ministers.) The proposed tour raised the critical question of expense. It would not do to do it on a fairly simple scale, as the Prince had done on his tour of the Colonies.

14. From New York.

His friends advocated that everything should be done on an Imperial scale, with ample provision for the exchange of presents demanded by Oriental courtesy – and no doubt for other little things too.

Between one and the other of them, between Queen Victoria and the Prince, backed up by his set, what could the Prime Minister do but compromise? Disraeli described the Prince, to one of his two Egerias, as 'a thoroughly spoilt child, who can't bear being bored', adding irresistibly, 'I don't much myself'.[15] To his other Egeria Dizzy wrote, 'I have had ceaseless correspondence with the Faery, [his private name for the Queen] who had refused Prince and Secy. of State to permit H.R.H. to hold an investiture of the Star of India, and things looked very black indeed. I had to interfere.' The Queen gave way to her Prime Minister, 'As you recommend me to do it I consent, but I don't like it.'

Disraeli proposed a vote of £60,000 for the Prince's personal expenses in addition to the costs of the journey. His friends thought that inadequate: they saw themselves accompanying him at official expense. So did the Queen. They got up a letter to *The Times*, which Disraeli describes as

> written by Randolph Churchill, under the dictation of Blandford and Bartle Frere. Under their inspiration he had prepared a Marlborough House manifesto, and utterly broke down, destroying a rising reputation. The letter is a mass of absurdities. It assumes the P. is to make presents to the 95 reigning Princes. If he visited them all, his tour wd. be six years, not six months. He will visit only about five.

Next came the question of who was to accompany him. The Queen wanted him suitably encased in an entourage of serious-minded personages. The Prince, in his determination not to be bored, insisted on half a dozen of his Marlborough House cronies – Lord Charles Beresford, Lord Carrington, the Duke of Sutherland, above all the Earl of Aylesford, a champion pig-sticker and polo-player, otherwise 'Sporting Joe'. Thereby came the fall. For Lord Aylesford had an attractive Welsh wife, to whom the Prince had been paying marked attention and even writing letters.

15. G. E. Buckle, *The Life of Benjamin Disraeli*, V. 429–30.

It would not do to leave Sporting Joe out of the party; the malicious said that the Prince was afraid to leave him behind.

As it happened, the Indian tour in the cold weather of 1875–6 was an immense success, as the Prince had felt it would be: he took care to make it so.

But Lord Aylesford had to return in the middle of it; for his frail lady had another admirer: Lord Blandford. He took the opportunity of Sporting Joe's absence to move his horses down to an inn not far from the Aylesfords' house for a good winter's hunting. Someone took the trouble to write Joe a letter to come home. Surprisingly enough he did.

The result was that he threatened to take proceedings that would incriminate Blandford, and the Prince backed his cause warmly. It was here that Lord Randolph came to his brother's rescue most effectively, but rashly, without counting the consequences, and in the event unwisely. Who was the Prince to intervene against his brother? He declared that if proceedings were taken he would publish the letters the Prince had written the lady. We can only infer that the lady had placed them at his disposal and that this was her way of defending her lover. In fact, there was a regular – or, rather, irregular – affair between them; for in the spring of 1876 Blandford refused to give up the lady: he preferred to part with his wife.[16]

For the Prince this was a terrible rebuff from a future subject, still more from a young man he had made his friend: deeply as he disapproved of Blandford's conduct, he had been made to withdraw by a threat. Lord Randolph's best friend could not approve of his action, so we must conclude that the Prince was more in the right: he was standing, if not for the proprieties, at any rate for the rules, of the game.

(Now we know why Queen Victoria was not amused by the proceedings of her son or the company he kept. Oddly enough, when he came to the throne he made a good king, dignified and conscientious, judicious and popular.)

But for Lord Randolph this had been a fatal step socially. The Prince let it be known that he would not set foot in any house that received him, and this meant complete social ostracism.

16. *Law Reports, Probate Division,* VIII, 1883, 19.

It was a bitter experience for a young couple, just as they were launched upon a brilliant course. One sees traces of the bitterness in Lady Randolph's sunny-natured *Reminiscences*. All the fashionable world held aloof from them, no longer invited anywhere: 'most people in the course of a lifetime get to know the real value of the Mammon of Unrighteousness, but few learn their lesson so early. We both profited by it. Personally I would never give up anything by which I really set store for the sake of its unsatisfactory approbation.'[17] But Lord Randolph was a young politician dependent on the world to make his way in it. There is no doubt that the iron entered into his soul; from this time a more corrosive strain appears in his wit. All this had put him wrong with society, and in the singular way in which these mixtures work out in human motivation – a dash of iron, a drop of poison – this experience gave an edge to his ambition, which had so far not declared itself, not even been aroused: it awoke in him a determination to make himself felt, and as he was impelled to declare war on humbug this took an increasingly restless, uncompromising and even Radical form.[18]

For the moment, to make themselves scarce and obtain some distraction, the Churchills went off on what was Randolph's first visit to America. They visited Niagara in a heat-wave and took refuge at Newport, which they found altogether more urban than Cowes. Thence they went to the Philadelphia Exhibition, which they were shown round by Jennie's uncle and much enjoyed. When they got back to London they found that the Duke had accepted the Irish Viceroyalty, largely in their interest; and Ireland, with few visits to London, was their refuge for the next four years.

This, however, was no solution for Blandford. In 1877 Lord Aylesford and his wife were separated. Next year Lady Blandford,

17. *Reminiscences of Lady Randolph Churchill*, 104.

18. cf. his son, 'I had no idea in those days of the enormous and unquestionably helpful part that humbug plays in the social life of great peoples dwelling in a state of democratic freedom'. – Winston S. Churchill, *My Early Life*, 70.

unable to obtain a regular income from her husband – we have seen that money was tight – got a deed of separation executed, securing a maintenance. However, Lady Blandford refrained from insisting on her rights: she – as they used to say – 'forgave him' on condition he 'sinned no more'. In July 1878 they began to try living together again until they found in April 1882 that they could stand it no longer.[19]

It must have been during this period that Lady Blandford thought up the best (or worst) of her practical jokes. One morning at breakfast the Marquis, on lifting the cover concealing his bacon and egg, was greeted by a small pink baby doll. Lady Blandford can hardly have known that in November 1881 Lady Aylesford gave birth to a son at 8 Avenue Friedland in Paris, whose reputed father was the Marquis.[20] But breakfast is no time for practical jokes. The Marquis departed: this time for good. In February 1883, on his wife's complaint of desertion, she was granted a divorce. It is evident that nothing could have made those two compatible.

These things must have grieved the last years of the pious old Duke, even if they did not cause him to question the gravity of marriage with a Deceased Wife's Sister. When he died in July 1883 both brothers received a shock: he had been for so long the dominating figure in their landscape. Especially for Randolph, who was deeply moved, gave himself up for hours to reading over his father's letters and went down to Blenheim to remember the past. 'It is very melancholy here – sad recollections at every moment. Nothing can be nicer than Blandford to everyone.'[21] At this moment of grief the brothers were drawn close together. The new Duke joined Randolph in Switzerland in August and they came home together. While abroad Lord Randolph had been infuriated by the opposition to his brother's election to the Carlton Club. 'And now how can anyone occupy a more unpleasant position than Blandford does? He has publicly changed his politics, to please me more than for any other reason, and owing to H. Chaplin's action his overtures to the Conservatives

19. *Law Reports*, loc. cit., 19–20.
20. *The Complete Peerage*, by G. E. C., new edn., I.
21. Winston S. Churchill, *Lord Randolph Churchill*, I. 267.

are spurned. . . .'[22] From which we can only infer that Blandford had enjoyed a spell of Liberalism: on acquaintance he becomes more and more like his ancestors, the fifth and sixth Dukes.

However, the new master of Blenheim had better fish to fry. He persuaded Lord Randolph to start up the Blenheim harriers again, and many a good day's hunting they had that autumn and winter. Together they pressed forward the Duke's scheme of bringing the railway from Oxford to Woodstock: which resulted in that delightful meandering single-track line across the meadows, with the little railway-station, closed in our time. The eighth Duke was a modern-minded man, and this we see with a vengeance in his next venture.

It was, ironically, the virtuous seventh Duke who set his son the worst of all possible examples in the dispersal of the Blenheim treasures. He had only to follow in his father's footsteps. His father had been driven by necessity, but there is no reason to suppose that he would ever have contemplated what his son proposed and proceeded to carry out – a clean sweep of all the Blenheim pictures, not to mention a trifle like the china and porcelain, which in itself took a three-day sale to disperse.

The eighth Duke was no fool, and for some time he had been watching the trends of sale prices, the immense figures given for favourite old masters. Perhaps he was influenced by the fabulous sums realized by the Hamilton Palace sales – some £400,000 in 1882 – the result of the doings of another miscreant duke. When the family realized what he proposed to do a stiff struggle was engaged, Lord Randolph taking the lead. The brothers had stood together in their fortunes hitherto; now there was a violent quarrel, an open breach, and no wonder.

For a couple of years before the great sales took place in 1886 it had been known that the new Duke intended to disperse the whole of the famous Blenheim collection. *The Times* said that this news had engaged the attention of the art world for the past two years.[23] Under the Chancery order obtained by the Duke's father, twenty-five of the finest pictures had been offered to the National Gallery for £400,000. This was a steep price, and

22. Winston S. Churchill, op. cit., I. 165.
23. *The Times*, 9 August 1886.

the nation acquired only the Ansidei Madonna for £70,000 and the equestrian portrait of Charles I for £17,500. The best prices had been obtained for sales by private contract; auction prices were generally below their standard.

As *hors-d'œuvre* before the feast the Teniers Gallery – 120 small copies by Teniers of great masters, which had hung round the billiard room at Blenheim – were exhibited for months at Davis's in the hope of selling them *en bloc*. They were of varying merit and interest and ultimately were sold one by one, mostly to Agnew's, at small prices. The total brought £2,031.[24] The first main portion, sold by Christie, Manson and Woods, 24 July 1886, contained all the Rubenses, some eighteen in all, a number of Van Dycks, a couple of Rembrandts, a Breughel, a fine Jordaens' 'Deposition', several Snyders, Teniers, Wouvermans, Cuyps.[25] *The Times* reported that, in a period of depression such as the present, prices had not reached the levels of the Hamilton Palace sales – whence the Berlin Gallery got so many of its pictures; nor were the European galleries represented as they had been then.[26] Some of the finest pictures had not reached the figures offered for them previously. All the same the total for the first day was considered handsome – £34,834 11s. Several of the best pictures had been sold privately for no very high sums compared with auction-room prices. Most of the canvases were purchased by private collectors, notably Lord Ardilaun, who bought several of the Rubenses. Sir John Millais bought the beautiful Van Dyck of 'Time Clipping the Wings of Cupid' for £241 10s. Among the art-dealers Agnew and Colnaghi led, Agnew bidding the highest, for the Rubens 'Venus and Adonis' – 7,200 guineas – to enthusiastic applause. Subsequently it was learned that this picture and the splendid Rubens 'Anne of Austria' had been bought in. The prices fetched by the Rubenses were considered very disappointing: like Rome they had been 'knocked down to the Didius Julianus of the hour for infinitely less than their value in all art-estimation'.[27]

24. *The Times*, 30 July 1886.
25. Sale Catalogue: Bodleian 1707 d. 6 (18).
26. *The Times*, 26 July 1886.
27. ibid., 2 August 1886.

The second portion consisted mainly of historical portraits. There were eight Van Dycks of Charles I's Court, a fine Mytens of Buckingham all in white, a Reynolds of a Marquis of Tavistock, a Gainsborough of the fourth Duke of Bedford, Gheerardts's portrait of the wicked Countess of Essex. In addition, Watteaus, Lancrets, Claudes, a Pater, a Poussin, a Stubbs and a group of Reynolds studies. No doubt this last group was collected by the connoisseur fourth Duke, as well as the Gainsborough portrait of his father-in-law. This last was bought for the National Portrait Gallery; the National Gallery of Ireland got a bargain in a fine William Dobson family group for £22. The two Lancrets sold for £27 and £11 respectively; two Watteaus for £35 and £11. The Mytens made more than expected; the Van Dycks and the portraits of the seventeenth-century school much more. Colnaghi bought the wicked Countess of Essex (I have come across her somewhere in America).

The third portion consisted mainly of Italian seventeenth- and eighteenth-century pictures: Carraccis, Marattis, four by Luca Giordano, six Ricci landscapes, Panninis, Carlo Dolcis, along with a Borgognone, Bassano, Tempesta; two Titians and a Veronese 'Europa'. As one would expect of the nineteenth century, these Italian baroque and mannerist pieces fetched very low prices: they were disconsidered then. But now! . . . Altogether they raised only £11,411 11s. 6d. There was one exception, Carlo Dolci's 'Madonna delle Stelle', which the late Duke had often been pressed to sell: Lord Dudley had offered 20,000 guineas for it. In those times of depression Agnew gave 6,600 guineas: top price, to much applause. In these August days were sold large collections of china and porcelain belonging to Blenheim. One of these, consisting of Chinese, Japanese and Chelsea porcelain, had not been formed by any Marlborough but had been 'presented to Blenheim by a Mr Spalding on certain conditions as an appendant to Blenheim'.[28] From 1813 onwards it had been exhibited in a special building near the Home Lodge: full of rare and old pieces, Mr Spalding's ranked among the finest collections. It was bought by dealers, Duveen's name appearing for the first time, for £2,326 8s. A second portion

28. *The Times*, 5 August 1886.

of the china, mainly English – Bow, Bristol, Derby, Wedgwood, Worcester – fetched £3,646 12s.[29] A third day devoted to old Chinese and Japanese porcelain brought the total for china up to £7,313.[30]

From *The Times* we gather that Sebastiano del Piombo's famous 'La Fornarina' had been sold to the Berlin Gallery for about 10,000 guineas; Rubens's 'The Graces' to Baron Rothschild for 25,000 guineas, his two magnificent portraits of himself and his wife to Baron Alphonse Rothschild for 55,000 guineas, the 'Andromeda' and 'Lot and his Daughters' to a Paris dealer for some 15,000 to 20,000 guineas each.[31] The Van Dyck, 'Mrs Morton and Mrs Killigrew', had been sold for a large sum just before the sale. So far the total sales had achieved some £350,000. *The Times* concluded with a justified rebuke: 'considering that the original cost of these treasures was something utterly insignificant compared with their present value, we cannot wonder that owners who are not enthusiastic lovers of art prefer to realize upon them as a luxury that can be dispensed with when the time comes'. The sale catalogue contained no less than 227 pictures: 'we must conclude that the Duke determined to have a great clearance sale', clearing out numbers of queer things that fetched next to nothing, along with the Rubenses and Van Dycks for which Blenheim was famous.

Most of these treasures, many of which had hung on the walls there since John and Sarah's day, left the country. It would be an interesting task, though it is no part of my purpose, to trace where these pictures went and where they have come to rest now.[32] Already on his visits around Europe Lord Randolph, who cared for these things, had the mortification of recognizing former belongings of Blenheim: at St Petersburg in 1881 an Italian cabinet his father had sold; at Berlin in 1888 'the picture gallery in which I observed three Blenheim pictures – the Fornarina by Raphael (now called a Sebastian del Piombo), the

29. *The Times*, 6 August 1886.

30. ibid., 10 August 1886.

31. ibid., 9 August 1886.

32. It would be an interesting subject of research for someone to undertake.

Andromeda of Rubens and the great Bacchanalian picture by Rubens . . .'[33]

As the result of these triumphant operations, over a period roughly equal to the campaigns of the great Duke, Blenheim now lay despoiled. The eighth Duke, who cared for none of these things, now had plenty of money to spend on what he did care for: science and agriculture. Most of the money went on equipping the farms, putting up farm buildings and, for himself – where the Titian gallery had been in old days – hot-houses.

There was still something wanting to his life – someone suggested to him that he might find it in America – a wife, with money. Here golden-hearted Mr Jerome came in handy: he had always been on good terms with this erring young Duke, who for his part was an admirer of the older man. In New York there was a very rich and good-natured widow, Mrs Hammersley, who was known for her habit of festooning the whole room at the back of her box at the theatre with orchids.[34] But she objected to her name Lilian because it rhymed with million, and insisted on her friends calling her Lily – with who knows what thoughts of rivalry with the lovely 'Jersey Lily'? The New Jersey Lily was not beautiful, but unlike Mrs Langtry, she had been left very far from poor.

Marlborough – he continued to be referred to as Blandford still in the family circle – went over in 1888 to have a look for himself. Leonard Jerome reports for us with his usual good humour.

The Duke has gone off this morning with Lawrence [*i.e.* Jerome's brother] and a party to the Adirondacks troutfishing, to be gone a week. I rather think he will marry the Hammersley. Don't you fear any responsibility on my part. Mrs H. is quite capable of deciding for herself. Besides I have never laid eyes on the lady but once. At the same time I hope the marriage will come off as there is no doubt she has lots of tin.[35]

33. *Reminiscences of Lady Randolph Churchill*, 166; Winston S. Churchill. *Lord Randolph Churchill*, II. 368.

34. She was the daughter of Cicero Price, Commodore of the U.S. Navy. Her wealth had come to her from her husband.

35. Anita Leslie, op. cit., 280–82.

Before the month was out Jerome reports, 'Well, Blandford is married! I went with him to the Mayor's office in the City Hall at one o'clock today and witnessed the ceremony. The bride was looking very well and all passed off quietly. I took charge of his cable to the Duchess [*i.e.* his mother], also sent one of my own to Jennie. I dine with them at Delmonico's this evening: a dinner given by Mr and Mrs Clews to the Duke and his bride. I shall go down to the *Aurania* in the morning to see them off. They had great difficulty in arranging the religious marriage. The clergy refused, he being a divorced man. However they found a parson of the Methodist persuasion who consented to perform the service. An hour ago it was all done.'

With his new bride to help, the Duke felt that some reparation was due to Blenheim. Central heating and electricity were installed. (One recalls Mrs Jeune's furs and hot-water bottles at mid-Victorian dinners in November.) The Long Gallery, robbed of its book-cases, had a Grand Willis organ installed in the bay Sarah had dedicated to Rysbrack's Queen Anne. There after dinner music was made. Leonard Jerome's old flame, Fanny Ronalds, came to sing – what but 'The Lost Chord'? Plunket Greene sang 'O Star of Eve'. We are in the flood-tide of Edwardian sentimentality.

Yet nothing assuaged this sad, strange man's ache at heart. All who knew the Duke testified to his talents, alas unfulfilled. Lady Randolph's brother-in-law was an admirer: 'I have known one or two quite first-class minds whose achievements have been nil. Take George, eighth Duke of Marlborough, an almost incomparable mind; indeed in receptivity, range and versatility, hardly to be matched.'[36] This may be an exaggeration; but there is Lord Ribblesdale – 'a youth of great promise marred by fate, shining in many branches of human endeavour, clever, capable of great industry, and within measurable distance of reaching conspicuous success in science, mathematics and mechanics'.[37] Something had gone wrong with him; sex was clearly a nuisance to him, but perhaps that was a symptom of some deeper unrest: he seems all his life, as to some extent his brother was, reacting

36. ibid., 274.
37. Lord Redesdale, *Memoirs*, II. 685.

against the too formidable, too righteous Victorian parents, wedded to standards impossible to achieve and perhaps not desirable to accept.

When Consuelo Vanderbilt came to Blenheim as Duchess she found the mantelpieces in the bedrooms inscribed with expressions of the dead Duke's rancour against life, which had somehow cheated him. 'One woke up in bed to find staring at one in large black letters, "Dust. Ashes. Nothing"; in another room, "They say. What say they? Let them say." – Which I gathered he lived up to', is her unsympathetic comment; for in these phrases one looks into the emptiness, the desolation, of a soul.[38]

He cannot have found happiness with Lily – or perhaps with anyone; but he at least had confidence in her. Suddenly one day in November 1892 he died of heart-failure: he was only forty-eight. It was a severe shock to Lord Randolph, already nearing his bourne, though five years younger: some nervous overstrain, some over-strung sensitivity, made life hard to bear for these two brothers.

His will – more personal than any of the Marlborough wills – gives us some insight into the heart of this unknown, disapproved man.[39] He made his wife Lily his executrix and left to her absolutely all the residue of his real and personal estate which he could dispose of. He also at the last had another friend: 'I bequeath to Lady Colin Campbell as a proof of my friendship and esteem the sum of twenty thousand pounds absolutely'. (No mention of Lady Aylesford or of her son.) Of his live or dead farming stock he left it to his son and heir to select £5,000 worth. The rest of his will recognized his obligation to Blenheim: a trust-fund of £5,000 to be invested and accumulate a sum at the end of twenty-one years to be applied to renovate the roof and outside of the Palace; generous bequests to his servants – £100 to each of them who had been in his service five years, £50 more if they had been ten years. He noted his wife's intention to devote £3,000 to the repair of Bladon church. Then comes the most

38. Consuelo Vanderbilt Balsan, *The Glitter and the Gold*, 66.

39. Somerset House, proved 4 February 1893; *The Complete Peerage*, VIII. 503, says at over £350,000 gross.

interesting clause, in which the dead man speaks his life-long maladjustment from the grave:

I dislike particularly the exclusiveness of family pride and I wish not to be buried in the family vault in Blenheim Chapel, but in any suitable place that may be convenient in which others of my own generation and surroundings are equally able with myself to find a resting place together.

After this glimpse into a saddened spirit it is pleasant to think that his widow found happiness in a second marriage and stayed in England, to be kind to the young subaltern who was the Duke's nephew. Lord William Beresford, later Marquis of Waterford, and 'Lilian Duchess had married in riper years', writes Sir Winston; 'but their union was happy, prosperous and even fruitful. They settled down at the beautiful Deepdene near Dorking, and bade me visit them continually.'[40] Here the young officer met people who exerted an influence upon his career, Colonel Brabazon, Sir Bindon Blood, the Prince of Wales.

I took a strong liking to Bill Beresford . . . and I was never tired of listening to his wisdom or imparting my own. Always do I remember his declaration that there would never be another war between civilized peoples. 'Often', he said, 'have I seen countries come up to the very verge, but something always happens to hold them back.' I did not accept this as conclusive; but it weighed with me, and three or four times when rumours of war filled the air, I rested myself upon it, and three or four times I saw it proved to be sure and true. It was the natural reflection of a life lived in the Victorian Age. However, there came a time when the world got into far deeper waters than Lord William Beresford or his contemporaries had ever plumbed.

All this must have been not without its effect on the mind of the young man who, barely twenty-one, now succeeded to the heritage of Blenheim and all its responsibilities. He had been born in November 1871 at Simla, where his father had left Lady Blandford to the kind offices of the Viceroy and Vicereine and gone off to enjoy the hospitality, the scenery, the pleasures of Kashmir. On her recovery she had to make her way home with the child and an ayah; but the boy was given

40. Winston S. Churchill, *My Early Life*, 105–6.

a traditional grand christening at the Chapel Royal, St James's. For his school Lord Blandford broke with tradition by sending him to Winchester: no member of the family had had contact with that monastic seminary since the early Churchills leased Minterne from it. From there Sunderland, as he was known – hence the familiar name 'Sunny' by which he was called all his life – was sent to Trinity College, Cambridge: another breach with tradition, for the Churchills had gone to Oxford all along. The boy thought himself bullied by his father; he is much more likely to have been neglected. In the year of his father's death a Chancery-case revealed that he had made an allowance of £400 to his son up to 1890, when he had ceased to pay it. The boy was then eighteen; the Court decided it had no power to make provision for the children of the Blandford marriage.[41]

And yet, how like his family this boy was! Intelligent, moody, pernickety rather than difficult – like his father; with something of his father's unrest of spirit; fastidious and fussy – for at bottom he was an aesthete, with a cult of perfection, whether in riding or architecture, buildings, landscape, dress or women. In him the taste, the connoisseurship of his Spencer ancestors burned bright and clear: it was the inspiration of his blood that drove him to sacrifice everything, his own personal happiness first, for the rehabilitation of Blenheim. It was the real passion of his life: in that he found such happiness as life held for him. It was incomplete.

This being so, and such the set of his mind and temperament, it was necessary to look for a wife, a great fortune.

On the other side of the Atlantic a very determined pair of eyes were on the look-out for him: those of Mrs William K. Vanderbilt, daughter-in-law of the old Commodore who had left his immense fortune equally between his two elder sons. Like Mrs Jerome's, Mrs Vanderbilt's ambitions were purely social, in her case concentrated on an only daughter, with a ferocious intensity – according to the daughter: Consuelo, named after her godmother who had become Duchess of Manchester. Mrs Vanderbilt had made up her mind early to marry her daughter, who was both lovely and well-educated, either to the Duke of

41. *Law Reports, Probate Division*, 1892, 148.

Marlborough's heir or the Marquis of Lansdowne's. Marlborough's heir was now the Duke and willing to sacrifice himself for the sake of Blenheim – in itself a sufficient indication of a remarkable nature in so young a man.

In the summer of her eighteenth birthday Consuelo was brought over for a brief visit to Blenheim. The boy was inhabiting the vast Palace practically alone. His unmarried sisters sometimes came to stay; his mother, Lady Blandford, was seldom asked. (It should be explained that though her husband had become Duke before their decree was made absolute, she preferred to remain Lady Blandford; while Lilian, otherwise Lily, though married to Lord William Beresford, retained her more honorific title as Lily, Duchess of Marlborough. No wonder foreigners find the vagaries of English aristocratic nomenclature incomprehensible. One has to be born to these things to understand them.) Consuelo immediately liked Marlborough's sister, Lady Lilian – who had no such objection to the name as Lily Duchess, nor the reason. There were two or three young men to join the party; but Consuelo felt that they were lost in so vast a house.

Next day, Sunday, the young Duke showed her his estate.

> We also drove to outlying villages, where old women and children curtsied and men touched their caps as we passed. The country round Blenheim is rural, with ploughed fields and stone fences. The villages are built of grey stone and the lovely old churches delighted me. Each cottage had its small garden gay with flowers. I realized that I had come to an old world with ancient traditions and that the villagers were still proud of their Duke and of their allegiance to his family.[42]

The country round about, the villages, the churches, the cottage gardens have not much changed: all that is wanting is the spirit of the thing, irretrievably broken in the revolution of our time. We are writing about, trying to evoke, a vanished world.

When Consuelo returned to Marble House, Newport, where even the gates were lined with sheet-iron, she found herself under the strict surveillance of her formidable mama, until Marlborough arrived on what he declared would be his one and only visit to America, to propose to her. 'It was in the comparative quiet of an evening at home that Marlborough proposed to me

42. Consuelo Vanderbilt Balsan, op. cit., 35.

in the Gothic Room, whose atmosphere was so propitious to sacrifice.'[43] Perhaps it is ungallant to reflect that the sacrifice was not all on one side. Marlborough was giving up the woman he loved for the sake of his house, his family – for Blenheim; in the way that royal personages are supposed to do, though not all are equal to the sacrifice.

The marriage was fixed for 5 November, when the Duke remembered that this was Guy Fawkes day and had it changed to 6 November. 'I could not understand why Guy Fawkes's attempt to blow up Parliament almost three centuries before should affect the date of our marriage, but this was only the first of a series of, to me, archaic prejudices inspired by a point of view opposed to my own.' That comic difference was a symptomatic pointer to what lay ahead: there was bound to be trouble between those two. There was too the significant difference between English and American in Marlborough's rooted objection to being married on Guy Fawkes day – impossible to explain: the one looking to the past, the other attitude a virgin soil. One can only say that the former is a richer soil, as indeed, for all Consuelo's beauty, spirit, warmth of heart, his was perhaps a subtler nature.

It does not appear from her reminiscences that, though a more generous and candid spirit, she wholly appreciated that. Each of them a remarkable person in his (and her) own right, they were temperamentally opposed and incompatible. Yet the marriage had its compensations. The girl of eighteen was born to be a duchess, and move an elegant and incomparable leader in an international society in its last days. England took her to its heart: 'I would stand all day in the street to see Consuelo Marlborough get into her carriage', said Barrie. As Duchess of Marlborough she was taken into the innermost of that society, given all it had to offer, sharing its experiences, a shining figure in its ritual and its *décor*. As she witnessed the coronation of Edward VII – after a lifetime as Prince of Wales becoming King at last[44] – her husband bearing the crown, she 'realized that she was more British than she knew'. There was all the magnificence of her visits to the Coronation Durbar in India, to the Imperial Court of St Peters-

43. Consuelo Vanderbilt Balsan, op. cit., 40.

44. 'Es ist zu spät', he is said to have said to Alexandra.

burg, before it vanished under the waters. There was – what she may have appreciated more, where she certainly did good work and was much loved – the devotion of those villagers and cottagers round Blenheim.

Marlborough gave her all this, and more: he gave her a Palace for a home, and children whom she adored. What, perhaps, in the end gives her the last word in the argument that has now entered into history: he could not give her love. And that, to a woman, is everything. To a man perhaps not so important.

After a prolonged honeymoon tour of the Continent Consuelo arrived at Blenheim to acclimatize herself to the stratified and congealed intricacies of English life, the arrogance of an aristocratic society. At Blenheim there was some distaste between the Churchills and the Hamiltons – Lady Blandford's clan. Consuelo thought her 'a typical *grande dame* of the late Victorian era – Disraeli had made her the heroine of one of his novels'.[45] In fact she is the Lady Corisande of his *roman à clef*, *Lothair*. 'Though the family likeness was still apparent in Lady Corisande,' wrote that old accomplished flatterer,

> in general expression she differed from her sisters. They were all alike with their delicate aquiline noses, bright complexions, short upper lips, and eyes of sunny light. The beauty of Lady Corisande was even more distinguished and more regular, but whether it were the effect of her dark-brown hair or darker eyes, her countenance had not the lustre of the rest, and its expression was grave and perhaps pensive.[46]

The clever Churchills thought Albertha a fool, and at Consuelo's presentation at Court she showed herself to be one. With Consuelo's beauty and extreme elegance it was not but to be expected that she would add lustre to the age-long ritual, the dazzling scene. Lady Blandford assured her, 'I must tell you that no one would take you for an American'. Really! – But this was but one instance of what Americans had to put up with from these aristocrats: the intolerable patronage and bad manners betraying a real *impolitesse du cœur*. One blushes for them. Nor is it an extenuating circumstance that it is but what

45. Consuelo Vanderbilt Balsan, op. cit., 54.
46. Lord Beaconsfield, *Lothair* (1885 ed.), 2.

we have all had to put up with, one way or another. A Russian prince one day said in Consuelo's hearing, 'De quel droit ces gens-là se permettent-ils de nous critiquer?' It enables one to understand, though one may regret, the Russian Revolution.

From all sides of the family it was impressed on the new arrival that she was, above all, the 'link in the chain': that her most important duty was to produce the next heir. This formed the riveting subject of her first interview with the formidable Dowager Duchess. She hoped to see Blenheim restored to its former glories and the prestige of the family upheld – this by way of prelude; for, after an embarrassing inspection of Consuelo's figure and extending an ear-trumpet, she came to the point. 'Your first duty is to have a child and it must be a son, because it would be intolerable to have that little upstart Winston become Duke. Are you in the family way?'[47] The old Duchess had never seen eye to eye with Lady Randolph: each of them too dominating and each of them a rival for the possession of Randolph, who escaped them both. It would have astonished that very certain old lady to learn that the 'little upstart Winston' would become chief among the glories of Blenheim, the abiding rock of the family's continuing prestige.

In time Consuelo did her duty and produced the heir, very suitably at Spencer House, the town-house of the Althorp branch. There followed the regular Chapel Royal christening, with the Prince of Wales as godfather: the child named John after the great Duke, William after his Vanderbilt grandfather, Albert Edward after the Prince.

Enough of this ladies' world.

Marlborough had now the wherewithal to embark upon his life's work of restoring the glories of Blenheim, in his grandmother's words: in other words, of rehabilitating it from the indignity to which it had been brought by her husband and her son, pious duke and impious alike. Naturally he began with the interior; we will begin with the exterior where his best efforts were made, his grandest effects achieved.

As the result of Capability Brown's work the Palace had lost its formal setting; it now rose up improbably from a sea of grass, shaggy and overgrown on every side. By a characteristic inspira-

47. Consuelo Vanderbilt Balsan, op. cit., 57.

tion Marlborough brought in a French architect and landscape-designer, Duchêne, who understood in his bones the essence of classic form, what the architecture of Vanbrugh intended and clamorously demanded. In 1900 they set to work on the grand northern entrance court which Brown had grassed over. It was a straightforward task for they had early prints to go on, showing how it had been: the *pavé*, the strip of coloured sand, the finished stone paving all round the edge at the foot of the walls, the terrace with steps approaching the house. The restoration of this Great Court of three acres was a triumph; if, with its square tubs of orange-trees formally placed, it has a French flavouring it is all the better for that: the French understand these things. The Palace makes its salute to Versailles, which is as it should be. Anyone who has once seen that front can never forget it; seen at night, flood-lit, in the dream of an earlier world, one forgets for a fraction of time the horror of ours.

The east side of the Palace presented a quite different problem. This was the side upon which the private apartments gave, Sarah's bow-window in the centre, from which she looked out without favour upon boundary walls. These had been swept away, the beds overgrown, all sense of form lost. The solution adopted by the Duke was ideally right: in this case a sunken garden from which Vanbrugh's east front rises up with heightened proportions and into which the windows look with all the more effect of colour and shape. A mermaid-fountain with a lily-pool to plash in, symmetrical flower-beds with elaborate patterns in box and figured box-edging. Again the idiom is slightly French; but then the inspiration of Vanbrugh's house is not so much English as Continental: the familiar eclecticism that is our idiom in this country.

The greatest problem of all was that of the western slopes from the Palace into the lake. The Duke was not able to approach this until the 1920s, after the first German war – with diminished resources, but with far greater experience of what was necessary. There was nothing to go upon, for Vanbrugh had been dismissed by Sarah before he had got round to the treatment of this western prospect, which he had recognized as far the finest from the house and planned an orangery to overlook.

The Duke conceived a series of water-terraces from the house all the way down to the lake, marrying the two by the imaginative use of water. 'The problem for M. Duchêne is to make a liaison between the façade of Vanbrugh and the water-line of the Lake made by Brown. To reconcile these conflicting ideas is difficult. The difficulty is not diminished when you remember that the façade of the house is limited and the line of the Lake is limitless. As an example, if you turn your back to the Lake and look at the façade, your parterre, basin etc. is in scale to the façade, but if you look at the same parterre from the rotunda to the Lake it is out of scale with the panorama.'[48] M. Duchêne's plan aroused the Duke's enthusiasm: 'it is certainly a stroke of genius on your part bringing the water-line up to the first terrace. I certainly should not have thought of this idea myself and I doubt any English architect would have.' Alas, the plan in full was found to be impracticable: 'I find in looking at old documents that the bed of the river runs at the water's edge. The depth is considerable and I fear the earth would slide into the middle of the Lake.'

He had to be content with two great terraces covering most of the slope to the lake and to the design of these he gave the utmost attention and thought. For hours he would stand there considering every detail, every alternative – rather like the first Marlborough standing on the bridge watching the house being built. At last he had found a use for the Bernini fountain: a second obelisk was executed to give symmetrical *points d'appui* on the terrace.

> I want you to work more in the spirit of Bernini than of Mansard or Le Nôtre. The value of the obelisks is this, that they give an architectural transition between a lateral line of stone and the perpendicular effect of the trees. Pray therefore do not despise them. I think we can get a magnificent effect. Something like the Trevi fountain or the Fontana Hispana in Rome.

When all was done – the Duke was afraid he might not live to see it finished – he was at last content. 'Pray tell M. Duchêne that the ensemble of the Terraces is magnificent and in my judge-

48. q. D. Green, *Blenheim Palace*, 205–6.

ment far superior to the work done by Le Nôtre at Versailles. The proportion of the house, the Terrace and the Lake is perfect.'[49] M. Duchêne was anxious that there should be movement in the water.

> I shall not contradict you. Bear in mind however that the situation is grandiose. Limpidity of water is pleasing and possesses a romance. You have got this effect in the basins and in the large area of water contained by the Lake. Be careful not to destroy this major emotion which Nature has granted to you for the sake of what may possibly be a vulgar display of waterworks which can be seen at any exhibition or public park. Turn all these matters over in your mind when you are at rest in the evening, for it is only by thought, constant thought, and mature reflection that artists have left their great works for the enjoyment of posterity.

We see from his letters what a remarkable man in his own right the ninth Duke was: the true successor of the art-patron of George III's reign. His work on the lake-front was the one major addition to the beauty of Blenheim since the lake itself. Would he have gone on to restore Henry Wise's Grand Parterre on the south front? There can be no doubt that he would have liked to. But he was now a sick man, too weary and discouraged by the way things had gone in his time, by the frustrations of his personal life. His cousin and friend – one notes points of similarity in style, 'Pray' this or 'Pray' that – pays well-deserved tribute to this gifted man, unhappy in his life:

> always there weighed upon him the size and cost of the great house which was the monument of his ancestor's victories. This he conceived to be almost his first duty in life to preserve and embellish. . . . As the successive crashes of taxation descended upon the Old World it was only by ceaseless care and management, and also frugality, that he was able to discharge his task. He sacrificed much to this – too much; but he succeeded; and at his death Blenheim passed from his care in a finer state than ever.[50]

Let us turn to the interior, where he was less successful. His own sternest critic, where aesthetic matters were concerned, he wrote: 'when I was young and uninformed I put French decoration into the three State rooms here. The rooms have

49. ibid., 217–18. 50. *The Times*, 2 July 1934.

English proportions . . . and the result is that the French decoration is quite out of scale and leaves a very unpleasant impression on those who possess trained eyes.'[51] It may be added that few possess such eyes; it was the very desire for perfection that made life so difficult for him.

However, within the house he pulled things together, after the disastrous Victorian interlude. The Long Gallery returned to being a library, book-cases re-installed, books collected once more, beautiful books bought: now one would not think that books had ever been missing from there. He employed a trained historical scholar to put his archives in order – and a good job was made of it, as I can testify. He salvaged the remains of the collections of china that had once bulged in the house, disposed the pieces to the best advantage. Tapestries were purchased, the pictures again added to – though nothing could bring back the wonderful Rubenses and Van Dycks. Not even his scientifically minded father had had the face to sell the bulk of the family portraits. The superb Reynolds canvas of his predecessor, the fourth Duke with his family, remained.

In 1905 Marlborough decided to give this a companion-piece with a portrait of his own family; nor did he make a mistake in calling in Sargent, in whom the Edwardians saw their age, their society, mirrored. This celebrated large canvas has the brilliance, the *panache*, demanded by its subject; it is not unworthy of the Reynolds. Once more the family is dominated by the Duchess, in this case markedly so with the Velasquez inflection of her beauty accentuated, her dominating height, the stylishness of the figure. She possesses the two children, the younger one of a Lawrence prettiness that betokened the distinguished connoisseur he, too, was to grow up to be. There are all the accessories: the two Blenheim spaniels, the bust of the great Duke looking down on them, the Blenheim standard with its fleurs-de-lys above. And then to one side, a little aloof from it all as if displaying it, is the Duke himself, the expression of a refined melancholy, disillusionment in the eyes.

The *train-de-vie* was what such a house, such a master dictated, with its boredom for the beautiful girl growing up with a

51. q. D. Green, op. cit., 204.

personality, a will of her own. There was the elaborate stratification of the household, sanctioned, like the ritual, by centuries: the Duke would not be the one to question it; for him it was the necessary order of life. There was still a groom of the chambers as there had been in the eighteenth century; the butler could not put a match to the fire, even if asked: a footman must be rung for to do that. As for their life when the doors were shut and they were alone together –

> how I learned to dread and hate these dinners, how ominous and wearisome they loomed at the end of a long day. They were served with all accustomed ceremony, but once a course had been passed the servants retired to the hall; the door was closed and only a ring of the bell placed before Marlborough summoned them. He had a way of piling food on his plate; the next move was to push the plate away, together with knives, forks, spoons and glasses – all this in considered gestures which took a long time; then he backed his chair away from the table, crossed one leg over the other and endlessly twirled the ring on his little finger. While accomplishing these gestures he was absorbed in thought and quite oblivious of any reactions I might have. After a quarter of an hour he would suddenly return to earth, or perhaps I should say to food, and begin to eat very slowly, usually complaining that the food was cold! As a rule neither of us spoke a word. I took to knitting in desperation and the butler read detective stories in the hall.[52]

But the immense house woke up at the weekends when there were parties. Then the Long Gallery came to life with music, for the Duke had an organist: C. W. Perkins. (In an obscure corner behind the organ are these tell-tale words: 'C. W. Perkins · how often : has thy genius · beguiled · my sad heart'. Whose were they? Marlborough's father's or his own?) Sometimes there were concerts given, like those in aid of the restoration of Woodstock church in October 1896, when Lady Randolph was among the eminent artists and would play a piano solo, C. W. Perkins give a recital and George Grossmith a humorous sketch; or in December 1897 when the Duke and Duchess, Lady Randolph, Ladies Lilian and Norah and Lord Churchill from Cornbury took part in a new musical burlesque.[53] From the musty

52. Consuelo Vanderbilt Balsan, op. cit., 60.
53. Bodleian, G. A. Oxon, C. 317 (19).

bills, with their old-fashioned provincial lettering, arises the aroma of those Edwardian days – as the announcement of a lecture in Woodstock Town Hall one day in 1892 by G. Bernard Shaw on 'The Progress of Social Democracy' foretells the sentence passed upon their order.

For some time the going was good, the years golden, the pace of life gentle and slow. On hot summer days the Indian tent would be set up under the cedars on the lawn.

> Sometimes we played tennis or rowed on the lake, and in the afternoon the household played cricket on the lawn. The tea-table was set under the trees. It was a lovely sight, with masses of luscious apricots and peaches to adorn it. There were also pyramids of strawberries and raspberries; bowls brimful of Devonshire cream; pitchers of iced coffee; scones to be eaten with various jams, and cakes with sugared icing. No one dieted in those days and the still-room maid, who was responsible for the teas, was a popular person in the household.
>
> Winston was then the life and soul of the young and brilliant circle that gathered round him at Blenheim. . . . Whether it was his American blood or his boyish enthusiasm and spontaneity, qualities sadly lacking in my husband, I delighted in his companionship.[54]

So also did the husband, it is agreeable to note: their affection and respect were mutual. It is a tribute to both that these cousins, so different in temperament, should have been drawn to each other. Political divergence, when Winston joined the Liberal Party and was vilified by the Conservatives, made not the slightest difference: it provided only the more fodder for friendly argument. In these very years Winston was writing his first big book, the biography of his father: when finished he dedicated it to his cousin 'in all faithful friendship'. It is clear, too, how much Sir Winston owed to the inspiration and encouragement of the Duke over his historical masterpiece, the vindication of their ancestor. That was a subject that must have been often discussed between them.

Sometimes there would be a more august visitor and a grander party: the Prince of Wales or the German Emperor, on one

54. Consuelo Vanderbilt Balsan, 103–4.

occasion the two together with the jealous problems of placing and seating that such a visitation provoked. The Kaiser lectured them all on the great Duke's battles: the Duchess was

> amused by his evident desire to shine, but William II seemed to me no more than the typical Prussian officer with the added arrogance and conceit his royal birth inspired. Indeed I was surprised at his undistinguished appearance, which was perhaps due to the fact that he was not in uniform, without which Germans usually appear at a disadvantage. He seemed to have inherited no English characteristics [which is not surprising considering that he had no English blood] and had neither the charm nor the wisdom of his uncle, the Prince of Wales. During the South African War, soon after this visit, his jealousy and hatred of England became evident.[55]

The South African War may be taken to announce the end of their care-free world – if ever any world can be said to be care-free. The Duke, who had political ideas and ambitions, had been made a Privy Councillor in 1894 and was Paymaster-General in Lord Salisbury's last government, from 1899 to 1902. In 1900 he went out to South Africa and was on Lord Roberts's Staff. On his return he was made a Knight of the Garter, as four of his predecessors had been; in Mr Balfour's administration he was Under-Secretary for the Colonies, 1903–5. But the long rule of the Liberals, which raised his cousin to power, kept him out. He made only a brief return to government in 1917 as Parliamentary Secretary to the Board of Agriculture.

Already his private griefs were thickening on him. We need not go into these: the story has been told by Consuelo Duchess – though we may remember that, since he is dead, we have not heard his side of the case. In the end, we may reflect – considering how incompatible their temperaments were – how much they together accomplished, and would certainly not have done without each other. No doubt it involved a sacrifice of personal happiness on both sides; but achievement always demands sacrifice. What remains now is the achievement; remarkable as it was, we have reason to be grateful for it. Consuelo Duchess did after all do her duty as a 'link in the chain': she

55. ibid., 101–2.

continued the family. She was a shining figure in the society she adorned with her gifts; warm-hearted and democratic in her feelings, she was loved in the neighbourhood of Woodstock, the heart of England. Then, too, there was Blenheim, saved, revivified, restored: as a work of art in its present state a national possession we owe in good part to them.

Chapter 10

The Rise and Fall of Lord Randolph

SUCH is the background against which we have to see the most tragic career in British politics of the nineteenth century:[1] that of Lord Randolph Churchill. What struck contemporaries so forcibly was the suddenness of his rise, to such a commanding height of leadership so young, the completeness of his fall. Politics is never without an element of the dramatic; but a couple of years, 1884 to 1886 – as disturbed and as decisive in their outcome as those we have observed in 1782 to 1784 – saw Lord Randolph's drama played out: ascent, apogee and fall.

The historian of the period tells us,

> aged only thirty-seven he was the youngest Chancellor of the Exchequer and leader of the House after Pitt. From the age of thirty-one his rise had been meteoric. On public platforms his party had no equal to him; in the election fight against Home Rule he had been its mainstay throughout the constituencies. He seemed predestined to be Prime Minister at no distant date; and might but for the events of the previous year [1885] have stepped into Disraeli's place already. Yet ere 1886 ended, from his sudden eminence he fell sheer.[2]

To suppose that Lord Randolph might have succeeded Disraeli immediately is, in my opinion, rather to exaggerate his power – as Lord Randolph did himself: chief reason for his fall. But it is clear that we must not underestimate him, when Lord Rosebery regarded him as 'incomparably the most formidable Tory in the House of Commons and probably in the country', and as 'one of the most remarkable men, with perhaps the most remarkable career, of my time' – strong tributes coming from that quarter.[3] He goes on to add that in all the century Lord Randolph's career was only less dramatic than that of Disraeli.

1. With the single exception of Parnell's.
2. R. C. K. Ensor, *England, 1870–1914* (*Oxford History of England*), 173.
3. Lord Rosebery, *Lord Randolph Churchill*, i, 14.

This gives us a clue to the inwardness of that brilliant, hectic, short life: Lord Randolph saw himself as Disraeli's successor in rejuvenating the Tory party, in renewing its contacts with the people, giving it a popular appeal, a programme with which to outbid and beat the Liberals. And not unreasonably. After Disraeli died there was no one among the Tories to take his place in the eye of the people. Lord Salisbury had no demagogic arts; in the House of Commons there was only blameless old Sir Stafford Northcote to lead the Tory remnant, and he was almost as much under the spell of the Grand Old Man, the incomparable Parliamentarian, as the Liberals themselves. 'In 1880 we were all thrown out of office by Mr Gladstone', writes Sir Winston – himself then aged six.[4] Mr Gladstone had returned from supposed retirement to active politics, and come back to power not only with an immense majority but with the conviction that the Almighty had put him there. He adduced 'the remarkable manner in which Holy Scripture has been applied to me for admonition and comfort. Looking calmly on this course of experience, I do believe that the Almighty has employed me for His purposes in a manner larger or more special than before.'[5]

These emanations of an exceptionally strong ego fortified what appeared to be an unchallengeable supremacy in Parliament and the country. It was this personal ascendancy of the grandest figure in the politics of the time that Lord Randolph went straight for – a young man who had hitherto not taken much of a part. In the next year or two, almost within a matter of months, the certainty and cohesion of the large Liberal majority were undermined, the moral authority of the government dissipated, the ascendancy of Mr Gladstone questioned and shaken in the House, if not yet in the country. All this was largely the work of Lord Randolph Churchill – an extraordinary achievement in one so young. He showed that in Parliament he was a match for the greatest of Parliamentarians; he went on to prove that in the country he could equal Mr Gladstone as a draw, as a compelling power with the mob – and even, at his best, draw larger crowds. Then, in a handful of years, all was over.

4. Winston S. Churchill, *My Early Life*, 21.
5. John Morley, *The Life of W. E. Gladstone* (ed. 1912), III. 2.

What kind of man was it, the strangeness of whose career made such an impression on his time? – certainly the complexity of his personality made him very little understood.

He was a little man, full of vibrant nervous energy, with large moustaches that endeared him to contemporary caricaturists, beneath which one glimpses the Churchill under-lip. Then there were the familiar prominent eyes – 'My, what poppy eyes those Churchills have!' said a tourist going the round at Blenheim. In short he was a good deal of a Churchill in appearance; Queen Victoria thought that he had a look of his grandfather; if so, he was like him in more ways than one. Lord Rosebery, his friend from Eton days, tells us:

> he was a born party leader, reminding one of Bolingbroke in the dashing days of Harry St John. He was brilliant, courageous, resourceful, and unembarrassed by scruple; he had fascination, audacity, tact; great and solid ability welded with the priceless gift of concentration; marvellous readiness in debate, and an almost unrivalled skill and attraction on the platform; for he united in an eminent degree the Parliamentary and the popular gifts.[6]

What then was lacking to rob these brilliant gifts of their full fruition?

It cannot be said that Lord Randolph was as wise as he was shrewd; that he was as good a strategist as he was a tactician; as dependable a colleague as he was an opponent. Though a very quick and piercing judge of a situation, his judgement was not really reliable. He was self-willed and impulsive, above all impatient. If he had only had patience all the rest would have come into line. But he had the defect of the artistic temperament, what we in our day of psychological jargon diagnose as the manic-depressive alternation – tremendous high spirits and racing energy on the upward bound, depression and discouragement on the down. This rhythm is present in a more or less marked degree with all persons of creative capacity, particularly in the arts. And clearly this strongly artistic strain we have observed in the stock came out in him, as it has done again in his son. But where in Sir Winston it has been accorded the foundation of rude

6. Rosebery, 74.

health, a rock-like character, Lord Randolph was betrayed by ill-health: nervous instability and over-excitement wore away a fragile, sensitive system, so that the tensions of politics were often accompanied, or relieved, by bouts of illness. We have to see Lord Randolph's political activities in that context; for some years before his death he was a failing man. He was dead at forty-six.

The large Liberal majority of 1880 might well have daunted the Conservatives, depressed as they were by Disraeli's retirement to the Lords; but almost immediately an issue was found that wrought the maximum confusion in the government ranks – the squalid affair of Bradlaugh, the militant rationalist Member who wished to make an affirmation instead of the usual oath on the Bible. That this affair should have reached the proportions it did, consumed parliamentary time and obstructed government business, was due to the ineptitude of Speaker Brand and the advantage taken of it by Lord Randolph. It seems to have been in badgering the government over this that the ginger-group of youngish men led by him came together on the Opposition benches. They were never more than four; but they made as much noise as forty and took up as much time as a hundred and forty.

They were always on their legs speaking, or protesting, or asking questions, or moving motions or amendments. There was Lord Randolph, pertinacious and marvellously quick to seize an advantage; there were Sir Henry Drummond Wolff and John Gorst with his invaluable legal equipment and longer experience. They were usually joined by young Arthur Balfour, who concealed beneath his lackadaisical manner a will of steel, a subtle intellect and a very cool detached judgement – for he was by blood a Cecil, a nephew of Lord Salisbury. They were for ever asking for explanations, for more information. Mr Gladstone, now seventy-one, could not resist that. Was there not a good deal of the Scotch pedagogue in him, the misplaced don? Was he not the Headmaster in the House? Night after night he would reply with unfailing courtesy, and at unfailing length, to these young men; until one night his lieutenant, Sir

William Harcourt, dared to protest to the G.O.M., 'if you speak again we shall be here till morning'.

Lord Randolph had got his measure. Though we need not suppose that religion meant much to him, he made the fullest use of it to embarrass Mr Gladstone over Bradlaugh. It was he again who insisted on their little group being accorded the name and consideration of a Fourth Party.

Lord Beaconsfield observed these beginnings with a certain amused sympathy. He could never forget that he had been young himself and not altogether respectable – unlike Mr Gladstone, who never had been young, while a touch of unrespectability would have made a man of him. Years ago Disraeli had reported to Queen Victoria of Lord Randolph's maiden speech,

> Lord Randolph said many imprudent things, which is not very important in the maiden speech of a young member and a young man; but the House was surprised and then captivated, by his energy and natural flow and his impressive manner. With self-control and study he might mount. It was a speech of great promise.[7]

Then came those bitter years when Lord Randolph was mostly out of the country.

Now in 1880 the old tired statesman wrote to encourage the young man, coupling with it a warning.

> I fully appreciate your feelings and those of your friends, but you must stick to Northcote. He represents the respectability of the party. I wholly sympathize with you all, because I never was respectable myself. . . . Don't on any account break with Northcote; but defer to him as often as you can.[8]

If Beaconsfield had lived he would have exercised a sympathetic restraining influence on Lord Randolph, who for his part never had any intention of deferring to a Stafford Northcote. The situation was intensely irritating to an impatient young man, for here was his own leader, the leader of the Opposition, deferring to Mr Gladstone, visibly unable to emancipate himself from the spell of those eagle eyes of his former chief at the Treasury. Sir Stafford was an amiable West Country gentleman; Lord Randolph was not altogether a gentleman, but he was a man of

7. G. E. Buckle, *Life of Disraeli*, V. 312. 8. ibid., VI. 589.

genius. It was maddening to sit under the authority of such nerveless leadership. Restive, audacious, self-willed, Lord Randolph soon began to show symptoms of gerontophobia: the old men were in the way. His campaign against the government became in large part a campaign against the leadership of his own party too: against the Old Gang in general, and the Goat (Northcote) in particular. These were Lord Randolph's own elegant terms expressive of his feelings. Meanwhile he set the pace.

Beaconsfield's visible exhaustion and withdrawal, followed shortly by his death, left the question of the leadership of the Conservative party open. It was by no means settled, and we must not ante-date the long ascendancy that Lord Salisbury ultimately won. For the present there was a dual leadership – Lord Salisbury in the Lords, Northcote in the Commons; and very unsatisfactory it was to impatient spirits like Lord Randolph. He exerted himself to have Lord Salisbury declared leader – with the irony usual in such things, for in the end it was Salisbury who destroyed him. But before the end of the year (1880) he had got him to come down to Blenheim and appear on the platform with him in his constituency at Woodstock. The aged eyes of Lord Beaconsfield, that perceived everything, saw how things were. His last judgement of Lord Randolph, delivered not long before he died to a Liberal who was expressing admiration of the young man's parliamentary instinct and his gifts, was prophetic as ever: 'Ah, yes, you are quite right: when they come in they will have to give him anything he chooses to ask for and in a very short time they will have to take anything he chooses to give them.'[9]

In those days before universal suffrage the attention of the nation was focused on the parliamentary arena with an intensity that today would be devoted to a football stadium or the pools, and it was not long before the nation noticed the form of the new performer. An aristocratic demagogue, a lord who was a good deal of a *gamin*, he touched people's imagination; he appealed especially to youth. Here was a new note: wit, cheek, imagination, insolence – he was great fun to listen to; there could not be a greater contrast with that other great master of the

9. Winston S. Churchill, *Lord Randolph Churchill*, I. 155.

demagogic art, the G.O.M. Only Lord Randolph dared to say what was what about him – or at any rate half what was what.

'Vanity of vanities,' says the Preacher, 'all is vanity.' 'Humbug of humbugs,' says the Radical, 'all is humbug.' Gentlemen, we live in an age of advertisement, the age of Holloway's pills, of Colman's mustard, and of Horniman's pure tea. The Prime Minister is the greatest living master of the art of personal advertisement. Holloway, Colman and Horniman are nothing compared with him. Every act of his, whether it be for the purposes of health, or of recreation, or of religious devotion, is spread before the eyes of every man, woman and child in the United Kingdom on large and glaring placards. . . . For the purposes of recreation he has selected the felling of trees; and we may usefully remark that his amusements, like his politics, are essentially destructive. Every afternoon the whole world is invited to assist at the crashing fall of some beech or elm or oak. The forest laments, in order that Mr Gladstone may perspire.[10]

It was immensely enjoyable; but underneath was a deadly ability, as we can see from the style of the invective. Mr Gladstone, for his part, was a gladiator worthy of him; he rode these waves undaunted, quite unquelled. One night, meeting Lady Randolph at dinner after one of Randolph's most effective performances against him, the old man inquired kindly, without irony, 'I hope Lord Randolph is not *too* tired after his magnificent effort'. If there was one thing that was irresistible about Gladstone it was his unfailing courtesy. Lady Randolph adored sitting by him at dinner. In fact the two people she most liked having beside her at dinner were Mr Gladstone, her husband's chief target, and Lord Salisbury, who ruined him. When Randolph was in India he wrote home to her, 'any Hindu who dies at Benares, and whose ashes are thrown into the Ganges, goes right bang up to Heaven without stopping, no matter how great a rascal he may have been. I think the G.O.M. ought to come here; it is his best chance.'[11]

The running against the government in these years, both in

10. q. ibid., 282–3.

11. *Reminiscences of Lady Randolph Churchill*, 119.

Parliament and in the country, was made by Lord Randolph. The serious side of what he had to say was this.

> 'Trust the people' – I have long tried to make that my motto: but I know, and will not conceal, that there are still a few in our party who have that lesson yet to learn and who have yet to understand that the Tory party of today is no longer identified with that small and narrow class which is connected with the ownership of land; but that its great strength can be found, and must be developed, in our large towns as well as in our country districts. . . . Trust the people, and they will trust you – and they will follow you and join you in the defence of that Constitution against any and every foe. I have no fear of democracy.[12]

These were rather questionable sentiments coming from a Tory at that time. Lord Salisbury had no intention of putting his trust in the people or in anything human. He was a philosophic sceptic, taken in by nothing in human affairs – and for the rest a profoundly religious man. He had always distrusted and feared democracy – had resigned office rather than approve Disraeli's Reform Bill enfranchising the urban working men. It was Lord Salisbury who reaped the benefit of Lord Randolph's trust in the people, who was the residuary legatee of the younger man's efforts.

Nevertheless, though Lord Salisbury was philosophically right, Lord Randolph was not wrong either. It was indispensable if the Tory party was to survive in the new circumstances, with a newly enfranchised electorate of several millions, with working men exercising the vote in the towns and soon to achieve it in the country, that the party should make both effective contact with, and appeal to, the mass of the people. It is perhaps Lord Randolph's chief claim to a place in history that he grasped this, alone among the Tory leaders, and also saw how it was to be done. The foundation upon which the constitution rested had completely changed:

> your new foundation is a great seething and swaying mass of some five million electors, who have it in their power by the mere heave of the shoulders, if they only act with moderate unanimity, to sweep away entirely the three ancient institutions and put anything they like in their place . . .

12. Winston S. Churchill, op. cit., I. 294–5.

This was what the Tory Democracy that Lord Randolph preached came to in essence – we need neither give it a greater importance as doctrine than it had, nor must we underrate it: the acceptance, generously and without reluctance, of the cardinal new fact of democracy in politics; the putting forward of a proper programme to appeal to it, a policy that took account of its interests. The seriousness of Lord Randolph's campaign and his platform has been often questioned – partly because he was a man dangerously devoid of humbug and of a cynical turn of wit. I do not think we need question his fundamental seriousness at all. He was the kind of person who – beneath the extravagant rhetoric, beneath the high spirits, the invective and the fun – meant what he said. There was enough bitterness in his experience of high life to make him mean it too, to give a cutting edge to his advocacy; and that won for him dangerous enemies on his own side. He was to drink of the cup of bitterness a great deal more deeply yet before he had finished.

So far as the new electorates were concerned things worked out with an unexpected twist. This came into evidence with the elections after Gladstone's Reform Bill of 1884. The working-class vote in the big towns came to provide a solid foundation for twenty years of Tory rule. To that extent Lord Randolph had been right and was a prime agent in making it so. The enfranchisement of rural labourers brought an accession of strength to the Liberals who now dominated the county constituencies. The unity of the landed interest in a Tory sense was broken. So much for the feudal view of the countryside entertained by the landowning class: a very direct disclaimer on the part of their dependants!

All over the country Lord Randolph was the star-turn of his party as a speaker. A follower of his wrote, 'the work of inspiring a beaten party with hope and courage was substantially left to one man'.[13] Meeting the people face to face was very far from Lord Salisbury's idea of pleasure: 'this duty of making speeches', he wrote to Queen Victoria, 'is an aggravation of the labours of your Majesty's servants which we owe entirely to Mr Gladstone'.[14] Now the womenfolk were able to lend a hand

13. ibid., 298.

14. *The Letters of Queen Victoria*, Third Series, ed. G. E. Buckle, I. 365.

and Lord Randolph was quick to perceive the use that might be made of the idea of the Primrose League, founded to keep Dizzy's memory green. Official orthodox Conservatives regarded this venture with distaste; most of their papers treated it with scorn and ridicule. It was only gradually that it took hold and conquered upper-class aversion. Wasn't it all very vulgar, a Conservative woman once asked Lady Salisbury. 'Of course, it's vulgar,' replied that common-sense lady, 'that's why we are so successful.'

Lord Randolph recruited his mother to become President, his wife as a member of the Ladies' Grand Council. Here was a platform on which the old Duchess and her daughter-in-law, who did not always see eye to eye, could unite. Together they battled and worked and canvassed for Randolph. He was so busy in Parliament and so much in request to speak in the big cities that sometimes the ladies had to carry the burden of the election for him in his own constituency at Woodstock. Driving about the leafy lanes of that delectable countryside, summer at its height, in their smart turn-out, the horses decorated with Randolph's racing colours, pink and brown, in at the gateways into the fields where the men were working, climbing the hay-ricks after shy or dumb voters – what a time they had! The rustic voters often did not know whether they were Conservative or Liberal, but only for which colours they voted, red or blue. Those were the days of old-fashioned gallantries, of election songs –

Bless my soul! that Yankee lady,
Whether day was bright or shady,
Dashed about the district like an oriflamme of war . . .

When Lady Randolph went to Birmingham to canvass for Mr Burdett-Coutts, she found that urban voters were apt to know a thing or two more. A waverer with whom Lady Randolph was pleading said that if he could get the same price as the beautiful Duchess of Devonshire had once given for a vote she could have his. Not a bit abashed the Yankee lady returned, 'Thank you very much: I'll let the Baroness Burdett-Coutts know at once'.[15]

15. *Reminiscences*, 124–30.

A much tougher struggle ensued with the Conservative party for the control of the party-machine. Its affairs and finances were governed by a Central Committee, virtually self-appointed, responsible to no one, utterly out of touch with the rank and file in the constituencies. Lord Randolph was very unpopular with the panjandrums of the party, entrenched in the central offices, at the Carlton Club as on the Opposition Front Bench. Several of them had taken a toss at his hands. The inseparable Sir Stafford Northcote and Sir Richard Cross had been guyed as 'Marshall and Snelgrove' – very insulting in those days when 'trade' was hardly respectable. Rich Mr W. H. Smith, of the bookshops, very much a *parvenu*, had expressed the thought that the inhabitants of Irish mud-cabins hardly qualified for a vote. He was treated to the following from Lord Randolph.

I have heard a great deal of the mud-cabin argument. I suppose that in the minds of the lords of suburban villas, of the owners of vineries and pineries, the mud-cabin represents the climax of physical and social degradation. But . . . the difference between the cabin of the Irish peasant and the cottage of the English agricultural labourer is not so great as that which exists between the abode of the right honourable member for Westminster [i.e. rich Mr W. H. Smith] and the humble roof which shelters from the storm the individual who now has the honour to address the Committee.[16]

He proceeded to add insult to injury by quoting Latin – it was unlikely that Mr Smith knew Latin:

Non ebur, neque aureum
Mea renidet in domo lacunar;
Non trabes Hymettiae
Premunt columnas ultima recisas
Africa.

Here was a by no means gentle art of making enemies. 'Vineries and pineries' stuck. But it was Mr Smith who had the last word.

Nevertheless, it was essential that the party-machine should be reconstructed effectively on a broad popular basis. Joseph Chamberlain was at this time showing how it could be done:

16. Churchill, op. cit., I. 345.

his Radical caucus at Birmingham was the foundation of his growing appeal as a national figure. Something similar in their position and temperaments drew these two, Chamberlain and Churchill, together. When Lord Randolph invited Radical Joe to dinner, the old Duke was scandalized. Was he not a republican? Had he not refrained from drinking the Queen's health at a public function in Birmingham, had doubts about driving in the same carriage as Mayor with the Prince of Wales? What company Randolph kept!

It is curious to think back over the lapse of time at the mutual attraction and exclusion of Joe Chamberlain and Lord Randolph – still more at the dichotomy exhibited in the careers of their sons. A good deal of recent English history has passed between the ranks of those two families.

Another Radical, who became a colleague and friend of Lord Randolph's son, has summed up the situation at that moment.

> The same general forces of the hour, working through the energy, ambition and initiative of individuals, produced the same effect in each of the two parties. The Radical programme of Mr Chamberlain was matched by the Tory Democracy of Lord Randolph Churchill; each saw that the final transfer of power from the ten-pound householder to artisans and labourers would rouse new social demands; each was aware that Ireland was the electoral pivot of the day, and while one of them was wrestling with those whom he stigmatized as Whigs, the other by dexterity and resolution overthrew his leaders as 'the Old Gang'.[17]

But this anticipates; it is sufficient to observe that the victory of Lord Randolph within the party-machine would necessarily bring him a large accession of power.

Where the Central Committee possessed all the power and the cash, the National Union of Conservative Associations represented the constituency parties, the active workers. It was to this national body that Lord Randolph appealed, and at the Birmingham Conference in 1883 he won their backing. His argument was a powerful one. 'The Conservative party will never exercise power

17. Morley, III. 152.

until it has gained the confidence of the working classes.'[18] From that he made the transition to the point that

> the great bulk of the Tory party throughout the country is composed of artisans and labouring classes.... No party management can be effective and healthy unless the great labouring classes are directly represented on the Executive of the party.

From this he drove home the conclusion that he wished to see 'the control and guidance of the organization of the Tory party transferred from a self-elected body to an annually elected body. I wish to see the management of the financial resources of our party transferred from an irresponsible body to a responsible body.'

Upon this the Conference passed a resolution directing a new Council to take steps to secure for the National Union its proper influence in the party organization. Impossible to recount here the complicated (and boring) party manoeuvres that ensued. Lord Randolph's supporters obtained a slight majority on the new Council, with himself as chairman. Lord Percy had been chairman of the Organization Committee, and Lord Salisbury continued to make his communications to him – and gave offence to the majority. On realizing this Lord Salisbury made a tactical retreat and wrote to Lord Randolph, 'I hope, however, that there is no chance of the paths of the Central Committee and the National Union crossing: for there is plenty of good work for both to do'.[19] One recognizes familiar language from that agile tactician: that was not the point.

It is clear that Lord Salisbury was not giving way. After some months of intrigue and counter-intrigue it transpired that all business relating to elections and candidates was to remain in the hands of the Central Committee – in other words, the Old Gang. At that Lord Randolph resigned his chairmanship and let it be known that he would withdraw from politics. Consternation in the Tory ranks; he was re-elected chairman unanimously. At the Sheffield Conference next year, in time for the general election, Lord Randolph won a complete victory. He was at the head of the poll; the Old Gang made every effort to maintain control, but in

18. Churchill, I. 308–9. 19. ibid., 316.

vain. The Central Committee was dissolved, the organization of the National Union on a democratic, representative basis was confirmed. Lord Salisbury and Lord Randolph were reconciled and met to form an alliance and plan strategy. But they met as two comparable powers – and observe that Lord Randolph had attained his object by a timely resignation.

In Parliament he continued to drive his furious pace. But there was calculation in his aggression: he considered it indispensable to attack, to destroy the personal ascendancy of Mr Gladstone if the Tory party were ever to regain the initiative. The Liberal plan for further extension of the franchise, with yet another Reform Bill, looked like putting the Tories in a permanent minority. An unfriendly critic on the Tory side bore reluctant witness to Lord Randolph's effectiveness. Whenever the Bradlaugh case came up, as it did again and again in this unhappy Parliament, he used it to distract the government and disrupt its majority. His speech on the Affirmation Bill was admitted

> even by his critics to be one of extraordinary brilliancy, research and accuracy. He after this performance established a reputation of powers of speech and controversy second only to Gladstone himself, and upon the reputation he had thus made became even more contemptuous than before in his treatment of his own Front Bench.[20]

It was not only Sir Stafford's deference to Gladstone that infuriated him, but his total lack of punch, the very conventionality of his character. This encouraged Lord Randolph to take a line of his own, and impose it: he did not care whether it was the party-line, approved by his accredited leaders, or no. In his inner mind they were not his leaders; his relations with Sir Stafford were purely formal and barely civil; he had undoubtedly passed sentence of exclusion upon him when his day came. The impression on his fellows may be gathered:

> on one side he was a genius, on the other a spoilt and naughty child; but in either capacity he always trampled on the weak and irresolute . . . as he rose in popularity so he became more dictatorial and un-

20. Lord George Hamilton, *Parliamentary Reminiscences and Reflections, 1868–85*, I. 208.

reasonable. . . . Provided he could embarrass the government, the after-effect of his action was of little concern to him. . . . Still, it must be admitted that Churchill's actions and speeches, impolitic and risky as they often were, did much to rehabilitate the Tory party as a fighting organization and a living force.[21]

In foreign affairs he was a Little Englander. He was opposed to our intervention in the Sudan, calling it a 'bondholders' war': a very advanced line for the time and one not calculated to please the bondholders. The view of Dilke, with whom Lord Randolph had broken, was that his fierce attacks on the Khedive of Egypt were 'without one atom of truth in them', and he regarded it as a curious example of his flightiness that when he went to Egypt a few years later, he was struck with wonder at the Khedive's refusal to receive him.[22] Even as a very young member Lord Randolph had been opposed to his party's pro-Turk policy. He was himself pro-Russian and pro-French – an alignment very much in advance of his time, though it may be said that his party ultimately came round to it with the Anglo-French entente of Lord Lansdowne and its sequel. This meant that he did not share his party's fears of a Russian advance on the North-West Frontier of India. Altogether Lord Randolph's temperamental leanings and prejudices were those of a Radical, except for the dominant question of the day: only Home Rule kept him a Tory.

On foreign policy even Mr Gladstone was sometimes more of a Tory, or, we may say, was more responsibly concerned for the vital interests of the country. In 1885 there was a Russian advance into Afghan territory: the Penjdeh 'incident'. Mr Gladstone asked at once for a credit of eleven millions, a very considerable sum in those days of financial responsibility, when money was worth something; he got a whole-hearted national response, a personal triumph in Parliament. Lord Randolph to Lord Salisbury:

Would you believe it? The whole Front Opposition Bench sat as mute as mummies – and the Prime Minister got his £11,000,000 at one gulp,

21. ibid., 200.
22. S. Gwynn and G. M. Tuckwell, *Life of Sir Charles Dilke*, II. 49.

without a remark of any sort or kind. . . . It never occurred to me for one moment that Sir S. N. would allow his intemperate remarks to pass unnoticed, or that the debate would collapse in such an ignominious manner for the Opposition.[23]

Lord Salisbury consoled him with engaging cynicism: 'I hope the papers will attribute the collapse to our exalted patriotism. At least, that is the only hope with which one can console oneself.' But may that not in fact be the simple explanation? Sir Stafford Northcote was a simple, straightforward, sincere man; he was not a good Leader of the Opposition.

The Irish question was coming more and more to dominate internal politics and with Mr Gladstone's conversion to Home Rule to divide and wreck the Liberal party. On this subject Lord Randolph had a special equipment and point of view of his own. Unlike most Tories he had a genuine sympathy with, and understanding of, the Irish character. He was in favour of concession, except for the ultimate one of Home Rule. He was liberal about extending the franchise and argued for the application of the Reform Bill of 1884 to Ireland. He put forward good cynical reasons for this course – after all, he knew Ireland. He argued that the Fenian proclivities of the towns would be more than counter-balanced by the increased power given to the peasantry. The incidents of agricultural life, he observed, are unfavourable to revolutionary movements, and the peasant is even more under the proper and legitimate influence of the Roman Catholic priesthood than the lower classes of the towns.[24]

A little later he exposed his calculations more clearly in a private letter.

It is the Bishops entirely to whom I look in the future to turn, to mitigate or to postpone the Home Rule onslaught. Let us only be enabled to occupy a year with the Education Question. By that time, I am certain, Parnell's party will have become seriously disintegrated. Personal jealousies, Government influences, Davitt and Fenian intrigues will all be at work on the devoted band of eighty: and the Bishops, who in their hearts hate Parnell and don't care a scrap for Home Rule, having safely acquired control of Irish education, will, according to my

23. Churchill, I. 382–3. 24. Morley, III. 108.

calculation, complete the rout. . . . My own opinion is that if you approach the Archbishop [Walsh] through proper channels, if you deal in friendly remonstrances and in attractive assurances . . . the tremendous force of the Catholic Church will gradually and insensibly come over to the side of the Tory party.[25]

In the end it was not so much the Irish Catholic bishops as the odious English Nonconformist conscience that ruined Parnell – with infinitely tragic consequences: the demand for Home Rule was stifled for two or three decades, to emerge in the murderous form of Sinn Fein with all the consequences of murder campaigns, arson and destruction, Black and Tans, civil war and ultimate separation of Ireland from the Commonwealth.

With slow rumination that powerful organ, Mr Gladstone's mind, was moving, righteously and rightly, to the acceptance of Home Rule. It may have been that that made him ready to accept a minor reverse on an item of the Budget as defeat for the government; Lord Randolph, who had planned it, jumping on his seat below the gangway and leading the cheers of the whole Conservative party. The immense Liberal majority had been at length breached. The Queen, with her usual common sense, expressed surprise that Mr Gladstone should regard a minor matter as a vital question. But he was determined to go – until an appeal to the country should decide who had its confidence. Meanwhile no one had any doubt whose victory it was.

The political situation was extraordinarily confused, partly because Parnell, alienated by the Liberals' application of coercion, was offering the votes of the Irish Nationalists to the Conservatives in return for – what? No one knew for what. Lord Randolph was playing Parnell for all he was worth. Until the political situation cleared one way or another, Lord Salisbury was called upon by the Queen to form a Caretakers' Government. He proposed to make Sir Stafford Northcote Chancellor of the Exchequer and Leader of the House of Commons. He offered Lord Randolph, who had never held office before, the India Office, then important among the Secretaryships of State. He then found that Lord Randolph would not accept so long as

25. Churchill, II. 4.

Northcote was to be Leader of the House. The wise old Duchess pleaded with her son:

I have been thinking very quietly and calmly over your position, and I think you might go to see Lord Salisbury to show him your friendly feeling while you maintain your own position. . . . He told you to consider his offer; so that, it seems to me, you are almost in duty bound to go to see him. There is no doubt he is in a very difficult position, and may say you require *not* any policy or special measure, but simply that he should *kill* an old friend whom *all* respect.[26]

But that was precisely what Lord Randolph did require of Lord Salisbury. For himself, he said,

I am very near the end of my tether. In the last five years I have lived twenty. I have fought Society. I have fought Mr Gladstone at the head of a great majority. I have fought the Front Opposition Bench. Now I am fighting Lord Salisbury. I have said I will not join the Government unless Northcote leaves the House of Commons. Lord Salisbury will never give way.[27]

As a matter of fact, when he learned that if Lord Randolph would not join the government neither would Hicks-Beach, Lord Salisbury had to give way. Not in the least anxious to form a government – a massive patience which he had developed by sheer force of character and intellect became a great asset to him – Lord Salisbury solved the dilemma by giving the Foreign Secretaryship, to which he himself had every claim, to Northcote and promoting him to the Lords.

While the matter hung in the balance Lord Salisbury informed the Queen of his troubles with Lord Randolph and asked 'if I had any insuperable objection to him, which I said I had not'.[28] The proposal that he should go to the India Office 'rather startled me, but the India Council would be a check on him'. On learning that he would not take office unless Sir Stafford were deposed from Leader – 'with due consideration to Lord Randolph Churchill', she did not think 'he should be allowed entirely his own terms, especially as he has never held office before'. When

26. Churchill, I. 143. 27. ibid., I. 415–16.

28. *The Letters of Queen Victoria*, Second Series, ed. G. E. Buckle, III. 663, 670, 679, 683.

at length all was arranged and Lord Randolph was sworn in as Secretary of State for India, in the Green Drawing-Room at Windsor on a dreadfully hot June day, the Queen was interested to observe that Lord Randolph was 'rather like his sisters, a little like his grandfather'. She had never seen this startling young politician before, now aged thirty-six, who was the talk of her kingdom. Now he was to preside over the government of her Indian Empire. It gave her to think; it gave her a headache later. Only a couple of years before, the Queen had taken the initiative in ending the rift between the rising politician and the royal family. The Prince of Wales made it up with Lord Randolph; Lady Randolph attended a Drawing-Room at the Queen's express wish. In July they were bidden to dine at Windsor. 'He is very quiet and has an extraordinary likeness to darling Leopold, which quite startled me . . . Lord Randolph talked sensibly.' She was evidently on hot bricks about him. Did she expect him to bite?

If so, he very shortly did. Lord Randolph had declared himself all along opposed to coercion in Ireland: it was this that had gained the Tories the support of the Nationalists, and he had been the chief procurer of it. Parnell demanded, as part of his price, an inquiry into the trials for murder that had taken place under the Coercion Viceroy, Lord Spencer. The Cabinet resolved against this as setting a very dangerous precedent. Lord Randolph dissented. Whatever his motive, whether out of just indignation or to please the Nationalists, he delivered a violent attack on Lord Spencer and his administration. The Queen was incensed at his language; she expressed her doubts about the policy of trying to govern Ireland without additional powers: it looked like trying to cajole the Nationalists, 'who she feels sure *everyone but* Lord Randolph in the Cabinet *must know* are totally *unreliable*'.[29] She hoped that Lord Salisbury would restrain Lord Randolph as much as he could. Poor Lord Salisbury was called on to explain. One sees the Queen as the most exalted, though not the most formidable, member of the Old Gang.

The result of this affair was unfortunate. Lord Spencer was deeply wounded by the attack; the breach between these two

29. ibid., III. 687.

leading members of the Spencer clan was never repaired. On Lord Spencer it had a somewhat paradoxical impact: he concluded that since it was not possible to govern Ireland without coercion, the only alternative was full Home Rule. When the split in the Liberal party came and the Liberal Unionists hived off, he was the only one of the great Whig magnates to remain with Mr Gladstone on his forlorn journey towards the setting sun and self-government in Ireland.

The Queen was now to experience in her own person, and her own sphere, something of what Lord Randolph could do. Since dear Lord Beaconsfield had made her Empress of India she took a personal interest in its affairs. Might there not be an opening there for her dear Arthur (the Duke of Connaught), who was so keen on his military career? She proposed him for the vacant Bombay command, which carried with it the Commandership-in-Chief and a seat on the Governor's Council. Lord Randolph thought not, on the ground that the post involved political functions, which it would be unsuitable for a member of the royal family to take part in.

At this the Queen consulted the Viceroy for his opinion and rather compromised Lord Salisbury by asking him to forward her telegram. He was in a fix; he could hardly have refused. Lord Randolph:

> I have for some time felt that the India Office, while I was there, had little influence with respect to other matters of great importance. But from what has passed between yourself and the Viceroy about the Duke of Connaught, it must be obvious to the Viceroy that I no longer possess the confidence of the Sovereign or of yourself.[30]

Lord Salisbury: 'I regret very much that you should think I have not shown you confidence. I have done my best to give effect to your wishes as far as I possibly could.' The boring explanations usual in such cases followed and the tangle was straightened out. But Lord Randolph got his way: the Duke of Connaught did not get the Bombay command while he was Secretary of State for India. It was left to Lord Salisbury to mollify the Queen, who could not see how she had offended 'because I had asked privately

30. Churchill, I. 506–7.

of Lord Dufferin, through Lord Salisbury, as to Arthur's fitness for Bombay'.[31] However, Lord Randolph 'has since returned to reason, "having taken calomel", as Lord Salisbury amusingly words it, and is not going to resign'.

A few days later Salisbury reported to the Queen the Cabinet decision to hold on to the Zulficar Pass in the delimitation of frontiers with Afghanistan. Lord Randolph had wished to settle without standing out for it; Salisbury and the majority of the Cabinet would not hear of it. 'He spoke of Lord Randolph, in general, as being a great difficulty, but that his state of health had much to do with it.' This jar between them could not but bring home to the Prime Minister the success of his junior partner's technique of resignation or threatened resignation.

For the rest Lord Randolph made an unexpectedly good departmental chief. In spite of his own feeling in presiding over the venerable Council of India 'like an Eton boy presiding at a meeting of the Masters', his officials paid tribute to his instinctive ability for the work. He was quick to seize the essential points, clear-minded and very hard-working. What surprised people was that such a man could be so conciliatory, sensitive and tactful. Officials found him skilful at devolving subordinate business and remarkably persuasive when he wanted anything. 'Few high officials can ever have been his superior, or indeed his equal, in the magical art of *getting things done*.'[32] When all was over between them Lord Salisbury singled out as Randolph's greatest gift that of attaching to himself the unlimited devotion of his subordinates. Like Chatham he does not seem to have had the art of working with equals.

Nor would it have been like him if his career at the India Office had not ended with a paradox. The Little Englander annexed Burma outright. Burmese government was in a frightful state of disintegration and decay: murders, massacres, outrages multiplied upon its own subjects; upon the foreign trading community vexations, insults, threats. The miserable ruler, King Theebaw, tried to play off the French against the British; this, at the threshold of India, was too much. He was presented with

31. *Letters of Queen Victoria*, ed. cit., III. 689.
32. Churchill, I. 480.

the demand to admit a British mission; Lord Randolph telegraphed that 'its dispatch should be concurrent with movement of troops and ships to Rangoon. If ultimatum is rejected, the advance on Mandalay ought to be immediate. On the other hand, armed demonstration might bring Burmese to their senses.'[33] It did. Neither Lord Salisbury nor the Government of India wished for annexation. But Lord Randolph's will prevailed: for the next half century the Burmese people experienced an intermission from murder, outrage and massacre as methods of government.

Lord Salisbury's conduct of his administration, firm and sagacious over foreign affairs, did much to recover the country's prestige abroad where Mr Gladstone had lost so much ground. No one was more appreciative of this than the Queen. But the internal difficulties of governing in a minority were insuperable, and Ireland exerted a distracting influence. Lord Randolph despaired of the parliamentary difficulties they met with and was anxious to be quit of the whole business. The Queen was tougher: 'the youngest member of the Cabinet must *not* be allowed to dictate to the others. It will *not* do, and Lord Salisbury must really put his foot down.'[34] It did not do: when Lord Salisbury found in turn that it was not possible to govern Ireland without coercion, Lord Randolph and his friend Hicks-Beach threatened resignation rather than accept it. They were wrong: in a few weeks it had to be resorted to. Lord Salisbury wrote Randolph a very wise, forbearing letter on the duty of government not being afraid to govern; he had gone all lengths to sacrifice his own opinion for the sake of unity in the Cabinet. 'Internally as well as externally our position as a government is intolerable. . . . I am feverishly anxious to be out,' and very shortly, in January 1886, he was.

Mr Gladstone was feverishly anxious to be in and the Liberals anticipated the result of the election with some confidence. They were wrong, and it was precisely the areas where Lord Randolph's appeal was strongest, the big cities, that put them wrong. The

33. q. Churchill, I. 523.

34. Lady Gwendolen Cecil, *Life of Robert, Marquis of Salisbury*, III. 283–4.

election was enlivened by a celebrated trope from him, comparing the Whig leader Lord Hartington to a boa-constrictor having to swallow the various morsels of the Radical programme that Mr Chamberlain handed out: 'the only difference between the boa-constrictor and the Marquis of Hartington is this – that the boa-constrictor enjoys his food [rabbits out of a hat] and thrives on it and Lord Hartington loathes his food and it makes him sick'.[35] The result of this was to make another enemy, and a very powerful one: leader of the Liberal Unionists to be. The result of the election – the newly enfranchised rural voters coming to Mr Gladstone's rescue – was a Liberal majority of 86, within which was a dissident wing of almost as many anti-Home Rulers; while Parnell's following of 86 held the balance in British politics. Mr Gladstone would, even apart from his inclinations, be forced to come out in favour of Home Rule.

What will happen now? a friend asked Lord Randolph. 'I shall lead the Opposition for five years,' he replied. 'Then I shall be Prime Minister for five years. Then I shall die.'[36] This turned out exactly right as to the term of life that remained to him: he must have had some inner knowledge that it would not be long. But the incalculable element in politics utterly falsified his other expectations.

The year 1886 was one of continuous political crisis. Mr Gladstone introduced his Home Rule Bill and in the struggle over it Lord Randolph took the lead on his side, urgent, aggressive, hectic. We find him in constant touch with Lord Salisbury by letter, and their correspondence affords a fascinating contrast. Where Randolph is urgent, Lord Salisbury is patient and wise; where the junior partner is all for aggression, his leader is much more *rusé*, waiting for the inherent difficulties of his opponents to overwhelm them; where Randolph wants action, Lord Salisbury is content to put the onus on others, to hold himself in reserve until he alone is the master of the situation. It is a masterly object-lesson; it was lost on Lord Randolph.

Over Home Rule Mr Gladstone divided his party for good.

35. Churchill, I. 464–5. 36. ibid., 473.

A large section of Liberal Unionists left the ranks. These consisted of two wings: there were the aristocratic Whigs led by Lord Hartington, whose views were naturally conservative and who were happier in association with Conservatives. The other wing, paradoxically, were those Radicals who followed Joseph Chamberlain, the catalytic effect of whose personality was to draw them out of their natural orbit, bring them too into association with the Tories, frustrate the natural development of a strong Radical Liberalism and distract the course of British politics for the next twenty years. There seems to have been something fatal in the Chamberlain touch throughout the last half century!

Lord Randolph expressed himself as ready to retire to make way for the Liberal Unionists: 'you will never get Whig support as long as I am in the government, and Whig support you must have. Very indifferent health makes me look forward irresistibly to idleness regained.'[37] Lord Salisbury: 'if retirements are required for the sake of repose and Whig combinations I shall claim to retire with you in both respects'. Politicians are apt to talk like that; but in the event one of them was indispensable, the other found to be expendable. At the height of the contest Lord Randolph went across to Ulster – which Mr Gladstone had not expected from his Irish Bill and had put under the rule of a Dublin Parliament – and in a flaming speech coined the slogan 'Ulster will fight, and Ulster will be right', which was to be revived with shattering effect in future years and with unexpected impact on his son.

In Parliament an intervention of Lord Randolph's had a decisive consequence. In the excitement of debate he managed to make Mr Gladstone commit himself to refusing to consider any substantial changes in the Bill as it was. That settled its fate. The Liberal dissidents voted against it; the government was defeated by 343 votes to 313.

The election that followed was an exceptionally critical one; both in the issue – for on it depended the political unity of the British Isles – and in its consequences for the future of parties. Few people at the time could have guessed that it would inaugurate a twenty-year long Tory ascendancy, when the natural

37. Churchill, II. 6–7.

thing, with the full extension of the franchise to the working-class, would have been to expect a dominant Liberalism with a Radical impulse. More than any other person, Joe Chamberlain was responsible for the distortions that followed – Tory Imperialism, a brash jingoism, the South African War, the poisoning of relations with Ireland. No wonder he was the most hated man in English politics.

The keynote of the election was set by Lord Randolph, and it was an intensely personal one, vulgar and very effective. Mr Gladstone was 'the Old Man in a hurry'. This phrase fastened on him and became historic, in the way that only a phrase that speaks a historic truth does. Though one can have no doubt, after all that has happened since, that Gladstone was profoundly right in his intuition that self-government was the only answer to the Irish question, it is probably true that he was over-hasty and premature. If those decades had been given to the Liberals it might have been dealt with gradually, the obstacle of the House of Lords and all. Joe Chamberlain the Radical ruined that hope.

In the strategy of the election Lord Randolph again held a key-place. He more than anyone saw to it that the Liberal Unionists were not opposed by Tories, that the split did the maximum damage to the Liberals. 'He had named the Unionist Party. He had been a principal agent in the electoral compact on which it was based. He was the link with Chamberlain.'[38] The results were decisive. Lord Salisbury's majority was a composite one, but with the Liberal Unionists it was 118; it gave him a foundation upon which to govern for the next six years, no one could have foretold how securely – and perhaps only Lord Salisbury could have held them together.

Lord Randolph now got his reward. He was at the zenith of his popularity and power – of his powers, too, we may add. The *Yorkshire Post* said that he had 'touched the popular imagination as the eloquence of few men has ever done';[39] other Tory papers followed suit; even *The Times* became more sympathetic with success. At Bradford an address was presented him by some two hundred and forty Conservative delegates. The Tory leaders

38. ibid., 129–30.
39. q. Lord Ronaldshay, *Life of Lord Curzon*, I. 108.

were very ready to accept the facts of the situation. Lord Salisbury offered him the Treasury with the Leadership of the House of Commons: at thirty-six he was the youngest since Pitt. John Tenniel in a famous *Punch* cartoon depicted him at the dispatch-box in the Leader's place, with the shade of Dizzy behind saying:

> You stand – at your age – where I stood after years
> Of waiting on Fortune and working on fools.

Dizzy's prophecy of some years before as to the future of Lord Randolph had now come true. A Liberal friend asked him, 'How long will your leadership last?' 'Six months,' he replied. 'And after that?' 'Westminster Abbey.' It lasted less than six months; there was no Westminster Abbey.

From the first the sage Lord Salisbury regarded it as an experiment, and Lord Randolph seems to have recognized that quite well. The Queen confided to her Journal, 'Lord Randolph, whom I felt to be a great experiment, Lord Salisbury said was very nervous, which was perhaps a good thing.'[40] Others too were doubtful. A friend wrote to young Curzon, who started his career as an enthusiastic follower of Lord Randolph and became his assistant private secretary, 'I must confess to being a wee bit anxious as to how he will lead. A leader requires angelic temper – this, I fear, Lord Randolph has not.'[41] A powerful enemy within the party, one of those who had to be removed from his propinquity to the Lords, wrote, 'I should be sorry to think that our future depended upon Randolph Churchill.'[42] He would need to be very circumspect.

And in the first brief September session he was. Even the Cecils had to admit that he surprised 'even his admirers by the dignity and unprovocative skill of his leadership'.[43] It was part of his duty to write nightly reports of the proceedings in the House to the Queen. Nothing could have been more dignified and proper – except that she was amused to find an offending morsel of tobacco in the official red box. From Balmoral she wrote him –

40. *The Letters of Queen Victoria*, Third Series, ed. G. E. Buckle, I. 171.
41. Ronaldshay, op. cit., I. 107.
42. A. E. Gathorne-Hardy, *Gathorne-Hardy*, II. 267.
43. Cecil, III. 317.

writing-paper deep-edged in black, though it was more than twenty years since the Prince Consort died:

> Now that the Session is just over, the Queen wishes to write and thank Lord Randolph Churchill for his regular and full and interesting reports of the debates in the House of Commons, which must have been most trying. Lord Randolph has shown much skill and judgement in his leadership during this exceptional session of Parliament.[44]

In addition to the Leadership there was the Treasury. That province had been for so long dominated by Mr Gladstone, where his financial orthodoxy was the prevailing religion, that Lord Randolph's arrival created consternation. 'I forget. Was I a bi-metallist when I was at the India Office?', he inquired gaily. It was like doubting the religion of the Gold Standard in the days of Montagu Norman. (His son was to entertain such doubts when his time came.) When it came to budgetary figures, 'I never could make out what those damned dots meant,' he said. Serious-minded officials, earnest Gladstonians, were shocked at such levity. But, indeed, Lord Randolph would have done better to act on the advice of an Irish friend and leave the Treasury to Goschen; not that he was incapable of running it, but that the double burden for one of his uncertain health and nervous excitement was too much.

His pre-eminence in the Commons and in the country made his position indisputable; and when he made his famous Dartford speech in October, outlining a whole programme of reform, he spoke, as Chamberlain noted, in the tone of a co-Premier.[45] That, however, was not Lord Salisbury's idea, nor was the programme of reform, in which he had no belief. And, in fact, in the ironical way in which things work out in politics, with Lord Randolph's arrival at leadership, the political situation underneath had changed against him. With the secession of the Liberal Unionists he, who had hitherto been indispensable, could now be dispensed with – if it came to the point. Lord Randolph had been most active in paving the way for co-operation with the Liberal Unionists; but when it came about, it immensely

44. Reproduced in Churchill, II. 154.
45. J. L. Garvin, *Life of Joseph Chamberlain*, II. 271.

strengthened Lord Salisbury's position as the pivot of power between the Tories and them. Some sense of this must have exasperated Lord Randolph – to arrive at the top and find that power was elsewhere; for exasperation was the keynote of his conduct in the following months. When to that was added the complete frustration of his ideas (he could not bear not to get his way), he was driven to despair, to make a desperate challenge.

The cool eye of the Cecils took in the situation. 'In dealing with Lord Randolph', Arthur Balfour's sister wrote, 'Lord Salisbury and his nephew were in the habit of taking long views.'[46] 'The line I took with Randolph Churchill', said his friend, young Balfour, who succeeded to his place, 'was based on the supposition that it was better to have him with us than against us.' The innermost thoughts of Lord Salisbury are revealed in the correspondence with his nephew – blood, however rarefied, is thicker than water – as they waited to catch Lord Randolph out.

> I am inclined to think that we should avoid, as far as possible, all 'rows' until Randolph puts himself entirely and flagrantly in the wrong by some act of party disloyalty which everybody can understand and nobody can deny. By this course we may avoid a battle altogether, but if a battle is forced upon us, we shall be forced to win it.[47]

Relations with Lord Salisbury were now of crucial importance – as his daughter recognizes from his point of view: 'that chief, meditating upon its [the government's] prospects, was in fact more occupied with a problem of personality than with one of political programmes'.[48] Lord Randolph did not hesitate to intervene in Lord Salisbury's sphere of foreign affairs, where the chief's judgement would be almost bound to be right. In the previous year Salisbury had engaged in a single-handed struggle to protect the union of Southern with Northern Bulgaria – against Russia and all the Continental powers. And against the wishes of the mercurial Randolph constantly protesting against our exasperating Russia, who had reversed her aggressive line since her war in Turkey, etc. Wise old monolith, how right Lord

46. B. E. C. Dugdale, *A. J. Balfour, 1848–1906*, 56–7.
47. ibid., 51. 48. Cecil, III. 316.

Salisbury was, and how much he deserved to be leader, when it came to the fundamental interests of the country! He stuck to his point and won against all Europe: Bulgaria achieved a certain measure of independence with unity.

Now in September 1886 there was another threat of a forward Russian move, and Lord Randolph was not in favour of resisting Russia's advance in the Balkans. Salisbury thought that if Russia attacked Constantinople, we should act in the Dardanelles. Lord Randolph did not mind about Constantinople. Lord Salisbury: 'You are naturally sarcastic about my Dardanelles, and I hope the matter will not come up in our time. But the possesion by Russia of Constantinople will be an awkward piece of news for the Minister who receives it.'[49] Not content with opposing the Prime Minister on a matter where he knew far better, Lord Randolph discussed matters with both the Russian and German ambassadors – quite beyond his sphere. Upon this the chief came down firmly and unmistakably.

> I am afraid you are prepared to give up Constantinople: and foreign Powers will be quick enough to find that divergence out. . . . I consider the loss of Constantinople would be the ruin of our party and a heavy blow to the country: and therefore I am anxious to delay by all means Russia's advance to that goal.

Who can doubt that the older and wiser man was right? Two world-wars have passed over us, and far too heavy a Russian domination has been imposed upon Eastern Europe. If Constantinople, gateway to the Mediterranean, had been given away then, it would have made the situation impossible.

Lord Randolph's ideas of internal policy were consistent with this Little Englandism, and they were Radical ones. At Dartford in October he stood on the pinnacle of his popularity – many thousands of Conservatives to greet him, a hundred addresses from all over the country, celebrations in the town all day, fireworks at night. There were no fireworks in the speech, but he promised a Bill to enable agricultural labourers to acquire freehold plots and allotments – with grateful acknowledgements to Mr Chamberlain. A Land Bill to make the transfer of land

49. Churchill, II. 160–2.

simple and cheap; a gradual transfer of the unpopular burden of tithe to the shoulders of the landlord. A reorganization of local government with changes in the incidence of local taxation; reform and simplification of House of Commons procedure. Lastly he proclaimed his intention of reducing public expenditure and taxation.

The most deadly opponent of Mr Gladstone was at work on a Gladstonian Budget. He was in fact bolder and more radical in his proposals than Mr Gladstone would have been. We need not go in detail into the damned dots, but indicate simply the principles of the thing. His aim was to lighten the burden on the lower middle classes, to transfer it from necessaries to luxuries. He was budgeting for a large surplus to distribute in lower taxes on tea and tobacco, and to provide funds for an important new system of local government grants: he really meant his promises of reform. To get his surplus he aimed at an increase in death-duties and house-duties – hardly palatable to Conservatives or to be expected from a Conservative administration. Income-tax, in accordance with correct Gladstonian principles, he proposed to lower – *O fortunatos nimium* – from 8d. to 5d. in the pound.

Such was his power that the Cabinet, strange to say, accepted his Budget in principle; but there was bound to be a struggle with the spending departments over the particular economies to be enforced, and his colleagues were nearing the end of their patience. Lord Randolph was in complete disagreement with his colleagues over Local Government reform: he wanted the Radical programme of the abolition of the Poor Law and Boards of Guardians, and placing relief of the poor under the County Councils and District Councils. All this was looking decades ahead. He thought that the Liberal Unionists would support him; but the Whig majority among them was more conservative than the Conservatives. Only the Radical wing under Chamberlain was in sympathy, and Lord Randolph should have concerted his moves with them. He and Chamberlain were taken with the idea of some central combination in politics between them, as his son played with the idea of a National party later on in our time. Sir Winston refers wishfully to 'that solid basis of agreement upon middle courses, which is shared by many sensible people and was in those days abhorrent to party machines. Need one add that the party machines always prove the stronger?'[50]

Lord Salisbury was full of forebodings: he thought that the Cabinet would break up. On his side Lord Randolph was despairing.

> Alas! I see the Dartford programme crumbling into pieces every day. The Land Bill is rotten. I am afraid it is an idle schoolboy's dream to suppose that Tories can legislate – as I did, stupidly. They can govern and make war and increase taxation and expenditure *à merveille*, but legislation is not their province in a democratic constitution. I certainly have not the courage and energy to go on struggling against cliques, as poor Dizzy did all his life.[51]

What he would have liked would be to bring Lord Salisbury – for whom he had a curiously filial feeling, affection and respect mingled with exasperation – over to his side; failing that, to force him. But Lord Salisbury was not the man to be forced.

The struggle with the tremendous *vis inertiae* of Conservatism at this time was wearing down Lord Randolph. The Queen noticed it when he came to dine at Windsor. 'We remained talking in the corridor till half past ten. Lady Randolph (an American) is very handsome and very dark. He said some strange things to me, which I will refer to later.'[52] She gave Lord Salisbury a full account of their conversation, saying that she thought Lord Randolph looked very ill and winding up shrewdly, 'it looked as if he was likely to be disagreeable and wanted the Queen to agree with him'. Lord Randolph had, according to Salisbury, thrown a fly at the Queen – ought not the Conservatives to agree with the Liberal Unionists as far as possible? She thought it a mistake for Conservatives to alter their principles. Lord Salisbury knew that Randolph was mistaken in thinking the Liberal Unionists were with him.

Salisbury warned Lord Randolph what would happen in a most interesting letter politically.

50. Winston S. Churchill, *Great Contemporaries*, 15.

51. Churchill, *Lord Randolph Churchill*, II. 223.

52. *The Letters of Queen Victoria*, Third Series, ed. G. E. Buckle, I. 223, 225.

> The classes and the dependants of class are the strongest ingredients in our composition, but we have so to conduct our legislation that we shall give some satisfaction to both classes and masses. This is specially difficult with the classes – because all legislation is rather unwelcome to them, as tending to disturb a state of things with which they are satisfied.[53]

He thought the policy of hitting the 'classes' hard and trusting the democracy to see one through would fail.

> I do not mean that the 'classes' will join issue with you on one of the measures which hits them hard, and beat you on that. That is not the way they fight. They will select some other matter on which they can appeal to prejudice, and on which they think the masses will be indifferent; and on this they will upset you.

The breach came over the Services. Lord Randolph was determined on economies on both Army and Navy. He managed to get Lord George Hamilton at the Admiralty to cut down his estimates by £700,000 – a very large sum then. Mr W. H. Smith at the War Office was made of sterner stuff. He would not give way, and if he were made to, he would go. With the crude finality of a *nouveau riche* in these aristocratic discussions, he put the issue: 'it comes to this – is he to be *the* Government? If you are willing that he should be, I shall be delighted, but I could not go on on such conditions.'[54]

When it came to the point Lord Salisbury was with the Services, as Lord Randolph expected. The outlook on the Continent was black, there was a distinct possibility of war: it was no time to be disarming. Lord Randolph was on his way to Windsor, when he told Lord George Hamilton quite casually that he meant to resign. But he said no word of it to the Queen, with whom he had a long and friendly conversation. On her writing-paper he wrote his resignation to Lord Salisbury – without a word of consultation with his friends, with Hicks-Beach who had made way for him and would certainly have dissuaded him;[55] without consulting his wise old mother, or

53. Churchill, op. cit., II. 224.
54. Cecil, III. 331.
55. cf. 'I should never have done it if Beach had been in London,' Lady Victoria Hicks-Beach, *Life of Sir Michael Hicks-Beach*, I. 301.

even his wife; without concerting any measures with sympathizers like Chamberlain. Lord Salisbury replied in a letter which, we now know, was not intended as an acceptance of resignation, but placed the onus squarely on Lord Randolph – acceptance of his, the Prime Minister's, decision. Lord Randolph was not the one to submit: he felt too much committed. He sent word of his resignation to the newspapers

When the final word reached Hatfield a ball was in progress; Lord Randolph's mother and sister were members of the house-party. Next morning Lord and Lady Salisbury were to be up early to see them off. The sagacious Prime Minister, knowing what to expect in *The Times* that morning – as skilful a tactician in small matters as in great – decided that they should oversleep. The guests departed without any awkward farewells.

We have an intimate glimpse of Lord Randolph at this moment from the pen of a Liberal M.P., afterwards Lord Esher. Going to call he found him

> lying on the sofa in his large grey library, smoking cigarettes, and completely prostrated by the excitement of the last two days. He said he was shunned like the pest and no one had been near him, not even those who owed everything to him. He was not in good spirits, and evidently doubtful of the result of his action.[56]

Only Chamberlain had been to dine with him and expressed himself very jealous: it was just the Budget he hoped to produce one day himself. The *Observer* revealed that it proposed to lower income-tax to 5d. in the £, to reduce tea and tobacco duties and relieve local taxation, while introducing graduated death-duties. This distinguished Liberal regarded it as a brilliant Budget, which would have won great popularity.

The resignation was for the moment a tremendous blow to the government – the suddenness of it, the unexpectedness by the public, in whose eyes Lord Randolph stood forth as the popular champion. Moreover, was he replaceable? On the Conservative side there was no one to replace him. For a few days the government rocked, and people expected it to fall. But it was precisely

56. M. V. Brett, *Journals and Letters of Viscount Esher*, I. 130–1.

in adverse circumstances that Salisbury's strongest qualities came to the fore.[57] He made the masterly move of once more offering to make way for Hartington; of course, the Liberal Unionists could not form a government.[58] But out of the manoeuvre he recruited their ablest financial brain, Goschen – superior in this sphere to anyone else in the House – as Chancellor of the Exchequer. At the Treasury, then, Lord Randolph was most successfully replaced – and this is the significance of his best known, but perhaps apocryphal, remark that he 'forgot Goschen'. For Leader of the House the Prime Minister turned to Mr W. H. Smith. It was Mr Smith of the vineries and pineries who had brought brilliant Lord Randolph down. He made a most successful Leader of the House. He received his reward: the family of Smith was ennobled, recruited to the peerage and, a more select accolade, intermarried with the Cecils. Had not the great Lord Burghley said, centuries before, 'What is gentility but ancient riches'?

For Lord Randolph the resignation was mortal; and a moment afterwards, in a flash of self-knowledge, he recognized that it was so. 'In inflicting on the Old Gang this final fatal blow, I have mortally wounded myself.'[59] He had indeed; there was to be no forgiveness, no remission for him. So far as the Tory party was concerned he had committed the irreparable offence: he had imperilled the unity of the party, and even its existence, for the sake of playing his own hand. Now that he was down all the antipathies he had provoked could come into the open; now that he had lost power it was safe for anybody to attack him. There was no protection, no quarter given; for his was the unpardonable offence. For the rest of his life Lord Randolph was a marked man; there was never any return. Lucifer had fallen from among the stars.

Salisbury's daughter has an admirable phrase to describe, fairly neutrally, the 'strongest force at work' against him: 'the instinctive British recalcitrance to an exaggerated personal

57. Chamberlain's opinion was – 'Salisbury is a bold man and is no doubt prepared for all the consequences'. – ibid., 129.

58. B. Holland, *Life of the Duke of Devonshire, 1833–1908*, 178

59. Churchill, II. 264.

claim'.[60] It is true that there is something un-English about the personality of Lord Randolph: he is much more like Celts we have known. Perhaps that is why he had an instinctive sympathy with the Irish and got on so well with them. And it may be by the same token that he was so exasperated, as Celts are apt to be, by the imperturbable impersonality of the English, a certain immobility that looks like sheer insensitiveness. Is it possible that the three generations of Stewarts from whom he was descended – mother, grandmother, great-grandmother – brought some such influence into his blood? For all his characteristics are so very much those of the Celt: the surface gaiety and effervescence, the melancholy and depression underneath; the mixture of extreme charm with aggression, of sensitiveness and tact with a biting tongue and willingness to wound; the very personal colouring of his judgement and of his reactions, the emotionalism; the quickness of perception, the lack of staying power; the quivering self-esteem, the genius and ultimate defencelessness.

He was up against a very powerful English type in Lord Salisbury, with the legions behind him. The Prime Minister made an interesting comment on the political reasons for his fall: he ascribed it to 'his resolution to make the interests of his Budget overrule the wishes and necessities of all the other Departments and, secondly, his friendship for Chamberlain which made him insist that we should accept that statesman as our guide in internal politics'.[61] Of the Prime Minister Lord Randolph never said anything harsher than 'What a fool Lord S. was to let me go so easily!' But Lord Salisbury was never at any time a fool about anything: it is fairly safe to say that the younger man never penetrated the reserves of wisdom, the recesses of subtlety, of the older man's mind. Yet he had a vast respect for it. Lord Salisbury had, he said, 'a mighty intellect'; to argue with him was like 'arguing with a rock'; and then, with a curiously feminine movement of mind, 'he might have made what he pleased of me'. That would have been a whole-time job, and Lord Salisbury had the country to govern, his party to manage.

Their last exchange was a very moving one. Old Sir Stafford Northcote, now Lord Iddesleigh, was dropped from the Foreign

60. Cecil, III. 335. 61. ibid., 336–7.

Office on the reconstruction of the government. By some misunderstanding he learned of his demotion before Lord Salisbury could see him and explain to him what he had in mind. When he came to see the Prime Minister at 10 Downing Street, the old man was suddenly struck down and died in his presence. Lord Randolph at once wrote a letter to which Salisbury's daughter describes as exemplifying 'the qualities which, in spite of all defects, made him so singularly attractive a character to his fellows'. Lord Salisbury responded even more remarkably.

> I had never happened to see anyone die before – and therefore, even apart from the circumstances, the suddenness of this unexpected death would have been shocking. But here was, in addition, the thought of our thirty years' companionship in political life, and the reflection that now, just before this sudden parting, by some strange misunderstanding, which it is hopeless to explain, I had, I believe, for the first time in my life, seriously wounded his feelings. As I looked upon the dead body stretched before me, I felt that politics was a cursed profession.[62]

In that, for once, the reserve is pierced and one looks into the heart of a man who knew all about the underlying tragic element in life.

The remaining years of Lord Randolph were an anticlimax to such a career. Mr Gladstone, with his immense experience of politics, judged that he was one of the rare cases of those who had committed political suicide. He noted in his Journal that the method of the resignation was an 'outrage' as against the Queen and also against the Prime Minister: 'this, of course, they will work against him'.[63] They did.

For the next three years, nevertheless, he remained a leading figure in politics, though an isolated one. He continued to speak at the top of his form. One of his speeches has a masterly passage about Podsnap and Podsnappery in politics – and that was one of his troubles: he was too candid: he had no humbug. Lourdes, for example, he thought 'a monument to *la bêtise humaine*'. His speeches continued to be reported in full, as only those of the Prime Minister and Mr Gladstone were. He remained always

62. Cecil, III. 345. 63. Morley, III. 275–6.

'news'. And not only in this country: when he journeyed on the Continent, visiting Berlin and St Petersburg, people wondered what he was up to now. But politics is about power: he was a political leader without power. He was left to eat his heart.

One observes his increasing realization of this in the accents of his letters. In 1887: 'when the Old Gang with their ideas are quite played out and proved to be utter failures, then, perhaps, people will turn to the young lot. Till this time comes, and I do not think it is far off, I must wait patiently.'[64] Politicians in his situation are apt to keep their courage up with that sort of reflection – he was writing to his mother. A little later: 'I own W. H. Smith has done better than I expected, for I expected a complete breakdown.' Mr Gladstone judged Lord Randolph's Budget speech of that year 'excellent'; but it was no consolation to the latter that the government was now adhering to his ideas on economy with regard to the Services. That, too, often happens.

In this year he and Chamberlain were attempting to co-operate. It ended in bitter disappointment for Lord Randolph. In Birmingham he had a large working-class following and his supporters wished him to stand for a seat there. Then he found that his friend Chamberlain not merely had no intention of sharing any power with him in his own preserve, but was not even willing to permit Lord Randolph's candidature for one of the seats. This ended those prospects of co-operation.

Over Ireland he came into open conflict with his party. So long as Parnell remained all-powerful there could be no peace in Ireland without Home Rule. The Tories were determined to snatch at any and every chance to ruin him; and by this time understandably sickened by the methods of Irish resistance – the maiming of cattle, arson and wanton damage – they wanted Ireland governed with a firm hand anyway. They now got it from, of all people, Randolph's junior associate in the Fourth Party, Arthur Balfour: the Prime Minister's nephew displayed unexpected courage and resource in the Irish Chief Secretaryship, while his debating ability in the House indicated that soon Lord Randolph would have an equal. The latter retained his

64. Churchill, II. 290–91.

sympathies with the Irish people and resented the strong hand – the imprisonment of Irish M.P.s, coercion – the Tories had always wanted. When the party snatched at the forged Pigott letters to discredit the Irish leader, and on the discovery of the forgery found themselves faced with the prospect of a Liberal and Nationalist victory, Lord Randolph, genuinely ashamed and shocked, assailed the Tory party in the most furious of his invectives. When he paused, exhausted – for he was already ill – no one in the ranks around him would so much as fetch him a glass of water.

His breach with his own party seemed complete: he should really have gone over to the Liberals. But he did not agree with them over Home Rule. This left him isolated and utterly impotent.

When he travelled abroad the Old Gang had their eye on him. In the winter of 1887–8 when he went to Russia and to Germany, and had conversations with the Tsar and with Bismarck, the Queen wrote to Lord Salisbury to see to it that foreign governments and the country knew that Lord Randolph was going simply on a private journey in no way charged with any message or mission from government, nor was likely to return to it.[65] Lord Salisbury did not need telling: he assured her that the information had been relayed to St Petersburg, Berlin and Vienna. *The Times* had been plainly instructed. The visit had been encouraged by the Prince of Wales, whose friendship now proved constant and strong.[66] He had highly approved of Randolph's appointment as Leader and Chancellor, and after his fall proved a good friend to him in adversity. They were constantly together at race-meetings, and of this the Queen disapproved, warning the Prince that intimacy with one 'so changeable and indiscreet' was compromising. On his return from Russia Lord Randolph reported at length on his conversations to the Prince. That would give no pleasure to Queen Victoria, who continued to withhold official papers from him on the ground that he was not sufficiently responsible. She was merely jealous, in the Hanoverian manner.

In his long conversation with the Tsar Lord Randolph observed

65. *The Letters of Queen Victoria*, Third Series, I. 367.
66. Sir Sidney Lee, *King Edward VII*, I. 529, 531, 682.

perfect propriety and loyalty to Lord Salisbury, whom the Tsar regarded as an enemy to Russia. On his return he duly reported his impressions to the Prime Minister, who forwarded an account to the Queen. But, he added, Lord Randolph did not mention some things which 'we know he said to Herbert Bismarck'. His policy is for us to line up with France and Russia: France will give way to us in Egypt, Russia will not molest us in India. 'It is odd that so clever a man should attach the slightest value to such a promise on the part of Russia.'[67] He had told his friends that the post of all others he would like is Viceroy of India. 'Of course it is impossible; his reputation for rashness is too pronounced. But it is odd that he should desire it. It is said that his pecuniary position is very bad.' One observes the accents of dislike: Lord Salisbury and Lord Randolph who should have been anticlastic were now antithetical.

In these circumstances of complete frustration he ceased to speak in the House and went more and more abroad. In 1891 he accepted an invitation from Cecil Rhodes to go to South Africa and travel up-country to Mashonaland, and he went in search of health and peace of mind. At once his journey was 'news', and the *Daily Graphic* offered him a large sum of money for a series of letters describing it. These were published next year as a book, *Men, Mines and Animals in South Africa*. Received in an unfriendly critical spirit, it is a characteristic production and makes interesting reading: vividly and well-written, though its manner is off-hand and disillusioned. The fact was his heart was in politics at home; as happens to politicians he could not do without the drug.

He left Dartmouth in the *Grantully Castle*, in which Mr Gladstone had performed his much-advertised 'periplus' round Britain, of which Randolph had made such fun in happier years. Arrived in South Africa he made amends by praising the magnanimity of Gladstone's peace giving up the Transvaal ten years before: it had won the confidence of the Cape Dutch, which Cecil Rhodes was now enjoying. Without it there would have been no confidence – though he had no illusions about the up-country Boers.

67. *The Letters of Queen Victoria*, Third Series, I. 383.

The Dutch settlers in Cape Colony are as worthy of praise as their relatives, the Transvaal Boers, are of blame. The former loyal, thrifty, industrious, hospitable, liberal, are and will, I trust, ever remain the backbone of our great colony at the Cape of Good Hope.[68]

He wished they might transmit some of their good qualities to 'their backward brethren in the Transvaal'. The Transvaal betrayed their bad and lazy farming, the thousands of acres carrying only a few hundred head of cattle; roads in a frightful state, even the main highway from Johannesburg to Pretoria, a mere thirty-five miles, in a shocking condition. There was the insolent denial by the Boers of all political or even municipal rights to persons other than of Dutch birth, in addition to their 'vicious and cruel sentiments to the native races'. These names, Pretoria, Potchefstroom, Mafeking, were soon to re-echo round the world.

At Mafeking he heard news that brought back all the old bitterness and at the same time made him long to be home.

So Arthur Balfour is really Leader – and Tory Democracy, the genuine article, at an end! Well, I have had quite enough of it all. I have waited with great patience for the tide to turn, but it has not turned, and will not now turn in time. . . . More than two-thirds, in all probability, of my life is over, and I will not spend the remainder of my years in beating my head against a stone wall. I expect I have made great mistakes; but there has been no consideration, no indulgence, no memory or gratitude – nothing but spite, malice and abuse. . . . All confirms me in my decision to have done with politics and try to make a little money for the boys and for ourselves.[69]

However, when the election came and the Liberals took office once more, though in a minority, he could not resist the drug: his party had need of him in Opposition and everybody thought that opposition would recover his powers. His disease was gaining upon him, and his articulation was not what it had been. It was noticed that Mr Gladstone, now over eighty – with his customary courtesy, his manners so much better than those of the aristocrats – was always in his place to hear what Lord Randolph had to say. He reported to the Queen on the Home Rule debate that his 'renewed participation in a great discussion, after

68. From the Preface. 69. Churchill, II. 452.

two years of absence or silence, excited interest in the House and was greeted with warm cheering by his own party'.[70] Mr Gladstone added that his criticisms were less incisive than Balfour's, 'perhaps owing to the fact that he did not for the moment seem to be at the highest level of his physical energies'. Harcourt thought that the speech regained some of his old influence with his party; but the truth was that he was going down-hill physically.

In these last years his views took an even more Radical turn. He had always had a peculiar, possibly a premature, sensitiveness about the way things were to go in society, perhaps with too little regard for the way they were at the moment. Now he sensed the emergence of the working-class as the foremost thing in the politics of the future. His views took on a collectivist tinge. He was anxious for the House of Commons to examine the demand for an eight-hour day; without further ado he expressed himself in favour of an eight-hour day for the miners – on this he was more radical than Mr Gladstone, who always remained an addict to Manchester doctrines. Lord Randolph wrote, with perceptive foresight:

> the Labour interest is now seeking to do for itself what the landed interest and the manufacturing capitalist interest did for themselves when each in turn commanded the disposition of State policy. Our land laws were framed by the landed interest for the advantage of the landed interest, and foreign policy was directed by that interest to the same end. Political power passed very considerably from the landed interest to the manufacturing capitalist, and our whole fiscal system was shaped by this latter power to its own advantage, foreign policy being also made to coincide. We are now come, or are coming fast, to a time when Labour laws will be made by the Labour interest for the advantage of Labour.[71]

We see that, on the essential point, neither Lord Salisbury nor Lord Randolph had much to learn from Karl Marx.

The Cecils, as we know from Lady Gwendolen's cool appraisal, never took Tory Democracy seriously. They thought it

> never precisely defined. With the majority of its supporters, the inspiring motive was tactical rather than political. It was not the creed of Conservatism that they doubted, but its power of appeal to the electorate.

70. *The Letters of Queen Victoria*, Third Series, II. 226, 231.
71. Churchill, II. 459.

The cry slackened almost to silence after victory, swelled recurrently after defeat, and was never louder than in the years which immediately followed the disaster of 1880. In every constituency there was a number of restlessly disappointed workers whose coveting of the catch-words which had served their opponents so victoriously as war-cries expressed itself in clamant aspirations after a 'democratic programme'. This section of opinion, of rather nebulous outline and – as Lord Randolph was to discover later to his loss – most unstable foundations

was stronger in the constituencies than in Parliament.[72]

This rather supercilious account of it, we take leave to think, is also rather too cynical: after all, there are the merits of the case. Lord Randolph's most enthusiastic supporters were Tory working men, and it is true they had not the power. But I think we have seen that there was a genuine Radicalism in his make-up and a tenacious consistency in his ideas: neither the one nor the other can be imputed to pure electioneering. And what of the merits of the case? In the heyday of upper and middle-class prosperity was he not right to seek to shift the burden of taxation on to their shoulders away from the people, to reform the Poor Law out of existence as has been done in our time, to better the conditions of the agricultural labourer, improve housing, control licensing and hours of work in the mines? These were all things that he wished not merely, passively, to see but actively to bring about.

From this point of view, now that it is all long over – though it made an immense perturbation in their day – we can see that his split with Lord Salisbury had a certain historical rightness. They did not mean the same thing. Lord Randolph both meant his Radicalism and thought it was the way to revivify the Tory party. The Tory party did not and therefore found him intolerable. As it happened, the orthodox Tories were right in the short run: the split in the Liberal party made it unnecessary to resort to Lord Randolph's ideas, while he himself could be dispensed with. Lord Salisbury's nephew, Balfour, took his place. Lord Randolph may be said to have had his delayed revenge with his son's going over to the Liberals in time for the great landslide of 1906 in their

72. Cecil, III. 84.

favour. What the Cecils thought of that may be gathered from Lady Salisbury's

My dear A. J. B.
D–n. D–n. D–n.[73]

It is possible that had he lived he would have moved over to the Liberal party – such is the conclusion that suggests itself from his son's biography – and that would have been a development consistent with his ideas. By the time of their victory he was long dead. After a last world-tour in 1894, in vain search of health, he came back to die in his mother's house, 24 January 1895. His friend Lord Rosebery, who knew him best, pays him the best tribute.

He had a faithful and warm heart; from childhood he had been the best of sons; and the whole soul of his mother was with him to the end. Nothing could exceed the pathos of her devotion to him in political adversity, or to his memory when he had passed away. . . . I see, as all the public saw, many faults; but I remember what the public could not know, the generous, lovable natur ‹ of the man. I cannot forget the pathos of the story; I mourn as all must mourn that he had not time to retrieve himself, not time to display his highest nature; I grieve, as all must grieve, that that daring and gifted spirit, should have been extinguished at an age when its work should only have just begun.[74]

Lord Salisbury lies on his tomb in Westminster Abbey, majestic and serene. Lord Randolph lies in the country churchyard at Bladon, among the grey slabs on the sunny south side of the church – Jennie beside him – just across from the park and the great house that gave him birth.

73. Dugdale, *Balfour*, 327. 74. Rosebery, 78, 183–4.

Chapter 11

The Backward Son: A Varied Apprenticeship

It would have been a great surprise to Lord Randolph to learn that his son would qualify for the Westminster Abbey burial he himself missed. Lord Randolph had been the kind of bright boy not unusual at school; his elder son was backward in an unusual way, not through lack of intelligence, but through sheer self-will and because his interest was not intelligently engaged or aroused. Where it was, he did well enough and even won a prize or two; but the ordinary classical grind of Victorian times both at his private and his public school – dominantly concerned with Latin and Greek, excruciatingly linguistic and grammatical – put him off. Even at this early stage he was not going to have it, and he did badly. It is obvious that Lord Randolph was disappointed in his offspring.

We may surmise that he was always rather a handful. Lady Randolph reports to her mother when he was five that he was a good boy and getting on with his lessons, 'but he is a most difficult child to manage'. After what we know of his father, and of his American grandfather, we need not wonder. The one person who could manage him, and that by unstinted love, was his nurse Mrs Everest – suitably named, we may suppose, for her task. His mother 'shone for me like the Evening Star. I loved her dearly – but at a distance. My nurse was my confidante. Mrs Everest it was who looked after me and tended all my wants. It was to her I poured out my many troubles, both now and in my schooldays.'[1] Not even she could always command obedience; once when he could not get his own way he threatened, as the wickedest thing he could think of – for Mrs Everest enjoyed a very Low Church form of piety – that he would go and 'worship idols'.

1. Churchill, *My Early Life*, 19.

The usual feminine jealousies intervened to complicate matters. His grandmother, the old Duchess, wanted him at Blenheim:

> I must say I am very disappointed at Winston's not being allowed to come here for a few days. I had made every arrangement to take great care of him knowing he is susceptible to colds, and I do not think there could have been as much danger as there is in going to Pantomimes in London. Besides I feel it's all an excuse of that horrid old Everest to prevent my having him and his being happy with his cousins without her. . . . I hardly ever see him, and must say I am very much vexed. He is not fit to go to Harrow if he is not fit for a visit here. The house is quite warm.[2]

Blenheim Palace in December, before the days of central heating! – it is evident that her ideas of warmth were of a Spartan Victorianism. It is also evident that Everest had defeated the Duchess – and perhaps this was one reason for her not liking the boy who remained right up to twenty-three, curious to think, heir presumptive to the dukedom and to Blenheim.

Affection for his nurse survived the adolescent cynicism of the atmosphere of a public school, or rather the young Winston was impervious to it. His cousin relates as a marked example of moral courage that when his old nurse came down to see him at Harrow in her poke-bonnet, he walked her all round the school and in public kissed her good-bye. He was a subaltern at Aldershot when she fell dangerously ill; he at once rushed up to London to be with her at the last: 'she had been my dearest and most intimate friend during the whole of the twenty years I had lived'.[3] He cites her life as having given him an impulse towards building the fabric of social insurance, sickness and old-age pensions he took part in under the Liberal government of 1906. On a more personal note we see early displayed the loyalty of his nature, the fidelity and good-heartedness so strong in his make-up: I think we may say, for a politician, so exceptionally strong.

School tore him away from Mrs Everest, and he did not like it. At home there had been the mechanical toys of the

2. A. Leslie, *The Fabulous Jeromes*, 270.
3. Churchill, op. cit., 87.

nursery, a magic lantern, a real steam-engine, and almost a thousand lead soldiers. (One sees those that are left still at Chartwell.) His cousin, Clare Sheridan – Clara Jerome's daughter – was much impressed.

> He filled me with awe. His playroom contained from one end to the other a plank table on trestles, upon which were thousands [*sic.*] of lead soldiers arranged for battle. He organized wars. The lead battalions were manoeuvred into action, peas and pebbles committed great casualties, forts were stormed, cavalry charged, bridges were destroyed – real water tanks engulfed the advancing foe.[4]

With all young animals the play-instinct foreshadows the future.

At his first private school he made the acquaintance of Latin, and a very funny account of the experience he gives. Declining *mensa* was not recommended in any way to his reason, so he declined to regard the subject with any respect and was frequently flogged. He makes a useful pedagogical comment: 'perhaps if I had been introduced to the ancients through their history and customs, instead of through their grammar and syntax, I might have had a better record'.[5] Taken away from this horrid school, which he hated and where he was made ill, he was sent to a less pretentious place where he was happy and learned things that interested him: history and poetry and French, above all, riding and swimming. And there were some delightful volumes of cartoons from *Punch*, which early aroused an interest in politics and recent history – even if their suggestions as to remoter history were apt to lead one a little astray. Mr Gladstone, for example, often appeared looking like Julius Caesar; it was long before the young Winston learned that Julius Caesar was not all what a virtuous Victorian like Mr Gladstone should be. From *Punch* too he gained his first interest in the American Civil War – not at all a bad source. Then there were the cartoons of his famous father, depicted always as a very little man though he was really of 'quite a passable stature'.

From here he went on to Harrow where he met the classics in even more august array. His first term was marked by a

4. Clare Sheridan, *Naked Truth*, 4. 5. Churchill, op. cit., 27.

collision with a sixth-former, a short, squat boy whom he took to be a junior and, coming up behind him, pushed into the swimming-pool. The boy turned out to be immensely strong and swift, head of his house, champion at gym and what not. An explanation with apology was necessitated: 'I mistook you for a Fourth Form boy. You are so small.' A sense of the inadequacy of this made him recover himself with, 'My father, who is a great man, is also small'. This was better received and formed the foundation of a life-long friendship with Leo Amery, colleagues as war-correspondents, in the House of Commons and in various Cabinets. It is nice to have all been at the same school together.

Latin, however, remained a stumbling block: either he could not, or more probably would not, learn it. So he learned English instead from an admirable master who taught it properly – as it was not taught in the public schools – to whom he confesses his indebtedness as a writer subsequently. Who can doubt that this was a better idea?

When in after years my school-fellows who had won prizes and distinction for writing such beautiful Latin poetry and pithy Greek epigrams had to come down again to common English, to earn their living or make their way, I did not feel myself at any disadvantage. Naturally I am biassed in favour of boys learning English. I would make them all learn English: and then I would let the clever ones learn Latin as an honour, and Greek as a treat.[6]

However, this kept him in the lower school; he never got into the upper: he stagnated in the bottom form until he went with the other dunces into the Army class. He was an odd case, for at the same time he won a prize for reciting twelve hundred lines of Macaulay's *Lays* without a mistake, could quote whole scenes from Shakespeare and had no hesitation in correcting the masters if they misquoted. He was building up a prodigious memory, subconsciously strengthening his tough mental aptitudes by feeding on what he liked and refusing what he did not like. He was evidently a fair terror. Mr Amery remembered him as a rather inky small boy, grubby and obstinate. Another

6. Churchill, op. cit., 31.

contemporary tells us that 'he consistently broke almost every rule made by masters or boys, was quite incorrigible, and had an unlimited vocabulary of "back-chat", which he produced with dauntless courage on every occasion of remonstrance'.[7] Not interested in football or cricket either, and making no pretence of it, he was pretty clearly not a popular figure.

'I was on the whole considerably discouraged by my school days,' he concludes. 'I am all for the Public Schools but I do not want to go there again.' He adds a comment not without malice, and another not without pathos.

> Most of the boys were very happy, and many found in its class-rooms and upon playing fields the greatest distinction they have ever known in life. . . . I would far rather have been apprenticed as a bricklayer's mate, or run errands as a messenger boy, or helped my father to dress the front windows of a grocer's shop. It would have been real; it would have been natural; it would have taught me more; and I should have done it much better. Also I should have got to know my father, which would have been a joy to me.[8]

In later years he has made it up with Harrow. In the autumn of 1940, after all the strain and glory of the events of that year, after the Battle of Britain had saved the country, he went back there as Prime Minister. Perhaps he felt some need for renewed contact with his youth, some unconscious sense of putting it right with his remote past: there could not have been a better moment for rehabilitation. Once more he sat there in the Speech Room with the other boys, singing the famous Harrow songs, tears in his eyes. Called on to speak – after half a century – he said, 'I like the song "Boy", although when I was at the school I did not advance to that position of authority which entitles one to make that call'.[9] He had only been a fag to other boys – perhaps a useful apprenticeship for doing the nation's chores. Reconciliation effected, he took pleasure and found solace in going back every year to his old school amid all the strain and anxieties of the war and post-war years. On one visit, in Novem-

7. *Churchill by his Contemporaries*, ed. Charles Eade, 19.
8. Churchill, *My Early Life*, 52–3.
9. *Sir Winston Churchill, a Self-Portrait*, ed. Colin R. Coote, 37.

ber 1942, just after the landings in North Africa, he paid tribute to what the Harrow songs had meant for him:

> You have the songs of Bowen and Howson (whom I remember well as house-masters here) with the music of John Farmer and Eaton Fanning. They are wonderful; marvellous; more than could be put into brick and mortar, or treasured in any trophies of silver or gold. They grow with the years. I treasure them and sing them with joy.

It is clear that he was a disappointment to his father, who decided that, since he was not clever enough to go to the Bar, the Army had better be his lot. But this also involved examinations: it took him three tries, and a special crammer's, to get him into Sandhurst. The monster in the path here was not Latin but mathematics – another, and more sympathetic, allergy. After his second attempt, when on holiday, he had a dreadful accident which might well have ended any further attempts at anything. He was playing a game with his cousins in a chine at Bournemouth when, to avoid capture, he jumped off a bridge hoping to catch the branches of a fir-tree and fell thirty feet to hard ground. He was very badly injured, with a ruptured kidney among other things, was for days unconscious and in bed for more than three months. 'It is to the surgeon's art and to my own pronounced will-to-live that the reader is indebted for this story [*My Early Life*]. But for a year I looked at life round a corner.'[10] I have heard it said, and it is probable enough, that it was this long illness that matured and ripened his faculties, gave him time to ponder, something to think about.

When he recovered he passed into Sandhurst, qualifying for a cavalry cadetship, which was easier than an infantry one, since life in the cavalry was so much more expensive. Lord Randolph, who was now heavily in debt, did not hold with this: 'he thought it very discreditable that I had not qualified for the infantry'. A certain embarrassment appears in the attitude of Lord Randolph towards his son. A quick and well-trained mind like his must have been baffled coming up against such an odd case: one sympathizes with his vexation at finding, after all the money spent on the boy's education, that he did not know what the

10. Churchill, *My Early Life*, 44.

Grand Remonstrance was. The boy, on the other hand, was genuinely puzzled why his father thought it so important. The time was coming when he would want to know all about it himself, and then he would appreciate its importance. What is so striking is the sudden, and belated, awakening.

This did not take place, alas, till the father was dead. On the son's side there had always been devotion and a partisan pride. He was aware of the tragedy of his father's life and of the bitterness and resentment that were gnawing at him. 'Although in the past little had been said in my hearing, one could not grow up in my father's house, and still less among his mother and sisters, without understanding that there had been a great political disaster.'[11] He longed to take up the cudgels on his behalf, most of all that his father would admit him to his confidence.

> But if ever I began to show the slightest idea of comradeship, he was immediately offended; and when once I suggested that I might help his private secretary to write some of his letters, he froze me into stone.... Had he lived another four or five years, he could not have done without me. But there were no four or five years!

He had just passed out of Sandhurst and was in his twenty-first year when his father died. 'All my dreams of comradeship with him, of entering Parliament at his side, and in his support, were ended. There remained for me only to pursue his aims and vindicate his memory.'

They were all living under the old Duchess's roof in Grosvenor Square at the time to save expense. On his South African tour Lord Randolph had made a very fortunate investment in the Rand. If he had lived he would have been a rich man from it; now, when sold, it was just enough to pay his debts – some £70,000. Jennie was provided for by her marriage settlement; but as for the young cavalry officer, 'I was now in the main the master of my fortunes'; in other words, he had his way to make for himself – as much as any working-class or middle-class lad moving out into the world, except that he had the advantage of all these connections, family and political, with Blenheim always

11. Churchill, *My Early Life*, 45, 60.

in the background. Then, too, there was his mother – worth a whole Army corps in herself:

> she soon became an ardent ally, furthering my plans and guarding my interests with all her influence and boundless energy. She was still at forty young, beautiful and fascinating. We worked together on even terms, more like brother and sister than mother and son. At least so it seemed to me. And so it continued to the end.[12]

In those days, the summer training season over, all good cavalry officers settled down to five months' hunting in the autumn and winter. This young subaltern could not afford that – besides, he had spent all his money on polo ponies. So he decided to go off and attend a war in progress. 'Rarity in a desirable commodity is usually the cause of enhanced value; and there has never been a time when war service was held in so much esteem by the military authorities or more ardently sought by officers of every rank.'[13] Spain was having trouble in Cuba, last of her American possessions. It was a guerrilla war on a considerable scale, with Spain having to keep a quarter of a million men at the end of the long Atlantic line; a war on the pattern that soon became familiar in South Africa, Malaya, Indo-China, Cyprus. And it ended in the intervention of the United States upon her first grand incursion into benevolent imperialism. Theodore Roosevelt, Colonel of the Rough Riders – perhaps the closest in temperament to Churchill of all modern figures – was in at the end; Lieutenant Churchill, his junior by sixteen years, was in at the beginning.

It was his father's old partner in the Fourth Party, Sir Henry Wolff, ambassador at Madrid, who got all the necessary passes and documents from the Spanish authorities. Arrived in Cuba young Churchill joined a mobile column under General Valdez at Sancti Spiritus, a place very unhealthy with yellow fever and smallpox. Here he got the experience he had travelled thousands of miles for, on money he could ill afford, of being under fire. The fire does not seem to have been much, but fire it was on several occasions as the column wound its way along like a

12. ibid., 76. 13. ibid., 88.

snake in the humid jungle. Once he received some shelter from the neighbouring hammock where hung a Spanish officer of substantial physique, 'indeed one might almost have called him fat. I have never been prejudiced against fat men.' The Lieutenant slept all the sounder. But he might easily have perished of yellow fever, or enteric, or smallpox, or typhoid. Instead, when the column got back to the coast Lieutenant Churchill, perfectly sound and better informed, sailed for home: his well-spent leave was up.

When he first left school for Sandhurst he had been kept for several months in the Awkward Squad, containing those who needed bringing up to scratch. When he passed out, it was with honours, and he was eighth in a batch of a hundred and fifty: his interest had been engaged and from this moment one sees him making firm strides. There was plenty of leeway to make up, and there were still apt to be the *contretemps* that are such a worry when one is young. Invited down to Deepdene by Lilian Duchess to meet the Prince of Wales, the subaltern was late; he had hoped to slip in unnoticed, but without him the party was thirteen. Edward couldn't bear unpunctuality; on the other hand, he wouldn't dream of sitting down thirteen at table; 'Don't they teach you to be punctual in your regiment, Winston?' he said severely. But it was here that he met Sir Bindon Blood, a foremost Indian Frontier commander, to whom he owed his next experience of action.

His regiment, the 4th Hussars, was posted to Bangalore in Southern India: excellent climate, 3,000 feet up, a bungalow wreathed in roses and purple bougainvillaea to share with one's friends, a butler, a boy to attend to one's wants, a syce to the ponies' – what more delightful for young men who were polo-addicts, for whom polo was the serious business of life? But there was one of them who found the long afternoon hours invaluable and it was then that he took his education in hand. He got his mother to send him packages of books. Someone had told him that his father admired Gibbon, had known whole pages by heart; so – 'all through the long glistening middle hours of the Indian day, from when we quitted stables till the evening shadows proclaimed the hour of Polo, I devoured Gibbon.

I rode triumphantly through it from end to end and enjoyed it all.'[14] Next followed Macaulay, with whom he was more closely engaged in later years – and emerged victor from the struggle. He had long loved the *Lays*, but had never read a page of the *History*. Now he galloped through Macaulay, *Essays* and all. It is not surprising that, when he came to write, the joint influences are Gibbon and Macaulay – though at the same time, from the very first, a personal voice is heard, idiosyncratic, already recognizable.

Four or five hours a day he read: Plato and Aristotle, Malthus and Darwin, Lecky and Winwood Reade. It was very remarkable: this was his university, out there in a cavalry regiment in a British cantonment, in the intervals of polo. And he began for the first time to envy the young men who had had no difficulties with Latin and who were at the university where there were scholars to tell them what to read and what was what about it. There was the problem of Ethics, for instance: what did it mean? No one to tell him on the parade-ground at Bangalore. He began to read books that challenged the religious views received – or customs observed – at Harrow. He came to a dominantly secular view. 'I adopted a system of believing whatever I wanted to believe, while at the same time leaving reason to pursue whatever paths she was capable of treading.'[15]

What one learns for oneself in this rough, tough fashion one is liable to hold on to more tenaciously. Another autodidact, picking up ideas for himself in the slums of Vienna not long after, became possessed of some very tenacious ideas. But the trouble with Hitler's demonic genius was that his *Weltanschauung* was at bottom uncritical: parts of it were utterly crazy, in the German manner, and he did not know whether it made sense intellectually or no. There is everything to be said for a strong tradition of tested common sense in a society and its schooling; and Churchill, though he was unaware of it at the time, imbibed that unconsciously at Harrow. Many years later when he went back, in the throes of the mortal struggle with Hitler, December 1940, he said – 'Hitler, in one of his recent discourses, declared

14. Churchill, *My Early Life*, 125.
15. ibid., 131.

that the fight is between those who have been through the Adolf Hitler schools and those who have been at Eton. Hitler has forgotten Harrow.'

While has was at home on leave in the hot weather of 1897 a chance of action suddenly appeared on his horizon. The Pathans of the North-West Frontier broke out in revolt against the retention of an outpost at Chitral in their country and the construction of the military road leading to it: like the Britons in Roman Britain they knew too well what it meant: *Pax Britannica.* Lieutenant Churchill was at Goodwood, but he at once telegraphed Sir Bindon Blood, who had been placed in command of the Field Force to suppress the irruption, reminding him of his promise. Duchess Lilian's husband, of the powerful Beresford clan, was also brought into play. At Bombay Sir Bindon left a message that, since he had no vacancies, Churchill might come up as a war-correspondent. While he was getting leave of absence from his regiment, to report the war for the *Pioneer* newspaper, his mother arranged for these letters to be published in England by the *Daily Telegraph* at £5 a column, paying all his own expenses. ('I have improved upon this figure in later life.')

Hence a thrilling experience, of which he made the most, and his first book: '*The Story of the Malakand Field Force, An Episode of Frontier War*. By Winston L. Spencer Churchill, Lieutenant, the 4th Queen's Own Hussars.' The title-page has a motto drawn from Lord Salisbury: 'They [Frontier Wars] are but the surf that marks the edge and the advance of the wave of civilization.' The book is dedicated to Sir Bindon Blood, to whom the author was indebted 'for the most valuable, and fascinating, experience of his life' – with charming ingenuousness, for the author was only twenty-three and would have some more valuable experiences before he had finished. (A certain ingenuousness has always been a part of that personality made in a simple mould, direct and sincere.)

A lot of men could have played their parts in such an expedition, gone through the dangers and had the adventures he had – thousands did on the North-West Frontier; but only a very promising one could have written this book at twenty-three.

He sees the Imperial theme – the influence of Gibbon is there:

looking at the road running broad and white across the valley; at the soldiers moving along it; at the political officers extending their influence in all directions; at the bridge and fort of Chakdara; and at the growing cantonment on the Malakand Pass, it needs no education to appreciate its significance. Nor can any sophistry obscure it.[16]

But to this he adds a romantic feeling, to which he can already give unforced expression. At Mardan, the entrance to the pass up which the Force went to action,

the passer-by should pause to see the guides' cemetery, perhaps the only regimental cemetery in the world. To this last resting-place under the palm-trees, close to the fields where they have played and the barracks in which they lived, have been borne the bodies of successive generations of these wardens of the marches, killed in action across the frontier line. It is a green and pleasant spot. Nor is there any place in the world where a soldier might lie in braver company.[17]

The scene is very well set and the descriptive passages throughout are vivid and well written: one sees the places. Even more striking is the way in which, with a shock of recognition, one meets the sage of half a century later – such is the force of personality, the continuity of style. Of a Hindu saint by the banks of the Indus: 'the longer his riparian reflections were continued, the greater his sanctity became'.[18] 'The religion of blood and war is face to face with that of peace. Luckily the religion of peace is usually better armed.' And naturally the personal accent, with such an individual, is stamped on every page: it could not be otherwise. Here he sees himself at both ends of the news:

how different are the scenes. The club on an autumn evening – its members grouped anxiously around, discussing, wondering, asserting; the noise of the traffic outside; the cigarette smoke and electric lights within. And, only an hour away along the wire, the field, with the bright sunlight shining on the swirling muddy waters; the black forbidding

16. Churchill, *The Story of the Malakand Field Force* (ed. 1898), 34–5.
17. ibid., 16. 18. ibid., 22, 41, 141.

rocks; the white tents of the brigade a mile up the valley; the long streak of vivid green rice crop by the river; and in the foreground the brown-clad armed men. I can never doubt which is the right end to be at. It is better to be making the news than taking it; to be an actor rather than a critic.

The letters to the *Daily Telegraph* had been well received in England, and now the book was an immediate success. The Prince of Wales, continuing his interest in Randolph's progeny, wrote him a letter of warm congratulation, adding 'you have plenty of time before you, and should certainly stick to the Army before adding M.P. to your name'.[19] More important, he was summoned for an interview with Lord Salisbury, who had read his book with much interest. There was 'the Great Man, Master of the British world, the unchallenged leader of the Conservative Party, a third time Prime Minister and Foreign Secretary at the height of his long career' in that spacious room in the Foreign Office 'in which I was afterwards for many years from time to time to see much grave business done in Peace and War'.

The young officer appreciated the tremendous air about the old statesman and the grave courtesy with which he met him, conducted him to a small sofa in the vast room and said that the book had enabled him to form a truer picture of the fighting in the Frontier valleys than from any of the documents which he had had to read. In dismissing Randolph's son he said, 'I hope you will allow me to say how much you remind me of your father, with whom such important days of my political life were lived. If there is anything at any time that I can do which would be of assistance to you, pray do not fail to let me know.' There very shortly was to come such an opportunity.

On his return to Bangalore he entertained himself in the long hot afternoons writing a Ruritanian romance, *Savrola*, which appeared in *Macmillan's Magazine* in 1897. In spite of his consistently urging his friends to abstain from reading it, it is well worth reading: not so much for the story, though that holds the attention, as for the light it throws upon the author and forward

19. Churchill, *My Early Life*, 171, 178–9.

upon coming events. In the way Nature has of imitating Art, with the climax of bombardment of an insurgent capital by the Fleet, it might be about recent happenings in Buenos Aires. The novel has a love-interest: the revolutionary leader Savrola is in love with the wife of the President who is defeated. But who but Churchill would describe the situation with the words – 'he was a young man, and Jupiter was not the only planet he admired'? His fellow-officers, to whom the book was dedicated, 'made various suggestions for stimulating the love interest which I was not able to accept'.[20]

We recognize the hero sixty years back: 'his highly wrought temperament exaggerated every mood and passion; he always lived in the superlative. . . . Under any circumstances, in any situation, he knew himself a factor to be reckoned with.'[21] The dreams of the youth reveal the man: here are the principles governing his life announced early. 'Would you rise in the world? You must work while others amuse themselves. Are you desirous of a reputation for courage? You must risk your life. Would you be strong morally or physically? You must resist temptations.' The naïveté, the egoism are patent and harmless; the fighting value of the convictions has received triumphant justification.

In 1898 Kitchener, the British Sirdar in command of the Egyptian army, judged that the moment was ripe for the re-conquest of the Sudan from the tyranny of the Dervish Empire. This was necessitated by the position of indirect rule, and certainly responsibility, we had taken on in Egypt as the result of Mr Gladstone's bombardment of Alexandria. Since that detonating event the squalid and corrupt rule of the Khedives in Egypt had gradually given way to the fostering care of Lord Cromer, with the usual results. A hitherto bankrupt state now had surpluses to spend on internal improvements; the delights of party faction-fights had to give way to irrigation, agriculture, growing cotton. This, of course, was Imperialism; but ordinary folk prospered better under it, as even Wilfrid Scawen Blunt, the romantic anti-Imperialist and friend of the Egyptian Nationalists, had to admit. With the revival of the country and the

20. ibid., 169. 21. Churchill, *Savrola* (ed. 1956), 62, 63, 124.

progress it was making, there was the obligation to recover the Egyptian position in the Sudan. Egyptian rule there had been rapacious and incompetent; but the Dervish Empire was worse, a fanatic military barbarism extending its sway dangerously. There were the French to forestall, and Gordon to avenge. (It was Lord Randolph who had first raised the question of General Gordon's safety in those months in 1885 when Gladstone would take no action.)

After the tragedy and humiliation of Khartoum 'the British people averted their eyes in shame and vexation from the valley of the Nile'. Now the position was to be rectified. Kitchener had already got as far as the confluence of the Nile and the Atbara, where his mixed army of British and Egyptians had destroyed the Khalifa's lieutenant in a fierce battle. There remained the difficult advance up the Nile – cataracts, rapids, desert, disease – to Omdurman and the final reckoning with the whole strength of the Dervish Empire. Lieutenant Churchill was 'deeply anxious to share in this'.

He found himself up against unexpected resistance. Hitherto in the Army he had had pretty much his own way. Now he met a prevalent attitude that what he needed was a long period of discipline and routine; harsh words like 'self-advertiser' began to be used about him – from which he was hardly ever to be free till late in life. Other junior officers of his rank were accepted, while he was refused. When his own time came he never rejected such requests for service: after all, 'they are only asking to stop a bullet'. Kitchener himself regarded the young applicant with disapproval and vetoed his appointment when recommended by the War Office. The fact was that he had been heard of; it was still more objectionable that he was successful, perhaps worst of all, that he made no attempt to conceal his desire to shine. Other human beings find this outrageous; it is usually found more tolerable to camouflage conspicuous talents; less confident persons adopt various methods of concealment. Henceforth he would always find, right up to 1940, this difficulty in his way in his relations with other people: too straight, too ingenuous, and taking no trouble to disguise his self-confidence or anything else. It is like the jealousy his ancestor

John Churchill had to contend with all his life; though a subtler man, artful and 'brimful of policy', the one thing he did not trouble to disguise was the superiority of his talents.

Lieutenant Churchill came home from India to argue his case. He brought Lord Salisbury's promise into play: not even the Prime Minister could prevail upon Kitchener. Only by chance did the subaltern learn that the Adjutant-General at home much resented Kitchener's interference with the posting of officers, and a direct appeal to him resulted in Churchill's being seconded to the 21st Lancers. A little late, he was nevertheless in time for the final phase of the campaign, in time for Omdurman. He was to go at his own expense, and if he got himself killed or wounded he was to be no charge to the British Army. Such terms justified his doubling the role of cavalry officer and war-correspondent again: this time he was to write a series of letters, at an improved fee, for the *Morning Post* and to this circumstance we owe his second war-book, *The River War*.

It is an altogether more mature and substantial book than the first, as the Sudan Campaign was an altogether more important affair than what was, after all, only 'an episode of Frontier War'. In fact it is a fine book, giving one a full account of the Mahdi's movement, of the Dervish Empire and its victories, its final struggle with the Anglo-Egyptian army, its collapse, the Fashoda incident and the pacification of the Sudan. Its evocation of the scene is masterly, the extraordinary country all sand and rock and scrub for hundreds of miles, only alive along the confines of the majestic river upon which all depends. There are many excellent descriptions, moments to remember, as when the sun goes down in the desert and 'the smell of grass was noticed by the alert senses of many, and will for ever refresh in their minds the strong impression of the night. The breeze which had sprung up at sundown gradually freshened and raised clouds of fine sand, which deepened the darkness with a whiter mist.'[22]

The personal element that gives the book character, colour and warmth is firmer, though not less in evidence than before. Good nature and magnanimity shine forth in the sympathetic

22. Churchill, *The River War* (ed. 1951), 232.

account he gives of the Mahdi: his sympathies are wholly with him and his followers against the miserable Egyptians, whose only aim had been to exploit the Sudanese. As for the expeditions they sent to recover their stranglehold: 'they came, they saw, they ran away'. It is with no reluctance that he relates that, when at Omdurman the 7th Egyptians began to waver and tried to bolt, they were turned round to face the right way by two companies of British behind them with fixed bayonets. Of many observations by this young man several remind us of the wisdom of the older. 'Few facts are so encouraging to the student of human development as the desire, which most men and all communities manifest at all times, to associate with their actions at least the appearance of moral right.'[23] 'All politics are a series of compromises and bargains, and while the historian may easily mark what would have been the best possible moment for any great undertaking, a good moment must content the administrator.' 'The human element – in defiance of experience and probability – may produce a wholly irrational result, and a starving, outmanoeuvred army win food, safety and honour by their bravery.' There is a reflection that points straight to far graver events in 1940, an early indication of the spirit, not without an element of calculation, that endured through such experiences as Dunkirk. Nor is the end of the story without a moral: 'it is pleasing to remember that a great crisis found England united. The determination of the Government was approved by the loyalty of the Opposition, supported by the calm resolve of the people.'

In action Lieutenant Churchill had two strokes of luck. On the day before Omdurman he was sent to report to Kitchener the advance of the Dervish army, which was expected to attack then and there. It was a dramatic confrontation, Kitchener riding alone in front of his staff, his two standard-bearers immediately behind him, and the irrepressible subaltern who was there contrary to his wishes. Nothing was said outside the matter in hand – but what an introduction for these two who were to be brought together, and clash, again in the first German war! Next day took place the battle he would not have missed for

23. Churchill, *The River War* (ed. 1951), 18, 101, 163, 318.

anything. 'Nothing like the battle of Omdurman will ever be seen again. It was the last link in the long chain of those spectacular conflicts whose vivid and majestic splendour has done so much to invest war with glamour. Everything was visible to the naked eye':[24] the Nile with its flotilla of gunboats (Lieutenant Churchill made the acquaintance of Lieutenant Beatty serving in one, a bottle of champagne thrown down to the thirsty shore); the *zeriba* behind which the small Anglo-Egyptian army was drawn up, back to the river; between them and the Mahdi's sacred city, the brown dome of his tomb rising above it, the hordes of the faithful, over fifty thousand of them in their battle-formations. In the battle he had the luck to be in the celebrated charge of the 21st Lancers: he was luckier still to get out of it alive, for there were two or three thousand Dervishes in the water-course the squadrons had to cross, and they had heavy casualties.

Lieutenant Churchill lived to tell the tale to much effect: letters, articles, books, appearances on lecture-platforms all in good time. On the proceeds he determined to leave the Army, live inexpensively with his mother at home and earn a better living with his pen than her Majesty could afford him. (From that day to this he has earned his own living by pen and tongue; though as a reward for virtue there descended upon him after the War of 1914–18 an ancient but considerable legacy under the will of his great-grandmother, the Duchess's mother.) First, however, he had to return to Bangalore to wind up his affairs and play in the team that won the Polo Tournament that year. On his way back to England he was able to submit the early chapters of *The River War*, with their account of Egyptian and Sudanese affairs, to the censure of Lord Cromer. He took the task seriously: 'one of the very few things which still interest me in life is to see young men get on'.

Churchill had been shocked by what he considered the brutal desecration of the Mahdi's tomb, knocking the knob off with a howitzer, and still more by Kitchener's carrying the prophet's head off as a trophy in a kerosene-can. No respecter of persons himself, he seems always – with no exaggerated rationalism of

24. Churchill, *My Early Life*, 186.

outlook – to have had a respect for their superstitions, their beliefs. This generosity of outlook much commended itself to Liberals as a weapon with which to beat Kitchener for winning Omdurman. *The River War* when it came out was then another score against this young man in the eyes of Kitchener – and a recommendation of him to the Liberals.

On his return to England he would have liked to go up to Oxford to go on with the formal education he had come, belatedly, to appreciate. That for a young man of his years and experience, with the books he had written, was something quite exceptional in those days, and there was no way to fit him in. He went so far as to make inquiries about how to get there: 'I was, I expect, at this time capable of deriving both profit and enjoyment from Oxford life and thought.'[25] Alas, the twin spectres of Latin and Greek guarded the gate and he could not bear the idea of going back to Greek irregular verbs after having commanded British regular troops. He could not see why he could not have gone and paid his fees (well earned by himself), listen to the lectures, argue with the professors and read the books. I think he might well have been disappointed, but he would certainly have enjoyed himself.

Nothing would have prevented him from enjoying himself: such zest, healthy and inexhaustible, is more like that of Leonard Jerome than it is of Lord Randolph, in whom there was a too highly-strung strain. His son enjoyed everything: soldiering, horses, polo, campaigning, good food and wine, writing. What fun it was writing a book! One lived with it; it went everywhere along with one. It was like building a house or planning a battle or painting a picture – all of which would come in time. As for the years, 'from the beginning of 1895 down to the present time of writing I have never had time to turn round. I could count almost on my fingers the days when I have had nothing to do. An endless moving picture in which one was an actor.' The most exciting experience of all, to date, was just ahead of him.

Before *The River War* could well get going the Boer War had got going instead: 'we all had other things to think about'.

25. Churchill, *My Early Life*, 216.

The events of the 1950s have thrown an illuminating searchlight into the genesis of the war in South Africa. We no longer have to accept the comfortable Liberal illusions as to British responsibility for it. It is true that Cecil Rhodes was disastrously impatient and that Dr Jameson made a shocking mistake, but what made the war certain was something more profound: the determination of the extreme Dutch Nationalists to impose their nationalism on South Africa.[26] As to that we are better informed today. Bringing it to a point was the readiness of the aged, but very agile, President Kruger of the Transvaal for a war of independence to achieve a United States of South Africa. Louis Botha, best and wisest of the Dutch, was opposed to the war; but mistakes on the British side – in particular, the understandable impatience of Milner, confronted with a monumental intransigence – played into the hands of the Transvaal extremists.

When the war broke out, the wonder is that the Boers – like Hitler in 1940 – did not win it at the first rush, for they had all the advantages.[27] Even with the first British reinforcements, the Boers were two to one in the field; their armies of mobile marksmen – and they were superb horsemen – were ideal for the veldt, their own terrain of which they took fullest advantage. Within their hill and mountain frontiers the Boer republics had the advantage of interior communications, of intelligence service, the sympathy of the countryside and hence facilities for surprise. Their Krupps guns, with Germans as usual to lend a hand, were superior to the types of British artillery then in use. Why, then, did the Boers not win? Because of a strategic misconception of the war at the beginning. The British were unprepared, fighting at the end of several thousand miles of supply-line (as in the 1770s) and made every conceivable mistake of generalship in the field. But their fundamental

26. cf. the following from an Orange Free Stater: 'the only thing we are afraid of now is that Chamberlain, with his admitted fitfulness of temper, will cheat us out of the war and consequently the opportunity of annexing the Cape Colony and Natal and forming the Republican United States of South Africa'. – q. L. S. Amery, *My Political Life*, I. 105.

27. cf. R. C. K. Ensor, *England, 1870–1914*, 252.

strategy was sound and, in the end, superior resources were bound to tell.

There was not much appreciation of all this at the outset of the war; mistakes were made, and there was much mutual ignorance, on both sides. Though Lord Salisbury's strong Cabinet had every desire to avoid war, there was an unpleasant atmosphere of swagger and bellicosity among the mob at the end of the 1890s. Though this is not to depreciate him, for he was a man of many-sided genius, it was the age of Kipling, the apogee of his fame; on one side he was the laureate of these impulses, his spirit spoke to theirs, expressed the spirit of the time – very rarely indeed, and hardly ever with a poet, has there been a writer more immediately in touch with the moods of a people, who so made himself their voice.

> Truly ye come of The Blood; slower to bless than to ban,
> Little used to lie down at the bidding of any man.

Not for nothing did he come from Nonconformist stock:

> Fair is our lot – O goodly is our heritage!
> (Humble ye, my people, and be fearful in your mind!)
>   For the Lord our God Most High
>   He hath made the deep as dry,
> He hath smote for us a pathway to the ends of all the Earth!

The war meant a grand opportunity for the most promising of British war-correspondents, and the *Morning Post* came forward with a higher offer than had yet been made in British journalism: £250 a month, plus all expenses, complete freedom of movement and expression.[28] What larks, indeed! Churchill

28. His vivid letters are reprinted in two volumes, *London to Ladysmith via Pretoria* and *Ian Hamilton's March*, 1900. These give one a more immediate sense of the war from our side than any other books I know, along with some illuminating shafts as to its origins. In the course of one of many discussions a Boer said to him, 'Is it right that a dirty Kaffir should walk on the pavement – without a pass too? That's what they do in your British Colonies. Brother! Equal! Ugh! Free! Not a bit. We know how to treat Kaffirs.' We see that theirs was the uncompromising, unyielding mentality

travelled out in the same ship as the Commander-in-Chief, Sir Redvers Buller, of whom the war-correspondent was to form an unfavourable opinion. For indeed Sir Redvers Buller was of a slow, monumental stupidity. Because he was a Liberal, because he was a West Countryman, and perhaps because he was so stupid and people could understand him, there was still a Buller cult in the West Country in my childhood: people thought that he was unfairly treated. It would have saved the lives of thousands and shortened the war if he had been thrown out earlier. Kipling spoke for the ordinary soldier when he wrote:

> The General 'ad 'produced a great effect',
>   The General 'ad the country cleared – almost;
> The General 'ad 'no reason to expect',
>   And the Boers 'ad us bloomin' well on toast!
> For we might 'ave crossed the drift before the twilight,
>   Instead o' sittin' down an' takin' root;
> But we was not allowed, so the Boojers scooped the crowd,
>   To the last survivin' bandolier an' boot.

Arrived at the frontier outpost of Estcourt in Natal, Churchill was able to set up his tent with Leo Amery, who had turned up as war-correspondent of *The Times*. At once there followed the adventure of the armoured train. A general had the idea of sending this helpless monster, with several hundred troops, into enemy country to reconnoitre – helpless, for remove a few feet

---

of the Southern States in the American Civil War. Churchill comments, 'probing at random I had touched a very sensitive nerve. We had got down from underneath the political and reached the social. What is the true and original root of Dutch aversion to British rule? . . . It is the abiding fear and hatred of the movement that seeks to place the native on a level with the white man. British government is associated in the Boer farmer's mind with violent social revolution. Black is to be proclaimed the same as white. The servant is to be raised against the master; the Kaffir is to be declared the brother of the European, to be constituted his legal equal, to be armed with political rights. The dominant race is to be deprived of their superiority; nor is a tigress robbed of her cubs more furious than is the Boer at this prospect.' – *London to Ladysmith*, 133–4.

of railway line and it would be stranded, like a whale on the coast of Patagonia. Something of this sort happened: two or three trucks left the line, the train came to a standstill while they were all under Boer fire. Churchill, ever to the fore, got out to investigate, formed a plan to clear the line, made his way up to the engine; there he left his pistol behind him. On his way back, scrambling along the cutting he found himself being headed off by a couple of Boer marksmen. He made a dash for cover, but in no time found himself covered by a Boer rifle. There was nothing for it but surrender: thus early in the war he was a prisoner. It did not mitigate matters at the time that his captor was Louis Botha: this was their first introduction. Some years later, when Botha was attending a banquet for Dominion Prime Ministers in Westminster Hall and his former prisoner was now Colonial Under-Secretary, the Boer leader paused to say to Lady Randolph, 'He and I have been out in all weathers'. In the years before 1914 whenever Botha came to London he always sought Churchill out, faithfully warned him what to expect of the Germans, enjoined on him to be prepared. When the war came his services to this country and the Commonwealth were immeasurable.

Nothing of all this could be glimpsed in that railway-cutting or in the prison-camp at Pretoria to which Churchill was removed. Naturally he made all the fuss possible: he was a Press correspondent, who had been taken unarmed.[29] (It seems merely a chance if he were without his pistol, and he was a very combative, if not combatant, correspondent.) But his importance, and his name, were appreciated by the Boers, who decided to retain him. Upon hearing this, Churchill decided that they

29. There is some conflict of evidence here. Field-Marshal Smuts's son says that the 'defiant young man' was brought before his father 'dishevelled and most indignant and claiming immunity as a non-combatant. It was pointed out, however, that he was carrying a pistol when captured and so he was sent on detention to Pretoria. . . . It appears that my father had developed quite a liking for the high-spirited young man he had interrogated and so, some days afterwards, he persuaded General Joubert that there was not much point in detaining him. . . . His release was therefore authorized, but before it could be put into effect he had escaped.' – J. C. Smuts, *Jan Christian Smuts*, 50–1.

should not. He was not, so far as he could help it, going to miss the entire war. He planned to escape, and he did.

> When by the labour of my 'ands
>   I've 'elped to pack a transport tight
> With prisoners for foreign lands,
>   I ain't transported with delight.
> I know it's only just an' right,
>   But yet it somehow sickens me,
> For I 'ave learned at Waterval
>   The meanin' of captivity.

Familiar as we have become with the escape-stories of the last war, Churchill's story of his escape never ceases to be thrilling – as exciting as *Kidnapped*, which he read with all the more interest while he lay concealed by the friendly mine-captain at Witbank. It should be read in his own words: how he boarded the coal-train moving east at night from Pretoria, got off it, wandered in the veldt, had fantastic luck in falling in with the one English household in the vicinity and a brave man who planned his escape in a hide-out among the bales of wool on a goods-train bound for Delagoa Bay. For years he could recite the names of the stations, that journey into freedom made such an impression: Witbank, Middelburg, Bergendal, Belfast, Dalmanutha, Machadodorp, Waterval Boven, Waterval Onder, Elands, Nooitgedacht and so on to Komati Poort. He turned up at Durban to find himself a popular hero. Today one of the most treasured possessions at Chartwell is the Pretoria poster offering a reward of £25 sterling

> to anyone who brings the escaped prisoner [*sic.*] of war
>
> CHURCHILL
>
> dead or alive to this office.

The story of his escape made him famous, thus young, all over the English-speaking world. It was a piece of individual pluck and audacity against the background of Black Week contemporaneously, the dreadful week in which three incompetent generals all suffered staggering defeats at Stormberg, Magersfontein and Colenso, which opened people's eyes to the seriousness of the situation and the magnitude of the effort required to retrieve it. Churchill's single-handed victory at once produced an equal current of reaction, of jealous disparagement. No doubt the self-advertiser had contrived it; it was held against him that he had escaped at all – who was he to escape? He had broken his parole; he had escaped alone, without bringing the others with him, etc. This surf of criticism was advanced against him for years – by the envious, by the third-rate, always those people with pretensions of their own who never achieve anything themselves. One knows the type well. Churchill had them at his heels all his life long, right up to 1940, when the nation in danger had need of such a man.

The situation was not improved by the tone he held towards the third-rate. In his dispatches home he told the truth. 'It is foolish not to recognize that we are fighting a formidable adversary. The high qualities of the burghers increase their efficiency. The individual Boer, mounted in suitable country, is worth from three to five regular soldiers.' That gave much offence, in clubs, dug-outs and such places: the brash young whipper-snapper was being disloyal now to the Army. Kipling, with the similar intuition of genius, knew better:

> Ah, there, Piet! – 'is trousies to 'is knees,
> 'Is coat-tails lyin' level in the bullet-sprinkled breeze;
> 'E does not lose 'is rifle an' 'e does not lose 'is seat.
> I've known a lot o' people ride a dam' sight worse than
>   Piet.

The war-correspondent did not hesitate to suggest a war-policy. 'We should collect overwhelming masses of troops. It would be much cheaper in the end to send more than necessary. There is plenty of work here for a quarter of a million men. More irregular corps are wanted. Are the gentlemen of England all fox-hunting? Why not an English Light Horse?'[30] In the end a quarter of a million soldiers had to be sent, the larger disparity he had mentioned – five British regulars to one Boer. To be thus corroborated does not make one more popular. It is probable that, great as was the *réclame* he collected, by the end of the war he had collected as much unpopularity in influential quarters, in

30. Churchill, *My Early Life*, 316.

the Army, among politicians, his equals and competitors. Simpler people are, of course, above such mean resentments.

Buller rewarded the young man's enterprise by giving him his wish – a commission in the newly recruited South African Light Horse. So there he was once more in the role that made people so envious, doubling the soldier with the correspondent. The rule against this had been specially made because of him; he was made the first exception. The General squared his conscience: 'you will have to do as much as you can for both jobs. But you will get no pay for ours'. Thus he returned to the Army under Colonel Byng (later Lord Byng of Vimy), who let him roam where he liked when they were not engaged in fighting and he 'lived from day to day in perfect happiness'.

The war proceeded on its slow course. Churchill was present at the fearful mess Buller made at Spion Kop, whence he announced that he had 'effected his retreat' – in the phrase Kipling took up. However, the new Lieutenant of the S.A.L.H. vastly enjoyed the two months' fighting for the relief of Ladysmith, in the course of which he came across his brother John. At home Lady Randolph had exerted herself to recruit benevolent American support to provide and equip a hospital-ship, the *Maine*, on which she served as a nurse. The first casualty she received was her younger son; the elder shortly joined them for a few good days together. Back at the front in Natal, Buller made his fourth attempt to relieve Ladysmith – this time in the right direction – and thus 'we all rode together into the long beleaguered, almost starved-out Ladysmith. It was a thrilling moment.'[31]

With Buller's supersession as Commander-in-Chief by Lord Roberts, Kitchener as his Chief-of-Staff, a transformation came over the war: henceforward it was fought on intelligent, and intelligible, lines. With his much larger forces concentrated, Roberts was moving forward from Cape Colony upon the Orange Free State, outflanking the Boer invasion of Natal. The Lieutenant of Light Horse at once transferred himself on to his other foot as war-correspondent and got leave of absence to take part in what was going forward on the now more active front. Lord

31. ibid., 341.

Roberts had been a friend of Lord Randolph, who had appointed him Commander-in-Chief in India over the head of Lord Wolseley. But neither Roberts nor Kitchener would recognize the existence of the too active, or too expressive, war-correspondent who broke all the rules – or rather, had a genius for getting his own way without actually breaking the rules. Nor would General French, to whose cavalry division the correspondent attached himself: there was a line-up of the generals against so irregular a case of a regular soldier who yet was irrepressible, could not be got at by discipline and reported home exactly what he thought about generals as well as everybody else.

This did not prevent him from enjoying himself as he marched north with Roberts's army: 'a jolly march, occupying with halts about six weeks and covering in that period between four and five hundred miles. The wonderful air and climate of South Africa, the magnificent scale of its landscape, the life of unceasing movement and of continuous incident' made a lasting impression, folded away in that astonishing treasure-house of memories.[32] Some of the incidents were somewhat equivocally amusing, asking for trouble, as before. Arrived at the outskirts of Johannesburg he could not wait to enter, though it had not yet been evacuated by the Boers. He bicycled straight down the main road into the city. It gave him a distinct sensation of adventure: 'according to all the laws of war my situation, if arrested, would have been disagreeable. I was an officer holding a commission in the South African Light Horse, disguised in plain clothes and secretly within the enemy's lines. No court-martial that ever sat in Europe would have had much difficulty in disposing of such a case. On all these matters I was quite well informed.'[33] However, the risk was taken: ambivalence has its rewards, it seems.

On his staff Lord Roberts had no less than three dukes – to the scandal of the Radical press – Norfolk, Westminster and Marlborough. It was decided to retrench Marlborough, who was despairing at the thought of being left behind in the advance. The effective war-correspondent managed to get his friend Ian Hamilton to take the Duke on to his staff. Thus it was that

32. Churchill, *My Early Life*, 459. 33. ibid., 362–3, 365.

the two cousins rode together at the head of an infantry column into Pretoria. These two made at once for the prisoner-of-war camp. 'We were only two, and before us stood the armed Boer guard with their rifles at the "ready". Marlborough, resplendent in the red tabs of the staff, called on the Commandant to surrender forthwith, adding by a happy thought that he would give a receipt for the rifles.' Thus happily, in appropriate family company, he returned to the starting-point of so many excitements and adventures.

Mr Churchill came back from South Africa to find himself, thus young, famous. Already the music-halls had caught up with him:

> You've heard of Winston Churchill;
>   This is all I need to say –
> He's the latest and the greatest
>   Correspondent of the day.

Across the Atlantic another Winston Churchill – who presumably, with that Christian name, was an offshoot of the old stock, for there were Churchills in Virginia quite early – was at the same time winning fame with his admirable novels. Our Winston at first liked to think that some of the literary tributes he received were due to a belated recognition of the merits of *Savrola*. Inevitably there was some confusion between these two literary aspirants and a pleasant correspondence followed in which the Transatlantic Churchill considered signing himself, 'The American', while the English – or, shall we say, the Anglo-American – Churchill solved the problem by affirming the Spencer along with the Churchill.

He returned in time for Chamberlain's Khaki Election of 1900, which gave the Unionists a thumping majority and the control of power for the next five years. He was asked to stand again for Oldham, which had rejected him on his first try before going out to South Africa. In that by-election Mr Balfour's Clerical Tithes Bill hung about his neck like a Deceased Wife's Sister, until the candidate threw the liability overboard – and found, to his surprise, that 'it is not the slightest use defending governments or parties unless you defend the very worst thing about which they are attacked'. Mr Balfour said, 'I thought he was a young man of promise, but it appears he is a young man of promises'. Having lost that election, he found that 'everyone threw the blame on me. I have noticed that they nearly always do. I suppose it is because they think I shall be able to bear it best.'[34]

Now he was received at Oldham like a conquering hero and when he told his audience the story of the Oldham man who had helped to conceal him in the Witbank Colliery, Lancashire shouted back, 'His wa-af's in the gallery'. Sensation. There was no resisting that. On winning the seat he was in request to lend a hand all over the country – in those leisurely days 'before the liquefaction of the British political system had set in', when a general election was spread over several weeks – and he appeared on both Chamberlain and Balfour's platforms and 'never addressed any but the greatest meetings'.[35]

After this there was the more remunerative experience of a lecture-tour – hardly ever less than £100 a night, with Lord Wolseley to take the chair in London, Lord Rosebery at Edinburgh, the Duke of Marlborough at Oxford. In America he had a more varied reception, depending on the place, for there was a good deal of pro-Boer feeling. When at Chicago the audience found that he had as much admiration and sympathy for the Boers as they had, their good nature prevailed and hostility turned to friendliness. At Boston a strong pro-British demonstration was staged; but the height for him was reached in New York, where he was thrilled to have for his chairman Mark Twain, beloved companion of his youth and of as many boys on this side of the Atlantic as on the other.

As the results of all his efforts, articles, books, lectures, he had £10,000 to invest and live on for the next few years, since in those days Members of Parliament were unpaid. That sum made the difference of ten years between his and his friend Amery's entry into Parliament. 'If I had not been caught, I could not have escaped, and my imprisonment and escape provided me with materials for lectures and a book which brought me in enough money to get into Parliament in 1900 – ten years before you!'[36]

34. Churchill, *My Early Life*, 240. 35. ibid., 373.
36. L. S. Amery, op. cit., I. 117.

He has always held strong views about the importance of chance in human affairs.

With all this behind him, though the youngest member of the House, with the expectations aroused from Lord Randolph's son, his maiden speech was awaited with attention, by himself with intense nervousness. For the truth is that he was not a good natural speaker. Not for him the deplorable fluency of so many people who have nothing to say. He had a great deal to say – there were inexhaustible resources pent up within him – but he had great difficulty in saying it. There was, as Amery notes, not only the lisp, but a tendency to stutter when excited and a voice that was harsh and unpleasing. How different the voice of the speaker before him in the debate, that of the Radical Lloyd George, already ten years a Member – that voice we still remember, the natural music of its cadences, the purity of the Welsh vowel-sounds, the soft caressing quality of it with its extraordinary range and variety of expression, the command in the voice of anger and scorn, humour and mischief, pathos and every kind of sympathy. In later years Churchill said of Lloyd George that 'at his best he could charm a bird off a tree'.

To Churchill speaking did not come naturally: he had to learn it like Demosthenes. (Somebody said that on the way back from South Africa on board ship he would practise his harangues, like Demosthenes, to the waves.) His speeches were carefully prepared, learnt by heart beforehand; that gave him a certain immobility in debate, for they could not be changed when the arguments he had to answer were different. The airy but agile Balfour, who prepared nothing, one day scored against him over this. Here, too, we notice a contrast with his father, who was a natural orator, fluent and precocious. On the night, however, everyone was kind; no one interrupted to put off the neophyte who, breathless and dripping with nervousness, stuck to it to the end, when 'the usual restoratives were applied and I sat in a comfortable coma till I was strong enough to go home'.[37] In fact the content of the speech was excellent, for it had been well got up; he had a line of his own: a very individual voice was heard and that was remarked on. The Speaker,

37. Churchill, *My Early Life*, 379–80.

for example, thought that Churchill spoke 'most effectively and marked himself out at once as a young man of great ability who would have to be reckoned with in the future'.[38]

Lloyd George's pro-Boer speech had been very scathing against the government; though Churchill spoke from the opposite side he insisted that 'no national emergency short of the actual invasion of this country itself ought in any way to restrict or prevent the entire freedom of Parliamentary discussion'.[39] It is interesting that this theme appeared thus early: he affirmed it again and again during the years 1940–45. A commonplace in itself, it was shrewd to assert it, for, though no doubt sincerely held, it was also flattering to the self-esteem of Parliament. He went on to speak of the war: 'from what I saw of the war – and I sometimes saw something of it – I believe that, as compared with other wars, especially those in which a civil population took part, this war in South Africa has been on the whole carried on with unusual humanity and generosity'. This was before the terrible experience of the concentration camps which were so ravaged by disease – the result of sheer military incompetence rather than any inhumanity.

A friendly feeling towards the Boers was evident in the phrase, 'if I were a Boer fighting in the field – and if I were a Boer I hope I should be fighting in the field' . . . Mr Chamberlain made an impatient movement on the Front Bench: 'that's the way to throw away seats', he muttered. The new member went further:

> I have often myself been very much ashamed to see respectable old Boer farmers – the Boer is a curious combination of the squire and the peasant, and under the rough coat of the farmer there are very often to be found the instincts of the squire – I have been ashamed to see such men ordered peremptorily by young subaltern officers, as if they were private soldiers.

His plea was that the government's policy should be 'to make it easy and honourable for the Boers to surrender'. Nothing should be left undone

> to bring home to those brave and unhappy men who are fighting in the field that whenever they are prepared to recognize that their small

38. Viscount Ullswater, *A Speaker's Commentaries*, I. 307.
39. Hansard, Fourth Series, LXXXIX. 407 foll.

independence must be merged in the larger liberties of the British Empire, there will be a full guarantee for the security of their property and religion, an assurance of equal rights, a promise of representative institutions and, last of all, but not least of all, what the British Army would most readily accord to a brave and enduring foe – all the honours of war.

Here was a new note, which was recognized by the Liberal speaker following him: 'the tone was different from what we sometimes hear with reference to this deplorable conflict'. We recognize it, the note of a chivalrous magnanimity continuous throughout his career. Before sitting down the new member had thanked the House for its kindness: 'it has been extended to me, I well know, not on my own account, but because of a splendid memory which many honourable members still preserve'. Chamberlain, who was the dominating figure in the House, paid his tribute to 'a speech which I am sure that those who were friends and intimates of his father will have welcomed with the utmost satisfaction in the hope that we may see the father repeated in the son'.

His father's image was constantly before his mind in this arena where he had been such a dazzling figure. The son took up his father's cause of retrenchment in a long speech a few months later.[40] He proceeded to cite Lord Randolph's views at length and his struggle with the Secretary of State for War:

in the end the government triumphed and the Chancellor of the Exchequer went down for ever and with him, as it now seems, there fell also the cause of retrenchment and economy. I suppose that was a lesson which Chancellors of the Exchequer were not likely to forget. . . . I am very glad that the House has allowed me, after an interval of fifteen years, to lift again the tattered flag I found lying on a stricken field. . . . If such a one is to stand forward in such a cause, no one has a better right than I have, for this is a cause I have inherited, and a cause for which the late Lord Randolph Churchill made the greatest sacrifice of any minister of modern times.

This speech marked the beginning of an effective campaign against the scheme for reorganizing the Army propounded by

40. Hansard, XCIII. 1563 foll.

Brodrick, Secretary of State for War.[41] The War Office wished us to continue as a military nation with a considerable expansion of the regular Army; the plan was inspired on German lines – six Army Corps, three for home defence, three to form an expeditionary force, if necessary, to Europe. The young speaker had an unanswerable objection to this: 'one is quite enough to fight savages, and three are not enough even to begin to fight Europeans'. The speech now took a remarkable turn: he had been in the House a very short time, but he was 'astonished to hear with what composure and how glibly Members, and even Ministers, talk of a European war'. They evidently had no idea of the great change that had overcome war and society. 'Democracy is more vindictive than Cabinets. The war of peoples will be more terrible than those of kings.' He enforced the point that the British Empire could never depend on the Army: 'the Admiralty is the only office strong enough to insure the British Empire ... the only weapon with which we can expect to cope with great nations is the Navy'. He ended by adducing the moral force which had been so strongly with us and had been a factor in our security in the past century, which it would be a fatal mistake to sacrifice for the aggressive gestures implied by 'the costly, trumpery, dangerous military playthings on which the Secretary of State for War has set his heart'.

The House was much impressed by this remarkable speech – which it had taken him six weeks to prepare and which he had learnt thoroughly by heart that he might not be thrown out of his stride; the Conservatives were startled, the Liberals wholly with him. It marked the beginning of his divergence from his party. Mr Brodrick replied with some acerbity: he expected that Parliament 'which was not afraid to part company with a brilliant statesman in 1886 will not sleep the less soundly because of the financial heroics' of the son.[42] He hoped that the son's 'judgement would grow up to his ability, when the hereditary qualities he possesses of eloquence and courage may be tempered also by discarding the hereditary desire to run Imperialism on the cheap'. At Cambridge he replied to Brodrick:

41. It is curious that there is no notice of St John Brodrick in the *D.N.B.*
42. Hansard, XCIV. 310 foll.

'We are all Imperialists nowadays. It is not only a political faith, but the prevailing fashion. I am an Imperialist, too – though I do not like the name – and perhaps I shall remain one when it is less fashionable, and from an electioneering point of view less profitable than at present.'[43]

This was the beginning of a duel with Brodrick that went on for the next couple of years. It seems that Brodrick had unwittingly had some part in Lord Randolph's fall; at any rate, consciously or unconsciously, the son was avenging him upon the War Office. In addition to this he was, on the whole, right. The cavalry officer was not blinkered by the regular soldier's point of view; his speeches were full of military images, but the speaker was not a militarist. Indeed, he was in the true tradition of British defence-policy, and as the campaign proceeded he did not fear to proclaim constructively what that should be. In the first place, reliance on the Navy. At some point, Brodrick was so unwise as to defend his scheme by the 'possibility of our, at any time, losing the command of the sea'. If that went, no amount of army reorganization could save us: that showed a fundamental failure to grasp our necessary strategy. The conception of the Army proper to our needs was that of a smaller, picked force distributed at strategic points within the Empire: while home-defence should make full use of volunteer forces.

At the outset Churchill was entirely alone in his campaign against the proposed Army reorganization, the only Conservative member who voted against it. As he went on, people began to see that his criticisms were justified; but 'political prophets are always unpopular, especially when they happen to be right'.[44] Nevertheless, his constituency supported him and he gradually gathered a band of young Conservatives who went into the lobby with him against Brodrick. It became clear that Brodrick's scheme was both financially burdensome and on unsound lines. His opponent was able to claim, 'now after two years I have no hesitation in saying that Mr Brodrick's scheme of 1901 is a total, costly, ghastly failure'. He did not spare Brodrick from ridicule, or his addiction to German models, methods, uniforms.

43. Churchill, *Mr Brodrick's Army*, 33. 44. ibid., 61, 62.

He did not spare the generals – we have seen that he was not popular with them in South Africa; he thought that not the least remarkable feature of the British Army was the number of its generals. He considered that there was a serious military prejudice against the Volunteers.

None of this endeared him in orthodox quarters either in the Army or the Conservative party. Brodrick's scheme was breaking down under the weight of criticism in the House and from its own impracticability. It was left to the Liberals when they came in, and to Haldane, to produce a better. As a move in his campaign Churchill published his speeches in a little book, *Mr Brodrick's Army*. He did not mince his language: he described the scheme as 'The Great English Fraud', and in his Preface he arrayed himself once more under his father's standard.

The summer of 1901 saw Unionism at the meridian of its political power and Blenheim chosen for its demonstration. There Chamberlain and Balfour appeared together on a hot August day on a platform beneath the Corinthian portico, supported by a score of lesser dignitaries and a hundred M.P.s. Thousands of people were gathered on Capability Brown's vast lawn to hear Chamberlain triumphing over the divided Liberals, taunting them in his characteristic way. But events were gradually bringing that party together again and providing matter for dissension within the Unionist majority. For one thing the war had by no means ended with the capture of Pretoria; it entered a new and more difficult phase of dispersed guerrilla warfare. The Boers were still holding out for nothing short of independence.

In regard to the conduct of the war Churchill expressed his dissatisfaction in a strong private letter to Chamberlain.

I am afraid you will not approve of the series of speeches I am making in the country . . . but I should like you to know what my line is . . . Kitchener is overworked, exhausts himself on many unimportant details, and is now showing signs of the prolonged strain. There is no plan worth speaking of in the operations except hammer, hammer, at random. The troops, which are numerous everywhere, are overwhelming nowhere. The thousands of superior men are intermingled with and consequently reduced to the level of the inferior soldiers. The mobility of the Army is that of the slowest mounted man. . . . What I want is that the government should localize, delimit and assign the functions of the C.-in-C. in Africa. Should reorganize the Remount and Intelligence Depts. Should lay the army by for a short period of rest and refreshment. Should organize a picked force. Should make some sort of peace: and make sure that we end the matter with the next bitter weather, whatever happens.[45]

Throughout 1902 we find Churchill concerning himself with every aspect of military questions; at one moment proposing to use 30,000 Indian troops to bring the war to a speedier end;[46] congratulating poor Mr Brodrick on abandoning 'the fatal and foolish theory of conscription'; dissociating himself from 'pious tributes to Ministerial infallibility'. Now he is horrified to find that the Military Intelligence Department had only sixteen or twenty officers, where the German had two hundred.[47] He made various suggestions for small economies, though he opposed that of bringing in business experts. Next he brings forward a motion for a Select Committee on the reduction of national expenditure. Mr Balfour, now Prime Minister, found this a bore and tried to forget it. He was not allowed to.

It was an arduous, industrious apprenticeship, for in spite of speaking frequently, 'in those days, and indeed for many years, I was unable to say anything (except a sentence in rejoinder) that I had not written out and committed to memory beforehand'.[48] Once now and again he makes the point, rather pathetically, that not having been to a university he had not had the experience of those young men in debating and discussion, in impromptu speaking of all kinds. He noticed this all the more because he was one of a group of younger members led by Lord Hugh Cecil – the Hughligans – whose mind was of a very academic dialectical turn, while the Hatfield of that generation and the next was a debating society in itself.

The year 1903 marked the beginning of the breach within the ranks of the Tories, the recovery of the Liberals, with Chamberlain's departure from Free Trade, coming out in favour of Imperial Preference. Churchill had several times tried to

45. Julian Amery, *The Life of Joseph Chamberlain*, IV. 40–41.
46. Hansard, CI. 473.
47. ibid., CV. 794.
48. Churchill, *My Early Life*, 378.

draw him on the subject in the House: it was acutely embarrassing to the government, which was deeply divided on the issue. Now Churchill came forward with an uncompromising Free Trade declaration – Oldham was Free Trade, his father had been, he was himself.

> This move means a change, not only in historic English parties, but in the conditions of our public life. The old Conservative Party, with its religious convictions and constitutional principles, will disappear and a new party arise like perhaps the Republican party of America – rich, materialist and secular – whose opinions will turn on tariffs, and who will cause the lobbies to be crowded with the touts of protected industries.[49]

He wrote to the Duke of Devonshire, leader of the Liberal Unionists, protesting against Chamberlain's Protectionist propaganda circulating through all the channels of the Conservative party. 'We are on the eve of a gigantic political landslide. I don't think Balfour and those about him realize at all how far the degeneration of the forces of Unionism has proceeded, and how tremendous the counter-current is going to be.'[50] This turned out a true prophecy.

In these years he was writing his biography of his father, devoting himself to it with his intense power of concentration and his artistic conscientiousness, collecting his letters – he already had his speeches by heart – seeing and consulting everybody who had known him well. The moral of his father's career cannot but have become increasingly clear to him: not to follow one's convictions into the party that agrees with them and will give effect to them is to condemn one's self to complete frustration. We have seen that intellectually Lord Randolph was genuinely Radical; he chose to remain inside the Conservative party, which had no further use for him and wasted his life: there was the real political suicide. In the course of writing his biography his son consulted Rosebery, who, to begin with, did not much approve of Winston – like a good many people, until they got to know him. The relationship between these two became rather touching: the young man avid to hear everything he

49. Hansard, CXXIII. 194.
50. B. Holland, *Life of the Duke of Devonshire, 1833–1908*, 319.

could learn about the famous father who had held himself so aloof from him, whom he had never got to know. One observes in his attitude to Rosebery something of a filial feeling, looking to him in place of the father he had lost. In these circumstances Rosebery became his mentor and that could not but have pulled him towards the Liberal party.

Others too had their influence.

> I found that Asquith and Grey and, above all, John Morley seemed to understand my point of view far better than my own chiefs. I was fascinated by the intellectual stature of these men and their broad and inspiring outlook upon public affairs, untrammelled as it was by the practical burden of events.[51]

A hardly less remarkable associate of his father met him at this moment for the first time: this was Wilfrid Scawen Blunt, poet, diplomat, Sussex squire, anti-Imperialist, breeder of fine Arab horses, opponent of the Egyptian occupation, of our Sudan ventures – and that had brought him into contact with Lord Randolph, also a Little Englander. Randolph's son interested Blunt intensely and he gives us the best impressions of him in these years, for they became fast friends. (Blunt, with the optimism of his kind, for long hoped to turn him into an anti-Imperialist too.) 'He is a little, square-headed fellow of no very striking appearance', wrote the tall and very striking poet,

> but of wit, intelligence and originality. In mind and manner he is a strange replica of his father, with all his father's suddenness and assurance, and I should say more than his father's ability. There is just the same *gaminerie* and contempt of the conventional and the same engaging plain-spokenness and readiness to understand. As I listened to him recounting conversations he had had with Chamberlain I seemed once more to be listening to Randolph on the subject of Northcote and Salisbury. About Chamberlain he was especially amusing, his attitude being one of mingled contempt and admiration, contempt for the man and admiration for his astuteness and audacity. In Opposition Winston I expect to see playing precisely his father's game, and I should not be surprised if he had his father's success. He has a power of writing Randolph never had. . . . He interested me immensely.[52]

51. Churchill, *My Early Life*, 381.
52. W. S. Blunt, *My Diaries, 1888–1914*, 489.

Here is a remarkably perceptive view so early: the poet's personal intuition was much better than his generalized judgement when it came to political affairs.

By 1904 Mr Balfour's Cabinet was breaking up and Churchill visibly preparing to move over to the Liberals. Balfour made no effort to retain him; years after Chamberlain said that he was 'the cleverest of all the young men, and the mistake Arthur made was letting him go'.[53] But no doubt it would have been impossible to stop him and, like Disraeli, he 'had his way to make'. Like the major figures in English politics, as opposed to the lesser ones, he was not a good party man: he transcended those narrow limitations. He wrote to a Liberal candidate at a by-election wishing him success in the common Free Trade cause. In the Budget Debate he supported an Opposition amendment, with a good deal of banter against his friend Austen Chamberlain, now Chancellor of the Exchequer. But he was not going to quote figures: 'it was quite enough to say that the government of the country cost half as much again as it did when the Unionist government in 1895 came into power. Was it governed half as well again?'[54] This was a mere debating point; in fact his quarrel with the government was now irreparable, and it had been essentially on the question of finance all along.

From this time he had to meet constant barracking from his own side. Several times the Conservatives tried to howl him down. Once when he rose to speak, as he now did very frequently, the Prime Minister left the Front Bench and all the Conservatives walked out of the House by a spontaneous demonstration, stopping at the door to jeer while Churchill stood waiting. It needed courage to persevere in these circumstances; what is more remarkable is that he retained his customary good-humour and courtesy.

Such a situation could not long endure. He accepted an invitation to stand at the approaching election as a Free Trade candidate for North-West Manchester, and crossed the floor of the House to sit beside Lloyd George. It was not long before

53. *The Autobiography of Margot Asquith*, II. 134.
54. Hansard, CXXXIV. 1479 foll.

he was moving an Opposition amendment about the tax on tea: he would have preferred to raise money by placing 2d. or 3d. on income-tax. In July he was joining with Lloyd George to attack the Prime Minister for not listening to representations from the mining industry against the coal-tax. Several times Balfour left the House when he rose to speak, and he was constantly faced with Conservative interruptions. Amery tells us that the Conservatives hated him, as the Liberals did Chamberlain for leaving them.[55] Chamberlain himself warned him from bitter experience, 'you must expect to have the same sort of abuse flung at you as I have endured. But if a man is sure of himself, it only sharpens him and makes him more effective.' All the same, even after his return to the fold twenty years later, there has always remained an irreducible element of antagonism to Churchill in the Conservative party, particularly in the party organization, where hidebound orthodoxy was at its most congealed. On the other hand, it is pleasant to think that in a few years it was precisely these contestants, Balfour and Churchill, Austen Chamberlain and Lloyd George, who became fast friends and held together in Coalition days. Churchill, bursting all the bonds, may be said to have had Coalitionism in his blood.

By this time he had lost his early diffidence, had himself become a marked figure in the House, was speaking – always with preparation – on every conceivable subject, frequently told by the Chair to keep to the matter in hand. These subjects ranged from Customs in the Isle of Man, Shop Hours, Reform of the Militia, Savings Banks, Sugar Duties, Chinese Labour in the Transvaal, all Army and most Budget questions, to the Tibet expedition. Clearly such energy, such industry, was crying out for office: a large machine would be required for such a dynamo.

Balfour had missed the opportunity to harness him to his government; now it was too late: the Cabinet itself was disintegrating under the contrary pressures of Chamberlain and the Conservative Free Traders. Chamberlain described Balfour's attempts to evade declaring himself, by frequently walking out of the House, as 'humiliating'. Churchill was more trenchant. 'The government are now doing penance for the disingenuousness

55. L. S. Amery, op. cit., I. 393.

of years. All their shams, all the shuffles, all their manoeuvrings, all their scurrying from the House of Commons, all their ingenious devices of the gag and the guillotine are of no avail.'[56] Balfour had inherited the greatest governing instrument possible from Lord Salisbury, which he had now wrecked in a couple of years, 'simply by weak and vacillating action, by not having the courage to state his opinions boldly on great controversies, he had wrecked his party, lost his friends and broken up his government'. This was followed by a series of personal attacks on the Prime Minister for 'the gross, unpardonable ignorance' he exhibited on public business, for his 'slip-shod, slap-dash, haphazard manner of doing business'.[57] The Prime Minister was often away from the House; Mr Churchill supposed, on one occasion, to write his philosophical Address to the British Association – and that may well have been so. The failing administration received a characteristic parting shot: 'the dignity of a Prime Minister, like a lady's virtue, was not susceptible of partial diminution'.[58]

All this, of course, was unfair: the small change of party controversy – and Churchill was now wholly with the other side. In truth, Balfour was never wanting in courage, personal or political; under the lady-like appearance there was the quality of steel. Moreover, his government had a fruitful legislative record: its Education Act (1902) was one of the grand constructive measures of a century: our educational system today is built on it. It simply was that after twenty years of Tory rule the country was looking to a new deal, the social reform that would have come twenty years earlier if Chamberlain had not apostatized from the Liberals.

During these years Churchill was labouring at his biography of his father – it would no doubt have surprised Lord Randolph to know who the author would be and what a fine, definitive job he would make of it. Lord Rosebery hailed it as 'among the first dozen, perhaps the first half-dozen, biographies in our language'.[59] Though this seems putting it rather high, we may content our-

56. Hansard, CXLIV. 582–3.
57. ibid., CXLIX. 995–6.
58. ibid., CL. 91 foll.
59. The Marquis of Crewe, *Lord Rosebery*, II. 497.

selves with remarking that the book was masterly: a very fine piece of work, firmly constructed, full in its documentation, just in its presentation of the subject and his companion figures, living and warm in its sympathies; a completely satisfying performance, no one has ever sought to impugn it. And this from a man of thirty who had been so backward in his beginnings. The book had the reception it deserved: it delighted the great world that read it and for whom it was written; at the same time they were again rather surprised that the author had it in him to produce a masterpiece.

The last stages in its composition were marked by a slight *contretemps* with Lord Rosebery, who intended to contribute his character-sketch to it. This contained the Etonian expression 'scug' to characterize Lord Randolph; and though Rosebery explained that the expression was harmless – it means a boy who does not play games, and is to that extent derogatory – Winston was not going to have it in his book. The mutual affection between him and his father's friend survived the strain. The book was written over some three years in the House, 'in spite of some political distractions', and in his bachelor rooms in Mount Street. There he worked away surrounded by his few treasured possessions: the entrance-hall hung with cartoons of his father, himself seated in the carved oak chair presented by the city of Manchester to Lord Randolph, dipping his pen into the immense inkstand that had been his father's. There were photographs of Lady Randolph, a portrait of the old Duchess and an engraving of the Duke playing chess – no doubt less objectionable than playing cards. Looking down on the work going forward was a print of the great Duke, whose biography also he would one day write. On the cabinet between the windows, in the most honoured place, stood a photograph of his old nurse.

Here Scawen Blunt came one day to visit him.

He is astonishingly like his father in manners and ways, and the whole attitude of his mind. He has just come in from playing polo, a short, sturdy little man with a twinkle in his eye, reminding me especially of the Randolph of twenty years ago. He took out his father's letters, which I had left with him six weeks ago, from a tin box and read them to me aloud while I explained the allusions in them and gave him a short account of the political adventures of the early eighties in which Randolph and I had been connected. There is something touching about the fidelity with which he continues to espouse his father's cause and his father's quarrels. He has been working double shifts this session in Parliament, and looks, I fancy, to a leadership of the Liberal Party and an opportunity of full vengeance on those who caused his father's death.[60]

The Liberal landslide of 1906 certainly saw full retribution upon the Tories; his life of his father did him full justice at last and put the record right. With his call to office under the Liberals and the appearance of his first masterpiece – the Preface dated from Blenheim – we may regard the long and arduous, but immensely varied and enriching, apprenticeship as over.

60. W. S. Blunt, op. cit., 518.

Chapter 12

Liberal Minister

FROM 1906 onwards the most fabulous, outsize career in our modern history begins to flow in full spate. We can no more describe it in detail, its ups and downs, its checks and chances, with the ever-mounting creative contribution to legislation, political action and the life of the nation, than we could the military campaigns of his ancestor. As with the great figure among the early Churchills, so with his descendant, the emphasis must be on the person and the personal, events forming the patterns in the tapestry.[1]

We observe a certain parallel in the significant rhythms of their careers. Just as John Churchill made his strenuous ascent from difficult, though not unpropitious, beginnings to be thrown back for a decade out of favour and out of office under William III, so the later Churchill's career has had its set-backs and remarkable recoveries. From 1906 to 1915 Winston Churchill's course was one of steady ascent and increasing importance as a minister and a national figure until, as First Lord of the Admiralty in 1914, he held one of the three or four key-positions in the conduct of the war. From that he fell almost sheer, and went off to fight as a soldier in France, until he was rescued by Lloyd George and brought back to be Minister of Munitions. The end of the Coalition in 1922 left him stranded once more and, for once, ill. ('In a twinkling of an eye I found myself without an office, without a seat, without a party, and without an appendix.'[2]) Saved from this dismal condition by Mr Baldwin, he was offered the Chancellorship – 'of the Duchy?' 'No – of the Exchequer.' As such he was a ruling figure until he separated from Mr Baldwin, opposed the Conservative party leadership and was out of office and of any power throughout the contemptible decade that led to war in

1. cf. *The Early Churchills*, 227.
2. W. S. Churchill, *Thoughts and Adventures* (ed. 1947), 162.

1939. His being out of office and the neglect of his counsels – indeed the opposite line was taken by the third-rate men who took his place – was a considerable factor in bringing the war upon us in the most unfavourable conditions. From 1940 to 1945 he was the chief instrument of our resistance and victory, as Marlborough had been from 1702 to 1711 – to be thrown out of office, as Marlborough was, before victory was quite complete and his own conditions for peace properly secured. Marlborough came back in his sixties when the Tories were ousted in 1714; Winston Churchill came back in his seventies when Labour lost power in 1951. Their lives are not dissimilar in their rhythms, the ebbs and flows of power, the recessions and strokes of fortune, their military inspiration and strategic concern for their country. Both of them were men of the sensible centre, one of them a Trimmer by nature, the other with Coalitionism in his blood; neither of them what is called 'a good party man'. Each of them might claim, though with a rather different emphasis, 'some men change their party for the sake of their principles; others change their principles for the sake of their party'.

I

The Liberal Prime Minister, Campbell-Bannerman, took the opportunity that Balfour had missed to make Churchill Under-Secretary of State for the Colonies. (Actually he was succeeding his cousin the Duke in the post, so Blenheim still had a voice, and a more powerful one, in the management of the Empire.) On this news the Prince of Wales wrote home to King Edward that Lord Elgin, the new Secretary of State, 'will have to look after him!'[3] But we do not hear of Lord Elgin again. Since he was skied in the Lords, the voice we hear is that of the Under-Secretary in the Commons; and since in these years the settlement of South Africa after the war was the foremost question in politics, Churchill came immediately to the fore with it.

On the personal side we see him henceforth from the interesting angle of his private secretary, Edward Marsh, whom he appointed somewhat irregularly and who accompanied him

3. Harold Nicolson, *King George V*, 93.

faithfully from office to office until they arrived together at the august, but somewhat uncongenial, portals of the Treasury. This partnership was in itself irregular: tribute to the dog-like, or perhaps more truly cat-like, devotion Winston aroused in this rather feminine type – in himself a remarkable man, who became a public-spirited patron and encourager of artists and writers. This faithful partnership took its rise from a party at which Marsh was put across Winston by a forceful aunt. The moral Marsh drew was never to miss parties. Actually he had already met Churchill and found him overbearing; but Lady Lytton assured him that 'the first time you meet Winston you see all his faults, and the rest of your life you spend in discovering his virtues'.[4] And so it proved.

Together they sallied off to Manchester to fight the election, where they explored the slums, Winston fascinated and horrified. He had never seen such places before: 'Fancy living in one of these streets – never seeing anything beautiful – never eating anything savoury – *never saying anything clever*!' Marsh was entranced to find that Winston had never so much as heard of lodgings. He soon fell completely for his new master and tells us that it was the officials who saw most of him who liked him best: they soon saw that there was no ill-will in his asperities or his impatience, no malice and hardly any guile – rare for a politician. And yet his manner of speaking in these early years was apt to arouse intense hostility. Marsh says that it was partly due to the difficulty he had in articulation, the harshness of utterance which could be very effective when aggression was called for, but which sounded aggressive when it was not intended.

A speech about Lord Milner in retirement, who had become a hero to the displaced Tories, gave much offence, particularly a phrase about 'this disconsolate pro-consul'. King Edward at Biarritz was alerted; when the Prime Minister attributed the party-rancour that had arisen to Milner's own intemperateness, 'I cannot consider Lord Milner's speech in the House of Lords was intemperate. If it was, what were Mr W. S. Churchill's speeches in the House of Commons?'[5] We observe King Edward's almost

4. Edward Marsh, *A Number of People*, 149–51.
5. Sir Sidney Lee, *King Edward VII*, II. 481–2.

paternal interest in his old friend's son, commenting like a headmaster on his form, pleased when he improves; performing his duty as a monarch in toning down asperities, helping to keep things together. Another phrase of Churchill's that became notorious and was frequently flung back at him was when he described some unwelcome statement as a 'terminological inexactitude'. The born writer's fondness for words and phrases became sometimes a liability to the politician.

More serious matters were to the fore and it fell to Churchill to put them to the King. There was the question of the new Transvaal Constitution: were the Boers to be granted complete self-government so soon after the war they had made? The Liberal government was in favour of taking the risk. The King at once put his finger on the crux of the matter in his letter to Churchill. Would this increase or diminish the chance of an English majority? Would it encourage immigration from England or choke it off? 'The King can well understand that the onus of all these discussions in Parliament was thrown upon your shoulders, and no doubt severe criticisms were made from both extremes, but his Majesty is glad to see that you are becoming a *reliable* minister and above all a serious politician' – here Edward VII took up the pen himself to add, '*which can only be attained by putting country before party*'. The junior minister replied with an immense letter of thirteen pages: too much for the King; he did not reply.

In July, however, Churchill concluded his speech recommending the Transvaal Constitution to Parliament with a magnificent appeal to the Tories, showing how much above mere party-spirit he was and foreshadowing the things to come. 'I will ask them whether they cannot join with us to invest the grant of a free constitution to the Transvaal with something of a national sanction. With all our majority we can only make it the gift of a party; they can make it the gift of England.'[6] They did not respond: to the party-Tory he was for long anathema. Later, he gave expression to his vision of the future of small nationalities – a subject on which Stalin, himself a sprig of one of them, was to specialize, with how different results! –

6. W. S. Churchill, in the House of Commons, 31 July 1906, *Liberalism and the Social Problem*, 44.

If the near future should unfold to our eyes a tranquil, prosperous, consolidated Afrikander nation under the protecting aegis of the British Crown, then, I say, the good as well as the evil will not be confined to South Africa . . . everywhere small peoples will have more room to breathe, and everywhere great empires will be encouraged by our examples to step forward – it only needs a step – into the sunshine of a more gentle and a more generous age.[7]

Then came the offer of the Cullinan diamond – the largest ever to come to light – to the British Crown by the Transvaal government as a peace-offering, a token of its loyalty within the Commonwealth. Small-minded people at both ends were opposed to this generous act, but the Under-Secretary through his friendship with his former captor, Botha, now Prime Minister of the Transvaal, was able to advance it. He had his way, and in recognition of his part in it he was presented with a replica of the diamond. When the object was taken round his luncheon-table on a silver salver for the guests to see, his aunt Lady Lilian, after one look at what she took to be a not very well-strained white jelly, replied, 'No, thank you'.

In the winter of 1907–8 Churchill and Eddie Marsh went off for a tour of the East African territories in their charge. In those spacious days the tour gave them four months off and commissions for the Under-Secretary to write a series of articles for the *Strand Magazine*, his private secretary for the *Manchester Guardian*. When Marsh applied to the Treasury for some item of equipment on the ground that Winston was taking one, Lord Chalmers replied, 'I dare say he is, but *you're* not a Blenheim spaniel'. Before leaving, Churchill finished an article for the *Daily News* with the question, 'Where is the statesman to be found who is adequate to the times?' and told Charles Masterman that if he were eaten by some horrible tsetse fly in East Africa this was his last message to the nation.[8] The statesman who was the answer was shortly to be found in East Africa, but he was taking no chances with the tsetse fly: Eddie Marsh observed him in the heat muffled up like Father Christmas. They had had a leisurely

7. W. S. Churchill, in the House of Commons, 31 July 1906, *Liberalism and the Social Problem*, 65.

8. Lucy Masterman, *C. F. G. Masterman*, 88.

journey out through the Mediterranean and Red Sea; the officers on board the *Venus*, who began with a strong prejudice against the Minister, ended up at his feet.

When the articles came out as a book, *My African Journey*, they contained some Radical sentiments. 'I have always experienced a feeling of devout thankfulness never to have possessed a square yard of that perverse commodity called "land".'[9] Something must have converted him by the time he set eyes on Chartwell and gradually acquired that delightful Kentish valley with its sidelong prospect away to the South Downs. 'I am clearly of opinion that no man has a right to be idle, whoever he be or wherever he lives.' This, which had a Radical ring in 1908, has quite a different application today.

The theme of the book is that of the immense possibilities of development, which thrilled Churchill's imagination. He spent hours at Ripon Falls watching the waters and revolving plans to harness them: 'so much power running to waste, such a coign of vantage unoccupied, such a lever to control the natural forces of Africa ungripped, cannot but vex and stimulate imagination. . . . And what fun to make the immemorial Nile begin its journey by diving through a turbine.'[10] His mind leaped forward at the prospect of controlling the system of Central African waters, the levels and flows, improving and co-ordinating the channels; he imagined the railway routes connecting up with steamers across the Great Lakes to form an uninterrupted chain of communication from Mombasa to Khartoum and thence to Cairo.

When he got to Khartoum he could see what British enterprise had accomplished in only the ten years since the Dervish empire had been shattered at Omdurman: Khartoum rebuilt in some splendour, quays giving upon the river, a fleet of steamers going up and down, a railway running more than a thousand miles to Cairo; in the immaterial realm, slavery abolished, the population restored and their education begun. In East Africa his hopes were upon Uganda as a most fertile and promising country, and he rejoiced that physical conditions were such as 'to prevent the growth in the heart of happy Uganda of a petty white

9. W. S. Churchill, *My African Journey*, 56, 63.
10. ibid., 132, 167.

community with the harsh and selfish ideas which mark the jealous contact of races and the selfish exploitation of the weaker'.[11] Such was the message not only of English enterprise but of English humanity.

Much of what he foresaw has come to pass in the half-century since he bicycled considerable stretches along the native tracks between the Great Lakes. Whole areas at that date had been depopulated by the ravages of sleeping sickness: not even he could foresee the work of recovery wrought by the achievements of twentieth-century medicine.

Along with this there went the inexhaustible capacity of his temperament for sheer enjoyment, and the book is full of vivid descriptions bringing the exotic scenery to the eye: the wonderfully coloured butterflies feeding upon the filth, the orchids, the flowers, the tangle of vegetation, the sunlight upon falls, the wild life, a whole river-bank that slid into the water at a shot – crocodiles packed together like sardines. There were the delights of shooting rhinoceros and pig-sticking: one wild pig with Winston's spear in him took refuge in a deep hole 'from which no inducements or insults could draw him'.[12] He had the pleasure of meeting (and shooting) one of the rare Burchell's White Rhinoceros: Eddie, who was caught at the encounter with only an umbrella, which he hoped to open with a bang, thought it looked rather a subfusc rhinoceros. However, the vegetation alone was such as to astonish; 'as for our English garden products, brought in contact with the surface of Uganda they simply give one wild bounce of efflorescence or fruition and break their hearts for joy'.

The fact was that they saw the world at its best – before 1914.

On Campbell-Bannerman's death Asquith formed his very able administration, on the personnel of which British politics subsisted almost up to the Second World War. Not afraid of superior talents, Asquith drew round him a government that included Lloyd George, Sir Edward Grey, Haldane and Lord Morley; and to these he proceeded to promote Churchill at thirty-three. There were people who were opposed to his inclusion in the Cabinet: such readiness to serve, such obvious ambition to work hard and make his contribution, called for

11. W. S. Churchill, *My African Journey*, 214. 12. ibid., 74, 89.

obstruction. There was a question whether he should go to the Local Government Board; but that had not the recommendation of a seat in the Cabinet. Churchill preferred the Board of Trade; he declined, he said, to be 'shut up in a soup-kitchen with Mrs Sidney Webb'. But he did not thus escape the Webbs; he walked straight into their parlour, where were spun so many plans for remaking English society on the Fabian model.

The grand opportunity for social legislation and reform which had been lost when Chamberlain dropped the Radical leadership over Home Rule now fell to this Liberal government and was grasped effectively and energetically by Lloyd George and Churchill. It was to this campaign for social services – labour exchanges, unemployment and sickness insurance benefits, old-age pensions with the concomitant campaign for economy on Army and Navy – that the fruitful partnership between these two dated.

The formidable Beatrice Webb had her eye on them for her own (entirely public-spirited) purpose. She had already met Churchill; her first impression can hardly be described as favourable:

> restless – almost intolerably so, without capacity for sustained and unexciting labour – egotistical, bumptious, shallow-minded and reactionary, but with a certain personal magnetism, great pluck and some originality – not of intellect but of character. More of the American speculator than the English aristocrat. . . . Bound to be unpopular – too unpleasant a flavour with his restless, self-regarding personality, and lack of moral or intellectual refinement. . . . No notion of scientific research, philosophy, literature or art: still less of religion. But his pluck, courage, resourcefulness and great tradition may carry him far unless he knocks himself to pieces like his father.[13]

I leave this as a monument to the superciliousness of the intellectual, the readiness to condemn on a very superficial acquaintance and little knowledge. Beatrice Webb was nothing if not cocksure – a quality that led the Webbs ultimately to their stupefying credulity about 'Soviet Communism', which completely took them in. John Burns, the old Labour leader who formed a (rather stupid) member of the government, had a better opinion of its youngest

13. Beatrice Webb, *Our Partnership*, ed. B. Drake and M. Cole, 269–70.

member: he thought Winston cleverer than his father and possessing a sounder political instinct.

Further acquaintance modified Mrs Webb's harsh judgement of Churchill; indeed for some time he became her white-headed boy, upon whom her chief hopes were placed. (I fear that with the Webbs, who judged by types rather than individuals, by the general rather than the concrete, their opinions of people went up and down according to whether they served their public purposes or not.) On Churchill's appointment to the Board of Trade they had him to dinner along with Masterman and Beveridge, the inventor of the scheme of Labour Exchanges. Churchill had agreeably

> swallowed whole Sidney's scheme for boy labour and unemployment. . . . He is most anxious to be friendly and we were quite willing to be so. . . . Winston has a hard temperament, with the American's capacity for the quick appreciation and rapid execution of new ideas, whilst hardly comprehending the philosophy beneath them. But I rather liked the man. He is under no delusions about himself.[14]

This from the woman who had rejected Chamberlain, though rather in love with him, on the ground that he had delusions about *him*self, was no small compliment.

Before succumbing completely to Beatrice's charms, Labour Exchanges, organization of labour and all, Winston took an important step towards fortifying himself: he decided to marry. We hear the news first from Wilfrid Blunt.

> Blanche Hozier writes from Blenheim that her daughter Clementine is to marry Winston Churchill. She says of him, 'yesterday he came to London to ask my consent, and we all three came on here. Winston and I spoke of you and of your great friendship with his father. He is so like Lord Randolph, he has some of his faults, and all his qualities. He is gentle and tender, and affectionate to those he loves, much hated by those who have not come under his personal charm.' It is a good marriage for both of them, for Clementine is pretty, clever and altogether charming, while Winston is what the world knows him, and a good fellow to boot.[15]

14. Beatrice Webb, *Our Partnership*, ed. B. Drake and M. Cole, 404.
15. W. S. Blunt, *My Diaries, 1888–1914*, 624, 627–8.

The poet made one of his rare visits to London to attend the wedding at St Margaret's, Westminster, on 12 September.

It was quite a popular demonstration. Lord Hugh Cecil Winston's best man, and the great crowd of relations, not only the church full, but all Victoria Street, though that may have partly been for the Eucharistic Congress. . . . At St Margaret's I arrived late when all the seats were taken, but Blanche Hozier found me one in the family pew. . . The bride was pale, as was the bridegroom. He has gained in appearance since I saw him last, and has a powerful if ugly face. Winston's responses were clearly made in a pleasant voice, Clementine's inaudible.

He tells us, in the concluding sentence of *My Early Life*, that he lived happily ever afterwards. (That autumn, too, saw another Churchill marriage: of Winston's brother, John, to Lady Gwendeline Bertie, who became mother of Clarissa, later wife of Sir Anthony Eden.)

The marriage was approved of by Mrs Webb for her own high reasons. In October

we lunched with Winston Churchill and his bride – a charming lady, well bred and pretty, and earnest withal – but not rich, by no means a good match, which is to Winston's credit. Winston had made a really eloquent speech on the unemployed the night before and he has mastered the Webb scheme, though not going the whole length of compulsory labour exchanges. He is brilliantly able – more than a phrasemonger I think – and he is definitely casting in his lot with the constructive state action.[16]

Now her mandibles close upon Lloyd George: 'a clever fellow, but has less intellect than Winston, and not such an attractive personality – more of the preacher, less of the statesman'. I think we may conclude that Lloyd George was less susceptible to the influence.

In fact Churchill showed himself much more audacious and energetic than the Webbs or even Beveridge hoped. At the dinner-party at which the Minister first met Beveridge, that superior young man from Balliol was not 'as much impressed by his cleverness as I expected to be, he was or appeared to be rather tired and

16. Beatrice Webb, op. cit., 416–17.

inconsecutive'.[17] He noticed, however, Churchill's horror of being called a Liberal. Stimulated by the Webbs and Beveridge, Churchill took Eddie Marsh off with him to Germany to study its system of Labour Exchanges on the spot. The Germans were astonished at the easy terms upon which the private secretary was with his official superior, never once clicking heels to attention. In the intervals of doing their home-work they toured the battlefields of the Franco–Prussian war in Alsace, Winston giving far more lucid explanations of the battles than he could yet give of the principles of Labour Exchanges.

He got it all mastered in time; the scheme was immense in its scope: there was the necessity for him to convert the Prime Minister and the Cabinet first. Having done that he obtained their assent to implement the Reports of the Royal Commission on the Poor Law and Unemployment six months before their publication – to young Beveridge's surprise. In November he gave a large breakfast at the Board of Trade to all the Labour M.P.s, at which he used the Webbs to explain the theory of the proposed Exchanges. Their purpose was to help the community and industry by organizing the supply of labour. This might have been done on a purely local basis, experimentally and sporadically, offering to supplement existing facilities with government assistance where desired. Instead of this he opted for a full-blown national system of Labour Exchanges, taking over the existing facilities and weaving them into the scheme. He had his eye on something further: their use for the purpose of a national system of unemployment insurance, if and when called into operation. As usual, he was beforehand: he asked Beveridge and Llewelyn Smith to try their hands at preparing a practical scheme of unemployment insurance. The scheme they drafted was that put into effect in 1911.

This was after Churchill had moved on to other spheres of activity. But what energy he generated: the Trade Boards Act, the Labour Exchanges Act, both in 1909. He made Beveridge Director of Labour Exchanges and these began to be set up from 1910 onwards. Beveridge cites Churchill's Presidency of the Board of Trade as a striking illustration 'of how much the personality of

17. Lord Beveridge, *Power and Influence*, 66.

the Minister in a few critical months may change the course of social legislation'.[18] And what fun he was to work for! These Oxford men found that 'the President has a mind about everything – and it's a mind one must attend to'. This rather surprised them, for to them he was still uneducated. One day at a dinner party he picked up a book: 'Matthew Arnold's poems – who's Matthew Arnold? – do you know anything about Matthew Arnold?' They had no difficulty in telling him all about Matthew Arnold. 'Oh,' said Winston, 'this public school education!' Then, shaking his fist, 'If ever I get my chance at it!'[19] He had not forgiven Harrow; but if Arnold had been an Harrovian he might perhaps have heard of him.

Anyhow, it was more important to have a genius for action. Beveridge pays tribute to it. In the midst of the first election campaign of 1910, when he was in demand as a speaker all over the country – and was notoriously generous in going to the help of his friends – Beveridge went to him one morning in bed, after an all-night journey, with a list of the first women divisional officers for the Labour Exchanges. 'Let there be women', he said and signed without further ado. Even Lord Esher, the King's confidant, who had started with a prejudiced view, was now ready to admit that Winston had 'very nearly, if not quite, a first-rate intellect'.[20] It is extraordinary the amount of prejudice he created and had to batter down in consequence. A homely dinner-party in Eccleston Square seems to have completed Lord Esher's conquest.

He has a charming double room on the first floor, all books. A splendid library. It was a birthday dinner. Only 6 people. But he had a birthday cake with 35 candles. And *crackers*. He sat all the evening with a paper cap, from a cracker, on his head. A queer sight, if all the thousands who go to his meetings could have seen him. He and she sit on the same sofa, and he holds her hand. I never saw two people more in love. If he goes out of office, he has not a penny. He would have to earn his living, but he says it is well worth it if you live with some-one you love. He would *loathe* it, but he is ready to live in a *lodging* – just

18. Lord Beveridge, *Power and Influence*, 87.

19. Masterman, op. cit., 128.

20. *Letters and Journals of Reginald, Viscount Esher*, ed. M. V. Brett, II. 307.

two rooms – with her and the baby! They have a cook now, two maids and a man. *She* ran down to the kitchen before dinner to see that it was all right. And an excellent dinner it was![21]

Their first baby to arrive, in the midst of all this activity in social legislation, was a girl – another Diana, a return to the eighteenth century for a name. Lloyd George was able to offer his congratulations as they sat on the Treasury Bench together. 'Is she a pretty child?' said the Chancellor of the Exchequer. 'The prettiest child ever seen,' said the President of the Board of Trade. 'Like her mother, I suppose?' said L.G. 'Not at all,' said Winston gravely, 'she's the very image of me.'

A sterner critic than Lord Esher loomed up in Mrs Webb. One day she and Winston met on the Embankment – chaste assignation. 'Well, how do you think we are doing, Mrs Webb?' '*You* are doing very well, Mr Churchill, but I have my doubts about your Cabinet: I don't believe they mean to do anything with the Poor Law.' This was because the government was not for accepting the Webbs' scheme of breaking up the Poor Law and bringing it to an end. 'Oh, yes, they do,' replied Churchill, 'we are going in for a *classified* Poor Law.'[22] This was not good enough for Mrs Webb; she recognized, however, that Lloyd George and Churchill were favourable to its supersession but were pledged to the introduction of their insurance schemes first. She gave them credit for this: 'The big thing that has happened in the last two years is that Lloyd George and Winston Churchill have practically taken the *limelight*, not merely from their own colleagues, but from the Labour Party. They stand out as the most advanced politicians.' She envisaged their young Fabian followers, 'fully equipped for the fray – better than the Labour men – enrolling themselves behind these two radical leaders'.

That was hardly likely, even if these early blissful beginnings of the Welfare State – to which these two men made such contributions – had not been shadowed by the sinister developments abroad, the threat constituted by twentieth-century Germany.

The curious thing is that Churchill, though he had the privilege of a personal invitation to the German Army manoeuvres in

21. ibid., 422–3. 22. Beatrice Webb, op. cit., 430, 465.

1906 and again in 1909, was slow to perceive it. He has always been a man of intense power of concentration; it is characteristic of him that, when engaged on a job, nothing else exists for him: in that sense, though a man of many ideas, a man of one idea at a time. And this provides the clue to the constantly recurring mistrust we find expressed as to his judgement. For such was his energy of mind and the battering force of his personality that he was apt to weigh down the weightier considerations on the other side.

Sir Edward Grey and the Foreign Office knew well how grave these were. They had had long experience of Germany's ill-will and continual attempts to exert pressure and force demands upon us. There had been ebullitions of it all through the Boer War, which went far beyond mere unfriendliness.[23] They were expressions of characteristic German *Schadenfreude* and of a deep-seated jealousy of this country, a determination to displace her, if possible. Childishly envious and on edge with inferiority complex as the Kaiser was – in this, that fatuous and somewhat winged peacock was a fair expression of his people – even he could assert that he was more friendly disposed than most Germans. Their ambassadors here, both Metternich and Lichnowsky, were convinced that British opinion was more friendly to Germany and her claims than ever German opinion was to Britain. To the Germans – apart from socialists and such people – to the dominant forces in the nation, Britain was the enemy *par excellence*, for Britain stood in the way: a war with Britain was 'in the logic of history'.

And this was the real purpose of the powerful navy they were determined to build.[24] By no stretch of imagination could it be described as merely defensive. As Grey pointed out, without any fleet at all Germany would still be the most powerful nation on the Continent. Metternich himself admitted that the Germans could not expect to possess both the strongest army and the strongest navy in the world. Again and again he warned his government faithfully that fear would not compel Britain to accept terms: he

23. cf. E. L. Woodward, *Great Britain and the German Navy*, 2.

24. Bebel said that they wanted it for use in an offensive war against England. ibid., 29.

was ultimately sacrificed for telling the Germans what they did not wish to hear. For, as Grey said, with the candour and sincerity of his nature, a margin of naval superiority was a matter of life and death for this country; for Germany it was not. Britain must maintain it at all costs, while willing to accept the fact of Germany's military pre-eminence.

The more one studies the history of those years the more it is brought home to one that nothing would deflect the German leadership from their naval challenge to Britain, and there is evidence that they could hardly desist from it in face of public opinion in Germany. Reasonable accommodation would have been regarded as capitulation. How familiar the attitude and mentality are from the 1930s: continuous from the 1900s! Every time the Liberal government here proposed a friendly slackening, it was taken for weakness; any offer for mutual reduction or slowing up of construction was regarded as an interference with Germany's sovereignty and her internal affairs. If Britain slackened her building, Germany took advantage of that fact to increase hers, hoping to overtake her.[25] In the end Britain had to make it clear beyond all doubt that she could never afford to risk her very existence by allowing Germany to outbuild her. Even so, when 1914 came – and even with the aid of France and Italy – our margin of naval security was only just sufficient.

At the turn of the century Germany had rejected Chamberlain's overtures for an alliance. Bülow was convinced that time was on Germany's side, that Britain would have to accept her terms, that she had no alternative. When an alternative was found in the Entente with France, an attempt was made to break it by a threat of force. The Tangier incident – when the Kaiser was sent off, against his better judgement, to Tangier to assert the German interest in Morocco against France and Britain – only had the effect of strengthening the Entente. The Emperor, who considered that British statesmen sometimes had 'lucid intervals', was sometimes permitted moments of perception himself; but he would never, or never dared to, give way on German naval ambitions. An American observer of the European scene, the ambassador in Britain, saw clearly what was the root of the trouble

25. cf. G. M. Trevelyan, *Grey of Fallodon*, 209, 214.

and where it was leading. When war came in 1914, he wrote: 'no power on earth could have prevented it. The German militarism, which is *the* crime of the last fifty years, has been working for this for twenty-five years. It is the logical result of their spirit and enterprise and doctrine. It *had* to come.'[26]

But in these years, when the threat was developing that was to overshadow our lives, Churchill was immersed in social legislation. There was a spirit of friendly rivalry between Lloyd George and him. 'Sometimes when I see Winston making these speeches I get a flash of jealousy,' said Lloyd George, 'and I have to say to myself, "Don't be a fool. What's the use of getting jealous of Winston?"'[27] In fact there was no doubt which was leader: in addition to his eleven years' seniority, his longer experience of Parliament, his greater flexibility and adaptability, his appeal to the masses with his brand of oratory, Lloyd George had the immense advantage of his standing within the Liberal party. He was the leader of the Radical wing, the second man in the party; Churchill was a recruit from Conservatism: he would have to work his passage.

Together, as advanced social reformers, they took the lead of the campaign for economy on arms, whether for the Army or Navy. In this Churchill was being faithful to his father's old line and consistent with his own; but it would soon cease to make sense. Meanwhile it gave much trouble to both Haldane at the War Office and McKenna at the Admiralty, and it vexed King Edward. At Swansea in August 1908 Churchill assured the miners that there was no German menace, that there was nothing to fight about except tropical plantations and coaling stations, and that even if Britain were defeated the status of the Colonies and India would remain unchanged.[28] How unwise this was, the experience of the first half of this century has taught us. He was young then, and he did not know. It is no part of a historian's purpose to show that his subject was always right, but rather how a great man learns from mistakes and matures with experience.

26. q. E. L. Woodward, op. cit., 438–9.
27. L. Masterman, op. cit., 129.
28. Sir Sidney Lee, op. cit., 654–5.

And what this makes clear is that Churchill had no anti-German prejudice: the facts themselves instructed him.

In 1905 the Admiralty was convinced that the Germans were accelerating their programme and that our security at sea could only be maintained by building six new dreadnoughts. This programme was strenuously resisted in the Cabinet by Lloyd George and Churchill, supported by Morley and young Harcourt. King Edward was annoyed at their intrusion into foreign affairs, which he considered the domain of the Prime Minister and the Foreign Secretary. We have a view of what the King's intimate adviser, Lord Esher, thought in his Diary: 'Winston works tremendously hard, but gets involved in subtleties. Ll. George realises that in 1912 we shall be in danger of having hardly a *one* power naval standard. Winston cannot see it. I pointed out to them that the great majority of the country is against them. To resign upon the point would ruin them.'[29] Eventually they accepted the inescapable facts of the situation; by 19 March 1909 Asquith was able to assure Grey that 'the course of things this week has been a complete débâcle for them and their ideas, and the two cannot help reflecting how they would have looked at this moment if they had resigned, with (as Winston predicted) 90 per cent of the Liberal party behind them'.[30]

The truth is that he was never an expert party-politician in the narrow sense and his judgement of party-reactions and manoeuvres has often been at fault and rather naïf. The Admiralty got its dreadnoughts and the country was, for the time, safe – until the German Navy Law of 1912 announced an immense increase: which it fell to Churchill as First Lord of the Admiralty – poacher turned gamekeeper – to meet. We need not blame him overmuch: at the Board of Trade and at the Home Office it was not his business to build battleships. When he went to the Admiralty his point of view changed: no one could have done better. Meanwhile, having brought him into line in time for the election campaign, the Prime Minister gave him a headmasterly certificate of conduct to the King, drawing his attention to 'the moderation of tone, and the absence of personalities and bad taste – as well as

29. Esher, II. 370.
30. Trevelyan, op. cit., 213.

the conspicuous ability – which have characterized Winston Churchill's campaign in Lancashire'.[31]

So too Lord Crewe and Grey thought, and agreed that Churchill 'has shown marked improvement during the elections of 1910, in grasp and tone'.[32] At this time they thought 'the other one' (Lloyd George) incorrigible. The fact was that, under the rhetoric necessary to keep his end up with the masses and in the party-hierarchy, Churchill was a moderate. Masterman found him ready to praise 'government by aristocracy and revealing the aboriginal and unchangeable Tory in him. . . . Winston, of course, is not a democrat, or at least, he is a Tory democrat.'[33] Lloyd George said, apropos of his Radical Budget of 1909 which provoked the Lords to reject it and so brought on the prolonged constitutional crisis and the two elections of 1910, 'if we put a special clause in the Budget exempting Sunny [Marlborough] from taxation, Winston would let us do what we liked'.

However, for the two electoral handicaps of 1910, he put forth a popular volume of selections from his speeches on the leading issues – the House of Lords, the Land, the Budget and Free Trade: *The People's Rights*. The House of Lords being the main issue, the statesman's thoughts are summed up under such headings as:

> Has the House of Lords ever done right in any of the great controversies of the last 100 years?

It did not appear that they had.

> The power of the Peers in Finance is only a power to wreck.
> The House of Lords is Representative of Nobody.

It was thought that the effect of his strictures upon the Lords in general, and upon dukes in particular, was somewhat diminished by this descendant of so many dukes, with a duke for his cousin, going to stay with him at Blenheim that Christmas.

Nevertheless he scrambled through the two elections of 1910 successfully, with no pretence of enjoying those orgies indispensable to democratic life. Having fought more parliamentary elections than any living member of the House of Commons – 'each taking at least three weeks, with a week beforehand when you are

31. Lee, op. cit., II. 669. 32. Esher, II. 445.
33. L. Masterman, 165, 173.

sickening for it, and at least a week afterwards when you are convalescing and paying the bills' – he reckoned that considerably more than a year of his life had been spent under these trying conditions.[34] There were the old jokes to endure trotted out for the thirty-third time, and 'nothing is so ludicrous as a large number of good people in a frantic state, so long as you are sure they are not going to hurt you'. Worst of all, there is the grief of one's supporters when defeated: 'men and women who have given weeks of devoted and utterly disinterested labour, with tears streaming down their cheeks and looking as if the world had come to an end!'

The resistance of the Lords to Lloyd George's Budget probably cost the Tories a hundred seats at the election of January 1910.[35] Now the Liberals were returned again, though dependent on Irish votes for a majority – which made the question of Home Rule once more a foremost issue in politics. At once Churchill won his well-earned promotion to a Secretaryship of State: he went to the Home Office. Here it fell to him to report the proceedings in the Commons to the King, who much enjoyed his Disraelian accounts of them – it would be nice to have them to read – though he had not much relished Churchill's allusions to the Crown in regard to the creation of peers in the course of the election.[36] This is the last we hear of the kindly, almost avuncular relations that subsisted between King Edward and his old friend's son, for in May the King died.

Whatever Churchill now said, nothing could mitigate the animosity of the Conservatives towards him or the rancour with which they pursued him. They hated him much worse than they hated Lloyd George, a more dangerous opponent, for he was a genuine Radical who had no use for the class-system: Churchill was a renegade from his class. One duke announced – rather comically, the image was so appropriate to the public's idea of a duke – that he would like to put them both in the middle of twenty couple of his hounds.[37] Conservative leaders in the Com-

34. W. S. Churchill, *Thoughts and Adventures*, 150, 152, 174.
35. R. C. K. Ensor, *England 1870–1914*, 418.
36. Lee, op. cit., II. 697, 704.
37. q. Virginia Cowles, *Winston Churchill*, 132–3.

mons said that his conversion to Radicalism coincided with his personal interests; a Cecil said that he was entirely without principle and 'ready to follow any short cut to the Prime Ministership'. (And, indeed, why should he not? Was that not what they were all out for? It was merely that he was obvious and direct, where they were oblique and devious.) A Lyttelton said, with some mixture of metaphor: 'He trims his sails to every passing air. One might as well try to rebuke a brass band.' There is brass, as there should be, in the Churchillian orchestra.

What is interesting is to observe that underneath this chorus of abuse, Churchill sat – like his ancestor the great Duke, and true to the tradition of his family – somewhat loosely to party. It was to this year 1910 that his first suggestions of a national coalition dated, a junction of parties to settle the Irish and constitutional issues that were becoming so embittered as to poison political life, and to prepare against the German menace now clearly visible to anybody of intelligence. In this endeavour he found a kindred spirit in F. E. Smith, later Lord Birkenhead. This brilliant lawyer had this quality, among others, in common with Churchill, that within the partisan claptrap there was a sound core of patriotic spirit. F. E. Smith's father had been a humble follower of Lord Randolph in the country; the son was at first unwilling to meet Churchill, who had left his father's party. But once they did meet they found each other: 'from that hour our friendship was perfect. It was one of my most precious possessions. It was never disturbed by the fiercest party fighting. It was never marred by the slightest personal difference or misunderstanding.'[38] Thus Churchill on that famous friendship. There was much else they shared too, the amenities, the pleasures, the excitements of life; those gay festive Christmases at Blenheim.

Now these younger men made their first attempt to bring their elders together. It is significant that Lloyd George and Balfour were willing. It was the second-rate who were not, in particular that very uninspiring man, Bonar Law, shortly to be leader of the Conservative party. A man of no imagination, he always had a rooted objection to Churchill.[39] It would have saved a great deal

38. The Earl of Birkenhead, *Frederick Edwin, Earl of Birkenhead*, I. 11.
39. Robert Blake, *The Unknown Prime Minister*, 55–6.

of bitterness, avoided many hazards, if only the parties could have come together to face them. Again and again in the mounting tension over Ireland – Home Rule, Ulster, Curragh and the whole dangerous road – Churchill made attempts across the party-barriers to achieve a settlement by coalition and agreement. They were always rejected until, during the war, the Conservatives made their own terms, the first of which was that Churchill should be kept out. He was their prime victim.

Meanwhile, at the Home Office 1910–11, he threw himself into his new job with characteristic zest. Wilfrid Blunt paid him tribute in an unexpected quarter. The old socialist leader Hyndman brought Blunt the information from Bebel and the socialist leaders in Germany that the dominant forces there meant aggression, and that war could not be prevented since German democracy was really powerless. This had no effect on Blunt in his comfortable Sussex squire's ivory-tower. Hyndman, who was in favour of compulsory military training in England, went on to ask about Churchill, of whom he had heard nothing good. Blunt told him that 'there were three things of value in him, great ability, honesty in politics, and a good heart'.[40]

Warmth of heart was evident in the enthusiasm with which he embarked at once on prison reform, calling for the programme Blunt had put forward, usefully for once, and himself making a tour of the prisons. He was moved by the number of boys in prison, with nothing of the criminal type about them and incarcerated for nothing much. It was scandalous that so many of them should be there, often for merely sleeping out: a way to create criminals. Where previous Home Secretaries had been content to administer the system as it was, Churchill, with his instinct for action, got powers to reform it. Blunt was pleased with him: 'he is quite thorough about the reforms and said he would have liked to adopt the whole of my programme only public opinion was not yet ready for it'. One reason why he wanted a coalition to deal with the House of Lords issue and end the interminable chaffer about it was to get on with the practical job of alleviating misery. 'If we could only get it shunted,' he would say to Masterman, 'think of all we could do: boy prisoners, truck,

40. Blunt, 707, 709.

feeble-minded.'[41] Eddie Marsh tells us that Churchill went to see Galsworthy's play *Justice* and was moved by it. Lady Randolph gave a dinner to bring them together. All not without its effect: Churchill got his powers enacted to initiate the modern era of prison reform. The pity is that no successor of similar courage and calibre has appeared in that office to carry the campaign to its proper conclusion and remove the most indefensible derogation from justice in this country, bringing it into accord with civilized standards in other countries.

When Churchill went down to stay with Blunt that autumn, 'he was dressed in a little close-fitting fur-collared jacket, tight leggings and gaiters, and a little round hat, which, with his half-mischievous face, made him look the exact figure of Puck'.[42] But he 'is going on energetically about prison reform, and will push it much beyond what he has already announced publicly. He means to arrange matters so that next year there will be 50,000 fewer people sent to prison than this year.' Someone else in conversation with him discovered the anguish the consideration of death-sentences – the most distasteful part of the Home Secretary's duties – cost him.

Other duties there were in plenty. Two celebrated affairs, Tonypandy and the Battle of Sidney Street, cost him much unpopularity and some obloquy. As the result of a strike in South Wales one district became greatly disturbed and there were riots. He might have moved in troops, as the Conservative party demanded; he contented himself with moving in a large number of Metropolitan police, keeping the troops in reserve. Order was preserved, and the general in charge attributed it entirely to these dispositions, which were Churchill's own idea. But this added unpopularity with Labour people, especially among the miners, to that which he already enjoyed with the Conservatives.

Nor was his own idea, of taking part in the Battle of Sidney Street, altogether a happy one. The trouble was that he could not keep away from trouble. Some suspicious Eastern European characters, who were armed, had barricaded themselves in a house in the East End and killed several of the police trying to round them up. It was thought that they were Anarchists; it is

41. L. Masterman, 176. 42. Blunt, 735.

certain that they were burglars. At any rate the Home Secretary in fur-lined coat and top hat, went down to the East End to have a look and could not resist conducting siege-operations. Unfortunately he was photographed in various attitudes and even appeared on cinema-reels. This was more than the conventional and respectable could stand in those days. The new king, George V, took exactly the same line as his father or grandmother would have done: what was a Cabinet minister doing down there in such a position, peeping round corners among the bullets? Mr Balfour asked a sarcastic question in the Commons. 'We are concerned to observe photographs in the illustrated newspapers of the Home Secretary in the danger-zone. I understand what the photographer was doing, but why the Home Secretary?' When he got back from the scene of action there was an irate civil servant to chide him for his misdemeanour. 'What the hell have you been doing now, Winston?' said Masterman, bursting into the Minister's room. '*Now* Charlie,' said the Minister with his imitable lisp. 'Don't be croth. It was such fun.'[43]

It must have been irresistible to serve such a Minister, who had the heart of a boy.

II

In the summer of 1911 Germany precipitated a dangerous crisis upon Europe, with the Agadir incident, which clearly foreshadowed the outbreak of war three years later. It seems clear that the Germans did not intend the war at that moment: their preparations were not yet complete, the widening of the Kiel Canal, to enable them to pass their fleet to and from the North Sea and the Baltic, would not be finished until August 1914. Their action in dispatching a cruiser to Agadir to assert their (largely non-existent) interests in Morocco was really to test the ground. Since their last similar action in 1906 they had forced a stinging defeat upon Russia, by supporting Austria's annexation of Slav Bosnia-Herzegovina. The result of that was that no Russian government could accept a further defeat at the hands of the Germans, and the Russians came to an understanding with

43. L. Masterman, 184.

Britain, compromising their differences. Now, since the Germans understood nothing in diplomacy save blackmail and bullying, this was to be put to the test of force.

The reaction surprised them. The Anglo-Russian Entente survived the shock and was strengthened by it, as the Anglo-French Entente had been in 1906. Holstein, the malign *éminence grise* of the Wilhelmstrasse – a man even more obtuse than Bülow and far more psychotic – believed that Britain would break any agreement she had entered into rather than be entangled in a Continental war. Those Radical and Pacifist elements in Britain did a grave disservice to peace, therefore, who gave him ground for thinking so. The unmistakable German threat shocked the more sensible among these elements into sense for the moment. Above all their leader, Lloyd George, whose underlying patriotism was stronger than the illusions he entertained. His Mansion House speech was a direct warning to the Germans that Britain would not purchase peace from them at any price and would defend her vital interests.

Churchill tells us that this came

> as a thunder-clap to the German government. All their information had led them to believe that Mr Lloyd George would head the peace-party and that British action would be neutralized. Jumping from one extreme to another, they now assumed that the British Cabinet was absolutely united, and that the Chancellor of the Exchequer of all others had been deliberately selected as the most Radical Minister by the British government to make this pronouncement.[44]

So like their clumsy stupidity, we may add, for the predominant sentiment of this Liberal government was pacific until it was overwhelmed by events in 1914.

Winston Churchill was among those who received a salutary shock and, being a sensible man, the impression remained. He was no longer to be found among those hampering the efforts of Grey at the Foreign Office, Haldane at the War Office, McKenna at the Admiralty, who were working to defend their country against a growing danger. He had hitherto been Lloyd George's closest associate in social reform and economy on the services;

44. W. S. Churchill, *The World Crisis* (1938 ed.), I. 33.

he had not been concerned with foreign affairs or defence. Henceforth he saw how the facts lay: the aggressive threat to Europe and ourselves constituted by Germany, the overriding necessity to prepare ourselves. This did not mean that he passed over to the aggressive. As to this we have the best testimony, that of Grey. Churchill

> followed the anxieties of the Foreign Office with intense interest. ... He followed all the diplomacy closely, but never either in Council or in conversation with me did he urge an aggressive line. It was only that his high-mettled spirit was exhilarated by the air of crisis and high events. His companionship was a great refreshment.[45]

The days had passed when Grey could regret chaffingly that the young Winston 'would soon be incapable of any post in the Cabinet but that of Prime Minister from sheer excess of mental energy'. The weary Foreign Secretary, longing for the country delights, the coolness of Fallodon in that hot summer in London, was grateful for the support of his younger colleague with all his superabundant energy. In the afternoons, after the anxieties of the day, they would go down to the Automobile Club together, where 'he would cool his ardour and I revive my spirits in the swimming-bath'.

That autumn – the immediate crisis over, the ultimate collision ever more certain – the Prime Minister saw fit to harness that dynamo of energy to the Admiralty. Asquith asked Churchill if he would like to become First Lord – actually a lower grade in the ministerial hierarchy. He answered, 'Indeed, I would'. It was a momentous task that he undertook, and at such an hour. For the whole security of Great Britain and the Empire, the existence of her people, then depended entirely on the Navy; and there is no doubt that the Navy needed to be revivified, brought up to date, magnetized, given new ideas. No one need doubt the courage, the unquestioning devotion of the senior fighting service from top to bottom of its ranks, but its very ascendancy for over a century had encrusted it with tradition, clogged it with conservatism, getting in the way of new methods proper to an increasingly technical age.

45. Viscount Grey of Fallodon, *Twenty Five Years, 1892–1916*, I. 238.

Sir John Fisher, who was First Sea Lord 1907–10, had already tackled the task and brought about tremendous changes. An extraordinary man of near-genius, who apprehended all the demands of a machine-age and envisaged revolutionary solutions to new problems – the essential factor of speed, gunnery of a quite different order of magnitude, the development of submarines and naval aircraft – he had been responsible for the introduction of the modern battleship, which had temporarily jeopardized our naval superiority and given the Germans a more equal chance. Fisher's work had demanded a superhuman effort and had been done at great cost: it divided the Navy from top to bottom; it created feuds and maddened Fisher. Moreover, when he retired on reaching seventy in 1910, it was not yet half done: the reconstruction of the Navy was but in its beginnings. Churchill writes, with magnanimity considering what ultimately happened between them in the fires of war:

> there is no doubt whatever that Fisher was right in nine-tenths of what he fought for. His great reforms sustained the power of the Royal Navy at the most critical period of its history. He gave the Navy the kind of shock which the British Army received at the time of the South African war. . . . But the Navy was not a pleasant place while this was going on. . . . Fisher was maddened by the difficulties and obstructions which he encountered, and became violent in the process of fighting so hard at every step.[46]

Churchill wished to bring back Fisher to carry forward the policy he had initiated; but though this proved impossible till the war came, he kept constant contact with the old sea-officer, whom he found 'a veritable volcano of knowledge and of inspiration; and as soon as he learnt what my main purpose was, he passed into a state of vehement eruption'. Thus began the famous unofficial partnership which ended so miserably under the stress of war. Years before they had taken to each other: when on a Mediterranean cruise in 1907 King Edward had found them 'most amusing together. I call them the "chatterers".'[47] The old Sea-Lord had found the young Minister keen to fight his battles for him: 'it was rather sweet: he said his perchant for me was that I painted with a

46. Churchill, op. cit., I. 54–5. 47. Lee, op. cit., II. 534.

big brush!'[48] Now it was from the astonishing old bachelor-Admiral who had found in the civilian head of the Admiralty a favourite son: 'Yours to a cinder', 'Yours till Hell freezes', etc. The day came between them when it did freeze.

Churchill's main purpose, and what he was sent to the Admiralty to accomplish, was to bring the Navy up to war-standard and the highest fighting efficiency in time of peace, when more than half the government and its supporters would hardly recognize the necessity or the reality of the danger. (Left Liberals always preferred to accept the information coming from German sources to their own government's.[49]) Churchill was therefore fighting on two fronts: on the naval front to bring it up to fighting form, on the political to get supplies to carry out his task. He was the man to do it, and no doubt that was why Asquith had replaced McKenna by him. There was a cetain irony in that Churchill had opposed McKenna's programme of dreadnoughts a few years before: McKenna had no love for Churchill after that; for his part Churchill never bore him any ill will. Asquith evidently appreciated that the Navy needed his dynamism.

The first necessity was the creation of a navy war staff – something parallel to the organization that Haldane was engaged in working out for the Army. Along with this went the necessity for co-ordinating plans for sending the British Expeditionary Force to France on the outbreak of war. Admiral Wilson, who had succeeded Fisher as First Sea-Lord, did not see the need for either of these, and shortly he went. For his Naval Secretary Churchill took – contrary to advice – Beatty, the youngest flag officer, whom he had met years before at Omdurman. There was general agreement about promoting Jellicoe, the cleverest of the Admirals, over the heads of several of those senior to him, to take supreme command when war came.

Thus equipped and supported, Churchill gave himself up to the crucial task in preparing England's defences for war. Always placable himself, he insisted on the absolute cessation of the vendetta Fisher had started. His policy was in the main Fisher's policy without his methods. But there was not time enough to carry through the titanic task to anything like the perfection

48. Lord Fisher, *Memories*, 183. 49. Woodward, op. cit., 243.

demanded by the technique of modern war: hence 'many untoward events' later. 'At least fifteen years of consistent policy were required to give the Royal Navy that widely extended outlook upon war-problems and of war-situations without which seamanship, gunnery, instrumentalisms of every kind, devotion of the highest order, could not achieve their due reward. Fifteen years! And we were only to have thirty months!'[50]

Thus began a new life of intense, and as usual single-minded, concentration upon a fresh subject. We may easily suppose that, new as he was to naval matters, they appealed more deeply to his nature than social reform. The main axis of his life's interest, whether as subaltern, Minister in his prime or Prime Minister, called back to office or in retirement, as historian or statesman, in action or in the bulk of his writing, has always been war, or in other words, the country's defence.

Eight months of every year were now spent afloat, inspecting naval bases, dockyards, ships, establishments, in the Admiralty yacht *Enchantress*. This was really a miniature liner of 4,000 tons with a Board Room, a good cellar and plenty of accommodation for guests, naval, political or simply social. Admiral Beatty could not bear these trips: he preferred to be either at sea with the Fleet, or else in the hunting-field.[51] Or perhaps he found it hard – like Brooke later – to support the unceasing battery of what Baldwin called 'Winston's 100 horse-power mind'; for he now talked nothing but the Sea and the Navy, forcing Beatty to think out every aspect of a naval war with Germany and perpetually discussing its problems. Elderly Asquith, who sometimes came on these excursions and whose mind was more cultivated than warlike, was to be found peaceably reading Baedeker with comments to an appreciative circle. So too Eddie, who says in his engaging way that in 1911 'we moved to the Admiralty', which he found the most agreeable of all their offices together; he records with enthusiasm those Whitsun cruises to inspect Gibraltar, Malta and anything else worth inspecting – Paestum, Spalato, Ragusa, Corfu.

In 1912 they were brought smartly to attention by the new

50. Churchill, I. 70.

51. W. S. Chalmers, *Life and Letters of David, Earl Beatty*, 112.

German Navy Law, providing for 'an extraordinary increase in the striking force of ships of all classes immediately available'.[52] Even the socialists in the Reichstag did not dare to oppose. Commenting on this aggressive measure Churchill said, 'the purposes of British naval power are essentially defensive. . . . The British Navy is to us a necessity and, from some points of view, the German Navy is to them more in the nature of a luxury.' This reflection provoked a storm of abuse in Germany – all the usual symptoms of their psychotic state. Haldane had been sent on a mission to Berlin to see if some agreement could not be reached on reduction of naval armaments. In the course of the discussion the Kaiser handed him the new naval programme. The unspeakable Tirpitz commented on his departure, 'after Haldane's visit, when our extravagant desire for an understanding led the English to believe for a time that they could treat us like Portugal, the government in London refused an agreement on neutrality'.[53]

In all the negotiations and discussions raised by the Liberal government to stop the race in naval armaments, the German demand was always the same: that England should remain neutral in a Continental war. In other words, that Germany should have a free hand in Europe to crush France and deal with Russia – leaving us to confront a German-controlled Europe. How could they suppose that we should be such fools? (Under the able conduct of our affairs before 1914 there was no likelihood of that; under the disgraceful conduct of our affairs in the 1930s we very nearly arrived at just that – only succeeded in extricating ourselves by the war of 1939, which the whole course of our action, or rather inaction, had brought upon us.)

The Liberal government's reply to the failure to get agreement was immediate and right: a speeding up and an increase of building, 'a maintenance of naval superiority known to be a matter of life and death to an island power, dependent upon imported foodstuffs'.[54] A further measure of immense importance which was decided on Churchill's Mediterranean cruise this year was an agreement with the French by which they concentrated their Navy in the Mediterranean, while we concentrated ours in

52. Churchill, I. 76–8. 53. q. Harold Nicolson, *King George V*, 194.
54. Woodward, 11.

the North Sea. That this was the consequence of his policy seems to have been lost on the ineffable Tirpitz, who wrote, even after the war should have opened his eyes: 'in order to estimate the strength of the trump-card which our fleet put in the hands of an energetic diplomacy at this time, one must remember that in consequence of the concentration of the English forces which we had caused in the North Sea, the English control of the Mediterranean and Far Eastern waters had practically ceased'.[55] Churchill expresses himself astonished at such incomprehension. Later, Tirpitz considers that 'seventeen years of fleet-building had, it is true, improved the prospects of an acceptable peace with England'. Churchill describes him as 'a sincere, wrong-headed, purblind old Prussian': one might equally well describe him as a crazy lunatic, if he had not been characteristic of the ruling forces in Germany.

The truth is obvious: nothing would stop them. The occult forces that ruled in Germany, the General Staff, Army and Navy – to whom the Kaiser was but a vain posturing mascot, with his fatuous letters to the Czar addressed from 'the Admiral of the Atlantic to the Admiral of the Pacific' – were determined on their all-out throw for *Weltmacht*. To think that a great nation's affairs should have been governed by such people! – many millions of simple good fellows perished because of it in the twentieth century and all our lives been darkened. Whole libraries of books have been and continue to be written on the origins of the war of 1914–18 or that of 1939–45. We really do not need to waste much time on them: the origins are perfectly clear, the determination of Germany's ruling forces, backed by most of the nation, to ride rough-shod over everybody else and achieve world power at whatever cost. Churchill sums up the situation completely though briefly:

> to create the unfavourable conditions for herself in which Germany afterwards brought about the war, many acts of supreme unwisdom on the part of her rulers were necessary. France must be kept in a state of continued apprehension. The Russian nation must be stung by some violent affront inflicted in their hour of weakness. The slow, deep, restrained antagonism of the British Empire must be roused by the

55. Churchill, I. 86–9.

continuous and repeated challenge to the sea-power by which it lived. Then and then only could those conditions be created under which Germany by an act of aggression would bring into being against her a combination strong enough to resist and ultimately to overcome her might.[56]

The German outbreaks against the peace of the world were continuous, two waves of the same movement. This passage relating to the war of 1914 may stand also for that of 1939 – except that the ineptitude of Baldwin and Chamberlain converted the unfavourable conditions for Germany in 1914 to favourable conditions in 1939; and where the methods of the Kaiser's Germany were those of bullying and blackmail, those of Hitler's Germany were criminal, of a bestiality hardly imaginable which yet must not be forgotten.

Churchill stuck to his job with all the energy of which he was capable: we may say that upon him and his work in these years rested the safety of the nation. 'The stakes were very high. If our naval defence were maintained we were safe and sure beyond the lot of any other European nation; if it failed, our doom was certain and final.'[57] From 1912 was carried through the conversion of the fleet from coal-burning to oil-burning, greatly increasing speed and mobility. In 1913 he twice made proposals for a 'naval holiday' to Germany. No response, save the ingenuous offer from Tirpitz of a ratio of construction which would have the effect of lowering 'the margin which the Admiralty had announced as necessary for British security'.[58] The alternative was the three programmes of 1912, 1913 and 1914, 'which comprised the greatest additions in power and cost ever made to the Royal Navy. . . . All through 1912 and 1913 our efforts were unceasing.'[59] By 1914 even Tirpitz was ready to acknowledge that Germany could not out-build Britain; he went so far as to urge that any further increase in the German Navy would be 'a great political blunder'.[60] The acknowledgement made nonsense of all his work, the whole course upon which he had led since 1900.

Impossible here even to sum up in detail the work Churchill

56. ibid., 13. 57. ibid., 116. 58. Woodward, 406.
59. Churchill, I. 102, 104. 60. Woodward, 431.

accomplished in those few years at the Admiralty – and unnecessary since he has described it himself: we may more usefully cite the impression it made upon a privileged observer, the King's confidant. Lord Esher began by expressing doubts as to his appointment as First Lord. He thought that he would have only one eye on the Navy, 'the other on the Radical tail'.[61] He very soon revised his opinion when he saw that Churchill meant business about the formation of a Naval Staff: 'the most pregnant reform which has been carried out at the Admiralty since the days of Lord St Vincent. . . . It is bound to have far-reaching results not only as regards the Navy but as regards our whole national and Imperial methods of preparing for war.' Lord Esher, who was himself a member of the Committee of Imperial Defence, expressed himself delighted with the details of Churchill's scheme. Later he wrote to Fisher, 'you must have been mightily pleased with Winston. He has done splendidly. It was a hard job for him too. What a tragedy it would be if this government were to be displaced by Bonar Law & Co.'

As to that we need not be in much doubt.

Churchill's intense preoccupation with the Navy did not mean that other things stood still. Within the country, too, events were moving to a grave crisis. Not for many years had there been such bitterness of party-spirit – the Churchills found themselves proscribed from many houses where they had formerly been welcome; once, after an attack on her friend Mrs Asquith, Mrs Churchill packed her bags and left Blenheim. Fortunately there was always the variegated and eccentric hospitality of Wilfrid Blunt's Sussex home. In October 1912 Churchill was there there with George Wyndham and began a political argument that went on from teatime all through dinner till midnight.

It was a fine night, and we dined in the bungalow, dressed in gorgeous Oriental garments, Clementine in a suit of embroidered silk, purchased last year in Smyrna, Winston in one of my Baghdad robes, George in a blue dressing gown, and I in my Bedouin robes. . . . Winston was very brilliant, and though he kept on at the madeira he also kept his head, and played with George's wild rushes like a skilled fencer with a greatly

61. Lord Esher, op. cit., III. 74, 77, 85.

superior fence. He is certainly an astonishing young man, and has gained immensely within the last two years in character and intellectual grip.[62]

This was a tribute coming from such a source, for Blunt was a pro-German along with his other fatuous fads; it was even more evidence of his tolerance that Winston could put up with him.

The Home Rule Bill brought party-dissension to a feverish pitch. Actually within the Cabinet Lloyd George and Churchill urged some measure of exclusion for Protestant Ulster. At Blenheim that summer of 1912 there was a big Unionist demonstration, attended by Bonar Law, F. E. Smith and Carson, with a hundred and twenty M.P.s and forty peers. The Unionist leader had the ill-judgement to appeal to force: 'in our opposition we shall not be guided by the considerations or bound by the restraints which would influence us in an ordinary constitutional struggle. . . . I can imagine no length of resistance to which Ulster can go in which I should not be prepared to support them.'[63] No wonder such a constitutionalist as Asquith had such a contempt for Bonar Law: this came very near to inciting the country to civil war. There were disorderly scenes in the Commons, such as have never been seen since; in one of them an Ulster M.P. hurled a book with accuracy and force at Churchill's head.

Yet Churchill remained a moderate. He maintained his friendship with F. E. Smith, in spite of the latter's extreme pro-Ulster stand. When Asquith wished to approach the Tories to see if some agreement were not possible, he used Churchill. It was only when Carson rejected Asquith's conciliatory offers that Churchill sent the 3rd Battle Squadron of the Fleet to Lamlash: a warning to Belfast. The unity of the United Kingdom was in danger of dissolution when the war broke out. Churchill had addressed a direct appeal to Carson: 'foreign countries never really understand us in these islands. They do not know what we know, that at a touch of external difficulties or menace all these fierce internal controversies would disappear for the time being, and we should be brought into line and into tune.'[64]

62. Blunt, op. cit., 812.
63. R. Blake, *The Unknown Prime Minister*, 130.
64. Churchill, I. 149.

Germans could hardly be expected to understand that, and perhaps it would not have mattered if they had. For their intention was already certain. The historian of these years tells us, 'it is clear that in January 1913 a decision was there [at Berlin] taken, that war between the Triple and Dual Alliances had become inevitable, and that Germany's business was to prepare for it instantly and bring it about when she was ready – in her time, not her enemies'. . . . Who made the decision at Berlin? The General Staff. There are reasons for thinking that from the inception the date worked towards was the beginning of August 1914.'[65] Herr Ballin, the distinguished head of the Hamburg–Amerika line, who knew opinion in England and America well, has left on record his conviction that 'even a moderately skilled German diplomatist could easily have come to an understanding with England and France, which could have made peace certain'.[66] When the full fatality of his people's atavistic impulses came home to him, the great shipping magnate sought a way out in suicide: an eloquent comment on the whole course upon which they were bent.

In England the situation was very different. Though the Conservatives were staunch – as they were not on the renewal of the menace in the thirties – they did not reciprocate Churchill's wish for a coalition to conduct the war. The Liberal Cabinet was overwhelmingly pacific: it looked at one time as if the majority would resign rather than do their duty and resist Germany. 'Nothing less than the deeds of Germany', says Churchill, 'would have converted the British nation to war.'[67] The delay meanwhile was agonizing to those who knew all that depended on it: above all to Grey, who knew the extent of our moral obligation to France, who fully realized what our own fate would be if we did not resist, and yet the hope of whose life, the maintenance of European peace, lay now in ruins.

The invasion of Belgium, the evident determination to smash France, resolved all doubts. The greatest of all Grey's services to his country was, ironically for such a man of peace, to have

65. R. C. K. Ensor, *England, 1870–1914*, 469–70.
66. Churchill, I. 158.
67. ibid.. 165.

brought the nation united into the war. He could at last speak all his mind to the Commons:

when he came to deal with the Belgian question, it became apparent for the first time that almost the whole House approved. The news that 'they have cheered him' was carried to the Foreign Office, causing inexpressible relief to those who knew better than the public that if we stood arguing together on the verge of war the Germans would be in Paris in a few weeks and England left shamed, friendless and foredoomed.[68]

Somehow, in reading of those days, it makes one weep – to think of all that was involved in it, our very existence, the nation unaware, the struggle Grey had had, all he had gone through. That night, as the lamps were being lit in the Park, Grey stood at the window of his room and said to a friend, 'the lamps are going out all over Europe; we shall not see them lit again in our life-time'. Nor, in a sense, have they ever been.

By good fortune, in those last days of July the fleet was mobilized on a war-footing at the conclusion of its summer manoeuvres. With anyone else than Churchill at the Admiralty it might have been dispersed in accordance with routine. In that last week on his own responsibility he kept it together. The outbreak of war found the strategic concentration of the Fleet in the North Sea accomplished, no longer open to the hazards of such a move. Grey himself, in quiet reflective fashion, recognizes the immense service that this was:

it was an accident that the end of the naval manoeuvres coincided with the diplomatic stage of a foreign crisis; the fact that full advantage was taken of this good fortune was due to the vigour and alertness of Churchill. . . . Undoubtedly the country owes much also to Churchill for the great advantage that war found us with a strong Fleet in an exceptionally good state of preparation.[69]

When, in the course of the disappointments and frustrations of the war, the Tories got their revenge upon Churchill for the years between, his old opponent Kitchener paid him the most moving of compliments, that which went most to his heart: 'there is one thing at any rate they cannot take from you: the Fleet was ready'.

68. G. M. Trevelyan, *Grey of Fallodon*, 265–6.
69. Grey, *Twenty-Five Years*, II. 64.

Chapter 13

The First World War

THERE is a revealing phrase that appears first in a letter Churchill wrote to Grey in the distress of the Dardanelles operations, and that would recur again and again at critical junctures in the second German war – adjuring him not to 'fall below the level of events'.[1] (The letter was not sent, for Grey never did.) The phrase is a clue to the man: it springs out of a rare imaginative perception of the historical quality of events as they are proceeding; further, it implies a duty not to be unworthy of them, to play one's part to the full. There goes along with this a willing acceptance of responsibility, unhampered by any unworthy preoccupation with the consequences to oneself. Churchill tells that he interpreted his duty as the head of the Admiralty before and in the first war thus: 'I accepted full responsibility for bringing about successful results, and in that spirit I exercised an unlimited power of suggestion and initiative over the whole field, subject only to the approval and agreement of the First Sea Lord on all operative orders'.[2]

What a contrast to the spirit of the men who were all-powerful in the thirties, whose main preoccupation, so far from being not to fall below the level of events, was to see that they did not fall out of office themselves! It is odd, considering the intellectual inferiority of their conduct of our affairs, they *they* should have thought themselves so indispensable. On the other hand, they could have observed the consequences to Churchill in his own career of his simple, rash and honest acceptance of responsibility. These men were cleverer, where their own interests were concerned; for we shall see that when things went wrong Churchill, with his *naïveté* of spirit and the unpopularity that genius often arouses, was made to bear the brunt of it, readily, enjoyably, vindictively.

1. Churchill, *The World Crisis*, I. 622. 2. ibid., 195.

The war began with the Germans, according to plan, overrunning Belgium, threatening to overwhelm France and making for the Channel ports to cut communications with Britain. The British Expeditionary Force – a solid, compact, efficient little army of six divisions, which had been built up by the able work of Haldane at the War Office – was in France, transported by the Navy without a single loss. As the Belgian forts fell with astonishing rapidity and the Channel ports were uncovered, Sir John French sent a despairing message to fortify Havre. Kitchener himself brought it over to Churchill at the Admiralty: 'I forgot much of what passed between us. But the apparition of Kitchener *Agonistes* in my doorway will dwell with me as long as I live. It was like seeing old John Bull on the rack!'[3]

Churchill considered himself 'sufficiently instructed to derive an immense refreshment of judgement from personal investigation'; in other words, he could not keep away from the scene of action, and the First Lord of the Admiralty crossed over to make a tour of the front that appeared to be crumbling.[4] Driven round by the Duke of Westminster, he witnessed the scenes 'that were afterwards to become commonplace: but their first aspect was thrilling'. As the German lunge threatened to envelop Antwerp he saw the strategic necessity to intervene and arrest it, if at all possible. For Antwerp was not only all that was left for a nucleus of Belgian national resistance, it was the true linch-pin of the Allied front. If a line from Antwerp to Lille could only have been held, it might have shortened the war by many months and many thousands of lives.

In this fearful emergency any action that offered a chance of staving off the disaster was worth trying – and Churchill was not thinking of reputation at such a moment. 'There is always a strong case for doing nothing, especially for doing nothing yourself.'[5] He was ready to go over at a few hours' notice, with what could be got together of a naval division and a few naval guns, to throw himself into Antwerp in the path of the oncoming Germans. But it was no Omdurman over again: these were a different sort of barbarian hordes, highly trained and technical, with vastly superior equipment, masters of the

3. Churchill, *The World Crisis*, I. 221. 4. ibid., 235. 5. ibid., 306.

art of modern war, inspired by the belief that the proper end of society is to make war.

> I now found myself suddenly, unexpectedly and deeply involved in a tremendous and hideously critical local situation which might well continue for some time. I had also assumed a very direct responsibility for exposing the city to bombardment and for bringing into it the inexperienced, partially equipped and partially trained battalions of the Royal Naval Division. I felt it my duty to see the matter through.[6]

The matter did not continue more than five days: there was no resisting the overwhelming forces the Germans brought to bear and which it was not realized they would have at their disposal. Meanwhile, the First Lord of the Admiralty was away from his post. It was not wise: 'no doubt had I been ten years older, I should have hesitated long before accepting so unpromising a task'. People said it was like the battle of Sidney Street over again. When Antwerp fell it was remembered against him; he would be made to smart for his gallant attempt to save it. Meanwhile, we may record at this moment of dejection his own golden rule in warfare: never to acquiesce in the will of the enemy, but to seek always to impose your will on him.

Other events came, through no fault of his own, to impair his authority. There was the torpedoing of the three old cruisers, *Aboukir*, *Cressy* and *Hogue*, while on patrol. It was true that they should not have been on patrol; but it was not Churchill's business to interfere with the routine operations of ships. Actually orders had been issued to withdraw them; before these were received the disaster had occurred. People then said that the First Lord had overridden the advice of the Admirals and sent the squadron to its fate. Next came the torpedoing of the *Audacious*. The British public has always been more sensitive to losses of ships than to any other losses in war. The indignation with which these sinkings were regarded partly reflects the over-confidence engendered by a century's complete security at sea: the public somehow expected the Navy to conduct war without breaking any of its ships. Losses had not yet come to be seen as in the nature of war: the public mind was still that of peace-

6. Churchill, *The World Crisis*, I. 316, 322.

time – and this was a factor in frustrating what should have been the grandest and most original contribution towards winning the war: the Dardanelles campaign. No credit accrued for successful actions, like that of the Heligoland Bight, or for the fundamental operation of bringing the Fleet up to its highest strength and efficiency: that was taken for granted, simply expected.

These untoward events coincided with a shocking press-campaign against Prince Louis of Battenberg, the admirable sailor who was First Sea Lord, on account of his German origin.[7] Prince Louis resigned and Churchill decided to do what he had wanted to do four years before and bring back Fisher, now aged seventy-four. King George V regarded this appointment with the utmost misgivings and appealed to Asquith to prevent it.[8] The King knew from experience the politics of the Navy and the distrust aroused by the personality of Fisher, who had risen from small beginnings and antagonized many people of social position and influence. Churchill overrode these objections: he held Fisher to be the greatest naval officer since Nelson; the Admiralty needed strengthening, and so did his own position. The old man came back, as full of energy, ideas and resource as ever. The unofficial liaison was regularized, so to speak. Since Fisher worked best in the early hours of the morning and Churchill worked far into the night, they made 'very nearly a perpetual clock', in Fisher's words.[9] He also said, referring to Churchill's minutes in red ink and his own in green, that they were 'the port and starboard lights'. Churchill comments, 'we had established a combination which, while it remained unbroken, could not have been overthrown by intrigue at home or the foe on the sea'. Alas, the day came when the combination ended in a fierce explosion, as was Fisher's way: it ended his career and brought Churchill's star plunging downwards into the night of exclusion from conduct of the war and even from office, relegating him to fighting in France, at his own desire, one of the hundreds of thousands of British soldiers now engulfed there.

7. Father of Admiral Earl Mountbatten and great-uncle of Prince Philip.
8. Harold Nicolson, *King George V*, 251–2.
9. Churchill, op. cit., I. 363.

It was all over the Dardanelles campaign, for the failure of which, since he was its initiator and whole inspiration, he was made the victim.

This abortive campaign, indeed the very conception of it, was for long the subject of acute controversy and a considerable literature has grown up about it. We cannot go into that here, and there is the less reason for doing so since there is now a definitive account of it in Mr Alan Moorehead's *Gallipoli*. For long it was regarded as a reckless gamble and Churchill, by implication, as the gambler. Then, when out of office after the war, he wrote *The World Crisis*, a large part of which was occupied by the issue; and this book had the rather rare effect of reversing opinion and vindicating himself. A conception, a project, a campaign that has the united judgement behind it of both Churchill and Attlee, who fought in it as a young officer, can hardly be regarded as unsound. Moorehead regards it as 'the most imaginative conception of the war, and its potentialities were almost beyond reckoning. It might even have been regarded, as Rupert Brooke had hoped, as a turning point in history.'[10]

The poet's imaginative perception was correct. The campaign certainly was a turning-point of the war: if it had succeeded, the war might well have been shortened by a year or two. It was no less a turning-point in history: success at that point would have saved Russia from defeat and perhaps from so extremist a Revolution with its malign consequences for millions of human beings. Moorehead sums up:

> . . . in its strictly military aspect its influence was enormous. It was the greatest amphibious operation which mankind had known up till then, and it took place in circumstances in which nearly everything was experimental: in the use of submarines and aircraft, in the trial of modern naval guns against artillery on the shore, in the manoeuvre of landing armies in small boats on a hostile coast, in the use of radio, of the aerial bomb, the land mine, and many other novel devices. These things led on through Dunkirk and the Mediterranean landings to the invasion of Normandy in the second world war. . . . Gallipoli was a mine of information about the complexities of the modern war of manoeuvre, of the combined operation by land and sea and sky; and

10. Alan Moorehead, *Gallipoli*, 364.

the correction of the errors made then was the basis of the victory of 1945. The next time, as Kitchener had once hoped, 'they got it right'.

This was no consolation to the men who endured the experience at the time. Still less to the man whose most cherished project it was, upon which rested his hopes of a speedy ending to the war, of imposing our initiative upon the enemy at a favourable point instead of allowing things inertly to settle down to a ghastly war of attrition. When Roger Keyes after the war steamed through the Dardanelles, which he had been prevented by his seniors in command from attempting to force, he was beside himself with emotion: 'My God, it would have been even easier than I thought; we simply *couldn't* have failed ... and because we didn't try, another million lives were thrown away and the war went on for another three years.'[11] For Churchill there was all the agony of watching things being mismanaged on the spot, of everything going wrong, himself trying to influence operations from afar at the Admiralty without being in command – thus exposing himself to being held responsible for the failure of others. And this was in fact what came about.

When Turkey came into the war, the plan at first was to rush the Dardanelles by a naval attack while they were weakly defended. Old battleships, which were anyway due to be scrapped in a few months, could be profitably expended in bombarding the forts. The Greeks were anxious to co-operate by taking the Gallipoli peninsula in flank. Admiral Carden on the spot was optimistic and put up a plan of operations that was decidedly promising. Churchill took it up and made it his own: here was the one chance of turning Germany's European flank, of making the war mobile instead of settling down to the static holocaust of the Western Front. Churchill got Fisher to agree to the plan, and then persuaded Kitchener on the basis of its being a purely naval operation. He turned his batteries on Cabinet and War Council; Lloyd George witnesses that when Churchill 'has a scheme agitating his powerful mind, as everyone who is acquainted with his method knows quite well, he is indefatigable in pressing it upon the acceptance of everyone who matters in

11. Alan Moorehead, *Gallipoli*, 363.

the decision'.[12] The War Council he carried 'with all the inexorable force and pertinacity, together with the mastery of detail he always commands when he is really interested in a subject'.

From the first everything began to go wrong to a degree hardly exampled in the history of war, even when we remember that all was experimental, ill thought out and ill prepared, in a field of combined operations – sea, land, air, submarine, mines – of which there was as yet no experience to hand and the techniques of which would not be worked out until the second German war. Even so, beyond the normal hazards of war, beyond all the mistakes that were made, the needless confusion created, everything seemed loaded against the operation, down to personal accidents. There is no doubt now that it could have succeeded, *might* have succeeded at a dozen turning-points, if chance had not been always against. This is what makes Gallipoli such sickening, such tragic reading – the heroism and sacrifice of individual men's lives, the confusion, the abdication of leadership at the head, and then every chance turning malign. The brilliant prospects offered by a Greek landing on the Gallipoli flank were vetoed by Russia – the power that stood to gain most from the opening of the Dardanelles, 'failing, reeling backward under the German hammer, with her munitions running short, cut off from her allies'.[13]

Then Admiral Carden, whose plan of a naval attack had been adopted, fell ill. He was succeeded by an incompetent commander, de Roebeck, who never believed in the operations, and after an initial check made scarcely any effort to go on – though the Turks were short of munitions and there were few forces in the peninsula. At home Fisher had never favoured the project: he had a wild scheme of his own for an impossible landing in the Baltic. It became clear that troops would be necessary; Kitchener had got the decision to send them reversed, the transports were countermanded. When at length the need was recognized there ensued weeks of delay, while the Turks, stiffened by Germans, fortified the peninsula under Liman von Sanders. At the Ad-

12. D. Lloyd George, *War Memoirs* (edn 1938), I. 234.
13. Churchill, I. 620.

miralty Churchill was in agony of mind: 'the mere process of landing an army after giving the enemy at least three weeks' additional notice seemed to me to be a most terrible and formidable hazard'.[14]

On the spot de Roebeck abdicated action and put the onus on the Army; the newest and most powerful battleship, *Queen Elizabeth*, which had been added to the armada, never fired a gun. Too late Kitchener undertook to storm the peninsula with the Army – on the assumption that the Navy would exert continuous pressure in support. But the Army was left to flounder and bog down in the sands of Gallipoli, now strongly held and fortified, where so many bleached bones lie. At home

> never again could I marshal the Admiralty War Group and the War Council in favour of resolute action. Never again could I move the First Sea Lord. 'No' had settled down for ever on our councils, crushing with its deadening weight what I shall ever believe was the hope of the world. Vain was it for Admiral de Roebeck a month later, inspired by the ardent Keyes, to offer to renew the naval attack. His hour had passed. I could never lift the 'No' that had descended, and soon I was myself to succumb.[15]

The fighting in the peninsula settled down to as grim a contest of attrition as the Western Front; all hope of mobility, of seizing the initiative, had passed. Even so the battles of July and August narrowly missed victory; just when the Turkish defenders had been worn down and at least were prepared to admit defeat the order for evacuation was sent out. But Churchill had now ceased to have any active part in the decisions.

We cannot here go into the operations, the hopes and despair of those agonizing months: we are concerned with their effect on the personal fortunes of Churchill. He was borne down with them. All the evidence shows, and it is completely in keeping with his character, that his mind was so set upon winning the war that he was hardly aware of the political repercussions going on around him, the undermining of his position. He knew that he was the target of a good many people's hatred. One day before the war he had opened his heart to his old friend Blunt

14. ibid., 647 15. ibid., 668.

on the subject: he bore no one any malice, yet he was the best-hated man in the country, the most mistrusted and traduced. Whatever the reasons for it, and they are complex – some inherent, some fortuitous – he could never command the popularity that came so easily, so unfairly to some men. Not until the country was in mortal danger in 1940, and he in his seventh decade, was this reversed. It is a very strange historical case: the more one thinks of it the stranger it becomes.

Lord Beaverbrook, who was in a position to know, says of this crisis in his fortunes:

> his attitude from August 1914 onwards was a noble one, too noble to be wise. He cared for the success of the British arms, especially in so far as they could be achieved by the Admiralty, and for nothing else. His passion for this aim was pure, self-devoted, and self-devouring. He thought of himself not as holding a certain position in relation to Liberal colleagues and a Tory Opposition, but as a National Minister secure of support from all men of good will.[16]

In short, the war was to him the only issue; he was above party-spirit, he ceased to be a party-man. It was honest, sincere, innocent of him. For he was confronted by people who had no good will for him, especially among the Tories who had never forgiven him for his defection. Now was their opportunity, their chance to get back at him was coming. Beaverbrook says that

> belief in the naval and military experts and intense opposition to Churchill were dominant articles in their creed. Churchill did not understand all this, largely because he shut himself up in the Admiralty and hardly ever went to the House of Commons except as a form. . . . His ambition was in essence disinterested. I do not say that he was always wise – but his patriotism burnt with a pure flame throughout. Hard fighter as he is in debate, he is a man devoid almost of rancour. A defeat does not sour him, even though it depresses him, nor does it turn him into a hater of the successful half of political mankind. And he possesses another virtue – exceptionally rare in politics – or, for that matter, almost anywhere. He is strictly honest and truthful to other people, down to the smallest details of his life.

He was now to find that these virtues are at times disadvantages. His old mentor and comrade, Fisher, turned traitor

16. Lord Beaverbrook, *Politicians and the War, 1914–1916*, I. 131–2.

to him; he not only went over into fierce opposition to the Dardanelles campaign while it was still at its most critical, he got in touch with the Tory Opposition, particularly Bonar Law, its most dangerous opponent and Churchill's personal enemy. Fisher now declared that he could no longer continue as Churchill's colleague and, without himself resigning, pulled down his blinds at the Admiralty and refused to serve at his post. Churchill addressed him a *cri de cœur*:

in order to bring you back to the Admiralty I took my political life in my hands – as you know well. You then promised to stand by me and see me through. If you go now at this bad moment and thereby let loose upon me the spite and malice of those who are your enemies even more than they are mine, it will be a melancholy ending . . .[17]

But the old Admiral insisted. He replied: 'YOU ARE BENT ON FORCING THE DARDANELLES AND NOTHING WILL TURN YOU FROM IT – NOTHING'. This explosion precipitated a Cabinet crisis. Mr Asquith's weakened government was forced to look to the Tories to strengthen itself by a coalition. Absorbed in his own problems, Churchill 'still had no knowledge whatever of the violent political convulsions which were proceeding around me and beneath me'. In the formation of the Coalition in May 1915 the Tories at last got their revenge: they insisted as an absolute condition on Churchill's exclusion from the Admiralty. All his experience there, all the work he had put in at that proud, cherished post were to go by the board. At that moment the news came to him that the German Fleet was coming out: 'the political crisis and my own fate in it passed almost completely out of my mind'.

The moment passed. He was to be excluded. Fisher presented an ultimatum to the government, revealing a state of advanced megalomania, demanding that he should have complete charge of the war at sea, together with the sole disposition of the Fleet and the appointment of all officers of all ranks whatsoever. His resignation was at once accepted. Admiral Wilson, the man whom Churchill had displaced on coming to the Admiralty, was to succeed Fisher as First Sea Lord. Then a strange

17. Churchill, II. 793–4, 797–8.

thing happened. Wilson, whom Churchill had disregarded, had been so much impressed by his work and devotion that he refused to be First Sea Lord under anybody else. Churchill was touched to tears by this testimony at such a point in his fortunes – and from such a quarter.

Lloyd George, who was a prime mover in the formation of the Coalition, hoped to see Churchill placed at the Colonial Office, 'where his energies would have been helpfully employed in organizing our resources in the Empire beyond the seas; and I cannot to this hour explain the change of plans which suddenly occurred'.[18] It seems to have been due not only to Bonar Law's sentence of exclusion but also to a loss of confidence in him on Asquith's part. He was made to take all the blame for the miscarriage of the Dardanelles, which Lloyd George considered as 'due not so much to Mr Churchill's precipitancy as to Lord Kitchener's and Mr Asquith's procrastination'. Churchill was now relegated to the Duchy of Lancaster,

> a post generally reserved either for beginners in the Cabinet or for distinguished politicians who had reached the first stages of unmistakable decrepitude. It was a cruel and unjust degradation. . . . The brutality of the fall stunned Mr Churchill, and for a year or two of the War his fine brain was of no avail in helping in its prosecution.

What the country lost by this we can infer from his adaptability of mind in regard to the techniques of war, when the mentality of the War Office was ossified by stupidity and tradition. Take the case of tanks – a cardinal invention in modern warfare. The War Office never saw the point and simply refused to carry on the experiments that led to their production. While at the Admiralty Churchill took the matter under his wing, though it was no business of his. (If people never ventured beyond their 'own business' the war would have been lost.) He took

> personal responsibility for the expenditure of the public money involved, about £70,000. I did not invite the Board of Admiralty to share this responsibility with me. I did not inform the War Office, for I knew they would raise objections to my interference in this sphere. . . . Neither did I inform the Treasury.[19]

18. Lloyd George, I. 139–42.
19. Churchill, I. 514, 525.

The experiments he had initiated and encouraged went slowly forward, hampered by every obstacle and discouragement in his absence. It took the High Command two years before they first brought a few tanks into action on the Somme. 'This priceless conception, containing if used in its integrity and on a sufficient scale, the certainty of a great and brilliant victory, was revealed to the Germans for the mere petty purpose of taking a few ruined villages.'

Perhaps we may reflect back here to the similar discouragements Marlborough experienced in the conduct of William III's war, the wooden unimaginativeness, the sticking to convention, the static slaughter – and the change that came about with the second war, the mobility, the far better generalship, the mastery. We observe a like contrast between the two wars of our time. And with this goes a further reflection. Churchill's instinct for war has often been suspect, by a confusion of thought, as if there was something inhumane about it. The exact converse is true. A war of manoeuvre and surprise would have been vastly less costly in lives.

> All such ideas had received their quietus. Good, plain, straightforward frontal attacks by valiant flesh and blood against wire and machine-guns, 'killing Germans' while Germans killed Allies twice as often, calling out the men of forty, of fifty, and even of fifty-five, and the youths of eighteen, sending the wounded soldiers back three or four times over into the shambles – such were the sole manifestations now reserved for the military art.[20]

These thoughts run like a recurring knell through Churchill's book, *The World Crisis*. There can be no doubt at all that he was right, nor that his conception of the war was the more humane.

Perhaps the conclusion one must draw from the Dardanelles campaign is that he could not hope to impose his conception without supreme power. His remaining in the government at all in such a humiliating position, after such a stunning fall, was only due to a sense of duty to the men still engaged in Gallipoli, to a desire to help forward in any way he could the operations in their last phase. He remained a member of the War

20. ibid., II. 929.

Committee of the Cabinet and was at first treated with consideration; after all, he had more experience and knowledge of war than any other civilian minister. He continued to press for reinforcements for the peninsula; his desire to go there himself was vetoed. Someone back from Gallipoli who saw him at this time thought he looked years older and very much depressed; at dinner he was dejected and silent, until he burst forth into a long harangue on the subject that obsessed him – into the sympathetic ears of his mother.[21] At the very moment when at last the fleet at the Dardanelles had got a competent commander, Admiral Wemyss, the decision was taken to evacuate. This was under the insistent pressure of Bonar Law, now in a position of decisive power in the government – though no one need suppose that that decent, melancholy, monochrome man had any instinct for war.

With the end of the Dardanelles and the reconstruction of the War Committee to include Bonar Law, Churchill was excluded. There was no place for him in the conduct of the war. He drew his own conclusions, decided 'to relinquish a well-paid sinecure office which I could not bear longer to hold at this sad juncture in our affairs', and go and fight in France.[22] On his resignation speech in the Commons, Bonar Law commented in his undistinguished way,

> I entered the Cabinet, to put it mildly, with no prejudice in favour of the right hon. gentleman. I have now been his colleague for five months. He has the defects of his quality and, as his qualities are large, the shadow which they throw is fairly large too; but I say deliberately, in my judgement, in mental power and vital force he is one of the foremost men in our country, and I am sure that every hon. member of the House wishes him success, and every kind of success in the new sphere in which he is engaged.[23]

These clichés can have given but cold comfort to a man in anguish.

It was in these tormented months that this extraordinary man became a painter – without ever having taken any interest

21. Moorehead, 172. 22. Churchill, II. 915.
23. Robert Blake, *The Unknown Premier*, 272.

in pictures before. But he felt the need for a distraction, an outlet. The sudden change from the intense executive activities of the Admiralty to the sinecure duties of a Chancellor of the Duchy of Lancaster left him gasping.

> Like a sea-beast fished up from the depths, or a diver too suddenly hoisted, my veins threatened to burst from the fall in pressure. I had great anxiety and no means of relieving it; I had vehement convictions and small power to give effect to them. I had to watch the unhappy casting-away of great opportunities, and the feeble execution of plans which I had launched and in which I heartily believed.[24]

Here was painting, an unknown territory in which to advance; after all, it was not unlike a campaign. Eddie Marsh tells us that he swooped upon a shop, and bought up practically the whole stock of easels, canvases, brushes, palettes, tubes. He soon discovered that 'painting a picture is like fighting a battle; and trying to paint a picture is, I suppose, like trying to fight a battle'.

For the first time in his life he seems to have been afflicted with diffidence: there was the canvas extended dauntingly before him, like the empty paper before the incipient writer awaiting the words. He hesitated. He never had any lessons. Lady Lavery bore down upon him, took the brush from his arrested hand.

> Splash into the turpentine, wallop into the blue and white, frantic flourish on the palette – clean no longer – and then several large, fierce strokes and slashes of blue on the absolutely cowering canvas. Anyone could see that it could not hit back. No evil fate avenged the jaunty violence. The canvas grinned in helplessness before me. The spell was broken. The sickly inhibitions rolled away. I seized the largest brush and fell upon my victim with Berserk fury. I have never felt any awe of a canvas since.

It was indeed an achievement to make himself, from such beginnings and at the advanced age of forty, into a recognized painter. He seems to have received some tips and wrinkles from Lavery, Orpen and Sickert; but for the most part he went his own wilful way, a boy at school again – the inspired autodidact. It was not until he happened to be painting one day on the

24. Churchill, *Thoughts and Adventures*, 234–6.

Côte d'Azur that he fell in with one or two painters who revealed to him the methods of French Impressionism. Thus he found himself as an artist: that is the kind of painter he became. It is astonishing, everything else considered, that he should arrive at exhibiting in the Academy – the Honorary Academician Extraordinary – and having his pictures collected by the galleries. When one observes his work in bulk, as one does at Chartwell, where staircase, corridors, passages are lined by his paintings, one sees something more significant – that his painting represents another, much less realized side to his nature, the gentler and more sensitive; it represents the feminine side in the complex that makes for genius.

At that time, Lord Beaverbrook tells us, Churchill was 'a character depressed beyond the limits of description. When the government was deprived of his guidance, he could see no hope anywhere.'[25] He turned with relief to the idea of a command in the field, ready to take his chance with the rest. The night before his departure Beaverbrook went to see him. 'The whole household was upside down while the soldier-statesman was buckling on his sword.' Downstairs, Eddie was in tears; upstairs, Lady Randolph 'in despair at the idea of her brilliant son being relegated to the trenches'. Mrs Churchill seemed to be the only person who remained calm and collected: she must have become used to such scenes.

In France Churchill's old enemy of Boer War days, Sir John French, offered him the command of a brigade, which his experience as a Regular well warranted. Churchill 'did not feel incapable of discharging the duties in question', but considered that he must first learn for himself the special conditions of trench warfare.[26] So he was posted off for instruction, as a Major, to a battalion of the Grenadier Guards – Marlborough's own regiment – in the line. There he received the somewhat frosty reception that might have been expected, not so much as a failed politician whose dizzy ascent from the stars looked like a parallel to his father, Lord Randolph's, but as a new boy at school once more. He was firmly put in his place; the colonel had not been

25. Beaverbrook, op. cit., II. 73–4.
26. Churchill, *Thoughts and Adventures*, 67–8, 71–2.

consulted in the matter of his coming to his battalion, etc. Before ten days were out his irresistible *bonhomie* prevailed, and 'I might as well have been an absolutely blameless Regular officer who had never strayed from the strict professional path. . . . It will always be a source of pride to me that I succeeded in making myself perfectly at home with these men and formed friendships which I enjoy today.'

One or two episodes in especial, while serving in the trenches, corroborated a conviction that had long held force in his mind – that the element of chance, luck, destiny, providence exerts a dominant and formative power upon a man's life. One day he was summoned out of the trenches for a rendezvous several miles behind the line with a general, whom he missed after all. It seemed so purposeless, until he got back, wet through in the rain, to find that he had missed another rendezvous: a shell-burst on the shelter had blown off the other occupant's head. It is such coincidences and escapes that build up in the fabric of human egoism the concept of destiny. Nevertheless, we have reason to be grateful for the hand that had been 'stretched out to move me in the nick of time from a fatal spot. But whether it was General —'s hand or not, I cannot tell.'[27]

He gives us the story of another such episode, when he had moved on to the command of the 6th Royal Scots Fusiliers in Flanders. He was then working upon a memorandum for the High Command on the secret projects in which he was so much interested, in particular the use of tanks for the offensive. Nor was this the only new development in warfare upon which his mind was working. He was using his interstices of leisure while at the Front to think out the methods of amphibious warfare that would come to dominate the second war. As he has told me himself, while Lloyd George was working his way back for him with the Tories, he was preparing a scheme for the capture of the Frisian island of Borkum. The essence of the plan was to use tanks to run ashore from specially constructed landing-craft on the beaches. How all this looked forward to the beaches of North Africa and Italy, Okinawa and the Pacific islands, and at length Normandy! There were the essential ideas – the

27. Churchill, *Thoughts and Adventures*, 78.

bullet-proof lighters, the tanks in large numbers, the flat-bottomed barges or caissons of concrete out of which came the mulberry harbours of 1944. Here is the sphere in which he regards himself as having made an original contribution to the art of warfare; it was 'by the mercy of providence' that he had not published this paper in *The World Crisis*, where it would certainly have been noticed and taken up by the Germans in their second war.

Lloyd George was so much impressed by this paper that he had it printed and circulated to the Admiralty and the War Cabinet. For by the end of 1916 he had arrived, not a day too soon, at the supreme direction of the war. The simple truth behind all the dissatisfactions and the political manoeuvres of that year was that Asquith was totally lacking in dynamism; the war, the country needed dynamic leadership and only Lloyd George could provide it. The war was proceeding in the most unsatisfactory fashion, and there was a growing danger of a peace by negotiation – which would in effect mean a German victory or a second bid when it suited them. In the field in France Churchill was as effectively frustrated as he had been at home. He should have been put on the staff at High Command, where his fertility in ideas, his invention and resource might have transformed the war. Suppose if tanks had been employed on the scale he conceived – it could have broken the stalemate on the Western Front. But Bonar Law would not hear of his having anything to do with the conduct of the war in France; he was not even allowed the command of a brigade he had been promised.

With the mounting dissatisfaction at home, champing for action, he allowed himself to be impelled back to Parliament by Carson and Beaverbrook to play his part among the ginger-groups calling for a new direction. But when Asquith fell, Lloyd George, who was anxious to harness Churchill's energies to his government, was not allowed to recruit him. He found himself confronted by Bonar Law's unshakable veto. When Lloyd George put the case for including Churchill even negatively – would he rather have Churchill against him? – the Tory leader replied, 'I would rather have him against us every time'.[28] Why were

28. Lloyd George, I. 636–7.

the Tories so bitter and implacable against him, when they were ready to accept Lloyd George? It was simple revenge for his desertion: 'had he remained a faithful son in the political household in which he was born and brought up, his share in the Dardanelles fiasco would have been passed over'. Then, too, 'it was interesting to observe in a concentrated form every phase of the distrust and trepidation with which mediocrity views genius at close quarters'. It was not for some six months, July 1917, that Lloyd George felt himself sufficiently strong to invite Churchill into his administration. And then it rocked the government, placed it in jeopardy according to Lloyd George; the Tory leaders were furious.

Since the war had become one of attrition a key-position was the Ministry of Munitions, which Lloyd George himself had created. Supplies were now all in all; other opportunities having been lost, we could only win by making full use of superior resources. This vast new war-time department had grown out of all proportion, proliferating sub-departments in all directions. Only an outsize Minister could grapple with it. Lloyd George was determined on Churchill. In consequence, 'at the Ministry of Munitions I worked with incomparably the largest and most powerful staff in my experience'.[29] But 'all the main and numberless minor decisions still centre upon the Minister himself. I found a staff of 12,000 officials organized in no less than fifty principal departments each claiming direct access to the Chief, and requiring a swift flow of decisions upon most intricate and interrelated problems.'

He set to work to change all this, and group the fifty departments into ten large units, each in charge of a head directly responsible to the Minister. The ten heads then formed a council like a Cabinet. 'The relief was instantaneous. I was no longer oppressed by heaps of bulky files. Every one of my ten councillors was able to give important and final decisions in his own sphere.... Once the whole organization was in motion it never required change.' As to the results Lloyd George is the best witness: 'owing to the energy which Mr Winston Churchill threw into the production of munitions, between March 1st and

29. Churchill, II. 1174–6.

August 1st the strength of the Tank Corps increased by 27 per cent, and that of the Machine Gun Corps by 41 per cent, while the number of aeroplanes in France rose by 40 per cent.'[30] He was at last making an effective contribution once more to winning the war.

With this vast machine running efficiently behind him he was able to tour the Front again with Eddie, whom we last saw crying at the foot of the stairs. Eddie had been so worked up over Jackie Fisher's falseness to Winston that he had torn up his signed photograph, 'Yours till Hell freezes', and now regretted it since the 'ever-placable' Winston had made it up with Fisher. Here, Beaverbrook noticed, was one of the sources of Churchill's charm: 'it lies so largely in his unexpectedness and in his belief that everybody takes everything as charmingly as he does'.[31] Beaverbrook was quite unable to fathom the mystery how Churchill could command such depths of devotion in Eddie. (The explanation is to have a loyal nature capable of devotion yourself.) At the Front Eddie was rather surprised at not feeling the least frightened at being under fire – Burchell's White Rhinoceros had been much worse. Together they visited Jack Churchill, now a Camp Commandant, of whom Winston observed, 'Jack is an extraordinary fellow – quite unborable.' There was a pleasant encounter when the American Winston Churchill came to drink coffee with the English one; another, crossed with more reflections, when they met Mr Asquith visiting his son at the Front. The Minister who provided the munitions was as pleased as Punch at the men recognizing and cheering him. Action had quite recovered his spirits. He specially went up to Arras to visit his old regiment, the Royal Scots Fusiliers, in the line. The spectacle of a daylight raid was found irresistible, though it put the time-table two hours out. 'Winston's disregard of time, when there's anything he wants to do, is sublime – he firmly believes that it waits for him.'[32] Perhaps in a way he was right.

The war was moving to its conclusion, though it could yield no satisfaction to contemplate. The generals' whole conception

30. Lloyd George, II. 1877. 31. Beaverbrook, II. 81.
32. Marsh, 250 foll.

of waging it, unimaginative and stupid, through the head-on offensives of 1915, 1916, 1917, with their fearful losses, never ceased to revolt him. When victory came, it came as a relief from exhaustion. 'I was conscious of reaction rather than elation.' The last words of his Memoirs of that war are, 'Surely, Germans, for history it is enough!'[33]

Yet, twenty-five years later, they attempted it all over again.

John Morley's prophecy that 'if there is a war Churchill will beat L. G. hollow' had been singularly falsified. The successful conclusion of the war raised Lloyd George to the heights of world fame; at Paris he figured as a world-statesman, along with President Wilson, and for the next three years he dominated British politics. The best Churchill could do for himself was to shelter under David's mantle. His first impulse after the prolonged conflict, which had been largely won by the blockade, was to rush a dozen food-ships to Hamburg, and this he urged upon Lloyd George. But the idea was too uncongenial to the public after what they had suffered at the hands of the Germans.

Upon the reconstruction of the Coalition government after the election Churchill might have gone back to the Admiralty – just where he was years before. But grave difficulties blew up in regard to demobilization and Lloyd George sent him to the War Office, the post of danger. This was to be combined with the Air Ministry. 'Whew!' wrote Sir Henry Wilson, Chief of the Imperial General Staff, in his diary, and inquired acidly on meeting his new chief why the Admiralty had not been thrown in as well. Why not, indeed? – it would have constituted the joint Ministry of Defence which he shortly came to think the answer to the problem, which he advocated all through the thirties and to some extent constituted in himself in the forties, and which in the fifties has at last come into existence, headed by his son-in-law.

The difficulties of demobilization were acute and dangerous. There were close on four million men under arms, clamouring to be released all at once. This could obviously not be done: the labour market was crowded with the intake from the munitions factories and there might easily be an uncontrolled mass of

33. Churchill, II, 1402.

unemployment. A rational scheme had been drawn up to release the key-men wanted in industry first; but these were the very men who had been called up to the forces last. There were demonstrations in Glasgow and Belfast, and several hundred men marched to Horse Guards Parade to vent their grievances. With the background of the Russian Revolution – and the initial hope offered to the working classes of the world by it – there was much underlying fear of social unrest in those years. (It accounts in part for Churchill's obsession about Bolshevism.) Now he accepted with speed: he scrapped the War Office plan, drew up another based on length of service and war-wounds and put it across the men with complete success. Always at his best in dealing with soldierly matters, he soon got the rate of demobilization flowing at 50,000 a day and the unrest subsided.

There remained the other side of the task, reconstituting quite a large Army for the various commitments with which the country was saddled: the occupation of Germany, Ireland and the Middle East. Churchill produced a plan and was soon able to report that volunteers were coming in at the rate of a thousand a day.[34] Next year he brought forward the government's scheme for reorganizing the Territorial Force.[35] It was like being Mr Brodrick, after the cataclysm.

What was new was the Air. 'Except for the year 1916, I was continually in control of one or the other branch of the Air Service during the first eleven years of its existence.'[36] We know that at the Admiralty he had been responsible for the creation of the Royal Naval Air Service; both he and Fisher had been very much alive to the possibilities of the new arm, so that the Navy started the war ahead of everyone in this field. At the Ministry of Munitions he was in charge of the design, manufacture and supply of all kinds of aircraft. Now, from 1919 to 1921, he was Air Minister as well as Secretary of State for War.

As such he had plenty of adventures; a long series of fatal accidents which he narrowly missed corroborated his conviction that Chance is not mere chance, but a kind of external power

34. *Annual Register, 1919*, 11. 35. ibid., *1920*, 8.
36. Churchill, *Thoughts and Adventures*, 133.

reaching out a hand to safeguard its favourites. It would certainly seem so. 'The young Pilot Instructor who gave me my first lesson at Eastchurch was killed the day after we had been flying together.'[37] A few weeks later he made a long and completely satisfactory flight in a new experimental sea-plane and sailed off happily to Sheerness in the *Enchantress*. No sooner had he arrived than he learned that the plane had nose-dived into the sea, killing all her officers.

As Minister of Munitions he had frequently to be on the other side of the Channel and he usually travelled by air. Thus he had a number of forced landings, and missed engagements. When Air Minister he flew more frequently than ever before, usually in a dual-control machine, 'and I had become capable, with supervision, of flying under ordinary conditions and performing the usual vertical turns'.[38] Once the plane caught fire: the pilot made an erratic fall of a thousand feet, surprising Churchill who did not know what was happening, and, by leaving the machine to take care of itself, had managed to stop the flames with a fire-extinguisher before they reached the petrol-tanks. 'I was extremely glad to find myself once more on *terra firma*.' On another occasion, when their plane crashed, the pilot and he looked so ridiculous hanging upside-down from the fuselage that, bruised and cut, they scrambled out laughing.

Evidently unkillable – or, perhaps, preserved for another purpose?

In these immediate post-war years his mind was obsessed by the dangers of Bolshevism, the threat that the Russian Revolution and the spread of international Communism constituted to the civilized world. For, remember, ideas were much more apt to go to his head than with any average politician.

> Of all the tyrannies in history, the Bolshevist tyranny is the worst, the most destructive, the most degrading. The miseries of the Russian people under the Bolsheviks far surpass anything they suffered even under the Tsar. The atrocities of Lenin and Trotsky are incomparably more hideous, on a larger scale and more numerous . . .[39]

37. ibid., 135–6. 38. ibid., 141, 144.
39. q. Virginia Cowles, *Winston Churchill*, 231.

Was that so very far out? Was it not very percipient, to become ever more hideously true under Stalin?

With his usual contempt for opinion and disregard of consequences, he made himself the leading spokesman against Communist Russia and thus came to be regarded as the fugleman of Reaction. Lloyd George disagreed with him and wanted to come to terms with the Russians: 'his ducal blood', he afterwards said of Churchill, 'revolted against the wholesale elimination of Grand Dukes in Russia'. There was much more to it than that. Churchill has always had a real detestation of tyranny, of dictatorship of any kind; his historical sixth sense enabled him to see that, once the safeguards of freedom have been removed, *anything* may be perpetrated; he sensed, with the sense of history that so distinguishes him among statesmen, the appeal the evil thing would have, the overtowering menace upon all our lives it would grow into, if left to itself to foster and spread.

His championship of this view, the ardour with which he pressed it, led to a grave misrepresentation of his positive action, which had ill consequences for himself. In fact he had no responsibility for the origins of our military intervention in Russia – and yet once more he had to take the blame for it in the public mind. When Lenin took Russia out of the war, we were still fighting the Germans; it was only natural that we should seek to stiffen what resistance we could to them inside Russia, safeguard the munitions and supplies we had sent to Archangel, prevent the oil-wells of Baku from falling into German hands. Hence the British forces at Archangel and in the Caucasus. It fell to Churchill to extricate our forces from these entanglements and bring them home. What he wanted to see was the anti-Bolshevik forces among the Russians prevail against the Communists.

They were a poor lot, as we know – Denikin, Kolchak and Co.; but Churchill managed to get the Supreme War Council in Paris to sanction supplying them, and proceeded on his dual path of sending them war-materials to stiffen them, while evacuating our forces. Nothing could stiffen them; to cover our withdrawal he thought it necessary to make a diversion and called for volunteers. This alarmed the British public, profoundly war-weary as it was and ready to believe any mischief of the man responsible for the Dardanelles. The Labour Movement in Britain, then much under the influence of idealistic expectations of the Russian Revolution, was strongly aroused and it was from that time that Churchill became the chief enemy in Labour's eyes.

Supplying the Russian counter-revolutionaries was a waste of breath and good supplies – like the Americans supplying the Chinese Nationalists. It all went down the drain. In the kingdom of the blind the one-eyed were kings and the Communists emerged from the scramble on top. Churchill expressed his conviction that the great powers 'would learn to regret the fact that they had not been able to take a more decided and more united action to crush the Bolshevist peril at its heart and centre before it had grown too strong'.[40] It may not have been practical politics, but are many practical politicians capable of taking such long-term views? Looking at the history of the world since, at the sufferings men had been made to endure by the Russian Revolution, can we say that he was wrong? Nevertheless, he disclaimed the sending of British troops to Russia; short of that he had 'done everything in his power to help the loyal anti-Bolshevist forces'.

For that he would have to pay with the prolonged distrust and hostility of all the forces of Labour, political and industrial, over the next two decades: he became the enemy *par excellence*. Not until the disastrous consequences of Tory appeasement of Hitler came home to us, and his own constant good record stood out clear in contrast, was he allowed to have worked his passage. Then – such are the ironies of politics – it was the Labour Movement that made Churchill Prime Minister in 1940; while it was his good record as an anti-Bolshevik that enabled him to put the alliance with Russia across the Tories in 1941. Twenty years before, speaking at Dundee in 1921, he urged that one tenth of the dose of Communism which had then shattered Russia would kill Great Britain stone dead.[41] Can we say that he was wrong? He lost that industrial seat for being right.

40. *Annual Register*, *1920*, 16. 41. ibid., *1921*, 101.

However, there were consolations at the War Office (and Air Ministry). Eddie had made friends with Ivor Novello, already famous as the composer of *Keep the Home Fires Burning*; and Lady Randolph arranged a lunch for the Minister to meet the young man, 'very spruce and taking in his smart new Air-Force uniform'.[42] At once there was brisk talk of old music-hall songs, of which Winston had a large repertory from Sandhurst days and where Ivor was a specialist, not caught out until the Minister said suddenly, 'Do you know, *you* ought to be in a home?' Everybody was taken aback, until the statesman scored with *You Ought to be in a Home* from old days. While at the War Office Churchill continued to play polo, but to preserve the serious character of the Minister's engagements-book it went under the French title of 'Collective Equitation'.

Shortly, in Eddie's phrase, 'our next move was in 1921 back to our primeval Colonial Office, where Winston was to cope with the complicated problems of the Middle East'. As to this Churchill confessed at his first interview with his expert adviser that he had a virgin mind; to which that official replied, 'I'm here to ravish it.' The fact was that the war, the break-up of the Turkish Empire and our own interests in that immense area made a most complex tangle. There had just been suppressed a dangerous rebellion in Iraq, but 40,000 troops at a cost of £30 millions a year were necessary to maintain order. This could not be borne; here was the danger-point and Churchill was moved to it.

He at once formed a Middle East Department at the Colonial Office to grapple with these problems, and, greatly to everybody's surprise, succeeded in recruiting Lawrence of Arabia to it.[43] For Lawrence had been bitterly disappointed, at the Paris Peace Conference, at the failure to recognize the help we had received from the Emir Feisal and his brothers in defeating the Turks and clearing them out of Arabia, Syria and Palestine.

42. Marsh, 370, 397, 399. Lady Randolph, vivacious and active to the last, died 29 June 1921, aged 67. Asquith paid tribute to her as 'an amazing reservoir of vitality and gay and unflinching courage', a woman who 'had lived every inch of her life up to the edge', and to Winston as 'best and most devoted of sons'. *H.H.A., Letters to a Friend, 1915–1922*, 192.

43. cf. *T. E. Lawrence, by his Friends*, ed. A. W. Lawrence, 196–8.

Now was his chance, in concert with Churchill, to rectify all this; it was in working together on this basis and to make a settlement of the Middle East that there came together these two men of genius, and their lasting friendship was founded. (We find Lawrence saying of Churchill in the doldrums of 1929, 'I want him to be Prime Minister somehow.') Now Churchill called a conference at Cairo and the tangle was sorted out.

If it was Lawrence's ideas that mainly prevailed, it was nevertheless a brilliant settlement for which Churchill was responsible. Against all the probabilities – and the Middle East was in an alarming state, out of which it was unlikely any settled order could be wrested – Churchill made a peace-settlement that endured up to the Second World War and beyond. It was a prime service to Britain; but because the country was then less conscious of Middle Eastern affairs – they were regarded as the specialist's field – and because he shortly after lost office, perhaps even because the settlement was so signally successful, the country lost sight of it.

What happened briefly was this. The injury done to Feisal's house was handsomely repaired by making him king of Iraq, while his brother Abdullah was made ruler of Trans-Jordan: two Arab succession-states placed under Arab rule friendly to ourselves. Iraq was no longer to be occupied by a British army, at £30 millions a year, but policed by the R.A.F. at £5 millions a year. The policy succeeded: Iraq was started on its course as the most successful and prosperous of the new Arab states. There was tremendous opposition to the proposals from the French, who took their revenge by giving Turkey support against Greece. There was opposition from the War Office, which could not believe that the R.A.F. could succeed where it had failed. Churchill, however, was optimistic: 'I had already noticed that when [Air-Marshal] Trenchard undertook to do anything particular, he usually carried it through.'

Even the self-tortured Lawrence declared himself contented, and was free to immure himself in the Army once more – his form of seclusion from the world. Churchill, he wrote, 'in a few weeks made straight all the tangle, finding solutions fulfilling (I think) our promises in letter and spirit (where humanly possible) without sacrificing any interest of our Empire or any interest of the peoples concerned'. And then he vanished, 'a small cloud of dust on the horizon'. Some years later he inscribed a copy of *The Seven Pillars of Wisdom*,

> Winston Churchill who made a happy ending to this show. And eleven years after we set our hands to making an honest settlement, all our work still stands: the countries having gone forward, our interests having been saved, and nobody killed, either on our side or the other. To have planned for eleven years is statesmanship.

Churchill's services were, however, not rewarded. When Bonar Law withdrew from Lloyd George's government in 1921, thereby gravely weakening it and preparing the way for a pure Tory administration, Churchill did not succeed to the Chancellorship of the Exchequer, though he was now the second man in the government and evidently expected it. A businessman, whom everyone has now forgotten, Sir Robert Horne, was appointed. Beaverbrook reported to Bonar Law abroad: 'Winston is very – very – very – very angry.'[44]

Nevertheless, he took his full share in the negotiations for an Irish settlement, long overdue – as he said in this year 1922, 'the mode and thought of men, the whole outlook on affairs, the grouping of parties, all have encountered violent and tremendous changes in the deluge of the world; but as the deluge subsides and the waters fall we see the dreary steeples of Fermanagh and Tyrone emerging once again'.[45] It was time the Coalition attempted a settlement, for only a coalition could carry it through, as Lloyd George and Churchill had long seen; the withdrawal of Bonar Law made a settlement more possible, on the other hand the Coalition was being undermined. It was a race for time. Churchill would have preferred to see the subjugation of Sinn Fein first, a generous grant of self-government afterwards – with South Africa in mind. (Would it have made much difference?)

He had some compunction about negotiating with Michael Collins, or 'shaking hands with murder', as it was called. And Collins proved difficult to deal with, moody and defiant: 'you

44. Blake, 427. 45. ibid., 417.

hunted me day and night. You put a price on my head.' 'Wait a minute,' said Churchill, 'you are not the only one.' He fetched down the Boer poster offering a reward for his capture. 'At any rate it was a good price – £5,000. Look at me – £25 dead or alive. How would you like that?' After that Collins conceived a real liking for Churchill. He went back to face death at the hands of his own countrymen, sending a farewell message, 'Tell Winston we could never have done anything without him'.

Subsequently it fell on him as chairman of the Cabinet Committee on Irish affairs to operate the Treaty, to help the Irish government establish itself and perform its function in spite of the murder-campaign with which it was dogged. At one point he had to issue a warning that if it continued the British government would have to regard the Treaty as violated and resume liberty of action.[46] On the other hand, he had to protect the integrity of Northern Ireland which insisted on remaining part of the United Kingdom. All this needed tactful yet firm handling, and people were surprised to find beneath the orator always at concert-pitch, who could be trusted to raise the temperature of an issue and make it too interesting, a patient, tireless, sagacious conciliator. Could it be that within one breast there were two men?

Both facets of this complex personality appear in the last months of the Coalition. There was the convinced Coalitionist – the man who for eleven years past, long before the war, had advocated a coming together of the men of good will to settle the outstanding issues of Ireland and the Constitution, and defend the country in danger. It may be opined that he was never altogether happy as a Liberal, any more than he was to be altogether happy as a Conservative returned to the fold. Such men as Churchill and Marlborough are not made to be defined or circumscribed by party-ties. (Today, in conversation, he does not speak like a Tory – he sits on Olympus, above all that.) After the cataclysm of the war, with the rise of the Labour Movement and socialism becoming the dominant issue in internal politics, he could not see that there was any real division of

46. ibid., 441. Asquith recorded that most people regarded this as a bid for Diehard support. *H.A.A., Letters to a Friend, 1922–1927*, 8–9.

principle between Liberals and Conservatives. Why could they not unite to combat socialism, which was as harmful to Liberalism as it was pernicious to the interests of the Empire? However, differences which are invisible or insignificant to really big men are all in all to small ones. Perhaps, without them, there would be the less reason for their existence. The Liberals, long an absurd anachronism in the circumstances of British political life, continued in holes and corners to encumber the scene.

Near the Dardanelles there blew up a crisis that brought down Lloyd George's government. Lloyd George was passionately pro-Greek and had sanctioned a Greek expansion in Asia Minor which brought about a war in which the Greeks were now being driven into the sea. Churchill had not shared these illusions, nor was he anti-Turk in this matter. Nevertheless, he was not prepared to see the victorious Turks under Kemal back in force in Europe. When they drew near to Chanak it happened to fall to him to draw up the ultimatum warning them off. He did so in no uncertain Churchillian terms: if they made any infraction of the neutral zone of the Dardanelles or crossed the European shores they would find themselves faced by the forces of the British Empire.

The interesting thing is that this strong language had its effect upon the Turks at once: they withdrew from Chanak and shortly signed an armistice. It was the British public that was alarmed: above all, no more war.

The back-bench Tories, long straining to free themselves, decided that this was the moment to get rid of Lloyd George – he had served his purpose and won the war – and get back to normal, peacetime, party government. In the disturbed circumstances of international affairs, since nothing had settled down in Europe, the best brains in British politics were in favour of continuing a national administration, retaining the world-wide prestige (and the genius) of Lloyd George. On Lloyd George's side was Churchill, among the Conservatives Balfour, Austen Chamberlain and Birkenhead: the best heads and hearts. On the other side were Bonar Law and Baldwin (the 'cabin-boy') and all the Cecils. A vote at the Carlton Club withdrew the Tory party from support; Lloyd George at once fell – and for ever. Bonar Law formed his administration and appealed to the country in the name of 'Tranquillity' – as if there could be any tranquillity in twentieth-century affairs! To lead people to suppose so was to mislead them. However, a Tory government 'of the second eleven', as Churchill called it, was installed. He himself, out on a limb, lost his seat. 'The avenging march of the mediocrities' had begun.[47]

47. The phrase is Guedalla's, op. cit., 223.

Chapter 14

Between the Wars

THE next decade hardly saw Churchill at his best. Nor the country either: the war had been too great a strain for Britain, and now she found herself wanting the ability and talent of the best of a generation massacred. To the historian the contrast between the grasp and distinction of the Liberal government before the war and the mediocrity of Conservative government after it is both pointed and poignant. Yet Churchill made an active and busy, a leading, figure in both. It must be that the times were unpropitious for him, in spite of the attainment (after some scuffling) of high office; that the environment was somehow uncongenial, in so many ways discouraging, as it was certainly confused in purpose and without leadership.

Something of what Churchill felt about it he expressed at the end of that decade in his Romanes Lecture of 1930.

> These eventful years through which we are passing are not less serious for us than the years of the Great War. The grand and victorious summits which the British Empire won in that war are being lost, have indeed largely been lost in the years which followed the peace. We see our race doubtful of its mission and no longer confident about its principles, infirm of purpose, drifting to and fro with the tides and currents of a deeply disturbed ocean. The compass has been damaged. The charts are out of date. The crew have to take it in turns to be Captain; and every captain before every movement of the helm has to take a ballot not only of the crew but of an ever-increasing number of passengers.

Even so, it was not inevitable, it was not absolutely essential, that the confused twenties should have been succeeded by the unrelieved disgrace and humiliation of the thirties. Perhaps now we can see it in historical perspective for what it was: a stage in the decline of the nation.

The war, the Coalition that had been necessary to see it through, and perhaps the profounder shifts underneath of a society in transformation, produced a period of political instability and confusion. Even when that was resolved with a steady Conservative majority in 1924, there was still uncertainty, hesitation and no real leadership. When leadership, of a kind, came with Neville Chamberlain it was in a fatally wrong direction: appeasement of Hitler. What a background these decades make for a Churchill! What a galling experience it must have been in the first decade to have to play second fiddle to a second-rate man, and how bitter in the next decade to have no place at all, to have less and less influence, while all the mistakes possible of omission and commission were made, Hitler handed his triumphs on a platter and the war rendered inevitable!

We can observe the effect upon Churchill in his restiveness, the implicit duel with Baldwin coming now into the open, the challenge to his leadership, Churchill's defeat and turning to expedients each more hopeless than the last to get rid of the incubus; in the end being reduced almost to despair. That he did not altogether despair was one of his prime services to the country: a lesser man might well have done so.

A series of unexpected accidents brought Mr Baldwin to the leadership of the Conservative party and made him the most powerful politician in the country for the best part of these two decades. In itself this was a surprising eventuality – a Worcestershire industrialist of a sound classical education (though also at Harrow) now turned country gentleman, a man who had never had to fight for anything, either for a living, or a seat in Parliament or office, and had made half a dozen speeches in the House in the years before the war, when Churchill was already a European figure making history. Those men of superior abilities, Asquith and Lloyd George, Birkenhead and Churchill, could never quite believe it and never acclimatized themselves to Baldwin's ascendancy, the cabin-boy made captain. It cannot have made it any the more tolerable to reflect, as Amery does, that if Churchill had remained with the Conservative party he would almost certainly have become its leader and Prime Minister in 1922.

All the same these superior men were astray in their estimate of Baldwin, for all was not so simple as meets the eye.[1] This so very typical Englishman, whose political fortune rested on typifying the English so nicely, was not an Englishman but a Celt. He had at heart that romantic dream of England which those who are not English are apt to entertain and find so profitable. Not for nothing was he a Macdonald on his mother's side – this affinity was to have important political consequences in 1931. 'Understand Baldwin?' said Lloyd George; 'of course you can't; he is one of us. He is a Celt.' Of his own mental processes Baldwin said, 'there is a cloud round my mind, it takes shape, and then I know what to say'.[2] The emphasis was all on intuition, perception, sympathy. For this strange man – he was very far from being the ordinary man he made himself out to be — was a good deal of a poet, like his Macdonald cousin, Kipling. He was a man of an exquisite tact and good feeling, infallible in personal matters; a shrewd committee-man and party-manager – Churchill said with some exaggeration, 'the greatest party-manager the Conservatives had ever had'[3] – a master of the art of persuasion. In the end, a nice man, moral and religious, respectable and kind.

Great countries require more than that their leaders should exemplify the domestic virtues. For, like Louis XV, who also had never had to fight for anything in his life, Mr Baldwin had the incurable vice of indolence; he had the inertia that went with a kind of fatalism, a scepticism that did not believe in *doing* anything. Thereby he nearly ruined his country. The most powerful politician in England, he took no single action to avert the war. When foreign affairs came up in Cabinet, 'wake me up when you are finished with that', he would say.[4] His biographer observes

1. To these we may add a very superior woman: Beatrice Webb wrote in November 1923: 'poor Mr Baldwin . . . is now regarded as a – politically speaking – "Natural". Today the poor man is perpetually saying that he is stupid, and everyone, whether Conservative, Liberal or Labour, now believes it! I am glad that idol – the honest but stupid man – is discredited.' – *Beatrice Webb's Diaries, 1924–1932*, ed. M. I. Cole, 251. This turned out to be the prelude to fourteen years of power, a longer period than anyone had enjoyed since Salisbury.

2. G. M. Young, *Stanley Baldwin*, 144.

3. Churchill, *The Second World War*, I. 26.

4. Young, 63, 77, 106.

that between him and Churchill there was a hopeless divergence of temper. 'Then comes Winston with his hundred-horse-power mind and what can I do?' Baldwin complained. 'I wish I had more energy; then I might have done something, and I have done nothing. But one must not expect to see results. I am always telling Winston that.' The English people felt when war came – as to which he had never even alerted them – that they had been taken in, betrayed by the man to whom they had given all their confidence, a trust such as few have been given in politics. And perhaps the instinct of the people, to which he paid so much lip-service, was not wrong. It was their own fault: they would not trust the man in whom trust would not have been misplaced.

I

'War is fatal to Liberalism', Churchill had declared many years earlier. This was perhaps only a rhetorical declaration, but it proved true. More important than the personal feud between the Asquith and Lloyd George wings into which the party had split, its social and class-foundations had given way so that it lost its *raison d'être* beyond any hope of revival. It became more evident with every year that passed that it was a waste of time, of good men, and a disservice to the country, to go on with it.

What was Churchill, now nearing fifty, to do in these circumstances?

In the election of 1922 he lost his seat at Dundee. When the inexperienced Baldwin precipitated an election in 1923 over Protection, an issue he believed in – he never made that kind of mistake again – Churchill as a Free Trader came out as a follower of Asquith, titular leader of the apparently reunited Liberals. Once more Churchill was rejected, this time by the electorate of West Leicester, in his search round the country for somewhere to represent. The result was that he was out of Parliament during the unsatisfactory episode of the first Labour government.

He had made himself anathema to the working-class with his campaign against Bolshevism in Russia, socialism at home, and it was fairly certain that henceforth no industrial seat would return him. This was the consequence of his attempts to make anti-socialism the basis of a centre-party at this time – his way out of the prevailing confusion among parties. Lord Esher saw the unwisdom of his campaign: 'I love the Labour party,' wrote the King's friend, 'so babyish and sanguine. It is all very well for Winston to taunt them with inexperience. Just the same things were said when the middle class was first admitted to high office.'[5] Labour people rewarded Churchill with long-held dislike.

A year out of Parliament enabled him to bring out the first two volumes, of four, of his War Memoirs, *The World Crisis*. It looked as if there was no future for him in politics; even his admirers Lloyd George and Birkenhead thought at this time that he would be remembered merely as a writer rather than a statesman. His book provoked even more furious controversy than his speeches or his actions: he raised the temperature of everything he touched. Balfour reported agreeably that he was reading Winston's autobiography disguised as a history of the universe. Everyone who could read was reading it. Lord Esher thought the character-sketches first-rate, but the book too full of documents and memoranda. The fact was that Churchill was bent on substantiating his case, particularly in regard to the Dardanelles. This let loose a flood of controversy. Everywhere at elections he was pestered by fatuous hecklers, 'What about the Dardanelles?' His reply, 'the Dardanelles might have saved millions of lives', naturally made no impression.

Esher noticed, with some irony, the magnanimity of Churchill's treatment of Fisher:

> of course, Jackie is the hero of the whole story. The one presiding genius over preparation for war! – and, had he been loose, the winner of the war in two years instead of four . . . Winston backed him up well from 1912. He had this merit that he listened to Jackie and chose his fighting sailors well.[6]

Later that year, ruminating about the book, there follows a reflection not without its poignancy: 'if Lloyd George and Winston and young commanders, *i.e.* Haig, Harrington, Roger Keyes had taken over the war in 1914, what would have happened?' As to

5. Esher, IV. 255–6. 6. ibid., 287, 290.

this Churchill had his own sad reflections. On Armistice Day 1924 he wrote to Beatty:

how I wish I could have guided events a little better and a little longer. Jutland would have had a different ring if the plans already formed in my mind after the Dogger Bank for securing you the chief command had grown to their natural fruition. I live a good deal in those tremendous past days.[7]

The book, when complete, ultimately proved unanswerable. Meanwhile it was encouraging to be writing away at half a crown a word: some consolation for being out of things. On the proceeds he brought Chartwell, destined to make a historic acquisition for the nation. Asquith had Churchill next to him at Princess Mary's wedding, and was amused to hear his plans for building and developing the little estate. A good deal of bricklaying there was done by Churchill himself, who learnt the art and joined the appropriate trade union. It did not reconcile trade unionists to him; bricklayers were not much interested in competitive records in bricklaying.

How to get back into politics?

In March 1924 there was a by-election in the Abbey division of Westminster, perhaps the most famous, certainly the most publicized, of constituencies. Though official candidates for all three parties were adopted, Churchill determined to break in and stand as an independent appealing to all who were anti-socialist to join together. The implication was – under his leadership. The response made this by-election a memorable one, which might have had decisive results. For, as usual, the impact of his personality had electric consequences. The Conservative Association was torn in two between the official candidate and him; so was the party leadership. Balfour came out in his favour; Baldwin against him. Thirty Conservative M.P.s appeared on his platform.

Dukes, jockeys, prize-fighters, courtiers, actors and business men, all developed a keen partisanship. The chorus girls of Daly's Theatre sat up all night addressing the envelopes and dispatching the election

7. W. S. Chalmers, *Life and Letters of David, Earl Beatty*, 401.

address. It was most cheering and refreshing to see so many young and beautiful women of every rank in life ardently working in a purely disinterested cause not unconnected with myself.... Incomparably the most exciting, stirring, sensational election I have ever fought. I must confess I thoroughly enjoyed the fight from start to finish.[8]

He was only just not elected, by forty votes out of forty thousand. But the defeat was decisive; if he had been elected he might have challenged the leadership of the anti-socialist forces. That now fell unquestionably to Baldwin, as everything did, without effort. In May Churchill addressed a large Conservative meeting at Liverpool, accepting the claim of the Conservative party as the bulwark against socialism and offering a small Liberal wing to co-operate with it. Baldwin was happy to accept the recruit, or rather the returned prodigal: it was a surrender to his terms. In September Churchill was adopted as candidate for the safe Conservative seat of Epping he has represented ever since. A few days later he was welcomed back by a large meeting of Scottish Conservatives at Edinburgh, presided over by Balfour. (It is pleasant to observe the constant good relations later prevailing between him and the leader he had flouted as a very young neophyte.) More than a year before, Churchill told Sir Robert Horne, the Conservative industrialist whom Lloyd George had appointed Chancellor of the Exchequer, 'I am what I have always been – a Tory Democrat. Force of circumstances has compelled me to serve with another party, but my views have never changed, and I should be glad to give effect to them by rejoining the Conservatives.'[9]

This he accomplished in time for the election of 1924, which settled the post-war instability of parties with a large Conservative majority. When he took office under Mr Baldwin as Chancellor of the Exchequer, a good many Conservatives took offence. It was in fact a shrewd move on Baldwin's part, whose prime purpose in politics was to keep Lloyd George out and to that end to re-absorb his chief supporters, Churchill, Austen Chamberlain, Birkenhead, individually. As for Churchill, he was at last, at ten

8. Churchill, *Thoughts and Adventures*, 162–3.

9. Lord Riddell, *Intimate Diary of the Peace Conference and After, 1918–1923* 409.

years older, in his father's place; Lady Randolph had faithfully preserved his father's robes as Chancellor for him to wear.

Did he make a good Chancellor of the Exchequer?

Views differ about that; opinion has not yet settled down into a definite form, and his work at that time has become overlaid in the public mind by the achievements of later years. It is noticeable that in the volume devoted to every aspect of his multifarious activity there is not a single chapter devoted to this.[10] And yet he was in charge of the Treasury for five crowded years, 1924 to 1929, and brought in no less than five Budgets. He has been condemned by Keynes and others for his return to the Gold Standard at the pre-war dollar-parity, and he has not said much in his own defence. It is probable that, like his father, he did not take to 'those damned dots' and that this department of state was less congenial to him than any of the numerous others he has occupied. There is something endearing about a head of that grim department who could say after dinner one evening, when it was over, 'everybody said that I was the worst Chancellor of the Exchequer that ever was. And now I'm inclined to agree with them. So now the world's unanimous.'[11]

The truth is far different. The economic historian of the period calls him dramatic, resourceful, ingenious.[12] If the return to the Gold Standard at such a high parity was a mistake fraught with ill consequences, he was much less responsible in the matter than the financial experts of the Treasury, above all the Governor of the Bank of England, Montagu Norman. The curious thing is that Churchill's instinct was rather against the measure, and in any other realm where he had confidence in his own judgement, he would have insisted on having his way – to the country's advantage. In the dim mysterious world of high finance – and it is extraordinary what a *mystique* it had in those days – he was not sure of himself. That was where he erred, oddly for him. Himself, he had no particular reverence for gold. 'Are we to be at the mercy of a lot of negro women scrabbling with their toes in the mud of

10. *Churchill, By his Contemporaries*, ed. Charles Eade.
11. Information for which I am indebted to Mr O. T. Falk.
12. cf. U. K. Hicks, *The Finance of British Government, 1920–1936*.

the Zambesi?' he inquired of his experts after a good dinner.[13] He would have done better to follow this up by telling the experts to go to the devil. As it was, he followed them, and was able to quote Keynes in his defence: 'if we are to return to gold, and in the face of general opinion that is inevitable, the Chancellor, the Treasury and the Bank have contrived to do so along the most prudent and far-sighted lines which were open to them'.[14]

To those forbidding portals the faithful Eddie accompanied him, to be relieved by the beauty of the room they occupied and to be the recipient of such confidences as – 'earned increments are sweet, but those unearned are sweeter'.[15] This was the last of their many offices together: Eddie remained with him till their final parting in 1929. Winston, with 'a natural desire to have everything handsome about him', wanted to make Eddie a K.C.M.G., which they interpreted to mean, for such was Eddie's function, Kindly Correct My Grammar. It was in this capacity that Eddie brought down an infuriated mob of grammarians upon Wintson's head by passing the word 'choate' which the latter deemed to exist: 'inchoate' existed, what more natural than to suppose therefor that there must be a word 'choate'? Winston did not know (Harrow again!); Eddie, who did know, thought it a useful addition to the language. He did not get his K.C.M.G.; he got a K.C.V.O. instead.

In tearing good spirits, with his usual energy and optimism, Churchill confronted the complicated problems, the arduous labour, of the new department he had desiderated three years before. In the international field there was the inextricable tangle of German Reparations and Inter-Allied War Debts. There was the question of the Gold Standard and dollar-parity. At home there were the depressed industries, especially coal, to dog the government and plague the country; and by consequence, strikes, unemployment, the demand for protection. All this in addition to, and with their repercussions upon, more strictly Budgetary problems. Nothing daunted, Churchill walloped into all these, lashing out about him, more or less at once. Asquith reported of him at

13. Information from Mr Falk.
14. *Annual Register, 1925*, 43.
15. Sir Edward Marsh, op. cit., 394, 407.

this moment: 'he is a Chimborazo or Everest among the sand-hills of the Baldwin Cabinet'.[16]

To fight the war and resist German aggression Britain had had to sell out a thousand million pounds' worth of investments built up in America by the enterprise and hard work of preceding generations, and to contract a debt of a similar magnitude. At the same time her allies had incurred a comparable debt to Britain. As Chancellor Churchill insisted on linking these two together: 'I thought that if Great Britain were thus made not only the debtor, but the debt-collector of the United States, the unwisdom of the debt-collection would become apparent at Washington'.[17] It did not become so to the lapidary Coolidge: 'they hired the money, didn't they?' was the extent of his contribution to the problem. 'This laconic statement was true,' comments Churchill, 'but not exhaustive.'

In January 1925 he had to plunge immediately into one of the Reparations Conferences that frequently punctuated those years. At Paris he showed himself sympathetic to the French point of view and consented to France accounting Germany with the cost of the Ruhr occupation – since the Germans were defaulting on Reparations. On the question of Inter-Allied debts he proposed that French payments to Britain should be independent of any sums received from Germany. The French shelved this unwelcome idea by a Cabinet crisis. In August there were further negotiations about the French debt with the pro-German Caillaux – who had narrowly escaped being shot as a traitor during the war. Caillaux's secretary 'leaked' to the press proposals which were far from being up to those Caillaux agreed with Churchill. When the French Cabinet accepted these 'France thereupon fell into the throes of a financial and political crisis which lasted till the end of the year, and, in spite of the agreement, Britain's prospects of receiving any payment from France on account of war-debt remained as uncertain as ever'.[18] The Germans solved their difficulties by importing as much American capital as ever they paid in Reparations; while in the 1930s they spent far more than both on

16. *H.H.A., Letters to a Friend, 1922–1927*, 123.
17. Churchill, *The Second World War*, I. 20.
18. *Annual Register, 1925*, 87.

re-armament. So much for Keynes's argument that they were unable to make reparation for the damage they had done – with which he did so much to undermine the moral authority of the Peace.

Lord Esher opined on Churchill's appointment, Gunpowder day 1924, 'I think Winston will be very economical and formidable at the Exchequer.'[19] At once he found himself, like his father, up against the service departments, in this case the Admiralty, which wanted a large cruiser-replacement programme. Early in January Beatty reports, 'yesterday I was vigorously engaged with Winston, and I think on the whole got the better of him. I must say, although I had to say some pretty strong things, he never bears any malice and was good-humoured throughout the engagement.'[20] On Churchill's return from Paris, Beatty had another wrangle of four hours with him and his Treasury myrmidons. After yet another:

> that extraordinary fellow Winston has gone mad. Economically mad, and no sacrifice is too great to achieve what in his shortsightedness is the panacea for all evils – to take 1s. off the Income Tax. Nobody outside a lunatic asylum expects a shilling off the Income Tax this Budget. But he has made up his mind that it is the only thing he can do to justify his appointment as Chancellor of the Exchequer.

The tussle went on day after day, with Beatty expecting a split in the Cabinet and the Conservative party. Occasionally the man of war had 'a rest from Winston for two days. . . . It takes a good deal out of me when dealing with a man of his calibre with a very quick brain. A false step, remark or even gesture is immediately fastened upon, so I have to keep my wits about me.' This is precisely what the soldier Brooke found in the Second World War and his Diary bears frequent witness to: we shall have to bear it in mind in considering the capital question of Churchill's judgement. Here it is enough to record the technique: bringing all the batteries to bear upon an opposing position by way of testing it and then giving way if necessary either to superior arguments or force of circumstances.

In this instance Baldwin came down against Churchill, if

19. Esher, IV. 297. 20. W. S. Chalmers, op. cit., 402–3, 405.

'came down' is the word for a feather-bed. But feather-beds are useful for smothering purposes. Beatty got his way and the cruiser-programme went through. Churchill bore no ill-will, and had reason to be grateful when the Germans renewed the war, as Foch was sure they would. (Of Versailles he had said, 'this is not peace: this is an armistice for twenty years'.)

Churchill was evidently anxious to strike the imagination with something dramatic in his first Budget and this he achieved with the announcement of the return to the Gold Standard. He raised death-duties on all estates save the very largest, while reducing super-tax and income-tax on the lower ranges. The intention seems clear: to encourage productive enterprise. He reimposed the McKenna protective duties, chiefly on imported motor cars; and in fact each year saw import duties grow up piece-meal at the hands of this Free-Trader. Industrial interests regarded a protective tariff as the only hope of reducing direct taxes, while he needed the money to finance the ambitious scheme of Contributory Pensions, including widows' pensions, which he was introducing: a further step in social welfare, which was continuous with his record in the matter from Liberal days.

The Budget created less sensation than expected. Snowden attacked it as 'the worst rich man's Budget of recent times', which it obviously was not, and taxed Churchill with having changed his mind on the shibboleth of Free Trade. 'There is nothing wrong with change, if it is in the right direction,' said Churchill. 'You are an authority on that,' retorted Snowden. 'To improve is to change; to be perfect is to change often,' concluded Churchill. This was the first of many slanging matches with Snowden, which became a feature of Budget debates year by year, a great attraction to average M.P.s and a bore to sensible men. There was no ill-will between the two duellists: Snowden once ended a rude exchange by abruptly telling Churchill he was really fond of him and wishing him a Merry Christmas, while Churchill assured Snowden in the midst of his attacks, 'the harder my opponent hits me the better I like him'.[21] Churchill's summing-up of his opponent's career is a warm-hearted tribute to someone with whom he genuinely disagreed, even if he has to say, reasonably enough, 'Gladstonian

21. Viscount Snowden, *An Autobiography*, 916.

Radicals are a very arrogant brood. To begin with they are quite sure they know all about everything. . . . The Treasury mind and the Snowden mind embraced each other with the fervour of two long-separate kindred lizards.'[22] The interesting thing is that Churchill excludes himself from this sacred enclosure: he had not 'the Treasury mind'.

The contrast between the two men is brought out in a remark by Snowden on his return to the Treasury in 1929, 'I found that Churchill had altered the position of all the furniture in the room. I at once had it replaced.' And perhaps equally by a remark of Churchill's who gaily assured Snowden on the same occasion that he had left him 'nothing in the till'. Looking over Churchill's tenure of the Treasury and his Budgets as a whole, one sees that he erred on the side of optimism. The country had indeed made a remarkable come-back after the war, but its international position in trade and finance was in some important respects impaired. He was able to claim that the return to gold made a great saving upon our purchases from the United States and on the payment of our war debt. But it had not brought about the restoration of international trade that had been hoped for; the basic industries remained depressed and in especial it dealt a heavy blow to the export of coal. (It is curious to reflect that there was then a redundancy of men in the mines.) In 1927 Churchill introduced a large measure of derating for industry and agriculture, partly consequent upon Neville Chamberlain's reforms in local government and partly designed to help productive industry. Both this and the new Pensions scheme proved more costly than was estimated, and Churchill was reduced to a variety of expedients to raise the money.

Twice he raided the Road Fund's substantial surpluses to stop up deficits. Another year he anticipated the collection of revenue. In 1926 he constructed a Betting Tax, which turned out a complete failure owing to 'the volatile and elusive nature of the betting population'.[23] (The fall in liquor consumption and revenue enabled him to contrast 'the results of regulated freedom corrected by high taxation with those which have flowed elsewhere from

22. Churchill, *Great Contemporaries*, 292–3.
23. *Annual Register, 1929*, 27–8.

Prohibition tempered by bootlegging'.) Even so his optimism might have been justified if it had not been for the disastrous events of 1926, the General Strike and the Coal Strike that lasted seven months and cost the country some £800 millions. As Churchill's Financial Secretary, Robert Boothby, pointed out, such a sum 'could have settled it, at any time, on fair terms. It left a legacy of bitterness which continues to this day.'[24] The miners have not ceased getting their own back or holding the community up to ransom.

Churchill bore some responsibility for the handicap the return to gold imposed on what was then an export industry; but it was an indirect one. The direct responsibility must be laid at the door of the government and its leader who failed to lead. A temporary subsidy was being paid to the miners because, in Baldwin's candid words, 'we were not ready'. When they were, the government forced a showdown. This precipitated the General Strike – an extraordinary nine days' wonder which ended in a humiliating fiasco for the Trades Union Congress that had never intended it. As Ernest Bevin emerged the one strong figure on the Labour side, so Churchill came out as the chief voice on the other. With his Bolshevist obsession he charged the T.U.C. with attempting to set up a Soviet. Nothing was further from their muddled thoughts. Mr Baldwin was more shrewd: he contented himself with outmanoeuvring Labour at every point, while taking care to speak so softly as always to be regarded as a friend.

Churchill's passion for action led him to take over the *Morning Post* plant, recruit a corps of volunteer type-setters and run a government *British Gazette* during this blessed intermission from newspapers. By the end of a week the *Gazette* had a circulation of over two millions. A run of the newspapers is now of some value. Its editor did not know what Baldwin considered the 'cleverest thing' he ever did: 'I put Winston in a corner and told him to edit the *British Gazette*.'[25]

The General Strike defeated, the Coal Strike went on all through the summer. The Prime Minister did nothing more, but went abroad as usual to Aix for August, leaving an intractable situation to Churchill. In his absence Churchill turned round

24. q. Cowles, 271. 25. Young, 116.

in favour of conciliation and tried to bring the coal-owners to a national conference. They were obdurate and he could not carry the Cabinet with him to force them. This was the kind of impasse that only Lloyd George could surmount: one sees what the country lost by the Tories' exclusion of him. It is evident that Churchill hoped to settle the strike over Baldwin's head, but there was no stealing a march on that bird. When he returned in the autumn – the miners still out – he addressed the Conservative Conference with much complacency, according to the *Annual Register*, and 'treated the coal-stoppage with a philosophical detachment'.[26] Some weeks later the Prime Minister 'adopted a more detached attitude than ever'. The miners were now drifting back to work; after seven months of misery and hunger they accepted surrender terms in November. We pay for that today.

In Parliament Churchill took far more trouble to present the government's case than the Prime Minister, who sat back and received the unearned increment for 'sympathy', though he had not raised a finger. Churchill answered MacDonald with truth that the government had not the powers to coerce the coal-owners to an agreement – an intellectually reputable answer, in contrast to the intellectual disreputability of Baldwin on such a crucial issue, lazy and disingenuous, yet always plausible. It is possible that left to himself Churchill would have enforced a solution; it is certain that Lloyd George would have contrived one. The shrewd party-manager of the Conservatives knew his party better than even to try.

All this darkened the economic outlook of the country and put out Churchill's plans for the future, already of too optimistic a cast – Baldwin did not share his optimism. In these circumstances Churchill's Budget speech of 1927 made up by its brilliance and audacity for the gloom of the deficit: a jeremiad had been expected, but people forgot the artist in him always liable to surprise.[27] He took pride in how little the strength and resources

26. *Annual Register, 1926*, 111, 132.

27. For its effect cf. Birkenhead: 'Winston's unpromising Budget has proved a great success. Everyone is enormously relieved that we can get through another year without adding anything to the income-tax and without any raid upon the Sinking Fund. Both the Press and the City are

of the nation had been affected by 'the shocking breakdown in our island's civilization': the country had continued to augment its capital, was still the chief creditor nation and financial centre of the world. (Alas! one reflects thirty years later.) However, there was no hope of a reduction of income-tax now and he had to face a Tory revolt against the Budget's attempt to prevent tax-evasion by private companies. He promised to administer the measure leniently, but all to no effect: the revolt went on and he had to introduce amendments later to pacify the rich. The selfishness of the moneyed classes in all this period has been well answered, and to some extent explains that of the working-class in ours.

Next year Churchill gave further offence to a section of the Conservatives by discountenancing their agitation for the protection of iron and steel. Nor, as the election of 1929 drew near, would he make an electioneering contribution by taking 6d. off the income-tax. He had more principle than many who make such a song about it, and the Budget gave no help to winning the election. An ominous fact was the growth of unemployment. Churchill laid the blame on the disturbances of 1926; it was still more the first symptoms of the economic blizzard that swept over the world destroying so many landmarks of the old order and levelling foundations for a cruel and dreary new one.

It seems that when Churchill left the Treasury in 1929 he was contemplating further measures of expansion, and that, we now know, would have been right – instead of the restrictive deflationary measures the National Government took to deal with the crisis in 1931–2, which were directly contrary to sense. Here, too, Churchill's instinct would have been sounder. We may sum up his Chancellorship fairly with the economic historian: the country would probably have done better with the careful financial orthodoxy of Snowden in the earlier years, and have profited by the unorthodox, expansionist bent of Churchill in the depression.[28]

---

enthusiastic. He made, as he always does on a great occasion, a very remarkable speech. The effect of the Budget has undoubtedly been to strengthen, at least for the moment, the position of the government.' – Birkenhead, op. cit., II. 291.

28. cf. U. K. Hicks, 15.

Such is the perversity of things that we enjoyed the exact opposite. As it was, the expenditures that produced the financial crisis of 1931 originated in the expansionist legislation of those earlier optimistic years – pensions and de-rating. In lightening the burdens on small incomes 'Churchill's zeal was almost a match for Snowden's'.[29] Not much credit is due for that: we always knew he had a good heart and anybody can ladle out money if it is there.

The election of 1929 put the Conservatives in a minority, and Churchill left office not to resume it again for the decade that ensued. Baldwin was hurt by the verdict of the electorate: he felt, as politicians are apt to do, their ingratitude for all he had done. But he was soon back again, in altered circumstances. The second Labour government, dependent on the divided Liberals for a majority, lasted no more than a couple of years. With complete helplessness it watched the unemployment figures mount up and up. There were only two things it could do: go off the Gold Standard and devalue the pound, or introduce a general protective tariff. It did neither, and was swept away by the financial panic of 1931: really the victim of the world-crisis that threw out the Republican party in America and, more malign, destroyed the Weimar Republic in Germany, preparing the way for Hitler.

II

The year 1931 was a turning-point for the world, certainly for Britain: our modern period begins here. It does not cease to be any the less heart-breaking looking at the 1930s in perspective, for it was to that time that we must date the responsibility for the relegation of this country, so long foremost, to a second-rate position in the world. It makes one sick to write about it. However, we must do our duty, if more briefly than history properly requires: it is rather more than one can stand.

Fortunately Sir Winston Churchill has both surveyed it himself, in a spirit that cannot be bettered, and has documented it fully as the events happened and the years rolled on. There is the admirable section, 'From War to War, 1919–1939', all the more forceful for its brevity, that is the prelude to his many-volumed

29. cf. U. K. Hicks, 236.

Memoirs of the Second World War; and there is the magnificent array of his speeches covering the thirties in the volume, *Arms and the Covenant*. He has imposed his pattern on the historiography of the time, and it is one with which historians will find little to disagree. It is unlikely to be changed by any challenge from the men of Munich. The only thing that surprises one is that these men should have the brazenness to defend themselves when they look round at the ruin they wrought for their country.

The real *raison d'être* of the so-called National Government of 1931 was to keep Labour out – and this they achieved with complete success. So complete a success had very ill consequences for the proper functioning of democratic government: the Labour party was in a hopelessly weak position in Parliament throughout, some of its ablest members were never in the House; its irresponsibility and unrealism were increased, the Movement was riddled with distrust and suspicion, very understandably, at the fraudulent appeals put across the electorate in 1931 and 1935, as in 1924 before. On the personal side the National Government was a coming together of MacDonald and Baldwin, two tired and disillusioned men, to keep out those dangerous activist brains of the first rank, Lloyd George and Churchill. In this they were lucky, for Lloyd George was ill at the time of the government's formation and Churchill already on bad terms with Baldwin. Though Lloyd George had better ideas than anyone for dealing with unemployment, that dynamic energy, unharnessed to office or responsibility, ran into the sand. In these circumstances the only intellectually formidable opposition to the government came from one man. It was a very remarkable performance – not the least so of all his performances, all the more strange when one looks back over it: a one-man Opposition.

During the Labour government he had parted company with Baldwin, and left the Conservative shadow-Cabinet, over India. This made it impossible for him to co-operate with the Left, for his appeal on India was to the extreme Right, the Tory Diehards, apart from whom he was now left isolated. There is no doubt that he was sincere in his Indian views, his detestation of a policy that could only terminate in the end of British rule and handing over to the Indians. Such a course was contrary to his deepest instincts and his earliest experience, as well as to his strategic sense. His antagonism was no less a challenge to Baldwin's leadership, an attempt to divide the party against him, to rally the old and true Tories to his side. And here he miscalculated: in the realm of party-manoeuvre he was no match for Baldwin, who was a past-master at it, and besides held all the trumps.

Something of his surprise and disappointment may be glimpsed from his speech to the Indian Empire Society he inspired, at a meeting at the Albert Hall, 18 March 1931, presided over by the Duke of Marlborough. 'One would have thought that if there was one cause in the world which the Conservative party would have hastened to defend, it would be the cause of the British Empire in India.'[30] Strangely enough they preferred to follow Baldwin in giving it away – it is always easier to give away – than to follow Churchill in defending it. He appealed to their sense of history, their pride in the past.

> The rescue of India from ages of barbarism, tyranny and intestine war, and its slow but ceaseless forward march to civilization constitute upon the whole the finest achievement of our history. This work has been done in four or five generations by the willing sacrifices of the best of our race. War has been banished from India; her frontiers have been defended against invasion from the north; famine has been gripped and controlled. . . . Justice has been given – equal between race and race, impartial between man and man. And by the new streams of health and life and tranquillity which it has been our mission to bring to India, the number of its people has grown even in our own lifetime by scores of millions.[31]

The appeal was in vain. The country was suffering from what he diagnosed himself as a disease of the will-power, a failure of confidence in itself. He related it specifically to the development of a democracy based on universal suffrage, and indeed it is clear that a democracy does not make a ruling power. He was convinced that the loss of India would mark the downfall of the British Empire and that we should be reduced to the scale of a minor power, like Holland in the eighteenth century.

30. Churchill, *India*, 117. 31. ibid., 30.

Nothing that he could say, no efforts that he made, were of any avail. The Conservative party conference of 1933 supported Baldwin against him by a majority of two to one; at that of 1934 the majority was nearly three to one. In the House of Commons he had only the Diehards with him; the bulk of the party were with the Labour and Liberal parties in supporting Hoare's Bill according India responsible government at the centre, a long step towards eventual self-government and independence. Churchill fought the Bill at every stage and all along the way: 'practically alone and with little effective support from his Diehard followers', Lord Templewood tells us,[32] 'he maintained the opposition not only in the House of Commons, but in meetings of the Conservative party and demonstrations in the country'. Once the Bill was passed Churchill announced with his usual good spirit that he intended 'to bury the hatchet . . . in face of the tasks and dangers that lay before the country'.[33] These had now become flagrantly obvious; but his declaration was not met in a similar spirit. His Indian campaign completed his alienation from the Conservative party and the determination of the men of the thirties to keep him out at all costs. 'He had gone about threatening to smash the Tory party on India,' said Baldwin, 'and I did not mean to be smashed.'[34]

In 1932, in New York, Churchill had a dangerous accident which very nearly brought to an end that inestimable life. He got out of his car on the wrong side, a thing that might happen to any visiting Englishman, proceeded to walk across Fifth Avenue and was mown down by one of those happily driven, jovial taxis – only it was a Winston Churchill that was beneath it. From this collision he emerged a very bad wreck; it took him two months to recover enough strength to go forward with the full lecture-tour of forty lectures all over the States that had been arranged for him. Even so he accomplished it, 'living all day on my back in a railway compartment, and addressing in the evening large audiences. On

32. Better known to history as Sir Samuel Hoare. Henceforth I shall for clarity call him by that name. Viscount Templewood (the Rt Hon. Sir Samuel Hoare), *Nine Troubled Years*, 102.

33. *Annual Register, 1935*, 63.

34. Young, 187.

the whole I consider this was the hardest time I have had in my life.'[35]

However, 'never say die' is the ruling principle of this life and those months of returning strength were of importance in enabling him to get to know his mother's country, which in so crowded a life he had so far not had much time to become acquainted with. We have a sketch of him from his American private secretary at this time, very convincing with all his foibles and old-fashioned prejudices.[36] For one thing he thought that women occupied too much of the American scene: American men 'just can't live without women all round them'. (Very unlike the life at Chartwell, we may add, which has something of a collegiate atmosphere, a hive of masculine activity, mitigated by intervals of family life.) Perhaps this reflected something of the smart he felt at being routed by Consuelo's mother, that formidable tartar, who for her part used to refer to him as 'that dreadful man'. However, people saw that 'there's a lot of the Yankee in Winston. He knows how to hustle and how to make others hustle too': he was always on the look-out for new and more effective ways of getting things done. This quality was soon to have supreme consequences for his country's survival. We can all recognize the authentic note in the observation on him in America: 'Mr Churchill's tastes are very simple. He is easily pleased with the best of everything.'

At home, apart from his growing anxiety over the way public affairs were going, especially after Hitler's advent to power, he had the enjoyable time of someone every moment of whose life is crowded with work and agreeable activity. At Chartwell he was building – cottages, terraces, policies, partly by his own hand – and making a garden. He was dictating articles which brought in plenty of money – more than office would have done. He was gathering his friends about him, technical advisers like Professor Lindemann on science, Ralph Wigram, the most promising brain in the Foreign Office, soldiers and airmen, for the stormy times that he saw were bound to close in on us now.

At the same time, with the help of expert advice – for it has

35. Churchill, *The Second World War*, I. 61.
36. Phyllis Moir, *I was Winston Churchill's Private Secretary*.

always been characteristic of him to make the best use of experts on their subjects – he was writing a historical masterpiece. It is only one more achievement in this titan's life to have written one of the grand historical works of the time, a book to place beside Trevelyan's *England in the Reign of Queen Anne* or Neale's trilogy on Elizabethan Parliaments. We have seen what an immense injustice Macaulay did to Marlborough's memory and how the power of his pen riveted this travesty of the man upon generations of readers – and also how paradoxical it was that the greatest of English soldiers should have come down to us so traduced and vilified.[37]

Churchill set himself to rectify this. He must have often discussed it with his cousin the ninth Duke, who kept the archives at Blenheim closed for his benefit. But it is possible that he might not have tackled it if it had not been that 'two of the most gifted men I have known urged me to it strongly'.[38] It is pleasant to note who these were. The first was Lord Rosebery, whose expert knowledge introduced him to Paget's exposure of Macaulay; the second was Balfour again, always encouraging to his former rebel. No effort was spared to make this work definitive: the archives in Paris, Vienna and London were searched for him, no less than the family records at Blenheim and Althorp. He himself in 1932 followed in Marlborough's tracks along the famous march from the Rhine to the Danube – in the course of which he narrowly escaped a meeting with Hitler.

The first volume came out next year, the year Hitler came to power. This was the really critical volume of the series, for it dealt with the first half of Marlborough's life, where Churchill had 'to plough through years of struggle and to meet a whole host of sneers, calumnies and grave accusations'. It became at once fairly evident that the amateur historian had reversed the great professional judgement, and for good. It seems that to begin with two, or at most three, volumes were intended. In the end there were four, spread across the thirties in which there was so much else to claim attention: a splendid tapestry depicting the age as well as the man, comparable to the series Marlborough

37. cf. *The Early Churchills.*
38. Churchill, *Marlborough, his Life and Times*, I, Preface, 6–8.

had had woven to depict the scenes of his life and hang at Blenheim.

One further reflection, which I owe to an earlier colleague of his: the contemplation of the problems involved in fighting the war of a Grand Alliance against an aggressor, as he saw them through Marlborough's eyes over these years, afforded a providential training for the comparable destiny awaiting Marlborough's descendant. The experience may be taken to have matured him as a statesman.

Perhaps this is the place to confront squarely, as the historian must, the question of Churchill's judgement. For it is a question. It comes up too often and in too many relations – Asquith and Lloyd George, Bonar Law and Baldwin, not to mention Brooke and others who came up against him in the second war – to be ignored. It is not enough to say that the lesser men were all wrong. What was at the bottom of their mistrust?

Lloyd George, Birkenhead and Beaverbrook, all friends who knew him best, have each made revealing contributions to the problem of this outsize personality and its effect upon others. Lloyd George wondered why it was that he was so unpopular with people.

> They admitted he was a man of dazzling talents, that he possessed a forceful and a fascinating personality. They recognized his courage and that he was an indefatigable worker. But they asked why, in spite of that, although he had more admirers, he had fewer followers than any prominent public man in Britain? Churchill had never attracted, he had certainly never retained, the affection of any section, province or town. . . . What then was the reason? Here was their explanation. His mind was a powerful machine, but there lay hidden in its material or its make-up some obscure defect which prevented it from always running true. They could not tell what it was. When the mechanism went wrong, its very power made the action disastrous, not only to himself but to the causes in which he was engaged and the men with whom he was co-operating. That was why the latter were so nervous in his partnership.[39]

It was this that Baldwin meant when he said, 'he is often right, but when he is wrong – my God!' And yet the problem is more subtle than this; for, after all, they were as often wrong

39. D. Lloyd George, *Memoirs*, I. 637–8.

as he was, and far more disastrously: Lloyd George about Hitler, and Baldwin as to what was necessary for the country's safety over the whole run of these years. The difference here must be that they at least gave the impression of being tellable, of being open to representations, where Churchill gave the *impression* – for it was not wholly true – of being untellable, intransigent, obstinately sticking to his own point of view. We have seen that there was this obstinacy in his character all the way along from childhood. And when right, it was a wholly good thing: it meant an unbreakable courage, resolution in adverse circumstances. It meant what the brilliant and sensitive Wigram said in his last message, himself shattered by the lunacy of appeasing Hitler and only too clear-eyed as to where it would all end: 'Winston has always, always understood, and he is strong and will go on to the end.'[40]

What was lacking was some intuitive tactile sense to tell him what others were thinking and (especially) feeling – the quality in which those feline Celtic natures, Lloyd George and Baldwin, were so gifted. Churchill was interested, in a very masculine way, only in the issue in itself, the merits of the case, not at all in its ambience. Baldwin was hardly at all interested in the issue itself, only in the personal ambience: he pondered the imponderables. Perhaps the defect in Churchill came from the very strength of the two natures mixed in him: the self-willed English aristocrat and the equally self-willed primitive American,[41] each with a hundred horse-power capacity for getting his or her own way. Or it came from the excessive force of the mixture: he lacked some ordinariness which ordinary people ordinarily have.

Beaverbrook sees very clearly the two natures: the winning seductive charm, the child-like spontaneity and naturalness – and the change to an intolerable peremptoriness, a ruthlessness called forth by opposition. Birkenhead has something to say about the contrast:

> to those who know him well it is very remarkable how complete is the public misconception of the man. He is looked upon as reserved,

40. Churchill, *The Second World War*, I. 155.

41. We recall how Jennie Jerome struck Lord D'Abernon as a beautiful panther.

insolent and even bullying. For these illusions his own demeanour is (unintentionally) much to blame. He has no small talk, and says everything which comes into his mind. Sometimes caustic and disagreeable things come into it though in private life this never happens. . . . He has indeed, in the intimacy of personal friendship, a quality which is almost feminine in its caressing charm. And he has never in all his life failed a friend.[42]

What a tribute! – his loyalty has indeed been a shining characteristic, absolute in itself, so much greater than with those who stress personal relations more.

The question of his judgement is bound up with this. The very excess of his mental energy has given him a certain obsessive quality: a man of one idea at a time, he has always been apt to be possessed by it to the exclusion of other considerations, particularly personal. It is a characteristic of genius to see things with such intensity that other things cease to exist; and those who work with him say that the concentration on the job in hand is such that nothing else does exist. (In this very unlike the supple Marlborough.) Perhaps this gives us some clue to why he has not been good as a party-politician, especially at personal manoeuvres, and reaches full stature with great issues, great arguments and events. Nor must we fail to note another singularity: that he should have gone on developing all his life so as to overcome these disabilities quite late, and reached maturity as a statesman, having begun so very young, only in his seventies.

Meanwhile, with Hitler's advent to power and Germany setting out on the path to her second attempt, events were catching up on this country with a vengeance.

First, the question of air-parity, which Churchill made his primary campaign. Its importance was this: only in the air could Germany hope to attain a rapid equality with, and then a predominance over, Britain and France; so everything depended on what we did about that. Churchill points out that 'if Great Britain and France had each maintained quantitative parity with Germany they would together have been doubly as strong, and Hitler's career of violence might have been nipped in the bud

42. q. Cowles, 253.

without the loss of a single life'.[43] He therefore obtained a solemn pledge from Baldwin that the National Government would 'see to it that in air strength and air power this country shall no longer be in a position inferior to any country within striking distance of its shores'. Mr Baldwin contributed a memorable phrase, which gave the impression that he meant business, that the frontiers of England were no longer the cliffs of Dover but on the Rhine.

Churchill pointed out at the time, what he has not ceased to bring home since, that Baldwin

> because of the mass of the people throughout the country who trusted his sober judgement and because he was head of the Conservative party with large majorities in both Houses, had only to make up his mind what was to be done in the matter, and Parliament would take all the steps that were necessary within forty-eight hours.[44]

But he never did make up his mind on this vital matter. At the end of 1934 Churchill learned from his own sources of information that Germany was already approaching equality in the air, and raised the matter once more in Parliament. Baldwin gave him a categorical denial that this was so or that it was likely to be so; he reassured the country – he was a past-master at reassurance – that in Europe alone we had a margin of 50 per cent. Next year he had to admit that he had been completely wrong and – not that he had misled the country but that – 'we were completely misled . . . it is the responsibility of the government as a whole, and we are all responsible, and we are all to blame'.[45] Churchill expected that this shocking admission exposing the country's danger would have immediate consequences – think what would have happened before 1914! Here he was wrong. The very frankness of Baldwin's confession doubled his popularity with a complacent House: one would have thought he had won a famous victory. Churchill 'felt a sensation of despair. To be so entirely convinced and vindicated in a matter of life and death to one's country, and not to be able to make Parliament and the nation heed the warning, or bow to the proof by taking action, was an experience most

43. Churchill, op. cit., I. 91.
44. *Annual Register, 1934*, 20.
45. q. Churchill, I. 96–7, 101.

painful.' He was not the only one to despair: with some, the despair has been lasting: fortunately for humanity, not with him: he was strong and would go on to the end. But 'the outbreak of the war found us with barely half the German numbers'.

Not content with this from government and Air Ministry, the Admiralty now added its own folly: an Anglo–German Naval Agreement which was not worth the paper it was written on. From the moment Hitler came in the Germans began constructing their pocket battleships, *Scharnhorst* and *Gneisenau*, 'in brazen and fraudulent violation of the Peace Treaty'; now, in direct contravention of the Agreement, they began laying down the *Bismarck*, which they made the most powerful battleship in the world. But the Agreement was worth a great deal to Hitler: it condoned their breach of the Peace Treaty, it drove a wedge between us and the French, it was a blow to the League and it encouraged Mussolini to go forward against Abyssinia. Churchill sums up: 'what had in fact been done was to authorize Germany to build to her utmost capacity for five or six years to come'.[46] What fools Hitler thought we all were! But there he was wrong: they were in the government, in Parliament and in the majority in the country who supported them. Those sections, however, were not exhaustive. Still, what a contrast in the conduct of our affairs under the Liberal government before 1914 and under the Conservative ascendancy that led to 1939!

There followed Mussolini's aggression against Abyssinia, his open defiance of the League and principally of this country. The Labour party, under the strong leadership of Ernest Bevin, threw over its pacifism, to implement the League with force if necessary and bring Mussolini to heel. Baldwin took the opportunity to catch the Labour party off-balance and force an election, on the pledge that he would resist aggression and uphold the League without any large increase in armaments. He won a thumping majority from a bemused country. 'Thus an administration more disastrous than any in our history', Churchill sums up, 'saw all its errors and shortcomings acclaimed by the nation. There was, however, a bill to be paid, and it took the new House of Commons nearly ten years to pay it.' On the personal side,

46. q. Churchill, I. 108–11.

'this remarkable Party Manager, having won the election on world leadership against aggression, was profoundly convinced that we must keep peace at any price'.[47] There had been some expectation before the election that Churchill would be recalled to the Admiralty, where he was certainly needed. Having won it, Baldwin lost no time in announcing that there was no intention to include him in the government. And having defeated the Labour party as the spokesman of collective security against aggression, he revealed his true mind, with cynical alacrity, in permitting Hoare to do his dirty deal with Laval.

At the revelation of this even Baldwin lost caste and the government rocked: instead of resigning himself he threw over Hoare, the Foreign Secretary, and brought in Eden who was really a Churchillian, a convinced supporter of collective security, in other words a Grand Alliance, to contain and restrain the aggressors. That was, in fact, the only hope of keeping the peace; even so, it needed enforcement and rearming. The Labour party had the sense to see the first, but had not the sense to see the necessity of the second. Churchill saw that the temper of the Labour party was changing, and that 'here was the chance of a true National Government'.[48] He happened to be abroad at the time and he thinks now that he ought to have returned: 'I might have brought an element of decision and combination to the anti-Government gatherings which would have ended the Baldwin regime.'[49] This is somewhat sanguine: nothing was more pervasive, more cohesive – or in the long run more disastrous to their world, their country and their order – than the sense of self-preservation among the Conservatives behind the men of the thirties. They marched together, the lot of them, on their melancholy, deliberate way to Munich and the war of 1939. I hope the survivors of them, when they look round, enjoy the world, the country, the order they made for themselves and us.

Hitler drew his conclusions from the disgraceful spectacle and shortly after, in March 1936, re-militarized the Rhineland. If this

47. ibid., 141.

48. ibid., 140. Note the implication of the word 'true': he thought Baldwin's National government false and fraudulent – as it was.

49. ibid., 144.

were accepted it meant that there was no further chance of controlling him: he would be free to complete his preparations and strike where and when he chose: only war would stop him. The country was now alarmed; but

> there was an immense measure of agreement open, and had His Majesty's government risen to the occasion they could have led a united people forward into the whole business of preparation in an emergency spirit. . . . It was astonishing to me that they did not seek to utilize all the growing harmonies that now existed in the nation.[50]

So far from that they altered nothing; thinking themselves indispensable, all their energy went into clinging on to power and keeping everybody else out; they kept the nation divided. Worst of all, they fatally accepted Hitler's move into the Rhineland. They even argued for it: 'wasn't it his own backyard?' was the cliché they used. I had it from Geoffrey Dawson, editor of *The Times* and immensely powerful in pushing in this fatally wrong direction. His All Souls friend, Lord Halifax, uses it today: 'to go to war with Germany for walking into their own backyard, which was how the British people saw it', he says.[51] He is mistaken: it was not the British people who saw it like that; the phrase came from his own circle, from Lothian and Geoffrey Dawson who put it across them. Lothian's friend, Lionel Curtis, assured me that 'Philip Lothian died in the knowledge that he had been wrong'. So were they all, all wrong, painstakingly, obstinately, determinedly wrong to the last.

But fancy anyone being wrong about Hitler even from the first! It is hard to conceive.

There was nothing now but to prepare for the war, see that it was met in the best possible circumstances, build up our alliances, strengthen our friends. Within the Foreign Office in December of that year, Churchill's friend, Wigram, died: his 'profound comprehension' of all that it meant and his inability to get the government to understand, let alone take the right action, was too much for him.

As a private citizen Churchill worked manfully to make up for

50. q. Churchill, I. 147–8.
51. The Earl of Halifax, *Fulness of Days*, 197.

the backwardness of the government in rearming, making the fullest use of his friendship with Professor Lindemann to keep abreast with the developments of science, especially in the air. What the country owes to this brilliant German-born friend of Churchill is incalculable. And here comes a very interesting thing, which the Germans were not aware of nor would have appreciated that such a thing was possible in the flexible and decent circumstances of English political life: at the same time as Churchill was attacking the government with severity over all other parts of the field, he was a member of the secret committee working hard to catch up in air-defence. They were only just in time. 'What would have surprised them [the Germans] was the extent to which we had turned our discoveries to practical effect, and woven all into our general air-defence system. In this we led the world, and it was operational efficiency rather than novelty of equipment that was the British achievement.'[52] It was this that just tipped the scale against superior numbers in the Battle of Britain.

He should, of course, have been made Minister of Defence. But that would not have pleased Hitler – and Hitler's likes and dislikes were a matter of careful concern to this government. Everyone expected that Churchill would be called in. Nothing reveals more the shocking levity of Baldwin's judgement in regard to the safety of the nation than his appointment of a mediocre Evangelical lawyer, Sir Thomas Inskip, whose real passion was the Prayer Book, as Minister of Defence. When he came down to All Souls he imparted to us that his Ministry of Defence consisted of himself, his private secretary, a typist and a charwoman. It was a characteristic piece of wool-pulling over the eyes of the public on the past-master's part thus to answer the anxious demand for a Ministry of Defence. Churchill pressed for a Ministry of Supply; he was answered that that was precisely what Sir Thomas Inskip was supplying.

However, at the end of that year, Baldwin surpassed himself over the sorry business of King Edward VIII and Churchill's fortunes were reduced to their lowest. People's qualities and their defects are intimately connected, and Baldwin, who could not be got to think out issues of policy on which the country's sur-

52. Churchill, I. 122.

vival depended, was at his most skilful in the personal business of getting rid of an unsuitable king. Not a step did he put wrong; he thought out every move, took subtle advantage of every mistake made on the other side, committed not a fault of tact and, it must be admitted, served his country well in the hypnotizing solo-dance he performed. He was enabled to retire in a cloud of equivocal glory – until profounder responsibilities on more important matters began to rain home.

Churchill's tactile sense, on the other hand, proved to be completely at fault. Never was the contrast between the two men more strikingly revealed. Churchill's intense loyalty of nature, the romantic appeal to his gallantry made by the plight of an unfortunate prince, were bound to put him on the side of the King. And not the less so because of the attitude of Mr Baldwin. If there was some idea of seizing on the issue to get rid of Baldwin, can we blame him? We have seen him turning now this way, now that in the vain hope of getting rid of the incubus. Would it not have been infinitely better, might it not have spared the nation the war, if he had only succeeded in ridding us of Baldwin, over India, or over the Hoare–Laval pact, over Air-Parity and Defence? The issue of the King – if that was how in part he saw it – was a last hope. It turned out a very nearly fatal miscalculation. He was the only political leader who had the courage to raise his voice on the King's behalf, but when he raised it

> it was on more than one occasion almost physically impossible to make myself heard. All the forces I had gathered together on 'Arms and the Covenant', of which I conceived myself to be the mainspring, were estranged or dissolved, and I was myself so smitten in public opinion that it was the almost universal view that my political life was at last ended.[53]

Neville Chamberlain was able to succeed to his inheritance with no breath of a challenge. Where Baldwin's sins had largely been those of omission, Chamberlain's were those of deliberate commission. For he really believed it was possible to do a deal with Hitler: that was the whole end of his policy and he meant to attain it. On his return from Munich he said that he had 'got

53. Churchill, I. 171.

the impression that here was a man who could be relied upon when he had given his word'.[54] Anyone who thought that was a fool indeed. But Neville Chamberlain, who was a good Minister of Health and an orderly minded head of a department, was a blinkered, opinionated, obstinate man with no knowledge whatever of Europe. Those men, his immeasurable superiors, Lloyd George and Churchill, described him accurately enough: the one, 'a good Lord Mayor of Birmingham in a lean year'; the other, 'he viewed world affairs through the wrong end of the municipal drain-pipe'.

It is sometimes thought that the best case made for the men of Munich is that given by Hoare in his Memoirs. If that is so there is no case at all. For what it comes to is that Chamberlain envisaged taking up each point at issue with Hitler and Mussolini one by one as a step to a general settlement. Exactly: at the end we should find ourselves with the whole balance of Europe turned against us and facing a Europe arrayed against us. This was the nightmare that had troubled Grey and that he so successfully countered.[55] As the result of the able conduct of our affairs before 1914 we went into the war with the whole balance of Europe with us against Germany; after two decades of dominantly Conservative rule we faced Nazi Germany alone and unprepared with a devitalized and defeatist France.

Why did they not see it? What is so difficult to understand is the ignorance of these men as to the life-interests of their country, the fundamental pattern of the Grand Alliance against any over-mighty aggressor that had been the sheet-anchor of our security throughout the ages – against Philip II, against Louis XIV and Napoleon, against the Germany of the Kaiser. It was all thrown away as against Hitler and Nazi Germany. Why? It is a searching question and one that goes to the heart of the decline of our country, and in our society. In part it was due to the decadence of the governing classes, a failure of confidence and

54. Keith Feiling, *The Life of Neville Chamberlain*, 367.

55. *V.* above, p. 396. The considerations there put forward on Grey's position make it clear that Lord Halifax's observation as to 'the misunderstanding of the British position there had been in 1914' (op. cit., 208) is unjustified.

nerve; in part to a muddlement of mind as between their class-interests and the interests of their country: they really thought that Hitler was their ally against Communism – no conception that a defeat by Nazi Germany, with the technical efficiency of its bestial barbarism, would be the end for this country anyway.

There went along with this a curious mentality on the part of the men of Munich, an interesting psychological phenomenon if it were not so distasteful: a complacent smugness about their course, a fatuous self-satisfaction, an astonishing conceit considering how wrong they were; they behaved extremely badly to those who opposed their fatal course – Churchill, Eden, Cranborne, Duff Cooper and others all had experience of this at their hands. When Eden revealed his disquiet at the course being taken – for the Foreign Office was never wrong in these matters, it was simply thrown over by an opinionated old man with no knowledge of foreign affairs – Chamberlain told him 'to go home and take an aspirin'. Actually he had an understanding with Mussolini's ambassador against his own Foreign Secretary. Duff Cooper tells us that Chamberlain was playing a part:

> while allowing his colleagues to suppose that he was as anxious as any of them to dissuade the Foreign Secretary from resigning, he had in reality determined to get rid of him, and had secretly informed the Italian ambassador that he hoped to succeed in doing so. Had I known this at the time, not only would I have resigned with Eden, but I should have found it difficult to sit in Cabinet with Neville Chamberlain again.[56]

Eden's resignation reduced Churchill to despair.

> I must confess that my heart sank, and for a while the dark waters of despair overwhelmed me. In a long life I have had many ups and downs. During all the war soon to come and in its darkest times I never had any trouble in sleeping. . . . But now on this night of February 20, 1938, and on this occasion only, sleep deserted me. From midnight till dawn I lay in my bed consumed by emotions of sorrow and fear.[57]

56. Duff Cooper, *Old Men Forget*, 215. cf. Churchill's reaction to all this, 'it makes one flush to read in Ciano's diary the comments which were made behind the Italian scene about our country and its representatives', op. cit., I. 266–7.

57. Churchill, I. 201.

Lord Halifax came to Chamberlain's rescue and the way to Munich was all clear.

Churchill's views on this disgraceful surrender are well known. At the time, with true strategic sense, they all focused upon the obvious necessity, 'We must get Russia in'. So far from this, 'no invitation was extended to Russia. Nor were the Czechs themselves allowed to be present at the meetings' at which their country was maimed for Hitler's benefit and handed over to his mercy.[58] Chamberlain made no attempt to bring over the balance of powers to our side, but simply relied on his own ability to 'do business' with a Hitler face to face. It is fairly clear that he had no idea what he was up against and that when he emerged from having made a complete surrender he really believed, what he told the crowd in Downing Street, that it was 'peace for our time'. When Churchill told the House of Commons 'we have sustained a total and unmitigated defeat', he was almost shouted down. Only some thirty to forty Conservatives were prepared to stand with him at this juncture, and they were made the target of attack by the Conservative machine – such was the Munich mentality. 'Each of us was attacked in his constituency by the Conservative party machine, and many there were, who a year later were our ardent supporters, who agitated against us.'

We are near the explanation of the psychological phenomenon of the Munich mentality: the men who were so wrong betrayed by their behaviour an uncomfortable consciousness at the back of their minds that they *were* wrong. That was why they were so determined to make everybody assent to what was crazy – to associate everyone with their guilt.

All they could do now was to go on downhill. In the privacy of his own circle Chamberlain would admit 'all depends on whether we can trust Hitler'. The impossibility of any such trust should have been evident all along – if our political leaders had been sufficiently educated to read *Mein Kampf* they would have known it all beforehand – but it took Hitler's breach of his word to *him*, Neville Chamberlain, the march on Prague and the swallowing up of Czechoslovakia to open his eyes. As Lord Halifax sagely observes, 'after March and the final rape of Prague, it was no

58. ibid., 242, 248, 258.

longer possible to hope that Hitler's purposes and ambitions were limited by any boundaries of race, and the lust of continental or world mastery seemed to stand out in stark relief'.[59] 'It was no longer possible to hope'! – it never had been possible to hope: to suppose that it was – there was the lunacy. After that there followed Chamberlain's scuttle to offer alliances and guarantees to anybody and everybody who would accept them – when it was too late and regardless of whether we could now render them any effective help. Lord Halifax observes, 'if the event showed that Hitler was not to be restrained, it was better that the nations under threat should stand and fight together than they should await German attack one by one'. Of course; but it would have been mere sense to have adopted that line all along, and it might not have been necessary to fight. Stand firm and the break would have come inside Germany – that was the policy of the Grand Alliance or collective security, under whichever name. Really, the intellectual devitalization of Lord Halifax's political chapters – as against the charm of Christmases at Hickleton or hunting over the Yorkshire wolds – leaves one amazed. Did these people never think things out, one wonders? If they did not, Churchill did – volumes of it.

He remains convinced that at this last moment war might have been averted. I do not know. Certainly the key to it was Russia. 'There can be no doubt', he says, 'that Britain and France should have accepted the Russian offer. . . . If, for instance, Mr Chamberlain on receipt of the Russian offer, had replied, "Yes. Let us three band together and break Hitler's neck," or words to that effect, Parliament would have approved, Stalin would have understood, and history might have taken a different course. At least it could not have taken a worse.'[60] In place of that, Chamberlain's 'reception of it was certainly cool, and indeed disdainful'. He was a fatal type. The Russians drew their own conclusions, reversed their policy and made their pact with Hitler. The war was upon us.

At this point Churchill has a magnanimous sentence upon his fellow-countrymen who had for so long disregarded his warnings:

59. Halifax, 204, 205. 60. Churchill, I. 284–5, 292.

'it is a curious fact about the British Islanders that as danger comes nearer and grows, they become progressively less nervous; when it is imminent, they are fierce; when it is mortal, they are fearless. These habits have led them into some very narrow escapes.'[61] What followed was a very narrow escape indeed – the narrowest since 1688, when Marlborough was at hand, or perhaps since 1588. As for their leaders throughout all this period, Churchill regards them as 'blameworthy before history'. 'That we should all have come to this pass makes those responsible, however honourable their motives, blameworthy before history.'[62]

On 3 September 1939 Neville Chamberlain broadcast to the nation that we were at war with Germany once more. Many of us remember that lugubrious, uninspiring discourse, all about himself: 'everything that I have worked for, everything that I have hoped for, everything that I have believed in during my public life has crashed into ruins'. – As if that were the most regrettable aspect of the matter! No historic conception of the day it was to arouse and steel the nation's resolve: the great Elizabeth's natal day, the day of Dunbar and Worcester, of Oliver's 'crowning mercy', the day when that mighty spirit went out in a thunderstorm.

Chamberlain had to take Churchill into his government. He came back to the Admiralty he had quitted a quarter of a century before: the Board had the imagination to send out the signal to the Fleet, 'Winston is back'. There were the familiar things about him once more, his old chair, the maps and charts, the map-case he had himself fixed in 1911, in the room he had last quitted when Fisher broke with him and all the hopes placed upon the Dardanelles foundered. From across the Atlantic there came a no less significant signal. President Roosevelt wrote, 'it is because you and I occupied similar positions in the World War that I want you to know how glad I am that you are back again in the Admiralty. . . . I am glad you did the Marlborough volumes before this thing started – and I much enjoyed reading them.'

Between Chamberlain and Churchill there could be no sympathy, and though Churchill had answered his call and come to the rescue of his government he complained that the Prime

61. ibid., 310. 62. ibid., 271. 63. q. ibid., 345.

Minister did not take him into his confidence. Chamberlain was indeed at sea, had no grasp of the situation. In April 1940 he told his Conservative followers, 'after seven months of war I feel ten times as confident of victory as I did at the beginning. . . . I feel that during the seven months our relative position towards the enemy has become a great deal stronger than it was.'[64] This was just before the avalanche fell upon us: Norway and Denmark overwhelmed, then Holland and Belgium, to be followed by France.

These events broke Neville Chamberlain's government at last. Even the Conservative party was beginning to turn, though in the final vote he still had a majority of eighty-one and could appeal to 'his friends' there – as if that were the question that counted at such a time. Roger Keyes came down to the House in full uniform as Admiral of the Fleet to record his vote against the men of Munich. Amery directed to them the words with which Cromwell had dismissed the Rump: 'you have sat here too long for any good you have been doing. Depart, I say, and let us have done with you! In the name of God, Go!' Lloyd George had his moment of revenge after nearly twenty years – Neville Chamberlain's prime motive in coming into politics had been to keep him out. The man who led the country to victory in 1918 now said that nothing could contribute more to victory in this war than that Chamberlain should go.

He still lingered, held on, hoping against hope, offering office to Amery, to the dissidents. At this moment when the avalanche descended – which we had done everything to bring down on us – nothing but a real National government would do instead of the humbugging simulacrum of the name which had bemused the country for now nine years. It is pleasant to record that it was the Labour party that at last gave Neville Chamberlain his *congé*: they would serve under Churchill but not under him. It is even pleasanter to think that Churchill owed his elevation to his old enemies the Labour people. His government, the Churchill–Labour government that fought the war and saved the country, was formed on an equal basis: a coming together of all the men of sense on both sides who had been kept out during that shame-

64. q. Cowles, 314.

ful decade. Even so, it is said that when Churchill led in his new government he got a very cool reception – it was Neville Chamberlain who got the cheers – from that unspeakable assembly, and that Churchill turned and said under his breath, 'any more of that and we'll have an election and wipe them out'. All the world knows what we owed to him in the years now to come, the forties; but it is questionable whether we did not owe him as much, all things considered, in those agonizing years of the thirties. Looking back over them in perspective one shudders to think where we should have been without him.

For himself, 'I was conscious of a profound sense of relief. At last I had the authority to give directions over the whole scene. I felt as if I were walking with destiny, and that all my past life had been but a preparation for this hour and for this trial.'[65]

The nation had found its true leader in time of danger, and that leader had at last found himself.

65. Churchill, I. 526–7.

Chapter 15

The Heroic Years

CHURCHILL's life was virtually synonymous with the history of the country during the heroic years 1940 to 1945, to a degree hardly paralleled in recent centuries – certainly to a greater extent even than with Lloyd George in the first war. Perhaps we should have to go back for a parallel to Pitt's leadership and inspiration in the Seven Years War; or, in more recent times, we may think of Lincoln's heroic Presidency, without whom the Civil War might never have been won. These years were the apogee of our country's history, when its purpose reached the fullest and ripest development. In its resistance to Nazi Germany – for what seemed at the time of going through it an age, alone – it rendered a grander service to Europe than even in its resistance to the Spain of Philip II, the France of Louis XIV and Napoleon, the Germany of Bismarck and William II; for though our existence was at stake, more was involved for others – the survival of European civilization.

Happy then is the man whose name is indelibly associated with the time he has himself described as 'their finest hour'.

That in itself carries with it an impossibility for the recorder of the family: it is out of the question to describe his life in detail in those years, give it its proper emphasis and proportion. He has himself told his story of the Second World War in six full volumes; and there are almost as many of his speeches, his words at the time. No English statesman has been so documented by himself – it stands in some contrast with the reserved Marlborough. Only Britain produced a leader capable equally of writing the history and of acting it. And there is something significant in that, for politics and literature are the two chief expressions of the English in the arts of life. In combining and expressing them Churchill may therefore be regarded as the most representative of Englishmen, as Luther is of the Germans in his combination of music and unreason.

Here, then, we must concentrate on Churchill's personal contribution in those years to winning the war, attempt to *préciser* what that was – in itself a formidable enough task.

We may say at the outset that for Britain in 1940 Churchill's contribution made the difference between defeat and resistance, or at any rate effective resistance. The slightest hesitation, the least faltering or any sign that we were prepared to consider terms – and we should have been done for. For, except for the Channel, we were defeated and Western Europe lay unexpectedly at Hitler's feet. At the moment Churchill was called to power, 10 May 1940, Holland and Belgium were being submerged and France, undermined and eaten out from within, was ready to crumble. All Englishmen who were alive at the time remember Churchill's words at that moment, the very tones of his voice, sombre and harsh, angry and defiant, thrilling with resolve to fight on or go down fighting. Indeed the whole story might be told in his words, to the best advantage, for never have words exerted a grander compulsion, a nobler impulse to such effect upon his hearers – or perhaps not since the words of Elizabeth and Drake in the summer of 1588, historic memories that came often to mind to sustain him.

On becoming, at last, their leader when all was crashing around them he told government, Parliament and people,

> I have nothing to offer but blood, toil, tears and sweat. We have before us an ordeal of the most grievous kind. We have before us many, many long months of struggle and of suffering. You ask, What is our policy? I will say: It is to wage war, by sea, land and air, with all our might and with all the strength that God can give us: to wage war against a monstrous tyranny, never surpassed in the dark, lamentable catalogue of human crime. You ask, What is our aim? I can answer in one word: Victory – victory at all costs, victory in spite of all terror, victory however long and hard the road may be; for without victory, there is no survival. Let that be realized: no survival for the British Empire; no survival for all that the British Empire has stood for, no survival for the urge and impulse of the ages, that mankind will move forward towards its goal. But I take up my task with buoyancy and hope. I feel sure that our cause will not be suffered to fail among men. At this time I feel entitled to claim the aid of all, and I say, 'Come, then, let us go forward together with our united strength'.[1]

1. Churchill, *Into Battle. Speeches*, ed. Randolph S. Churchill, 208.

Even now, nearly two decades after, with the dust lying upon so much ardour along the dreary way, one can hardly see for tears in transcribing those words that bring back that glorious, unforgettable summer, the long hot days full of catastrophe and suspense, the country's sudden and complete uncovering, the mortal danger we stood in. Consider the situation he had to confront: the French army crumbling at the moment he was engaged in forming his government, himself flying to and from Paris attempting in vain to stiffen resistance while recruiting his ministry at home. It was not contemplated that France would collapse: it is fairly clear that he envisaged the second German war in terms of the first, the large French army, in which he placed his trust, holding the Germans until British man-power and resources were fully mobilized and engaged. When the Germans began their break-through, Churchill asked the French High Command, as a soldier naturally would, where were their reserves, the mass of manoeuvre to deploy in this situation? He was told there were none. It was one of the worst surprises he had ever had in his life. And there was the British Army – small, it is true, but all we had, with its equipment – increasingly exposed to being cut off on the northern flank, under a French command that believed all was irremediably lost. But 'where were we British anyway, having regard to our tiny contribution – ten divisions after eight months of war, and not even one modern tank division in action?'[2]

However, to the British people on the eve of the decision in France:

> Today is Trinity Sunday. Centuries ago words were written to be a call and a spur to the faithful servants of Truth and Justice: 'Arm yourselves, and be ye men of valour, and be in readiness for the conflict; for it is better for us to perish in battle than to look upon the outrage of our nation and our altar. As the Will of God is in Heaven, even so let it be.'[3]

At this moment, the hand of the great President in Washington, who understood all that was at stake, was stretched out to sustain him; and to him he could confide his innermost thoughts.

2. Churchill, *The Second World War*, II. 44.
3. Churchill, *Into Battle*, 212.

I do not need to tell you about the gravity of what has happened. We are determined to persevere to the very end, whatever the result of the great battle raging in France may be. We must expect in any case to be attacked here on the Dutch model before very long, and we hope to give a good account of ourselves. But if American assistance is to play any part it must be available soon.[4]

And again, 'our intention is, whatever happens, to fight on to the end in this Island, and, provided we can get the help for which we ask, we hope to run them very close in the air battles in view of individual superiority'. Here a factor of extreme importance, an element indispensable to winning the war and Churchill's own vital contribution, is already adumbrated: the effect of his courage and confidence upon Roosevelt, persuading him that we were not a lost cause – against all the evidence – but worth supporting. A German victory would leave America unprepared and exposed to a hostile Europe on the Atlantic front, when she already had a hostile Japan facing her across the Pacific. We were a risk doubly worth taking; but Churchill's relations with the President, his own American blood enabling him to feel along with the Americans, clinched it as a Chamberlain could never have done.

On the eve of the battle of Dunkirk, on which the fate of the Army depended, for it was there surrounded on every side but the sea, there was a service of Intercession and Prayer at Westminster Abbey. 'The English are loth to express their feelings, but in my stall in the Choir I could feel the pent-up, passionate emotion, and also the fear of the congregation, not of death or wounds or material loss, but of defeat and the final ruin of Britain.'[5] In fact, we all remember that these were glorious moments in which to be alive; Churchill not only voiced them but embodied the hour. When he let drop almost casually in Cabinet – many of whom had supported Baldwin and Chamberlain all the way along – the words, 'of course, whatever happens at Dunkirk, we shall fight on', there occurred an extraordinary demonstration of emotion unexampled in the long history of British Cabinets. One resolve united government and people, was

4. Churchill, *The Second World War*, II. 49–51.
5. ibid., 87–8.

incarnate in one man, for so long unheard, disconsidered, disregarded.

All the same, by the light of cool reason it is difficult to see how, if the Army had been destroyed at Dunkirk, we could have fought on. But now Europe witnessed one of these miraculous transformations – perhaps the last and finest in our history – which sea-power can accomplish. Overhead the R.A.F. contested the air with the Luftwaffe above the entrenched army within its contracting perimeter. The very night after the service in Westminster Abbey, 'a great tide of small vessels began to flow towards the sea, first to our Channel ports, and thence to the beaches of Dunkirk and the beloved Army'.[6] That is the only time in our history that I can remember the Army being described as 'beloved'; yet strangely enough that was discovered to be what was at the bottom of all our hearts. Only Churchill could have said it.

And now the advantage of being a seafaring people came to the rescue – the crest of a wave going back a long way beyond 1588. The brunt of the Dunkirk evacuation was borne by the Navy, especially by the destroyers and minesweepers; but everybody else who had a boat joined in, fishing trawlers and drifters, tugs and motor-boats, yachts and pleasure-boats, old Thames steamers and river-craft of every kind. The great majority of the ships in that Armada in reverse, that plunged into the inferno of those waters, were little boats. One-third of them all were lost; but the bulk of the Army was saved. We remember them as they came back from the Channel and passed through the ports and railway-stations, where civilians brought them food and cigarettes – blackened, dirty, disarmed, but not at all dismayed by their ordeal: in fact, in high spirits, their general reaction, 'Give us the arms and we'll give Jerry some of his own back.'[7] (Notice that their attitude towards the odious people who had let loose this inferno a second time upon Europe was not even unfriendly. But note Churchill on leaving to meet the President on 4 August 1941: 'it is twenty-seven years ago

6. Churchill, *The Second World War*, II. 89.

7. These were the very words I heard from a group of them passing through a southern railway-station.

today that the Huns began their last war. We must make a good job of it this time. Twice ought to be enough.'[8] They *knew*.)

When it was known that the bulk of the Army was saved an immense feeling of an almighty deliverance spread through the nation. Anyone would have thought that it had been a great victory, instead of a very narrow escape; but the English apparently take more pleasure in narrow escapes. Churchill noticed that 'the sense of fear seemed entirely lacking in the people', and that was true. Simple folk at the time were relieved after the fall of France – they felt that now they could go forward and fight the war better by themselves. That, of course, was pure ignorance; the intelligent realized that we were in mortal peril. The importance of Dunkirk was that now the bulk of the trained men were safe we could build a bigger Army anew upon their cadres. But the whole of their equipment had been lost, all the *matériel*, artillery, machine-guns, automobiles, rifles that had at least been brought together in the improvident years. It would take years to train and equip an Army capable of re-entering Europe. Meanwhile the country was stripped bare militarily: there was the Navy and the R.A.F., for the rest, very few guns, hardly even rifles and only one armoured regiment in the country. Could we hold on? Could we hold out? Could we resist invasion?

Here again Churchill's resolve, his very character, was of inestimable value: everybody knew he would not give in. In reporting the issue of Dunkirk to the House he made his famous declaration, which owed something to his memory of Clemenceau's word in 1918:[9]

we shall go on to the end, we shall fight in France, we shall fight on the seas and oceans, we shall fight with confidence and growing strength in the air, we shall defend our island, whatever the cost may be, we shall fight on the beaches, we shall fight on the landing grounds, we shall fight in the fields and in the streets, we shall fight in the hills; we shall never surrender, and even if, which I do not for a moment believe, this island or a large part of it were subjugated and starving, then our Empire

8. Churchill, op. cit., III. 381.

9. 'I will fight before Paris, I will fight in Paris, I will fight behind Paris.' cf. Romier, *History of France*, trans. Rowse, 452.

beyond the seas, armed and guarded by the British Fleet, would carry on the struggle, until, in God's good time, the New World, with all its power and might, steps forth to the rescue and the liberation of the Old.[10]

It was this spirit that turned the scale with the President and his Secretary of State, and impelled them to their resolution of turning over the mass of arms that could be spared from the minimum requirements of the American Army: half a million rifles from 1918, cartridges, machine-guns, field-guns. Cordell Hull says quite simply, 'the President and I believed Mr Churchill meant what he said. Had we had any doubt of Britain's determination to keep on fighting, we would not have taken the steps we did to get material aid to her.'[11] Without that we should not have been able to resist in case of invasion.

For Churchill especially the fall of France was a harassing experience: he had always been the most French in sympathy of British political figures, had maintained his confidence in the French Army, alongside of whom he had fought on the Western Front in 1916. Now that Pétain had surrendered to Hitler, Churchill had to take an agonizing decision: to eliminate what remained expendable of the French Navy at Oran. With our backs to the wall, with the Italian Fleet now in the war against us in the Mediterranean, we simply could not take the risk of the French Fleet there being added to our enemies. They were given the choice of coming over to us or being put out of action. It was a terrible decision to take, and controversy rages about it still. There is no doubt that it was Churchill's and, though Vichy was able to exploit anti-English feeling by it, he was sure that the French people would understand the hard measures that were necessary for our common salvation. They certainly have forgiven him for it – taken him to their hearts as no other foreign statesman. Moreover, the action at Oran brought home to all the world that the British government would stop at nothing to make sure the command of the sea and continue the war. After the Battle of Britain and our own agony that autumn,

10. Churchill, *Into Battle*, 223.
11. Cordell Hull, *Memoirs*, I. 774–5.

Churchill was able to address the French people with a personal appeal, assuring them that all would come right in the end, and this, in spite of everything, went home to their hearts.

> Good-night then: sleep to gather strength for the morning. For the morning will come. Brightly will it shine on the brave and true, kindly upon all who suffer for the cause, glorious upon the tombs of heroes. Thus will shine the dawn. *Vive la France!* Long live also the forward march of the common people in all the lands towards their just and true inheritance, and towards the broader and fuller age.[12]

The country was now expecting invasion. Hitler was expecting our surrender; but, as the Duke of Windsor said, he 'did not know Winston'. He had previously met a number of feebler specimens among our politicians, and a lunatic fringe of pacifists, appeasers, defeatists, do-gooders, whose total efforts had done much to bring the war down on us. At the surrender of France the Führer of the German people danced his extraordinary jig of joy, but this was somewhat premature after all: he danced his last jig in the macabre environment of the underground Bunker in Berlin. Dizzy with success, the Führer waited a little, even made a peace-offer of which no notice was taken, and then, somewhat at a loss and rather belatedly, gave the orders for the assault on Britain to be set in motion.

All that fine summer while we were waiting, the lorries crashed down to the coast night and day; gun-emplacements, hide-outs, machine-gun posts, trenches, tank-traps, barriers were feverishly constructed – one comes across them in quiet English countryside still – the American rifles and ammunition handed sparely out. By the end of the summer those of us living on the exposed coast, looking across to France, felt not quite so naked. From the centre an utterly new spirit went forth vibrating through the country. Week by week the Prime Minister assembled his full Cabinet, as a member of it has told me, to inject his resolution into them, tell them what he expected and what he demanded of

12. Churchill, *Into Battle*, 297. I should add his immense service to France in getting de Gaulle away in 1940, in protecting him and forwarding his cause throughout the war.

them. A message from him went through the country's governing machine:

> the Prime Minister expects all his Majesty's servants in high places to set an example of steadiness and resolution. They should check and rebuke the expression of loose and ill-digested opinions in their circles, or by their subordinates. They should not hesitate to report, or if necessary remove, any persons, officers, or officials, who are found to be consciously exercising a disturbing or depressing influence, and whose talk is calculated to spread alarm and despondency. Thus alone will they be worthy of the fighting men who, in the air, on the sea, and on land, have already met the enemy without any sense of being outmatched in martial qualities.[13]

How different a spirit from that of the thirties! An admirable historian friend of mine bears witness to the change of spirit within the governing machine, where he served, with Churchill's advent to power. Before, he says, one could not see that the war could be won; after a short time, though one still could not see, one began to feel that it might be. It was like Pitt in 1758 – of whom he is no great admirer. He does not know how it was done. It is not difficult to understand, if one allows oneself to.

Actually, though the danger was acute, the outlook grim and no one could tell what the upshot would be, Churchill's confidence was a reasoned one: it was not mere bravado. He reckoned that in our own skies, over the island and its waters, the R.A.F. could beat the much larger German Air Force; and upon that condition the Navy could hold the seas around us and destroy the enemy setting their course for us. He has himself told me he was sure they could not land. But if they had landed every inch would be contested. No surrendering London as Paris had been surrendered: 'you may rest assured that we should fight every street of London and its suburbs. It would *devour* an invading army, assuming one ever got so far. We hope however to drown the bulk of them in the salt sea.'[14] If they got so far as to land he intended to use the grim, inspiriting slogan, *You can always take one with you.* In these 'white-hot weeks' he had two brave spirits very close to him, Ernest Bevin

13. Churchill, *The Second World War*, II. 211. 14. ibid., 235, 246.

and Beaverbrook; if the government had had to disperse over the country, he has told me, he had an idea of a triumvirate with them. The government would never leave the island. Of those summer weeks, while German planes sneaked across our coasts, spying out the land, probing our defences, and the country steadied itself for the trial, he writes, 'this was a time when it was equally good to live or die'.

Meanwhile, the withdrawal of the French Navy left us perilously strained at sea, especially in destroyers, what with the losses at Dunkirk, and from U-boats, aircraft and mines. Laid up in American harbours were fifty old destroyers from the first war, now unused. All that summer Churchill exerted his powers of persuasion with the President to sell, give or hand them over. 'Mr President, with great respect I must tell you that in the long history of the world this is a thing to do *now*.'[15] The President was nothing loth: his difficulties were political and they seemed insuperable. After all, he was supposed to be neutral; we all remember the crazy neutrality-legislation that hampered the cause that was in essence as much America's as ours. But the President was not a superlative politician for nothing – immensely Churchill's superior in these arts: after the Battle of Britain was fought and won Roosevelt thought up a way of releasing the destroyers, in return for the lease of bases on British territory around American shores. It may well be considered that the United States had the better of this bargain; but the aid those destroyers gave was inestimable in 1940, while resources were so strained and before new building came in. It was one of the factors that enabled us to hold out, and Churchill's gratitude to the President for his confidence in him has always been profound and unshaken. But already he was looking further than the personal factor:

> this process means that these two great organizations of the English-speaking democracies, the British Empire and the United States, will have to be somewhat mixed up together in some of their affairs for mutual and general advantage. For my own part, looking out upon the future, I do not view the process with any misgivings. I could not stop

15. Churchill, *The Second World War*, II. 356.

it if I wished; no one can stop it. Like the Mississippi, it just keeps rolling along. Let it roll on – full flood, inexorable, irresistible, benignant, to broader lands and better days.[16]

In August and September the Battle of Britain was fought out in the skies, the country saved in the lives of our fighter-pilots. If an invasion was to be attempted it was indispensable for the Luftwaffe to establish an ascendancy over the R.A.F., and this by a narrow margin it failed to do.[17] With his irresistible desire to be on the spot, Churchill was at the headquarters of the chief defending Group at Uxbridge on the culminating day of the battle, 15 September – like Waterloo, he recalled, fought on a Sunday. In his Memoirs he describes this critical air-battle, which proved the turning-point; after that the Luftwaffe gave up the attempt and turned to bombing: the invasion was off. With his mind always sustained, as well as enriched, from the wells of history, Churchill thought of Drake and his little ships in 1588 while action raged in the skies. Even more striking is the knowledge he shows of the complicated technical matters involved. And then we are reminded of his experience earlier at the Air Ministry, his constant interest in developments in the air, his learning to pilot an aircraft, his part in our air rearmament, unbeknown to the Germans, just in time for the war. His work with Lindemann had a share in achieving that operational efficiency by which the R.A.F. survived and triumphed, 'the like of which existed nowhere in the world' at that time.[18] When the issue was decided he was able to sum it up in an unforgotten phrase in the Commons: 'never in the field of human conflict was so much owed by so many to so few'.

Defeated in battle, the Germans turned to the methods of indiscriminate *Blitzkrieg* which had won such results in Poland and Norway, upon friendly Rotterdam. That autumn they made London their target. It was difficult to miss, and Londoners were treated to the fascinating, dangerous, unbelievable spectacle

16. Churchill, *The Second World War*, II. 362.

17. For an interesting account of the German bafflement at the result see the American observer, William L. Shirer, *Berlin Diary* (New York, 1941), 553–7.

18. Churchill, *The Second World War*, II. 294, 300.

of their city going up in flames. The King and Queen had a narrow escape from a salvo of bombs which fell on Buckingham Palace, giving them the exhilaration of feeling that they were sharing the dangers equally with their subjects. It was difficult to restrain the Prime Minister from going up on the roofs at night to have a look. As the blitz grew heavier he went to visit the worst-damaged quarters: he seemed to be everywhere, the familiar bulky figure clambering over the smoking ruins, cheering the bombed-out with his sympathy, his jokes, his spirit.

Early on one day in Peckham, where there had been a large amount of damage in a very poor district from a land-mine, a crowd surrounded his car when he was recognized, 'cheering and manifesting every sign of lively affection, wanting to touch and stroke my clothes. One would have thought I had brought them some fine substantial benefit which would improve their lot in life. I was completely undermined, and wept. Ismay, who was with me, records that he heard an old woman say: "You see, he really cares. He's crying."'[19] It was that that put him into the people's hearts: none of the middle-class fear of emotion, their inhibition in expressing it: the old aristocrat was much nearer the people in spirit. And in his reactions too, direct and natural, uncomplex and understandable. When the Peckham crowd had shown him round the crater and the devastation, 'Give it 'em back', they cried, and 'Let *them* have it too.' 'I undertook forthwith to see that their wishes were carried out; and this promise was certainly kept.' It was a regular feature of those days and of the winter of bombing that followed to see groups of the bombed and houseless telling him 'Stick it, Winnie' – as if he needed the adjuration. The spirit in Britain was certainly very different from what the malign *Schadenfreude* of Hitler and Goebbels fancied, the characteristic German mixture of envy and spite.

At the end of that wonderful year an unexpectedly complete victory came to cheer the company of the faithful. At the moment of the fall of France, Mussolini, fearful he would be too late to join in the spoils, entered the war, begging Hitler that Italian aircraft might share in the attack on Britain. Churchill,

19. ibid., 307–8.

who had never had any animus against Mussolini – in that mistaken, in my view – sent him a personal message, half-appeal, half-warning. But Mussolini was convinced that we were finished. At the height of our preparations against invasion Churchill took the daring resolution to counter the Italian attack on Egypt and Suez by sending half the tanks we had left, two armoured regiments, to reinforce our garrison there. Thus stiffened, Wavell's small army inflicted an overwhelming defeat upon the Italian Army, several times its size, that was invading Egypt. At Sidi Barrani five Italian divisions were destroyed; 38,000 prisoners were taken for the loss of 133 British killed. By mid-December Egypt was completely cleared of the enemy. It must be said that the Italians showed up very badly – which only proves how easily they could have been dealt with in 1935 and the disastrous run of events thereafter stopped.

By the end of the year 1940 a remarkable transformation had come over the outlook for us. The Battle of Britain had defeated all serious threat of invasion; Suez was firmly held and one of the Axis partners had been started on the road of defeat, humiliatingly and without reversal. If only France had continued the fight from North Africa the duration of the war would have been halved.

For us the year 1940 must ever rank with that other *annus mirabilis* 1588. Transcendent as were the services yet to come from Churchill, 1940 must rank as his finest hour, along with the nation's, for in that year his contribution made the difference between defeat and survival.

At the same time, though we had survived, one could not see how it would all end, how we were to win, alone against a German-controlled Europe. My own view at the time, the argument I steadily put forward to depressed friends, was that our fundamental interest against German domination was one with Russia and the United States: the moment that latent common interest became realized in action we were safe, though the fighting still remained to be done. This conception of our common interests – it was what was implied by 'collective security' and should have dominated our policy in the ignorant thirties – was clear enough in the Foreign Office[20] and must have been present to Churchill's mind. He put it rather differently, on one occasion saying that the mistakes of our enemies would come to our aid; they would certainly be taken full advantage of.

There is a most revealing conversation that he had in 1937 with Ribbentrop, the egregious creature whom Hitler sent to London as ambassador. Ribbentrop made Churchill the suggestion that bemused so many Chamberlainites: a German guarantee of the British Empire in the outside world in return for a free hand for Germany in Europe. Churchill said Britain would never disinterest herself in the Continent to the extent of accepting a German domination of Central and Eastern Europe. Ribbentrop replied, 'in that case war is inevitable. The Führer is resolved. Nothing will stop him and nothing will stop us.'[21] (That short interchange should have been enough to enlighten Chamberlain's government as to Germany's real intentions – as if, even so, it should have been necessary!) Though a mere private Member of Parliament whom not more than twenty Tories would follow then, Churchill gave Ribbentrop a solemn warning, which Germans would have done well to take heed of – it was really the same warning their ambassadors had given them before 1914, which they would not listen to.

> When you talk of war, which no doubt would be general war, you must not underrate England.... Do not judge by the attitude of the present Administration. Once a great cause is presented to the people, all kinds of unexpected actions might be taken by this very government and by the British nation.

He repeated, 'do not underrate England. She is very clever. If you plunge us all into another Great War, she will bring the whole world against you like last time.' But Ribbentrop, so like a German, wouldn't take telling: he rose in heat and said, 'Ah, England may be very clever, but this time she will not bring the world against Germany'.

20. Once and again in those years a word of encouragement reached me from the Foreign Office in my own small campaign on these lines, cf. my *End of an Epoch*.

21. Churchill, *The Second World War*, I. 175.

But this was just what was now about to happen.

In the spring of 1941 we find Churchill very early alerted about Hitler's troop-movements against Russia, correctly assessing his intentions, ready to pounce and take the utmost advantage of this transformation of the war. As early as 3 April he transmitted a warning personally to Stalin through our ambassador, Sir Stafford Cripps. He got no reply. The extraordinary thing was that, thought the Soviet leaders were well aware of the conflict between German and Russian interests, and between Nazism and Communism, they preferred to 'trust' Hitler rather than the Western democracies. Like calls to like, gangster to gangster, thug to thug. Both were tyrannies, both were barbarous and cruel – even if one were ultimately rational, the other ultimately insane; both had their hands imbrued in men's blood; neither of them had any belief in truth, or honesty, or common decency. And so Stalin preferred Hitler's assurances to Churchill's warning – with the result that, when the German assault came, a considerable part of the Soviet Air Force was destroyed on the ground and the Russians were caught at a great disadvantage. Molotov's wonderful reaction to the German ambassador was – 'your aircraft have just bombarded some ten open villages. *Do you think that we deserved that?*'[22]

With the German attack on Russia, Britain no longer stood alone: she had an ally in fact, if unwilling and surly. Actions speak louder than words; facts are stronger than tempers. It was Churchill's immense service to clinch the alliance at once, without hesitation or leaving a moment for mistrust or doubt to fester. No one was in so strong a position to reconcile doubters to our new ally. This was the beginning of our deliverance and there must be no faltering about it. There were plenty of doubters where Russia was concerned – understandably enough. The year before, when Russia was engaged in her war against Finland,

22. It is not absolutely certain that Molotov has no sense of humour, or if so, here is his one recorded joke. On his visit to Ribbentrop in Berlin, November 1940, a British air-raid was laid on for their benefit. They had to finish their conversations in an air-raid shelter. 'England', said Ribbentrop, 'is finished. She is no more use as a power.' 'If that is so,' said Molotov, 'why are we in this shelter, and whose are these bombs which fall?'

there had been people so lunatic as to urge our helping the Finns and taking on Russia in addition to Germany. And indeed, at bottom, it was anti-Communism that had split the mind of the governing class in Britain and ruined all hope of a coherent policy before the war – made them give the game away to Hitler as to Mussolini and Franco.

There was no confusion of mind, no hesitation with Churchill; in the struggle with Nazi Germany the existence of the nation was at stake: if one is in mortal combat with a tiger, and a crocodile or great bear comes to one's aid, is it sense to reject it? The very day of the German attack on Russia, 21 June, Churchill broadcast to the nation making clear all the implications of the new state of affairs – more, grappling them to our use. Anyone else might have hesitated; it was over this that Chamberlain's government had hesitated and brought on the Soviet–German Pact and the war. It is to be noticed that much of the argument of the broadcast was addressed to the doubters; but no one could address them so compelling an argument as he with his long record of anti-Bolshevism.

> No one has been a more consistent opponent of Communism than I have for the last twenty-five years. I will unsay no word that I have spoken about it. But all this fades away before the spectacle which is now unfolding. . . . I have to declare the decision of His Majesty's government – and I feel sure it is a decision in which the great Dominions will in due course concur – for we must speak out now at once, without a day's delay. I have to make the declaration, but can you doubt what our policy will be? We have but one aim and one single, irrevocable purpose. We have resolved to destroy Hitler and every vestige of the Nazi régime. . . . Any man or state who fights on against Nazidom will have our aid. . . . It follows therefore that we shall give whatever help we can to Russia and the Russian people. . . . The Russian danger is therefore our danger, and the danger of the United States, just as the cause of any Russian fighting for his hearth and home is the cause of free men and free peoples in every quarter of the globe.[23]

There is the argument in as many sentences: it could not be better put, considering all the susceptibilities, the awkwardnesses, his own past record of intervention in Russia, the so recent

23. Churchill, *The Second World War*, III. 331–2.

indifference of our new-found ally to our survival. The broadcast gave also something of the pattern the future would take. One great wing of the Grand Alliance was taking shape; it could hardly be doubted now that the other would form in due course. Of all Churchill's services in following up his promise of aid to Russia, putting up with Stalin's surly responses and insults, himself, though the older man, journeying to Moscow to get relations on to a better footing, at length establishing a not ungenial if uneasy camaraderie for the purpose of the war, nothing exceeds his firm initial grappling of Russia to our side and the unequivocal ending of our isolation.

All through 1941 President Roosevelt was gradually bringing the United States towards a full and open share in the Grand Alliance. In the New Year he sent his most intimate confidant to Churchill with the message: 'the President is determined that we shall win the war together. Make no mistake about it. He has sent me here to tell you that at all costs and by all means he will carry you through, no matter what happens to him – there is nothing that he will not do so far as he has human power.'[24] Churchill and his government were deeply grateful for all the support, moral and material, that they received from the President and his country in this time of tribulation. The remarkable correspondence between their two leaders continued with ever-growing intimacy – there had been absolute and entire confidence from the first, such as was perhaps only possible between two leaders of English-speaking peoples – with favourite quotations from the Bible and exchanges of verse. The President sent by Wendell Willkie Longfellow's verse –

> Sail on, O ship of State!
> Sail on, O Union, strong and great!
> Humanity with all its fears,
> With all the hopes of future years,
> Is hanging breathless on thy fate.

With the transformation of the war by the entry of Russia, and with the growth of the aid to her without which she would not have been able to withstand Germany's onslaught – as in 1917 – Roosevelt and Churchill both felt the need of a meeting,

24. Churchill, *The Second World War*, III. 21, 24.

to know each other's full minds and plan their future course of action. A rendezvous was arranged for August in Placentia Bay, Newfoundland, the President arriving in the *Augusta*, the Prime Minister in the *Prince of Wales.* Churchill has a poignant description of the scene that summer morning in the quiet sunlit bay, when the President came aboard the *Prince of Wales* with all his staff and several hundred representatives of all ranks for Sunday service,

> the close-packed ranks of British and American sailors, completely intermingled, sharing the same books and joining fervently together in the prayers and hymns familiar to both. I chose the hymns myself – 'For Those in Peril on the Sea' and 'Onward, Christian Soldiers'. We ended with 'O God, our Help in Ages Past', which, Macaulay reminds us, the Ironsides had chanted as they bore John Hampden's body to the grave. Every word seemed to stir the heart. It was a great hour to live. Nearly half those who sang were soon to die.[25]

Churchill brought with him the original draft of the Atlantic Charter – his own composition, he records with glee as a riposte to the tales of his reactionary, Old World, imperialist outlook. As the upshot of their talks the President and he issued a full declaration of war-aims and sent a joint message to Stalin. The Americans made an important further move towards entering the war by taking over the America–Iceland stretch of the Atlantic, a considerable help when the Battle of the Atlantic was at its height, losses from U-boats were enormous and the Navy still under continuous strain. There was nothing more Hitler could do about it.

But at Pearl Harbor on 7 December the Japanese took a hand. As Churchill says, madness carries with it the advantage of surprise – as we had found with Hitler. As the Germans in 1940 had gained by it the (temporary) domination of Europe, so now Japan by a sudden treacherous stroke had gained the (temporary) command of the Pacific. It is difficult for a sceptical historian to appreciate why people will attempt these things in history: they so rarely last. The immediate disaster was grievous, though it might have been even worse: the aircraft-carriers were away on other duties, and it was by them ultimately

25. ibid., 384.

that the Japanese Navy was defeated. Meanwhile the American Pacific Coast was exposed: Churchill's reaction was at once to think of sending the *Prince of Wales* and the *Repulse* from Singapore across the Pacific to reinforce what was left of the American Fleet. The next thing he heard was that they were at the bottom of the sea. When he heard the news, 'I was thankful to be alone. In all the war I never received a more direct shock.'[26] Years afterwards, he has spoken to me of the horror of that moment, and indeed we all of us felt its heart-sick anguish.

Churchill's instinct, as always, was for action and he decided that he must go to Washington at once to establish complete understanding for the conduct of the joint war. For the Americans were now in it up to the neck: Hitler had characteristically given orders to sink all American shipping wherever found, three days before declaring war upon the United States, and there followed innumerable sinkings off the Atlantic coast. But the fact that America was now fighting beside us gave us the certain assurance of victory, whatever further disasters and trials we should have to endure together. And at this grim moment Churchill had a message for the American people based on our own long endurance: it was the message he had given us on Trinity Sunday, 1940: 'Arm yourselves, and be ye men of valour, and be in readiness for the conflict'. Not that the Americans needed any steeling of their resolve: the mood was one of cold anger at these dastardly blows and no one need doubt their fighting toughness – the Germans were so stupid to ignore and belittle that as they did, unteachably, in the second war as in the first.

However, Churchill himself was a visible embodiment of courage and resistance when the world was falling around one; he felt one with the Americans, they too were his own people. As he put the point in that wonderful speech to Congress we all remember listening to, for it was relayed to us across the Atlantic: 'I cannot help reflecting that if my father had been an American and my mother British, instead of the other way round, I might have got here on my own.'[27] And then, chuckling, 'in that case

26. Churchill, *The Second World War*, III. 551.
27. Churchill, *The Unrelenting Struggle*, 333.

I should not have needed any invitation, but if I had, it is hardly likely that it would have been unanimous'. The revealing moment came with the question – the accent stern, angry, defiant: 'what sort of people do they think we are?' and the roar of response that came from the representatives of the whole American nation assembled there. For, a foreigner and yet one of their own, he had touched the dominant chord in the assembly, he had voiced the will-power of the nation. After that, he was never a foreigner in the United States again; the American people took him to their hearts, for good, as the British had done in the stress of 1940.

For himself that Christmas in the White House was crammed with work, both future planning and current business, speeches to prepare for the Canadian Parliament as well as for Congress – he does not know how he got through it all. From it there issued the Anglo–American accords: directives for the joint war, the offensives planned, operations decided. There were consolations – not only warmth and kindness on every hand, but the ever-present sense of history, of making history in the present continuous with the living past. When he wheeled the President in his chair in the drawing-room of the White House inhabited by memories of John Adams and Andrew Jackson, Lincoln and Woodrow Wilson – he thought of himself as Sir Walter Ralegh spreading his cloak before Queen Elizabeth. On Christmas Day the President and he went to church together, and found peace in the simple service and well-known hymns. 'Certainly there was much to fortify the faith of all who believe in the moral governance of the universe.'[28]

Though the ultimate configuration was now secure, the disasters and set-backs of the winter of 1941–2 reacted upon Churchill's position. We were all suffering from the sickness of hope deferred. In North Africa the entry of Rommel's Afrika Corps reversed Wavell's brilliant victories against the Italians: it was sickening to see the loss of Libya and Cyrenaica after they had been so largely won. In the Far East the loss of Malaya and the fall of Singapore were even more shattering: Australia was now

28. Churchill, *The Second World War*, III. 594.

exposed – and reproachful, though there was nothing more we could have done. In these circumstances the campaign in Britain, voiced by Aneurin Bevan and the Left, for opening up a Second Front in Europe for the relief of Russia was nothing short of wicked: it could not be mounted without at least a year's preparation in landing-craft, tanks, *matériel*, training; to try it prematurely was the one way to lose the war, and to fail, as it would have done, would mean hundreds of thousands of casualties for nothing. It is difficult to have any patience with politicians who would trifle with men's lives. Nor did Churchill need any pushing on the subject of a Second Front: all along he had been only too anxious to open one up, he was often tempted by the thought of a return to Norway, at this time his mind was set on 1943 as the target for the Second Front. If there was any ground for criticism it was that he was too impatient, too anxious for immediate results, always in favour of the offensive. The campaign for a Second Front simply had the effect of weakening him in his dealings with Stalin, exposed him to further recriminations when he was doing all he could for Russia, sending vast stores of equipment we badly needed ourselves through the Arctic convoys with their frightful losses.[29]

A sense of dissatisfaction with the conduct of the war was spreading and the Press was full of suggestions that, though he should remain Prime Minister, he should cease to be Minister of Defence and leave the direction of the war to others. It was ominously like 1916 again. At this moment Sir Stafford Cripps chose to return from his embassy in Moscow, bearing himself, as Churchill says, 'as if he had a message to deliver'.[30] (The phrase persuades one that the joke, 'there, but for the grace of God, goes God' – one of many that circulated throughout the dark

29. Sir James Grigg who, as Secretary of State for War, was in a position to know writes, 'Winston "fell over backwards" – to use an Americanism – in loyalty to our allies. He always tried to appreciate their view, he continually pressed the British forces and commanders to take more than their share of the joint sacrifices; he insisted on sending supplies to Russia that we sadly needed ourselves, he almost worried the life out of the Chiefs of Staff to find some means of bringing indirect aid to the Russians in the dark days of 1942.' – P. J. Grigg, *Prejudice and Judgment*, 393.

30. Churchill, *The Second World War*, IV. 69.

days of the war to rejoice us – must be authentic.) The Prime Minister invited him to join the government as Minister of Supply; but this was not good enough: he held himself in majestic reserve. Churchill called for a vote of confidence, and won it, with unexpected completeness, by 464 to 1 – the one, plus his two tellers, being members of the idiot I.L.P. The President cabled his congratulations: 'it is fun to be in the same decade with you'.

Upon this Churchill gained the adhesion of Sir Stafford Cripps by inviting him to become Leader of the House of Commons, where he was not very successful. This involved a reconstruction of the government, though the Prime Minister's personal position was no longer involved. He did not suffer from any desire to be relieved of his responsibilities: 'all I wanted was compliance with my wishes after reasonable discussion'.[31] In the Far East the Japanese progress continued: Burma was invaded, India now threatened. In June, Churchill was in Washington for his second visit, when the President handed him a telegram with the news of the fall of Tobruk with 25,000 prisoners: 'I was the most miserable Englishman in America since Burgoyne.' The root of the trouble was the failure in tanks. The Americans were better than their word: they put three hundred Sherman tanks at once at his disposal, and these played their part in Rommel's defeat in the end. He came home to face a vote of censure – which was lost from the start by its seconder, Admiral Sir Roger Keyes, insisting that it would be a deplorable disaster if the Prime Minister had to go: he wanted him to sack his Chiefs of Staff. The vote was supported by a mere twenty-five – exactly the same number as had voted against the younger Pitt's conduct of the war in 1799. This was very consoling to the historically minded Prime Minister; the vote gave equal pleasure to the President. Harry Hopkins cabled, 'your strength, tenacity, and everlasting courage will see Britain through, and the President, you know, does not quit'.[32]

31. ibid., 78.

32. Churchill, *The Second World War*, IV. 366. The Nazis had regarded these difficulties with great hope and put their money on Cripps. cf. Goebbels, 11 February 1942: 'the Führer agrees that Cripps is a real treasure for

Such was the sum of our internal political difficulties in the Second World War, in striking contrast with the first. There was no further question about Churchill's position. On Chamberlain's resignation, to die, in 1940 Churchill had at last become Leader of the Conservative party, and this gave him an inexpugnable position, for the Conservatives retained the immense majority over all parties they had won by Baldwin's fraud in 1935. There was some question whether the truly national leader Churchill had become ought to be a party-leader at all; but after the experience of the first war there could be no doubt for him. Supported by loyal colleagues from all parties – the Chamberlainites now at a discount, one of them relegated to Madrid, another to Washington, a third to the Woolsack, others demoted or dropped – he was left free from the daily routine of internal administration to devote his energies wholly to the war.

So far we have been considering mainly Churchill's contribution in the realm of politics and morale – one might almost say, the spirit. We must now confront the much-debated question of his specifically military contribution.

Here the essential thing, we observe, is that his instinct was all for action; he was always on the aggressive. In the darkest days of defeat he was thinking of the come-back, ways and means of bringing the war home to the enemy, no mere resistance but a resumption of the offensive as early as possible. He was impulsive, impatient, self-willed, as he always had been; but if he had not been like that we should not have held out and might never have won through. That quality, though morally of the utmost value, led to some mistakes, though these are not to be compared with the positive achievement.

---

us, to be guarded carefully. His latest effusions have created such a sensation in neutral countries that we may in future expect all sorts of good things from this white-headed boy.' 13 February 1942: 'Cripps continues to carry on agitation on behalf of the Bolsheviks. For us he is a propagandist whom we simply could not pay with money. . . . It is claimed that Hore-Belisha and Cripps intend to found a new anti-Churchill party. It would be best, of course, if Churchill were defeated and Hore-Belisha took his place. Today we would most heartily welcome a Jew as Prime Minister.' – *The Goebbels Diaries*, trans. Louis P. Lochner, 42, 44. One sees what a fantasy-world these maniacs inhabited.

He was always urging his generals on to action. His mood was very much like Chatham's, who chose Wolfe because, where other officers had difficulties, he found expedients. That was what Churchill liked; he hated obstruction, difficulties being created: he suspected inertia. At the beginning of his close and long co-operation with Brooke as Chief of the Imperial General Staff – to whom we owe our most intimate portrait of him in directing the war – there was a midnight scene when the Chief of Air Staff objected to Churchill promising to send Russia ten squadrons from North Africa at the end of the Libyan offensive. This course was both too risky and too magnanimous. There was an outburst: 'we were told we did nothing but obstruct his intentions, we had no ideas of our own and, whenever he produced ideas, we produced nothing but objections, etc. etc. . . . God knows where we should be without him, but God knows where we shall go with him!'[33] But, note: next day he came round to their view: he did not overrule them. He hated negativeness, troops standing by idle, unemployed. 'Those damned planners of yours', he one day said to Brooke, 'plan nothing but difficulties.' And again a year later when Montgomery's offensive against Rommel was delayed:

he started all his worst arguments about generals only thinking about themselves and their reputations and never attacking until matters were a certainty; of never being prepared to take any risks, etc. . . . At the root of it all lay his everlasting desire to speed up the date of all attacks irrespective of the effect such measures might have on the preparations.

Again, note: when Brooke told him so, he accepted the rebuke and adjusted his orders to the Chief of Staff's view.

Here is a marked contrast with Hitler and one that underlines the superiority of democratic methods. Hitler too was a man of intense fertility in ideas – we must not deny that evil spirit this justice. But no one dared contradict the Führer; his ideas did not have to go through the sieve of equal discussion; he frequently overruled his professional advisers and contributed largely by his mistakes to Germany's defeat. Churchill never

33. q. from Brooke's Diary, Sir Arthur Bryant, *The Turn of the Tide*, 298–9, 505.

overruled his Chiefs of Staff when they were united in their judgement. But he submitted them to the gruelling test of all-in argument day and night. Tough men of action quailed before the ordeal, as Beatty had done. The large-hearted and very able C.I.G.S., Dill, preferred the gentler clime of Washington, where the President did not interfere with professional military matters. Churchill, as an old professional, interfered with everything. Brooke complained that hardly six hours went by but he was called up by the Prime Minister; he could not bear the night sessions Churchill liked, the interminable discussions wore him down.

However, the end of it all was this, in C. M. Woodhouse's just summing-up:

> what he did, and had every right to do, was to test the firmness of their judgement to the uttermost limits of endurance, so that no conceivable possibility became recognized as an impossibility until it had been through the fire over and over again. That is not ignorance of strategy; it is leadership, and a peculiarly British kind of leadership – the kind that beat Hitler.[34]

Over any specific issue,

> it would not be so certain that the policy was correct if Sir Winston had not insisted, with all his superlative and appalling powers of advocacy, on the examination of half a dozen other policies as well. . . . The last word rests with Sir Winston: 'in war you do not have to be nice – you have only to be right'.

Then, too, he had so much of his own to contribute, not only ideas and expedients, but his share in specialized techniques. We have seen the pride he takes in the suggestions he made during the first war for landings on Borkum, landing-craft for tanks, cement-caissons out of which developed the mulberry harbour, the technique of amphibious warfare. There is his striking readiness to listen to the promptings of science in every field; he owed a great deal to his close friendship with Professor Lindemann, nevertheless such flexibility of mind is all the more remarkable in so inflexible a man.

34. The Hon. C. M. Woodhouse, 'How Vital Was Churchill?', *The National and English Review*, 1957, 119–23.

There remains the final question of grand strategy about which there has been so much controversy. It is clear that Brooke did not think highly of Churchill as a strategist:

> Winston never had the slightest doubt that he had inherited all the military genius of his great ancestor, Marlborough. His military plans and ideas varied from the most brilliant conceptions at the one end to the wildest and most dangerous ideas at the other. To wean him away from these wilder plans required superhuman efforts and was never entirely successful in so far as he tended to return to these again and again.[35]

The root of the difference was that between the intuitive mind of the artist, and the logical methods, carefully calculating and working out pros and cons, of the military scientist. General Marshall in Washington had the same professional distrust of the brilliant amateur and an even greater fear of what he considered Churchill's diversionary predilections. The two professionals, however, were at logger-heads with each other. Brooke stood for the concentric strategy of making the best use of our sea-power to close in on Germany from the perimeter, beginning with the Mediterranean. Churchill was at one with him on that; however much he tested and tried Brooke at home, when it came to the Combined Chiefs of Staff in Washington we find Churchill standing firmly with Brooke, as we see from Hopkins's *White House Papers*. On the other hand, Churchill sympathized with the American desire for the invasion of Europe as early as 1943: it turned out to be impossible for simple reasons of logistics. It is difficult to see that he was wrong on either of these prime issues – though he may have been wrong about Norway, Greece and Singapore.

The main charge made against Churchill all his life, as we have seen, was on the ground of his judgement. People feared the peremptoriness in him, the strongheadedness, the impetuousness like that which had taken him over the bridge as a boy at Bournemouth. He did not take us over the bridge, after all, in the second war: he controlled his impulsiveness to a remarkable degree, put up with a long catalogue of defeats and disappointments in an exemplary manner, and fought the war with

35. q. Bryant, 415.

the least expenditure of lives – only a quarter of those lost in the holocaust of the first. Most important – and a discriminating test of judgement – he chose the right men. He chose Brooke and Montgomery and Alexander, Mountbatten and Slim. No one has made that point, yet it is the last quality of the statesman, without which everything else goes wrong. Like Chatham, like Elizabeth I, he chose right.

The co-operation of Churchill and Brooke, the man of intuitive genius and the brilliant strategical brain, was the right one: they were complementary to each other and produced historic results. Brooke wrote, 'he is quite the most difficult man to work with that I have ever struck, but I would not have missed the chance of working with him for anything on earth'.[36] There were certainly compensations: there was a great deal of fun and it was a source of never-ending interest watching and studying him. At Chequers, March 1941:

> P.M. suffering from bronchitis, came down to dinner in his 'siren-suit', a one-piece garment like a child's romper-suit of light blue. He was in great form and after dinner sent for his rifle to give me a demonstration of the 'long port' which he wanted to substitute for the 'slope'. He followed this up with some bayonet exercise!

In June 1942 they were flying to America, 'at a time when the Atlantic had not been so very frequently flown, we were both somewhat doubtful why we were going, whether we should get there, what we should achieve while we were there, and whether we should ever get back'. This did not depress the Prime Minister, who arrived 'dressed in his zip-suit and zip-shoes, with a black Homburg hat on the side of his head and his small gold-tipped malacca cane in his hand. Suddenly, almost like Pooh-Bear, he started humming, "We are here because we're here – We're here because we're here".' The only person who could call him to order was his butler-valet, Sawyers. For Washington Winston had changed into a Panama hat turned up all round: the Prime Minister looked like a small boy going down to the beach to dig in the sand. Sawyers refused to let him get off the plane: 'the brim of your hat is turned up, does

36. q. Bryant, 39, 253, 399, 411.

not look well, turn it down!' The Prime Minister, rather red in the face, turned it down. Sawyers, standing aside to let him pass: 'That's much, much better!'

In August 1942 they were in Cairo, where the Australians were delighted to see him. They would have been still more so if they could have seen him in some of his off-moments – after a long day motoring in clouds of sand, addressing the troops, talking with officers, taking a second bathe in the sea (contrary to doctor's orders) and being rolled over by the waves, coming in upside-down doing the V-sign with his legs. Or resting in an improbable bed in Cairo, in a Moorish alcove with a religious light shining on either side, the bed with light-blue silk covering six inches deep in lace; 'and there in the bed was Winston in his green, red and gold dragon dressing-gown, his hair, or what there is of it, standing on end, the religious lights shining on his cheeks, and a large cigar in his face!'[37] Or there was the march-past of the famous 51st (Highland) Division, the wild music of the pipes bringing a lump into Brooke's throat while the tears streamed down Winston's face. Or Winston in bed with pneumonia, looking very ill but protesting at the reduced number of papers reaching him when his temperature was only 100° and he was quite ready to joke. No wonder Brooke thought him the most wonderful man he had ever met and doubted if any historian of the future would ever be able to paint him in his true colours.

These journeys told on Churchill more than he knew. After the strain of the Casablanca Conference and his tour of North Africa, the Eighth Army, Cyprus and Cairo by air and home again to an English February, he had a bad bout of pneumonia. I well remember the country's anxiety at the news. The doctor described the disease as 'the old man's friend'. Winston asked innocently, 'Why?' 'Because it takes them off so quietly.' He noticed with some disapproval the marked diminution in the number of official papers that reached him; however, he consoled himself with *Moll Flanders*. (Defoe has long been an admiration of his and provided something of a model for his

37. q. ibid., 563, 578, 584. For a detailed description of the P.M. dressing, too long to quote, v. 587.

Memoirs.) An unknown gentleman kindly presented him with a lion, with good wishes for his recovery. 'I do not want the lion at the moment either at Downing Street or at Chequers, owing to the Ministerial calm which prevails there. But the Zoo is not far away, and situations may arise in which I shall have great need of it.'[38] President Roosevelt sent him, with orders to obey the doctor, a photograph of an American Civil War General Churchill, a direct descendant of the Dorset Churchills, with a marked resemblance to Winston.

In spite of his being senior to both Roosevelt and Stalin, it fell to him to make the journeyings between both Washington and Moscow. And this in spite of Roosevelt's conviction that he could 'personally handle Stalin better than either your Foreign Office or my State Department. Stalin hates the guts of all your top people. He thinks he likes me better, and I hope he will continue to do so.'[39] In August 1942 Churchill paid his first visit to Moscow, flying via Cairo and Teheran, to establish a personal relationship with Stalin, who was so inaccessible, and see if they could not achieve some harmony, a measure of trust for the common purpose of defeating Hitler. Stalin's responses so far had been curt and ungracious: no recognition of the drain upon us of the Arctic convoys. Nothing but the Second Front would do.

Churchill had the unpleasant task of informing him that there could be no Second Front in 1942 – or at any rate, no invasion of Europe. The atmosphere of this first meeting was very glum. Then Churchill imparted to him the joint Anglo-American plans for the landings in North Africa, the assault upon 'the soft under-belly' of the Axis powers, himself drawing the picture of a crocodile and unfolding the maps. Stalin's interest was very much excited and in the shortest space grasped all the strategic implications. Churchill was much impressed. 'It showed the Russian Dictator's swift and complete mastery of a problem hitherto novel to him. Very few people alive could have comprehended in so few minutes the reasons which we had all so long been wrestling with for months. He saw it all

38. Churchill, *The Second World War*, IV. 652–4. 39. ibid., 177.

in a flash.'[40] At the end of Churchill's exposition Stalin, quite moved, said, 'May God prosper this undertaking.' The atmosphere improved; the relationship – one of comradeship in the struggle against Hitler, mutual wariness about what would happen thereafter – was established. There is no disingenuousness in Churchill; 'I was very active in the intervention,' he said to Stalin, 'and I do not wish you to think otherwise. Have you forgiven me?' Stalin replied, 'all that is in the past, and the past belongs to God'. With Stalin, who had had the advantage of a seminary education, the word 'God' was frequent upon the lips.

Anglo-American co-operation was a very different matter. When Eisenhower and Mark Clark came to London 'we talked all our affairs over, back and forth, as if we were all of one country'.[41] When Churchill was on his third visit to Washington in May 1943 and one day passed through the town of Frederick with the Roosevelts, he inquired about Barbara Frietchie and her house. Harry Hopkins came out with the lines everybody knows,

'Shoot, if you must, this old grey head,
But spare your country's flag', she said.

No one else could say any more of Whittaker's poem, so Churchill started,

Up from the meadows rich with corn,
Clear in the cool, September morn,
The clustered spires of Frederick stand
Green-walled by the hills of Maryland . . .

and went on to the end, while they all joined in the chorus – *She said.* He took a schoolboy pleasure in this demonstration, for which he received full marks from the President of the United States; but then we remember his schoolboy accomplishment of reciting hundreds of verses at pleasure. Gettysburg he had already seen and knew the story of the Civil War, its battles and its heroes, in detail such as perhaps few Americans do. That story was very familiar to Englishmen of his generation, but with Churchill, after all, it was part of the family tradition.

40. ibid., 433–4, 443. 41. ibid., 472, 711–12.

In August he was back on the American continent for the first Quebec conference planning the invasion of Normandy. After the hard work was over, 'I remained for a few days in the Citadel, pacing the ramparts for an hour each afternoon, and brooding over the glorious panorama of the St Lawrence and all the tales of Wolfe and Quebec.'[42] With the fall of Mussolini the Axis was beginning to break, but there remained the Germans to be got out of Italy – a far tougher proposition. The new situation brought with it further problems and he went down to Washington to discuss them. When the President left for his home at Hyde Park, he put the White House at Churchill's disposal with a characteristic generosity. Thus the Prime Minister was enabled to preside over the Combined Chiefs of Staff – the most remarkable instrument of Anglo–American co-operation to emerge from the war – in the Council Room of the White House. What could be more appealing to the historic sense, or more striking evidence of entire mutual confidence?

The last phase of the war was, perhaps, bound to bring out divergence between the Allies, both with regard to the operations and the shape of things after the war. But it is always sad to watch the dissolution of an historic comradeship. Earlier, in 1942, over India – a question which Roosevelt envisaged in terms of the American War of Independence – Churchill wrote, 'anything like a serious difference between you and me would break my heart'.[43] Differences were now widening between them, though there seems to have been no derogation from their mutual respect or even – on Churchill's side – of affection. The great President was at heart a lonelier man, less accessible and more inscrutable, far more of a politician and a subtler nature; moreover, he had carried an inhuman burden, in circumstances of intense physical strain, for years: he was nearing his end.

The root of the strategic difference between Churchill and the Americans was the old distrust of his 'diversions' from the main ground of attack. They had the rules of classic strategy on their side; they had also a factor not fully known to either of us: the Germans were working at their V-bombs and rockets, which next year would put London and the southern counties

42. Churchill, *The Second World War*, V. 106. 43. ibid., IV. 195.

once more under a strain like that they had endured in 1940–41. The Americans turned out to be right in wanting to hurry up the direct assault upon Hitler's Europe planned for Normandy. They wanted to put everything into that and nothing to be deflected from it. But the British had a fine army fighting the Germans in Italy: if it could be sufficiently reinforced it would fight its way through to Vienna, whence the Western powers would be able to influence events in Central Europe and the Balkans. Churchill had his eye on the balance of forces there at the end of the war, and wanted the West to end it in no unfavourable position. 'I was very anxious to forestall the Russians in certain areas of Central Europe. The Hungarians, for instance, had expressed their intention of resisting the Soviet advance, but would surrender to a British force if it could arrive in time.'[44] Would it not have been better for us all, Hungarians included, if he could have had his way?

Stalin favoured the American plan of an advance up the Rhône valley to aid the assault on Normandy – naturally: anything to keep us out of the Balkans. The Americans were rather slow to appreciate the point of this: they were much more conscious of British 'imperialism' than of Russian. Roosevelt felt that he was committed to this project and did not wish to prejudice his good relations, or what he considered his influence, with Stalin. To be just, he may not have been wholly mistaken – if he could have remained alive to exert the influence. This became a prime issue at the Teheran conference in November, at which Roosevelt and Stalin met for the first time. The Russians arranged for the President to share his compound. Churchill, who was unwell with a return of his pneumonic symptoms, felt a little left out. Perhaps the President thought it more important to establish relations with Stalin on a friendly footing for post-war purposes. When Churchill took up these arguments somewhat warmly with Stalin, to his surprise he found the President arbitrating between them rather than supporting him. The shadow of Poland was coming to loom between them. It had an even greater significance.

As D-Day approached and all the preparations along the

44. ibid., VI. 131.

Channel came to a head for the liberation of Europe, the return to France from which we had been driven in 1940, the end of the long nightmare, the Prime Minister could not contain his anxiety, or conceal his intention, to be there on the day for which he had laboured with all his might so long. The King, who as a young man had been present at the battle of Jutland, wished to be there too. The Prime Minister did not favour this risk. The King thought that if it was not right for him to go, neither was it for Churchill. The Prime Minister had a reply to that: he considered that in his capacity as Minister of Defence it was his duty to go. The King's secretary came to his master's rescue: he thought that 'his Majesty's anxieties would be increased if he heard his Prime Minister was at the bottom of the English Channel'. Still Churchill did not give up: it took a letter from the King, just as he was setting out, to stop him. He must have been sad.

Those days before and after D-Day in the summer of 1944 were indeed unforgettable to all of us who lived through them. It was like the summer of 1940 again, but this time with the burning hope that all would be put right at last. The mood of the whole country was a mood of prayer: everyone understood what was at stake: everyone had somebody involved in it, in danger. No one knew what the casualties would be – the word went round fifty-fifty. By now people were steeled to bad news, the V-bombs were falling on London; this was the last hope, this the moment for which all had waited and many had died. People that day stood in the streets waiting every hour for news, strangers speaking familiarly to each other. Every morning at dawn people in the south of England awoke to hear the planes go over to aid the landings. Not to be there was like not being there on St Crispin's day.

'How I wish you were here', wrote Churchill to the President. As soon as Montgomery launched his offensive Churchill went over to see for himself how things were going and encourage the men. He visited every sector within our restricted foothold and ended up with the field hospital where casualties were coming in. One poor fellow was on the operating table, and Churchill was about to slip away when the soldier said he wanted him.

The Prime Minister came to his side; the wounded man smiled wanly and kissed his hand.

At Yalta death's hand was already upon the President. Himself unwell, Churchill went by plane to meet him in Valletta harbour.

> As the American cruiser steamed slowly past us towards her berth alongside the quay wall I could see the figure of the President seated on the bridge, and we waved to each other. With the escort of Spitfires overhead, the salutes, and the bands of the ships' companies in the harbour playing 'The Star-spangled Banner' it was a splendid scene.[45]

The President was looking frail and ill. A young British sailor who saw him disembarking told me how harrowing it was to see the effort it cost him to move, the sweat pouring down his face: he was going, careless of the personal cost, to his death. However, he took full part in the sessions of the conference, seven out of eight of which were devoted to Poland. At the end a joint declaration was issued: 'we re-affirm our common desire to see established a strong, free, independent, and democratic Poland'. We know how that promise was kept.

Churchill did not see the President again. When he said good-bye to him he felt that his contact with life was already slender, his mind remote. The Prime Minister returned to the rejoicings over the crossing of the Rhine and victory in sight. But

> Britain, though still very powerful, could not act decisively alone. I could at this stage only warn and plead. Thus this climax of apparently measureless success was to me a most unhappy time. I moved among cheering crowds, or sat at a table adorned with congratulations and blessings from every part of the Grand Alliance, with an aching heart and a mind oppressed with forebodings.[46]

In April came the news of the President's death. It struck him as a physical blow. And so it did the people of Britain. No leading figure outside this island has ever meant so much to ordinary simple folk within it: he was a figure beside everyone's hearth. They all felt, not obscurely, that he had come to their rescue. That

45. Churchill, *The Second World War*, VI. 299, 338. 46. ibid., 400.

day an intense sense of the presence stilled, the image of the friend gone from the world, was with us all: every English house was a house of mourning.

The days of the government that had saved Britain from being so nearly lost were numbered. It is fairly clear that its best members did not wish it to break up, neither Churchill nor Bevin, Eden nor Attlee. Victory against Hitler was won. On Victory day one saw Churchill at the head of the House of Commons lead them proudly in procession, head high, across Parliament Square to give thanksgiving in St Margaret's, their parish church. Those leaders knew how much remained to do, the problems left by the defeat of Hitler, a Europe in dissolution, ready for the strongest and most unscrupulous to take advantage of, the Russian advance into the centre of the Continent. It would have been better for Britain and the world if the government could have kept together a little longer, utilizing its experience and authority. But the forces of party and the pressure of lesser men had their way.

Stalin never had any doubt that the Conservatives would win. At Yalta he had asked politely who could be a better leader than he who had won the victory. Churchill explained that we had two parties in England and that he belonged to only one of them. 'One party is much better,' said Stalin with conviction.[47] Later, at Potsdam, with the certainty that attaches to Russian orthodoxy, Stalin was able to assure Churchill that he would have a majority of about eighty. After all he had considerable experience of foretelling the results of elections in Russia. Churchill himself was not unconfident – he even hoped to reconstitute the coalition with which he had saved England, to save Europe if possible – until the night before the results were declared. He awoke with an intuitive certainty, that was almost a stab of physical pain, that he was beaten. 'The power to shape the future would be denied me. The knowledge and experience I had gathered, the authority and goodwill I had gained in so many countries, would vanish.'

The day confirmed this foreboding. There was an immense majority for the Labour party – or rather, against the twenty-

47. Churchill, *The Second World War*, VI. 344, 549, 583.

year rule of the Conservatives that had brought us to such a pass. It was in keeping with the fatuity of human affairs that the man who had delivered us should have to pay the penalty for them. He did not wait to meet Parliament; at the end of the day he handed in his resignation to the King. 'The verdict of the electors had been so overwhelmingly expressed that I did not wish to remain even for an hour responsible for their affairs.'

Epilogue

THUS passed the most famous five years in all our history.

It is impossible to describe the events of the thirteen years that have followed: they have not yet entered into history, or, rather, become suitable fodder for historiography. We lack the documents, the precise annotated information; we do not know the inner facts. Anyway, we need not envy the chronicler of a squalid age.

The initial relapse to party-politics threw Churchill off his balance; in the changed circumstances, the war-time comradeship over, we do not find him at his best. On the withdrawal of the Labour people from the coalition he formed a 'caretaker government' to carry on over the election and until the results were known. But his appeal to the country struck an unfortunate note, and one that was unworthy of him. Instead of keeping people's minds firmly to the tasks ahead of them, the dangers that would follow, none knew better, from the advance of Soviet Russia in Europe, the increasing rift between East and West, the still overriding need for unity in the nation, he tried to alert the electors to the internal Bolshevik danger coming from the Labour party.

This was very unconvincing, and indeed unfair of him: his friends and opponents, Attlee and Bevin – did they look like Bolsheviks? Attlee considered that this line was due to Lord Beaverbrook's influence and, himself yielding to no one in his admiration for Churchill, points out how necessary it is that the latter should have people about him strong enough to counter an impulsive wrong idea. With characteristic under-statement Attlee says, 'I feel that the line I took was more in accord with the mood of the electors.'[1] Churchill persisted and tried to take advantage of an intervention by Laski, the asinine Chairman of the Labour Party,[2] to place Attlee in a bad tactical position. 'I was generally

1. C. R. Attlee, *As It Happened*, 140, 144–5.

2. 'Whose political judgement was not very good', says Attlee. This, too, is an under-statement.

thought', says Attlee, with meek effectiveness, 'to have had the better of the exchanges.' The truth is that Churchill was not a match for Attlee as a party-tactician. When the large Labour majority over the Conservatives became clear – some 393 members to a Conservative minority of 213, smaller than at any since 1906 – it is said that Churchill muttered, 'they should have had Baldwin to lead them, and they wouldn't have lost the election'. This may not be apocryphal: it has the right ring, comic, magnanimous, rueful. (And we may add – maybe, but *he* would have lost the country.) It is really rather irresistible in so great a man to be so bad at the mere party-game that occupies so much of the minds of lesser men. And even here, strange to say, he has improved his form, come to maturity – in his late seventies!

Actually these manoeuvres may have contributed little enough to the result of the election of 1945 anyway. The vast majority of the service-men voted Labour. One of the new Labour Ministers, Ellen Wilkinson, told me that on her tour of our Occupied Zone in Germany when she asked a young soldier exactly why he had voted Labour, he replied blissfully, 'Well, you know, miss – anything for a change!' And that was about it. In my own constituency the working people assured me that they had voted Labour, but were very sorry that Mr Churchill had been defeated. This not only goes to show the good-heartedness rather than the logical sense of the British elector, but that there may be more sense in him than logic. What the country needed at this juncture was the continuance of the Churchill government, with a larger Labour wing.

At such a rebuff anyone else might have given up; there was the long unhappy twilight of Lloyd George's career as a warning; plenty for him to write about, plenty to paint. Not so Churchill. He was Leader of the Opposition, a new job for him, in diminished circumstances, in a House full of new faces that knew not David. People wondered how he would do, how he would accommodate himself to this raw, untutored assembly. They were rather restive at first and, not knowing the great days, inclined to be disrespectful. But the comrades of 1940, who knew who had saved the country, were not wanting in respect, neither Attlee nor Bevin, Morrison nor Dalton; and soon the new House listened with attention to what the 'Old Man' had to say. Though he was not constant in attendance upon the routine business of the House – he had better things to do with his time – he yet spoke on many occasions and on all the leading issues, giving full measure of his experience, warning, advice.

The dominant issues left by the war, as we know too well, were those of an Atomic world, the illimitable prospects of destruction opening up from nuclear fission, the world-advance of Communism, the conflict between East and West, the throttling of liberties over all of Eastern, and much of Central, Europe. Here he was much better apprised than most people what to expect. He knew Stalin's record of duplicity and cruelty in the treatment of Poland, the determination to throttle any Polish independence or freedom. It was the more agonizing that we could do nothing about it, since we owed Poland a debt of honour. Churchill's only consolation was the thought that 'this is not the end of the story'. Nor is it, indeed; it never is: then why do people go on trying these things in history? It was followed by the extinction of any independence in Rumania, Bulgaria, Hungary; Yugoslavia at that time was an obedient satellite; half Austria and all Eastern Germany were in the Russian grip; notice was served on the West with the Communist *coup* in Czechoslovakia, the stifling of her independence, the brutal dragooning of Benes, the murder of Jan Masaryk. It had been a profound mistake at the end of the war to allow the Russians so far forward into the heart of Europe; if only Berlin had been the frontier between East and West, Europe would have been able to breathe more freely.

Churchill himself says that the Americans were slow to grasp what it all meant, and for the first six months Bevin was left to stand in the breach alone. He knew the Communists – had had them to deal with all his life; he was at one on the subject with Churchill. At Churchill's last meeting with his Conservative Cabinet he had spoken sombrely of the country's outlook with a large socialist majority; but he concluded with one consoling thought – Bevin was to be Foreign Secretary, an Englishman and a patriot firm as a rock, in whose hands the country's interests were safe. And so it proved.

One thing we can affirm of these next years: no statesman out of office, except possibly Gladstone, has exerted such an influence by his words alone. And now Churchill's words excited as much attention, if not more, in America. In March 1946 he made there his Fulton speech, which had a wider reverberation round the world than any of his speeches. It was not altogether welcome: he used President Truman's encouragement to give 'true and faithful counsel' to direct the attention of the world to the full implications of Stalin's course of action while it was still in its early stages. 'I shall certainly avail myself of this freedom, and feel the more right to do so because any private ambitions I may have cherished in my younger days have been satisfied beyond my wildest dreams.'[3]

His dominant theme was that the American monopoly of the atomic bomb for a year or two gave the Western world only 'a breathing space to set our house in order'. From Stettin to Trieste an iron curtain had been drawn across the Continent, all communications of the spirit broken off. At the end of the fighting the American and British armies had withdrawn westwards along a front of four hundred miles, in some places to a depth of 150 miles – territory which the Western democracies had conquered, but handed over to the Russians to occupy. In most countries, except those of the Commonwealth and the United States, 'the Communist parties or fifth columns constitute a growing challenge and peril to Christian civilization'. He did not believe that a new war was inevitable or that Soviet Russia desired war. 'What they desire is the fruits of war and the indefinite expansion of their power and doctrines.' From what he had seen of the Russians, he was convinced that what counted with them was strength; they despised weakness, especially military weakness. The Western democracies needed then to stand together, organize their forces and parley from a position of strength. To this end he advocated the continuance of the war-time facilities between America and the Commonwealth for the mutual use of naval and air bases all over the world. This would double the mobility of American forces and greatly expand the strength of the British. 'Eventually there may come – I feel eventually there will come – the principle

3. Churchill, *The Sinews of Peace. Post-War Speeches*, ed. Randolph S. Churchill, 93 foll.

of common citizenship, but that we may be content to leave to destiny, whose outstretched arm many of us can already clearly see.'

Not content with announcing imperative measures of common defence he described – as so rarely – the ends for which these exist, what we mean by the cause of democracy, why it is worth defending and what it has to offer to the world.

All this means that the people of any country have the right, and should have the power, by constitutional action, by free unfettered elections with secret ballot, to choose or change the character or form of government under which they dwell; that freedom of speech and thought should reign; that courts of justice, independent of the executive, unbiased by any party, should administer laws which have received the broad assent of large majorities or are consecrated by time and custom. Here are the title-deeds of freedom which should lie in every cottage home. Here is the message of the British and American peoples to mankind.

This speech had a bad reception in Britain, and not a very good one in America: people do not like to be told home-truths. This did not discourage him: he had been through that before.

Last time I saw it all coming and cried aloud to my own fellow-countrymen and to the world, but no one paid any attention. Up till the year 1933 or even 1935, Germany might have been saved from the awful fate which has overtaken her and we might all have been spared the miseries Hitler let loose upon mankind. There never was a war in all history easier to prevent by timely action than the one which has just desolated such great areas of the globe. It could have been prevented in my belief without the firing of a single shot, and Germany might be powerful, prosperous and honoured today; but no one would listen and one by one we were all sucked into the awful whirlpool.

It is probable that no speech by a politician out of office and power has exerted such an influence on events. For it is to this that we must date the alerting of the democracies to their danger and their mental preparedness to take steps in their own defence. America and Britain, with their essentially civilian outlook, had been far too anxious to return to a peace-time basis and had gone too far, too soon, in unscrambling and dispersing their war-time forces. As Stalin's intentions were progressively revealed, all this was ended. The democracies began to equip themselves once more for their defence; America set up her advanced air-bases in the island, once more the pivot of their joint security. All this went back to the Fulton speech: it cannot be said that it was premature or, alas, unnecessary.

In this, as with regard to world affairs generally, Bevin and Churchill were in much agreement. And it must be said that the Labour government did far better in resisting Stalin than the pre-war Conservatives had done in resisting Hitler. Where Churchill disagreed with them, as he always had done, was over socialist economics. The war left us economically exhausted: capital investments abroad eaten up; immense material damage within the country, large cities ruined, areas laid waste; industry run down, railways worn out, nothing replaced or kept up for years, except war-industries; the people suffering from under-nourishment, listless and weary. And that continued to be so for years after the war.

In these circumstances it would be a mistake to expect too much from them. The transition to a Welfare State was inevitable. Churchill had no quarrel with that; indeed, we have seen that he had had a large and generous hand in its early beginnings years before. What he did not believe in was the end and aim of socialist doctrine: a planned and regulated society controlled by the state; the economic life of the country held in the strait-jacket of a bureaucracy; a level of taxation penalizing enterprise, the operation of incentive throughout society undermined and rendered null. In short, he feared that a socialist society would not be a free society; intellectually he remained, what he had always been, a liberal.

The bulk of the burden the country was bearing was due to the war: we owe it to the Germans. And without American aid on an immense scale, and of an unprecedented generosity – let us hope that we are a better investment than China – we could not have carried on or begun to revive. It was natural enough, after such long endurance, that the people should take, with or without leave, a five-day week – though the deplorable Germans, to whom these miseries were due, were working all hours to restore their shattered country. But on top of these burdens, at a time when there was so much destruction to replace, and when the prime necessity was therefore work, enterprise, incentive, the socialist government saw fit to burden the economy with larger instalments of the Welfare State than the country could possibly afford, social services, a vast transformation and expansion in education, expensive health services, pensions, socialized medicine, what not. It was too much, all at once and at such a time. Its cost was crippling, at the expense of savings, of proper capital-investment, of capital-formation, of the future. For a socialist society, *unless forced,* eats the seed-corn.

This is the theme of speech after speech of Churchill's, as crisis upon crisis over foreign exchange succeeded each other throughout the Labour government, gold and dollar reserves were lost, the value of the pound undermined, down to a third what it had been before the war, and the long fever of inflation gained head, from which we are not likely to recover. I do not see how Churchill's arguments can be gainsaid. On the financial crisis of September 1949:

in these last four lavish years the socialist government have exacted upwards of £16 thousand millions and spent them – over four times as much every year as was the cost of running the country in our richer days before the war. They have used up every national asset or reserve upon which they could lay their hands; they have taken 40 per cent of the national income for the purposes of governmental administration. Our taxation has been the highest in the world. Large incomes are virtually confiscated. The exertions and rewards of the most active class of wage-earners and craftsmen have been burdened in times of peace by the harsh direct taxation which in war, when we are fighting for life, may be a matter of pride to bear, but which in victory is at least a disappointment, and I believe has been a definite deterrent to production. . . . As has been well said, we ate the Argentine railways – £110 millions – last year as a mere side-dish. . . . We have been given or loaned – and have spent – £1750 thousand millions by the United States. We have been helped to the extent of over £30 millions by Canada, Australia and New Zealand. . . . In all history no community has ever been helped and kept by gratuitous overseas aid, that is to say, by the labour of other hard-working peoples, to anything approaching the degree which we have been under the present socialist government. And where are we at the end of it all?[4]

4. Churchill, *In the Balance. Speeches 1949 and 1950,* ed. Randolph S. Churchill, 87.

The answer was – in a crisis which necessitated an emergency session of Parliament to sanction fixing the pound, as against its pre-war rate of $4·86, at $2·70.

As the election drew near Churchill stated the choice before the nation:

> between two ways of life; between individual liberty and state domination; between concentration of ownership in the hands of the state and the extension of a property-owning democracy; between a policy of increasing restraint and a policy of liberating energy and ingenuity; between a policy of levelling down and a policy of finding opportunity for all to rise upwards from a basic standard.[5]

These may be political clichés; the realities in Britain are sufficiently dreary and disheartening: a kindly and slack society without the sense of quality of enterprise, without colour or discrimination, subtlety or spirit, neither desiring nor valuing historic achievement.

Let us turn, for a moment, from the distasteful subject.

Churchill, with his old-fashioned energy, his prodigious Victorian vitality, had better things to do. Now in his seventies, he was writing his Memoirs of the Second World War. The first volume was ready a couple of years after the fall of his government, in spite of distractions as Leader of the Opposition and a few other little things; it was published in 1948. He modestly refuses to describe it as history, in the austere sense of the word, 'for that belongs to another generation. But I claim with confidence that it is a contribution to history which will be of service to the future.'[6] Once more, as with his Memoirs of the First World War, there would be controversy,

> but it would be wrong not to lay the lessons of the past before the future. . . . One day President Roosevelt told me that he was asking publicly for suggestions about what the war should be called. I said at once 'The Unnecessary War'. There never was a war more easy to stop than that which has just wrecked what was left of the world from the previous struggle.

5. Churchill, *In the Balance, Speeches 1949 and 1950*, ed. Randolph S. Churchill, 169.

6. Churchill, *The Second World War*, I. vii–ix.

He follows this up with the theme of this volume occupying a page to itself, 'How the English-speaking Peoples through their Unwisdom, Carelessness and Good Nature Allowed the Wicked to Re-Arm'.

We see that he is a believer in the practical value of the study of history, in drawing its morals and learning its lessons. All the sages of the past have thought that, from Erasmus and Francis Bacon downwards; the lesser academics of today know better. But what is the point of history if we do not learn from it, relate it to life? It is no abstract, pure geometry. Thereafter followed a volume each year until the last, a sixth, which appeared in 1954, when he was Prime Minister again. The theme of that is 'How the Great Democracies Triumphed, and so Were Able to Resume the Follies which Had so nearly Cost Them their Life'.[7]

In his seventy-seventh year, in November 1951, Churchill became Prime Minister and Minister of Defence once more. There had been nothing to equal this since Gladstone.

Labour's ascendancy had been undermined by the constant weakening of the economic position and a consequent failure of confidence, by the death of their real leader Bevin and by the squabbles and divisions endemic in the party, but which he and Attlee had managed to hold in check. In return for Churchill's warnings as to the danger from Soviet imperialism and the necessity to rearm, he was under constant attack from the more irresponsible Labour people at this time as a 'war-monger'. It was exactly what had been said about him by Chamberlainite Conservatives in the 1930s, and it was the exact reverse of the truth. 'One can break one's heart only once', he had said at the time of Munich; but there is every evidence that he was deeply wounded at the renewal of this wicked charge. 'I do not hold that we should re-arm in order to fight,' he had to explain; 'I hold that we should re-arm in order to parley.'[8] If we had remained disarmed and weak there was nothing to stop Stalin occupying all Europe. He was already trying it out in the Far East, when the Americans had withdrawn from Korea: the real reason for the Korean War: the objective was Japan. If President Truman had not had the

7. ibid., VI. ix. 8. *Annual Register, 1951*, 59.

courage to resist then and there, the world-balance against Communism would have been lost. Churchill, naturally, saw the whole thing; political lunatics, naturally, not.

However, it was generally thought that this charge made the difference of twenty seats to the Conservatives: they were returned to power with a small majority of only twenty-five – difficult to work on. Churchill's Cabinet leaned definitely to the liberal Conservative side: the Churchillians, not the Chamberlainites – this still remained the primary division in the party – were in the ascendant. On the last day of the year the Prime Minister departed in a gale for America, determined to achieve solvency, warning his countrymen that 'Britons should not expect the Americans to solve their domestic problems', and carrying with him the decision to repay in full the first instalments of the American loan.[9]

All through the first year of his second government the financial situation remained one of feverish debility and intermittent crisis. Immense losses of gold and dollar reserves continued: the truth was that the war and the Welfare State together had seriously impaired the country's economic viability. In 1952 the government was at its lowest strength: if there had been an election Labour would certainly have been returned to power. A member of Churchill's Cabinet has told me that only the old man's will-power kept them together and saw them through: a new-comer himself and a heroic fighting man in the war, he was deeply impressed by the spectacle and the experience. Walter Lippmann paid tribute from the other side: he was 'after all the old champion, their champion and our champion. What he has to give, which is his genius and the steadfastness of his people is, on any decent reckoning, the equal of anything he can get in return.'[10] Lippmann hoped that 'the alliance would not degenerate into an American empire, surrounded only by satellites and dependencies'.

At the end of this year Churchill went off again for talks with Truman and the incoming President Eisenhower, and for a December holiday in the West Indies. He clearly liked going; but though the use of American bases in Britain was continued, he could not persuade the Americans to contribute a token force in

9. *Annual Register, 1951*, 194. 10. ibid., *1952*, 2–3.

the Suez Canal zone. Not till a year later was the real reason for the visit disclosed: the hydrogen bomb was now well on the way, and he was much concerned at Britain's lack of information. The advance of nuclear fission, the increasing possibilities of destruction for the human race, the urgent necessity for an understanding with Russia, some assured basis for peace – these were the thoughts that obsessed his mind in these last years of office. He longed to bring about a meeting of the three leaders at the summit, as in the days of the war, when pulling together for a common end had been possible in spite of divergences. Now, more than ever, it was a dire necessity. He longed to end his career, not as a 'war-monger' but as a harbinger of peace to the nations. Again and again he suggested a meeting with the Russian leaders. Time pressed – certainly for him. He strained every nerve to bring it about, but American opinion was now, in a changed atmosphere, consistently unfavourable; nor were the Russians willing.

King George VI had died in 1952, still a comparatively young man, but worn out by work, the strain of the war-years, of service to the country. It was thought that the Prime Minister's tribute not even he had surpassed. In May 1953 came the coronation of Queen Elizabeth II, and that moment coincided with a recovery of the country's spirits. Not until then did the mood of weariness and war-exhaustion lift from the people; everybody noticed a new buoyancy, the old gaiety and cheerfulness return to the English after too long an endurance. Not even the Russian menace, and their comparative proximity to it, repressed them. The Coronation junketings helped. One saw him at that marvellous spectacle in the Abbey, leading the procession of the Commonwealth Prime Ministers, pausing to say a word to Lady Churchill in the pew in front before taking his place in his stall in the choir, a billowing figure in the plumes and robes of a Knight of the Garter – a Low cartoon of himself. For over-night he had accepted the Garter he had refused in 1945. He had forfeited the majestic simplicity of Mr Churchill – somehow one hardly becomes acclimatized to 'Sir Winston', for all its pleasant long-retarded chime with his ancestor, the Cavalier Colonel. On his way out from the astonishing hieratic scene we had all witnessed – its poignancy multiplied a hundredfold for those in whose minds re-echoed the memories in that place of Victoria, of the young George III and his friend the fourth Duke, of Anne and Sarah and Marlborough, of Elizabeth I and the medieval kings going right back to the Conqueror – one saw him hang back surveying the scene on which the improbable sacrament, the enacted dream of the ages had taken place, looking at it for the last time, then moving on in the procession past the spot where Arabella and her brother are buried, on and out.

The strain of that year was too much for him; in July he had a severe stroke, paralysing all one side of his body, arm and leg. The secret was very well kept, for at the moment his designated successor Eden was desperately ill, undergoing one of those liver-duct operations of which the Americans have perfected the technique, without which he could not have lived. People only knew that he was suffering from strain – as well he might be – and was resting down at Chartwell. Hardly anyone was admitted to see him; he was out of action for four months – until people wondered whether he would come back. Not the least of his marvels is his recovery, at such an age, from so severe a thrombosis and coming back to carry on as Prime Minister. In October he returned to public life, to speak to the Conservative Conference. Then it was, 'would the Old Man prove to be his old self again?' His speech provided a triumphant and a moving affirmative:

> if I stay for the time being, bearing the burden at my age, it is not because of love for power or office. I have had an ample share of both. If I stay it is because I have the feeling that I may, through things that have happened, have an influence on what I care about above all else – the building of a sure and lasting peace.[11]

On his return to the House the better side, the latent good nature, of British politics was made evident. The Opposition declared that it had been 'a duller place in his absence'. After Stalin's death in March Churchill suggested a private conference of the Western allies as a preliminary to conferring with the Russians. The Opposition contrasted the humanity of his approach to the pettifogging difficulties made by his colleagues while he was away. We may say that from this time the Opposition took

11. *Annual Register, 1953*, 49.

him to their hearts as in the great years, 1940 to 1945 – only with a few leading Chamberlainites has the rancour remained. Labour had forgiven him everything; they nothing. But he was a figure now above the storm, above party.

In June he spent a weekend at Washington with President Eisenhower. 'I come from my fatherland to my mother's land.'[12] He praised the amenities of a Federal system: England 'was once a Heptarchy and it might be a good thing if it were to become a heptarchy again'. There was evidently no response for a meeting with the Russians in that quarter. In July he made a private proposal for an exploratory meeting to Molotov: he got an answer to something different. He was holding on, hoping against hope that something might be possible, some assurance of peace to humanity on which he might go out.

In November he paid his annual visit to Harrow, where a verse was added to the School song in his honour:

> Sixty years on – though in time growing older,
> Younger in heart you return to the Hill.

In retrospect perhaps it had not been so bad after all: Time, so long a time, had put it right. At the end of the month his eightieth birthday was celebrated in unparalleled manner by Parliament – members of all parties joining in – and the nation. Addresses, honours, presents showered. The House of Lords had a happy thought: two silver jugs that had belonged to General Charles Churchill, the great Duke's brother, engraved with his crest and coat of arms and that of his wife, Mary Gould. There was a unique ceremony in Westminster Hall, where both Houses of Parliament assembled to do him honour. His portrait was presented to him, with a felicitous speech by his friend and opponent Attlee, who, as an old soldier in the Dardanelles campaign, did not hesitate to praise it as 'the only imaginative strategic concept of the war'.[13] In Churchill's reply the whole country heard the familiar voice for the last time, on a grand occasion: 'there has never been anything like it in British history and, indeed, I doubt whether any of the modern democracies abroad have shown such

12. *Annual Register, 1954*, 24.
13. *The Times*, 1 December 1954.

a degree of kindness and generosity to a party politician who has not yet retired and may at any time be involved in controversy'. Going back to 1940 – all people's minds and emotions were there again –

> I have never accepted what many people have kindly said, namely, that I inspired the nation. Their will was resolute and remorseless, and, as it proved, unconquerable. It fell to me to express it, and if I found the right words, you must remember that I have always earned my living by my pen and by my tongue. It was the nation and the race dwelling all round the globe that had the lion's heart. I had the luck to be called on to give

– and here we heard, for the last time, the old harsh defiant note – 'the roar'.

It was all in inverted commas now, mellowed and mute. All the same it was impossible to listen without emotion to the V-sign given out upon the drums, Elgar's march accompanying him as he walked down the full length of Westminster Hall out at the great west door to the crowd awaiting him in Parliament Square.

The nation had subscribed its present: a very large sum which the Prime Minister proposed to turn into a trust for the endowment of Chartwell – his creation as it stands, with all its treasures – 'as a museum containing relics and mementoes of my long life'. So the nation will have something far more personal and idiosyncratic, if on a much smaller scale, befitting a more egalitarian society, than the magnificent impersonality, at once so eloquent and so reserved, that commemorates John Churchill in Blenheim.

Still he did not resign. He evidently enjoyed the comedy of keeping people guessing; his colleagues might be on tenterhooks, but the Opposition relished the situation – they had become fond of their old enemy and were loth to let him go. In January and February 1955 he presided, for the last time, over the Conference of Commonwealth Prime Ministers. At last he had given up hope of bringing about the meeting he so much desired. His last message on the subject upon which humanity's future rests was that for the next three or four years superiority in hydrogen bombs should give us a breathing-space; that deterrence might well prove the road to disarmament; it might be that 'safety would be the sturdy child of terror and survival the twin-brother of annihilation. . . . Meanwhile, never flinch, never weary, never despair'.[14] In that lies all our attenuated hope.

On 4 April he entertained the Queen to dinner at 10 Downing Street, where once more he assembled his war-time colleagues of both parties. In proposing the Queen's health he was able to say that he had enjoyed drinking that toast as a cavalry subaltern 'in the reign of your Majesty's great-great-grandmother'. What a world away that was, the world of Queen Victoria and Mr Gladstone, Lord Salisbury and Lord Randolph, the hot afternoons at Bangalore in which he had read Gibbon and Macaulay, the first experience of war on the North-West Frontier and of writing it up in *The Story of the Malakand Field Force*, the Empire and the Raj apparently secure as ever. It was an immense span of experience for one life to hold. Queen Victoria's great-great-grandfather was George II, and his was James I: we are back in the age of the first Elizabeth, from which it all sprang.

His life has been fortunate beyond belief in coinciding with the finest hour in the country's long history – its apogee, and the moment when its separateness is coming to an end, in the fearful danger of our age, and is merging in that of the English stocks across the world. Here, too, his has been a chosen life, prophetic of the future; for he has drawn strength equally from the two main branches of those stocks on either side of the Atlantic and in himself has drawn them together.

We have observed again and again in the story of the family how singularly it reflects the history of the country. Apart from those out-riders on the flanks, those party-men on the Right and on the Left, the Cavalier Colonel and Lord Robert, who are exceptions, the tradition of the family has been essentially centripetal. Undoctrinaire and undogmatic, however strong their personalities, they have been Trimmers in the true sense of the word – in the sense in which so many of the most intelligent men in politics have been: standing somewhat loosely to party, they have been to be found usually where the interest of the country was to be found.

14. *Annual Register, 1955*, 6.

Though the two peaks with which the family has culminated in its two grand periods, the great Duke and our war-time Prime Minister, stand in some contrast of character, Sir Winston does sum up richly in his life many of the themes of the family exposed in this book. There is the overriding interest in politics and military affairs of the Churchills; the artistic inheritance of the Spencers coming out in him not only as a writer, but in painting. He is no less an artist than politician, a Spencer than a Churchill. And we see in him how the conscious ideal of a family tradition can have a decisive effect in moulding a life – the desire to complete his father's broken career, the aristocrat who was a tribune of the people; the return to his mother's soil for renewal and inspiration, to a remoter past with the determination to be the Marlborough in the Grand Alliance of his time.

The miracle is to have achieved it all.

Index

Index

Abdullah, Emir, 441
Aboukir, cruiser, 418
Abyssinia, 472
Adelaide, Queen, 209, 257
Admiralty, Board of, 139, 141, 370, 416, 417, 418–27, 472, 481, 482
Afghanistan, 309, 315
Africa, East, 385–7; —, North, 496, 503, 507, 511, 512; —, South, 333–4, 356–64
Agadir incident, 403–5
Agnew, art dealer, 240, 275, 276
Aiguillon, Duc d', 85
Ailesbury, Lord, 17
Aix-la-Chapelle, Peace of, 67
Alexandria, 351
All the Talents, Ministry of, 183
Almack's Club, 135
Althorp House, 19, 26, 35, 67, 467
Amelia, Princess, 155
America, 114, 116, 252, 257–8, 366, 455, 465–6, 493–4, 496, 500–3, 512, 524–6; American Revolutionary War, 115, 138–48
Amery, L. S., 341, 359, 366, 377, 482
Amherst, Jeffrey, Lord, 81
Amiens, Peace of, 179, 181
Anglo-German Naval Agreement, 472
Anne, Queen, 2, 27, 101
Antwerp, 417–18
Arbuthnot, Mrs, 208, 215
Archangel, 438
Ardilaun, Lord, 275
Argyll, Duke of, 199, 201
Armisted, Mrs, 179, 181
Army, reorganization, 369–73; World War I, 417, 430–2, 433; World War II, 486–9, 496, 504, 505, 507–10, 514–16
Arnold, Matthew, 392
Ashe House, 1, 4
Ashley, Cropley, 202
Asquith, Herbert Henry, 375, 387, 405, 407, 408, 413, 419, 425, 426, 432, 434, 443, 449, 451, 454–5
Atlantic Charter, 501
Atomic bomb, 523, 524, 531
Attlee, C. R., Earl, 420, 518, 521–2, 529, 533
Auckland, William Eden, Lord, 95, 139, 147, 159, 160–1, 175, 187, 188, 189–92, 193, 206
Audacious, H.M.S., 418
Augusta, U.S. cruiser, 501
Austen, Jane, 167
Australia, 503–4
Austria, 187, 403; Austrian Succession, War of the, 44–51
Aylesford, Earl of, 270–71; —, Lady, 240, 271

Baldwin, Stanley, Earl, 381, 444, 447–9, 451–2, 455, 456, 459, 460, 463–5, 468–9, 471–3, 475–6, 522
Balfour, A. J., Earl, 293, 298, 322, 331, 334, 336–7, 373, 374, 376, 377–8, 382, 403, 450, 451, 467
Balkans, the, 323, 515
Ballin, Albert, 414
Bampton Lectures, 196
Banbury, 71
Bangalore, 346, 355, 535
Bangor diocese, 137, 148–9
Barrie, Sir James, 284
Bartolozzi, F., 171, 239
Bateman, Lord, 28–9; —, Lady, 27, 28–30, 31, 45, 55
Bath, 63, 92, 103, 104, 132–3, 163, 169
Battenberg, Prince Louis of, 419

Beatty, Admiral, Earl, 355, 407, 451, 456
Beauclerk, Topham, 124–5, 169–70; —, Lady Diana (born Spencer, then Lady Bolingbroke), 41, 48, 83, 89, 93, 107–8, 118, 124–5, 162, 168–73, 196; —, Lord Vere, 63
Beaverbrook, Lord, 424, 430, 432, 434, 468, 469, 493, 521
Bebel, August, 394
Beckley, James, 133
Bedford, 4th Duke of, 35, 39, 57, 58–9, 66, 68, 70, 78, 98, 110, 114, 115–19; —, Diana Spencer, 1st wife of, 5, 8, 25, 28–9, 35; —, Gertrude, 2nd wife of, 106, 107–9, 113, 173, 200, 201; —, estates, 237
Belgium, 414–15, 417–18
Benes, President, 523
Beresford, Lord Charles, 270; —, Lord William, 281, 283
Berlin, 189, 277, 414, 491, 523; — Gallery, 277
Bernini, Giovanni, 288
Bertie family, 119; —, Lady Gwendeline, 390
Beveridge, Lord, 389, 390–1
Bevin, Ernest, 459, 472–3, 492, 518, 521, 522, 523, 526, 529
Birkenhead, F. E. Smith, Earl of, 400, 413, 447, 450, 452, 460–1n., 469–70
Birmingham, 214, 304, 306, 331, 477
Bismarck, battleship, 472
Bismarck, Prince, 266; —, Herbert, 333
Bladon, 129, 280, 337
Blandford, Albertha, Lady, 256, 262–3, 271, 272–4, 281, 283, 285; —, George Spencer Churchill, Lord, *see* Marlborough, 8th Duke of; —, George Spencer, Lord, *see* Marlborough, 5th Duke of; —, John Churchill, Lord, 2; —, William Godolphin, Lord, 2, 5, 14–16, 18, 26, 38
Blenheim Palace, 4, 5, 7, 36, 47, 91' 103, 109, 126–34, 143, 163–5, 169, 191, 194–8, 206–9, 231–2, 237–40, 246–50, 279–81, 283–4, 339, 372, 398; household expenses, 73–4, 131–2; Library, 6–7, 238, 248–9, 290; royal visits to, 155–7, 209, 231–2; sales, 248–50, 274–5; Settled Estates Act, 249; theatricals, 132, 162, 194–5
Blood, General Sir Bindon, 346, 348
Blunt, Wilfrid Scawen, 351, 375, 379–80, 389–90, 401–2, 423
Boccaccio, the Valdarfer, 204, 207–8
Bolingbroke, 3rd Viscount, 93, 105, 106, 118, 119, 125, 179; —, Lady, *see* Lady Diana Beauclerk
Bolton, Duke of, 58
Bombay, 314, 348
Boothby, Sir Robert, 459
Borkum, island of, 431, 508
Boscawen, Admiral, 77; —, Mrs, 135
Bosnia-Herzegovina, 403
Boston, Massachusetts, 366
Botha, General, 357, 360, 385
Boufflers, Marquise de, 176
Bournemouth, 343, 509
Bouverie, Mr, 178, 182, 184; —, Mrs, 182, 184; —, Diana, 184
Braddock, General, 77
Bradlaugh, Charles, 299, 308
Brand, Speaker, 298
Brighton, 134, 163, 167, 190; — Pavilion, 134, 167, 168, 199
Brington church, 25
Britain, Battle of, 342
British Expeditionary Force, 417
British Gazette, 459
Brodrick, W., Lord Midleton, 370–73
Brooke, Field-Marshal, Lord Alanbrooke, 456, 507–11
Brooke, Rupert, 420
Brooks's Club, 134–5, 175–6, 177 180, 184, 186

Brown, 'Capability', 128–30, 131, 288
Bryant, Jacob, 87–8, 94–7, 164, 239
Buccleuch, Duke of, 237
Buckingham Palace, 167, 495
Buckinghamshire, 237
Bulgaria, 322, 523
Buller, General Sir Redvers, 359, 363
Bülow, Prince, 395
Burchell's White Rhinoceros, 387, 434
Burdett-Coutts, Baroness, 304
Burghley, Lord, 328
Burgoyne, General, 137, 177, 195, 505
Burke, Thomas H., 245, 252
Burma, 315–16, 505
Burney, Fanny, 156, 169
Burns, John, 388–9
Bute, 3rd Earl of, 3, 101, 105, 111–13, 116
Butt, Isaac, 242
Byng, Field-Marshal Lord, 363

Caillaux, Joseph, 455
Cairns, Lord, 248
Cairo, 386, 511, 512
Cambridge University, 94, 282
Campbell, Lady Colin, 280
Campbell-Bannerman, Sir Henry, 382, 383, 387
Canada, 81, 148, 503, 514
Cancale bay, 84–5
Canning, George, 160, 223
Canterbury, revenues of Archbishop, 225; — of Cathedral Chapter, 226
Carden, Admiral, 421, 422
Carlton Club, 273, 305, 444; — House, 167, 177, 181
Caroline, Queen, 35–6, 59–61
Carson, Lord, 413, 432
Carteret, Lord (later Earl Granville), 34–5, 49, 51
Catholic Emancipation, 213–14, 223
Cavendish, Lord Frederick, 245, 252
Cecil family, 262, 320, 322, 328; —, Lord Hugh, 225, 253, 373, 390, 444
Chamberlain, Joseph, 305–6, 318, 319, 323, 324, 327, 331, 357n., 365, 368, 369, 375, 376, 377, 378, 388, 389, 395; —, Neville, 458, 476–83; —, Sir Austen, 375–7
Chambers, Sir William, 127–8
Chandos, sloop, 47
Charlemont, Earl of, 169
Charles II, King, 124
Charlotte, Princess Royal, 257
Charlotte, Queen, 101, 155–6, 158, 172
Chartwell, 4, 340, 361, 386, 430, 451, 466, 532, 534
Chatham, *see* Pitt, William the elder
Chequers, 510
Cherbourg, 85
Chesterfield, Lord, 57
Chicago, 366
Child, Sarah, 198–9
Christie's saleroom, 240, 275–7
Church of England, Reform of, 225–6, 227–30; —, revenues, 225–6, 228–9
Churchill, Lord Alan Spencer, 221; —, Lord Alfred Spencer, 219, 221, 222; —, Lord Almeric Spencer, 221; —, Arabella, 531; —, General Charles, 533; —, Lord Charles Spencer, 218; —, Lady Clementina Spencer, 221; Diana, 393; —, Francis, Lord Churchill of Wychwood, 132, 205–6, 207; —, Henrietta, *see* Marlborough; —, Lord Henry Spencer, 197; —, John, 1; —, Colonel John, 363, 390, 434; —, Lord John Spencer, 218; —, Lady Lilian Spencer, 291, 385

Churchill, Lord Randolph Spencer, 3, 4, 74, 231, 238, 258, 259, 273, 274, 307–9, 330–32, 338, 340, 342, 343–4, 350, 352, 363, 364, 369, 371, 374–5, 378–80, 389, 452; character, 261–2, 271–2, 295–8, 328–9, 337; at Eton and Oxford, 260–2; and Fourth Party, 298–301, 331; and Home Rule, 295, 310–11, 313, 317–18, 331–2, 334–5; in Ireland, 241–4; marriage, 238, 263–4, 268; and party machine, 305–8; and Prince of Wales, 240, 270–2; and reform, 335–6; resignation, 326–9; as Secretary of State for India, 313, 314–16; and Tory Democracy, 301–3, 335–6; travels, 332–4; Treasury and Leadership of Commons, 319–26; —, Lady Randolph (Jennie Jerome), 238, 240, 242, 243–4, 247–8, 258, 263–4, 266–9, 272, 301, 304, 313, 325, 337, 338, 363, 379, 402, 430, 440, 453

—, Winston, American novelist, 365, 434; —, Sir Winston, Cavalier Colonel, 1–2, 165n., 222, 244, 531, 536

—, Sir Winston Spencer, 240, 244, 247, 259, 264, 292–3, 296, 324–5; birth, 268; in Cuba, 345; in E. Africa, 385–7; and Edward VII, 383–4, 397, 399; in Egypt, 351–6; and India, 346–51, 464–6; marriage, 389–90; as painter, 428–30; schooldays, 338–43, 347; and South Africa, 356–64, 368–9, 372–3, 382, 384–5; in United States, 465–6, 502–3, 515, 510, 513, 514, 524–5, 530–31; political career, 253–4, 365–80, 381–415, 446–66, 481–3; Admiralty, 381, 405–12, 415–16, 435, 436, 481; Air and Naval parity, 470–1, 475; and Army reorganization, 370–3; Board of Trade, 388–93; Chancellor of the Exchequer, 381, 453–62; Colonial Office, 382–7, 440–3; judgment, 468–70; Ministry of Munitions, 433–4; Transvaal constitution, 384–5; War Office and Air Ministry, 436–7, 494–5; books by, 292, 348, 350–1, 353–6, 372, 374–5, 378–9, 386–7, 420, 427, 450, 462–3, 467, 528–9; Romanes Lecture, 446; World War I, 416–45; World War II, 484–519; and Dunkirk, 487–9; and France, 485–91; and invasion, 491–3; military contribution, 506–10; personal contribution, 484–96; and President Roosevelt, 481, 486–7, 490, 493, 500–3, 505, 512, 513–15, 517, 528; and Russia, 498–500, 504, 512–13, 515, 517, 518; and Stalin, 512–13, 515, 518; —, Clementine, Lady, wife of Sir Winston —, 389–90, 412, 430, 531; — family, characteristics of, 3–4, 535–6

Ciano, Count, 478n.

Civil War, American, 484, 513

Clagett, Nicholas, Bishop of St David's, 31–4

Clemenceau, Georges, 489

Clifden, Lord, 162; —, Dowager Lady, 161

Cobham, 79; —, Lord, 58

Cockerell, Sir Charles, 208

Collins, Michael, 442–3

Colnaghi, art-dealer, 276

Communism, 437–9, 499, 523, 524, 529–30

Connaught, Duke of, 314

Conservative party, 296, 298, 300, 302–8, 319–20, 331–2, 335–6, 374, 376–7, 381, 384, 399–400, 413, 414, 447, 471; — attitude to Sir Winston Churchill, 399–400, 424, 425, 432–3, 444–5, 451–2, 460–61, 463–5, 479, 482, 506

Constantinople, 323

Conway, Field-Marshal, 195
Conyngham, Lady, 210; —, Lady Elizabeth, 210
Coolidge, President, 455
Cooper, Duff, 478
Cornbury, 70, 130, 205
Cornwall, borough owners of, 154n.
Cornwallis, Lord, 145
Cowdray, 186
Cowes, 263, 266
Coxe, Archdeacon, 94, 95, 136–7, 139
Creevey, Thomas, 182, 184, 186
Creighton, Bishop Mandell, 262
Crimean War, 226, 227
Cripps, Sir Stafford, 498, 504–5, 505–6n.
Croker, J. W., 217
Cromer, Lord, 351, 355
Cromwell, Oliver, 482
Cuba, 345
Cullinan diamond, 385
Cumberland, Duke of, 69, 80
Curzon, Lord, 320
Cyrenaica, 503
Czechoslovakia, 479, 523

D-Day, 515–16
D'Abernon, Lord, 244
Daily Telegraph, 348, 350
Dardanelles, 323, 420–28, 444, 450, 533
Dartford programme, the, 323, 325
Dashwood family, 72; —, Sir Henry, 200, 201; —, Sir James, 74, 103
Davitt, Michael, 245, 310
Dawson, Geoffrey, 474
Deceased Wife's Sister Bill, 273, 365
Declaration of Independence, 137
Deffand, Marquise du, 123–4, 171, 175
Defoe, Daniel, 511
De Gaulle, General, 491n.
Delany, Mrs (previously Mrs Pendarves), 35, 39, 42
Denbigh, Lord, 105
Denikin, Marshal, 438
Derby, Earl of, 234, 237
De Roebeck, Admiral, 423
Dettingen, battle of, 47, 48–50
Devonshire, 4th Duke of, 112; —, the Bachelor Duke of, 210; —, 8th Duke of, 374; —, Georgiana, Duchess of, 171, 181, 304; — House, 180
Dijon, 22
Dill, Field-Marshal Sir John, 508
Disraeli, Benjamin, Lord Beaconsfield, 232–5, 236, 240, 242, 245–6, 260, 268, 270, 285, 295, 296, 298, 299, 300, 320, 325, 376
Dodington, Bubb, Lord Melcombe, 111–12
Doncaster Races, 215
Dorset, Duke of, 74
Dresden, 188–9
Dublin, 74, 236, 242, 244–5
Duchêne, M., landscape-designer, 287–8
Dudley, Lord, 276
Dundee, 449
Dunkirk, 79, 487–9
Durham, Richard Trevor, Bishop of, 95, 97, 104, 136; — church revenues, 225, 229
Dutch, the, 45, 48

Eden family, 155; —, Sir Anthony, 390, 473, 478, 532; —, Clarissa, Lady, 390; —, William, *see* Lord Auckland
Edward VII, King, 284, 383–4, 397, 399, 406; as Prince of Wales, 231–2, 240, 249, 253, 256–7, 260–61, 292, 306, 332, 346, 350
Edward VIII, King, 475; as Duke of Windsor, 491
Egmont, Lord, 36, 77 and n., 92
Egremont, Lord, 166, 179
Egypt, 309, 351–5, 496, 511
Eisenhower, General and President, 513, 530, 533

Elgin, Earl of, 382
Elizabeth I, Queen, 481, 510; Elizabeth II, 531, 533
Ellenborough, Lord and Lady, divorce of, 216–17
Enchantress, Admiralty yacht, 408, 437
Epping, 452
Erskine, Lord, 202
Esher, Viscount, 327, 392, 397, 412, 456
Essex, ship, 85
Eton College, 7–8, 90–91, 96, 159–60, 207, 210, 221, 260–61, 315, 379
Eugénie, Empress, 264, 266
Everest, Mrs, 338–9

Fane, Mr, 17
Farinelli, Carlo, 60
Feisal I, Emir, 440
Fenians, the, 233, 245
Ferdinand, Prince of Brunswick, 86–7
Ferrers, Earl, 98
Fielding, Henry, 60
Finland, 498–9
Fish, Captain, 10–13, 17–23
Fisher, Admiral Lord, 406, 407, 419, 422, 424–5, 434, 450
Fleury, Cardinal, 10, 44
Florence, 122
Foch, Marshal, 457
Foster, Lady Elizabeth, 171
Fox, Charles James, 141, 143, 144, 145, 146, 147, 150–52, 158, 171, 172, 175–84, 185, 186, 190; —, H. E., 208; —, Henry, 1st Lord Holland, 43, 47, 60, 62–5, 68, 75–9, 101, 108, 112, 114, 141; —, Sir Stephen, 62
France, 10, 43–4, 49, 80, 83–5, 138, 140, 145, 148, 179, 266, 395, 409, 410, 415, 455; World War I, 414–15, 430–33, 434; World War II, 485–91, 492, 516; French Revolution, 175, 179, 188, 189
Frederick Maryland, 513
Frederick, Prince of Wales, 59–61, 63, 69, 91
Frederick the Great, 44, 138
French, Field-Marshal Sir John, 364, 417, 430
Frere, Sir Bartle, 270; —, John Hookham, 160
Frietchie, Barbara, 513
Fulton speech, Sir Winston Churchill's, 524–6

Gainsborough, Thomas, 102, 170, 175, 276
Gallatin, M., tutor, 8–11
Gallipoli, 420–3
Galloway family, 201, 220
Galsworthy, John, 402
Garlies, Lord, 118
Garrick, David, 135, 169
Geneva, 8–11
George I, King, 5, 57
George II, King, 14, 35–6, 42, 51, 57–8, 59–61, 63, 75–6, 102
George III, King, 3, 69, 94, 95, 98, 101–2, 104–5, 110–18, 120, 139, 142, 146–7, 166, 167, 178, 188, 190; character, 99–102; madness, 157–9; visit to Blenheim, 155–7
George IV, King, character, 167–8; as Prince of Wales, 157, 158, 163, 166–8, 178, 179, 198
George V, King, 382, 403, 419
George VI, King, 495, 516, 519, 531
Germaine, Lord George, 139; —, Lady Betty, 109
Germany, 16, 47–51, 83, 86–7, 391, 454–5; —, appeasement of, 473–81; — pre-1914, 393–7, 403–11, 414–15; World War I, 416–19, 421, 422, 425, 427, 432, 434–5; World War II, 484–501, 513–15
Gettysburg, 513
Ghent, 45
Gibbon, Edward, 139, 169, 171, 177, 190, 347, 349

Gibraltar, 145, 148
Gladstone, Sir John, 184; —, William Ewart, 233, 235, 243, 246, 250–51, 296–7, 298–9, 300–301, 303, 308–12, 316–19, 321, 324, 330, 331, 333, 334–5, 340, 351–2, 524
Glover, Matilda, 219–20
Godolphin, Sidney, 1st Earl of, 2, 5, 14; —, Francis, 2nd Earl of, 2, 5, 6, 7, 26–7, 54
Goebbels, Dr, 495, 505–6n.
Goldsmith, Oliver, 169
Gordon, General, 352
Gordon-Cumming, Sir William, 268, 269
Gorst, Sir John, 298
Goschen, Viscount, 321, 328
Gould, Mary, 533
Gower, Lord, 113, 119
Graham, Sir James, 218
Grantully Castle, S.S., 333
Grasse, Comte de, 145
Greece, 421–2, 444
Grenville, George, 115, 116; —, Lord, 188, 193
Greville, Robert Fulke, 158
Grey, Earl, 185
Grey, Sir Edward, 375, 387, 394–5, 398, 405, 414–15, 477
Grimston, Lord, 15
Gronow, Captain, 204–5, 210
Gunning, General, wife and daughters, 199–202
Gustav IV, King of Sweden, 192

Hague, The, 48, 187–8, 190
Haldane, Lord, 372, 404, 407, 409
Halifax, George Savile, Marquis of, 2; —, Edward Wood, Earl of, 474, 477n., 479–80
Hamilton, Emma, Lady, 164; —, Lord George, 326; —, James, Duke of, 199; —, Sir William, 164; — Palace, 274
Hampton Court, 220
Hanbury-Williams, Sir Charles, 62
Handel, G. F., 48, 59–60
Hanover, 17, 44
Harcourt, 1st Earl, 92, 98; 2nd Earl, 155; —, Sir William, 299, 335
Harrow School, 339, 340–43, 347, 392, 447, 533
Hartington, Lord, 317, 318, 328; later Duke of Devonshire, 374
Hatfield House, 327
Hatzfeldt, Count, 266
Hauk, Minnie, 265
Havana, 111
Heligoland Bight, battle of, 419
Herbert, Lord, 137, 162; — family, 95
Herschel, Sir William, 157
Hertford, Countess of, 39, 43
Hervey, Lord, 57, 58, 61
Heytesbury, 154, 160
Hicks-Beach, Sir Michael, 253, 312, 326
Hitler, Adolf, 347–8, 447, 462, 466, 467, 469, 470, 472, 473–4, 475, 476–80, 501, 508, 525
Hoare, Sir Samuel (Lord Templewood), 465, 473, 476, 477
Hobhouse, J. C., 215
Hoechst, 47–8
Holkham, 180
Holland, 3rd Baron, 194; —, Elizabeth, Lady, 178, 182, 188–90, 194; — House, 180
Holstein, Baron von, 404
Home Rule, 310, 317–18, 331, 413
Hopkins, Harry, 505, 509, 513
Horne, Sir Robert, 442, 452
Hornsby, Dr, 165
Howe, Admiral Earl, 83, 85; —, General, 137
Hozier, Blanche, Lady, 389
Hull, Cordell, U.S. Secretary of State, 490
Hume, Joseph, Radical M.P., 216, 217, 225
Hungary, 515, 523
Hunter, Kitty, 124

Hurd, Bishop, 154
Huxley, T. H., 232
Hyde Park, 81, 83
Hyder Ali, 145
Hyndman, H. M., 401

India, 145, 230, 269–71, 309, 314–16, 346–50, 463–5, 505, 514; — Bill, Fox's, 150
Inskip, Sir Thomas, 475
Iraq, 440–42
Ireland, 74, 105, 145, 236, 240–46, 310–11, 313–14, 331–2, 442–3
Italy, 17, 23, 495–6

Jackson, Dean Cyril, 160
Jameson, Dr, 357
Japan, 487, 501, 505, 529
Jellicoe, Admiral Lord, 407
Jerome, Clara, 268–9, 340; —, Clara Hall, 264, 266; —, Jennie *see* Lady Randolph Churchill; —, Lawrence, 272; —, Leonard, 238, 263–8, 269, 278–9, 338, 356; — family, 3–4, 264
Jeune, Mrs, 223–4, 231
Johannesburg, 364
Johnson, Dr, 102, 115, 169
Jones, Dean, 268
Joseph II, Emperor, 121

Keate, Dr, 210
Keck, Anthony, 102–3, 118; —, Lady Susan, 72
Kemal Atatürk, 444
Keppel, Admiral Lord, 140–1, 142; —, Colonel, 232
Kew, 159
Keyes, Admiral Sir Roger, 421, 450, 482, 505
Keynes, J. M., Lord, 453–4, 455
Khartoum, 352, 386
Kiel Canal, 403
Kimbolton, 173
Kingston, Duke of, 23
Kipling, Rudyard, 358, 359, 362, 363, 448
Kitchener, Field-Marshal Lord, 351–3, 354–6, 364, 372, 415, 417, 421, 422–3, 426
Knightley, Lady, 223
Knock, 250
Knollys family, 119
Korean War, 529
Kruger, Paul, 357
Krumpholtz, Madame, 203

Labour party, 382, 393, 439, 450, 459, 463, 465, 473, 482, 521–2, 529
Ladysmith, 363
Laguerre, Louis, 268
Lamb, Matthew, 23–4, 54, 55
Lambeth Palace, 155, 159
Langley Park, 40–41, 46, 68, 73, 91, 93, 158
Laski, Professor, 521
Laval, Pierre, 473
Lavery, Sir John, 429; —, Lady, 429
Law, Bonar, 400, 412, 425, 426, 428, 432, 442, 444, 445
Lawrence, T. E., 440–42
Leeds, 5th Duke of, 161
Leitrim, Lord, murder of, 241
Lenin, N., 438
Lennox, Lady Caroline, 62; —, Lady Sarah, 101, 105, 107–9
Lenôtre, André, 288, 289
Leopold, Duke of Lorraine, 11, 12
Les Saintes, battle of, 148
Liberal party, 296, 303, 308, 310, 317–20, 396, 397, 399, 407, 449; — and Sir Winston Churchill, 443–4
Libya, 503, 505, 507
Lichnowsky, Prince, 394
Liddell, Dean, 223, 231
Liman von Sanders, General, 422
Limoges enamels, 248, 250
Lincoln, President Abraham, 484
Lincolnshire, 110, 176
Lindemann, Professor (Lord Cherwell), 466, 475, 494
Lippmann, Walter, 530

Lisbon, 7
Little Marble Hill, 170
Lloyd George, D., 367, 376–7, 381, 387, 390, 393, 396–8, 399, 400, 404, 412, 413, 421, 426, 431–4, 435, 438, 442, 444, 447–8, 449, 450, 452, 460, 463, 468–9, 482, 484, 522
London, 61, 122, 142, 168, 492, 514, 516; —, Bishop of, revenues, 225, 228; —, Blitz on, 494–5
Londonderry, Marquis of, 231; —, Marchioness of, 234
Longfellow, H. W., 500
Lorne, Lord, 199, 200
Lorraine, Court of, 9–13
Lothian, Philip, Lord, 474
Louis XV, King, 90, 448
Louisbourg, 77
Lourdes, 330
Lowth, Bishop, 154
Lowther, Sir James, 92
Lunéville, 12
Luther, Martin, 484–5
Lyttelton, Lord, 44, 142, 175
Lytton, Lady, 383

Macaulay, T. B., 197, 341, 347, 467, 501
Macclesfield family, 70, 73; —, Lady, 231
MacDonald, J. R., 460, 463
McKenna, Reginald, 404, 407
Mafeking, 334
Maine, hospital ship, 363
Malakand Pass, 348–9
Malaya, 503
Malmesbury, 1st Earl of, 174; —, 3rd Earl of, 235
Malta, 517
Manchester, 189, 228, 236, 379, 383; —, Duchess of, 173; —, Consuelo, Duchess of, 258
Marble House, Newport, Rhode Island, 283
Maria Theresa, Empress, 120
Marie Antoinette, Queen, 250
Marlborough, John Churchill, 1st Duke of, 1–2, 4, 14–15, 20, 26, 38, 44–5, 56, 76, 90, 111, 182, 208, 239, 254, 288, 379, 381, 382, 509; Sir Winston Churchill's life of, 467; —, Sarah, 1st Duchess, 1–2, 5–40, 46–7, 52–6, 57, 64, 65, 67, 79, 90, 93, 126, 127, 176, 254, 257, 287; —, Henrietta, 2nd Duchess of, 2, 5, 30; —, Charles Spencer, 3rd Duke of, 2, 4, 7–8, 35; army career, 44–52, 63–4, 83–8; assassination threat, 81–3; financial difficulties, 31–4, 37–40, 52–6, 94; marriage, 27–8, 31–4; political career, 57–78; tour abroad, 8–23; —, Elizabeth Trevor, 3rd Duchess, 27–9, 30, 32–3, 37, 41–3, 45–51, 86–8, 94–7, 106, 136; —, George Spencer, 4th Duke of, 2–3, 42, 83, 87–8, 90–91, 93, 95–6, 97–8, 104–5, 106, 110, 165, 170, 191; and Blenheim, 122–34; gem collection, 133, 239–40, 248; marriage, 106–9; and politics, 112–13, 115–20, 138–44, 149, 150–4; social life, 132–7; —, Caroline Russell, 4th Duchess of, 107–9, 132, 134, 135, 137, 151, 155–6, 157, 161–2, 164–5, 172, 191, 194; —, George Spencer Churchill, 5th Duke of, 132, 133, 136, 159–60, 161, 174, 196, 212, 219, 239; extravagance, 203–5, 207–9; Gunning scandal, 198–201; marriage, 201; politics 206, 217–18; and Mary Ann Sturt, 202–3; —, Lady Susan Stewart, 5th Duchess of, 201, 203, 209, 211, 220; —, George Spencer Churchill, 6th Duke, 209–21; marriages, 220; will of, 220–21; John Winston Spencer Churchill, 7th Duke, 7, 221, 260–61, 263, 266–7, 273, 306, 380; and Blenheim, 223–4, 231–3, 237–40,

246–50; character of, 222–3; and Church reform, 224–30, 236; death and will, 254–5; and Ireland, 236, 240–46, 250–52, 272; —, Frances, 7th Duchess, 223, 231, 233, 234, 237, 242, 246, 247–8, 254, 261, 269, 286, 312, 327, 337, 339, 344, 379; —, George Charles Spencer Churchill, 8th Duke of, 254–5, 259–60, 262–3, 270–74, 278–9; Blenheim sales, 274–8; will, 280–1; —, Lilian, Duchess of, 278–9, 280, 281, 283, 346, 348; —, Charles Richard John, 9th Duke of, 281–2, 364, 366, 382, 464, 467; and Blenheim, 286–94; marriage, 282–3; —, Consuelo Vanderbilt, 9th Duchess of, 258, 280, 282–6, 290–94; —, John Albert Edward William, 10th Duke, of 286
Marlborough House, 56, 61, 92, 93, 161, 164, 173, 257, 268, 270
Marsh, Sir Edward, 382–3, 385, 387, 391, 402, 408, 429, 430, 434, 440, 454
Marshall, General, 509
Masaryk, Jan, 523
Masham, Lord, 40, 57; —, Lady, 27, 40
Masterman, C. F. G., 389, 401, 403
Maynooth College, 223
Melbourne, 1st Viscount, 166; —, 2nd Viscount, 166
Metternich, Prince, 394
Microcosm, The, 160
Middle East, the, 440–2
Millais, Sir John, 275
Milner, Lord, 357, 383
Minorca, 77
Minterne, 4
Molotov, V. M., 498 and n., 533
Montagu, Mrs, 115, 135; —, Lord, 186
Montgomery, Field-Marshal Lord, 507, 516
Moore, John Archbishop of Canterbury, 94–5, 103, 121–3, 125, 136–7, 139–40, 142, 143–4, 146, 148–9, 155, 156, 157, 159–61, 164, 166, 174, 176, 202
Morley, Lord, 375, 435
Morning Post, 358
Morocco, 395
Moscow, 500, 512
Müller, Professor Max, 224
Munich, 473, 480, 529
Mussolini, Benito, 472, 478, 495–6, 514

Naples, 122
Napoleon Bonaparte, 182, 183
Nares, Professor, 195–7, 204
Natal, 359, 363
National Gallery, 274
Navy, Royal, reconstitution (1911–14), 405–11; World War I, 416–19, 424–5; World War II, 481–2, 488, 490, 492–3
Nelson, Lord, 164
Netherlands, 45, 48, 65, 161, 187–8
Newcastle, Duke of, 68, 69, 71, 73, 76, 77, 86, 87, 104, 112, 114
Newport, Rhode Island, 272, 283
New York, 263–5, 278, 366, 465; *New York Times*, 265
Norfolk, 180; —, Duke of, 237; House, 61
Norman, Montagu, Lord, 453
Normandy, invasion of, 514, 515–16
North, Lord, 139, 141, 143, 146, 149
Northcote, Sir Stafford, 296, 299–300, 305, 308, 310, 311–12, 329–30
Northumberland, Duke of, 135
North-West Frontier, 348–9
Norway, 482, 494, 509
Nova Scotia, 69
Novello, Ivor, 440

Observer, 327
O'Connell, Daniel, 216

Ohio, 77
Oldham, 366, 374
Omdurman, battle of, 353, 354–5, 386
Oran, action at, 490
Ossory, Lord, 178
Oxford, city, 70–3, 103–4, 119–20, 131, 184, 206, 366; races, 131; university, 70, 156, 174, 197, 220, 222–3, 356; colleges: All Souls, 474, 475; Christ Church, 5–6, 96–7, 160, 222, 262; Merton, 194, 262; Oriel, 222; St John's, 222; Sheldonian Theatre, 156
Oxfordshire, 110, 130, 237; — election of 1754, 70–3; — election of 1761, 102–4; —, representation, 74, 174

Paget, Lady (Minnie Stevens), 258, 269
Paine, Thomas, 189
Pantheon, Oxford Street, 204
Paris, 10, 16, 17, 19–21, 24, 122–3, 175–6, 181–2, 189, 210, 264, 266, 415, 455, 456; —, Peace of, 1763, 114, 119, 148; —, Peace Conference of 1919, 435, 441
Parker, Lord, 73
Parnell, C. S., 241, 242, 243, 310, 311, 313, 317, 331–2
Pearl Harbor, 501
Peckham, 495
Peel, Sir Robert, 223
Pelham family, 67; —, Henry, 75
Pembroke, Henry, Earl of, 101, 124, 138–9, 142–4, 157; —, Elizabeth Spencer, Countess of, 42, 48, 89, 90–1, 92, 101, 106, 123–4, 142–3, 158, 173, 184–5
Perceval, Spencer, 206
Perkins, C. W., 291
Pétain, Marshal, 490
Peyton, Henry, 218
Pigott, Richard, 332
Pitt, William the elder, Earl of Chatham, 44, 57, 67, 75–81, 83–4, 110–12, 116–18, 138, 141, 484, 492, 507; —, William the younger, 141, 149, 150–52, 153–4, 156, 160, 164, 172, 174, 179, 181–2, 187, 193, 205–6
Placentia Bay, Newfoundland, 501
Poland, 87, 494, 515, 517, 523
Poor Law, 115
Portland, Duke of, 133
Potsdam, 189; — Conference, 518
Potter, Archbishop, 61
Prague, 45, 479
Pretoria, 334, 360, 365
Primrose League, 304
Prince of Wales, battleship, 501, 502
Princeton, 264
Prussia, 189, 192–3; —, King of, 189; —, Prince Royal, 189; —, Prince Henry, 192, 193–4
Punch, 320, 340

Quebec Conference, first, 514
Queen Elizabeth, battleship, 423
Ranelagh, 107
Rebellion of 1745, 66
Reebkomp, Augustus, 124
Reform, Parliamentary, 215–16, 217–18
Reform Bill of 1832, 3, 120; — of 1867, 233; — of 1884, 303, 310
Repulse, battle cruiser, 502
Reynolds, Sir Joshua, 133, 137, 290
Rhineland, 474
Rhodes, Cecil, 333
Ribbentrop, J. von, 497, 498n.
Richmond, 3rd Duke of, 62; —, 4th Duke of, 106, 139; — Park, 158, 184
Ripon Falls, 386
Ritz, Madame de, 189
Roberts, Field-Marshal Lord, 293, 363–4
Robinson, John, 154
Rochefort expedition, 80

Rockingham, Marquis of, 112, 116, 146–7
Rodney, Admiral Lord, 145, 148
Rome, 121
Rommel, Marshal, 503, 505, 507
Romney, George, 138, 170, 175
Ronalds, Fanny, 265, 279
Roosevelt, President F. D., 481, 486, 487, 490, 493, 500–3, 505, 508, 512, 513, 514, 515, 516–18
Roosevelt, President Theodore, 345
Rosa, Salvator, 137
Rosebery, Lord, 262, 268, 295–6, 297, 337, 366, 374–5, 378, 467
Rotterdam, 494
Roxburghe, Duchess of, 255; — Club, 204, 239
Royal Air Force, 437, 475, 489, 492, 494
Royal Scots Fusiliers, 431, 434
Royal Society, 165n.
Russell, Lord John, 216; Russell family, 184, *and see* Bedford
Russia, 138, 309, 323, 332–3, 403–4, 420, 422, 480, 496, 518; post-war, 523, 524, 531; Revolution of 1917, 436, 437–9; World War II, 498–501, 504, 512, 515
Rysbrack, J. M., 254

Sackville, Lord George, 86
St Albans, 8, 11, 15–16
St Eustatius, 145
St George's, Hanover Square, 35
St James's Palace, 59, 60, 61; — church, Piccadilly, 15, 61; — Street, 177
St-Malo, 83–5
St Margaret's, Westminster, 390, 518
St Petersburg, 277, 284–5, 332
Salisbury, Marquis of, 233, 293, 296, 298, 300, 301, 302, 307, 309–10, 312–16, 317, 319–30, 332–3, 336, 337, 350, 378, 448n; —, Marchioness of, 256, 304, 327, 337
Sandhurst, 344, 346
Sandwich, Earl of, 114, 139, 141
Saratoga, 137, 138, 177, 179
Sargent, J. S., 290
Savannah, 140
Sawyers, Sir Winston Churchill's valet, 510–11
Saxony, Prince Anthony of, 189
Scarbrough, Lord, 13
Scarpelain and McCarty, livery makers, 163
Schwarzenberg, Prince, 216
Selwyn, George, 177, 178
Seven Years' War, 75, 77–81, 83–7, 99–100, 110–14
Sévigné, Madame de, 17, 23
Shaftesbury, Earl of, 211–12, 223, 225, 229–30
Shaw, George Bernard, 292
Shelburne, Earl of, 146–9, 178
Sheridan, Clare, 340
Sidi Barrani, battle of, 496
Sidney Street, 'Battle of', 402–3, 418
Silesia, 44
Simla, 281
Singapore, 503
Sinn Fein, 442
Smith, Sir Llewelyn, 391; —, Rev. Sydney, 167; —, W. H., 305, 326, 328, 331
Smuts, Field-Marshal J. C., 360n.
Snowden, Philip, Viscount, 457–8, 462
South African War, 293, 356–63, 368, 372–3
Spain, 65, 111, 138, 140
Spalding, Mr, 276
Spencer, Lady Caroline, 132, 162; —, Lord Charles, 41, 74, 96–7, 102–3, 108, 110, 112, 115, 117–18, 131, 134, 139–40, 141–2, 144, 146–7, 152–4, 162, 173–4, 195; —, Lady Charlotte, 132, 162–3, 194, 195–7; —, George John, 3rd Earl, 207–8; —, Lord Henry, 132, 160–61, 187–94, 205; —, John,

2, 7–8, 26, 28–9, 34–7, 54, 55, 66–7; tour abroad, 8–23; —, John Poyntz, 5th Earl, 252, 313–14; —, Lord Robert, 42, 97, 102–4, 120–22, 131, 135, 139, 143–4, 145–7, 172–3, 174–86; —, William Robert, 171; — family, characteristics of, 3–4, 8, 10, 11, 19, 35–6, 536; — House, 286
Spion Kop, 363
Staël, Madame de, 165
Stair, Earl of, 44, 49–51, 66
Stalin, Joseph, 384, 498, 500, 512–13, 515, 518, 523, 525, 526, 529, 532
Stamp Act, 115
Stanhope, Charles, 24
Stockholm, 190–92
Stratford, Dr, 5–6
Strawberry Hill, 163
Sturt, Mary Ann, 202–3
Sudan, 309, 351–2
Suez, 496, 531
Sunderland, Anne Churchill, Countess of, 3, 5; —, Charles, 3rd Earl of, 5–6, 24–5, 38; —, Charles, 5th Earl of, *see* 3rd Duke of Marlborough; —, Robert Spencer, 2nd Earl of, 25; —, Robert Spencer, 4th Earl of, 6–7, 12, 15, 20, 23–4, 38–9; — Library, 6–7, 238, 249
Sweden, 190–92
Switzerland, 182, 203, 273

Tangier incident, 395
Tavistock, 184
Teheran, 512, 515
Temple, Earl, 111, 113
Tenniel, John, 320
Tetbury, 132–3
Thesiger, Frederick, Lord Chelmsford, 218
Thomas, Rev. Vaughan, 207, 209
Tibbett, William, 132, 133
Times, The, 224, 240, 249, 270, 274, 275, 277, 319, 327, 332, 359, 474
Tirpitz, Admiral von, 409, 411
Tobruk, 505
Tonypandy, 402
Tory party, 70–73
Townshend, Jack, 97
Trade and Plantations, Board of, 139, 177
Trafalgar, battle of, 205
Transjordan, 441
Transvaal, 334, 357, 384–5
Trenchard, Air Marshal Lord, 441
Trevor, 1st Lord, 27; —, 2nd Lord, 32–3, 91; — family, 38
Trimmer, defined, 2, 382, 535
Truman, President Harry S., 524, 529, 530
Turkey, 322, 421–3, 440
Turner, Charles, 131, 133; —, Sir Edward, 73
Turton, Captain, 73
Twain, Mark, 366

Uganda, 386–7
Ulster, 318, 413
United States, 345, 455, 458, 462; World War II, 487, 490, 493, 500–503, 505, 508, 509, 510–11, 512–16; post-war period, 523–6, 527–8, 529–31, 533
Utrecht, 18; —, Peace of, 27, 45, 111
Uxbridge, 494

V-bombs, 514
Valmy, battle of, 179
Vanbrugh, Sir John, 127, 128, 129, 287, 288
Vanderbilt, Consuelo, *see* Marlborough; —, Commodore, 265, 282; —, Mrs W. K., 282–3, 466
Versailles, 24, 287, 289; —, Treaty of, 455, 472
Vichy, 490

Victoria, Queen, 225, 233, 234, 236–7, 246, 249, 256, 260, 265, 269–70, 271, 311, 535; — and Lord Randolph Churchill, 297, 299, 312–15, 316, 320–1, 325–6, 330, 332–3
Vienna, 120–1, 188, 347, 515
Villiers, Lord, 120
Voltaire, 21

Waldegrave, Lord, 69
Walpole, Horace, 36, 76, 78, 83, 99–100, 108, 110, 115, 127, 133, 159, 163, 170, 171, 175, 195; —, Horatio, 63; —, Sir Robert, 5, 16, 34, 36, 42, 44, 52–3, 54, 58–9, 63–5
Wanley, Humphrey, 6
Wareham, 184
Washington, 455, 502–3, 508, 510, 514, 533
Washington, President George, 145, 264
Waterloo, battle of, 3, 206, 210
Wavell, Field-Marshal Lord, 496, 503
Webb, Beatrice and Sidney, 388–91, 393
Wellington, Duke of, 208
Westminster, 518; —, Duke of, 417; — Abbey, 82–3, 320, 487, 531–2; election, 451; — Hall, 106, 533–4
Westphalia, 47
Weymouth, Lady, 35
Wheate, Sir Thomas, 15
Wheatfield, 110, 139, 162, 173, 195
Whig party, 70–3
White House, the, 514
Whiteknights Park, 197, 203, 207, 208
White's Club, 175
Whittier, John Greenleaf, 513
Wigram, Ralph, 466, 469, 474
Wilberforce, Bishop Samuel, 230, 232, 235, 238
Wilkes, John, 113, 114
Wilkinson, Ellen, 522
William II, German Emperor, 292–3, 394, 395, 409, 410, 411
William III, King, 101, 381
Wilson, Admiral, 407, 425–6; —, General Sir Henry, 435; —, President Woodrow, 435
Wimbledon, 36
Winchester, Bishop of, revenues, 225–6; — School, 282
Windsor, 63, 164, 260; — Castle, 232, 260, 313, 325, 326; — Lodge, 8, 30–1, 35; — Little Lodge, 36–8
Wise, Henry, 128–9, 232, 289
Witbank Colliery, 361, 366
Woburn, 108–9, 180
Wolfe, General, 507
Wolff, Sir Henry Drummond, 298
Wolseley, Field-Marshal Lord, 364, 366
Woodstock, 14–16, 29, 71, 72, 74, 102, 128, 130, 131, 154, 160, 165, 184, 187, 205, 212, 218, 247, 267, 292, 294, 300, 304; —, vicar of, 72
Woolbeding, 185–6
Wordsworth, William, 183
World War I, 414–35; — II, 484–517
Wyatt, James, 129, 204
Wychwood Forest, 70, 130, 131
Wyndham, George, 412

Yalta Conference, 517, 518
York, Archbishop, revenues of, 225–6
Yorktown, 145–6, 179
Young, Arthur, 106, 127
Yugoslavia, 523

Zambezi, 453–4
Zanetti collection of gems, 133
Zorndorf, 87

MORE ABOUT PENGUINS

A. L. Rowse

THE USE OF HISTORY

'It achieves . . . the clarity and the distinction which only a mind of high intellectual calibre can impose without losing the charm of a spontaneous intimacy.

'This little book may well be a pointer for a very wide public to a branch of knowledge which, without disastrous consequences, we cannot afford to neglect. The weight of popular opinion in favour of material and scientific learning must be shifted if man is ever to become – as he surely could – the master rather than the slave of matter. It is only by our knowledge of the human mind that we may learn to control that knowledge of things which has proved and is proving so dangerous to us all.

'But leaving aside these gloomier and more solemn thoughts, history is a delightful study, and Mr Rowse a delightful guide' – C. V. Wedgwood.

'Admirable . . . is Mr Rowse's insistence that history is to be found in things, in places, and not merely in print' – C. Northcote Parkinson

G. M. Trevelyan

BRITISH HISTORY IN THE NINETEENTH CENTURY AND AFTER: 1782–1919

Between 1780 and 1920 Britain underwent the most rapid change of character any country had ever experienced until then. Despite the most stable political structure in Europe the nation changed with startling speed. The first industrial state was created; the world shrank under the impact of steam power and the electric telegraph; man's scientific, social, and political attitudes were revolutionized; an Empire grew at the same time as a parliamentary aristocracy transformed itself into a parliamentary democracy. And Britain, almost alone, was without violent revolution.

G. M. Trevelyan's famous study of the period is focused on the political stage, on which the central themes of the century were played out by such actors as Pitt and Gladstone, Wellington and Queen Victoria, Disraeli and Parnell. The author employs his gift for divining the logic of events to show how developments in science, industry, economics, and social theory made themselves felt on the conduct of the nation's affairs.

Alan Moorehead

DARWIN AND THE BEAGLE

When H.M.S. Beagle sailed out of Plymouth in 1831 on survey, she carried a naturalist named Charles Darwin, who had been fortuitously appointed at the age of twenty-two. Destined for the church, Darwin was happily prepared to champion the Book of Genesis.

But everything he encountered on the voyage – from the primitive people of Tierra del Fuego to the famous finches of the Galapagos Islands, from earthquakes and eruptions to fossil seashells gathered at 12,000 feet in the Andes – conspired to wean the young scientist from the simple faith of Beagle's commander, Captain Fitzroy, and force upon him the subversive conclusions of *The Origin of Species.*

Perfectly told by Alan Moorehead and magnificently illustrated from contemporary sources, *Darwin and the Beagle* is the exciting story of a five-year circumnavigation which was to change the course of human thought.

'Mr Moorehead's admirable prose style, his entrancing narrative . . . are beyond praise . . . No praise can be too high for the production with its colour plates' – *The Times Literary Supplement*

Also available

No Room in the Ark
The White Nile

A. L. Rowse

THE EARLY CHURCHILLS

From obscure beginnings in the West Country to the death of Sarah, the remarkable first Duchess of Marlborough, A. L. Rowse traces the foundations of one of England's greatest families.

Here we meet the original Sir Winston Churchill, the Cavalier colonel, described by his famous descendant as 'one of the most notable and potent of sires'; his daughter Arabella, mistress of James II and mother of the martial Duke of Berwick; his eldest son John, the Duke of Marlborough, who curbed the ambitions of Louis XIV; and other Churchills who left their mark on English history.

The Early Churchills – to quote the *Listener* – 'sets a model for family history . . . a brilliant example'